Communications
in Computer and Information Science

2579

Series Editors

Gang Li ⓘ, *School of Information Technology, Deakin University, Burwood, VIC, Australia*

Joaquim Filipe ⓘ, *Polytechnic Institute of Setúbal, Setúbal, Portugal*

Zhiwei Xu, *Chinese Academy of Sciences, Beijing, China*

Rationale

The CCIS series is devoted to the publication of proceedings of computer science conferences. Its aim is to efficiently disseminate original research results in informatics in printed and electronic form. While the focus is on publication of peer-reviewed full papers presenting mature work, inclusion of reviewed short papers reporting on work in progress is welcome, too. Besides globally relevant meetings with internationally representative program committees guaranteeing a strict peer-reviewing and paper selection process, conferences run by societies or of high regional or national relevance are also considered for publication.

Topics

The topical scope of CCIS spans the entire spectrum of informatics ranging from foundational topics in the theory of computing to information and communications science and technology and a broad variety of interdisciplinary application fields.

Information for Volume Editors and Authors

Publication in CCIS is free of charge. No royalties are paid, however, we offer registered conference participants temporary free access to the online version of the conference proceedings on SpringerLink (http://link.springer.com) by means of an http referrer from the conference website and/or a number of complimentary printed copies, as specified in the official acceptance email of the event.

CCIS proceedings can be published in time for distribution at conferences or as post-proceedings, and delivered in the form of printed books and/or electronically as USBs and/or e-content licenses for accessing proceedings at SpringerLink. Furthermore, CCIS proceedings are included in the CCIS electronic book series hosted in the SpringerLink digital library at http://link.springer.com/bookseries/7899. Conferences publishing in CCIS are allowed to use Online Conference Service (OCS) for managing the whole proceedings lifecycle (from submission and reviewing to preparing for publication) free of charge.

Publication process

The language of publication is exclusively English. Authors publishing in CCIS have to sign the Springer CCIS copyright transfer form, however, they are free to use their material published in CCIS for substantially changed, more elaborate subsequent publications elsewhere. For the preparation of the camera-ready papers/files, authors have to strictly adhere to the Springer CCIS Authors' Instructions and are strongly encouraged to use the CCIS LaTeX style files or templates.

Abstracting/Indexing

CCIS is abstracted/indexed in DBLP, Google Scholar, EI-Compendex, Mathematical Reviews, SCImago, Scopus. CCIS volumes are also submitted for the inclusion in ISI Proceedings.

How to start

To start the evaluation of your proposal for inclusion in the CCIS series, please send an e-mail to ccis@springer.com.

Riccardo Guidotti · Ute Schmid · Luca Longo
Editors

Explainable Artificial Intelligence

Third World Conference, xAI 2025
Istanbul, Turkey, July 9–11, 2025
Proceedings, Part IV

 Springer

Editors
Riccardo Guidotti ⓘ
University of Pisa
Pisa, Italy

Ute Schmid ⓘ
University of Bamberg
Bamberg, Germany

Luca Longo ⓘ
Technological University Dublin
Dublin, Ireland

ISSN 1865-0929   ISSN 1865-0937 (electronic)
Communications in Computer and Information Science
ISBN 978-3-032-08329-6   ISBN 978-3-032-08330-2 (eBook)
https://doi.org/10.1007/978-3-032-08330-2

© The Editor(s) (if applicable) and The Author(s), under exclusive license
to Springer Nature Switzerland AG 2026. This book is an open access publication.

Open Access This book is licensed under the terms of the Creative Commons Attribution 4.0 International License (http://creativecommons.org/licenses/by/4.0/), which permits use, sharing, adaptation, distribution and reproduction in any medium or format, as long as you give appropriate credit to the original author(s) and the source, provide a link to the Creative Commons license and indicate if changes were made.
The images or other third party material in this book are included in the book's Creative Commons license, unless indicated otherwise in a credit line to the material. If material is not included in the book's Creative Commons license and your intended use is not permitted by statutory regulation or exceeds the permitted use, you will need to obtain permission directly from the copyright holder.
The use of general descriptive names, registered names, trademarks, service marks, etc. in this publication does not imply, even in the absence of a specific statement, that such names are exempt from the relevant protective laws and regulations and therefore free for general use.
The publisher, the authors and the editors are safe to assume that the advice and information in this book are believed to be true and accurate at the date of publication. Neither the publisher nor the authors or the editors give a warranty, expressed or implied, with respect to the material contained herein or for any errors or omissions that may have been made. The publisher remains neutral with regard to jurisdictional claims in published maps and institutional affiliations.

This Springer imprint is published by the registered company Springer Nature Switzerland AG
The registered company address is: Gewerbestrasse 11, 6330 Cham, Switzerland

If disposing of this product, please recycle the paper.

Preface

Over the last decade, Explainable Artificial Intelligence (XAI) has developed into an ever-growing research field dedicated to approaches that make AI systems—especially those based on machine-learned black box models—more transparent, interpretable, and comprehensible to humans. The demand for XAI methods rises with the growing number of application areas for AI methods, from image-based medical diagnostics to personalised recommenders to scientific discovery. In the context of the European AI Act, requirements for trustworthy AI systems have been defined, including human agency and oversight, robustness, fairness, and transparency. Trustworthiness is crucial for critical application domains, such as healthcare, industrial production, and finance. XAI methods can help meet these requirements.

A growing variety of XAI methods has emerged over the last decade. Initially, a strong focus has been placed on feature relevance methods for classification models applied to images and tabular data. These methods are beneficial for model developers to assess the quality of learned models, particularly in addressing issues such as overfitting to training data or unwanted biases. Soon, the importance of non-expert users of AI systems was recognised, especially professionals in the respective application domain of an AI system and end-users who interact with AI systems in a private context. Consequently, the need for XAI methods that consider the specific information needs of these user groups has been recognised. This has resulted in a rich set of XAI methods, including counterfactual or contrastive explanations, prototype-based explanations, and concept-based explanations. Furthermore, it has been recognised that XAI must be an interdisciplinary endeavour to consider the cognitive demands of the explainees and design helpful human-AI interfaces.

While most XAI research has focused on local, post-hoc explanations for classifiers, XAI methods have expanded to unsupervised learning and generative AI approaches. Additionally, methods for explaining inherently interpretable AI models and providing global explanations are investigated. Methods of explanatory interactive learning broaden the scope of XAI research, shifting from explanation to understanding and revision. Over recent years, the need to systematically evaluate XAI methods has been recognised. To support understanding the output of a model, an explanation needs to be faithful concerning its inferential mechanisms.

To bring together the growing number of researchers dedicated to developing and evaluating XAI methods, the World Conference of Explainable Artificial Intelligence (xAI) was established in 2023. This conference aims to connect researchers from AI, computer science, cognitive science, human-computer interaction, social sciences, law, philosophy, and practitioners from all continents to share and discuss knowledge, new perspectives, experiences, and innovations in XAI. The Third World Conference on Explainable Artificial Intelligence (xAI 2025) took place in Istanbul, Turkey, from July 9 to 11, 2025. It attracted 224 submissions worldwide for the main track, as well as over

60 submissions for the late-breaking work and demo tracks. The conference also had a doctoral consortium, and 14 doctoral proposals were accepted.

Split over five volumes, the proceedings aggregate the best contributions received and presented at xAI 2025, describing recent approaches, methods, and techniques for explainability. The acceptance rate has been roughly 40 per cent, with 96 accepted papers for the main track. The accepted contributions were selected through a rigorous, single-blind peer-review process. Each article received at least three reviews, with an average of four reviews per paper, from more than 300 scholars in academia and industry. All accepted research contributions are included in these proceedings and their authors were invited to give oral presentations.

Several thematic sessions were organised, each proposed and chaired by various researchers. A parallel track was organised for work in progress, specifically preliminary novel research studies relevant to xAI, which were presented as posters during the event. A demo track was held, where researchers from academia and industry presented their software prototypes, focusing on explainability or real-world applications of explainable AI-based systems. A doctoral consortium was organised, with lecturers for PhD scholars who submitted their doctoral proposals on future research in XAI. Finally, two panel discussions were organised with renowned scholars in XAI, offering multidisciplinary views while inspiring the attendees with tangible recommendations to tackle challenges toward designing responsible, trustworthy AI-based technologies through explainable AI.

We would like to thank the volunteers who helped in the xAI 2025 organising committee, our local chair, Berrin Yanikoglu, and Pınar Karadayı Ataş. Thank you to the doctoral consortium chairs, Przemysław Biecek and Slawomir Nowarczyk, and the late-breaking work and demo chair Gitta Kutyniok. Also, a special thank you goes to Wojciech Samek, the keynote speaker for xAI 2025. A word of appreciation goes to the proposers of the special tracks and those who chaired them during the conference, and to all the senior chairs, including Charlie Abela, Christopher Anders, Omran Ayoub, Pietro Barbiero, Przemysław Biecek, Enrico Ferrari, Pascal Friederich, Francesco Giannini, Paolo Giudici, Julia Herbinger, Verena Klös, Tuwe Löfström, Gianmarco Mengaldo, Maurizio Mongelli, Anna Monreale, Grégoire Montavon, Francesca Naretto, Ann Nowe, Ruairi O'Reilly, Roberto Pellungrini, Alan Perotti, Salvatore Rinzivillo, Christin Seifert, Francesco Sovrano, Lenka Tětková, Giulia Vilone, Philipp Wintersberger, and Bartosz Zieliński. A word of appreciation goes to all the moderators and panellists of the two engaging sessions "Integrating XAI in industry processes challenges for responsible AI" and "From Explanations to Impact". Special thanks go to the researchers and practitioners who submitted their work, the various program committee members who provided valuable feedback during the peer-review process, and all who attended the event, making it a fantastic networking opportunity to share findings and learn from one another as a community.

July 2025

Riccardo Guidotti
Ute Schmid
Luca Longo

Organization

Programme Committee Chairs

Riccardo Guidotti — University of Pisa, Italy
Ute Schmid — University of Bamberg, Germany

Doctoral Consortium Chairs

Przemysław Biecek — Warsaw University of Technology, Poland
Slawomir Nowarczyk — Halmstad University, Sweden

Late-Breaking Work and Demo Chair

Gitta Kutyniok — LMU Munich, Germany

Local Chairs

Berrin Yanikoglu — Sabancı University, Turkey
Pınar Karadayı Ataş — Istanbul Arel University, Turkey

General Chair

Luca Longo — Technological University Dublin, Ireland

Steering Committee

Sebastian Lapuschkin — Fraunhofer Heinrich Hertz Institute, Germany
Paolo Giudici — University of Pavia, Italy
Luca Longo — Technological University Dublin, Ireland
Christin Seifert — University of Marburg, Germany
Grégoire Montavon — Freie Universität Berlin, Germany

Programme Committee

Ad Feelders	Utrecht University, Netherlands
Adrian Byrne	CeADAR UCD/Idiro Analytics, Ireland
Alan Perotti	CENTAI Institute, Italy
Alberto Fernández	University of Granada, Spain
Alberto Freitas	University of Porto, Portugal
Alberto Tonda	INRAE, France
Alessandro Antonucci	IDSIA, Switzerland
Alessandro Renda	Università degli Studi di Firenze, Italy
Alex Freitas	University of Kent, UK
Alexander Schulz	Bielefeld University, Germany
Alexandros Doumanoglou	Information Technologies Institute, Greece
Amparo Alonso-Betanzos	University of A Coruña, Spain
André Artelt	Bielefeld University, Germany
André Panisson	CENTAI Institute, Italy
Andrea Apicella	University of Naples Federico II, Italy
Andrea Campagner	Università degli Studi di Milano-Bicocca, Italy
Andrea Passerini	University of Trento, Italy
Andrea Pazienza	NTT DATA Italia SpA & A3K Srl, Italy
Andrea Pugnana	University of Pisa, Italy
Andreas Holzinger	University of Natural Resources and Life Sciences, Vienna, Austria
Andreas Theissler	Aalen University of Applied Sciences, Germany
Andres Paez	Universidad de los Andes, Colombia
Andrew Lensen	Victoria University of Wellington, New Zealand
Angela Lombardi	Politecnico di Bari, Italy
Angelica Liguori	ICAR-CNR, Italy
Ann Nowe	Vrije Universiteit Brussel, Belgium
Anna Monreale	University of Pisa, Italy
Annalisa Appice	Università degli Studi di Bari Aldo Moro, Italy
Antonio Mastropietro	Università di Pisa, Italy
Antonio Moreno	Universitat Rovira i Virgili, Spain
Antonio Jesús Banegas-Luna	Universidad Católica de Murcia, Spain
Anurag Koul	Microsoft Research, USA
Arianna Agosto	University of Pavia, Italy
Aris Anagnostopoulos	Sapienza University of Rome, Italy
Astrid Rakow	German Aerospace Center (DLR) e.V., Germany
Athanasios Voulodimos	University of West Attica, Greece
Autilia Vitiello	University of Naples Federico II, Italy
Axel-Cyrille Ngonga Ngomo	Paderborn University, Germany
Barbara Hammer	Bielefeld University, Germany

Bartosz Zieliński	Jagiellonian University, Poland
Benoît Frénay	Université de Namur, Belgium
Bernard Zenko	Jožef Stefan Institute, Slovenia
Bettina Finzel	Otto-Friedrich-Universität Bamberg, Germany
Björn-Hergen Laabs	Universität zu Lübeck, Germany
Bruno Martins	INESC-ID - Instituto Superior Técnico, University of Lisbon, Portugal
Bruno Veloso	University of Porto & LIAAD - INESC TEC, Portugal
Carlo Metta	University of Florence, Italy
Carlos Soares	University of Porto, Portugal
Caroline Petitjean	Université de Rouen - LITIS EA 4108, France
Carsten Schulte	University of Paderborn, Germany
Caterina Senette	IIT-CNR, Italy
Cèsar Ferri	Universitat Politècnica de València, Spain
Charlie Abela	University of Malta, Malta
Chiara Renso	ISTI-CNR Pisa, Italy
Chirag Agarwal	University of Illinois Chicago, USA
Christian Lovis	University Hospitals of Geneva, Switzerland
Christin Seifert	University of Marburg, Germany
Christoph Schommer	University of Luxembourg, Luxembourg
Christophe Labreuche	Thales R&T, France
Christopher Anders	Technische Universität Berlin, Germany
Christos Dimitrakakis	University of Neuchâtel, Switzerland
Ciara Heavin	University College Cork, Ireland
Clemens Dubslaff	Eindhoven University of Technology, Netherlands
Corrado Mencar	Università degli Studi di Bari Aldo Moro, Italy
Damiano Verda	Rulex Innovation Labs Srl, Italy
Dariusz Brzezinski	Poznań University of Technology, Poland
Dave Braines	IBM United Kingdom Ltd., UK
David Leake	Indiana University, USA
David H. Glass	University of Ulster, UK
Diego Borro	CEIT and University of Navarra, Spain
Dino Ienco	IRSTEA, France
Domenico Talia	University of Calabria, Italy
Donato Malerba	Università degli Studi di Bari Aldo Moro, Italy
Duarte Folgado	Associação Fraunhofer Portugal Research, Portugal
Edel Garcia	CCG, Portugal
Eliana Pastor	Politecnico di Torino, Italy
Elio Masciari	University of Naples Federico II, Italy
Elvio Gilberto Amparore	Università di Torino, Italy

Emmanuel Müller	TU Dortmund University, Germany
Enea Parimbelli	University of Pavia, Italy
Enrico Ferrari	Rulex Innovation Labs Srl, Italy
Erasmo Purificato	Joint Research Centre, European Commission, Italy
Fabian Fumagalli	Bielefeld University, Germany
Fabio Fassetti	University of Calabria, Italy
Fabrizio Angiulli	University of Calabria, Italy
Fabrizio Marozzo	University of Calabria, Italy
Federico Cabitza	Università degli Studi di Milano-Bicocca, Italy
Florije Ismaili	South East European University, North Macedonia
Floris Bex	Utrecht University, Netherlands
Francesca Naretto	Scuola Normale Superiore, Italy
Francesco Flammini	University of Florence, Italy
Francesco Giannini	Scuola Normale Superiore, Italy
Francesco Guerra	Università di Modena e Reggio Emilia, Italy
Francesco Marcelloni	Università di Pisa, Italy
Francesco Sovrano	University of Zurich, Switzerland
Francesco Spinnato	University of Pisa, Italy
Françoise Fessant	Orange Labs, France
Frederic Jurie	University of Caen Normandie, France
Gabriella Casalino	Università degli Studi di Bari Aldo Moro, Italy
Ganna Grynova	University of Birmingham, UK
Georgiana Ifrim	University College Dublin, Ireland
Gesina Schwalbe	University of Lübeck, Germany
Gianmarco Mengaldo	National University of Singapore, Singapore
Giovanna Dimitri	University of Siena, Italy
Giovanni Ciatto	University of Bologna, Italy
Giulia Vilone	Technological University Dublin, Ireland
Giulio Rossetti	KDD Lab ISTI-CNR, Italy
Giuseppe Casalicchio	Ludwig-Maximilians-Universität München, Germany
Giuseppe Manco	ICAR-CNR, Italy
Giuseppe Marra	KU Leuven, Belgium
Gizem Gezici	Scuola Normale Superiore, Italy
Gjergji Kasneci	Technical University of Munich, Germany
Grégoire Montavon	Freie Universität Berlin, Germany
Grzegorz J. Nalepa	Jagiellonian University, Poland
Guido Bologna	University of Applied Sciences and Arts of Western Switzerland, Switzerland
Hamed Ayoobi	Imperial College London, UK

Heike Buhl	Paderborn University, Germany
Hendrik Baier	Eindhoven University of Technology, Netherlands
Henning Müller	HES-SO and University of Geneva, Switzerland
Henrik Boström	KTH Royal Institute of Technology, Sweden
Henrique Lopes Cardoso	University of Porto, Portugal
Heta Gandhi	Nurix Therapeutics, USA
Howard Hamilton	University of Regina, Canada
Ilir Jusufi	Blekinge Institute of Technology, Sweden
Iordanis Koutsopoulos	Athens University of Economics and Business, Greece
Isacco Beretta	Università di Pisa, Italy
Isel Grau	Eindhoven University of Technology, Netherlands
Jaesik Choi	Korea Advanced Institute of Science and Technology, South Korea
Jan Arne Telle	University of Bergen, Norway
Jane Courtney	Technological University Dublin, Ireland
Jaromir Savelka	Carnegie Mellon University, USA
Jasper S. van der Waa	TNO, Netherlands
Jaumin Ajdari	South East European University, North Macedonia
Jenny Benois-Pineau	LaBRI Université de Bordeaux, CNRS, France
Jérôme Guzzi	IDSIA, Switzerland
Jerzy Stefanowski	Poznań University of Technology, Poland
Jesús Alcalá-Fdez	University of Granada, Spain
João Gama	Porto University, Portugal
Jörg Hoffmann	Saarland University, Germany
Johannes Fürnkranz	Johannes Kepler University Linz, Austria
Johannes Langer	University of Bamberg, Germany
John Gilligan	Technological University Dublin, Ireland
John Lawrence	University of Dundee, UK
Jonathan Ben-Naim	Institut de Recherche en Informatique de Toulouse (IRIT-CNRS), France
Jonathan Dunne	IBM, Ireland
Jose Juarez	Universidad de Murcia, Spain
Jose M. Molina	Universidad Carlos III de Madrid, Spain
Jose Paulo Marques dos Santos	University of Maia, Portugal
Josep Domingo-Ferrer	Universitat Rovira i Virgili, Spain
Juan Corchado	University of Salamanca, Spain
Juan A. Recio-Garcia	Universidad Complutense de Madrid, Spain
Julia Herbinger	Ludwig-Maximilians-Universität München, Germany
Julien Delaunay	Université Rennes, France

Juri Belikov	Tallinn University of Technology, Estonia
Kary Främling	Umeå University, Sweden
Katharina Rohlfing	University of Paderborn, Germany
Katharina Weitz	Fraunhofer Heinrich Hertz Institute, Germany
Kirsten Thommes	Padeborn University, Germany
Konstantinos Makantasis	University of Malta, Malta
Kristoffer Wickstrøm	UiT The Arctic University of Norway, Norway
Larisa Soldatova	Goldsmiths, University of London, UK
Lars Kai Hansen	Technical University of Denmark, Denmark
Lenka Tětková	Technical University of Denmark, Denmark
Luca Ferragina	University of Calabria, Italy
Luca Oneto	University of Genoa, Italy
Lucas Rizzo	Technological University Dublin, Ireland
Lucie Charlotte Magister	University of Cambridge, UK
Luis Galárraga	Inria, France
Luis Macedo	University of Coimbra, Portugal
Luís Rosado	Fraunhofer Portugal AICOS, Portugal
Maguelonne Teisseire	Irstea - UMR Tetis, France
Malika Bendechache	University of Galway, Ireland
Manuel Mazzara	Innopolis University, Russia
Marcelo G. Manzato	University of São Paulo, Brazil
Marcilio De Souto	LIFO/University of Orléans, France
Marcin Luckner	Warsaw University of Technology, Poland
Marco Baioletti	Università degli Studi di Perugia, Italy
Marco Podda	University of Pisa, Italy
Marco Polignano	Università degli Studi di Bari Aldo Moro, Italy
Maria Kaselimi	National Technical University of Athens, Greece
Maria Riveiro	Jönköping University, Sweden
Marija Bezbradica	Dublin City University, Ireland
Mario Brcic	University of Zagreb, Croatia
Mario Giovanni C. A. Cimino	University of Pisa, Italy
Mark Hall	Airbus, UK
Markus Löcher	Berlin School of Economics and Law, Germany
Marta Marchiori Manerba	Università di Pisa, Italy
Martin Atzmueller	Osnabrück University, Germany
Martin Gjoreski	Università della Svizzera italiana, Switzerland
Martin Holeňa	Czech Academy of Sciences, Czechia
Martin Jullum	Norwegian Computing Center, Norway
Marvin Wright	Leibniz Institute for Prevention Research and Epidemiology - BIPS & University of Bremen, Germany
Massimo Guarascio	ICAR-CNR, Italy

Mathieu Roche	Cirad, TETIS, France
Mattia Cerrato	Johannes Gutenberg University Mainz, Germany
Mattia Setzu	University of Pisa, Italy
Maurizio Mongelli	CNR-IEIIT, Italy
Mauro Dragoni	Fondazione Bruno Kessler, Italy
Md Shajalal	University of Siegen, Germany
Megha Khosla	Delft University of Technology, Netherlands
Meiyi Ma	Vanderbilt University, USA
Melinda Gervasio	SRI International, USA
Mexhid Ferati	Linnaeus University, Sweden
Michail Mamalakis	University of Cambridge, UK
Michelangelo Ceci	Università degli Studi di Bari Aldo Moro, Italy
Miguel Couceiro	Inria, France
Miguel A. Gutiérrez-Naranjo	University of Seville, Spain
Miguel Angel Patricio	Universidad Carlos III de Madrid, Spain
Mirna Saad	Scuola Universitaria Professionale della Svizzera Italiana, Switzerland
Myra Spiliopoulou	Otto von Guericke University Magdeburg, Germany
Nick Bassiliades	Aristotle University of Thessaloniki, Greece
Nicolas Boutry	EPITA Research Laboratory (LRE), Le Kremlin-Bicêtre, France
Niki van Stein	Leiden University, Netherlands
Nikolay Tcholtchev	Fraunhofer FOKUS, Germany
Nikos Deligiannis	Vrije Universiteit Brussel, Netherlands
Nikos Karacapilidis	University of Patras, Greece
Nirmalie Wiratunga	Robert Gordon University, UK
Nuno Silva	INESC TEC & ISEP - IPP, Portugal
Oliver Eberle	Technische Universität Berlin, Germany
Oliver Ray	University of Bristol, UK
Omran Ayoub	Scuola Universitaria Professionale della Svizzera Italiana, Switzerland
Özgür Lütfü Özcep	University of Hamburg, Germany
Pance Panov	Jožef Stefan Institute, Slovenia
Paola Cerchiello	University of Pavia, Italy
Paolo Giudici	University of Pavia, Italy
Paolo Pagnottoni	University of Insubria, Italy
Paolo Soda	Umeå University, Sweden
Pascal Friederich	Karlsruhe Institute of Technology, Germany
Pascal Germain	Inria, France
Paulo Cortez	University of Minho, Portugal
Paulo Lisboa	Liverpool John Moores University, UK

Paulo Novais	University of Minho, Portugal
Pedro Sequeira	SRI International, USA
Peter Kieseberg	St. Pölten University of Applied Sciences, Austria
Peter Vamplew	Federation University Australia, Australia
Philipp Cimiano	Bielefeld University, Germany
Prasanna Balaprakash	Oak Ridge National Laboratory, USA
Przemysław Biecek	Polish Academy of Sciences, University of Wrocław, Poland
Renato De Leone	Università di Camerino, Italy
Ricardo Prudêncio	Universidade Federal de Pernambuco, Brazil
Riccardo Cantini	University of Calabria, Italy
Richard Jiang	Lancaster University, UK
Rita P. Ribeiro	University of Porto, Portugal
Rob Brennan	University College Dublin, Ireland
Roberta Calegari	Alma Mater Studiorum–Università di Bologna, Italy
Roberto Capobianco	Sapienza University of Rome, Italy
Roberto Interdonato	CIRAD - UMR TETIS, France
Roberto Pellungrini	University of Pisa, Italy
Roberto Prevete	University of Naples Federico II, Italy
Rocio Gonzalez-Diaz	University of Seville, Spain
Romain Bourqui	Université Bordeaux 1, Inria Bordeaux-Sud Ouest, France
Romain Giot	LaBRI Université de Bordeaux, CNRS, France
Rosa Lillo	Universidad Carlos III de Madrid, Spain
Rosa Meo	University of Turin, Italy
Rosina Weber	Drexel University, USA
Ruairi O'Reilly	Munster Technological University, Ireland
Ruben Laplaza	École Polytechnique Fédérale de Lausanne, Switzerland
Ruggero G. Pensa	University of Turin, Italy
Rui Mao	Nanyang Technological University, Singapore
Sabatina Criscuolo	University of Naples Federico II, Italy
Salvatore Greco	Politecnico di Torino, Italy
Salvatore Rinzivillo	ISTI-CNR Pisa, Italy
Salvatore Ruggieri	Università di Pisa, Italy
Sandra Mitrović	IDSIA, Switzerland
Sang Won Baae	Stevens Institute of Technology, USA
Santiago Quintana Amate	Airbus, UK
Sebastian Lapuschkin	Fraunhofer Heinrich Hertz Institute, Germany
Severin Kacianka	Technical University of Munich, Germany
Shahina Begum	Mälardalen University, Sweden

Shai Ben-David	University of Waterloo, Canada
Shujun Li	University of Kent, UK
Silvia Giordano	Scuola Universitaria Professionale della Svizzera Italiana, Switzerland
Simon See	Nvidia, Singapore
Simona Nisticò	University of Calabria, Italy
Simone Piaggesi	University of Bologna, Italy
Simone Stumpf	University of Glasgow, UK
Slawomir Nowaczyk	Halmstad University, Sweden
Sriraam Natarajan	University of Texas at Dallas, USA
Stefano Bistarelli	Università di Perugia, Italy
Stefano Mariani	Università di Modena e Reggio Emilia, Italy
Stefano Melacci	University of Siena, Italy
Stéphane Galland	Université de Technologie de Belfort-Montbéliard, France
Sylvio Barbon Junior	University of Trieste, Italy
Szymon Bobek	AGH University of Science and Technology, Poland
Takafumi Nakanishi	Musashino University, Japan
Tania Cerquitelli	Politecnico di Torino, Italy
Telmo Silva Filho	University of Bristol, UK
Teodor Chiaburu	Berliner Hochschule für Technik, Germany
Thach Le Nguyen	University College Dublin, Ireland
Thomas Guyet	Inria, France
Thomas Lukasiewicz	University of Oxford, UK
Tiago Pinto	Universidade de Trás-os-Montes e Alto Douro/INESC-TEC, Portugal
Tjitze Rienstra	Maastricht University, Netherlands
Tomáš Kliegr	Prague University of Economics and Business, Czechia
Tommaso Turchi	University of Pisa, Italy
Tran Cao Son	New Mexico State University, USA
Tuan Pham	Queen Mary University of London, UK
Tuwe Löfström	Jönköping University, Sweden
Udo Schlegel	University of Konstanz, Germany
Ulf Johansson	Jönköping University, Sweden
Vân Anh Huynh-Thu	University of Liège, Belgium
Vedran Sabol	Know-Center GmbH, Austria
Verena Klös	Carl von Ossietzky Universität Oldenburg, Germany
Vincent Andrearczyk	HES-SO, Switzerland
Vincenzo Moscato	University of Naples, Italy

Vincenzo Pasquadibisceglie	Università degli Studi di Bari Aldo Moro, Italy
Weiru Liu	University of Bristol, UK
Werner Bailer	JOANNEUM Research, Austria
Wojciech Samek	Technical University of Berlin, Germany
Yazan Mualla	Université de Technologie de Belfort-Montbéliard, France
Zahraa S. Abdallah	University of Bristol, UK

Contents – Part IV

XAI in Computer Vision

Comparing XAI Explanations and Synthetic Data Augmentation Strategies in Neuroimaging AI 3
  Danilo Danese, Giuseppe Fasano, Angela Lombardi, Eugenio Di Sciascio, and Tommaso Di Noia

Superpixel Correlation for Explainable Image Classification 27
  Vahidin Hasić, Amar Halilović, and Senka Krivić

On Background Bias of Post-Hoc Concept Embeddings in Computer Vision DNNs 45
  Gesina Schwalbe, Georgii Mikriukov, Edgar Heinert, Stavros Gerolymatos, Mert Keser, Alois Knoll, Matthias Rottmann, and Annika Mütze

Explaining Vision GNNs: A Semantic and Visual Analysis of Graph-Based Image Classification 72
  Nikolaos Chaidos, Angeliki Dimitriou, Nikolaos Spanos, Athanasios Voulodimos, and Giorgos Stamou

Counterfactuals in XAI

HalCECE: A Framework for Explainable Hallucination Detection Through Conceptual Counterfactuals in Image Captioning 87
  Maria Lymperaiou, Giorgos Filandrianos, Angeliki Dimitriou, Athanasios Voulodimos, and Giorgos Stamou

Diffusion Counterfactuals for Image Regressors 112
  Trung Duc Ha and Sidney Bender

Mitigating Text Toxicity with Counterfactual Generation 135
  Milan Bhan, Jean-Noel Vittaut, Nina Achache, Victor Legrand, Annabelle Blangero, Nicolas Chesneau, Juliette Murris, and Marie-Jeanne Lesot

Guiding LLMs to Generate High-Fidelity and High-Quality Counterfactual Explanations for Text Classification 158
  Van Bach Nguyen, Christin Seifert, and Jörg Schlötterer

Exploring Ensemble Strategies for Graph Counterfactual Explanations 177
Mario Alfonso Prado-Romero, Bardh Prenkaj, and Giovanni Stilo

Explainable Sequential Decision Making

Leveraging XAI Techniques for Context-Aware Energy Consumption
Forecasting 205
Brígida Teixeira, Tiago Pinto, and Zita Vale

ConformaSegment: A Conformal Prediction-Based, Uncertainty-Aware,
and Model-Agnostic Explainability Framework for Time-Series
Forecasting 218
*Fatima Rabia Yapicioglu, Meltem Aksoy, Tuwe Löfström, Fabio Vitali,
and Alberto Rigenti*

FLEXtime: Filterbank Learning to Explain Time Series 243
*Thea Brüsch, Kristoffer Knutsen Wickstrøm, Mikkel N. Schmidt,
Robert Jenssen, and Tommy Sonne Alstrøm*

From Text to Space: Mapping Abstract Spatial Models in LLMs During
a Grid-World Navigation Task 268
Nicolas Martorell

Class-Dependent Perturbation Effects in Evaluating Time Series
Attributions 292
Gregor Baer, Isel Grau, Chao Zhang, and Pieter Van Gorp

Explainable AI in Finance & Legal Frameworks for XAI Technologies

XAI In Fraud Detection: A Causal Perspective 317
Katiuscka van Veen, Faizan Ahmed, and Maurice van Keulen

Detecting Fraud in Financial Networks: A Semi-supervised GNN
Approach with Granger-Causal Explanations 330
Linh Nguyen, Marcel Boersma, and Erman Acar

Legal Requirements, Trust Issues and Engineering Challenges -
A Multi-disciplinary Case for User-Specific Explainability 354
Merle Fairhurst, Katharina Kaesling, and Verena Klös

Explainable Fairness in Mortgage Lending 378
Golnoosh Babaei, Paolo Giudici, and Lunshuai Wu

Cyber Risk Management with Time Varying Artificial Intelligence Models 399
  Paolo Giudici, Marco Pirra, and Rasha Zieni

Author Index 419

XAI in Computer Vision

Comparing XAI Explanations and Synthetic Data Augmentation Strategies in Neuroimaging AI

Danilo Danese[✉], Giuseppe Fasano, Angela Lombardi[✉], Eugenio Di Sciascio, and Tommaso Di Noia

Department of Electrical and Information Engineering, Politecnico di Bari, 70125 Bari, BA, Italy
{danilo.danese,giuseppe.fasano,angela.lombardi,eugeniodi.Sciascio, tommasodi.noia}@poliba.it

Abstract. Brain age, a biomarker of neurological health, is widely used in neuroimaging for early detection of neurodegenerative diseases. While deep learning models have shown promise in brain age prediction from MRI, data imbalance and model interpretability remain key challenges.

This study investigates the impact of data augmentation (DA) on both predictive accuracy and explanation stability in convolutional neural networks (CNNs) for brain age prediction. We compare three training strategies: (i) a baseline model, (ii) a model augmented with real MRI scans from OASIS-3, and (iii) a model trained with synthetic data generated by a diffusion model. Model performance is evaluated using mean absolute error (MAE), while interpretability is assessed through Explainable AI (XAI) methods, including DeepSHAP, Grad-CAM, and Occlusion.

Our findings indicate that synthetic augmentation improves predictive accuracy, particularly for underrepresented age groups (individuals aged 40-80 years), while real-data augmentation provides more stable feature attributions. However, differences in XAI methods suggest that explanation reliability varies across training strategies.

These results highlight the trade-offs between accuracy and interpretability in AI-driven neuroimaging, emphasizing the need for balanced augmentation strategies to develop clinically trustworthy models.

Keywords: XAI · Brain Age Prediction · Data Augmentation

1 Introduction

Understanding the relationship between brain structure and aging is a key challenge in computational neuroscience, with significant implications for neurological health assessment and early disease detection [8]. One approach that has gained increasing attention is brain age prediction, which refers to the estimation of an individual's biological brain age based on neuroimaging data, typically using structural MRI scans. This estimated brain age is then compared to the individual's chronological age. A significant discrepancy—often referred to as the brain age gap—can indicate atypical brain aging and may serve as an early biomarker for neurological or psychiatric conditions [16].

Predicting brain age is relevant because it provides a quantifiable and interpretable measure of brain health at the individual level. It enables the identification of accelerated or delayed brain aging, which has been linked to cognitive decline, neurodegenerative diseases, and mental disorders [3]. As such, brain age can support early diagnosis, disease monitoring, and the development of personalized medical interventions [4,12,38].

Deep learning, particularly Convolutional Neural Networks (CNNs), has demonstrated exceptional performance in brain age prediction by capturing complex spatial patterns in structural and functional neuroimaging data [14]. CNNs excel in extracting hierarchical features from brain scans, allowing models to learn age-related structural variations in an end-to-end fashion. However, while these models achieve high predictive accuracy, their decisions remain opaque, raising concerns about their clinical applicability and reliability [23,32].

A significant challenge in brain age prediction using deep learning is the heterogeneity of publicly available neuroimaging datasets. These datasets often lack desirable statistical properties, such as a uniform distribution of the target variable, age, which can lead to biased model training and reduced generalizability. Additionally, datasets are typically aggregated from multiple sites, introducing significant variability in imaging parameters, acquisition protocols, and scanner characteristics [30,46]. This heterogeneity complicates model training and interpretation, as differences in data characteristics can influence both predictive performance and the reliability of model explanations.

To address this limitation, XAI methods have been increasingly adopted to provide insights into model decision-making. XAI techniques offer a means to interpret which features contribute most to predictions, making AI-driven decisions more transparent and understandable for clinicians and neuroscientists [1,48]. In the context of brain age prediction, interpretability is crucial for verifying that the model is basing its predictions on meaningful neurobiological features rather than spurious correlations [32]. Beyond clinical validation, XAI plays a fundamental role in regulatory compliance, ensuring that AI models adhere to ethical guidelines and fairness standards [11]. Furthermore, XAI aligns with the Human-Centered AI (HCAI) paradigm, which emphasizes the development of AI systems that prioritize human interpretability, usability, and trustworthiness, making AI-based diagnostics more accessible and reliable [31,37].

Despite the importance of interpretability, the stability of XAI-based explanations under different data manipulations, particularly augmentation, remains an open question. Data augmentation (DA) techniques are essential in deep learning for neuroimaging, allowing models to learn from different variations of brain scans and reducing overfitting. Traditional augmentation methods include spatial transformations and intensity perturbations, but more recent approaches leverage generative models such as diffusion models and autoencoders to synthesize realistic brain structures [26]. These methods not only enhance model performance but also introduce potential shifts in feature importance maps, raising concerns about the consistency of explanations across augmented versions of the same brain scan. If XAI methods produce inconsistent explanations under different augmentation strategies, their reliability in guiding clinical decisions becomes questionable.

In this exploratory study, we compare the explanations derived from different XAI methods when CNN-based brain age prediction models are trained with different augmentation strategies applied to a multisite dataset. We systematically assess how different augmentation techniques influence explanation stability and whether certain augmentation strategies lead to more consistent feature attributions.

2 Related Work

2.1 XAI in Brain Age Prediction

Deep learning models, particularly CNNs, have been extensively applied to brain age prediction, leveraging their ability to learn hierarchical features from neuroimaging data. However, the interpretability of these models remains a key concern, necessitating the integration of XAI techniques [47]. Post hoc XAI methods aim to highlight the most influential regions in an input image that contribute to the model's decision. These methods include relevance maps and saliency maps, which generate visual explanations by attributing importance to different regions of the input. Specific techniques such as Grad-CAM [41], Layer-wise Relevance Propagation [5], DeepSHAP [33], and Occlusion [53] provide different approaches to computing and visualizing these attributions, facilitating human understanding of AI-driven predictions.

While relevance maps and saliency maps are widely used in natural image classification, their application in medical imaging presents unique challenges. Unlike natural images, where feature importance aligns with human intuition (e.g., highlighting the eyes in cat images), neuroimaging-based explanations lack an intuitive baseline, even for experts. This limitation can introduce biases in interpretation, such as confirmation bias, where researchers selectively validate results based on preconceived expectations [24]. To mitigate this, recent studies emphasize the need for quantitative evaluations of relevance maps, linking them to interpretable neurobiological features [20].

Gradient-based methods, such as Grad-CAM, have been employed to visualize the contribution of specific brain regions in CNN-based age prediction models [54]. These methods have been particularly useful in identifying cortical and subcortical regions associated with age-related changes. Similarly, Deep SHAP combines SHAP values with deep learning frameworks to estimate feature importance across multiple layers, providing robust attributions [9]. Occlusion-based methods, on the other hand, systematically mask regions of the input image to observe the impact on model predictions, helping to pinpoint critical areas for classification [49]. However, most studies focus on group-level explanations, averaging heatmaps across multiple subjects [29].

Most studies in the literature primarily analyze group-level relevance maps, which help identify generalizable patterns but fail to capture the nuances of individual variability. As a result, the specific characteristics of explanations at the individual level remain underexplored. A more detailed investigation of these individual differences is essential to improve the reliability and clinical relevance of AI-generated explanations for personalized decision-making.

2.2 Data Augmentation with Generative AI

Despite the increasing availability of large datasets, many fields still struggle with limited labeled data. Healthcare presents a particularly challenging case, where researchers often work with small patient cohorts, while analyzing high-dimensional data such as neuroimaging 3D scans containing millions of voxels. This combination creates poor population representation and makes traditional statistical analyses [7]. Deep learning models, which have shown remarkable success across various applications, require extensive training data to generalize effectively and avoid overfitting [18]. When working with small datasets, DA becomes a crucial technique to improve model performance by synthetically expanding the training set.

The simplest form of DA applies basic transformations to existing images, such as adding Gaussian noise or cropping, while maintaining the original labels [28]. Though useful, these techniques have limitations: some transformations may provide little information value or even introduce bias [42]. Evaluating the relevance of augmented data becomes particularly challenging with complex datasets, often requiring expert assessment. Imbalanced datasets present another challenge, as they tend to bias algorithms toward overrepresented classes. Oversampling techniques create synthetic samples by interpolating minority class data points. Some methods [21,36] refine this by generating samples near decision boundaries using nearest neighbours or support vector machines to reduce misclassification. However, they struggle to scale in high-dimensional spaces [6,15].

Geometric transformations remain fundamental in medical image augmentation. Affine transformations preserve structural integrity, making them suitable for tasks like lesion alignment. Meanwhile, elastic deformations simulate anatomical variability and motion artifacts, enhancing model robustness in segmentation tasks [35]. Erasing transformations, which obscure image regions by replacing them with fixed values or noise, can help models learn more robust features [10]. However, excessive modifications risk distorting critical pathological details, reducing clinical applicability. In neuroimaging, these can distort critical brain structures, disrupt symmetry, or alter intensity distributions essential for diagnosis. For example, flipping a brain image might break its left-right symmetry, making it less useful for deep learning training and making it anatomically inconsistent. Moreover, pixel's color adjustments, can alter intesity distributions of gray and white matter, losing clinically relevant information [50].

These limitations push the field toward more specialized approaches that preserve anatomical accuracy. Synthetic sample generation offers a more advanced approach to DA, where instead of simple image manipulations, these methods create entirely new data points, increasing dataset diversity and addressing class imbalances.

2.3 Generative Models for Data Augmentation

Deep generative models [18] aim to learn the underlying probability distribution of data by mapping a low-dimensional latent variable $z \in \mathbb{R}^d$, sampled from a prior distribution $p(z)$, to a high-dimensional data point $x \in \mathbb{R}^D$ via a function $g : z \to x$. The objective is to ensure that the generated sample $g(z)$ is similar to a true data sample taken from $p(x)$. While various models differ in their learning strategies, they all must handle a fundamental trade-off: achieving fast sampling, producing high-quality outputs, and covering the full diversity of the data distribution. This challenge is often referred to as the *generative learning trilemma* [51]. In recent years, three key architectures have emerged in the field of deep generative models: Generative Adversarial Networks (GANs), Variational Autoencoders (VAEs), and, more recently, Diffusion Models.

GANs. [19] consist of two competing neural networks: a generator G and a discriminator D. The generator maps a latent variable z sampled from a prior distribution $p(z)$ to a synthetic data sample, while the discriminator attempts to distinguish real data from generated samples. The training process follows a minimax game, where the generator aims to deceive the discriminator, and the discriminator learns to improve its classification accuracy. GANs have demonstrated effectiveness in generating high-quality medical images, making them a valuable tool for augmenting datasets across modalities such as MRI, CT, and X-ray [2,52]. However, they present challenges, including training instability and mode collapse, where the generator produces limited variations of samples.

VAEs. [27] take a probabilistic approach to generative modeling, learning a latent representation of the data through Bayesian inference. They approximate the intractable posterior $p(z|x)$ with a simpler distribution $q_\phi(z|x)$ and optimize the evidence lower bound (ELBO), which balances reconstruction accuracy and regularization:

$$\mathcal{L}_{\text{VAE}} = \mathbb{E}_{z \sim q_\phi(z|x)}[\log p_\theta(x|z)] - D_{\text{KL}}(q_\phi(z|x) \,\|\, p(z)) \tag{1}$$

where the first term represents the reconstruction loss, ensuring the generated samples resemble real data, while the Kullback-Leibler (KL) divergence term regularizes the latent space by encouraging similarity to the prior distribution. VAEs offer stable training and broad data coverage but often generate blurry images due to their probabilistic nature [27]. To mitigate these limitations, several variations have been developed to improve stability and control over the generated data.

Diffusion models (DMs). [40] take a different approach by modeling the data generation process as a gradual diffusion (or noise injection) followed by a learned denoising process. The forward diffusion process gradually adds Gaussian noise to a data sample x_0, leading to a sequence of latent variables:

$$q(x_t|x_{t-1}) = \mathcal{N}\big(\sqrt{\alpha_t}\, x_{t-1},\, \beta_t \mathbf{I}\big),$$
$$q(x_{1:T}|x_0) = \prod_{t=1}^{T} q(x_t|x_{t-1}), \qquad (2)$$

where $\beta_t \in [0,1]$ is the noise variance at step t, and $\alpha_t = 1 - \beta_t$.

The reverse (denoising) process is learned to recover the original data from pure noise. This is formulated as:

$$p_\theta(x_{0:T}) = p(x_T) \prod_{t=1}^{T} p_\theta(x_{t-1}|x_t), \qquad (3)$$

with the reverse transitions modeled as:

$$p_\theta(x_{t-1}|x_t) = \mathcal{N}\big(\mu(x_t, t),\, \Sigma(x_t, t)\big). \qquad (4)$$

Training involves maximizing an ELBO similar to that in VAEs, aligning the learned reverse process with the true denoising distribution.

Diffusion models have recently shown exceptional performance in generating high-quality, realistic images, achieving superior sample quality and mode coverage compared to both GANs and VAEs. However, they typically require a large number of steps for the reverse process, resulting in slower sample generation compared to the latter. Since their introduction, DM have been improved in efficiency and generative quality. In [22], the authors introduced denoising diffusion probabilistic models (DDPMs), which optimize a variational lower bound and leverage a reparameterization trick for more effective sampling. Subsequent works have addressed key limitations of DDPMs, including computational inefficiency and slow inference. [45] proposed score-based generative models, which reformulate the diffusion process as a stochastic differential equation, leading to more flexible sampling strategies. Several architectures [51] have been designed to tackle the generative learning trilemma, helping diffusion models secure their place as the leading choice in the field. Different strategies have been explored to speed up sampling, improve training stability, and balance the trade-off between efficiency and quality, even in the medical field [17]. At the same time, hybrid approaches [44] combining diffusion with other generative techniques have further strengthened their position as the preferred choice for high-quality synthesis.

3 Materials

3.1 OpenBHB

In this work, we used the OpenBHB[1] dataset, which includes 3,984 T1-weighted brain MRI scans from healthy individuals across 10 public datasets: IXI, ABIDE

---
[1] baobablab.github.io/bhb/dataset.

1, ABIDE 2, CoRR, GSP, Localizer, MPI-Leipzig, NAR, NPC, and RBP [13]. These scans were collected from 62 international sites, encompassing diverse populations from North America, Europe, and Asia. Variations in scanner types, acquisition protocols, and demographic factors such as age and sex within the training data can significantly impact the generalizability of machine learning models trained on neuroimaging data. The dataset covers a wide age range, from adolescents to older adults, with an average age of approximately 24.92 years (± 14.29). The sex distribution is relatively balanced, with 52.38% of male participants. The number of sites contributing to each dataset varies significantly, ranging from a single site in datasets such as IXI and MPI-Leipzig to 20 sites in ABIDE I, highlighting the dataset's diverse origins. Due to the heterogeneous structure of OpenBHB, it is well suited to support challenges in brain age prediction and to address potential biases arising from differences in imaging characteristics and acquisition sites.

OpenBHB offers separate training and validation sets, along with a private test set. For our study, we used the publicly available data, treating the training set as our training data and the validation set as our test data. This approach helps assess our algorithms' ability to generalize across different studies and populations, addressing potential biases from imaging characteristics and acquisition sites. The validation set in OpenBHB is divided into two parts: an internal test set with data from the same sites as the training set, and an external test set with data from five new sites not included in the training set. Both sets are created using stratified sampling based on age and sex, with the internal set also considering site differences. This setup allows us to evaluate models' performance on both familiar and new settings, testing their generalization capabilities.

The MRI scans in OpenBHB were obtained using 1.5 T and 3 T scanners, with varying manufacturers and acquisition parameters. The dataset provides three data types derived from these scans: Voxel-Based Morphometry (VBM), Surface-Based Morphometry (SBM), and quasi-raw (minimally preprocessed) data. Our study focused on the quasi-raw T1-weighted images and SBM indices obtained using FreeSurfer.

3.2 OASIS-3

The OASIS-3[2] dataset is a publicly available neuroimaging resource that compiles longitudinal MRI and PET imaging data along with clinical and cognitive assessments. It includes participants recruited through the Washington University Knight Alzheimer Disease Research Center, spanning a period of 15 years. The dataset comprises individuals across the adult lifespan, ranging in age from 42 to 97 years, including both cognitively healthy individuals and patients diagnosed with Alzheimer's disease (AD).

For our study, we focused exclusively on cognitively normal individuals and utilized only MRI scans. Our subset consists of 1,314 cognitively normal participants, with a mean age of 71.10 years (± 8.93), a minimum age of 42 years,

---

[2] sites.wustl.edu/oasisbrains/home/oasis-3.

and a maximum age of 97 years. The dataset was initially designed to support research in healthy aging and neurodegenerative disorders, offering extensive structural MRI data that enables the study of brain morphology across different age groups. The MRI scans in OASIS-3 were acquired using 3 T scanners, with variations in acquisition protocols and scanner manufacturers.

3.3 UK Biobank

In this study, we utilized synthetic brain MRI scans generated by a pretrained diffusion model [39]. This model was trained on a large dataset from the UK Biobank[3] (UKB), a population-based study that tracks the health and well-being of volunteer participants across the United Kingdom. Specifically, the diffusion model was trained using T1-weighted MRI scans from 31,740 healthy individuals, aged between 44 and 82 years, with an average age of 63.6 ± 7.5 years. The dataset includes 14,942 male participants, representing 47% of the total sample.

To enhance the realism and anatomical variability of the generated images, the model was conditioned on key brain morphology features, including ventricular cerebrospinal fluid volume and brain volume normalized for head size. Prior to conditioning, these variables were normalized using min-max scaling to ensure consistency in model training and generation. We generated 3,000 synthetic brain MRI scans by conditioning the Diffusion Model from [39] on age, ensuring a uniform distribution across the range of 44 to 82 years. This approach enabled the synthesis of anatomically plausible brain images while preserving population-level age variability. An overview of the data distribution is presented in Fig. 1.

4 Methodology

Our methodology follows a structured pipeline designed to investigate the impact of data augmentation on XAI-based explanations in brain age prediction. The key steps in our pipeline include:

- Dataset preprocessing: standard preprocessing steps such as bias field correction, spatial normalization, and intensity standardization are applied to ensure consistency across imaging data;
- Data augmentation strategies: three training setups are explored: (i) a baseline model trained on the original dataset, (ii) a model augmented with real data from an additional neuroimaging dataset (i.e., OASIS-3), and (iii) a model trained using synthetic brain MRIs. The synthetic data is generated through diffusion model inference, which synthesizes anatomically plausible brain scans by conditioning on age, thereby increasing data diversity and mitigating dataset imbalance;

---

[3] www.ukbiobank.ac.uk.

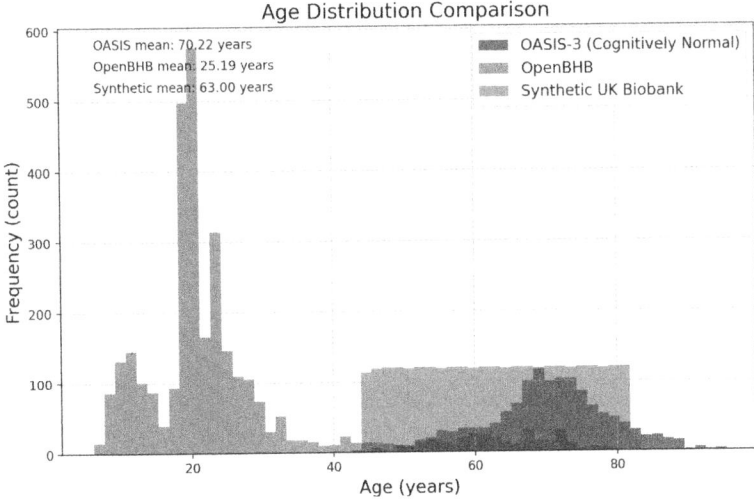

Fig. 1. Overview of the three datasets: OpenBHB contains healthy real patients; OASIS-3 has been subsampled to include only healthy subjects; Diffusion Model Synthetic samples conditioned on age, data derived from the UK Biobank.

- CNN model training: a 3D CNN architecture, optimized for neuroimaging data, is trained separately for each dataset configuration. Standard optimization techniques, including learning rate scheduling and data balancing, are employed to enhance model performance;
- CNN model test: CNN models trained using different training strategies are evaluated on an independent dataset of adult subjects to assess their performance and generalization ability, particularly in predicting brain age for an underrepresented age group in the original dataset;
- Explainability analysis: post hoc XAI methods, including Grad-CAM, Deep SHAP, and Occlusion, are applied to evaluate feature importance across different training setups. These explanations are compared across the three training setups, examining differences in feature attribution and stability of explanations under augmentation conditions. Additionally, the biological relevance of the features is analyzed at a regional level by assessing the correlation between the contribution of different brain regions and the target variable, i.e., the subjects' age.

These steps are further detailed in the following sections to provide a comprehensive understanding of the methodology and its implications.

4.1 Preprocessing

We followed a standardized pipeline on established neuroimaging tools to obtain minimally preprocessed neuroimaging data. First, we applied bias field correction using the ANTs[4] toolkit to mitigate artifacts, ensuring uniform intensity profiles across the images. Next, affine registration with 9 degrees of freedom (excluding shear transformations) was performed using FSL FLIRT[5] to align each scan to the MNI152 [34] template, standardizing spatial orientation across subjects. BET[6] was then applied to remove non-brain tissues (e.g., skull, cerebrospinal fluid), isolating brain structures for downstream analysis. The preprocessed images underwent spatial downsampling to optimize computational efficiency while retaining diagnostically relevant features. Each dimension of the 3D MRI volumes was reduced by 50%, resulting in final dimensions of $91 \times 109 \times 91$ voxels. This step balances computational resource demands with preservation of macroscopic anatomical features critical for brain age prediction. Finally, z-score normalization was performed to standardize intensity values across the dataset. For each scan, the mean (μ) and standard deviation (σ) of voxel intensities were computed, and intensity values were transformed as $z = x - \mu\sigma$. This standardization ensures consistent intensity ranges across scans, reducing variability caused by differences in scanner hardware or acquisition protocols. The pipeline has been applied to the real neuroimaging data of OASIS-3, aligning with the minimal preprocessing of OpenBHB.

4.2 Diffusion Model Inference

For synthetic data generation, we utilized the pipeline proposed in [39]. This model was trained on brain imaging data from 31,740 participants in the UK Biobank, using high-resolution 3D T1-weighted MRI scans with a voxel size of $1\,\text{mm}^3$. Each volume had dimensions of $160 \times 224 \times 160$ voxels. The inference process was computationally efficient, fitting within 4GB of VRAM.

To ensure compatibility with our experimental setup, the generated synthetic volumes were resized to $91 \times 109 \times 91$ voxels and normalized accordingly. The framework allows the generation of synthetic brain volumes conditioned on age, which is fundamental for our task. Specifically, we generated 3,000 synthetic samples, with ages linearly distributed between 44 and 82 years, following the age distribution of the UK Biobank dataset.

4.3 Selection of the CNN Model and Training

In this study, we employed a well-known convolutional architecture tailored to solve computer vision problems, which came from the family of densely connected convolutional networks (DenseNet) [25]. Notably, we chose the DenseNet-121 architecture, which we modified in a 3D version of the 2D design proposed in the original paper. Other slight changes were made to the architecture to accommodate the resolution of the input volumes, leading to a final number of parameters equal to 11 million.

---

[4] github.com/antsx/antspy.
[5] web.mit.edu/fsl_v5.0.10/fsl/doc/wiki/FLIRT.html.
[6] web.mit.edu/fsl_v5.0.10/fsl/doc/wiki/BET.html.

The choice of DenseNet-121 is justified by the findings of our previous work [9], in which we exploited the OpenBHB dataset to train and compare various CNNs on the brain age prediction task. The comparison proved DenseNet-121 as the most-performing architecture among the investigated ones. We also implemented the same setup for the training phase, involving the Stochastic Gradient Descent optimizer and the cosine annealing scheduler with warm restarts. The scheduler was configured with an initial learning rate of 0.01 and a starting period of 17 epochs that doubled after each cycle. The mini-batch size and the number of training epochs were set equal to 16 and 100 respectively.

We trained three different versions of the DenseNet-121 with the same training setup but different datasets.

- First, we trained the model with the OpenBHB dataset, and we considered this version as the baseline model[7];
- A second version of the DeseNet-121 was trained with the OpenBHB training set integrated with the volumes from the OASIS-3 dataset;
- Finally, the last version of the model was trained with the OpenBHB dataset augmented with the synthetic data generated by the diffusion model previously described.

Both augmentations were involved in increasing the number of samples belonging to the underrepresented training class of individuals over 40 years old. Considering the three configurations previously described, we were able to explore how XAI outputs relative to a model are influenced by the integration of real and synthetic data in the training process.

4.4 XAI

In this work, we conducted an explainability analysis considering three well-known XAI algorithms tailored for convolutional architectures: DeepSHAP, Grad-CAM, and Occlusion.

DeepSHAP is a DeepLift-inspired [43] variant of SHAP (SHapley Additive exPlanations) [33] designed for CNNs. SHAP is an established post-hoc, model-agnostic technique that allows the analysis of a single tabular instance treated by a trained model. Applying a process based on the cooperative game theory of Shapley, SHAP assigns scores to the features according to their relevance in the final prediction. While SHAP is a feature-attribution technique, DeepSHAP exploits the peculiar architecture of the convolutional models to compute SHAPs for the pixels or voxels of the input. As SHAP, DeepSHAP also needs a reference sample from the training set to compute pixel attributions. This sample is often referred to as the mask or background.

Occlusion [53] is a post-hoc, model-agnostic method based on a straightforward perturbation approach. Given an input image, a sliding window cyclically masks regions, and the difference in the output of the model per masking is

---

[7] The pre-trained weights of our DenseNet-121 are made available at the link: https://huggingface.co/SisInfLab-AIBio/BrainAge_DenseNet.

registered. The technique allows for controlling the granularity of the explanations since both the window size and the stride of the sliding can be customized.

Grad-CAM (Gradient-weighted Class Activation Mapping) [41] is a gradient-based, post-hoc technique that produces saliency maps. Each saliency map shows the regions of the input image that the model focuses on to compute the prediction. Compared to the previously described method, Grad-CAM works on a single input instance without cyclically perturbing it, leading to a faster and less computationally intensive process.

We implemented a pipeline to systematically compare XAI outputs per method across different versions of the trained model. Since the target of the augmentation was the class of participants over 40 years old, we only considered the $N = 71$ test samples from this class. The pipeline consisted of the following two modules:

- Generation module that computes the model explanation per method and processes it for further analysis.
- Analysis module that compares XAI outputs across different models per method.

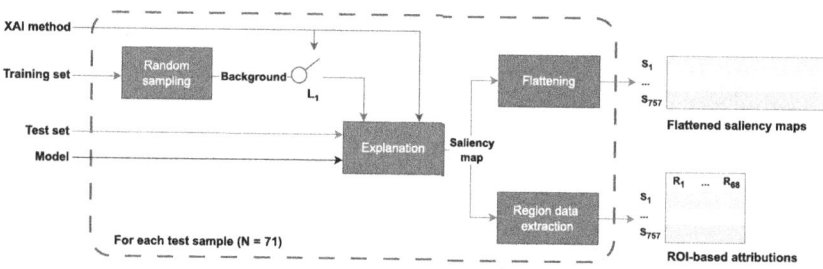

Fig. 2. Generation module of the XAI pipeline. The L_1 switch is closed when the considered method is DeepSHAP.

Generation Module. The processes carried out by the generation module are shown in Fig. 2. Considered an XAI method, the first step consisted of the computation of the voxel attributions per model for each of the $N = 71$ test instances. Then, the saliency maps are processed to follow two different analysis paths in the subsequent module. The two transformations are conducted as follows:

- flattening phase: the 3D saliency maps were reshaped into 1D vectors, resulting in a total of 71 attribution vectors per model per method;
- Region data extraction phase: the Desikan-Killiany atlas was used to aggregate voxel-wise attribution scores into 68 anatomical brain regions. For each region, the total attribution score was computed. This process resulted in a table with 71 rows (corresponding to test observations) and 68 columns (representing brain regions) for each model and method.

To compute SHAP values, DeepSHAP was provided with a background of 200 training instances. For each execution of DeepSHAP, the background consisted of a different random sample of the training data. On the other hand, Occlusion was configured with a sliding window of dimensions $7 \times 8 \times 7$ and a $15 \times 17 \times 15$ stride. The value of the first voxel of each image, corresponding to a void voxel, was set for the voxels occluded by the window.

It is important to note that a methodological adjustment was needed for the application of Grad-CAM. According to the authors of the method [41], we should expect that the last convolutional layer of a CNN encoder typically provides the best balance between abstract feature representation and spatial detail, despite its lower resolution compared to the input image. In our case, the last convolutional layer of DenseNet-121, located at the end of the fourth block, had a resolution of $2 \times 3 \times 2$. This was too low to retain enough spatial information from the original $91 \times 109 \times 91$ input volume. As a result, we had to select a different layer for Grad-CAM. The last layer of the third block, with a resolution of $5 \times 7 \times 5$ was still too limited, so we opted for the last layer of the second block, which had a resolution of $11 \times 14 \times 11$. To capture the importance of voxels across multiple layers, we computed the saliency map of a test instance for each convolutional layer between the input layer and the last layer of the second block, upsampled them to the same resolution, and averaged them in one final saliency map.

Analysis Module. As depicted in Fig. 3, this module examines and compares the processed outputs of the previous model on two different levels:

- **Inter-model analysis.** This level of analysis quantifies the effect of different data augmentation strategies on the explanations provided by the models. For each XAI method considered:
    - Let be v_n^i and v_n^j the vectors of attribution computed with the same XAI method on the n-th test instance with models f_i and f_j respectively;
    - For each pair of models (i, j), the Pearson correlation coefficient $\rho(v_n^i, v_n^j)$ is computed;
    - The process is repeated across all $N = 71$ test instances, and the mean correlation $\bar{\rho}_{ij}$ is computed, considering only statistically significant correlations (significant threshold $\alpha = 0.05$).

    A high $\bar{\rho}_{ij}$ value indicates that the two models provide similar explanations for the same input images, whereas a low value suggests that augmentation has altered the features the model relies on for predictions.
- **Intra-model analysis.** This level of analysis assesses the biological relevance of XAI explanations by evaluating the correlation between brain region attributions and chronological age.
    - Consider the ROI-based table T_k^i for a model f_i and XAI technique E_k, which contains the attributions for 68 brain regions for each test subject;
    - For each brain region, the Pearson correlation coefficient is computed between the attribution value and the subject's chronological age, resulting in a vector of 68 correlation coefficients P_k^i;

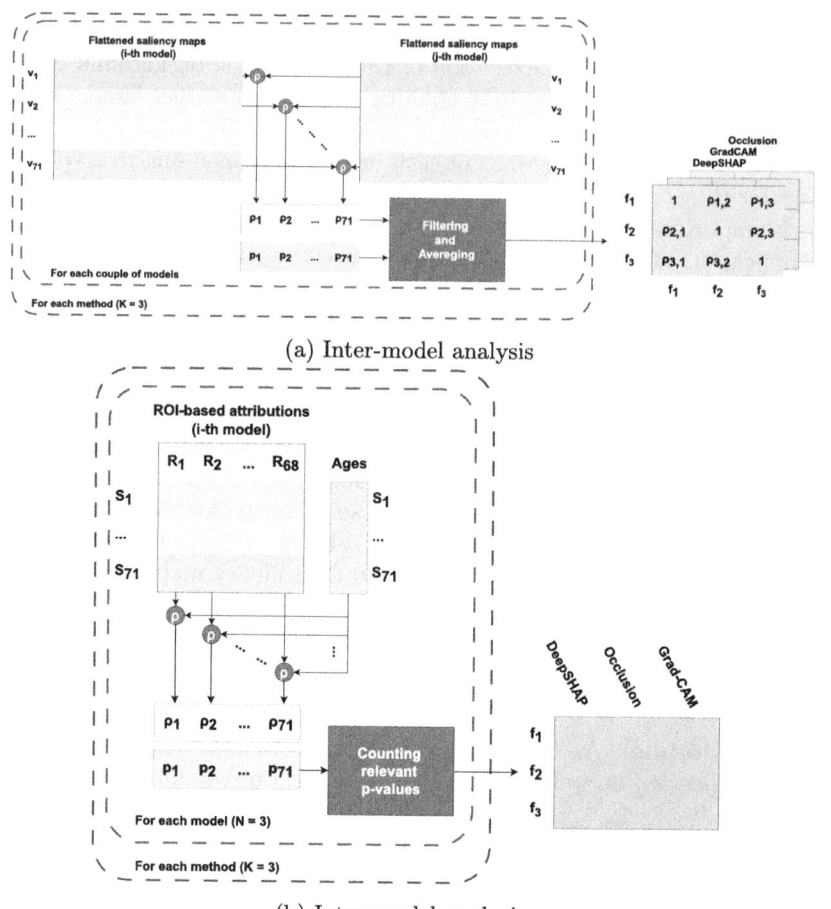

Fig. 3. Approaches of the analysis module (a) **Inter-model analysis** and (b) **Intra-model analysis**.

- The number of statistically significant correlations is then counted, applying the Bonferroni correction to account for multiple comparisons.

More statistically significant correlations suggest that the XAI explanations capture biologically meaningful age-related patterns.

5 Results and Discussion

5.1 Training Results

The values of MAE for the trained models on the test set are collected in Table 1. We focused on the performance relative to the test samples of individuals older than 40 years old since this group was the target of the augmentation.

Table 1. Performance of the different approaches for test samples with over 40 years old.

Approach	MAE
Baseline	11.57
Real-data augmentation	10.26
Synthetic-data augmentation	**5.47**

The baseline model exhibited the highest prediction error among the investigated models ($MAE = 11.57$), likely due to the long-tail effect caused by the data distribution in OpenBHB. Specifically, in a training set of over 3,000 samples, fewer than 400 instances correspond to individuals over 40 years old. In contrast, the model trained with synthetic data augmentation demonstrated the best performance ($MAE = 5.47$), achieving an error nearly half that of the baseline model.

Interestingly, the model trained with real-data augmentation yielded a slightly lower error than the baseline ($MAE = 10.26$), yet it performed significantly worse than the model trained with synthetic augmentation. The distinct distributions of the augmented data may have played a crucial role in the observed performance gap between the two augmented models.

Overall, these findings suggest that incorporating generated brain images as an augmentation strategy effectively enhances CNN performance in brain age prediction, particularly for underrepresented age groups. Reshaping the original data distribution through synthetic samples appears to be a key factor driving this improvement.

5.2 Impact of Augmentation

Inter-model Analysis. In this preliminary work, we investigated how real and synthetic data augmentation influence model explanations generated by different XAI techniques, including DeepSHAP, Occlusion, and Grad-CAM.

Our analysis reveals significant variations in feature attribution patterns across the three trained models for each XAI method. Figure 4 presents the correlation heatmaps summarizing these relationships.

– DeepSHAP (Fig. 4a) exhibits consistently low inter-model correlation values, indicating that feature attribution patterns are poorly preserved across training setups. In particular, the correlation between the baseline and real-data augmented models is minimal, suggesting that real-data augmentation does not effectively retain the original attribution distribution. The correlation further decreases between the baseline and synthetic-data augmented models, suggesting that synthetic augmentation induces even more substantial shifts in the focus of the model. Interestingly, the correlation between the two augmented models (real and synthetic) is relatively higher, implying that both augmentation strategies may modify the feature attribution in a similar direction despite differences in data origin;

- Grad-CAM (Fig. 4b) exhibits the lowest overall inter-model correlations among all XAI methods. This suggests that Grad-CAM explanations are highly sensitive to variations in training data distribution, potentially limiting their reliability for assessing feature importance when different augmentation strategies are applied;
- Occlusion (Fig. 4c) shows the highest inter-model correlation values, indicating more stable feature attributions across different training strategies. This higher stability may be attributed to the size of the occlusion window, which smooths out fine-grained details and emphasizes broader regions of importance. As a result, Occlusion-based explanations may be less affected by small-scale perturbations introduced by different augmentation strategies.

Across all XAI methods, we consistently observe that the correlation between explanations from the baseline and real-data augmented models is higher than that between the baseline and synthetic-data augmented models. This suggests that synthetic augmentation leads to a more profound shift in the model's learned features compared to real-data augmentation.

Intra-model Analysis. Table 2 provides insights into how different augmentation strategies impact the biological relevance of model explanations. Specifically, it reports the number of brain regions where feature attributions show significant correlations with chronological age, revealing substantial variations across models and XAI methods.

- Occlusion identifies a markedly higher number of age-associated brain regions in both augmented models (66 regions for real-data augmentation, 52 for synthetic data augmentation) compared to the baseline model (16 regions). This substantial increase suggests that data augmentation improves the model's ability to capture biologically meaningful age-related patterns across the brain. The broader spatial focus observed with Occlusion-based explanations may be attributed to the smoothing effect of the occlusion window, which aggregates information over larger regions rather than emphasizing fine-grained voxel-level details;
- DeepSHAP exhibits a more consistent pattern across models, with a similar number of significantly correlated regions (8, 9, and 4 for the baseline, real-data, and synthetic-data augmented models, respectively). The slight reduction in age-correlated regions for the synthetic-data augmented model, despite its superior predictive performance, suggests that this model may focus on a smaller but more predictive subset of brain regions, potentially improving generalization;
- Grad-CAM reports the fewest significant correlations overall, with no age-associated regions detected in the baseline model and only modest increases in the augmented models (6 regions for real-data augmentation and 1 for synthetic-data augmentation). This aligns with Grad-CAM's weaker inter-model correlations, further indicating that its feature attributions may be more sensitive to training data variations and less robust for identifying biologically meaningful patterns.

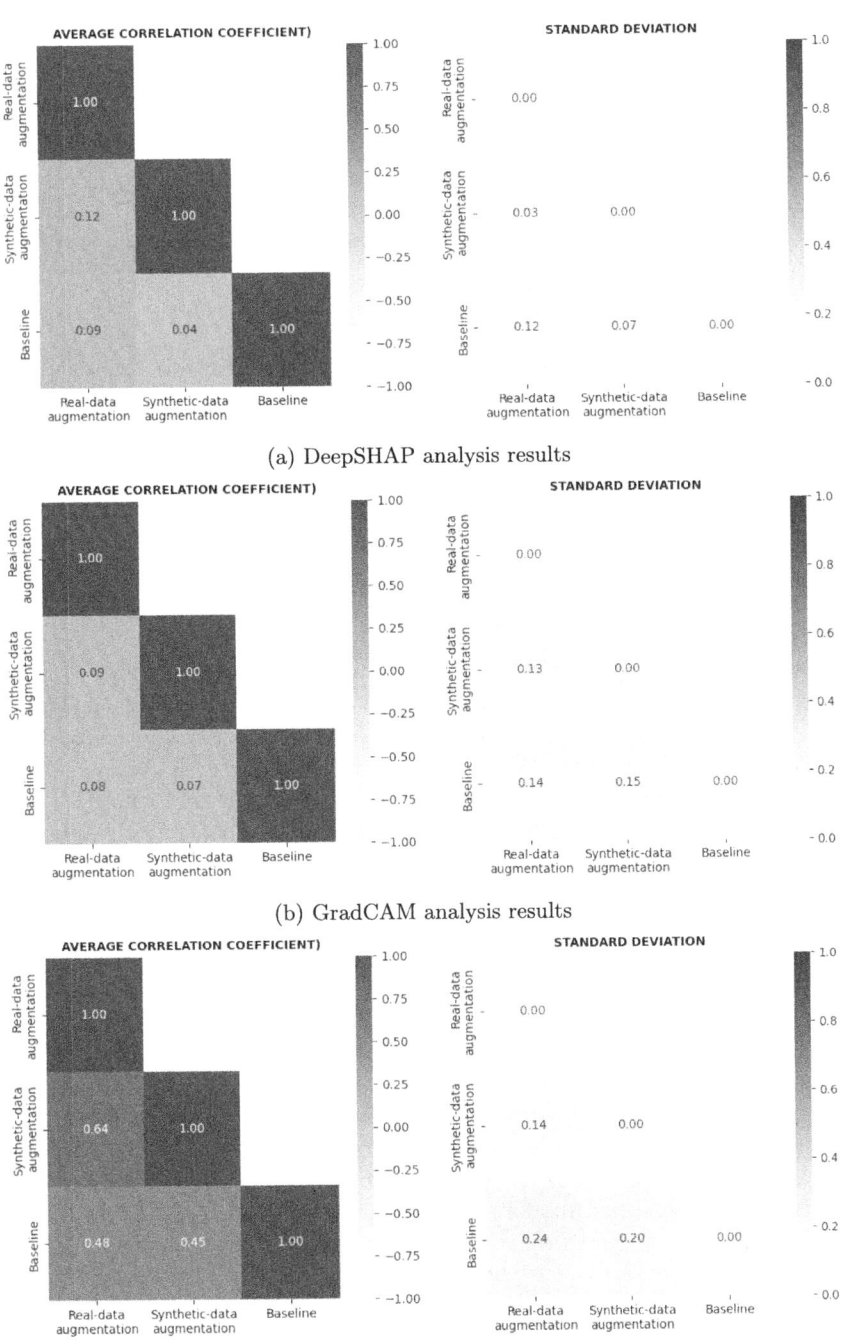

Fig. 4. Heatmaps of correlations between explanation distribution from different approaches per XAI method: (a) **DeepSHAP**, (b) **GradCAM** and (c) **Occlusion**.

These findings highlight how different XAI methods exhibit varying degrees of sensitivity to augmentation strategies when analyzing the biological relevance of model explanations. While Occlusion captures broader patterns, DeepSHAP appears to focus on a more selective subset of brain regions, and Grad-CAM provides the least stable correlations across models.

Table 2. Number of significant correlations between region-based feature attributions and chronological age per model.

Approach	Features		
	DeepSHAP	GradCAM	Occlusion
Baseline	8	0	16
Real-data augmentation	9	6	66
Synthetic-data augmentation	4	1	52

5.3 Stability and Reliability of XAI Explanations

The substantial variations in XAI outputs across different training strategies highlight a key challenge: model explanations are highly dependent on the training data distribution, potentially compromising their reliability for clinical interpretation.

Among the different XAI methods, Occlusion consistently identified a larger number of brain regions associated with chronological age, likely due to its broader feature aggregation. In contrast, Grad-CAM produced the least stable explanations, exhibiting weak inter-model correlations and identifying fewer age-related regions. DeepSHAP showed an intermediate behavior, capturing biologically relevant features while maintaining some degree of consistency across models.

A clear trade-off emerges between interpretability and performance. Synthetic data augmentation led to a substantial improvement in model accuracy but introduced significant shifts in feature attribution, raising the question of whether the model is truly learning age-related patterns or is instead incorporating biases introduced during the generation of synthetic data. On the other hand, real-data augmentation resulted in more stable explanations, preserving a portion of the baseline model's feature attributions. However, this stability came at the cost of lower predictive accuracy, suggesting that while real-data augmentation maintains consistency in interpretability, it does not enhance performance as effectively as synthetic augmentation.

These findings indicate that synthetic augmentation fundamentally reshapes the learned feature space, yet its impact on explanation stability requires further investigation. Ensuring that performance improvements do not come at the expense of clinically irrelevant or biased attributions remains a critical concern for the deployment of AI models in neuroimaging applications.

5.4 Biases and Limitations

Several factors may introduce biases into the results, influencing both model predictions and their interpretability:

- Demographic and sampling biases from the UK Biobank dataset: the diffusion model used for synthetic data generation was trained on UK Biobank data, which has a specific demographic composition. As a result, the synthetic images may inadvertently reflect biases present in the original dataset, potentially leading the brain age prediction model to learn population-specific patterns that lack broader biological generalizability;
- Occlusion's high correlation values and methodological constraints: the relatively high inter-model correlations observed with occlusion-based explanations could be partly influenced by the chosen window size and stride parameters, rather than solely reflecting true biological feature importance. Future work should explore how different occlusion configurations impact attribution stability;
- Architectural modifications to DenseNet: while necessary to accommodate 3D neuroimaging data, the modifications made to DenseNet-121 could introduce architectural biases, altering feature extraction patterns compared to standard 2D implementations. Further comparisons with alternative 3D architectures would help assess the generalizability of these results;
- Age-specific biases introduced by augmentation strategies: since both augmentation approaches focused on increasing samples for individuals over 40 years old, the model may have learned to rely more heavily on aging-specific features rather than capturing general biomarkers of neurobiological aging. This could reduce its ability to generalize across younger populations, highlighting the need for balanced age distributions in training data.

6 Conclusions

This study examined the interplay between DA and XAI methods in the context of brain age prediction, emphasizing both predictive performance and interpretability. Our findings highlight the trade-offs inherent in different augmentation strategies: while synthetic data augmentation significantly improved model accuracy, it also introduced shifts in feature attributions that warrant further investigation to rule out dataset-induced biases. In contrast, real-data augmentation produced explanations more consistent with the baseline model but failed to yield substantial performance gains, underscoring the challenge of balancing accuracy with interpretability.

Moreover, our comparison of XAI techniques revealed notable differences in their stability across training configurations. Occlusion provided the most consistent and biologically meaningful explanations, while DeepSHAP exhibited moderate stability, and Grad-CAM struggled with feature resolution limitations. These variations emphasize the need for rigorous evaluation of explainability methods when deploying AI models in neuroimaging applications.

Ultimately, our results suggest that augmentation is not merely a tool for improving model performance but also a factor influencing the reliability of AI-driven explanations. Future work should explore how different augmentation paradigms shape feature attributions and whether certain strategies introduce biases that impact the clinical applicability of these models. The ability to balance predictive power with biologically grounded, trustworthy explanations will be crucial for advancing AI-driven neuroimaging toward real-world implementation.

Acknowledgement. This work was partially supported by the following projects: "LIFE: the itaLian system wIde Frailty nEtwork"; DEMETRA: "Development of an ensemble learning-based, multidimensional sensory impairment score to predict cognitive impairment in an elderly cohort of Southern Italy" (CUP D99J22001970006) Missione 6/componente 2/Investimento: 2.1 "Rafforzamento e potenziamento della ricerca biomedica del SSN", funded by European Commission NextGenerationEU; We acknowledge the CINECA award under the ISCRA initiative (Project IsCc1_SynBrain), for the availability of high performance computing resources and support; "IDENTITA - rete Integrata meDiterranea per l'osservazione ed Elaborazione di percorsi di Nutrizione".

Disclosure of Interests. None.

References

1. Ali, S., et al.: Explainable artificial intelligence (XAI): what we know and what is left to attain trustworthy artificial intelligence. Inf. Fusion **99**, 101805 (2023)
2. Antoniou, A., Storkey, A.J., Edwards, H.: Data augmentation generative adversarial networks. CoRR abs/1711.04340 (2017). arXiv:1711.04340
3. Baecker, L., Garcia-Dias, R., Vieira, S., Scarpazza, C., Mechelli, A.: Machine learning for brain age prediction: introduction to methods and clinical applications. EBioMedicine **72** (2021)
4. Ball, G., Kelly, C.E., Beare, R., Seal, M.L.: Individual variation underlying brain age estimates in typical development. Neuroimage **235**, 118036 (2021)
5. Binder, A., Montavon, G., Lapuschkin, S., Müller, K., Samek, W.: Layer-wise relevance propagation for neural networks with local renormalization layers. In: Villa, A.E.P., Masulli, P., Rivero, A.J.P. (eds.) ICANN 2016, Part II. LNCS, vol. 9887, pp. 63–71. Springer, Cham (2016). https://doi.org/10.1007/978-3-319-44781-0_8
6. Blagus, R., Lusa, L.: SMOTE for high-dimensional class-imbalanced data. BMC Bioinform. **14**, 106 (2013). https://doi.org/10.1186/1471-2105-14-106
7. Button, K., et al.: Power failure: why small sample size undermines the reliability of neuroscience. Nat. Rev. Neurosci. **14** (2013). https://doi.org/10.1038/nrn3475
8. Cole, J.H., Franke, K.: Predicting age using neuroimaging: innovative brain ageing biomarkers. Trends Neurosci. **40**(12), 681–690 (2017)
9. Bonis, M.L.N., et al.: Explainable brain age prediction: a comparative evaluation of morphometric and deep learning pipelines. Brain Inform. **11**(1), 33 (2024)
10. Devries, T., Taylor, G.W.: Improved regularization of convolutional neural networks with cutout. CoRR abs/1708.04552 (2017). http://arxiv.org/abs/1708.04552

11. Díaz-Rodríguez, N., Ser, J., Coeckelbergh, M., Prado, M.L., Herrera-Viedma, E., Herrera, F.: Connecting the dots in trustworthy artificial intelligence: from AI principles, ethics, and key requirements to responsible ai systems and regulation. Inf. Fusion **99**, 101896 (2023)
12. Dinsdale, N.K., et al.: Learning patterns of the ageing brain in MRI using deep convolutional networks. Neuroimage **224**, 117401 (2021)
13. Dufumier, B., Grigis, A., Victor, J., Ambroise, C., Frouin, V., Duchesnay, E.: OpenBHB: a large-scale multi-site brain MRI data-set for age prediction and debiasing. Neuroimage **263**, 119637 (2022)
14. Feng, X., et al.: Estimating brain age based on a uniform healthy population with deep learning and structural magnetic resonance imaging. Neurobiol. Aging **91**, 15–25 (2020)
15. Fernández, A., García, S., Herrera, F., Chawla, N.V.: SMOTE for learning from imbalanced data: progress and challenges, marking the 15-year anniversary. J. Artif. Intell. Res. **61**, 863–905 (2018). https://doi.org/10.1613/JAIR.1.11192
16. Franke, K., Gaser, C.: Ten years of Brainage as a neuroimaging biomarker of brain aging: what insights have we gained? Front. Neurol. **10**, 789 (2019)
17. Friedrich, P., Wolleb, J., Bieder, F., Durrer, A., Cattin, P.C.: WDM: 3d wavelet diffusion models for high-resolution medical image synthesis. In: Mukhopadhyay, A., Öksüz, I., Engelhardt, S., Mehrof, D., Yuan, Y. (eds.) DGM4MICCAI 2024. LNCS, vol. 15224, pp. 11–21. Springer, Cham (2024). https://doi.org/10.1007/978-3-031-72744-3_2
18. Goodfellow, I., Bengio, Y., Courville, A.: Deep Learning. MIT Press (2016). http://www.deeplearningbook.org
19. Goodfellow, I.J., Pouget-Abadie, J., Mirza, M., Xu, B., Warde-Farley, D., Ozair, S., Courville, A.C., Bengio, Y.: Generative adversarial nets. In: Ghahramani, Z., Welling, M., Cortes, C., Lawrence, N.D., Weinberger, K.Q. (eds.) Advances in Neural Information Processing Systems 27: Annual Conference on Neural Information Processing Systems 2014, December 8-13 2014, Montreal, Quebec, Canada. pp. 2672–2680 (2014). https://proceedings.neurips.cc/paper/2014/hash/5ca3e9b122f61f8f06494c97b1afccf3-Abstract.html
20. Guo, K.H., et al.: Anatomic interpretability in neuroimage deep learning: Saliency approaches for typical aging and traumatic brain injury. Neuroinformatics 1–16 (2024)
21. Han, H., Wang, W.-Y., Mao, B.-H.: Borderline-SMOTE: a new over-sampling method in imbalanced data sets learning. In: Huang, D.-S., Zhang, X.-P., Huang, G.-B. (eds.) ICIC 2005. LNCS, vol. 3644, pp. 878–887. Springer, Heidelberg (2005). https://doi.org/10.1007/11538059_91
22. Ho, J., Jain, A., Abbeel, P.: Denoising diffusion probabilistic models. In: Larochelle, H., Ranzato, M., Hadsell, R., Balcan, M., Lin, H. (eds.) Advances in Neural Information Processing Systems 33: Annual Conference on Neural Information Processing Systems 2020, NeurIPS 2020, December 6–12, 2020, virtual (2020). https://proceedings.neurips.cc/paper/2020/hash/4c5bcfec8584af0d967f1ab10179ca4b-Abstract.html
23. Hofmann, S.M., et al.: Towards the interpretability of deep learning models for multi-modal neuroimaging: finding structural changes of the ageing brain. Neuroimage **261**, 119504 (2022)
24. Hofmann, S.M., et al.: The utility of explainable AI for MRI analysis: relating model predictions to neuroimaging features of the aging brain. Imaging Neuroscience (2025)

25. Huang, G., Liu, Z., Van Der Maaten, L., Weinberger, K.Q.: Densely connected convolutional networks. In: Proceedings of the IEEE Conference on Computer Vision and Pattern Recognition, pp. 4700–4708 (2017)
26. Islam, T., Hafiz, M.S., Jim, J.R., Kabir, M.M., Mridha, M.: A systematic review of deep learning data augmentation in medical imaging: Recent advances and future research directions. Healthcare Anal. 100340 (2024)
27. Kingma, D.P., Welling, M.: Auto-encoding variational Bayes. In: Bengio, Y., LeCun, Y. (eds.) 2nd International Conference on Learning Representations, ICLR 2014, Banff, AB, Canada, April 14-16, 2014, Conference Track Proceedings (2014). http://arxiv.org/abs/1312.6114
28. Krizhevsky, A., Sutskever, I., Hinton, G.E.: Imagenet classification with deep convolutional neural networks. Commun. ACM **60**(6), 84–90 (2017). https://doi.org/10.1145/3065386
29. Levakov, G., Rosenthal, G., Shelef, I., Raviv, T.R., Avidan, G.: From a deep learning model back to the brain–identifying regional predictors and their relation to aging. Hum. Brain Mapp. **41**(12), 3235–3252 (2020)
30. Lombardi, A., Amoroso, N., Diacono, D., Monaco, A., Tangaro, S., Bellotti, R.: Extensive evaluation of morphological statistical harmonization for brain age prediction. Brain Sci. **10**(6), 364 (2020)
31. Lombardi, A., et al.: A human-interpretable machine learning pipeline based on ultrasound to support leiomyosarcoma diagnosis. Artif. Intell. Med. **146**, 102697 (2023)
32. Lombardi, A., et al.: Explainable deep learning for personalized age prediction with brain morphology. Front. Neurosci. **15**, 674055 (2021)
33. Lundberg, S.M., Lee, S.I.: A unified approach to interpreting model predictions. In: Proceedings of the 31st International Conference on Neural Information Processing Systems. NIPS'17, Red Hook, NY, USA, pp. 4768–4777. Curran Associates Inc. (2017)
34. Mazziotta, J.C., Toga, A.W., Evans, A., Fox, P., Lancaster, J.: A probabilistic atlas of the human brain: theory and rationale for its development: The international consortium for brain mapping (icbm). NeuroImage (Orlando, Fla.) **2**(2), 89–101 (1995)
35. Nalepa, J., Marcinkiewicz, M., Kawulok, M.: Data augmentation for brain-tumor segmentation: A review. Frontiers Comput. Neurosci. **13**, 83 (2019). https://doi.org/10.3389/FNCOM.2019.00083
36. Nguyen, H.M., Cooper, E.W., Kamei, K.: Borderline over-sampling for imbalanced data classification. Int. J. Knowl. Eng. Soft Data Paradigms **3**(1), 4–21 (2011). https://doi.org/10.1504/IJKESDP.2011.039875
37. Panigutti, C., et al.: Co-design of human-centered, explainable AI for clinical decision support. ACM Trans. Interact. Intell. Syst. **13**(4), 1–35 (2023)
38. Peng, H., Gong, W., Beckmann, C.F., Vedaldi, A., Smith, S.M.: Accurate brain age prediction with lightweight deep neural networks. Med. Image Anal. **68**, 101871 (2021)
39. Pinaya, W.H.L., et al.: Brain imaging generation with latent diffusion models. In: Mukhopadhyay, A., Öksüz, I., Engelhardt, S., Zhu, D., Yuan, Y. (eds.) DGM4MICCAI 2022. LNCS, vol. 13609, pp. 117–126. Springer, Cham (2022). https://doi.org/10.1007/978-3-031-18576-2_12
40. Rombach, R., Blattmann, A., Lorenz, D., Esser, P., Ommer, B.: High-resolution image synthesis with latent diffusion models. In: IEEE/CVF Conference on Computer Vision and Pattern Recognition, CVPR 2022, New Orleans, LA, USA, June

18-24, 2022, pp. 10674–10685. IEEE (2022). https://doi.org/10.1109/CVPR52688.2022.01042
41. Selvaraju, R.R., Cogswell, M., Das, A., Vedantam, R., Parikh, D., Batra, D.: Gradcam: Visual explanations from deep networks via gradient-based localization. In: 2017 IEEE International Conference on Computer Vision (ICCV), pp. 618–626 (2017)
42. Shorten, C., Khoshgoftaar, T.M.: A survey on image data augmentation for deep learning. J. Big Data **6**, 60 (2019). https://doi.org/10.1186/S40537-019-0197-0
43. Shrikumar, A., Greenside, P., Kundaje, A.: Learning important features through propagating activation differences. ICML **70**, 3145–3153 (2017). https://proceedings.mlr.press/v70/shrikumar17a.html
44. Song, Y., Dhariwal, P., Chen, M., Sutskever, I.: Consistency models. In: Krause, A., Brunskill, E., Cho, K., Engelhardt, B., Sabato, S., Scarlett, J. (eds.) International Conference on Machine Learning, ICML 2023, 23-29 July 2023, Honolulu, Hawaii, USA. Proceedings of Machine Learning Research, vol. 202, pp. 32211–32252. PMLR (2023). https://proceedings.mlr.press/v202/song23a.html
45. Song, Y., Durkan, C., Murray, I., Ermon, S.: Maximum likelihood training of score-based diffusion models. In: Ranzato, M., Beygelzimer, A., Dauphin, Y.N., Liang, P., Vaughan, J.W. (eds.) Advances in Neural Information Processing Systems 34: Annual Conference on Neural Information Processing Systems 2021, NeurIPS 2021, December 6-14, 2021, Virtual, pp. 1415–1428 (2021). https://proceedings.neurips.cc/paper/2021/hash/0a9fdbb17feb6ccb7ec405cfb85222c4-Abstract.html
46. Tafuri, B., et al.: The impact of harmonization on radiomic features in Parkinson's disease and healthy controls: a multicenter study. Front. Neurosci. **16**, 1012287 (2022)
47. Tanveer, M., et al.: Deep learning for brain age estimation: a systematic review. Inf. Fusion **96**, 130–143 (2023)
48. Velden, B.H., Kuijf, H.J., Gilhuijs, K.G., Viergever, M.A.: Explainable artificial intelligence (XAI) in deep learning-based medical image analysis. Med. Image Anal. **79**, 102470 (2022)
49. Wood, D.A., et al.: Accurate brain-age models for routine clinical MRI examinations. Neuroimage **249**, 118871 (2022)
50. Wu, G., Suk, H.I.: Deep learning in medical image analysis. Ann. Rev. Biomed. Eng. **19** (2017). https://doi.org/10.1146/annurev-bioeng-071516-044442
51. Xiao, Z., Kreis, K., Vahdat, A.: Tackling the generative learning trilemma with denoising diffusion GANs. In: The Tenth International Conference on Learning Representations, ICLR 2022, Virtual Event, April 25-29, 2022. OpenReview.net (2022). https://openreview.net/forum?id=JprM0p-q0Co
52. Yi, X., Walia, E., Babyn, P.S.: Generative adversarial network in medical imaging: a review. Med. Image Anal. **58** (2019). https://doi.org/10.1016/J.MEDIA.2019.101552
53. Zeiler, M.D., Fergus, R.: Visualizing and understanding convolutional networks. In: Fleet, D., Pajdla, T., Schiele, B., Tuytelaars, T. (eds.) ECCV 2014, Part I. LNCS, vol. 8689, pp. 818–833. Springer, Cham (2014). https://doi.org/10.1007/978-3-319-10590-1_53
54. Zhang, Y., et al.: Improving brain age prediction with anatomical feature attention-enhanced 3D-CNN. Comput. Biol. Med. **169**, 107873 (2024)

Open Access This chapter is licensed under the terms of the Creative Commons Attribution 4.0 International License (http://creativecommons.org/licenses/by/4.0/), which permits use, sharing, adaptation, distribution and reproduction in any medium or format, as long as you give appropriate credit to the original author(s) and the source, provide a link to the Creative Commons license and indicate if changes were made.

The images or other third party material in this chapter are included in the chapter's Creative Commons license, unless indicated otherwise in a credit line to the material. If material is not included in the chapter's Creative Commons license and your intended use is not permitted by statutory regulation or exceeds the permitted use, you will need to obtain permission directly from the copyright holder.

Superpixel Correlation for Explainable Image Classification

Vahidin Hasić[1(✉)], Amar Halilović[2], and Senka Krivić[1]

[1] Faculty of Electrical Engineering, University of Sarajevo, Sarajevo, Bosnia and Herzegovina
{vahidin.hasic,senka.krivic}@etf.unsa.ba
[2] Institute of Artificial Intelligence, Ulm University, Ulm, Germany
amar.halilovic@uni-ulm.de

Abstract. Explainable AI (XAI) is essential for fostering trust in the predictions of deep neural networks (DNNs), especially within the domain of image classification. SHAP (SHapley Additive exPlanations), a theoretically sound method rooted in game theory, stands as a prominent XAI technique for attributing feature importance. However, SHAP's inherent computational complexity, which grows exponentially with the number of features, restricts its practical application. Although numerous approximation methods have been proposed, they often deviate from the original SHAP formulation, potentially sacrificing accuracy and theoretical fidelity. In this paper, we introduce CorrSHAP, a novel approach that leverages image superpixel correlations to significantly accelerate SHAP value estimation while preserving the rigor of the original formulation. CorrSHAP efficiently quantifies the interdependence of superpixels within an image, enabling the SHAP calculation to consider only interdependent superpixel combinations. This targeted approach significantly reduces the computational burden without compromising the faithfulness of the explanation. Evaluation results demonstrate that CorrSHAP outperforms the comparable Monte Carlo SHAP method in explanation faithfulness, achieving this in a fraction of a second, with a 55-fold speed improvement. The source code is available on the link (https://github.com/vhasic/CorrSHAP).

Keywords: Explainable AI · Image classification · SHAP · Concept-based explanations · Pearson Correlation

1 Introduction

Recent advances in deep learning have revolutionized image classification, leading to models that achieve unprecedented accuracy on a wide range of tasks. Despite these successes, the opaque nature of deep neural networks (DNNs) has raised concerns about interpretability, trust, and accountability [33]. The black-box behavior of these models makes it difficult for practitioners and end users,

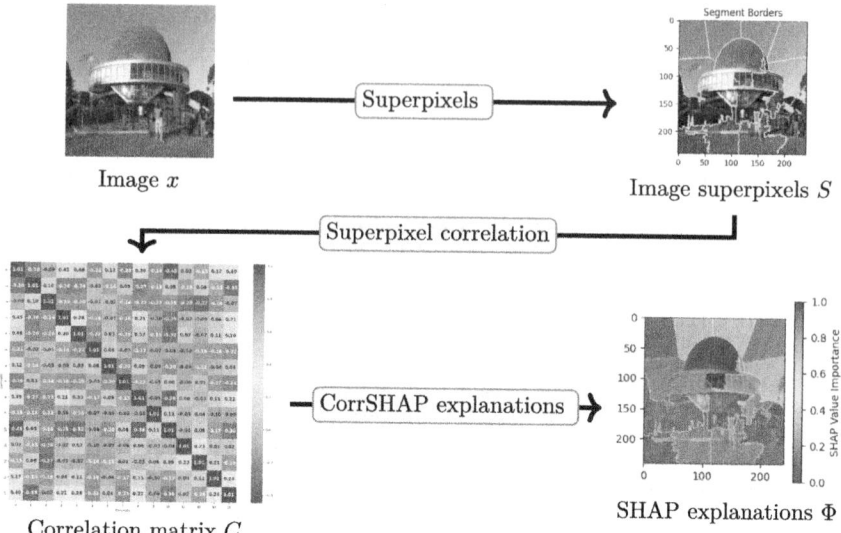

Fig. 1. Framework of the proposed CorrSHAP method. Input image x is segmented into superpixels S. Superpixels are vectorized and centralized into vectors V. Correlation matrix C between superpixels is calculated using cosine similarity between individual vectors. For each superpixel, we take correlated superpixels, where correlation is higher than threshold $|C_{ij}| > \tau$, and perform perturbations on all combinations to calculate superpixel attribution.

usually laymen, to understand the rationale behind individual predictions, a critical barrier to wider adoption in real-world applications.

The field of eXplainable Artificial Intelligence (XAI) [11] has seen significant advancements, particularly in developing methods to interpret deep learning models' predictions. XAI has been applied to different research areas and problems, as well as image classification [2]. Among different XAI methods, SHAP (SHapley Additive exPlanations) [18] has emerged as a prominent technique for feature attribution explanations. Built on cooperative game theory, SHAP assigns an importance value to each feature by considering its contribution across all possible feature subsets. While effective in providing rigorous attributions, SHAP suffers from computational inefficiency. Lack of interpretability is also a problem when SHAP is applied to high-dimensional data such as images [19].

One promising avenue for enhancing image interpretability is to shift the focus from pixel-level explanations to region-based representations. Superpixels are groups of perceptually similar pixels and offer a natural and semantically meaningful partition of an image. Analyzing higher-level structures and relationships within the image becomes feasible by aggregating local information into superpixels. In this context, examining the superpixel correlations can reveal how different regions contribute to the classification decision. For example, certain correlated superpixel groups may capture object parts or contextual elements crucial for distinguishing between classes [29].

SHAP, when applied to images, provides feature attributions by estimating the contribution of individual input features, i.e., pixels, in the case of image classification models. However, pixel-level attributions often lack interpretability due to their fine granularity, resulting in complicated explanations for humans to understand and analyze. Additionally, generating these attributions can be computationally expensive, especially for high-resolution images with many features, be it pixels or groups of pixels (superpixels). We propose the Correlation SHAP (CorrSHAP) method to speed up SHAP calculation by calculating the correlation between image superpixels and perturbing only correlated ones to calculate SHAP values.

The main contribution of this paper is a novel superpixel-based correlation method, CorrSHAP, that efficiently calculates SHAP values while being black-box. The proposed method is not limited to superpixels and generalizes to other semantically meaningful image regions or concepts. CorrSHAP achieves better faithfulness while offering a 55-times speedup in SHAP value calculations compared to Monte Carlo SHAP.

2 Related Work

The demand for trust and transparency in machine learning models has propelled a stream of research into XAI techniques, particularly in the context of image classification. Early approaches focused on generating saliency maps that highlight the regions of an image most influential to a model's decision, such as Gradient-weighted Class Activation Mapping (Grad-CAM) [26] and Integrated Gradients [28], which compute pixel-level importance scores based on gradient information, providing intuitive visualizations of model attention. However, they often suffer from issues such as noise and lack of spatial coherence, making it challenging to extract semantically meaningful insights. Furthermore, they keep pixel-based level explanations, which do not correspond to higher-level semantic image features, such as identifiable objects or concepts on images.

Another important line of work in explainable image classification elevates interpretable image representation from pixels to so-called superpixels, i.e., groups of pixels. Superpixels have long been employed in computer vision as a means to reduce computational complexity and improve spatial coherence in image analysis. Superpixels are generated by image segmentation (superpixelization). There are three major groups of image segmentation methods: more traditional cluster-based [1,9,15,32], graph-based segmentation methods [27], and more recent learning-based [17,22]. As we are not concerned with interpretable representation optimization, we stick to cluster-based segmentation and use Simple Linear Iterative Clustering (SLIC) [1] throughout the rest of this paper. By grouping pixels into superpixels, models can operate on regions that better align with human perception, enabling explanations that are both localized and semantically rich. The majority of works that employ superpixels are perturbation-based methods, including notable Local Interpretable Model-agnostic Explanations (LIME) [23] and Anchors [24]. These methods perturb segments (superpixels) of an image and observe the impact on the classifier's output. Differences between outputs for different perturbations serve as explanations. While effective and relatively easy to understand, the perturbation approach can be computationally intensive and may generate explanations that are sensitive to the segmentation granularity [13]. Additionally, the majority of perturbation-based methods do not guarantee optimal explanations and are based on approximations. SHAP has been proposed as an overarching theoretically-sound explanation approach based on cooperative game theory. However, it heavily suffers from computational complexity [18].

Recent research has significantly advanced SHAP and Shapley value calculation by tackling computational complexity, proposing efficient approximations, and broadening application domains. Huang and Marques-Silva [14] refine complexity claims by proving that computing SHAP scores is P-hard for commonly used classifiers while extending polynomial-time computation to non-binary decision trees. Complementing this, SHAP-IQ [10] introduces a unified, sampling-based method for approximating any-order Shapley interactions with guarantees of unbiasedness, consistency, and tight approximation bounds. Other studies [3] highlight that the exact computation of SHAP explanations is intractable for many models, emphasizing fundamental limitations in current approaches. Application-focused contributions include a SHAP-based method for interpretable object detection in satellite imagery [16] that leverages pixel-wise attributions to visualize inference, regulate training, and improve data selection, as well as adaptations of SHAP values for deep learning-based image semantic segmentation to yield fine-grained, human-intuitive insights at both pixel and region levels. Other advancements such as h-Shap [30] an efficient, hierarchical extension for image explanations and Faith-Shap [31] which generalizes Shapley values to capture feature interactions via weighted regression.

Correlation analysis has been utilized in various domains to uncover dependencies among features. In XAI, understanding how different regions or features interact can yield insights that go beyond isolated importance scores. Correlations have been explored in tabular and textual data. However, leveraging correlation analysis in the context of image classification, especially at the level of superpixels, remains underexplored. Our approach builds on this idea by explicitly modeling the relationships between superpixels, thereby providing explanations that capture the synergistic effects of spatially distributed regions.

3 Methodology

Given an input image $x \in \mathbb{R}^{H \times W \times K}$, where H, W, and K denote height, width, and channels, respectively, and a pretrained image classification CNN model $f : \mathbb{R}^{H \times W \times K} \to \mathcal{Y}$ parameterized by θ, such that $f_\theta(x) = \hat{y}$ (where $\hat{y} \in \mathcal{Y}$ is the predicted class), the goal of CorrSHAP is to efficiently compute SHAP values [18]. We achieve this by exploiting intersegment correlations, significantly reducing the computational burden of Shapley value calculation.

CorrSHAP partitions the input image x into a set of N distinct, non overlapping segments (superpixels). This segmentation is represented by a set of binary masks $M = \{m_i \mid m_i \in \{0,1\}^{H \times W}\}$. Pixel values of 1 in m_i indicate inclusion in the segment, and 0 indicates exclusion. This segmentation adheres to two constraints: (1) Non-overlap: $m_i \cap m_j = \emptyset$ for all $i \neq j$, ensuring that each pixel belongs to at most one segment; and (2) Complete coverage: $\bigcup_i m_i = \{1\}^{H \times W}$, ensuring that every pixel is assigned to a segment. Any segmentation algorithm satisfying these properties can be employed in CorrSHAP.

We examine three approaches to obtain a one-dimensional vector representation for superpixels treated as image features: (1) raw pixel vectorization, (2) feature map vectorization, and (3) gradient vectorization.

Raw Pixel Vectorization (Option 1). The simplest and fastest way to vectorize the image is raw pixel vectorization. Each superpixel i is isolated by multiplying the input image x with its corresponding binary mask m_i, resulting in a superpixel image $s_i = x \odot m_i$, where $\odot$ signifies the Hadamard product. This superpixel image s_i is flattened into a vector $v_i \in \mathbb{R}^d$, where d is the product of the image dimensions $d = H \cdot W \cdot K$ (Eq. 1).

$$v_i = \text{flatten}(s_i) = \text{flatten}(x \odot m_i)$$
$$v_i \in \mathbb{R}^d, x \in \mathbb{R}^{H \times W \times K}, m_i \in \{0,1\}^{H \times W \times K}, d = H \cdot W \cdot K. \quad (1)$$

Feature Map Vectorization (Option 2). The classification model f is decomposed into two functions: $g : \mathcal{X} \to \mathcal{Z}$, mapping the input to an intermediate feature space $\mathcal{Z}$, and $h : \mathcal{Z} \to \mathcal{Y}$, mapping the feature representation to the output, such that $f(x) = h(g(x))$. We obtain feature maps $g(s_i)$ by passing the superpixel images s_i through the feature extraction component g. These feature maps are flattened to obtain the vector representations $\mathbf{v}_i$, as shown in Eq. 2.

$$v_i = \text{flatten}(g(s_i))$$
$$f(x) = h(g(x)), g : \mathcal{X} \to \mathcal{Z}, h : \mathcal{Z} \to \mathcal{Y}. \quad (2)$$

Gradient Vectorization (Option 3). Inspired by [4], who demonstrated the effectiveness of network gradients to capture superpixel similarity from a DNN perspective, we propose a gradient-based vectorization method. The gradient of the output of the network with respect to its parameters is computed for each superpixel image s_i. These gradients are flattened to yield the vector representation (Eq. 3).

$$v_i = \nabla_\theta f_\theta(s_i). \quad (3)$$

To quantify the relationships between superpixels, a correlation matrix is computed. Each superpixel vector $\mathbf{v}_i$ is centralized by subtracting the mean vector $\bar{\mathbf{v}}$ across all superpixels, as defined in Eq. 4.

$$\mathbf{v}'_i = \mathbf{v}_i - \bar{\mathbf{v}}, \quad \text{where } \bar{\mathbf{v}} = \frac{1}{N} \sum_{j=1}^{N} \mathbf{v}_j. \quad (4)$$

The Pearson correlation (Eq. 5) between two vectors $\mathbf{v}_i$ and $\mathbf{v}_j$ is defined as:

$$\text{corr}(\mathbf{v}_i, \mathbf{v}_j) = \frac{\sum_{k=1}^{n}(v_{ik} - \bar{v}_i)(v_{jk} - \bar{v}_j)}{\sqrt{\sum_{k=1}^{n}(v_{ik} - \bar{v}_i)^2}\sqrt{\sum_{k=1}^{n}(v_{jk} - \bar{v}_j)^2}}, \quad (5)$$

where n is the dimensionality of the vectors, v_{ik} is the k-th element of $\mathbf{v}_i$, and $\bar{v}_i$ represents the mean of $\mathbf{v}_i$. Due to the centralization of the superpixel vectors ($\bar{v}_i = 0$ for all i), the Pearson correlation simplifies to cosine similarity (Eq. 6).

$$\text{corr}(\mathbf{v}'_i, \mathbf{v}'_j) = \frac{\mathbf{v}'_i \cdot \mathbf{v}'_j}{\|\mathbf{v}'_i\| \|\mathbf{v}'_j\|}. \quad (6)$$

A correlation matrix $C \in \mathbb{R}^{N \times N}$ is constructed, where each element C_{ij} represents the cosine similarity between centralized superpixel vectors $\mathbf{v}'_i$ and $\mathbf{v}'_j$: $C_{ij} = \cos(\mathbf{v}'_i, \mathbf{v}'_j)$.

The original SHAP framework explains predictions by assigning each feature an importance value based on its average marginal contribution across all possible feature subsets. However, evaluating contributions across all 2^n possible feature subsets renders exact SHAP computation prohibitively expensive. In the proposed method, the SHAP values are computed using the same formula as the original SHAP but by considering only coalitions of correlated superpixels, significantly reducing the computational complexity compared to the exhaustive approach. Superpixels i and j are considered correlated if $|C_{ij}| > \tau$, where τ hyperparameter represents correlation threshold. Thus CorrSHAP employs a modified SHAP attribution formula:

$$\hat{\phi}_i = \sum_{S \subseteq \mathcal{N} \setminus \{i\}} \frac{|S|!(|\mathcal{N}| - |S| - 1)!}{|\mathcal{N}|!} \left[f_x(S \cup \{i\}) - f_x(S) \right], \quad (7)$$

Algorithm 1. Correlation SHAP (CorrSHAP)

Input: Model f, Image x, ImageSegmentation q, Option ω
Output: SHAP superpixel attribution values $\hat{\phi}$
1: $g \leftarrow$ FeatureExtractor(f) {$f(x) = h(g(x))$}
2: $\mathcal{N} \leftarrow q(x)$ {Image segmentation}
3: **if** $\omega = 1$ **then**
4:    $V \leftarrow$ flatten($\mathcal{N}$) {Raw pixel vectorization}
5: **else if** $\omega = 2$ **then**
6:    $V \leftarrow$ flatten($g(\mathcal{N})$) {Feature map vectorization}
7: **else if** $\omega = 3$ **then**
8:    $V \leftarrow \nabla_\theta f_\theta(\mathcal{N})$ {Gradient vectorization}
9: **end if**
10: $V' \leftarrow$ Centralize(V) {Vectors centralization}
11:
12: $C = \{\cos(\mathbf{v}'_i, \mathbf{v}'_j) \mid \mathbf{v}'_i, \mathbf{v}'_j \in V'\}$ {Superpixel correlation matrix calculation}
13: $\hat{\phi} \leftarrow SHAP(\mathcal{N}, C)$ {Calculate SHAP values}
14: **return** $\hat{\phi}$

where $\hat{\phi}_i$ is the approximated SHAP value for superpixel i, $\mathcal{N}$ is the set of all superpixels ($|\mathcal{N}| = N$), S is a subset of correlated superpixels excluding i, and $f_x(S)$ is the model prediction when only superpixels in S are present (other superpixels are masked to zero).

This formulation efficiently computes exact SHAP values using superpixel correlations, substantially reducing computational cost. The proposed Corr-SHAP method is visualized in Fig. 1, and the steps are shown in Algorithm 1.

4 Results and Discussion

We conducted a comprehensive ablation, qualitative, and quantitative evaluation of the proposed Correlation SHAP (CorrSHAP) method. We compared CorrSHAP, using all three proposed vectorization approaches, to Monte Carlo SHAP (MCSHAP) [20]. Experiments used two common superpixel algorithms: Quickshift [32] and Simple Linear Iterative Clustering (SLIC) SLIC [1].

4.1 Experimental Setup

For our experiments, we used several pre-trained models from the PyTorch library, specifically: ResNet-50, ResNet-18 [12], MobileNetV2 [25], and Vision Transformer (ViT-B/16) [8]. These models represent a diverse range of architectural approaches, from convolutional neural networks of varying depths and computational efficiency to a transformer-based architecture. We evaluated these models on a subset of the ImageNet-1k dataset [7], consisting of 1000 randomly sampled images from the validation set. All experiments were performed on AMD Ryzen 7950X, 64 GB of RAM, and an NVIDIA GeForce RTX 4090 GPU, providing a consistent hardware platform for performance analysis.

4.2 Metrics

In our experiments, we evaluated CorrSHAP's explanations on faithfulness and computational efficiency (execution time) metrics.

Faithfulness quantifies the extent to which the importance assigned to superpixels accurately reflects their true contribution to the model's prediction [6]. Following established practice [21], we employed the Area Under the Curve (AUC) for both insertion and deletion metrics. These metrics operate by iteratively inserting or removing superpixels, ordered by their assigned importance of Shapley values. The insertion metric assesses how rapidly the model's confidence in the correct class, y, increases as influential superpixels are added. Conversely, the deletion metric measures the rate at which the model's performance degrades as important superpixels are removed. The explanation method might excel at identifying crucial features for a prediction (high insertion AUC) but struggle to identify features that, if removed, would significantly harm the prediction (high deletion AUC, which is undesirable) or vice-versa. Thus, insertion and deletion are evaluated separately. Let $s^{(i)}$ represent the image with the

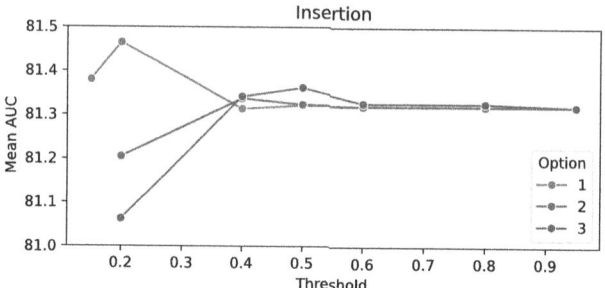

(a) Mean AUC insertion performance depending on threshold.

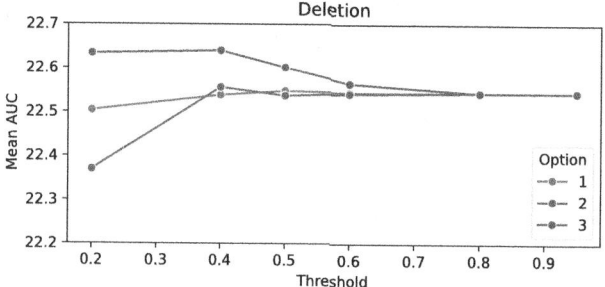

(b) Mean AUC deletion performance depending on threshold.

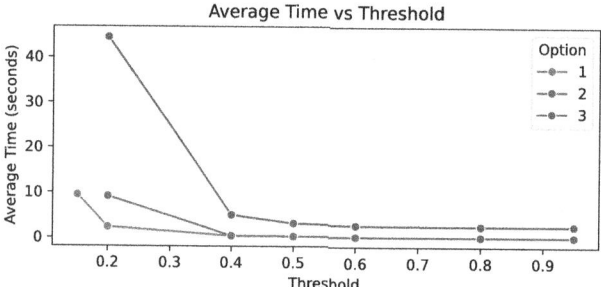

(c) Execution time depending on threshold.

Fig. 2. Performance analysis as a function of the threshold τ. **Option 1** - raw pixel vectorization, **Option 2** - feature map vectorization, and **Option 3** - gradient vectorization. Lower AUC deletion, higher AUC insertion scores, and lower execution time indicate superior performance. The execution time decreases sharply until $\tau = 0.5$, without sacrificing method faithfulness. Further reductions in τ yield diminishing returns in performance. Consequently, $\tau = 0.5$ was selected as the optimal threshold for subsequent experiments.

i-th most important superpixel (according to CorrSHAP) either inserted (for insertion) or removed (for deletion). The AUC is computed by integrating the curve of $f(s^{(i)})$ as i ranges from 0 to the total number of superpixels. Higher AUC scores for insertion and lower AUC scores for deletion indicate superior faithfulness.

Execution time measures the time in seconds that the explanation method takes to calculate the attributions for an image.

4.3 Ablation Study

The proposed CorrSHAP method introduces a single hyperparameter τ, which serves as a threshold to determine the correlation of the concept. Specifically, τ is applied to the computed correlation matrix to identify significant concept relationships. To understand the influence of τ on CorrSHAP performance, we conducted a ablation study. This study systematically explores the behavior of CorrSHAP across a range of τ values. The objective is to identify near-optimal settings for τ in a diverse set of datasets and tasks. We evaluated the impact of τ on two key performance metrics: faithfulness of the explanations and execution time.

Our choice of the threshold parameter τ, is motivated by its connection to the Pearson correlation coefficient, which provides a statistical measure of association. The Pearson correlation coefficient lies within the range $[-1, 1]$, with its magnitude interpreted according to established guidelines for the strength of correlation [5] (Table 1). To comprehensively evaluate CorrSHAP across varying degrees of superpixel dependence, we selected a set of τ values that represent the midpoints of these commonly used correlation strength categories. Specifically, we used $\tau \in \{0.2, 0.4, 0.5, 0.6, 0.8, 0.95\}$. These values correspond to thresholds delineating weak, moderate, and strong correlations, respectively.

Table 1. Interpretation of Pearson correlation coefficient.

Size of Correlation	Interpretation
.90 to 1.00 (−.90 to −1.00)	Very high positive (negative) correlation
.70 to .90 (−.70 to −.90)	High positive (negative) correlation
.50 to .70 (−.50 to −.70)	Moderate positive (negative) correlation
.30 to .50 (−.30 to −.50)	Low positive (negative) correlation
.00 to .30 (.00 to −.30)	Negligible correlation

Our analysis reveals different performance trends for mean AUC insertion and deletion between the three options as a function of the correlation threshold, τ. Figures 2a and Fig. 2b show the insertion and deletion of AUC for different values of τ. For option 1, the mean AUC insertion demonstrates a slight initial decrease with increasing τ to approximately 0.4, after which it recovers slightly to 0.5 and plateaus. Conversely, options 2 and 3 exhibit a monotonic increase in mean insertion AUC up to 0.5, followed by a stable plateau. Regarding the mean deletion AUC, faithfulness improves with increasing τ until 0.5 for option 3. Options 1 and 2 experience a marginal decrease, eventually stabilizing around 0.5. The execution time, as shown in Fig. 2c, exhibits a sharp initial decrease with increasing τ until around 0.4, beyond which it remains relatively constant. This suggests that larger τ values effectively reduce the number of superpixels considered for combinatorial perturbation. Together, these results demonstrate that CorrSHAP substantially reduces execution time while maintaining explanation faithfulness. This outcome indicates the effectiveness of our correlation method in accurately assigning correlations to superpixels. Consequently, we can restrict the computation of superpixel attributions for explanations to a smaller subset of correlated superpixels. Based on these observations, we selected $\tau = 0.5$ as the optimal value for subsequent experiments.

4.4 Qualitative Evaluation

We conducted a qualitative evaluation of CorrSHAP through several analyses: visualization of correlation matrices, visualization of correlated superpixels, and visual comparison to MCSHAP. We visualize the correlation matrices generated by each of the three proposed variants of CorrSHAP. We also present illustrative examples of the concepts exhibiting the highest correlation with a given target concept, according to each CorrSHAP variant. Finally, we compare the concept-based explanations generated by CorrSHAP with those produced by the competing method, MCSHAP.

Figure 3 shows the correlation matrices produced by each variant of the CorrSHAP method, along with visualizations of the two concepts exhibiting the highest correlation with the most influential superpixel. For this analysis, we generated superpixels from a randomly selected ImageNet-1k image, classified as "jeep", using the SLIC algorithm. Our method identified superpixel 5 as the most influential. Analyzing the correlation matrix, we can see that most of the superpixel correlations are negligible or low. Thus, the proposed methods achieve high computation efficiency without losing performance by computing SHAP values only for moderately or highly correlated superpixels.

We compare the explanations generated by the proposed CorrSHAP method and Monte Carlo SHAP (MCSHAP) [20] using random images from the ImageNet -1k dataset. MCSHAP approximates exact Shapley values by averaging a feature's marginal contribution across a sampled subset of all possible feature permutations rather than exhaustively considering every permutation as required by the original SHAP. This sampling drastically reduces computation, making SHAP estimation feasible for complex models, but introduces approximation error dependent on the number of samples. If the total number of feature permutations is less than or equal to the number of Monte Carlo samples, the algorithm is equivalent to the original SHAP. Figure 4 visualizes a qualitative comparison of explanations generated by CorrSHAP and MC-SHAP. CorrSHAP explanations are more aligned with human perception. For instance, in the "apiary" image, CorrSHAP identifies the dome as the most important superpixel,

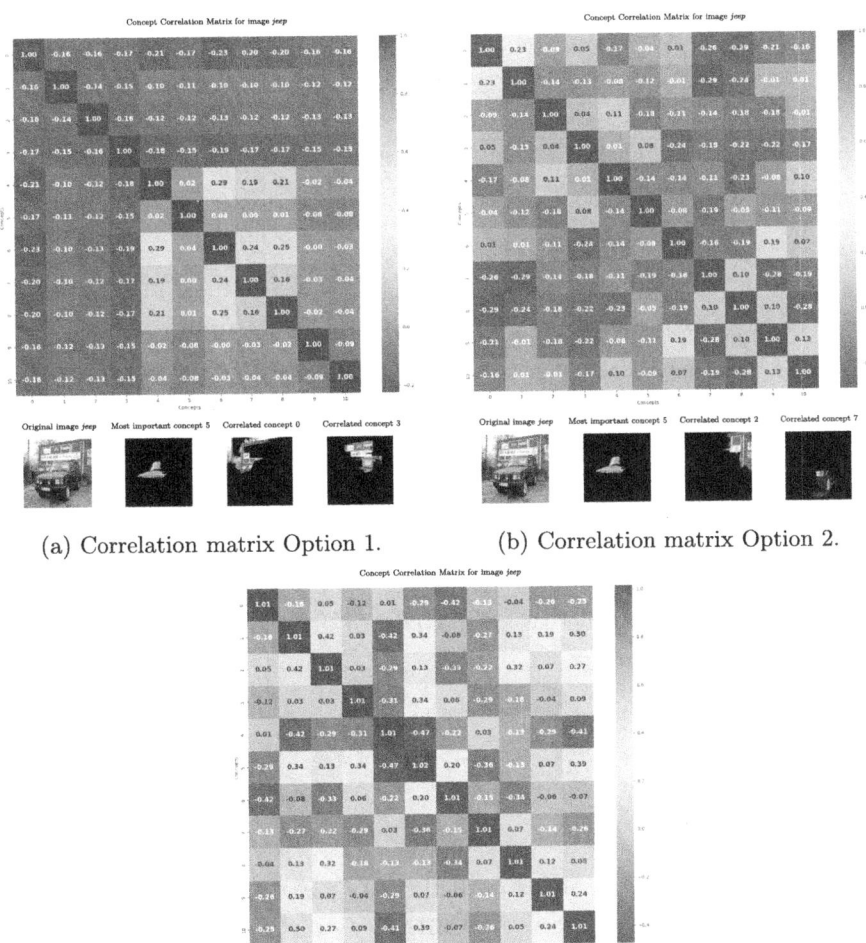

(a) Correlation matrix Option 1. (b) Correlation matrix Option 2.

(c) Correlation matrix Option 3.

Fig. 3. Correlation matrices for CorrSHAP variants, showing the two most correlated superpixels with superpixel 5 in a "jeep" image. Correlation values generally range from ±0.1 to ±0.3, indicating weak superpixel correlations. Diagonal elements (self-correlation) are, in some cases, 1.01 due to rounding errors.

whereas it is not among the top three for MCSHAP. Similarly, for the "elephant" image, MCSHAP highlights a background superpixel as the second most important superpixel, while CorrSHAP highlights superpixels that represent parts of the elephant itself.

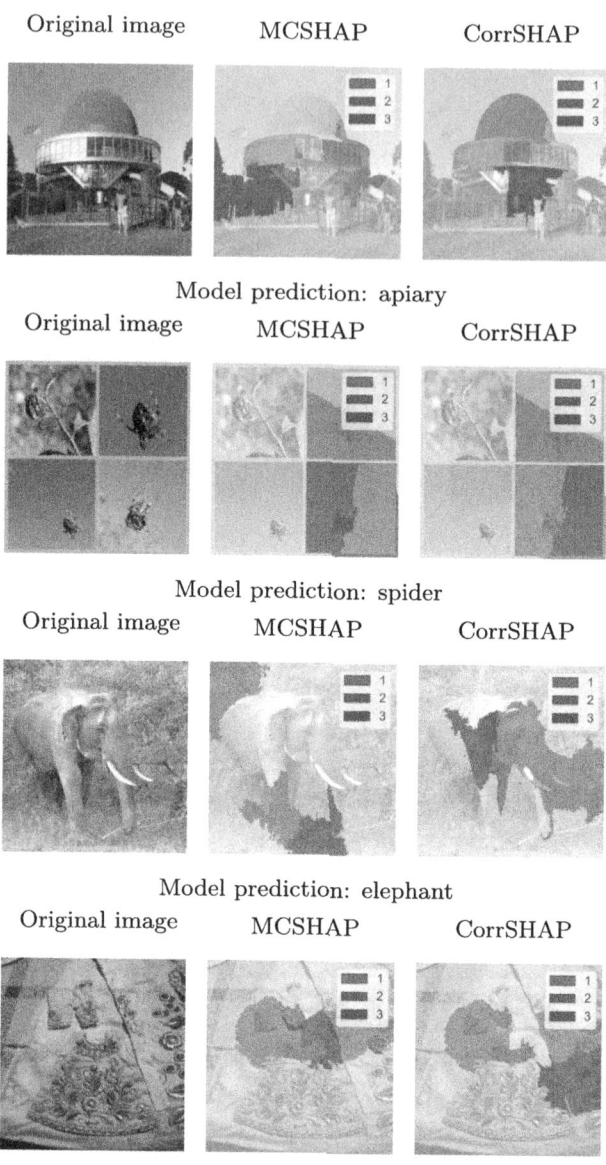

Fig. 4. Qualitative comparison of explanations generated by CorrSHAP and MCSHAP. Visual inspection reveals that CorrSHAP's explanations are more consistent with human perception of important image features (like in the *elephant* image explanation).

Table 2. Quantitative evaluation of explanation methods using metrics AUC Insertion, AUC Deletion, and execution time. Methods (CorrSHAP versions 1–3 and MCSHAP) are compared across architectures (MobileNet-v2, ResNet-18, ResNet-50, ViT-b16) and superpixel algorithms (Quickshift and SLIC).

Model	Superpixels	CorrSHAP 1	CorrSHAP 2	CorrSHAP 3	MCSHAP
Area Under the Curve (AUC) Insertion ↑					
MobileNet-v2	Quickshift	80.4	80.37	80.29	**80.89**
	SLIC	**78.12**	78.13	78.15	77.79
ResNet-18	Quickshift	60.21	60.23	60.21	textbf61.60
	SLIC	54.66	54.65	54.65	**55.41**
ResNet-50	Quickshift	**82.63**	82.61	82.63	82.27
	SLIC	**81.20**	81.20	81.20	80.66
ViT-b16	Quickshift	80.83	80.83	80.74	**81.84**
	SLIC	76.36	76.33	76.41	**76.82**
Area Under the Curve (AUC) Deletion ↓					
MobileNet-v2	Quickshift	**20.14**	20.14	20.16	20.93
	SLIC	**19.48**	19.48	19.48	21.40
ResNet-18	Quickshift	8.25	8.25	8.25	**8.03**
	SLIC	9.06	9.06	9.06	**9.01**
ResNet-50	Quickshift	**22.79**	22.79	22.79	24.16
	SLIC	**22.36**	22.36	22.39	23.79
ViT-b16	Quickshift	17.20	17.17	17.13	**16.86**
	SLIC	20.53	20.53	20.53	**20.48**
Execution Time (seconds) ↓					
MobileNet-v2	Quickshift	**0.42**	0.54	1.15	16.13
	SLIC	**0.74**	0.89	1.86	14.98
ResNet-18	Quickshift	**0.43**	0.50	1.09	7.85
	SLIC	0.66	**0.51**	1.91	13.82
ResNet-50	Quickshift	**0.46**	0.58	2.76	25.16
	SLIC	**0.78**	0.93	5.93	36.49
ViT-b16	Quickshift	**0.40**	0.52	5.41	7.26
	SLIC	**0.73**	1.01	10.53	18.00

4.5 Quantitative Evaluation

To ensure a fair comparison between the evaluated methods, we employed a consistent superpixel segmentation across all experiments. We utilized Quickshift and SLIC superpixel algorithms. For Quickshift, the hyperparameters were configured as follows: kernel size $\sigma = 10$, maximum distance $\tau = 400$, and ratio $\rho = 0.2$. For SLIC, we set the target number of segments to $K = 15$, the compactness parameter to $C = 20$, and the spatial smoothing parameter to $\sigma_s = 0$.

While the exact number of superpixels generated varied per image, the average number of superpixels was approximately nine.

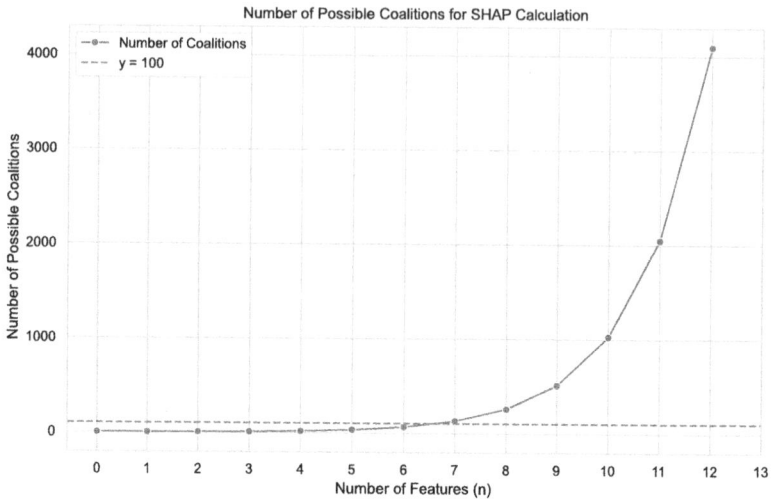

Fig. 5. Number of Possible Coalitions for SHAP Calculation. The graph illustrates the exponential growth in the number of possible coalitions as the number of features (n) increases. The y-axis represents the number of possible coalitions, calculated as (2^n). A red dotted line is drawn at y = 100 to highlight the threshold of 100 coalitions used for MCSHAP. The plot demonstrates the rapid increase in computational complexity with adding each feature, emphasizing the challenges in SHAP value calculations. (Color figure online)

For the Monte Carlo SHAP (MC-SHAP) explanation method, we used $N = 100$ random samples to approximate Shapley values. We deliberately selected superpixel hyperparameters that resulted in a relatively low number of superpixels. This choice served two purposes: (1) to accelerate experimental execution without significantly compromising the generalizability of our findings and (2) to enable scenarios where MC-SHAP effectively evaluates all possible feature subsets. Specifically, when the number of generated superpixels, denoted as S, was less than 7 ($S < 7$), the number of possible combinations (2^S) remained below our MC-SHAP sample size ($N = 100$). In these cases, the MC-SHAP approximation has more samples than a possible number of combinations, so it converges to the exact Shapley values, providing ground truth for comparison (Fig. 5).

Table 2 presents the results of our quantitative analysis. The proposed Corr-SHAP method outperforms MCSHAP in most of the scenarios evaluated. While MCSHAP exhibits a slight performance advantage when the number of superpixels in an image is low, this is due to its exhaustive consideration of feature subsets. For instance, with an image containing $n = 7$ superpixels, MCSHAP implicitly evaluates a large proportion of the possible $2^n - 1$ feature combinations. Specifically, when $n = 7$, the total number of combinations is $2^7 - 1 = 127$. As MCSHAP considers 100 combinations, it covers $\frac{100}{127} \approx 78.7\%$ of the entire combination space. CorrSHAP achieves comparable AUC results, with a maximum observed difference of $\Delta AUC = 1.39$, while evaluating only four combinations. This represents a mere $\frac{4}{127} \approx 3.1\%$ of the possible combinations for the $n = 7$ case. This demonstrates the significantly superior computational efficiency of CorrSHAP, achieving near-optimal performance with a dramatically reduced execution time.

CorrSHAP demonstrates superior faithfulness while achieving a speedup of 55x, with the precise performance gain dependent on both the underlying model and the superpixel segmentation algorithm employed. We considered a full SHAP calculation, but its computational cost proved prohibitive for practical application. For instance, with $n = 27$ superpixels, a scenario observed in several images segmented using the Quickshift algorithm, the number of possible feature subsets is $2^{27} - 1 = 134,217,727$. Evaluating Shapley values for all these combinations would require days of computation for a single image, rendering a full SHAP analysis infeasible.

5 Conclusion

This paper introduces a novel idea for concept explanations with concept correlation. It proposes CorrSHAP, a novel approach that leverages the correlation between image superpixels to greatly accelerate the computation of SHAP explanations while maintaining the faithfulness of the full SHAP. CorrSHAP transforms image superpixels into centralized vector representations and employs the modified Pearson correlation approach to quantify superpixel relationships. This correlation measure enables a drastic reduction in the number of feature subsets required for accurate SHAP value calculation. The concept of region correlation extends beyond SHAP values. It can be readily integrated into other explanation methods, such as LIME, which currently does not account for superpixel dependencies. Furthermore, the principle of region correlation is not limited to explainability as it holds potential for applications in other domains, such as image segmentation.

CorrSHAP is model-agnostic and shows great performance in qualitative and quantitative evaluations while offering a substantial leap in computational efficiency, with an execution time 55 times faster than the method employing a similar conceptual framework. This enables our method to be practical and applicable in real-world scenarios.

Future work will explore alternative correlation measures beyond Pearson correlation and cosine similarity. We also plan to integrate our superpixel correlation approach into established explanation methods, including KernelSHAP, GradSHAP, and LIME. While our current method utilizes superpixel correlation for efficiency without modifying the underlying SHAP algorithm, this approach means strict adherence to properties like completeness and symmetry cannot always be guaranteed due to the non-exhaustive sampling of coalitions. Addressing this limitation by developing compensatory mechanisms is a key direction for future research. Finally, we envision the development of interactive visualization tools that empower users to explore superpixel relationships and gain real-time insights into model predictions, which will facilitate a deeper understanding of model behavior.

Acknowledgement. This work is funded by the Austrian Federal Ministry of Climate Action, Environment, Energy, Mobility, Innovation and Technology, the Austrian Federal Ministry of Digital and Economic Affairs, and implemented by austria wirtschaftsservice (aws) and the Austrian Research Promotion Agency (FFG) in the frame of the Important Project of Common European Interest (IPCEI) on Microelectronics and Communication Technologies (ME/CT).

References

1. Achanta, R., Shaji, A., Smith, K., Lucchi, A., Fua, P., Süsstrunk, S.: Slic superpixels compared to state-of-the-art superpixel methods. IEEE Trans. Pattern Anal. Mach. Intell. **34**(11), 2274–2282 (2012)
2. Bennetot, A., Franchi, G., Ser, J., Chatila, R., Diaz-Rodriguez, N.: Greybox XAI: a neural-symbolic learning framework to produce interpretable predictions for image classification. Knowl.-Based Syst. **258**, 109947 (2022)
3. Broeck, G., Lykov, A., Schleich, M., Suciu, D.: On the tractability of Shap explanations. J. Artif. Intell. Res. **74**, 851–886 (2022)
4. Charpiat, G., Girard, N., Felardos, L., Tarabalka, Y.: Input similarity from the neural network perspective. In: Advances in Neural Information Processing Systems, vol. 32 (2019)
5. Cohen, J.: Statistical Power Analysis for the Behavioral Sciences. Routledge (2013)
6. Colin, J., Fel, T., Cadène, R., Serre, T.: What i cannot predict, I do not understand: A human-centered evaluation framework for explainability methods. Adv. Neural. Inf. Process. Syst. **35**, 2832–2845 (2022)
7. Deng, J., Dong, W., Socher, R., Li, L.J., Li, K., Fei-Fei, L.: Imagenet: a large-scale hierarchical image database. In: 2009 IEEE Conference on Computer Vision and Pattern Recognition, pp. 248–255. IEEE (2009)
8. Dosovitskiy, A., et al.: An image is worth 16x16 words: transformers for image recognition at scale. In: 9th International Conference on Learning Representations, ICLR 2021, Virtual Event, Austria, May 3–7, 2021 (2021)
9. Felzenszwalb, P.F., Huttenlocher, D.P.: Efficient graph-based image segmentation. Int. J. Comput. Vision **59**, 167–181 (2004)
10. Fumagalli, F., Muschalik, M., Kolpaczki, P., Hüllermeier, E., Hammer, B.: Shap-iq: Unified approximation of any-order shapley interactions. In: Advances in Neural Information Processing Systems, vol. 36 (2024)
11. Gunning, D., Stefik, M., Choi, J., Miller, T., Stumpf, S., Yang, G.Z.: Xai—explainable artificial intelligence. Sci. Robot. **4**(37), eaay7120 (2019)

12. He, K., Zhang, X., Ren, S., Sun, J.: Deep residual learning for image recognition. In: Proceedings of the IEEE Conference on Computer Vision and Pattern Recognition, pp. 770–778 (2016)
13. Hu, L., Wang, K.: Computing shap efficiently using model structure information. arXiv preprint arXiv:2309.02417 (2023)
14. Huang, X., Marques-Silva, J.: Updates on the complexity of shap scores. In: Proceedings of the Thirty-Third International Joint Conference on Artificial Intelligence, pp. 403–412 (2024)
15. Jiang, H., Jang, J., Kpotufe, S.: Quickshift++: provably good initializations for sample-based mean shift. In: International Conference on Machine Learning, pp. 2294–2303. PMLR (2018)
16. Kawauchi, H., Fuse, T.: Shap-based interpretable object detection method for satellite imagery. Remote Sens. **14**(9), 1970 (2022)
17. Kirillov, A., et al.: Segment anything. In: Proceedings of the IEEE/CVF International Conference on Computer Vision, pp. 4015–4026 (2023)
18. Lundberg, S.: A unified approach to interpreting model predictions. arXiv preprint arXiv:1705.07874 (2017)
19. de Mijolla, D., Frye, C., Kunesch, M., Mansir, J., Feige, I.: Human-interpretable model explainability on high-dimensional data. arXiv preprint arXiv:2010.07384 (2020)
20. Mitchell, R., Cooper, J., Frank, E., Holmes, G.: Sampling permutations for shapley value estimation. J. Mach. Learn. Res. **23**(43), 1–46 (2022)
21. Petsiuk, V.: Rise: randomized input sampling for explanation of black-box models. arXiv preprint arXiv:1806.07421 (2018)
22. Ravi, N., et al.: Sam 2: segment anything in images and videos. arXiv preprint arXiv:2408.00714 (2024)
23. Ribeiro, M.T., Singh, S., Guestrin, C.: "why should i trust you?" explaining the predictions of any classifier. In: Proceedings of the 22nd ACM SIGKDD International Conference on Knowledge Discovery and Data Mining, pp. 1135–1144 (2016)
24. Ribeiro, M.T., Singh, S., Guestrin, C.: Anchors: High-precision model-agnostic explanations. In: Proceedings of the AAAI Conference on Artificial Intelligence, vol. 32 (2018)
25. Sandler, M., Howard, A., Zhu, M., Zhmoginov, A., Chen, L.C.: Mobilenetv2: inverted residuals and linear bottlenecks. In: Proceedings of the IEEE Conference on Computer Vision and Pattern Recognition, pp. 4510–4520 (2018)
26. Selvaraju, R.R., Cogswell, M., Das, A., Vedantam, R., Parikh, D., Batra, D.: Gradcam: visual explanations from deep networks via gradient-based localization. In: Proceedings of the IEEE International Conference on Computer Vision, pp. 618–626 (2017)
27. Shi, J., Malik, J.: Normalized cuts and image segmentation. IEEE Trans. Pattern Anal. Mach. Intell. **22**(8), 888–905 (2000)
28. Sundararajan, M., Taly, A., Yan, Q.: Axiomatic attribution for deep networks. In: International Conference on Machine Learning, pp. 3319–3328. PMLR (2017)
29. Tang, J., Tong, H., Tong, F., Zhang, Y., Chen, W.: Exploiting superpixel-based contextual information on active learning for high spatial resolution remote sensing image classification. Remote Sens. **15**(3), 715 (2023)
30. Teneggi, J., Luster, A., Sulam, J.: Fast hierarchical games for image explanations. IEEE Trans. Pattern Anal. Mach. Intell. **45**(4), 4494–4503 (2022)
31. Tsai, C.P., Yeh, C.K., Ravikumar, P.: Faith-shap: The faithful shapley interaction index. J. Mach. Learn. Res. **24**(94), 1–42 (2023)

32. Vedaldi, A., Soatto, S.: Quick Shift and Kernel Methods for Mode Seeking. In: Forsyth, D., Torr, P., Zisserman, A. (eds.) ECCV 2008. LNCS, vol. 5305, pp. 705–718. Springer, Heidelberg (2008). https://doi.org/10.1007/978-3-540-88693-8_52
33. Zhang, Y., Tiňo, P., Leonardis, A., Tang, K.: A survey on neural network interpretability. IEEE Trans. Emerg. Top. Comput. Intell. **5**(5), 726–742 (2021)

Open Access This chapter is licensed under the terms of the Creative Commons Attribution 4.0 International License (http://creativecommons.org/licenses/by/4.0/), which permits use, sharing, adaptation, distribution and reproduction in any medium or format, as long as you give appropriate credit to the original author(s) and the source, provide a link to the Creative Commons license and indicate if changes were made.

The images or other third party material in this chapter are included in the chapter's Creative Commons license, unless indicated otherwise in a credit line to the material. If material is not included in the chapter's Creative Commons license and your intended use is not permitted by statutory regulation or exceeds the permitted use, you will need to obtain permission directly from the copyright holder.

On Background Bias of Post-Hoc Concept Embeddings in Computer Vision DNNs

Gesina Schwalbe[1](✉)[iD], Georgii Mikriukov[2,3][iD], Edgar Heinert[5][iD], Stavros Gerolymatos[4][iD], Mert Keser[3,6][iD], Alois Knoll[6][iD], Matthias Rottmann[7][iD], and Annika Mütze[5][iD]

[1] University of Lübeck, Lübeck, Germany
gesina.schwalbe@uni-luebeck.de
[2] Hochschule Anhalt, Köthen, Germany
georgii.mikriukov@hs-anhalt.de
[3] Continental AG, Hanover, Germany
{georgii.mikriukov,mert.keser}@continental-corporation.com
[4] University of Liverpool, Liverpool, UK
s.gerolymatos@liverpool.ac.uk
[5] University of Wuppertal, Wuppertal, Germany
{heinert,muetze}@uni-wuppertal.de
[6] Technical University of Munich, Munich, Germany
muetze@uni-wuppertal.de
[7] Osnabrück University, Osnabrück, Germany
matthias.rottmann@uos.de

Abstract. The thriving research field of concept-based explainable artificial intelligence (C-XAI) investigates how human-interpretable semantic concepts embed in the latent spaces of deep neural networks (DNNs). Post-hoc approaches therein use a set of examples to specify a concept, and determine its embeddings in DNN latent space using data driven techniques. This proved useful to uncover biases between different target (*foreground* or concept) classes. However, given that the *background* is mostly uncontrolled during training, an important question has been left unattended so far: Are/to what extent are state-of-the-art, data-driven post-hoc C-XAI approaches themselves prone to biases with respect to their *backgrounds*? E.g., wild animals mostly occur against vegetation backgrounds, and they seldom appear on roads. Even simple and robust C-XAI methods might abuse this shortcut for enhanced performance. A dangerous performance degradation of the concept-corner cases of animals on the road could thus remain undiscovered. This work validates and thoroughly confirms that established Net2Vec-based concept segmentation techniques frequently capture background biases, including alarming ones, such as underperformance on road scenes. For the analysis, we compare 3 established techniques from the domain of background randomization on > 50 concepts from 2 datasets, and 7 diverse DNN architectures. Our results indicate that even low-cost setups can provide both valuable insight and improved background robustness. The code is available at: https://github.com/gesina/bg_randomized_loce.

1 Introduction

With the advance of deep neural networks (DNNs) into safety-critical application areas, like medical imaging or automated driving perception, a pressing need to explain the inner workings of trained DNNs has arisen [24,29,33,51]. To this end, an increasingly popular class of introspection methods utilizes concept-based explainable artificial intelligence (C-XAI): Their common aim is to verify and explore the internal representation of *concepts* from natural language within DNN latent spaces [35,53,60]. For verification purposes, special focus was placed on post-hoc supervised C-XAI techniques based on TCAV [30] and Net2Vec [15]. These reveal, for already trained DNNs, whether and how user-defined concepts are represented in the DNN intermediate outputs [1,59].

As a shared basic principle, they use few positive and negative examples of a concept to train a simple, usually linear [30] model. This model, which we refer to as the *concept embedding (CE)*, shall distinguish between intermediate outputs of image regions with or without the concept of interest. Performance and similarity of CEs provides valuable insights into the semantic structure and potential biases of the DNN's latent space [30,50]. Prominent examples from the computer vision domain are gender bias (tie cooccurring with male [30]), dependence on object size [45,59], and nonconformity to symbolic rules [19].

CEs even give rise to very intuitive interpretations: They capture the most activating neurons/filters for a concept; and represent the latent space vector pointing into the direction of "more" concept, e.g., looks more "animalish". However, in this work, we choose a model-based definition to highlight a crucial caveat: Supervised CEs are data-driven, and therefore prone to mirror biases inherent to the concept data and to the DNN intermediate outputs. In particular, the C-XAI results may be sensitive to bias of the DNN-learned concepts with respect to their backgrounds, e.g., large animals rarely occur against a background of roads. If unexplored, these biases may conceal important flaws of the DNN's generalization capability, e.g., failing to detect animals crossing the road. This would be no surprise: Recent work by Janoušková et al. [25] demonstrated on the example of fungal classification, how background information can significantly influence model decision-making. Substrate features were often leveraged by models even when they were not explicitly part of the target class. Apart from full DNNs, bias exploration of CEs has so far been restricted to bias between different foreground concepts [1,30,59] or adversarial concepts [46] not foreground-vs.-background; and only few works have briefly touched upon background randomization for CEs, but not with background robustness in mind [45].

Meanwhile, a rich field of research has been established around reducing background biases during the training phase of a DNN: Many techniques for background randomization, mostly via image manipulation, are available to average out any background dependencies. Early simple ones crop and paste an image's foreground onto new backgrounds [67]. Diverse techniques complement this, allowing for diversification of backgrounds, generation of new ones [52], and enhanced realism of pasting [27]. Even factorization of influence factors like shape, texture and color, is possible [48]. In this work, we leverage a set of standard background randomization techniques to, for the first time, systematically explore and measure background biases of a broad spectrum of post-hoc supervised C-XAI methods, computer vision DNNs, and datasets.

The questions at hand are whether (1) despite being linear, CEs do fall for (natural) background biases; and (2) this can be uncovered (and avoided) using background randomization techniques, increasing chances to find otherwise hard-to-discover biases in DNN models and data. In this paper, we thoroughly investigate and confirm these questions for the specific but common case of concept segmentation, i.e., a region-wise classification of DNN intermediate outputs. This region-based setting makes the problem particularly handy: No strict (and costly to obtain) realism of the full image composition is needed anymore, only of spatially local patches. We therefore use and compare 3 low-cost background randomization techniques, and test these both for use in testing (for bias discovery) and training (for bias confirmation and removal) of the CEs. This even allows to unravel sources of bias: If performance still drops for CEs trained with background randomization, this indicates a bias intrinsic to the DNN's representations. Our main findings and contributions are as follows:

- a **method and workflow to both reveal and assess background biases of concept embeddings** in DNN latent spaces, and simultaneously **counteract data-biased concept-based explanations**, using established background randomization techniques;
- a broad study proving effectiveness of our method: standard DNNs and concept datasets exhibit clear and potentially dangerous background biases, which can at least partly be mitigated using local-to-global C-XAI techniques;
- an ablation study showing that insightful results can already be obtained very **cheaply** with as little as a **single round of background replacements and a single late DNN layer**.

2 Related Work

2.1 Concept-Based XAI

Concept-based explainable AI summarizes DNN introspection techniques that associate DNN internal units like filters with human-understandable concepts from natural language. In the visual domain these can be object or subobject classes, as well as object attributes (material, texture, etc.) [2], complete scenes [75], and more general language synonym sets [14,15]. First methods in the subfield associated concepts with single neurons or CNN-filters. An example for this is simple unsupervised feature visualization [49,50]. By now, the field has grown to a wide range of problems, with a growing amount of research interest and reviews on the topic [28,35,36,53,60], as detailed in the following. One branch focuses on ante-hoc enforcement of alignment between intermediate units and given concepts [32,58] respectively automatically learned interpretable prototypes [6,12,71] (see, e.g., [36, Fig. 4] for a graphical overview). These, however, require control over the training process and special care to avoid leakage of non-concept information into the units' meanings [22,43]. In many applications, post-hoc analysis of already trained feature spaces poses an alternative. While a plethora of methods by now allow to explore learned concepts of models in an unsupervised fashion [13,18,54,69,74], verification typically relies on finding specific, user-predefined concepts from given rules [1,19,59]. Good results were achieved using complex latent-space-to-concept mappings, like neuralizing flows [10] or non-linear SVM classifiers [7]. However, simple linear mappings are claimed to be more intuitive for explanations [30].

An early representative of this direction is the assignment of concepts to (singular) filters by Bau et al. [2]. The problem setting later evolved to more general assignment of concepts to latent space *vectors*. This was first done in a supervised manner by Kim et al. in TCAV [30] for concept classification, and in parallel for concept segmentation by Fong et al. as the Net2Vec framework [15], and later regression [20]. Here, we extend this line of concept segmentation research. To this end, we build on several proposed extensions of this framework, including less costly preprocessing [45,59], and more stable losses [61]. Most recently, Mikriukov et al. introduced a local-to-global version of Net2Vec, LoCE [44], to analyze how concepts manifest differently across individual samples. This additionally captures the variance in concept representations and supposedly their dependence on surrounding context, such as background information.

2.2 Background Randomization

To randomize image backgrounds, one typically first identifies the foreground canvas. This process often relies on existing segmentation labels, but can also involve AI-based approaches, such as foundational segmentation models [31,41] or foreground-prediction models [62,73].

A straightforward approach for background randomization is to paste the identified foreground onto a different background image. This technique has been used for background augmentation [57], to analyze the influence of foreground and background information on classification models [72], and to introduce out-of-distribution objects into semantic segmentation street scenes [3]. As progress has been made in the field of image generation [40,56], prompt-based generation of artificial backgrounds has been considered [37,42]. These methods come with the limitations of the generative models, which include the generation of undesired foreground objects within complex backgrounds. Another approach leaves the natural domain and corrupts backgrounds either with simple distortions, such as Gaussian noise [47] or by style transfering the background with paintings, thereby changing the texture and color of backgrounds [66]. Finally, some datasets contain naturally occurring adversarial samples, where unusual foreground-background combinations challenge model robustness [5,21,25,34]. However, these datasets are not appropriate for a controlled study of specific foreground-background relationships, and the adversarial combinations they contain are not random.

To study the randomization of naturally occurring backgrounds and assess the individual limitations of each technique, we apply both straightforward past-

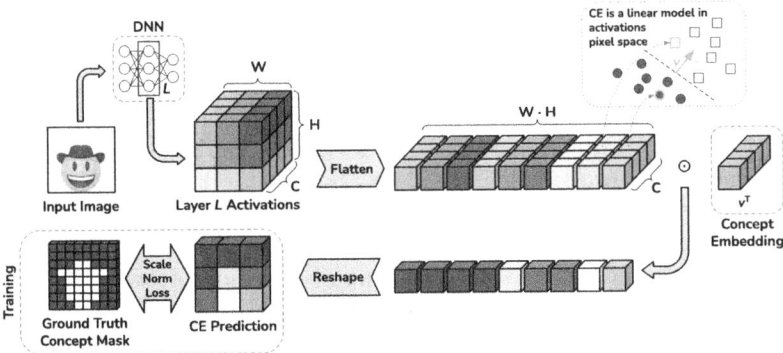

Fig. 1. Illustration of training and inference of global and local concept embeddings (here for concept cowboy smiley): A CE is a linear classifier on activation map pixels, represented by its normal vector v in latent space. To infer the model on a new *input image*, (1) the *activations* for the desired layer L are collected, (2) each pixel is classified using dot product with the CE, which yields a heatmap of concept presence as *CE prediction*. For training, (3) this is compared against a *ground truth concept mask* to update the CE weights via gradient descent.(Color figure online)

ing and artificial background generation independently. Furthermore, to increase background variability within a single image, we experiment with placing foregrounds on Voronoi-patch-based backgrounds, where each cell contains a different background, following the approach of [48].

3 Background: Global and Local Post-Hoc Concept Segmentation

Post-hoc supervised C-XAI aims to find a latent representation for a user-defined language concept inside an already trained DNN. In particular, the motivating question is: *Does the DNN latent space encode (enough) information about a concept?* Here, we use two main and closely related methods: Net2Vec and local concept embeddings (LoCE).

Global Concept Embeddings. Starting with Net2Vec, the main ingredients in the beginning are a trained DNN, a selected layer therein, and a labeled image dataset defining the concept via segmentation masks. They now rely on three tricks to answer the above question (cf. illustration in Fig. 1):

1. The question is reformulated to: Is it possible to predict the presence of my concept in an image solely from the latent space outputs of the image at that layer? If this is the case, then the latent space does encode information about the concept (the mutual information is high). This makes it essentially a **learning problem**: Can one train a well-performing classifier to predict (segment) presence of the concept?

2. The input image already contains enough information about the concept, since human labelers can decide its presence/segmentation. If the DNN would therefore be the identity function, the previous point would in principle still confirm that the DNN has "knowledge" about the concept. To counteract this counterintuitive situation, a strict **model bias** must be imposed. The choice here is a **linear model**, due to its good interpretability.
3. Lastly, to make it a **segmentation instead of a classification task**, Net2Vec suggested making the **classification per activation map pixel** instead of the complete activation map. Given an activation map of size Channels × Height × Width thus yields Height × Width activation map pixels, each a vector of dimensionality Channels=:C. As we now extract concepts from pixels instead of whole feature maps, the linear classification problem is drastically simplified: It becomes the training of the kernel of a singular 1×1 convolution.

This kernel takes the role of the normal vector to the linear hyperplane separating concept from non-concept activation map pixels in that pixels space. In particular, it is itself also a vector of size C (the concept vector); the one pointing in the direction of the concept pixels. This makes the vectors easy to compare.

Measuring CE Performance. Note that this formulation makes obtaining CEs simply a machine learning problem: The classifier for a concept (with the concept's CE as parameters) can be trained on a training set; and later be used for inference on new samples. In our case new samples are activation map pixels of new images. So, a CE can be used to segment the learned concept in a new image. Such obtained segmentation masks can be tested against a ground truth after rescaling, measuring how well the CE captured information about the concept.

The segmentation test performance of a CE depends both on the quality of the concept training data used to obtain the CE, as well as the quality of concept encoding of the DNN latent space. We unravel this here to distinguish between background bias originating from (1) the concept training data (removable by randomizing the concept training data's backgrounds), and (2) from the DNN itself (not removable).

Local and Globalized Local Concept Embeddings. The main adaptation done by the LoCE approach [44] compared to Net2Vec is quite simple: Instead of training one CE on the *complete* concept dataset, one trains one CE per *single sample* in the concept dataset (the *local CE, LoCE,* of that image). A single LoCE thus captures the information about how the occurrences of its concept in *its specific image* can be differentiated from the background in *that image*; as compared to a Net2Vec CE, which captures how to differentiate *any* concept instance from *any* background. The distribution of the LoCEs in latent space captures as much of the variance of the separation problem as possible. LoCEs can later be combined again via averaging, again obtaining a CE that is valid for a complete concept, not only instances from one image. We here call such an average the *globalized LoCE* (GloCE) of the concept. Mikriukov et al. [44] showed that this is similar but in general not equal to the Net2Vec (i.e., directly global) CE trained on the same concept data. Therefore, we investigate them separately (*and later in this work show that they better capture background biases*).

Layer Selection. It is known that the quality of information about a given concept typically smoothly evolves across several layers, gradually increasing until an optimum (set of) layer(s) [15,16,55]. Also, colors and textures are typically better embedded in early layers, whereas more complex concepts are optimally embedded in later layers [15]. Similar to [44], this work adopts a structured approach to layer selection by extracting activations at the level of full network blocks rather than after individual within-block layers. Blocks act as meaningful processing units, providing consistent checkpoints for analyzing internal representations. For CNNs, selected convolutional block outputs are used; for transformers, encoder outputs are analyzed. In multi-branch architectures (e.g., object detectors), one representative branch is selected to trace feature progression.

4 Approach

Concept embeddings are obtained using (concept) training data, and therefore can themselves easily be prone to biases. In this paper, we are specifically interested in *background biases*. These are *any dependencies of the CE's performance on non-object-level features that are unrelated to the quality of the CE's concept*; e.g., a fox should still be a fox independent of whether it is on the road or on a field. Non-object-level feature here refers to a feature not part of the concept objects, i.e., one of the features in input image pixels that do not belong to the image's semantic canvas. *Such features are commonly also referred to as scenery or background* [75]. The primary use of CEs is also what makes their biases so interesting: By design, they represent a piece of knowledge encoded in the internal representations of their DNN under scrutiny. If a CE is biased, e.g., better detects foxes in fields than on streets, this might indicate a flaw in the DNN's encodings. In that case, background information leaks into evidence collection for the concept fox.

In this work, we specifically investigate the following questions:

1. Given trained CEs, *does a change of the background distribution impact their performance when testing?* In other words: Are there preferred or hard-to-deal-with backgrounds?
2. *Does the CE training extract different information about the concept if the background distribution is changed during training?* Which divides into:
    – *Do different (here: uniformly randomized) backgrounds lead to different concept vector representations?* This quantifies the background bias of the CE, both coming from the concept data or the DNN itself.

– *Do CEs trained on randomized backgrounds exhibit a different / better performance distribution over backgrounds?* An improvement indicates removable background bias originating from the concept training data. Remaining performance issues can indicate a bias of the DNN itself.

At the heart of answering them are two main ingredients: Being able to control the background distribution of test and training datasets; and the actual training and evaluation of the CEs (cf. Sect. 3). In the following, we first detail our approaches to control the background distribution via background randomization techniques, and then summarize the used CE techniques and metrics.

4.1 Techniques for Background Randomization

Image-Level Background Randomization. In order to extract background-debiased and thus broader CE class distributions, we randomized the backgrounds of each foreground in three ways, always preserving the original canvas specified by the foreground class mask.

Foreground. All methods have in common that the foregrounds of the concepts of interest must be given, i.e., a dataset of images together with segmentation masks defining which parts of an image belong to which of the foreground concepts. For this we employed two well-known concept segmentation datasets as a foreground dataset: The Pascal VOC dataset [11] with 20 classes, and the ImageNetS50 dataset [17], a subset of ImageNet1k [8] with 50 classes that has foreground class masks for each of its 64431 train and 752 validation images.

Background Annotations and Filtering. Another preliminary for our methods is that a dataset of labeled backgrounds must be available, such that the distribution of backgrounds can be controlled. Assuming both a foreground and a set of background samples are given, we randomly select a background, resize and crop both images to size 256 × 256. We further employ two filtering criteria: We exclude background images for which the foreground class itself was in the top 5 predictions of an ImageNet pretrained Vision Transformer (`vit_base_patch16_224` [9,70]); and for generation of several background variants we draw background classes without replacement, such that a highly diverse set of background variants is created. The pasting is also common to all methods: We created additional images by replacing all non-foreground pixels with random realistic scenes from the backgrounds.

Background Generation. We here investigate three different techniques for generating the background. As the simplest version, we directly use a 10% subset of the Places205 dataset [75], a large-scale scene collection of 205 categories, containing 247k images (`Places`). For the testing, we manually selected and

Table 1. Tested background supercategories with corresponding Places205 classes. Superclasses were selected to be visually homogeneous (*Note: crowded background sceneries were excluded to not interfere with the **person** concept class.*).

architecture:	abbey, aqueduct, arch, attic, basilica, building_facade, office_building
indoors:	bedroom, dining_room, hotel_room, kitchen, kitchenette, living_room
at_water:	bayou, canyon, coast, creek, dock, islet, marsh, ocean, pond
machinery:	engine_room
open_lands:	badlands, butte
forest:	bamboo_forest, forest_path, rainforest
botanical:	botanical_garden, cottage_garden, formal_garden, orchard, topiary_garden
field:	golf_course, wheat_field, fairway
snow:	crevasse, iceberg, mountain_snowy, ski_slope, snowfield
road:	crosswalk, highway

clustered 24 background categories into 10 diverse, each visually homogeneous supercategories (for details see Table 1).

In an attempt to increase the variability of background randomization per image and thus reduce the amount of required samples, we used a Voronoi-patching approach similar to [48] (`Voronoi`). In this work, we generate a Voronoi diagram [68] based on 8 uniformly sampled points (cf. Fig. 2a for illustration). Each cell is filled with a randomly shifted cutout either from a chosen or a randomly sampled background image.

Lastly, we investigate whether the need for manual background labeling can be overcome by using generative AI. We leverage Würstchen[1] [52], a highly efficient text-to-image diffusion model, to create semantically rich backgrounds. A diverse set of background categories—including `cloudscape`, `space`, `jungle`, `desert`, `arctic`, `volcanic`, `ocean`, and `abstract patterns`—was defined, with each category described using detailed text prompts emphasizing realism and atmospheric characteristics. The generator synthesized 100 high-resolution (1024 × 1024) images per category using controlled diffusion, ensuring diverse and contextually relevant textures.

4.2 Measuring Background Robustness

In order to benchmark and compare the CEs, we employ two main perspectives: A model-based one relying on black-box performance measurement; and a representation-based one, measuring similarity of the underlying concept vectors.

Performance Measurement. With respect to the model-based perspective, a CE can be simply considered as a linear classifier that can predict a segmentation mask on new samples. In these terms, robustness translates into robust performance, i.e., generalization to novel kinds of samples such as the ones with

---

[1] Implementation: https://huggingface.co/warp-ai/wuerstchen, using default parameters.

randomized backgrounds. To measure the quality of an output mask M against the ground truth M_{gt}, we use Intersection over Union (IoU), also known as the Jaccard index, defined as

$$\text{IoU}(M, M_{\text{gt}}) := \frac{M \cap M_{\text{gt}}}{M \cup M_{\text{gt}}} \in [0, 1] \tag{1}$$

We note that measuring performance on unseen samples does not make sense for LoCEs: These are not trained to generalize. Instead, we globalize them: Given a set of LoCEs that represent one concept in a latent space, we define their globalized LoCE (GloCE) as the model / hyperplane defined by the mean of their representing concept vectors.

Representation Comparison. As an alternative to black-box test statistics, we use one of the core advantages of linear models: Being represented by vectors, we compare CEs c_1, c_2 pairwise by calculating the cosine similarity of their underlying concept vectors v_1, v_2. With $\|\cdot\|$ denoting the Euclidean norm, this is defined as

$$\text{CosSim}(v_1, v_2) := \frac{v_1^T v_2}{\|v_1\| \cdot \|v_2\|} \in [-1, 1] \tag{2}$$

and intuitively measures the angle between the two vectors, resulting in -1 for opposite, 0 for orthogonal, and 1 for parallel vectors. This can be used to directly compare a pair of LoCEs that was trained on the same image.

5 Experiments

In this section, we detail the exact setup and results of our background robustness analysis. The latter is split into three parts, following the questions posed in Sect. 4: (1) Whether a *performance* drop is measurable when testing on manipulated background distributions *(yes, for some concepts and backgrounds)*, (2) whether training on background randomized samples results in different *concept representations* (yes, they do quite strongly), and lastly (3) in how far the background-randomized training changes the performance of CEs *(visibly beneficial at low cost)*. In the latter, we include an ablation study showing that neither a large number of randomized image variants is necessary, nor more than one layer per model in order to obtain relevant results. Some examples of CE inference are provided in Fig. 2.

5.1 Experiment Settings

Concept Datasets. As previously mentioned, we use the ImageNetS50 dataset [17], which features segmentations of 50 object classes, each with 10 carefully selected training and 10 validation images. We note that CE training is few shot on images: The CEs have a very small amount of to-be-trained parameters

(a) **Examples** of an original ImageNetS image (*left*) with random Places205 background (*center left*), a Voronoi-style background (*center right*) and an image with Würstchen-generated background (*right*):

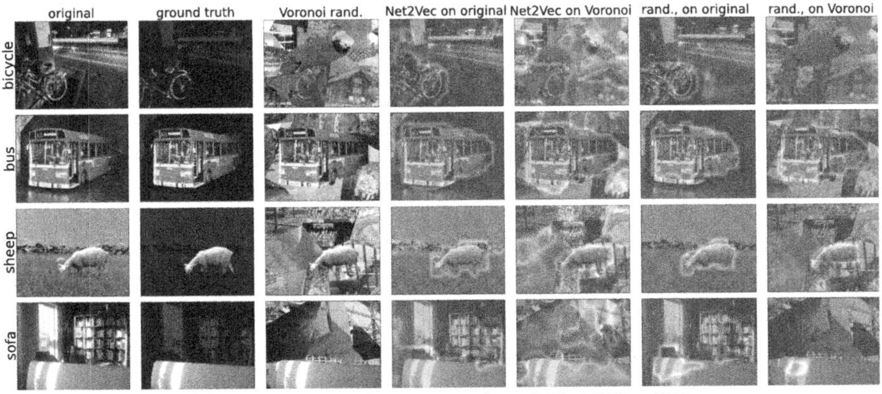

(b) Exemplary inference results of **Net2Vec** CEs.

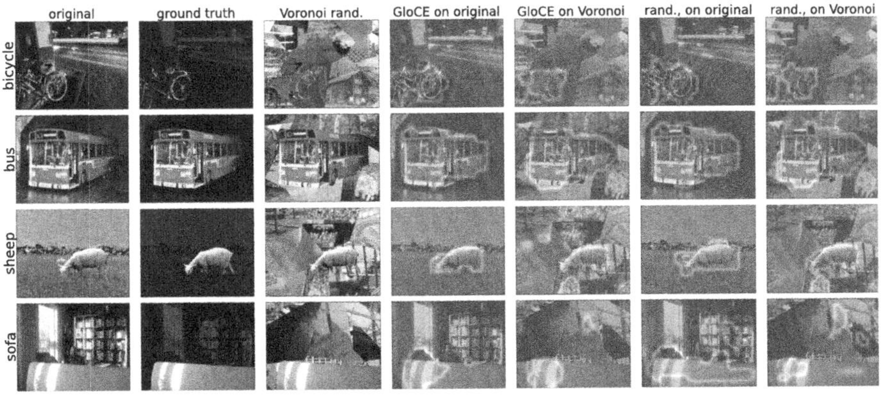

(c) Exemplary inference results of **GloCEs**.

Fig. 2. Exemplary results for Net2Vec CE and GloCEs and 4 Pascal VOC concepts. For each concept, the heatmaps resulting from inference of a CE trained on vanilla data and one trained with simple Places205 background randomization (rand.) are shown side-by-side, each for the vanilla original and a Voronoi randomized version of a (randomly chosen) test sample. Ground truth masks (*2nd column*) and predicted heatmaps (*columns 4–7*) are shown via overlays: *dark/blue* means 0, *no darkening/red* means 1. Figure 2a visualizes all three considered background randomization techniques. (Color figure online)

Table 2. Overview of used early, middle, and last layers per DNN. Used shorthands: m=model, bb=backbone, enc=encoder, f=features.

	early	middle	late
detr:	`m.bb.conv_enc.m.layer4`	`m.input_projection`	`m.enc.layers.5`
vit:	`conv_proj`	`enc.layers.encoder_layer_6`	`enc.layers.encoder_layer_11`
swin:	`f.0`	`f.3`	`features.7`
efficientnet:	`f.4.2`	`f.6.0`	`f.7.0`
mobilenet:	`f.7.block.2.0`	`f.12.block.3.0`	`f.16.0`
yolo:	`4.cv3.conv`	`14.conv`	`23.cv3.conv`
vgg:	`f.7`	`f.21`	`f.28`

(typically ≤ 500), while each single image gives rise to an activation map of spatial size at least $16 \times 16 = 256$ pixels, each serving as one CE training input (cf. Fig. 1). This amounts to at least $5\times$ the number of samples compared to the number of parameters in the vanilla case. Apart from that, we also use a subset of 20 concepts from the Pascal VOC dataset with each 50 / 20 randomly selected train / validation samples (see Tables 3, 4, 5 for the class list). For evaluation on background-randomized test samples, each 10 variants per foreground are created by random background sampling.

DNNs and Layers. We follow prior work on LoCEs[2] in [44], regarding the choice of a diverse set of CNN and Vision Transformer (ViT) architectures, using: CNN classifiers VGG16[3], MobileNetV3-L[10] [23] (MobileNet), and EfficientNet-B0[10] [65] (EffNet); classification transformers ViT-B-16[10] [9] (ViT), SWIN-T[10] [38] (SWIN); and object detectors YOLOv5s[4] (YOLO), with residual backbone, and DETR[5] with ResNet50 [64] backbone. For each we select an early, middle, and late layer to process (see Table 2).

CE Training. We consider two major paradigms for concept segmentation: The global one, derived from Net2Vec [15], and the local one from the LoCE framework [44]. As a third set, we derive from the LoCEs their respective GloCE where necessary for evaluation. Net2Vec CEs are trained with weighted binary cross-entropy loss (as compared to the less stable original intersection-based loss [59]) with a weighting factor for class balancing as defined in the original paper [15], AdamW optimizer [39] at batch size of 512 (LoCE) or 256 (Net2Vec) for 30 (ImageNet) or 20 (Pascal VOC) epochs. As tested in [44,59], we skip the activation map thresholding from the original NetDissect approach [2], and reduce costs further by not upscaling the activation maps to full image size, but instead scaling both activations and ground truth masks to the common size of

---
[2] https://github.com/continental/local-concept-embeddings
[3] https://pytorch.org/vision/stable/models
[4] https://pytorch.org/hub/ultralytics_yolov5/
[5] https://huggingface.co/facebook/detr-resnet-50

80 × 80 pixels (comparable to the choice made in [44]). For the vanilla data, each CE is trained on 50 samples; and for the background-randomized samples, we explore generating each 1, 4, 8, and 32 variants per image (results in Fig. 3). LoCEs are trained with the same settings except for batch size, which is 1 since every LoCE only is trained on one input sample.

5.2 Testing for Background Bias

One of our main questions is whether the (foreground) performance of a CE depends on the backgrounds. To answer this, we test the generalization performance of the CEs on images with foregrounds from the concept test set, but backgrounds randomized using images from the Places dataset. This allows to compare IoU performance for:

- the unchanged original image background (vanilla);
- each of the defined Places background superclasses (see Table 1); and
- on an approximately uniform sample of backgrounds, serving as the baseline (denoted as any category).

If a CE's performance on an individual background class decreases compared to any background this means that the CE is negatively biased with respect to that background (detecting it there is harder); and vice versa. This captures whether a background faces suspiciously bad (or good) performance compared to the other backgrounds. Tables 3, 4, 5 show for each pair of concept and background class the relative change of IoU results compared to the any results for that concept (IoU values averaged over all test samples and late layer CEs of all models). Note that the vanilla test values could also serve as a baseline here. This would, however, not change the *relative* differences.

Findings. The following interesting background biases are directly visible:

- **Some backgrounds are generally difficult** for all concepts: machinery generally poses a difficult background category (possibly due to the rich texture), while open lands and field seem to be easier to distinguish from foregrounds. Alarmingly, one of the *categories consistently causing drops in segmentation quality are road scenes*.
- **There are concept-specific biases:** Animals like red fox (Tables 4, 5), and furniture like grand piano and park bench (Tables 4, 5) or dining table (Tables 3, 4, 5) have a boost in performance on fields and open lands, but a **noticeable drop in detection accuracy on urban scenes like** road **and** architecture, which may pose a safety risk in certain applications. This is counterintuitive: Animals should better fit into vegetation, making a foreground-background differentiation more difficult (cf. the drop of frog and hamster for botanical backgrounds, Tables 4, 5). Thus, this most probably originates from a **Clever Hans effect**, i.e., the CE uses the background as additional evidence for the foreground class, even though it is unrelated.

Table 3. Background bias (Pascal VOC concepts): The values show in % how much the average test IoU of vanilla CEs increases (marked *blue*, higher absolute is darker) respectively decreases (marked *red*, higher absolute is darker) on specific background categories compared to performance on arbitrary backgrounds. Test samples are created via simple background pasting (4 random variants per test sample). CEs are global Net2Vec CEs (*top*) respectively globalized LoCEs (*bottom*) for the shown Pascal VOC concepts and late model layers, IoUs averaged over 7 models.

(a) **Net2Vec** results

VOC Concept	arch.	at water	botanical	field	forest	indoors	mach.	open l.	road	snow	vanilla
aeroplane	-3.43	8.45	-1.53	11.26	-1.01	-19.92	-26.90	12.07	-0.19	11.65	12.98
bicycle	-3.13	11.62	-2.38	10.92	0.95	-10.13	-35.00	18.19	0.29	9.46	-12.33
bird	-0.84	5.40	1.84	7.07	10.75	-8.95	-18.70	7.37	-1.97	3.79	21.19
boat	-11.32	13.98	4.22	18.03	14.01	-23.55	-37.89	21.12	-10.92	3.91	11.46
bottle	-2.75	6.61	2.24	8.80	8.45	-9.55	-29.56	15.83	-8.15	6.21	-18.10
bus	-4.56	1.89	2.03	4.75	3.76	-14.84	-21.54	3.75	-3.42	2.50	0.03
car	-5.75	5.42	1.79	10.85	8.63	-17.81	-27.54	10.32	-6.81	4.63	-6.22
cat	2.24	-1.06	-2.48	-1.89	-1.73	8.41	-0.32	-4.15	2.08	-2.14	10.61
chair	-13.53	10.85	3.43	13.89	15.98	-24.60	-34.30	11.30	-6.56	10.42	-16.95
cow	-3.64	6.05	1.30	8.78	4.86	-19.05	-17.87	5.44	0.19	7.86	14.66
dining table	-2.76	-0.98	-1.17	-0.17	2.13	-5.30	-2.69	-1.29	-3.42	-0.97	2.59
dog	-2.30	3.13	2.55	3.45	3.64	-7.56	-13.17	2.75	-1.05	4.29	-2.55
horse	-1.20	2.94	1.92	7.95	5.82	-12.46	-15.12	4.00	-0.05	0.46	7.94
motorbike	-6.31	5.68	4.84	9.37	3.67	-11.66	-16.75	9.02	-0.20	4.24	16.17
person	0.46	-0.20	2.78	1.06	1.34	-1.68	-6.85	-2.33	-2.25	-2.05	-6.25
potted plant	1.68	2.23	-16.46	0.79	-6.50	2.04	-10.67	9.16	2.43	7.37	-0.37
sheep	-2.30	3.08	1.06	6.96	5.61	-7.35	-10.42	-0.61	1.20	-1.16	17.52
sofa	-0.31	-0.91	2.17	1.59	3.72	2.22	-8.39	-5.43	-2.21	-7.59	10.98
train	-7.81	6.44	0.55	14.82	3.65	-22.76	-32.48	16.62	-4.91	11.40	12.15
TV monitor	1.40	-2.18	-1.12	3.07	2.12	5.42	0.03	1.61	-1.19	0.18	4.52

(b) **GloCE** results

VOC Concept	arch.	at water	botanical	field	forest	indoors	mach.	open l.	road	snow	vanilla
aeroplane	-5.22	7.33	2.86	12.08	9.45	-14.94	-31.94	10.75	-1.74	5.54	17.30
bicycle	-7.45	6.13	3.02	12.49	5.40	-4.26	-24.77	11.02	4.25	-0.76	15.53
bird	-4.69	9.41	8.79	12.62	21.83	-13.78	-18.61	15.76	-2.17	3.70	30.17
boat	-11.76	18.54	5.91	20.33	15.61	-27.56	-43.19	20.59	-3.83	6.59	22.18
bottle	-12.42	13.62	11.44	17.25	18.52	-3.89	-29.34	27.99	-2.64	14.34	23.80
bus	-5.51	2.57	2.14	6.20	3.70	-10.90	-17.12	3.84	-0.66	2.28	4.13
car	-8.05	4.65	5.45	12.84	10.75	-15.59	-22.29	10.68	-2.45	3.64	14.53
cat	-0.76	-0.85	-3.60	-1.53	-0.53	6.86	-0.50	-6.23	0.53	-1.09	31.45
chair	-11.04	12.13	16.13	20.07	22.32	-23.69	-38.75	15.84	6.70	5.48	-45.87
cow	-4.91	2.41	-0.24	7.56	5.36	-14.44	-22.92	4.45	0.50	1.54	17.71
dining table	-4.22	-0.84	2.24	3.23	8.12	0.35	-6.70	-1.42	-6.21	-6.46	16.10
dog	-2.69	2.68	1.33	4.86	4.16	-2.98	-13.41	1.93	0.22	2.57	7.41
horse	-0.16	2.16	2.02	7.04	4.60	-10.07	-17.42	3.66	1.87	-0.96	9.54
motorbike	-1.06	6.22	3.06	9.29	5.40	-7.07	-21.33	10.36	0.40	4.13	5.25
person	2.75	4.60	3.78	3.88	2.51	-4.27	-10.70	1.96	1.90	-0.30	-14.76
potted plant	-1.31	1.26	-20.94	-1.62	-13.39	7.07	-3.92	7.41	7.23	6.00	-9.68
sheep	-9.62	4.08	0.66	11.15	6.97	-15.01	-20.24	3.81	-2.21	2.79	38.64
sofa	-9.18	0.10	4.34	5.96	8.54	-0.10	-23.92	-7.21	-2.37	-10.61	35.46
train	-6.38	2.41	2.68	9.97	8.23	-16.90	-30.78	10.53	-4.39	3.44	19.65
TV monitor	-3.87	-3.57	5.36	3.43	7.06	5.74	-11.32	2.24	-5.44	-3.49	15.60

Table 4. Background bias (ImageNetS50 concepts, Net2Vec): The values show in % how much the average test IoU of vanilla CEs increases (marked *blue*, higher absolute is darker) respectively decreases (marked *red*, higher absolute is darker) on specific background categories compared to performance on arbitrary backgrounds. Test samples are created via simple background pasting (4 random variants per test sample). CEs are global Net2Vec CEs for the shown ImageNetS concepts and late model layers, IoUs averaged over 7 models.

VOC Concept	arch.	at water	botanical	field	forest	indoors	mach.	open l.	road	snow	vanilla
African elephant	-6.15	1.36	2.25	5.50	3.49	-12.59	-15.77	1.83	-2.15	0.07	10.38
agaric	-2.30	2.62	1.44	1.81	7.29	-12.00	-9.21	2.55	-3.31	0.26	11.83
airliner	-0.00	5.83	5.75	8.25	8.72	-6.06	-17.26	6.24	-2.36	1.05	1.85
American black bear	-0.73	0.62	9.11	2.16	10.11	-5.47	-8.63	0.43	-1.46	-3.34	16.15
ashcan	-1.57	3.32	3.30	5.12	3.39	-9.38	-16.62	3.29	-1.52	2.92	1.99
ballpoint	-7.20	4.64	1.45	10.28	5.11	-17.88	-31.99	14.32	-8.65	10.67	18.84
beach wagon	-3.10	1.26	1.68	3.99	2.43	-6.88	-13.68	3.40	-3.73	0.81	1.54
boathouse	-14.50	14.26	5.66	19.27	9.97	-18.29	-23.63	18.08	-9.59	13.59	11.24
bullet train	6.15	3.60	6.14	6.87	10.62	-13.04	-21.78	0.78	0.63	-4.96	15.59
carbonara	-0.03	-0.58	-6.90	-1.46	-6.66	5.51	1.02	-1.28	3.21	1.19	5.32
cellular telephone	-3.52	5.58	2.47	6.95	4.26	-7.16	-18.59	8.51	-5.45	6.80	5.71
chest	-4.23	2.02	2.30	3.03	4.00	-6.27	-8.90	2.37	-2.22	2.81	1.79
clog	-0.59	4.30	0.59	1.67	2.58	-6.54	-15.05	2.34	-0.55	2.48	1.96
container ship	-6.68	11.74	0.43	17.30	8.45	-14.74	-26.55	14.36	-4.27	12.41	19.54
digital watch	-5.76	4.31	0.24	5.45	4.15	-9.10	-20.19	4.76	-5.77	5.35	3.25
dining table	-4.56	-0.52	4.79	2.81	13.17	-9.59	-7.35	-1.85	-5.17	2.21	-1.49
dog (kuvasz)	1.13	-0.92	-0.31	3.50	1.79	1.78	-3.64	-2.97	1.72	-5.20	-0.13
giant panda	2.00	0.41	0.74	-0.20	4.89	-1.13	-2.37	1.47	-0.09	-1.51	0.52
gibbon	-0.25	1.10	0.78	2.45	4.97	-5.17	-8.93	0.73	0.41	1.25	5.88
goldfinch	0.20	4.57	4.34	4.78	11.24	-12.28	-16.04	5.61	-4.00	3.58	7.58
goldfish	-3.66	1.55	1.55	3.34	6.47	-6.26	-14.02	-3.71	-1.65	-1.06	-4.26
golf ball	-3.51	0.85	-0.80	5.58	6.92	-7.67	-14.84	1.61	-4.71	-2.78	10.25
grand piano	-7.42	1.60	6.28	6.39	5.11	-13.55	-23.87	6.14	-6.15	3.00	-12.25
hamster	-0.96	-0.80	-3.20	-0.70	-0.45	1.80	-0.51	0.21	0.14	1.09	0.16
iron	-4.30	3.79	2.41	6.93	5.85	-10.20	-20.62	6.72	-4.55	4.09	6.39
lab coat	-0.15	2.62	-0.53	4.86	-2.62	-2.36	-16.23	1.61	0.56	-3.35	0.68
ladybug	-2.20	3.33	3.37	11.19	18.42	-19.36	-31.38	-0.12	-9.54	1.03	10.22
lemon	3.90	-2.07	-0.21	-1.55	0.49	0.32	2.52	-2.65	-0.40	-3.04	-16.42
mixing bowl	0.06	1.24	-0.56	0.39	-0.79	-2.12	-3.12	1.23	0.37	1.20	-0.85
motor scooter	-1.06	4.47	2.29	5.24	4.21	-6.94	-23.61	5.09	-1.12	2.13	-4.60
padlock	-2.61	5.85	1.54	8.78	6.29	-9.29	-16.47	5.01	-1.00	5.53	-3.90
park bench	-11.21	5.87	5.03	9.03	7.67	-18.71	-22.86	8.39	-7.17	5.89	3.93
purse	-1.50	2.51	-2.90	3.47	0.56	-0.88	-7.05	3.07	1.21	4.31	9.09
red fox	-0.27	3.71	1.49	3.47	4.12	-9.95	-15.43	2.68	-0.91	5.76	8.08
Siamese cat	0.66	-1.03	0.51	-0.32	0.30	1.76	-3.78	-2.42	-0.56	-2.53	-0.55
street sign	-8.32	9.05	2.61	9.51	6.61	-12.90	-19.70	8.28	-9.70	8.44	-6.09
streetcar	-3.89	7.49	3.87	6.12	5.13	-16.59	-26.04	13.12	-4.11	7.75	-3.67
sulphur butterfly	-4.89	-0.04	0.71	4.13	5.48	-6.45	-16.25	0.98	-6.84	-3.44	6.92
table lamp	-2.19	5.14	1.13	6.02	3.75	-14.23	-15.44	5.65	-3.13	1.76	-7.82
television	2.00	2.06	1.52	4.03	5.31	-4.08	-10.13	3.19	-1.92	4.36	-3.88
tiger shark	-2.66	3.23	3.22	6.84	5.66	-6.06	-17.23	1.83	-2.22	-0.74	18.55
toilet seat	1.05	3.04	4.54	4.08	5.93	-5.25	-11.14	5.34	-1.10	0.12	-3.00
tree frog	-0.26	4.15	-4.22	5.48	1.49	-7.43	-14.46	2.20	-1.11	3.81	1.73
umbrella	-3.59	3.41	-1.07	4.67	0.57	-3.64	-12.66	2.44	-3.07	-0.49	-13.84
vase	-3.38	6.34	-3.50	5.52	0.52	-10.40	-22.52	3.65	1.34	2.98	-9.59
water bottle	-1.05	0.52	-3.20	2.33	-1.32	-7.70	-20.06	5.53	-0.40	3.15	-13.07
water tower	-8.22	7.35	3.10	9.19	2.17	-19.73	-26.49	10.61	-3.92	8.08	10.31
wild boar	-0.13	1.68	1.86	6.12	5.13	-6.90	-12.30	2.77	0.74	1.43	10.91
wood rabbit	-3.21	2.40	1.20	6.23	6.37	-7.17	-13.62	-0.08	-2.72	1.90	9.41
yawl	-9.05	7.79	3.12	9.13	6.41	-20.47	-26.81	13.41	-5.82	7.56	-0.79

Table 5. Background bias (ImageNetS50 concepts, GloCE): The values show in % how much the average test IoU of vanilla CEs increases (marked *blue*, higher absolute is darker) respectively decreases (marked *red*, higher absolute is darker) on specific background categories compared to performance on arbitrary backgrounds. Test samples are created via simple background pasting (4 random variants per test sample). CEs are globalized LoCEs for the shown ImageNetS50 concepts and late model layers, IoUs averaged over 7 models.

VOC Concept	arch.	at water	botanical	field	forest	indoors	mach.	open l.	road	snow	vanilla
African elephant	-7.24	1.37	0.89	5.36	2.90	-11.71	-17.22	2.36	-2.81	-1.38	14.26
agaric	-2.28	1.26	0.62	0.78	4.59	-10.91	-9.36	1.99	-3.29	-0.47	5.88
airliner	-1.84	5.51	1.19	6.00	4.22	-9.47	-20.92	7.13	-0.65	4.64	14.79
American black bear	-0.84	1.12	7.02	1.91	8.82	-4.50	-5.61	1.82	-1.95	-1.34	20.81
ashcan	-3.58	4.79	2.02	6.82	4.66	-13.45	-21.24	5.61	-2.89	5.44	-3.12
ballpoint	-4.99	6.21	1.17	7.34	5.78	-17.18	-28.86	14.23	-9.76	7.81	11.99
beach wagon	-3.07	1.65	1.37	3.76	2.15	-4.80	-12.74	3.19	-2.87	1.23	2.26
boathouse	-22.17	20.00	11.11	24.24	18.61	-35.95	-38.94	23.14	-13.19	14.99	26.42
bullet train	2.19	-2.64	-0.81	0.01	5.33	-8.41	-12.90	-1.77	2.03	-6.39	21.35
carbonara	-1.20	0.74	-5.74	1.46	-5.98	2.09	-3.34	0.32	2.05	1.55	3.59
cellular telephone	-3.56	8.38	2.55	9.57	7.82	-10.31	-18.08	12.06	-3.40	8.96	13.79
chest	-3.07	1.82	1.79	2.17	2.71	-5.14	-7.00	1.97	-1.42	2.91	3.10
clog	-0.49	5.03	2.57	2.65	5.12	-7.18	-11.19	3.16	-3.00	1.82	10.20
container ship	-8.47	15.59	1.39	14.94	9.11	-14.82	-24.93	13.42	-1.27	13.89	42.57
digital watch	-7.08	3.66	0.61	5.59	4.42	-8.35	-18.43	4.62	-4.88	6.27	6.64
dining table	-9.56	-0.03	8.05	4.85	20.64	-10.50	-4.53	3.65	-4.68	5.13	39.02
dog (kuvasz)	0.08	0.10	1.11	4.01	2.51	-4.42	-5.20	-2.73	0.50	-5.12	2.06
giant panda	1.75	0.12	2.52	0.32	5.01	-1.40	-3.90	1.37	-1.27	-2.46	3.80
gibbon	-1.56	0.27	-0.95	1.12	3.20	-3.86	-7.15	-0.59	-1.06	2.86	7.26
goldfinch	2.47	3.58	1.76	4.03	7.34	-9.12	-5.78	2.67	-2.66	2.69	12.22
goldfish	-2.45	4.12	0.64	4.40	5.75	-15.78	-12.69	0.76	-3.84	0.84	-3.71
golf ball	-4.31	1.92	-1.56	5.12	3.41	-11.61	-10.58	3.86	-5.87	-2.14	13.29
grand piano	-8.48	1.62	3.42	4.10	3.89	-7.43	-10.73	5.70	-4.49	4.52	-11.17
hamster	-1.35	-1.49	-2.52	-1.46	-1.69	1.66	1.80	-2.21	0.02	-0.26	13.88
iron	-5.37	6.58	2.70	8.06	5.93	-13.45	-16.15	9.56	-2.75	6.52	-0.57
lab coat	-0.67	0.45	-0.01	1.66	-0.92	-1.68	-8.97	-0.02	-0.31	-5.09	0.21
ladybug	-2.66	6.25	-2.39	8.27	12.38	-22.10	-20.22	9.64	-7.76	7.93	15.50
lemon	0.79	0.24	-0.89	-0.08	1.21	-2.25	0.59	0.36	-2.27	1.13	-19.31
mixing bowl	0.52	0.35	-0.85	0.05	-0.81	-2.21	-1.86	-0.01	0.28	1.04	1.15
motor scooter	-0.28	3.24	1.04	4.35	3.58	-4.81	-20.80	4.00	-0.48	0.22	-3.48
padlock	-8.23	4.70	3.32	6.19	13.74	-18.22	-8.38	8.89	-2.29	7.59	-4.61
park bench	-12.42	8.60	8.85	12.61	11.88	-21.73	-25.62	9.55	-7.14	6.03	15.86
purse	-2.01	3.12	-2.92	3.85	-0.83	-1.87	-9.60	3.02	0.57	4.06	6.76
red fox	-3.10	6.05	3.89	4.79	7.14	-12.69	-15.84	4.07	-2.42	8.90	21.08
Siamese cat	0.94	-0.55	-0.63	0.32	0.03	2.53	-2.23	-2.45	-0.71	-2.26	6.85
street sign	-2.41	2.34	4.19	3.65	6.67	-8.84	-11.30	3.67	-5.28	-0.95	-4.13
streetcar	-2.30	4.50	5.11	5.50	5.25	-10.65	-18.14	7.57	-0.20	2.59	8.26
sulphur butterfly	-3.04	0.37	-1.10	2.37	3.11	-12.05	-8.94	2.13	-3.94	1.05	1.56
table lamp	-1.87	4.13	-1.64	1.71	2.60	-7.92	-11.15	4.74	-3.37	3.28	-5.66
television	1.19	0.94	1.04	1.94	2.99	-2.53	-7.90	5.39	-1.51	6.57	-2.32
tiger shark	-3.10	5.41	2.78	6.82	6.43	-9.53	-10.57	3.57	-4.25	2.36	19.91
toilet seat	3.39	0.93	2.32	1.29	4.10	1.75	-3.85	1.47	0.33	-2.20	5.56
tree frog	-1.06	5.06	-4.86	3.97	2.04	-8.17	-7.44	5.33	-0.54	5.81	9.46
umbrella	0.47	3.05	-2.56	1.95	6.10	-4.49	-10.43	0.66	-2.60	-3.83	-2.13
vase	-6.07	6.83	-1.16	6.58	1.47	-9.80	-23.88	5.99	-1.78	4.32	-9.68
water bottle	-5.38	2.42	-4.21	1.72	-0.78	-10.23	-23.10	5.84	-3.55	2.40	-13.30
water tower	-6.21	7.72	1.21	6.43	3.46	-20.76	-26.11	9.24	-5.83	7.11	7.51
wild boar	-0.40	2.23	4.13	4.55	6.02	-8.31	-11.07	2.95	0.07	0.61	16.84
wood rabbit	-2.93	1.61	-1.19	3.21	4.11	-4.85	-8.97	-1.94	-1.84	1.35	11.30
yawl	-11.32	12.36	5.23	12.78	9.26	-29.96	-32.80	14.67	-6.21	11.11	3.67

- **Many (though not all) biases are intuitive**: CEs for indoor pets like cat (Tables 3, 4, 5) or hamster (Tables 4, 5) get a boost on indoor scenes, while wild animals and cattle (e.g., fox, boar, elephant in Tables 4, 5; horse, cow, sheep in Table 3) and vehicles see—partly severe—drops in performance. However, some clearly urban concepts like street signs and streetcar (Tables 4, 5) or trains (Table 3) also drop clearly on road and architecture scenes, which cannot be fully explained by label noise. This shows that **some biases can hardly be anticipated**, and the ones uncovered here require further investigation.

5.3 Background Bias in Concept Representations

To answer the question, whether a change in background distribution also changes the global(ized) concept representation, we train both new LoCEs and Net2Vec CEs for each of the 3 background randomizations in order to compare them to standard CEs with no background randomization.

Ablation Study. We first conducted an ablation study with respect to the benefit of the number of layers and background variants per foreground image. Naively, one could assume that both layer selection and high number of background variants are vital to capture the full spectrum of effects and performance / similarity variance. However, this would make CE validation difficult in practice, because considering many layers and background variants heavily increases testing effort. Fortunately, our findings do not confirm the naive assumption:

Number of variants per background: In the global and globalized cases, the number of backgrounds is not crucial. Increasing the number of background variations for the given foregrounds has no—initially even a slight adverse—effect on IoU (see Fig. 3). This emphasizes that the considered C-XAI methods are few-shot analysis methods.

Layers: The effects of background randomization are **very similar across layers**. The only notable difference is, as expected for more complex object concepts, that early layers have consistently lower IoU values than the later ones. Results are summarized in Table 6. This means that for analysis of background bias it should be sufficient to stick with a single later layer, thus substantially reducing the cost of CE training.

Models: The same holds for model architectures: Both cosine similarities (cf. standard deviation in Fig. 4) and IoU differences (cf. standard deviation in Fig. 5) indicate similar trends across models. This is pretty much irrespective of their architecture, training task, and dataset. Expectedly, larger object detector models with more complex tasks tend to exhibit richer latent space semantics, i.e., higher IoU scores.

CE Method: Net2Vec turned out to yield slightly worse IoU results at the same amount of training time (cf. Table 6). Also, GloCEs show slightly stronger relative deviation between vanilla and randomized trained versions (cf. the stronger coloring in Table 3), attesting them slightly better bias-capturing capabilities. Improving convergence, e.g., by increasing the number of epochs, did not change above tendencies.

This means, **already a minimal setup of a single variant per foreground and a single layer per model can provide valuable insights into the robustness and bias of CEs.**

Table 6. Average IoU performance of global and globalized CEs per layer depth. Results are averaged over concepts and models, best per row marked **bold**. Note that GloCEs outperform global ones consistently.

	early	middle	late
GloCE	0.27±0.26	0.40±0.27	**0.48±0.25**
Net2Vec	0.23±0.23	0.38±0.26	**0.45±0.26**

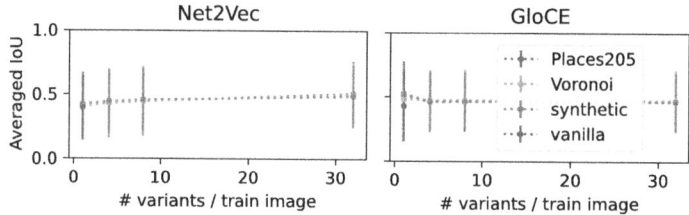

Fig. 3. Averaged IoU of CEs for different background randomization techniques4 at increasing amounts of training image variants. Variants are created by pasting a train image's foreground onto different backgrounds, using a plain *Places205* background, a *Voronoi* version, or a *synthetic* background. The *vanilla* baseline (single variant, no randomization) is marked in red. The mean is taken over concepts from ImageNetS50 and Places205, for each the late layer of 7 models.

Cosine Similarities. The pairwise cosine similarities show for all CE methods that significantly different vectors are learned, as shown in Fig. 4. Interestingly, this is the case pairwise between *all* available methods, only with a slight trend of stronger similarity between the two Places205 based techniques. The dissimilarity between these two underscores the **non-negligible effect of using shape randomization for concept segmentation**.

Finally, local methods yield much more dissimilar vectors for the different techniques. However, this is mostly averaged out when globalizing, i.e., averaging, confirming previous results [44], that **local overfitting of LoCEs well captures the full variance of a concept representation**. Also, when using

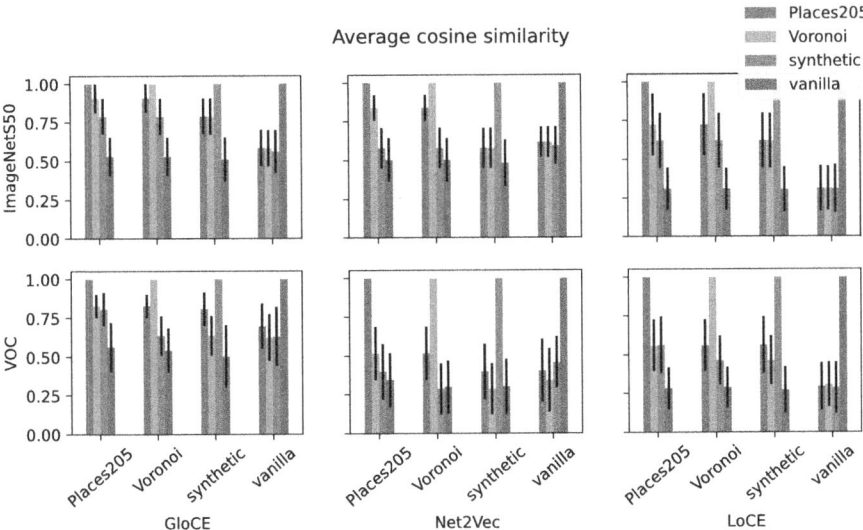

Fig. 4. Pairwise cosine similarities between CEs of the same concept and layer but from different train data randomization schemes. Cosine similarities are calculated for matching pairs of CEs for the same layer (late layers only) and concept, then averaged. Bars indicate left to right averaged similarity to CEs trained on *Places205* (*blue*), *Voronoi* (*orange*), *synthetic* (*green*), *vanilla* (*red*) data. Standard deviation is indicated via error bars (black). For visual reference, cosine similarities of CEs with themselves are reported (value of 1). (Color figure online)

cosine similarity as a measure of stability, **local-to-global methods seem to overtake purely global ones** in demanding settings, like this one with large background variance.

5.4 Performance Changes

As to be expected, both global methods receive a boost in generalization to background-randomized data if trained on such. Interestingly, they simultaneously show a comparatively small to no loss in performance on vanilla test data, maintaining the level of vanilla-trained models; and thus **CEs with background randomized training data outperform the vanilla ones clearly on mixed test datasets**. This holds throughout all considered layer depths, most clearly visible in early layers. Results on late layers are shown in Fig. 5. Interestingly, also the more sophisticated Voronoi approach, which brings in way more background information per image, is no clear winner with respect to performance. This is good news for scalability: The simple randomization techniques employed here already focused on a cost-effective setup. If already such a simple and easy-to-employ technique can reveal interesting insights, these could serve many practical use-cases instantly.

Lastly, we revisit the per-background-class testing setup in Sect. 5.2. The CEs arising from background-randomized training can be understood as a baseline for the performance achievable using background-agnostic training. While the previous comparison rather revealed consistently under- or overperforming background categories (column-wise results), here we find consistency on concept side (row-wise results): Concepts like cow (Table 3); dog, dining table (Tables 3, 4, 5); and motorbike and person (Tables 4, 5) consistently show major improvements when using background randomization during training. This indicates that (1) these concepts probably had an issue with background bias in the concept training data; and (2) **solely testing on background randomized data will not reveal all flaws related to background bias, but background-randomized CEs can help to add these insights.**

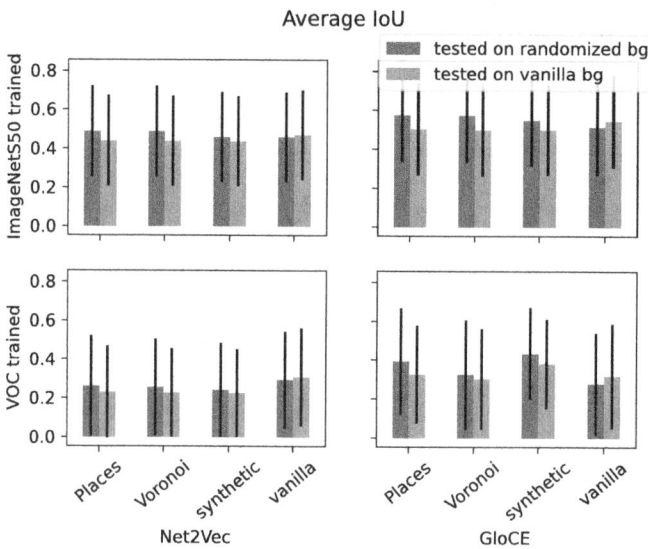

Fig. 5. IoU on bg-randomized test images (simple bg pasting from Places validation dataset) versus non-randomized ones. Compared are different training schemes: Pasting the test image foregrounds onto single unchanged or *Voronoi* backgrounds from the *Places* training data, onto *synthetic* backgrounds, or keeping the original backgrounds (*vanilla*). Results are shown for Net2Vec (*left*) and GloCE (*right*) CEs trained for concepts from Pascal VOC (*top*) and ImageNetS50 (*bottom*), averaged over all concepts and 7 DNNs.

5.5 Discussion and Future Work

Limitations: Label Noise. Our real-image background dataset does not feature segmentation labels for the concepts. Thus, we reside to filtering out background images that could possibly contain the concept of interest, which would invalidate the original concept mask. This, however, is error prone, and might change the distribution of the background images in a category (e.g., most indoor scenes contain a chair, cf. Table 3). We obtained the same trends, just generally lower IoU values, without the filtering, suggesting that the distribution change does not invalidate results per se. Nevertheless, practical application could consider scene datasets with segmentation labels for the concepts instead.

Additional Models and Datasets. It should be noted that clearly the setup could be widened even further, e.g., including more background datasets to investigate biases with respect to backgrounds not part of Places205 or our synthetic background classes, and in other domains like medical diagnostics. Also, checking results on most recent models, like later YOLO and DETR versions, would indicate whether next generation architectures show different trends. However, with >50 concepts from two quite different datasets, and 7 diverse state-of-the-art models, we are confident that the results generalize to most standard models and yield also interesting results for further background classes.

Distribution Perspective. Some interesting future work would be to further leverage the distribution nature of LoCEs: Our results suggest that they encode a lot of valuable information about variance and concept corner cases. Hence, instead of sole cosine similarity between vectors, one could compare the distributions. For this, different techniques to model the distribution out of a set of samples could be investigated: Apart from the Gaussian mixture modeling in [44], also simpler techniques like PCA might already be sufficient. Comparison of distributions instead of vectors would then hopefully give some hints on typical indicators for flawed concept representations in latent spaces; eventually opening doors to fix them in a post-hoc targeted manner, or incorporate findings about skewed distributions into the training objective.

Downstream Tasks: Model Fixing. Finally, a valuable future direction would be to further assess the actual practical impact of background-biased concept embeddings: Do the identified background biases allow the construction of DNN failure cases? And how useful is this information to fix the DNN? These questions need to be answered on the way to practical application of this method.

6 Conclusion

This paper revisited concept-based XAI techniques for post-hoc concept segmentation. Our guiding question, namely, whether state-of-the-art techniques exhibit a background bias, was finally answered affirmative: Across models, layers, concepts, and datasets we were able to identify notable drops in performance of concept segmentation models when changing the background distributions. E.g., wild animals being less well detected on roads. Gladly, we were able to show that any such flaws can be dug out with relatively cheap and simple background randomization techniques, as presented in this work. This hopefully motivates readers to introduce beneficial background randomization techniques also into other data-driven explainability techniques; and finally eases investigation of DNN biases encoded in their latent spaces.

Acknowledgments. G.S. acknowledges support through the junior research group project "chAI" funded by the German Federal Ministry of Education and Research (BMBF), grant no. 01IS24058. The authors are solely responsible for the content of this publication. E.H., A.M. and M.R. acknowledge support through the junior research group project "UnrEAL" by the German Federal Ministry of Research, Technology and Space (BMFTR), grant no. 01IS22069. S.G. acknowledges support by a studentship from the School of Electrical Engineering, Electronics and Computer Science, at the University of Liverpool, UK.

References

1. Achtibat, R., et al.: From attribution maps to human-understandable explanations through concept relevance propagation. Nat. Mach. Intell. **5**(9), 1006–1019 (2023). https://doi.org/10.1038/s42256-023-00711-8
2. Bau, D., Zhou, B., Khosla, A., Oliva, A., Torralba, A.: Network dissection: quantifying interpretability of deep visual representations. In: Proceedings of the 2017 IEEE Conference of Computer Vision and Pattern Recognition, pp. 3319–3327. IEEE Computer Society, Honolulu, HI, USA (2017). https://doi.org/10.1109/CVPR.2017.354
3. Blum, H., Sarlin, P.E., Nieto, J., Siegwart, R., Cadena, C.: The fishyscapes benchmark: measuring blind spots in semantic segmentation. Int. J. Comput. Vis. **129**(11), 3119–3135 (2021)
4. Carion, N., Massa, F., Synnaeve, G., Usunier, N., Kirillov, A., Zagoruyko, S.: End-to-end object detection with transformers. In: European Conference on Computer Vision, pp. 213–229. Springer (2020)
5. Chan, R., et al.: Segmentmeifyoucan: a benchmark for anomaly segmentation. arXiv:2104.14812 (2021)
6. Chen, C., Li, O., Tao, D., Barnett, A., Rudin, C., Su, J.: This looks like that: deep learning for interpretable image recognition. In: Advances in Neural Information Processing Systems 32. vol. 32, pp. 8928–8939. Vancouver, BC, Canada (2019)
7. Crabbé, J., Schaar, M.: Concept activation regions: a generalized framework for concept-based explanations. Adv. Neural. Inf. Process. Syst. **35**, 2590–2607 (2022)
8. Deng, J., Dong, W., Socher, R., Li, L.J., Li, K., Fei-Fei, L.: Imagenet: a large-scale hierarchical image database. In: 2009 IEEE Conference on Computer Vision and Pattern Recognition, pp. 248–255. IEEE (2009)
9. Dosovitskiy, A., et al.: An image is worth 16x16 words: transformers for image recognition at scale. In: 9th International Conference Learning Representations. OpenReview.net (2021)
10. Esser, P., Rombach, R., Ommer, B.: A disentangling invertible interpretation network for explaining latent representations. In: Proceedings of the 2020 IEEE Conference on Computer Vision and Pattern Recognition, pp. 9220–9229. IEEE, Seattle, WA, USA (2020). https://doi.org/10.1109/CVPR42600.2020.00924
11. Everingham, M., Gool, L.V., Williams, C.K.I., Winn, J., Zisserman, A.: The Pascal visual object classes (VOC) challenge. arXiv preprint arXiv:0909.5206 (2010)

12. Feifel, P., Bonarens, F., Koster, F.: Reevaluating the safety impact of inherent interpretability on deep neural networks for pedestrian detection. In: Proceedings of the 2021 IEEE/CVF Conference on Computer Vision and Pattern Recognition, pp. 29–37 (2021). https://doi.org/10.1109/CVPRW53098.2021.00012
13. Fel, T., et al.: CRAFT: concept recursive activation factorization for explainability. In: Proceedings of the IEEE/CVF Conference on Computer Vision and Pattern Recognition, pp. 2711–2721 (2023)
14. Fellbaum, C. (ed.): WordNet: An Electronic Lexical Database. Language, Speech, and Communication, A Bradford Book, Cambridge, MA, USA (1998)
15. Fong, R., Vedaldi, A.: Net2Vec: quantifying and explaining how concepts are encoded by filters in deep neural networks. In: Proceedings of the 2018 IEEE Conference on Computer Vision and Pattern Recognition, pp. 8730–8738. IEEE Computer Society, Salt Lake City, UT, USA (2018). https://doi.org/10.1109/CVPR.2018.00910
16. Fuchs, F.B., et al.: Neural stethoscopes: unifying analytic, auxiliary and adversarial network probing. arXiv preprint arXiv:1806.05502 (2018)
17. Gao, S., Li, Z.Y., Yang, M.H., Cheng, M.M., Han, J., Torr, P.: Large-scale unsupervised semantic segmentation. TPAMI (2022)
18. Ghorbani, A., Wexler, J., Zou, J.Y., Kim, B.: Towards automatic concept-based explanations. In: Advances in Neural Information Processing Systems. vol. 32, pp. 9273–9282. Vancouver, BC, Canada (2019)
19. Giunchiglia, E., Stoian, M., Khan, S., Cuzzolin, F., Lukasiewicz, T.: ROAD-R: the autonomous driving dataset with logical requirements. In: IJCLR 2022 Workshops. Vienna, Austria (2022)
20. Graziani, M., Andrearczyk, V., Müller, H.: Regression concept vectors for bidirectional explanations in histopathology. In: Understanding and Interpreting Machine Learning in Medical Image Computing Applications. LNCS, pp. 124–132. Springer (2018)
21. Hendrycks, D., Zhao, K., Basart, S., Steinhardt, J., Song, D.: Natural adversarial examples. In: CVPR (2021)
22. Hoffmann, A., Fanconi, C., Rade, R., Kohler, J.: This looks like that... does it? Shortcomings of latent space prototype interpretability in deep networks. arXiv preprint arXiv:2105.02968 (2021)
23. Howard, A., et al.: Searching for mobilenetv3. In: Proeedings of the IEEE/CVF International Conference on Computer Vision, pp. 1314–1324 (2019)
24. ISO/TC 22/SC 32: ISO/AWI PAS 8800(En): Road Vehicles — Safety and Artificial Intelligence. ISO, wd01 edn. (2022)
25. Janoušková, K., Gavrus, C., Matas, J.: Segment to recognize robustly - enhancing recognition by image decomposition. arXiv preprint arXiv:2411.15933 (2024)
26. Jocher, G.: Yolov5 by ultralytics (2020). https://doi.org/10.5281/zenodo.3908559, https://github.com/ultralytics/yolov5
27. Keser, M., Savkin, A., Tombari, F.: Content disentanglement for semantically consistent synthetic-to-real domain adaptation. In: 2021 IEEE/RSJ International Conference on Intelligent Robots and Systems (IROS), pp. 3844–3849. IEEE Press, Prague, Czech Republic (2021). https://doi.org/10.1109/IROS51168.2021.9635948
28. Keser, M., Schwalbe, G., Nowzad, A., Knoll, A.: Interpretable model-agnostic plausibility verification for 2D object detectors using domain-invariant concept bottleneck models. In: Proceedings of the IEEE/CVF Conference on Computer Vision and Pattern Recognition, pp. 3891–3900 (2023)

29. Keser, M., Shoeb, Y., Knoll, A.: How could generative ai support compliance with the EU AI act? A review for safe automated driving perception. In: 2024 IEEE International Conference Vehicular Electronics and Safety (ICVES), pp. 1–6 (2024). https://doi.org/10.1109/ICVES61986.2024.10928135
30. Kim, B., et al.: Interpretability beyond feature attribution: quantitative testing with concept activation vectors (TCAV). In: Proceedings of the 35th International Conference Machine Learning. Proceedings of Machine Learning Research, vol. 80, pp. 2668–2677. PMLR, Stockholmsmässan, Stockholm, Sweden (2018)
31. Kirillov, A., et al.: Segment anything. In: Proceedings of the IEEE/CVF International Conference on Computer Vision, pp. 4015–4026 (2023)
32. Koh, P.W., et al.: Concept bottleneck models. In: International Conference on Machine Learning, pp. 5338–5348. PMLR (2020)
33. Koopman, P., Edge Case Research, Underwriters Laboratories: UL4600: Standard for Safety of Autonomous Products. Edge Case Research (2019)
34. Lau, F., Subramani, N., Harrison, S., Kim, A., Branson, E., Liu, R.: Natural adversarial objects. arXiv preprint arXiv:2111.04204 (2021)
35. Lee, J.H., Lanza, S., Wermter, S.: From neural activations to concepts: a survey on explaining concepts in neural networks. Neurosymbolic Artif. Intell. J. (2024)
36. Lee, J.H., Mikriukov, G., Schwalbe, G., Wermter, S., Wolter, D.: Concept-based explanations in computer vision: where are we and where could we go? In: eXCV Workshop at ECCV 2024. Milano, Italy (2024)
37. Li, Y., Dong, X., Chen, C., Zhuang, W., Lyu, L.: A simple background augmentation method for object detection with diffusion model. In: European Conference on Computer Vision, pp. 462–479. Springer (2024)
38. Liu, Z., et al.: Swin transformer: hierarchical vision transformer using shifted windows. In: Proceedings of the IEEE/CVF International Conference on Computer Vision, pp. 10012–10022 (2021)
39. Loshchilov, I., Hutter, F.: Decoupled weight decay regularization. In: International Conference on Learning Representations (2018)
40. Lugmayr, A., Danelljan, M., Romero, A., Yu, F., Timofte, R., Van Gool, L.: Repaint: inpainting using denoising diffusion probabilistic models. In: Proceedings of the IEEE/CVF Conference on Computer Vision and Pattern Recognition, pp. 11461–11471 (2022)
41. Lukáš Picek, L.N., Matas, J.: Animal identification with independent foreground and background modeling. arXiv preprint arXiv:2408.12930 (2024)
42. Lynch, A., Dovonon, G.J.S., Kaddour, J., Silva, R.: Spawrious: a benchmark for fine control of spurious correlation biases. arXiv preprint arXiv:2303.05470 (2023)
43. Marconato, E., Passerini, A., Teso, S.: GlanceNets: interpretable, leak-proof concept-based models. In: Advances in Neural Information Processing Systems, vol. 35, pp. 21212–21227 (2022)
44. Mikriukov, G., Schwalbe, G., Bade, K.: Local concept embeddings for analysis of concept distributions in vision DNN feature spaces. Int. J. Comput. Vis. (2025)
45. Mikriukov, G., Schwalbe, G., Hellert, C., Bade, K.: Evaluating the stability of semantic concept representations in CNNs for robust explainability. In: Longo, L. (ed.) Explainable Artificial Intelligence - First World Conference, xAI 2023, Lisbon, Portugal, July 26–28, 2023, Proceedings, Part II. Communications in Computer and Information Science, vol. 1902, pp. 499–524. Springer (2023). https://doi.org/10.1007/978-3-031-44067-0_26

46. Mikriukov, G., Schwalbe, G., Motzkus, F., Bade, K.: Unveiling the anatomy of adversarial attacks: concept-based XAI dissection of CNNs. In: Longo, L., Lapuschkin, S., Seifert, C. (eds.) Explainable Artificial Intelligence, pp. 92–116. Springer (2024). https://doi.org/10.1007/978-3-031-63787-2_6
47. Moayeri, M., Pope, P.E., Balaji, Y., Feizi, S.: A comprehensive study of image classification model sensitivity to foregrounds, backgrounds, and visual attributes. In: 2022 IEEE/CVF Conference Computer on Vision and Pattern Recognition, pp. 19065–19075 (2022)
48. Mütze, A., Grabowsky, N., Heinert, E., Rottmann, M., Gottschalk, H.: On the influence of shape, texture and color for learning semantic segmentation. arXiv preprint arXiv:2410.14878 (2024)
49. Nguyen, A., Yosinski, J., Clune, J.: Understanding neural networks via feature visualization: a survey. In: Explainable AI: Interpreting, Explaining and Visualizing Deep Learning. LNCS, pp. 55–76. Springer (2019). https://doi.org/10.1007/978-3-030-28954-6_4
50. Olah, C., Mordvintsev, A., Schubert, L.: Feature visualization. Distill **2**(11), e7 (2017). https://doi.org/10.23915/distill.00007 https://doi.org/10.23915/distill.00007
51. European Parliament: Proposal for a regulation of the European parliament and of the council laying down harmonised rules on artificial intelligence (Artificial Intelligence Act) and amending certain union legislative acts (2021)
52. Pernias, P., Rampas, D., Richter, M.L., Pal, C., Aubreville, M.: Würstchen: an efficient architecture for large-scale text-to-image diffusion models. In: 12th International Conference of Learning Representations (2024)
53. Poeta, E., Ciravegna, G., Pastor, E., Cerquitelli, T., Baralis, E.: Concept-based explainable artificial intelligence: a survey. arXiv preprint arXiv:2312.12936 (2023)
54. Posada-Moreno, A.F., Surya, N., Trimpe, S.: ECLAD: extracting concepts with local aggregated descriptors. Pattern Recogn. **147**, 110146 (2024)
55. Rabold, J., Schwalbe, G., Schmid, U.: Expressive explanations of DNNs by combining concept analysis with ILP. In: KI 2020: Advances in Artificial Intelligence. LNCS, pp. 148–162. Springer (2020). https://doi.org/10.1007/978-3-030-58285-2_11
56. Rombach, R., Blattmann, A., Lorenz, D., Esser, P., Ommer, B.: High-resolution image synthesis with latent diffusion models. In: Proceedings of the IEEE/CVF Conference on Computer Vision and Pattern Recognition, pp. 10684–10695 (2022)
57. Ryali, C.K., Schwab, D.J., Morcos, A.S.: Characterizing and improving the robustness of self-supervised learning through background augmentations. arXiv preprint arXiv:2103.12719 (2021)
58. Sawada, Y., Nakamura, K.: Concept bottleneck model with additional unsupervised concepts. IEEE Access **10**, 41758–41765 (2022). https://doi.org/10.1109/ACCESS.2022.3167702
59. Schwalbe, G.: Verification of size invariance in DNN activations using concept embeddings. In: Artificial Intelligence Applications and Innovations. IFIP Advances in Information and Communication Technology, pp. 374–386. Springer (2021). https://doi.org/10.1007/978-3-030-79150-6_30
60. Schwalbe, G.: Concept embedding analysis: a review. arXiv preprint arXiv:2203.13909 (2022)
61. Schwalbe, G., Wirth, C., Schmid, U.: Enabling verification of deep neural networks in perception tasks using fuzzy logic and concept embeddings. arXiv preprint arXiv:2201.00572 (2022)

62. Siméoni, O., Sekkat, C., Puy, G., Vobecký, A., Zablocki, É., P'erez, P.: Unsupervised object localization: observing the background to discover objects. In: 2023 IEEE/CVF Conference on Computer Vision and Pattern Recognition, pp. 3176–3186 (2022)
63. Simonyan, K., Zisserman, A.: Very deep convolutional networks for large-scale image recognition. In: Proceedings of the 3rd International Conference on Learning Representations. San Diego, CA, USA (2015)
64. Simonyan, K., Zisserman, A.: Very deep convolutional networks for large-scale image recognition. In: 3rd International Conference on Learning Representations, Conference Track Proceedings (2015)
65. Tan, M., Le, Q.: Efficientnet: rethinking model scaling for convolutional neural networks. In: International Conference on Machine Learning, pp. 6105–6114. PMLR (2019)
66. Theodoridis, J., Hofmann, J., Maucher, J., Schilling, A.: Trapped in texture bias? A large scale comparison of deep instance segmentation. In: European Conference on Computer Vision, pp. 609–627. Springer (2022)
67. Tobin, J., Fong, R., Ray, A., Schneider, J., Zaremba, W., Abbeel, P.: Domain randomization for transferring deep neural networks from simulation to the real world. In: Proceedings of the 2017 IEEE/RSJ International Conference on Intelligent Robots and Systems, pp. 23–30 (2017)
68. Torquato, S.: Cell and random-field models. In: Random Heterogeneous Materials: Microstructure and Macroscopic Properties, pp. 188–209. Interdisciplinary Applied Mathematics, Springer, New York, NY (2002)
69. Vielhaben, J., Bluecher, S., Strodthoff, N.: Multi-dimensional concept discovery (MCD): a unifying framework with completeness guarantees. Trans. Mach. Learn. Res. (2023)
70. Wightman, R.: Pytorch image models (2019). https://github.com/rwightman/pytorch-image-models, https://doi.org/10.5281/zenodo.4414861
71. Willard, F., et al.: This looks better than that: better interpretable models with ProtoPNeXt. arXiv preprint arXiv:2406.14675 (2024)
72. Xiao, K.Y., Engstrom, L., Ilyas, A., Madry, A.: Noise or signal: the role of image backgrounds in object recognition. In: International Conference on Learning Representations (2021)
73. You, Z., Kong, L., Meng, L., Wu, Z.: Focus: towards universal foreground segmentation. arXiv preprint arXiv:2501.05238 (2025)
74. Zhang, R., Madumal, P., Miller, T., Ehinger, K.A., Rubinstein, B.I.P.: Invertible concept-based explanations for CNN models with non-negative concept activation vectors. In: Proceedings of the 35th AAAI Conference on Artificial Intelligence, vol. 35, pp. 11682–11690. AAAI Press, virtual (2021)
75. Zhou, B., Lapedriza, A., Xiao, J., Torralba, A., Oliva, A.: Learning deep features for scene recognition using places database. Adv. Neural Inf. Process. Syst. **27** (2014)

Open Access This chapter is licensed under the terms of the Creative Commons Attribution 4.0 International License (http://creativecommons.org/licenses/by/4.0/), which permits use, sharing, adaptation, distribution and reproduction in any medium or format, as long as you give appropriate credit to the original author(s) and the source, provide a link to the Creative Commons license and indicate if changes were made.

The images or other third party material in this chapter are included in the chapter's Creative Commons license, unless indicated otherwise in a credit line to the material. If material is not included in the chapter's Creative Commons license and your intended use is not permitted by statutory regulation or exceeds the permitted use, you will need to obtain permission directly from the copyright holder.

Explaining Vision GNNs: A Semantic and Visual Analysis of Graph-Based Image Classification

Nikolaos Chaidos[✉], Angeliki Dimitriou, Nikolaos Spanos,
Athanasios Voulodimos, and Giorgos Stamou

National Technical University of Athens, Athens, Greece
{nchaidos,angelikidim,nspanos}@ails.ece.ntua.gr, thanosv@mail.ntua.gr,
gstam@cs.ntua.gr

Abstract. Graph Neural Networks (GNNs) have emerged as an efficient alternative to convolutional approaches for vision tasks such as image classification, leveraging patch-based representations instead of raw pixels. These methods construct graphs where image patches serve as nodes, and edges are established based on patch similarity or classification relevance. Despite their efficiency, the explainability of GNN-based vision models remains underexplored, even though graphs are naturally interpretable. In this work, we analyze the semantic consistency of the graphs formed at different layers of GNN-based image classifiers, focusing on how well they preserve object structures and meaningful relationships. A comprehensive analysis is presented by quantifying the extent to which inter-layer graph connections reflect semantic similarity and spatial coherence. Explanations from standard and adversarial settings are also compared to assess whether they reflect the classifiers' robustness. Additionally, we visualize the flow of information across layers through heatmap-based visualization techniques, thereby highlighting the models' explainability. Our findings demonstrate that the decision-making processes of these models can be effectively explained, while also revealing that their reasoning does not necessarily align with human perception, especially in deeper layers. The code is available at https://github.com/nickhaidos/Vision-GNNs-Explainer.

Keywords: Graph Neural Networks · Image Classification · Explainability

1 Introduction

Image classification has long been dominated by powerful yet opaque models, raising questions about their decision-making processes. As these models achieve unprecedented accuracy, the need for transparency has become critical. To bridge this gap, techniques such as Grad-CAM [16], saliency maps [17], and occlusion experiments [20] have provided insights into how image models prioritize image regions, illuminating the internal logic behind classification decisions.

These methods have both advanced our grasp of deep models' inner workings and highlighted challenges in aligning machine explanations with human intuition.

Building on this rich history of interpretability, a new frontier is emerging with Graph Neural Networks (GNNs). Unlike Convolutional Neural Networks (CNNs) or Vision Transformers (ViTs) that operate on pixel grids, GNN-based approaches reimagine images as collections of interrelated patches - nodes connected by edges that encode semantic or spatial similarity. This graph-based perspective has

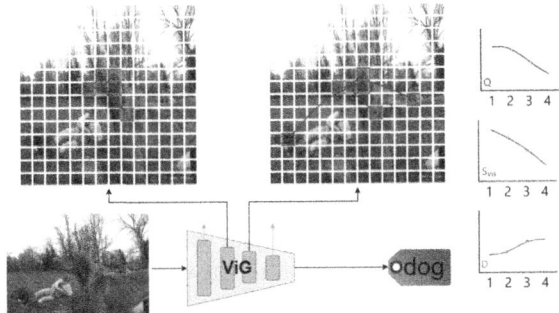

Fig. 1. Visual depiction of ViG's representation of a "dog" image at different layers (2, 3). Subgraphs refer to the central green patch and its neighbors (red patches) at that layer. Diagrams represent object-based modularity (Q), visual similarity (S_{vis}) and spatial distance (D) with dots corresponding to the 2nd and 3rd layer. (Color figure online)

proven to be efficient thanks to lightweight GNN models that ultimately process the graph representations of images for classification. Recent research has already explored several ways to further accelerate the process by focusing on the optimal construction of the graph - for example, by comparing dynamic and static graphs or applying directional constraints [13,14]. Furthermore, claims have been made that GNN-based image classification can potentially provide sufficient interpretability for model decisions [4] by offering explainability insights that mirror the way humans naturally perceive and organize visual information. However, their inner workings remain largely unexplored, leaving open questions about semantic consistency and the reliability of explanations across different layers.

The seminal approach by Han et al. [4] (Vision GNN (ViG)) introduces the foundations of graph-based approaches, redefining image classification by structuring images as graphs rather than grids. In ViG, an image is first divided into non-overlapping patches that serve as nodes, while edges are formed based on spatial proximity or learned feature similarities. Whereas CNNs mainly rely on local receptive fields, ViG propagates information through message passing, allowing for flexible and dynamic interactions between distant regions in the image. This approach not only reduces computational complexity but also captures richer contextual dependencies. Given its merits and its inherent inclination toward explainability, as hinted by its authors, ViG is a natural choice for a study on interpretability among other GNN-based vision models [5,13,14].

To this end, in this paper we present the first explainability analysis of the ViG model, investigating whether its graph-based structure inherently leads to interpretable decisions. While graphs are often considered inherently interpretable - by providing a clear mapping of nodes to object parts and their relationships - we aim to rigorously evaluate this assumption both visually and numerically. Specifically, we examine whether patches belonging to the same object tend to connect with semantically similar or spatially close ones, illuminating the model's inner workings. Our approach leans toward a white-box analysis, leveraging feature representations at each layer to assess the extent to which the subgraphs formed around each patch remain localized and whether they stay within the object defining the image's class. To quantify this, we measure visual and embedding-based similarity between interconnected patches, their spatial proximity, and the graph's node separation quality, correlating these factors with the classification label at different layers. Additionally, we introduce a heatmap-style visualization to track how key patches - particularly those belonging to the main object - relate to their neighbors across layers, offering a more granular view of information flow within the model. To examine robustness and consistency with human understanding, we not only perform experiments on a subset of the standard ImageNet [15] dataset but also ImageNet-a [6], which contains commonly misclassified adversarial examples. This enables us to explore how the explainability approach holds up when applied to images that may be more challenging to classify, providing deeper insights in diverse scenarios.

An illustrative example of our approach can be seen in Fig. 1. To elaborate, given an image of dogs in a park, the ViG model correctly classifies it under the "dog" category in ImageNet by progressively representing the image as a dispersed graph of patches, rather than strictly localized pixel groups as CNNs do. Our explainability method provides both visual and numerical insights into this decision. We visualize patch interconnections to examine whether the GNN-based vision model learns to associate *visually* and *semantically* similar patches, regardless of their spatial distance. In Fig. 1, for instance, a green patch corresponding to a dog's face initially connects only to adjacent body parts of the same dog (2nd layer output). However, by the 3rd layer, it becomes linked to more distant red patches corresponding to other dogs' faces. This finding is further reflected in metric diagrams: spatial distance (D) increases from layer 2 to layer 3, while visual similarity (S_{vis}) and node separation quality (Q) decrease. These and additional metrics, detailed in later sections, serve as indicators of the model's decision-making process, ultimately helping to assess how reliably its classifications align with human perception.

In summary, this paper makes the following contributions: (1) We introduce the first explainability analysis of GNN-based image classification approaches, (2) We propose an evaluation of graph node separation along with semantic, visual, and spatial coherence analysis across layers, combined with heatmap visualizations to track patch interactions, and (3) We conduct a comparison of interpretability between standard and adversarial examples to assess robustness and generalizability.

2 Related Work

Graph Neural Networks in Vision. GNNs have gained traction as an alternative to CNNs/ViTs for vision tasks, offering greater flexibility in modeling non-

Euclidean relationships between image regions and enhancing efficiency. In this direction, ViG [4], introduced a graph-based representation where image patches serve as nodes, with edges encoding semantic and spatial relationships, demonstrating competitive performance against ViTs and CNNs. Feature embeddings are propagated through multiple GNN layers via message passing, and a classification head processes the final node embeddings to predict the final label. ViG's innovation includes a **dynamic graph** update mechanism, contrasting with previous approaches that rely on static superpixel graphs [1,3]. Expanding on this, Vision HGNN [5] proposed a hypergraph-based approach to capture higher-order feature interactions, further improving recognition accuracy. Recent efforts have also focused on enhancing the efficiency of GNNs for mobile applications, as seen in MobileViG [13], which employs sparse attention on a static graph to reduce computational overhead while maintaining high accuracy. Additionally, GreedyViG [14] introduces dynamic axial graph construction to optimize graph structure adaptively for further efficiency. Such performance-driven design choices lead to more spatially constrained models that are less capable of capturing semantic relationships. As a result, their interpretability is likely to be the same as - or even lower than that of ViG. Despite their merits, none of these works explore the explainability prospects of their efforts. To address this gap, we focus on ViG to investigate how its graph structure can reveal which interconnected image regions contribute to classification, providing visual and quantitative insights into the model's decision-making process.

Image Classification Visualization Techniques. A relevant foundational approach follows the use of Class Activation Maps (CAMs) [21], which highlight regions of an image that significantly influence the model's predictions. Building on CAMs, Grad-CAM [16] improved them by enhancing localization, followed by Grad-CAM++ [2], which further refined interpretability. Eigen-CAM [12] improved robustness by reducing reliance on gradients. Additionally, [17] introduced class saliency maps, highlighting influential pixels via gradient-based analysis. While our approach shares similarities with these well-known techniques, such as highlighting key image regions, we do not aim to directly compare our method to theirs. Unlike traditional classifiers, which rely on pixel-level feature extraction, our approach leverages a higher-level GNN backbone, and the nature of the explanation derived from the constructed graph, rather than individual pixels, offers a fundamentally distinct form of interpretability.

Explainability in Graph Neural Networks. Recent research has explored multiple approaches to enhance GNN explainability. GNNExplainer [19] is a post-hoc method which identifies key subgraphs and features through mutual information, while PGExplainer [11] uses probabilistic masking for instance-level and global explanations. GraphLIME [7] adapts LIME for localized insights, and PGM-Explainer [18] leverages probabilistic models through perturbations to obtain instance level explanations. Collectively, these methods advance GNN explainability, but still leave a significant gap in the explainability of dynamic graph-based models, and specifically to Vision GNNs, which we aim to address.

3 Background

3.1 Notation

Let $G = (V, E)$ denote a directed graph, where $V = \{v_1, ..., v_N\}$ is the set of N nodes and $E \subseteq V \times V$ is the set of edges. Each node v_i is associated with a feature vector $\mathbf{x}_i \in \mathbb{R}^D$, where D is the feature dimension. The complete set of node features is denoted as $\mathbf{X} = [\mathbf{x}_1, \mathbf{x}_2, ..., \mathbf{x}_N]^T \in \mathbb{R}^{N \times D}$. The graph structure can be represented by an adjacency matrix $\mathbf{A} \in \mathbb{R}^{N \times N}$, where $A_{ij} = 1$ if there exists an edge from node i to node j, and 0 otherwise. For a node v_i, we denote its set of incoming neighbors as $\mathcal{N}(i) = \{j | (j, i) \in E\}$.

We use the superscript l to denote layer-specific quantities throughout the network, where $G^l = (V, E^l)$ represents the graph, $\mathbf{A}^l \in \mathbb{R}^{N \times N}$ the adjacency matrix, and $\mathbf{x}_i^l \in \mathbb{R}^D$ the feature vector of node i at layer l. For the input image $\mathbf{I} \in \mathbb{R}^{H \times W \times 3}$, we later partition it into $N = 196$ patches, where each patch $\mathbf{P}_i \in \mathbb{R}^{16 \times 16 \times 3}$ is positioned at coordinates (r_i, c_i) in a 14×14 grid. For classification outputs, we denote the ground truth class label as $y \in \{1, ..., C\}$, the model's output logits as $\hat{\mathbf{y}} \in \mathbb{R}^C$, and the predicted class probabilities after softmax as $\mathbf{p} \in [0, 1]^C$.

3.2 Vision GNN Architecture

ViG [4] processes an input image $\mathcal{I} \in \mathbb{R}^{H \times W \times 3}$ as follows:

Patch Embedding. The image is first resized to 224×224 and then partitioned into $N = 14 \times 14 = 196$ non-overlapping patches, where each patch $P_i \in \mathbb{R}^{16 \times 16 \times 3}$ is passed through 2D convolutions to obtain initial node features $\mathbf{x}_i \in \mathbb{R}^D$ (where D is the hidden dimension hyperparameter). Learnable positional encodings $\mathbf{e}_i \in \mathbb{R}^D$ are added to preserve spatial information.

Dynamic Graph Construction. At each layer l, a graph $\mathcal{G}^l = (\mathcal{V}, \mathcal{E}^l)$ is constructed by connecting each node to its K nearest neighbors in the embedding space, based on cosine similarity between node features. This yields a layer-specific adjacency matrix $\mathbf{A}^l$ (or adjacency list $\mathcal{E}^l$), which we focus on later.

Message Passing. The proposed Grapher module performs information exchange through message passing. Specifically, the max-relative graph convolution module [9] is chosen for its efficiency, which is formulated as:

$$\mathbf{x}_i' = [\mathbf{x}_i, max(\{\mathbf{x}_j - \mathbf{x}_i | j \in \mathcal{N}(\mathbf{x}_i)\})] W_{update} \quad (1)$$

where the bias term is omitted. The final update is implemented across multiple heads and the authors apply linear transformations before and after the graph convolution to avoid over-smoothing.

Classification. The final prediction is obtained by applying global average pooling over the node features from the final layer, followed by a linear classifier. For analysis purposes, we can apply this classification head to intermediate layer representations to study the evolution of the model's decision-making process.

4 Analysis Framework

4.1 Datasets

Our analysis is conducted primarily on ImageNet ILSVRC 2012 [15], using a subset of 10,000 validation images to establish baseline metrics and patterns. For a more comprehensive understanding of the model's behavior, we extend our analysis to ImageNet-a [6], which collects 7,500 natural adversarial images that are commonly misclassified by models that perform competitively on ImageNet.

4.2 Designed Metrics

We introduce five quantitative metrics to analyze the evolution of graph structure and decision-making process across layers:

1. Embedding Similarity (S_{emb}^l): For layer l, we compute the average cosine similarity between connected patches:

$$S_{emb}^l = \frac{1}{|\mathcal{E}^l|} \sum_{(i,j) \in \mathcal{E}^l} \frac{\mathbf{x}_i^l \cdot \mathbf{x}_j^l}{\|\mathbf{x}_i^l\| \|\mathbf{x}_j^l\|} \quad (2)$$

where $\mathcal{E}^l$ is the edge set at layer l and $\mathbf{x}_i^l$ represents the embedding of node i at layer l. By quantifying the similarity of learned representations between connected patches, we assess if the model links semantically related regions. Higher values indicate stronger semantic coherence in the graph structure.

2. Spatial Distance (D^l): We measure the average Manhattan distance between connected patches:

$$D^l = \frac{1}{|\mathcal{E}^l|} \sum_{(i,j) \in \mathcal{E}^l} (|r_i - r_j| + |c_i - c_j|) \quad (3)$$

where (r_i, c_i) represents the grid position of patch i. This metric helps us understand if the model maintains local connectivity or gradually forms long-range connections, revealing how the receptive field evolves across layers.

3. Visual Similarity (S_{vis}^l): For connected patches, we compute the average pixel-space similarity:

$$S_{vis}^l = \frac{1}{|\mathcal{E}^l|} \sum_{(i,j) \in \mathcal{E}^l} \cos(P_i, P_j) \quad (4)$$

where P_i and P_j are the flattened RGB values of patches i and j. By comparing the raw RGB values between connected patches, this metric quantifies the level at which the model maintains connections between visually similar regions, therefore tracking how the model transitions from low-level visual features to higher-level semantic representations.

4. Layer-wise Classification (p^l): For each layer l, we compute:

$$p^l = Pred(\mathbf{X}^l) \quad (5)$$

where $Pred$ is the final classification head of the model, and $\mathbf{X}^l$ is the node feature matrix at layer l. Only the probability of the ground-truth class y is tracked. This metric reflects how confidence in the ground-truth class evolves across layers.

5. **Object-based Graph Modularity** (Q^l): Given a binary mask M indicating the image patches that include the ground-truth object, we compute the graph modularity score:

$$Q^l = \sum_{c=1}^{2} \left[\frac{L_c}{|\mathcal{E}^l|} - \left(\frac{k_c^{in} k_c^{out}}{2|\mathcal{E}^l|} \right)^2 \right] \quad (6)$$

where L_c is the number of intra-community links for each community c (object or background), k_c^{in} and k_c^{out} are the sums of incoming and outgoing degrees of the nodes in a community, respectively. For this metric, we start by partitioning the graph into two sets of patches, those that belong to the main object, and those that do not. To automate this pipeline, we utilize GroundingDino [10] along with SAM [8], to compute the object binary masks. Then, we use graph modularity, to measure how much the edges of the graph stay localized within each group, or cross between them. This is a particularly insightful metric in our

Table 1. Analysis metrics across model layers on **ImageNet** (top) and **ImageNet-a** (bottom). Top three values for each dataset per metric are indicated by **bold** (highest), * (second), and † (third).

	Layers	S_{vis}^l	D^l	S_{emb}^l	Q^l	p^l	Top-1 Acc.
ImageNet	1-2	**0.700**	3.525	**0.949**	**0.236**	0.005	0.008
	3-4	0.640*	3.672	0.936*	0.234*	0.009	0.018
	5-6	0.556†	5.394	0.908†	0.204†	0.019	0.045
	7-8	0.513	5.848	0.889	0.186	0.049	0.133
	9-10	0.451	6.593	0.854	0.160	0.118	0.281
	11-12	0.421	7.142†	0.842	0.146	0.244†	0.449†
	13-14	0.357	8.160*	0.845	0.119	0.379*	0.600*
	15-16	0.306	**8.858**	0.900	0.088	**0.486**	**0.686**
ImageNet-a	1-2	**0.700**	3.537	**0.953**	0.095*	0.001	0.000
	3-4	0.643*	3.651	0.940*	**0.096**	0.001	0.001
	5-6	0.563†	5.398	0.912†	0.079†	0.001	0.002
	7-8	0.521	5.890	0.893	0.071	0.002	0.003
	9-10	0.463	6.638	0.859	0.058	0.003	0.004
	11-12	0.434	7.165†	0.846	0.052	0.004†	0.007†
	13-14	0.371	8.128*	0.845	0.040	0.007*	0.012*
	15-16	0.320	**8.845**	0.877	0.030	**0.018**	**0.027**

use case, since it allows us to monitor how the edges' separation quality of the generated graph evolves, across different layers.

Visual Explanation through Connection Heatmaps: To qualitatively analyze the model's attention patterns, we visualize the connection structure for specific patches across different layers. For a selected patch (green), we create a heatmap showcasing the generated incoming edges of this patch (red), where the intensity represents the embedding-based similarity score between connected patches. As demonstrated in Fig. 2, this approach reveals how a selected patch on the ship's hull (green) forms connections with varying intensities of red, where brighter red indicates stronger embedding similarity. This visualization aids in understanding how the model gradually builds connections between different regions of the image.

5 Results

5.1 Quantitative Results

Results correspond to experiments conducted on the ViG-Small variant of the Vision GNN [4]. Across all three datasets consistent patterns emerge in how the model's graph structure evolves through the intermediate layers. In the standard ImageNet validation set (Table 1), we observe a clear trade-off between local and global feature integration. Early layers (1–4) maintain high visual ($S_{vis}^l > 0.6$) and embedding similarities ($S_{emb}^l > 0.9$) with relatively short spatial distances ($D^l < 4$), indicating a focus on **local feature extraction**. As the network deepens, these metrics gradually shift, with spatial distances increasing significantly ($D^l \approx 8.8$ in final layers) while visual similarity decreases ($S_{vis}^l \approx 0.3$), indicating a more explorative behavior, that also increases the effective receptive field of each patch. The emergence of class-specific representations in deeper layers is supported by the sudden increase in embedding similarity (S_{emb}^l) during the final two layers, suggesting a convergence towards more **semantically meaningful features**. This evolution correlates with improving classification accuracy, reaching 68.6% in the final layers.

This progressive transformation of the graph structure closely mirrors the hierarchical feature learning observed in traditional CNNs. Similar to how CNN kernels gradually expand their receptive field to capture increasingly complex patterns, ViG systematically builds connections across larger spatial distances while transitioning from low-level visual features to more abstract class-specific representations. Compared to the fixed kernel sizes of a CNN, however, this dynamic graph construction offers an inherently interpretable view of how the model processes information - each edge in the graph explicitly reveals which image regions the model considers relevant for feature extraction, effectively providing a self-documenting receptive field that adapts to the input content.

When comparing the metrics between ImageNet validation and ImageNet-a datasets (Table 1), the most striking difference appears in the graph modularity scores (Q^l), which are significantly lower for adversarial images (starting at

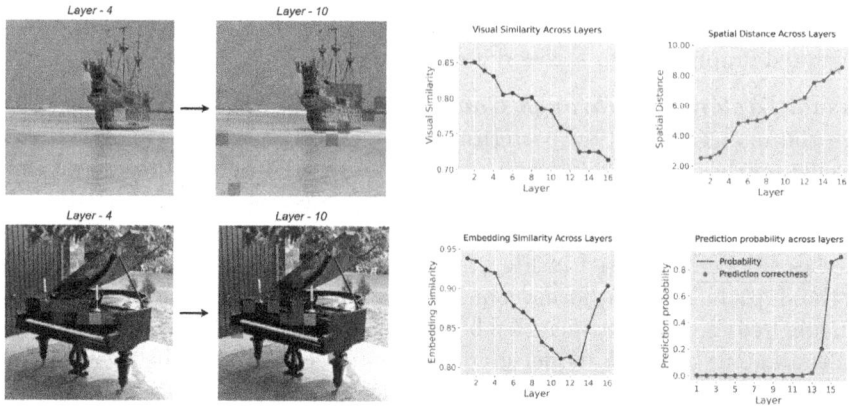

Fig. 2. Heatmap Visualization of intermediate graphs (layers 4 and 10), for two ImageNet images, and metric evolution across all layers Visual Similarity, Spatial Distance (top image) and Embedding Similarity and Prediction probability (bottom image). (Color figure online)

0.095 compared to 0.236 for standard images). This suggests that the model struggles to maintain coherent graph structures that separate object regions from the background in challenging cases. This degradation in graph structure is reflected in the dramatically reduced classification performance, with top-1 accuracy dropping from 68.6% to just 2.7% and correct class probability (p^l) falling from 0.486 to 0.018 in the final layers. While the model's performance shows that it still encounters the same pitfalls as models trained on large-scale datasets (strong intra-domain performance but limited generalization ability) we showcase that our framework still reliably provides insights even in failure cases.

5.2 Qualitative Results

To complement our quantitative analysis, we visualize the evolution of graph connections across selected cases and interpret the results using our proposed metrics. As shown in Fig. 2, examining the top image of a ship reveals how the model's connection patterns differ from layer 4 to layer 10. In the earlier layer, connections (shown in red) from the selected patch (in green) remain largely concentrated within the main object's structure, maintaining high visual similarity with neighboring patches (indicated by the intensity of the red patches). By layer 10, these connections extend further spatially, reaching into the background regions, while maintaining stronger similarities with patches that belong to the ship. This aligns with our quantitative observations in the adjacent diagrams that showcase increasing spatial distance and decreasing visual similarity as we observe deeper layers in the model. The bottom example of a piano further illustrates this progression while also demonstrating a particularly interesting pattern in the final layers - the sharp increase in prediction probability coincides with a notable spike in embedding similarity during the last three layers.

A Semantic and Visual Analysis of Graph-Based Image Classification   81

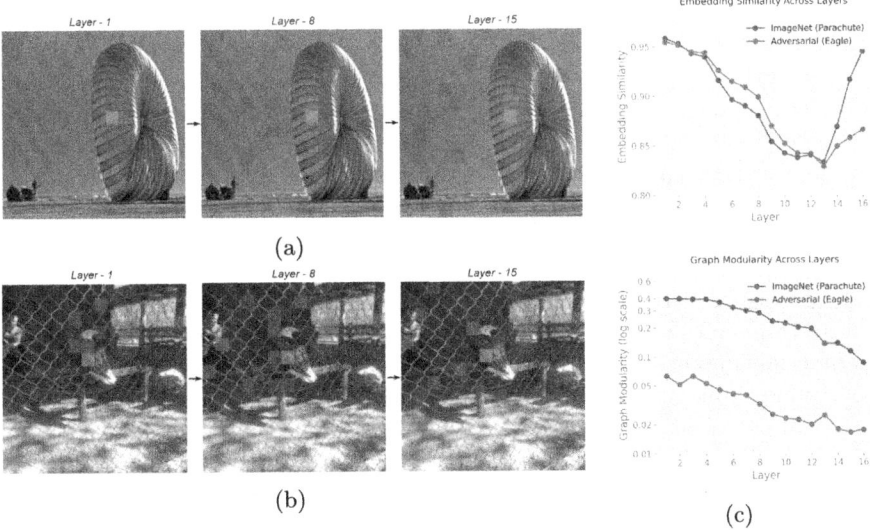

Fig. 3. Heatmap Visualization of intermediate graphs (layers 1, 8 and 15), for intradomain ImageNet (a) and adversarial ImageNet-a (b) images, and metric evolution across all layers for Embedding Similarity and Graph Modularity (c).

This correlation supports our earlier quantitative findings about the model's convergence toward class-specific representations in deeper layers, suggesting a crucial phase where the model consolidates its classification decision. Notably, this critical decision-making phase occurs precisely when visual similarity between connected patches is at its lowest, revealing that the model's most confident predictions emerge from representations that diverge significantly from human visual intuition.

Comparing the in-domain ImageNet image (Fig. 3(a)) with an adversarial image from the ImageNet-a dataset (Fig. 3(b)) reveals important differences in how the model builds and maintains connections. The adversarial example shows significantly more dispersed connectivity patterns even in early and middle layers, with connections constantly extending beyond the main object. This behavioral difference is quantitatively captured in the Graph Modularity diagram (Fig. 3(c)), where the adversarial example shows consistently lower modularity scores across all layers, indicating weaker separation between object and background regions. Furthermore, the adversarial image is misclassified as a dog breed, which is also reflected in the Embedding Similarity diagram. In this diagram, the characteristic spike in similarity during the final layers (associated with convergence to class-specific features, as shown in the Quantitative section) is notably diminished in the adversarial case. While the in-domain example shows a sharp increase in embedding similarity in layers 15–16 (reaching 0.95), the adversarial case exhibits a much more modest increase (only reaching 0.86), indicating potential difficulties in forming consistent class-specific representations.

6 Conclusion

In this work, we presented the first comprehensive explainability analysis of graph-based image classification with Vision GNNs, proposing novel quantitative metrics and visualization techniques to understand how these models process and encode visual information. Our analysis revealed that the model exhibits a clear progression from local to global feature processing across layers, demonstrated by increasing spatial distances and evolving similarity patterns between connected patches. Through experiments on both the standard ImageNet dataset and adversarial variations, we showed that our proposed metrics and visualization techniques can provide valuable insights into the model's behavior and decision-making, even in cases where classification fails. However, our approach has certain limitations, such as its white-box access of specific model architectures and potential computational overhead. Future research should explore how this method can be further leveraged to enhance the interpretability and performance of Vision GNNs, potentially guiding architectural improvements and integrating these metrics into a re-training stage to refine model performance.

Acknowledgments. This work was supported by the Hellenic Foundation for Research and Innovation (HFRI) under the 5th Call for HFRI PhD Fellowships (Fellowship Number 19268). We acknowledge the use of the Amazon Web Services (AWS) platform for providing the infrastructure to build and test our experimental setup.

Disclosure of Interests. The authors have no competing interests to declare that are relevant to the content of this article.

References

1. Avelar, P.H., Tavares, A.R., da Silveira, T.L., Jung, C.R., Lamb, L.C.: Superpixel image classification with graph attention networks. In: 2020 33rd SIBGRAPI Conference on Graphics, Patterns and Images (SIBGRAPI), pp. 203–209. IEEE (2020)
2. Chattopadhyay, A., Sarkar, A., Howlader, P., Balasubramanian, V.N.: Grad-CAM++: improved visual explanations for deep convolutional networks. In: 2018 IEEE Winter Conference on Applications of Computer Vision (WACV), pp. 839–847 (2018). https://doi.org/10.1109/WACV.2018.00097
3. Fey, M., Lenssen, J.E., Weichert, F., Müller, H.: SplineCNN: fast geometric deep learning with continuous b-spline kernels. In: Proceedings of the IEEE Conference on Computer Vision and Pattern Recognition, pp. 869–877 (2018)
4. Han, K., Wang, Y., Guo, J., Tang, Y., Wu, E.: Vision GNN: an image is worth graph of nodes. In: NeurIPS (2022)
5. Han, Y., Wang, P., Kundu, S., Ding, Y., Wang, Z.: Vision HGNN: an image is more than a graph of nodes. 2023 IEEE/CVF International Conference on Computer Vision (ICCV), pp. 19821–19831 (2023), https://api.semanticscholar.org/CorpusID:267024787
6. Hendrycks, D., Zhao, K., Basart, S., Steinhardt, J., Song, D.: Natural adversarial examples. In: CVPR (2021)

7. Huang, Q., Yamada, M., Tian, Y., Singh, D., Yin, D., Chang, Y.: Graphlime: Local interpretable model explanations for graph neural networks (2020). https://arxiv.org/abs/2001.06216
8. Kirillov, A., et al.: Segment anything. In: Proceedings of the IEEE/CVF International Conference on Computer Vision, pp. 4015–4026 (2023)
9. Li, G., Müller, M., Thabet, A.K., Ghanem, B.: DeepGCNs: can GCNs go as deep as CNNs? 2019 IEEE/CVF International Conference on Computer Vision (ICCV) pp. 9266–9275 (2019), https://api.semanticscholar.org/CorpusID:201070021
10. Liu, S., et al.: Grounding DINO: Marrying DINO with grounded pre-training for open-set object detection. In: European Conference on Computer Vision, pp. 38–55. Springer (2024)
11. Luo, D., et al.: Parameterized explainer for graph neural network (2020). https://arxiv.org/abs/2011.04573
12. Muhammad, M.B., Yeasin, M.: Eigen-cam: Class activation map using principal components. In: 2020 International Joint Conference on Neural Networks (IJCNN), pp. 1–7. IEEE (2020)
13. Munir, M., Avery, W., Marculescu, R.: Mobilevig: graph-based sparse attention for mobile vision applications. In: 2023 IEEE/CVF Conference on Computer Vision and Pattern Recognition Workshops (CVPRW), pp. 2211–2219 (2023). https://api.semanticscholar.org/CorpusID:259317049
14. Munir, M., Avery, W., Rahman, M.M., Marculescu, R.: GreedyViG: dynamic axial graph construction for efficient vision GNNs. In: 2024 IEEE/CVF Conference on Computer Vision and Pattern Recognition (CVPR), pp. 6118–6127 (2024). https://api.semanticscholar.org/CorpusID:269757862
15. Russakovsky, O., et al.: Imagenet large scale visual recognition challenge. Int. J. Comput. Vision **115**, 211 – 252 (2014). https://api.semanticscholar.org/CorpusID:2930547
16. Selvaraju, R.R., Cogswell, M., Das, A., Vedantam, R., Parikh, D., Batra, D.: Gradcam: visual explanations from deep networks via gradient-based localization. In: Proceedings of the IEEE International Conference on Computer Vision (ICCV), pp. 618–626 (2017). https://doi.org/10.1109/ICCV.2017.74
17. Simonyan, K., Vedaldi, A., Zisserman, A.: Deep inside convolutional networks: visualising image classification models and saliency maps. arXiv preprint arXiv:1312.6034 (2013)
18. Vu, M.N., Thai, M.T.: PGM-explainer: Probabilistic graphical model explanations for graph neural networks (2020). https://arxiv.org/abs/2010.05788
19. Ying, R., Bourgeois, D., You, J., Zitnik, M., Leskovec, J.: Gnnexplainer: generating explanations for graph neural networks (2019). https://arxiv.org/abs/1903.03894
20. Zeiler, M.D., Fergus, R.: Visualizing and understanding convolutional networks. In: Fleet, D., Pajdla, T., Schiele, B., Tuytelaars, T. (eds.) ECCV 2014. LNCS, vol. 8689, pp. 818–833. Springer, Cham (2014). https://doi.org/10.1007/978-3-319-10590-1_53
21. Zhou, B., Khosla, A., Lapedriza, A., Oliva, A., Torralba, A.: Learning deep features for discriminative localization. In: Proceedings of the IEEE Conference on Computer Vision and Pattern Recognition, pp. 2921–2929 (2016)

Open Access This chapter is licensed under the terms of the Creative Commons Attribution 4.0 International License (http://creativecommons.org/licenses/by/4.0/), which permits use, sharing, adaptation, distribution and reproduction in any medium or format, as long as you give appropriate credit to the original author(s) and the source, provide a link to the Creative Commons license and indicate if changes were made.

The images or other third party material in this chapter are included in the chapter's Creative Commons license, unless indicated otherwise in a credit line to the material. If material is not included in the chapter's Creative Commons license and your intended use is not permitted by statutory regulation or exceeds the permitted use, you will need to obtain permission directly from the copyright holder.

Counterfactuals in XAI

HalCECE: A Framework for Explainable Hallucination Detection Through Conceptual Counterfactuals in Image Captioning

Maria Lymperaiou[✉], Giorgos FIlandrianos, Angeliki Dimitriou, Athanasios Voulodimos, and Giorgos Stamou

National Technical University of Athens, Athens, Greece
{marialymp,geofila,angelikidim}@ails.ece.ntua.gr,
thanosv@mail.ntua.gr, gstam@cs.ntua.gr

Abstract. In the dynamic landscape of artificial intelligence, the exploration of hallucinations within vision-language (VL) models emerges as a critical frontier. This work delves into the intricacies of hallucinatory phenomena exhibited by widely used image captioners, unraveling interesting patterns. Specifically, we step upon previously introduced techniques of conceptual counterfactual explanations to address VL hallucinations. The deterministic and efficient nature of the employed conceptual counterfactuals backbone is able to suggest semantically minimal edits driven by hierarchical knowledge, so that the transition from a hallucinated caption to a non-hallucinated one is performed in a black-box manner. HalCECE, our proposed hallucination detection framework is highly interpretable, by providing semantically meaningful edits apart from standalone numbers, while the hierarchical decomposition of hallucinated concepts leads to a thorough hallucination analysis. Another novelty tied to the current work is the investigation of role hallucinations, being one of the first works to involve interconnections between visual concepts in hallucination detection. Overall, HalCECE recommends an explainable direction to the crucial field of VL hallucination detection, thus fostering trustworthy evaluation of current and future VL systems.

Keywords: Hallucination detection · Explainable Evaluation · Counterfactual Explanations · Vision-Language Models · Image Captioning

1 Introduction

In the ever-evolving landscape of artificial intelligence, the appearance of hallucinations has emerged as a significant concern. While neural models showcase remarkable linguistic and/or visual prowess and creativity, their outputs

---

M. Lymperaiou, G. FIlandrianos and A. Dimitriou—Contributed equally.

occasionally veer into unpredictable directions, blurring the line between factual accuracy and imaginative fabrication. Hallucinations as a research topic have recently received attention in NLP, with Large Language Models (LLMs) producing unfaithful and inaccurate outputs, despite their sheer size in terms of trainable parameters and training data volume [2,28,43,54].

The nature of hallucination is tied with difficulty in their detection for several reasons, one of them being the variability in hallucination types. [54] recognize three hallucination categories: Input-Conflicting Hallucinations refer to unfaithful LLM generation in comparison to what the input prompt requested. Context-Conflicting Hallucinations involve inconsistencies within the generated output itself. Finally, Fact-Conflicting Hallucinations violate factuality, providing false information in the output.

Even though LLM hallucinations have captivated significant interest in literature, multimodal settings, such as vision-language (VL) hallucinations, have not been adequately explored yet. Especially during the timely transition towards Large VL Models (LVLMs) [1,3,30,36], impressive capabilities in VL understanding and generation are unavoidably accompanied by unfaithful outputs that are even more difficult in detection compared to LLM hallucinations due to intra-modality ambiguity and alignment challenges.

The literature on hallucinations of VL models so far addresses some fundamental research questions regarding evaluation [14,24,31, 42,47,52] and mitigation [20,27,34, 40,43,55]. Nevertheless, it grapples with inherent limitations, notably in terms of the interpretability and granularity of metrics employed, hindering a comprehensive understanding of the nuanced challenges posed by hallucinatory phenomena in VL models. We argue that the current VL hallucinations research gaps emphasize the need for an *explainable evaluation* strategy [33], which not only interprets inner workings behind hallucination occurrence, but also paves the way towards effective

Fig. 1. Example of hallucination on image captioning. The generated caption c misses an accurate relationship between the man and the dog. The concept "laptop" should replace the concept "dog" in the generated caption, while the relationship "next to" should be added to connect the concepts "dog" and "man".

hallucination mitigation approaches. At the same time, we recognize some related endeavors in recent VL evaluation literature [32], even though the term "hallucination" is not explicitly used.

In this work, we set the scene for an **explainable evaluation framework** of VL hallucinations by applying our approach to image captioning, a task associated with hallucination challenges, as in Fig. 1. We borrow techniques from prior work in VL hallucination evaluation, specifically targeting image generation from language [32], showcasing their effortless applicability in the reverse task of language generation from text. Since most current hallucination evaluation research focuses on object hallucination, i.e. the appearance of extraneous objects or, on the contrary, objects consistently missing in the generated output, while only a few assess role hallucinations [49], referring to spatial relationships or actions, we aim to construct a unified framework named HalCECE, incorporating both of them through their projection on **graph edits**. In our proposed HalCECE framework, we retain fundamental properties of conceptual counterfactuals [10] and graph-driven edits [8], which will be analyzed in subsequent sections. Overall, we present the following contributions:

– We propose the adoption of explainable evaluation in image captioning hallucination detection contrasting typical captioning evaluation metrics.
– We decompose concepts existing in captions to allow fine-grained evaluation and quantification of hallucination.
– We substantiate our findings by applying our proposed evaluation framework to various image captioners of increasing model size.

2 Background

Image Captioning. stands as a pioneering task in machine learning, bridging the visual and linguistic modalities so that an accurate intra-modality communication can be established. Real-world AI systems rely on image captioning to provide textual descriptions for visually-impaired people, facilitate indexing and retrieval of images based on textual requests and enable image-language alignment for advanced interaction between humans and computers. To this end, hallucinations arise as a crucial concern that impede the effective usage of visual descriptions in practice [12].

With the advent of VL transformers, the field of image captioning has made substantial strides, with models such as BLIP [23], BLIP-2 [22], Llava [29,30], BEiT [48], GiT [46] and others achieving state-of-the-art results in the low-billion parameter regime. Despite scaling up towards billion trainable parameters [1,3,36], which serves as a general criterion for language generation quality, many image captioners often come across hallucinations in the generated text, the detection and mitigation of which becomes even more challenging under closed-source scenarios, as in the case of GPT-4 [36] and Claude [1] models.

Hallucinations in VL models refer to the appearance of non-existent concepts in the generated modality. Evaluation of complex VL systems for language generation from images has largely exploited metrics focusing on linguistic quality, such as BLEU [37], ROUGE [25], CIDEr [45] and others, which have been widely used for benchmarking. Association between intra-modality concepts, i.e. the agreement of visual and linguistic cues has only recently been addressed, under the spotlight of VL hallucinations.

Recent research has showcased some interesting endeavors towards capturing hallucinations, targeting different aspects of the problem, and employing varying techniques. With a focus on objects, detection of VL hallucinations was initially performed using the CHAIR (Caption Hallucination Assessment with Image Relevance) metric [42]. The per instance $CHAIR_i$ is defined as:

$$CHAIR_i = \frac{|Hallucinated\ Objects|}{|All\ Predicted\ Objects|} \quad (1)$$

Furthermore, the per sentence $CHAIR_s$ is formed as:

$$CHAIR_s = \frac{|Sentences\ with\ hallucinated\ objects|}{|All\ sentences|} \quad (2)$$

Despite its simplicity, CHAIR acts as a first, immediate measure for object hallucinations, inspiring more refined consequent approaches.

The FAITHSCORE metric addresses different types of VL hallucinations in a fine-grained way by breaking down the caption in subcaptions, from which atomic facts are extracted [14]. Similarly, ALOHa [38] leverages an LLM to identify groundable objects within a candidate caption, assess their semantic similarity to reference objects from both captions and object detections, and utilize Hungarian matching to compute the final hallucination score. Nonetheless, the subcaption process leverages LLMs, which also hallucinate themselves.

The dialog-based evaluation process of POPE [24] suggests answering "yes/no" to questions regarding the existence of an object in an image. Objects are extracted from images based on ground truth annotations or segmentation tools, filling question templates, while an equally sized set of non-existent objects provides negative samples to measure the confidence of prompted models against "yes/no" answer bias. Then, the agreement between answers with ground truth objects is measured. Also using a question-answering pipeline to evaluate object hallucinations, NOPE [31] regards LLM-constructed questions with negative indefinite pronouns (e.g. nowhere, none etc.) as ground truth answers.

Involving LLMs in the hallucination detection pipeline, [47] are the first to recognize VL hallucination patterns, driving the construction of prompts for ChatGPT to generate relevant hallucinated instances. Fine-tuning LLama [44] on such hallucinations provides a proficient module for capturing VL hallucinations.

Model performance on standard text generation metrics may be negatively correlated with hallucination occurrence, while the choice of image encoding techniques and training objectives employed in the pre-training stage can be definitive [5]. Statistical factors accompanying object hallucinations were analyzed in [56], examining frequent object co-occurrences, uncertainty during the generation process, and correlations between hallucinations and object positioning within the generated text.

3 Explainable Hallucinations Evaluation

Many of the contributions analyzed above harness LLMs at some point of the hallucination evaluation process. These approaches inevitably induce uncertainty related to the prompt used, while simultaneously facing the possibility of LLMs also hallucinating and ultimately hindering the robustness and trustworthiness of the affected module, and thus the evaluation framework itself. In our framework, we deviate from the usage of LLMs, sacrificing the simplicity they provide in order to enhance the determinism and reliability of the evaluation process.

Other than that, both metrics evaluating linguistic quality, as well as metrics for VL hallucinations lack explainability aspects, since they do not suggest the *direction of change* towards dehallucinated generation. This direction of change should primarily be **measurable** and **meaningful**, while its optimal usage prescribes notions of **optimality**, translated to semantically *minimal changes*, as well as the *fewest possible number of edits* leading to the desired outcome. We will analyze these desiderata:

Measurable change refers to assigning a well defined numerical value for comparative reasons. This requirement demands the connection of concepts to be changed with similarity features within a unified structure, such as their distance on a semantic space or within a semantic graph.

Meaningful change refers to performing operations that are sensible in the real world, such as substituting an object with another object and not with meaningless sequences of characters. For example, swapping the concept "cat" with the character sequence "hfushbfb" does not hold a useful meaning. Moreover, even substituting objects with actions breaks meaningfulness, e.g. replacing the concept "cat" with the concept "swimming" within the same sentence violates the well-defined rules of linguistic syntax.

Optimal change refers to employing a strategy which guarantees that valid and measurable changes are the best ones to be found among a possibly infinite set of valid and measurable changes. For example, replacing "cat" with "person" is meaningful for a human, while also being measurable if we place the concepts "cat" and "person" in a semantic graph structure. However, an alternative suggestion could be replacing "cat" with "dog", as they are both animals, or even "cat" with "tiger" since they are both felines. In this case, optimal edits require finding the most *semantically similar concept* to the source one. Such similarity requirements can be imposed by structured knowledge bases, deterministically ensuring **semantically minimal edits**. Furthermore, the number of such edits should be controlled, since infinitely performing minimal changes should be naturally excluded from the proposed framework. For example, the transition "cat"→"dog" should not consider extraneous changes, if not required to approach the ground truth sample. Therefore, the set of all proposed changes should be minimized in terms of overall semantic cost, ultimately resulting in *fewest possible semantically minimal edits*.

To address these challenges, we leverage the framework first proposed in [10], where counterfactual explanations are provided via edits satisfying our desiderata. This framework was later adopted for the evaluation of image generation models [32], where a source set S contains the ground truth concepts as extracted from the generated modality (in our use case being textual captions) and a target set T contains ground truth concepts as extracted from the input modality (in our case being annotated images provided to the captioner).

We wish to perform the $S \to T$ transition using the fewest possible semantically minimal and meaningful edits, which is achieved via the guarantees offered by the WordNet hierarchy [35]: concepts from S, T are mapped on WordNet synsets, which correspond to sets of cognitive synonyms. Distances of synsets within the hierarchy translate to semantic differences in actual meaning. Finding the minimum path between two synsets entails semantically minimal differences between corresponding concepts. WordNet is a crucial component of this implementation, since it guarantees **measurable** (WordNet distance is a numerical value), **meaningful** (WordNet synsets correspond to lexical entities of the English language) and **semantically minimal** (shortest WordNet distance between two concepts is found using pathfinding algorithms [7]) concept edits. The algorithm of [10] uses bipartite matching to minimize the overall cost of assignment between S and T concepts, ensuring the optimal $S \to T$ transition.

By breaking down the $S \to T$ transition, the following three edit operations e are allowed for any source $s \in S$ and target concept $t \in T$ [10,32]:

- **Replacement (R)** $e_{s \to t}(S)$: A concept $s \in S$ is replaced with $t \notin S$.
- **Deletion (D)** $e_{s-}(S)$: A concept $s \in S$ is deleted from S.
- **Insertion (I)** $e_{t+}(S)$: A concept $t \in T$ is inserted in S.

Especially in the case of image captioning, we impose higher importance in **D** and **R** edits; the rationale behind this decision is that since hallucinations refer to the presence of irrelevant or extraneous concepts, they should be deleted or replaced to match the ground truth ones. Moreover, in many cases, captions purposefully provide a higher-level description of an image, therefore several visual concepts are omitted, sacrificing coverage for brevity. In that case, **I** suggests the addition of visual concepts to the caption, which may not be always necessary. In our framework, we also include **I** calculations, but we do not consider them in the overall transformation cost; instead, we provide them as *suggestion* for the user to choose whether they may be incorporated in more verbose captions.

3.1 The Role of Roles

In Fig. 1, the captioning model (BLIP) confuses the spatial relationship between the man and the dog, showcasing the importance of *role hallucinations*, which were not widely addressed in prior work, since object hallucinations were their primary concern. Additionally, roles should be addressed *in conjunction to objects*, and not on their own, since this more simplistic approach would result in under-detection of hallucinations. For example, if we apply the counterfactual explanations algorithm of [10] on sets of roles, the proposed edits for Fig. 1 would be {**I**("next to")}, referring to the addition of the role "next to" that connects the dog and the man. However, if we consider *triples* of two objects connected with a role, the resulting edits would be: {**R**(["dog", "on", "lap], ["laptop", "on", "lap"]), **I**(["dog", "next to", "man"])}, which is a more valid set of edits, if we view the human-written ground truth caption and the image itself.

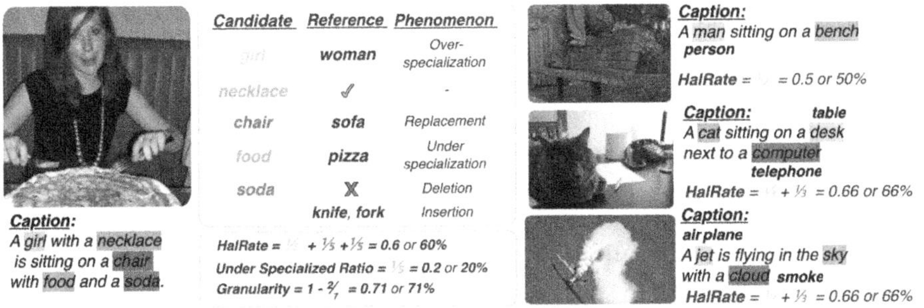

Fig. 2. An example of detected hallucination of objects in image captioning from our framework is presented, depicting each phenomenon along with the proposed metrics. Objects in yellow represent an overspecialized phenomenon, in purple a replacement, and in red a removal. Those in green are correct objects, and those in blue are the underspecialized objects (which do not constitute hallucinations, as the caption contains a more generic concept to the ground truth one). As shown, the hallucination rate is calculated as the sum of the rate of each hallucination phenomenon independently. (Color figure online)

To perform the transition to editing triples instead of standalone concepts, we require scene graphs instead of objects to acquire a conceptual representation of the image [8]. Regarding the caption, we also parse the sentence in a graph structure. Given two graphs G_T representing the image and G_S corresponding to a possibly hallucinated generated caption c, we search for the minimum cost set of **R**, **D**, **I** edits (applied on objects and roles) that transform $G_S \rightarrow G_T$, i.e. convert a -possibly- hallucinated graph to a non-hallucinated one.

This cost of transformation is calculated using Graph Edit Distance (GED) between G_S, G_T. Denoting as $c(e_i)$ the cost of an operation $e_i \in \{\mathbf{R}, \mathbf{D}, \mathbf{I}\}$ and $P(G_S, G_T)$ the set of n edit paths to transform $G_S \rightarrow G_T$, GED is formed as:

$$GED(G_S, G_T) = \min_{(e_1,\ldots,e_n) \in P(G_S, G_T)} \sum_{i=1}^{n} c(e_i) \quad (3)$$

The shortest paths $P(G_S, G_T)$ are calculated using deterministic pathfinding algorithms, such as Dijkstra [7], ensuring optimality of edits e_i.

However, GED is an NP-hard algorithm, meaning that it cannot be calculated efficiently in its basic, brute-force format. For this reason, we employ some approximations, such as the Volgenant-Jonker (VJ) algorithm [15], which allows for GED calculation in polynomial time.

4 Hallucination Detection Framework

Object Hallucinations. In Fig. 2 we illustrate the hallucination analysis provided by our framework. We formulate the object hallucination detection problem as follows: each caption c has generated objects $S = \{s_1, s_2, \ldots, s_n\}$, and each image contains the ground truth objects $T = \{t_1, t_2, \ldots, t_m\}$. We find the **R**, **D**, **I** sets of object edits to perform the transition $S \rightarrow T$, as analyzed in Sect. 3.

In order to evaluate different granularities of hallucinations, i.e. presence of more generic or more specific concepts compared to the ground truth one, we utilize the Least Common Ancestor (LCA) within the WordNet hierarchy. Specifically, LCA denotes the closest ancestor synset between two synsets in WordNet; we closely examine the case where the LCA between two synsets contains one of the synsets itself: for example, given two synsets v and w, if $LCA(v, w) = v$, then v is a hypernym (more generic concept) of w.

Based on these, we analyze the following *hallucination phenomena:*

- **Deletion (D)**: When an object $s_i \in S$ must be deleted; e.g., in Fig. 2, the concept "soda" is in the generated caption c but not in the image.
- **Replacement (R)**: When an object $s_i \in S$, is replaced with a different object t_j, where $LCA(s_i, t_j) \neq s_i$, and $LCA(s_i, t_j) \neq t_j$ (meaning that no object is a hypernym of the other). For instance, the caption references a "chair", but the image contains a "sofa".
- **Over-specialization (O)**: When an object $s_i \in S$ is replaced with a different object t_j, where $LCA(s_i, t_j) = t_j$, i.e. t_j is a more general concept than s_i in the hierarchy. For example, the caption states that the image contains a "girl", but the image depicts a "woman"; in this case, the caption erroneously overspecified this term, since "girl" is subcategory of "woman".

Based on these phenomena, we measure the degree of hallucination for a caption c as the number of objects that exhibit at least one of the aforementioned phenomena. Thus, the metric for counting hallucinations in captioning, denoted as $Hal(S,T)$, is defined as the sum of the cardinalities of the sets of **D**, **R**, **O**:

$$Hal(S,T) = |\mathbf{D}(S,T)| + |\mathbf{R}(S,T)| + |\mathbf{O}(S,T)| \qquad (4)$$

The hallucination rate *HalRate* reveals the percentage of hallucinated objects over the total number of objects $|S|$ in c, and it is mathematically expressed as:

$$HalRate(S,T) = \frac{Hal(S,T)}{|S|} \qquad (5)$$

We incorporate additional semantic metrics on these properties, such as quantifying the semantic distance between hallucinatory and ground truth concepts.

- **Similarity of Replacements**: We employ Wu-Palmer similarity [50] to measure the semantic similarity of replacements based on the position of synsets in WordNet. This way, we measure how close the replaced terms are in order to gain further understanding of the behavior of the captioner. For example, semantically related replacements receive a higher Wu-Palmer similarity score, denoting more "justified" hallucination occurrences.

An additional facet of HalCECE lies in its capacity to explore phenomena beyond hallucination. This is exemplified through the following measures:

- **Granularity**: Defined as 1 minus the ratio of **Insertions (I)** over the number of ground truth image objects. In essence, it represents the percentage of objects that c attempts to encapsulate compared to the image objects:

$$Granularity(S,T) = 1 - \frac{|\mathbf{I}(S)|}{|T|} \tag{6}$$

- **Under-Specialization (U)**: Quantifies the instances of underspecialized objects, where an object $s_i \in S$ from c is replaced with a different object t_j, and $LCA(s_i, t_j) = s_i$, meaning that the caption object is more generic than the corresponding image object. For instance, if the caption indicates the presence of "food", but the image portrays a "pizza", the caption is not incorrect (because a "pizza" is a sub category of "food") but could benefit from greater specificity. The ratio is computed as the division of the number of under-specialized objects by the total number of objects in c, reflecting the proportion of objects in the generated captions that are underspecialized.

In our analysis, we incorporate both the **average number of objects per caption** and the **average number of WordNet ancestors (hypernyms)** associated with each of these objects for all data instances. This approach provides a comprehensive perspective on the content of each caption c.

Role Hallucinations. Our framework is directly extended to incorporate edge-level hallucinations. On top of objects included in T and S, images and captions also describe object interactions. As explained, role hallucination is measured using *triples* and not simply relations which would disregard adjacent objects and their transformations. To this end, we denote the sets of triples corresponding to captions and image annotations respectively as $S^r = \{(s_i, r_j^s, s_k), \ldots\}$ and $T^r = \{(t_i, r_j^t, t_k), \ldots\}$. A visual representation of roles within captions can be found in Fig. 3. Examples of caption triples are "horse *over* obstacle" and "people *sitting at* table". To measure role hallucinations, i.e. the transition from $S^r \to T^r$, we employ an adjusted version of aforementioned equations. Edit sets **D** and **R** are calculated by considering triples instead of objects as following:

- **Deletions (D)**: When an edge r_j^s between two objects s_i, s_k must be deleted. Notably, this edit set includes deletions induced as "collateral damage" due to object deletions or replacements, as well as hallucinated relations between correctly detected objects in c. In Fig. 3, the role "eating" between "people" and "food" is deleted because "food" is hallucinated by the captioner.
- **Replacement (R)**: When an edge r_j^s between two objects s_i, s_k is replaced with another edge r_w^t. For example, in Fig. 3 the role "jumping" between "person" and "horse" is hallucinated and needs to be replaced with "riding". Despite "jumping" being a valid relation between "horse" and "obstacle", or even "person" and "obstacle", it is definitely not correct in the presented configuration, placing a great focus on leveraging roles as part of a triple.

It is noteworthy that the definition of over-/under- specialization is not applicable for roles, as edges describe actions, topology or "part of" relations, steering away from hierarchies. To combat this, we leverage the annotation information provided by humans to correctly match caption relations to ground truth ones and map them to WordNet. When captioners produce previously unseen relations (in terms of ground truth), we weight them accordingly, so that they can be easily inserted or deleted during GED computation; they are not likely to be replaced with other roles though, since we lack semantic content. To detect if they are part of **R**, we deploy an extra post-hoc reasoning step and check if a relation r_j^s between the same two objects has been deleted and another r_w^t has been added. Given the previous analysis, role hallucinations are measured as:

$$Hal(S^r, T^r) = |\mathbf{D}(S^r, T^r)| + |\mathbf{R}(S^r, T^r)| \tag{7}$$

while *HalRate* and *Granularity* are simply adjusted to be:

$$HalRate(S^r, T^r) = \frac{Hal(S^r, T^r)}{|S^r|} \tag{8}$$

$$Granularity(S^r, T^r) = 1 - \frac{|\mathbf{I}(S^r)|}{|T^r|} \tag{9}$$

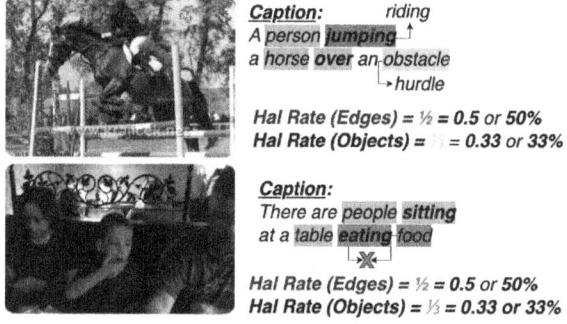

Fig. 3. An demonstration of the edge integration into HalCECE. The edges are highlighted in **bold**, and the different colors correspond to those of Fig. 2.

5 Experiments

Dataset and Models. To evaluate HalCECE on images connected with both captions and scene graphs, we experiment on the intersection of Visual Genome (VG) [17] and COCO [26]. VG contains handcrafted scene graph annotations incorporating objects, attributes and roles. On the other hand, COCO scenes are connected with 5 captions per image, provided by humans. We restrict our experimentation on the COCO validation set (splits are provided by the dataset creators), which demonstrates 2170 common instances with VG; a few of those are eliminated, if the corresponding objects cannot be aligned with WordNet.

We initially experiment with non-proprietary captioners, evaluating both smaller and larger models, since smaller ones can be more easily deployed by every researcher. Specifically, we apply our method on variants of GiT [46] and BLIP [21,23], namely *GiT-base* (trained on 10 million image-text pairs), *GiT-large* (trained on 20 million image-text pairs) and *GiT-base/large-coco* (fine-tuned on COCO captions); also *BLIP-base* (using ViT [9] base encoder), *BLIP-large* (ViT large encoder), *BLIP2-flan-t5-xl* (Flan-T5 [4] is used as the language decoder) and *BLIP2-opt-2* (using OPT [53] 2.7B as the language decoder). We attempt unconditional and conditional image captioning (related experiments will be denoted as *unc/cond*), where captioners are fine-tuned to estimate conditional and unconditional distributions over captions respectively [16]. Moreover, we experiment with *ViT-GPT2* [19], which leverages ViT as the encoder and GPT2 [41] as the decoder. Finally, we provide results on two proprietary foundational models of the Claude family [1] prompted for captioning, namely *Claude-sonnet*[1] and *Claude-haiku*[2]. This way, we prove the real power of HalCECE on closed-source models where our white-box competitors are not applicable. All parameter counts for these models are detailed in Appendix 6.

Since prompting LVLMs can define the length of the generated captions, we attempt to generate both longer captions (20–30 words), as well as shorter ones (10 words max), which are comparable to the captions produced from the rest of the captioners. This way, we get the opportunity to explore HalCECE on longer descriptions, something that is not available in smaller VL models. We name the respective experiments using L for *long* generations and S for *short* ones.

Concept Sets Construction. We construct the linguistic S, S^r and visual concept sets T, T^r, corresponding to source and target concept sets respectively with the goal of transforming $S \to T$ and $S^r \to T^r$. Linguistic sets are formed by extracting graphs from text via the Scene Graph Parser tool[3], while visual sets are constructed using ground truth annotations from COCO and VG.

Experimental setup Non-proprietary pre-trained captioners are loaded from Huggingface[4] using their respective model cards and their inference is executed on a 12GB NVIDIA TITAN Xp GPU. No further training is performed. Proprietary Claude models are accessed via Amazon Web Services (AWS) using API calls (Bedrock service). Prompts for Claude models are presented in App. 6.

5.1 HalCECE Results

Based on the hallucination detection framework analyzed in the previous section, we present our findings as following: Tables 1, 2, 3 contain averaged results per captioner involving the hallucination phenomena introduced above. In addition, Figs. 4, 5 demonstrate the distributions of values per hallucination phenomenon in our dataset, addressing object and role hallucinations respectively. These plots refer to GiT-base as a proof-of-concept, since it is one of the best-performing captioners according to our reported explainable metrics.

---

[1] anthropic.claude-3-5-sonnet-20241022-v2:0.
[2] anthropic.claude-3-haiku-20240307-v1:0.
[3] https://github.com/vacancy/SceneGraphParser.
[4] https://huggingface.co/models?pipeline_tag=image-to-text.

Table 1. Object hallucinations (mean values) on the $VG \cap COCO$ validation subset. **Best** and **worst** results are denoted. Numbers in parenthesis denote absolute #objects.

Model	#objects	#ancestors	HalRate (#hal. objects)↓	Granul.	U↓
GiT-base-coco	3.13	27.93	35.56% (1.13)	17.0%	4.06% (0.13)
GiT-large-coco	3.15	27.97	33.93% (1.1)	17.0%	3.92% (0.12)
GiT-base	1.76	16.57	26.41% (0.48)	9.0%	3.27% (0.06)
GiT-large	1.74	16.28	**25.38% (0.46)**	9.0%	3.31% (0.06)
BLIP-base-unc	2.53	22.55	34.28% (0.91)	13.0%	4.48% (0.12)
BLIP-base-cond	3.23	29.5	58.48% (1.87)	17.0%	2.96% (0.1)
BLIP-large-unc	3.63	32.73	39.2% (1.45)	19.0%	3.47% (0.13)
BLIP-large-cond	4.22	37.5	53.04% (2.24)	22.0%	**2.84% (0.12)**
BLIP2-flan-t5-xl	2.57	23.16	33.13% (0.89)	14%	4.05% (0.11)
BLIP2-opt-2	2.78	24.89	33.28% (0.96)	15.0%	4.19% (0.12)
ViT-GPT2	2.95	26.51	38.76% (1.18)	16.0%	4.47% (0.14)
Claude sonnet-L	6.85	58.94	58.91% (4.05)	36.0%	4.71% (0.33)
Claude haiku-L	7.12	58.66	**64.31% (4.64)**	39.0%	5.4% (0.39)
Claude sonnet-S	3.35	30.48	47.16% (1.6)	17.0%	4.67% (0.16)
Claude haiku-S	2.95	25.49	54.36% (1.62)	16.0%	**6.74% (0.19)**

Table 2. Continuation of Table 1. More object hallucination phenomena on $VG \cap COCO$ validation subset. Numbers in parenthesis denote absolute #objects.

Model	D↓	O↓	R↓	Similarity of R↑
GiT-base-coco	4.38% (0.15)	3.01% (0.09)	28.18% (0.89)	0.56
GiT-large-coco	4.4% (0.16)	2.46% (0.08)	27.06% (0.87)	0.55
GiT-base	**2.11% (0.05)**	**2.17% (0.04)**	22.12% (0.4)	**0.61**
GiT-large	2.46% (0.05)	2.41% (0.04)	**20.51% (0.36)**	0.6
BLIP-base-unc	3.78% (0.11)	2.65% (0.07)	27.86% (0.73)	0.57
BLIP-base-cond	**23.07% (0.72)**	2.76% (0.09)	32.66% (1.05)	0.52
BLIP-large-unc	6.13% (0.24)	3.48% (0.13)	29.59% (1.08)	0.56
BLIP-large-cond	19.27% (0.81)	2.46% (0.11)	31.3% (1.32)	0.52
BLIP2-flan-t5-xl	4.27% (0.12)	3.16% (0.08)	25.7% (0.69)	0.56
BLIP2-opt-2	3.64% (0.11)	2.8% (0.08)	26.84% (0.77)	0.57
ViT-GPT2	3.45% (0.11)	3.16% (0.09)	32.14% (0.97)	0.6
Claude sonnet-L	15.79% (1.05)	2.51% (0.19)	40.61% (2.81)	0.52
Claude haiku-L	17.3% (1.28)	2.69% (0.2)	**44.33% (3.15)**	**0.49**
Claude sonnet-S	7.1% (0.25)	**5.42% (0.18)**	34.63% (1.16)	0.57
Claude haiku-S	7.78% (0.24)	4.59% (0.13)	41.99% (1.26)	0.52

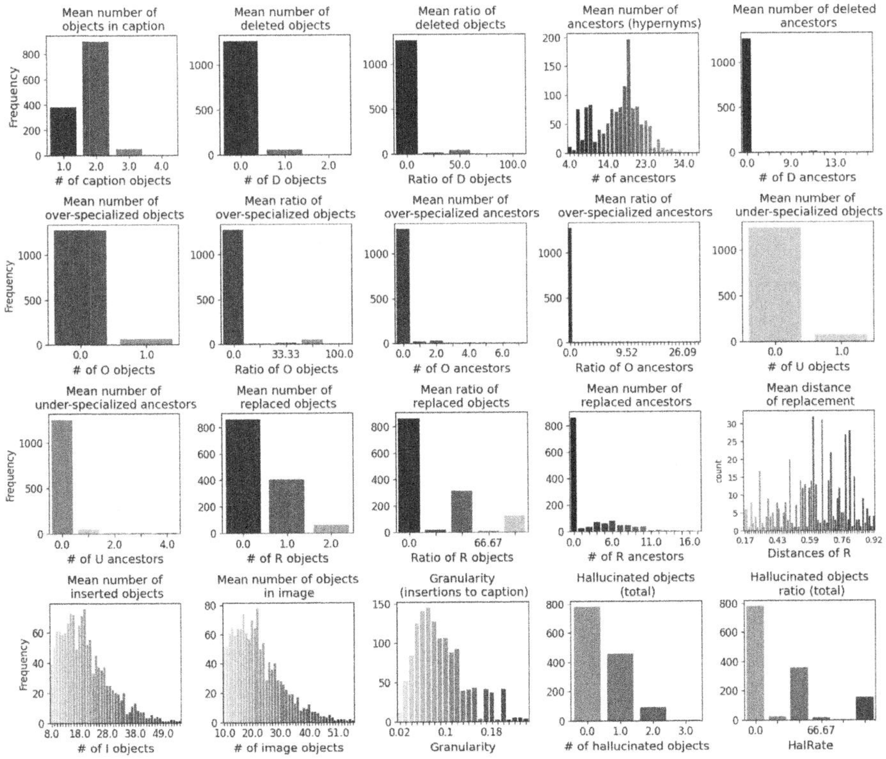

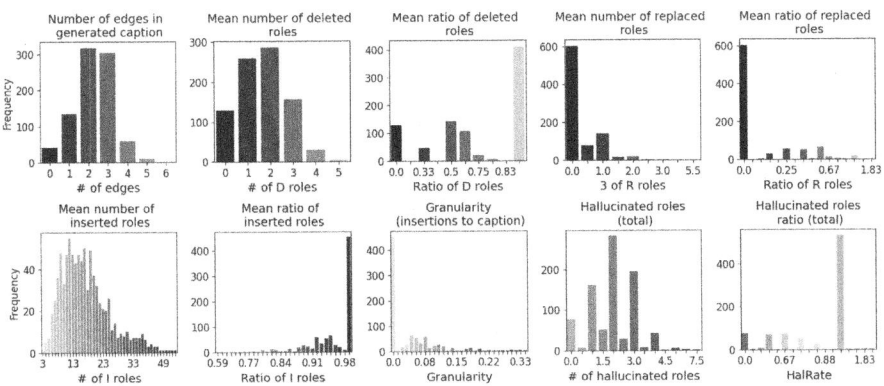

Fig. 4. Statistics of our proposed explainable metrics on *object hallucinations* by GiT-base on the $VG \cap COCO$ validation set.

Fig. 5. Statistics of our proposed explainable metrics on *role hallucinations* by GiT-base on the $VG \cap COCO$ validation set.

Table 3. Role hallucinations (mean values per image) on the $VG \cap COCO$ validation subset. Numbers in parenthesis denote absolute #roles.

Model	#roles	D↓	R↓	HalRate (#hal. roles)↓	Granul.
GiT-base-coco	1.92	65.32% (1.37)	14.06% (0.29)	79.38% (1.66)	3.93%
GiT-large-coco	1.94	65.33% (1.36)	13.75% (0.29)	79.09% (1.65)	4.08%
GiT-base	0.73	44.05% (0.47)	11.98% (0.13)	56.03% (0.59)	1.8%
GiT-large	0.69	39.15% (0.42)	11.58% (0.12)	50.63% (0.54)	1.89%
BLIP-base-unc	1.44	61.2% (1.01)	13.04% (0.2)	74.23% (1.22)	3.01%
BLIP-base-cond	2.14	90.96% (1.93)	4.22% (0.1)	95.18 (2.03)	1.48%
BLIP-large-unc	2.28	68.32% (1.67)	13.2% (0.31)	81.52% (1.98)	4.38%
BLIP-large-cond	2.98	86.6% (2.54)	6.68% (0.22)	93.28% (2.77)	2.99%
BLIP2-flan-t5-xl	1.62	69.26% (1.16)	14.2% (0.22)	83.47% (1.38)	3.25%
BLIP2-opt-2	1.79	68.87% (1.25)	14.37% (0.25)	83.24% (1.51)	3.65%
ViT-GPT2	1.86	71.05% (1.36)	16.46% (0.28)	87.5% (1.64)	3.42%
Claude sonnet-L	3.9	80.71% (3.17)	9.8% (0.39)	90.51% (3.56)	7.1%
Claude haiku-L	3.99	80.25% (3.29)	10.31% (0.38)	90.56% (3.67)	6.28%
Claude sonnet-S	2.1	75.19% (1.62)	11.85% (0.25)	87.04% (1.87)	5.24 %
Claude haiku-S	1.85	74.31% (1.39)	13.71% (0.14)	88.02% (1.53)	4.99%

In all cases, a rather high percentage of hallucinations for all semantics (objects, roles and derived phenomena) is observed; almost $1/3^{rd}$ of the caption objects present some form of hallucinations, while for roles several occurrences contain some hallucinatory inaccuracy, even exceeding 90% in HalRate.

Replacements (**R**) represent the most common type of object edit e, indicating that captioners often generate hallucinated objects that are still related to the source (e.g., "daybed" instead of "couch"), rather than entirely unrelated hallucinated objects. Replacements of relevant objects are preferable to deletions for HalCECE, as the paths leading to another concept within WordNet are often shorter than the path to the root node (*entity.n.01*), which corresponds to the Deletion (**D**) edit. However, for unrelated objects, where the distance between these two is greater than the cost of first deleting the one and then inserting the other, replacement is not preferable. This is because concepts appearing in captions usually lie lower in the hierarchy, being specific enough to describe depicted objects. This level of conceptual granularity is imposed during the pre-training of captioners, which utilize descriptive captions, such as the ones of COCO or similar datasets comprising image-text pairs. On the contrary, role hierarchy is much shallower, justifying the higher number of **D** edits in comparison to **R** edits (Table 3). This finding is further reinforced by the fact that objects connected in c often are not immediate neighbors in the ground truth, meaning that a completely new edge will need to be inserted.

A comparison between model families regarding object hallucinations (Tables 1, 2) reveals interesting insights: GiT variants consistently hallucinate less, achieving best results across most metrics compared to other model families; note the colored cells of respective Tables. On the other hand, Claude variants are accompanied with more hallucinations (note the colored cells). This may occur due to the fact that Claude models are not explicitly pre-trained on image captioning using COCO captions or similarly distributed image-text pairs, therefore they tend to hypothesize the existence of out-of-distribution concepts.

This elevated hallucination tendency is more expected on longer captions (20-30 words), since the model is forced to be more verbose, possibly adding extraneous concepts to meet the length requirements; this is verified by the reported results, even though shorter captions are not devoid of object hallucinations as well. Additionally, as expected, longer descriptions demonstrate roughly twice the Granularity, indicating greater object coverage. Furthermore, shorter generations are accompanied by higher over-specialization (**O**) rates, indicating that Claude models become excessively specific when attempting to condense visual information within a restricted word budget. Another notable observation is that Haiku variants (either prompted for short or longer captions) tend to be more generic, as denoted by the inflated under-specialization (**U**) percentages in comparison to Sonnet variants, despite being prompted with the same instructions. Other than that, Haiku variants require more conceptual replacements (**R**) to assimilate the ground truth captions compared to Sonnet ones; it is possible that those **R** edits can be attributed to substitutions with concept *hyponyms*, so that the **U** rates are also reduced.

A comparatively worse performance in terms of hallucinations is observed when conditional generation is employed over unconditional one in BLIP variants. This can be attributed to over-reliance over linguistic priors [51], amplifying possible biases or noise. HalCECE is able to highlight such discrepancies regarding the generation strategy selected, suggesting straightforward mitigation strategies (in that case being the usage of unconditional caption generation). It also breaks down the source of hallucinations, as indicated in Tables 1, 2: the rate of hallucinations (HalRate) is significantly higher than their unconditional counterparts, even though the **U** percentages are the lowest, meaning that specificity is not the culprit of hallucinations. On the contrary, the higher percentage of **D** and **R** edits denotes the presence of extraneous objects that have to be removed and substituted accordingly.

Regarding role hallucinations and comparison between models, similar trends emerge. Larger models exhibit more hallucinations overall, while GiT variants consistently produce fewer, performing best across most metrics. The primary differences across model families emerge in deletions rather than transformations, exemplified by BLIP-base-cond, which has the lowest **R** but the highest overall hallucination rate. This suggests that some models are more prone to omitting role-related information rather than altering it. Notably, Claude models demonstrate greater Granularity in role assignments, which may contribute to their higher hallucination rates. These findings align with object hallucination trends, reinforcing the idea that pre-training differences and generation strategies significantly impact hallucination tendencies across models.

Overall, it is evident that larger models cannot guarantee reduced hallucination rates. On the contrary, lower rates and fewer conceptual edits are observed in smaller captioners, such as the ones from GiT family. Even though this may sound surprising at a first glance, the source of hallucinations can be the data annotations rather than the capacity of the model itself. This means that when the visual input is ambiguous or the vision-language grounding is weak, larger models might rely more on their strong language priors, extensively stored during pre-training, thus producing fluent but unfaithful details. In the interest of image captioning, this can manifest as hallucinations -objects or actions that are statistically likely in language but *not* actually present in the image. Additionally, larger models may overfit to noisy or spurious correlations in the training data, further amplifying hallucinated content. For example, larger vision-language models may generate more detailed captions that sound plausible yet include elements unsupported by the visual evidence [6,51]. This suggests that the balance between visual grounding and language fluency can be more challenging to maintain as model size increases. In the following section we delve into possible discrepancies between linguistic capacity and hallucinations.

5.2 Linguistic Metrics may be Misleading

Apart from our proposed hallucination evaluation metrics, we report language generation metrics, and specifically *ROUGE* [25], *BLEU* [37], *Google BLEU*[5], *Mauve* [39] and perplexity (*PPL*) [13] to reveal agreements and disagreements.

ROUGE metrics measure recall and structural overlap between ground truth and generated captions. Specifically, *ROUGE1* compares individual words (unigrams), *ROUGE2* evaluates agreement between two-word sequences (bigrams), while *ROUGEL* considers the longest common subsequence (LCS) between ground truth and generated text to decide upon their agreement. All these metrics are extracted by comparing the generated caption with each one of the 5 COCO captions at a time, and then obtaining their average score. Finally, the *ROUGELsum* variant regards LCS scores across multiple ground truth references (in our case being all 5 COCO captions per image), offering similar results to ROUGEL.

BLEU and *Google BLEU* assess unigram precision between the ground truth and the generated caption, once again considering averaged values.

Mauve provides a broader perspective on the text quality and naturalness, measuring the distributional differences between the ground truth and the generated text embeddings. It is less sensitive to exact wording and better reflects semantic similarity and stylistic variability. In technical terms, we opt for GPT2 as the decoder to obtain embedding representations, following the default setup[6].

All those metrics range between [0,1] with higher values being better.

Perplexity (PPL) quantifies how "surprised" a language model is when it sees the next word in a sequence, providing a measure of confidence in accurately predicting the next word. This higher confidence is associated with more predictable,

---

[5] https://huggingface.co/spaces/evaluate-metric/google_bleu.

[6] https://huggingface.co/spaces/evaluate-metric/mauve.

fluent and coherent textual generations, reflected in lower PPL scores. A perfect PPL score equals to 1, while no upper bound exists. **What is the issue with language generation metrics?** While these widely used metrics provide useful signals—primarily around fluency, style, and surface-level similarity—they can be misleading indicators of overall quality in text generation, often failing to capture semantic accuracy, contextual appropriateness, and hallucinations, as expressed via factual inconsistencies [11,18].

For example, n-gram overlaps reward surface-level similarity, totally excluding semantically equivalent expressions or even word ordering variability. For example, if an image contains the concept "cat", n-gram metrics will assign the *same penalty* over captions that contain either the concepts "kitten" or "ship" in place of "cat". On the contrary, HalCECE will provide a significantly higher **R** cost to the "cat" → "ship" edit in comparison to the "cat" → "kitten" one. Even semantically adaptive metrics, such as *Mauve*, are not oriented towards factual inconsistencies, as reflected on disagreements between the visual and the linguistic modalities. This means that a caption can be perfectly natural and well-written, achieving high *Mauve* scores, while also containing several objects or roles not existing in the corresponding image. Similarly, *PPL* penalizes inarticulate generations but totally ignores semantic disagreements between modalities. Overall, apart from the n-gram overlap metrics, the rest are by design *not explainable*; their reliance on linguistic distributions sacrifices senses of semantic interpretability, leading to obscure and dispersed evaluation practices in the first place. Finally, in all cases, linguistic metrics require ground truth captions in order to function, contrary to HalCECE which only requests standalone concepts.

Based on the above, the motivation behind our explainable and conceptual hallucination detection framework is further verified by the unsuitability and opaqueness of common text generation evaluation practices. Therefore, the language generation metrics are incapable of providing proper hallucination signals on their own, and in several cases -e.g. when n-grams are employed to measure agreement- they can even be *misleading*. These arguments will be analyzed with the support of language generation metric results, as presented in Table 4.

Analysis. The results presented in Table 4 reveal interesting patterns, notably indicating that linguistic metrics are unsatisfactory overall, primarily because exact agreements with ground truth captions are not achieved in most cases. Specifically, even though n-gram-based metrics (i.e. *ROUGE* and *BLEU* variants) can explain their reported low scores, they lead to over-penalization of generations, since they do not respect semantical equivalence between concepts, contrary to HalCECE. On the other hand, *Mauve* and *PPL* are unable to explain themselves, despite being more semantically consistent, a gap that HalCECE is able to fill be breaking down the source of semantic disagreements.

Interestingly, linguistic metrics across models present some unexplainable variability. For example, BLIP2-opt-2 is one of the top-scorers regarding n-gram metrics, though it significantly fails according to *Mauve*. This is somehow contradictory, since the same model presents a higher exact match capability over

Table 4. Language generation evaluation metrics on the *VG∩COCO* validation subset.

Models	ROUGE1↑	ROUGE2↑	ROUGEL↑	ROUGELsum↑
GiT-base-coco	0.152	0.021	0.145	0.145
GiT-large-coco	0.152	0.022	0.146	0.146
GiT-base	0.139	0.01	0.134	0.134
GiT-large	0.127	0.01	0.122	0.122
BLIP-base-unc	0.16	0.021	0.153	0.154
BLIP-base-cond	0.352	0.116	0.317	0.317
BLIP-large-unc	0.134	0.017	0.126	0.126
BLIP-large-cond	0.402	0.163	0.361	0.361
BLIP2-flan-t5-xl	0.435	0.179	0.402	0.402
BLIP2-opt-2	0.44	0.187	0.404	0.404
ViT-GPT2	0.406	0.153	0.370	0.370
Claude sonnet-L	0.133	0.008	0.117	0.117
Claude haiku-L	0.141	0.011	0.125	0.125
Claude sonnet-S	0.062	0.002	0.058	0.058
Claude haiku-S	0.123	0.009	0.114	0.114
	BLEU↑	Google BLEU↑	Mauve↑	PPL↓
GiT-base-coco	0.0005	0.051	0.186	68.305
GiT-large-coco	0.0005	0.051	0.192	63.629
GiT-base	0.0001	0.027	0.131	1541.317
GiT-large	0.0001	0.025	0.13	1475.033
BLIP-base-unc	0.0004	0.037	0.141	461.076
BLIP-base-cond	0.024	0.099	0.058	506.732
BLIP-large-unc	0.0003	0.033	0.132	67.632
BLIP-large-cond	0.056	0.133	0.064	127.578
BLIP2-flan-t5-xl	0.046	0.132	0.067	211.738
BLIP2-opt-2	0.055	0.139	0.009	130.29
ViT-GPT2	0.051	0.131	0.068	69.605
Claude sonnet-L	0.0001	0.029	0.174	71.307
Claude haiku-L	0.0002	0.029	0.174	42.032
Claude sonnet-S	0.0	0.032	0.174	358.33
Claude haiku-S	0.0004	0.047	0.174	170.585

the rest, but also the lowest semantic agreement at the same time. This confusion is resolved via HalCECE, which places the hallucination performance of BLIP2-opt-2 somewhere in the middle in comparison to the other captioners, as demonstrated in Tables 1, 2.

Comparisons between model families indicate that BLIP variants score higher in n-gram-related metrics (i.e. *ROUGE* and *BLEU* variants), revealing a comparatively increased adherence to ground truth captions. On the contrary, Claude models present the lowest scores regarding most n-gram metrics, revealing their reduced tendency to follow ground truth distributions. This fact was also reported in HalCECE results and related analysis of Tables 1, 2, attributing the source of disagreeing semantics to their generic pre-training. Nevertheless, the percentages occurring from HalCECE are less strict, thanks to its semantic-driven foundations: hallucination rate (assimilating a recall-related scenario, where the ratio of generated concepts over all relevant concepts is measured) reaches a maximum of 64.31% (Claude haiku-L at Table 1), while *ROUGE* variants, expressing recall-related agreement as well, reach up to 12.5% of conceptual agreement according to *ROUGEL/ROUGELsum* scores of Table 4 for the same model, which equals to a minimum of 87.5% hallucination rate. At the same time, *ROUGE* scores, despite being able to highlight which concepts are responsible for the reported disagreements, they cannot suggest *what needs to*

Table 5. Correlation between the linguistic metrics and the object hallucination metrics provided by HalCECE.

	#obj.	#ancest.	HalRate	Granul.	U	D	O	R	Sim. R
ROUGE1	−0.15	−0.06	−0.04	−0.05	−0.05	−0.03	−0.03	−0.03	−0.03
ROUGE2	0.05	−0.04	−0.15	−0.15	−0.09	−0.06	−0.02	−0.06	−0.02
ROUGEL	−0.04	−0.03	0.0	0.0	−0.01	−0.02	−0.03	−0.02	−0.03
ROUGELsum	−0.04	−0.03	−0.01	−0.02	−0.02	−0.02	−0.03	−0.03	−0.03
BLEU	−0.01	−0.03	−0.08	−0.08	−0.06	−0.05	−0.03	−0.05	−0.03
Google BLEU	−0.02	−0.03	−0.04	−0.05	−0.04	−0.03	−0.02	−0.03	−0.02
Mauve	−0.02	−0.02	−0.02	−0.02	−0.02	−0.02	−0.02	−0.02	−0.02
PPL	−0.06	−0.02	0.03	0.01	−0.01	−0.03	−0.05	−0.03	−0.05

Table 6. Correlation between the linguistic metrics and the role hallucination metrics provided by HalCECE.

	#roles	D	R	HalRate (#hal. roles)	Granul.
ROUGE1	−0.1	0.05	0.03	0.04	0.03
ROUGE2	0.18	0.01	0.07	−0.03	0.02
ROUGEL	−0.01	0.03	0.01	0.05	0.03
ROUGELsum	0.01	0.03	0.02	0.04	0.03
BLEU	0.07	0.02	0.05	−0.01	0.02
Google BLEU	0.04	0.02	0.03	0.01	0.02
Mauve	0.02	0.02	0.02	0.02	0.02
PPL	−0.09	−0.01	−0.05	0.01	−0.03

be changed, in order to reach a dehallucinated state; conversely, a lookup in HalCECE recommendation prescribes that the 5.4% of Haiku caption concepts are too generic, the 2.69% are erroneously specific, while the 17.3% and 44.33% of caption concepts should be deleted and replaced respectively (Tables 1, 2). Finally, *PPL* is highly uninformative when it comes to hallucinations: the high *PPL* scores corresponding to GiT-base captions denote significantly uncertain generations, even though the same captioner is associated with a low HalRate. On the contrary, Claude Haiku L presents the lowest *PPL*, despite being one of the models associated with the highest HalRate. This inverse trend indicates that *PPL* is a completely unsuitable evaluation measure with regard to hallucination detection, rendering any hallucination-related insights driven by *PPL* severely misleading.

To sum up, we calculate the correlation between the linguistic metrics and object/role hallucination metrics as calculated from HalCECE. Related results are presented in Table 5 for object hallucination metrics, and Table 6 for role hallucination metrics, denoting weak correlations (close to 0) between the two metric categories in both cases. Ultimately, we conclude that linguistic metrics cannot provide any useful information regarding the presence of hallucinations in image captioning, as detected from HalCECE.

6 Conclusion

In conclusion, our novel HalCECE framework designed for detecting hallucinations in image captioning represents a pioneering stride towards explainable evaluation of ever evolving VL models. By delving into the hallucination mechanisms, we decompose related phenomena based on conceptual properties enabled by the incorporation of external hierarchical knowledge. Our proposed method imposes semantically minimal and meaningful edits to transit from hallucinated concepts present in captions to non-hallucinated ground truth ones, employing the explanatory power of conceptual counterfactuals. Moreover, previously overlooked role hallucinations are analyzed, revealing that widely-used image captioners tend to generate erroneous object interconnections more often than not. Overall, we view our current analysis as a crucial first step in the direction of accurately detecting hallucinations in VL models in a conceptual and explainable manner, paving the way for future hallucination mitigation strategies.

Acknowledgments. We acknowledge the use of Amazon Web Services (AWS) for providing the cloud computing infrastructure that allowed the usage of Claude models. This work was supported by the Hellenic Foundation for Research and Innovation (HFRI) under the 3rd Call for HFRI PhD Fellowships (Fellowship Number 5537) and also under the 5th Call for HFRI PhD Fellowships (Fellowship Number 19268).

Disclosure of Interest. The authors have no competing interests to declare that are relevant to the content of this article.

Appendix

A. Proprietary Model Prompting. Regarding long generations, the prompt provided to Claude models is:

```
Provide me a descriptive caption of this image in English.
The caption should contain between 20 and 30 words.
```

As for short generations, the prompt is:

```
Provide me a short caption of this image in English in up to 10 words.
```

B. Parameter Count. Since no official parameter count exists for many of our captioners, we provide estimates based on public sources and model documentation, unless official information is available. These numbers may vary depending on the exact model version and any further fine-tuning or architectural modifications.

- GiT base: ∼110 million parameters
- GiT large: ∼330 million parameters
- BLIP base: ∼123 million parameters
- BLIP large: ∼430440 million parameters
- BLIP2opt2.7: 2.7 billion parameters (official)
- BLIP2flant5 (XL version): ∼3 billion parameters
- ViTGPT2: ∼200 million parameters (combining a ViTBase encoder and GPT-2 Small decoder)
- Claude haiku & Claude sonnet: Both are based on Anthropic's Claude model, which is estimated to have ∼52 billion parameters

C. Limitations. Our benchmark relies on ground truth annotations to construct conceptual edits, which may limit its use in annotation-scarce settings, though this is less critical given the benchmark—not a supervised model—is the main contribution. Additionally, edge cases like ambiguous or partially occluded images, where even humans may disagree, are not extensively discussed and present an avenue for deeper analysis.

References

1. Anthropic: The claude 3 model family: Opus, sonnet, haiku. https://api.semanticscholar.org/CorpusID:268232499
2. Bai, Z., et al.: Hallucination of multimodal large language models: A survey (2024). https://arxiv.org/abs/2404.18930
3. Chu, X., Su, J., Zhang, B., Shen, C.: Visionllama: a unified llama backbone for vision tasks (2024). https://arxiv.org/abs/2403.00522
4. Chung, H.W., et al.: Scaling instruction-finetuned language models (2022). https://arxiv.org/abs/2210.11416
5. Dai, W., Liu, Z., Ji, Z., Su, D., Fung, P.: Plausible may not be faithful: Probing object hallucination in vision-language pre-training. ArXiv abs/2210.07688 (2022). https://api.semanticscholar.org/CorpusID:252907639
6. Datta, S., Sundararaman, D.: Evaluating hallucination in large vision-language models based on context-aware object similarities (2025). https://arxiv.org/abs/2501.15046

7. Dijkstra, E.W.: A note on two problems in connexion with graphs. Numer. Math. **1**(1), 269–271 (1959)
8. Dimitriou, A., Lymperaiou, M., Filandrianos, G., Thomas, K., Stamou, G.: Structure your data: Towards semantic graph counterfactuals (2024). https://arxiv.org/abs/2403.06514
9. Dosovitskiy, A., et al.: An image is worth 16x16 words: Transformers for image recognition at scale (2021)
10. Filandrianos, G., Thomas, K., Dervakos, E., Stamou, G.: Conceptual edits as counterfactual explanations. In: AAAI Spring Symposium: MAKE (2022)
11. Fischer, T., Remus, S., Biemann, C.: Measuring faithfulness of abstractive summaries. In: Schaefer, R., Bai, X., Stede, M., Zesch, T. (eds.) Proceedings of the 18th Conference on Natural Language Processing (KONVENS 2022), pp. 63–73. KONVENS 2022 Organizers, Potsdam, Germany (12–15 Sep 2022). https://aclanthology.org/2022.konvens-1.8/
12. Ghandi, T., Pourreza, H.R., Mahyar, H.: Deep learning approaches on image captioning: a review. ACM Comput. Surv. **56**, 1 – 39 (2022). https://api.semanticscholar.org/CorpusID:246430542
13. Jelinek, F., Mercer, R.L., Bahl, L.R., Baker, J.K.: Perplexity–a measure of the difficulty of speech recognition tasks. J. Acoustical Soc. Am. **62**(S1), S63–S63 (2005). https://doi.org/10.1121/1.2016299
14. Jing, L., Li, R., Chen, Y., Jia, M., Du, X.: Faithscore: Evaluating hallucinations in large vision-language models (2023). ArXiv abs/2311.01477 (2023). https://api.semanticscholar.org/CorpusID:265019245
15. Jonker, R., Volgenant, A.: A shortest augmenting path algorithm for dense and sparse linear assignment problems. Computing **38**(4), 325–340 (1987)
16. Kornblith, S., Li, L., Wang, Z., Nguyen, T.: Guiding image captioning models toward more specific captions (2023)
17. Krishna, R., et al.: Visual genome: Connecting language and vision using crowdsourced dense image annotations. Int. J. Comput. Vis. **123**, 32 – 73 (2016). https://api.semanticscholar.org/CorpusID:4492210
18. Kryscinski, W., McCann, B., Xiong, C., Socher, R.: Evaluating the factual consistency of abstractive text summarization. In: Webber, B., Cohn, T., He, Y., Liu, Y. (eds.) Proceedings of the 2020 Conference on Empirical Methods in Natural Language Processing (EMNLP), pp. 9332–9346. Association for Computational Linguistics, Online, November 2020. https://doi.org/10.18653/v1/2020.emnlp-main.750, https://aclanthology.org/2020.emnlp-main.750/
19. Kumar, A.: The illustrated image captioning using transformers. ankur3107.github.io (2022). https://ankur3107.github.io/blogs/the-illustrated-image-captioning-using-transformers/
20. Leng, S., Zhang, H., Chen, G., Li, X., Lu, S., Miao, C., Bing, L.: Mitigating object hallucinations in large vision-language models through visual contrastive decoding (2023)
21. Li, J., Li, D., Savarese, S., Hoi, S.: Blip-2: bootstrapping language-image pre-training with frozen image encoders and large language models. In: Proceedings of the 40th International Conference on Machine Learning, ICML'23, JMLR.org (2023)
22. Li, J., Li, D., Savarese, S., Hoi, S.C.H.: Blip-2: Bootstrapping language-image pre-training with frozen image encoders and large language models. In: International Conference on Machine Learning (2023). https://api.semanticscholar.org/CorpusID:256390509

23. Li, J., Li, D., Xiong, C., Hoi, S.: Blip: Bootstrapping language-image pre-training for unified vision-language understanding and generation (2022)
24. Li, Y., Du, Y., Zhou, K., Wang, J., Zhao, W.X., rong Wen, J.: Evaluating object hallucination in large vision-language models. ArXiv abs/2305.10355 (2023). https://api.semanticscholar.org/CorpusID:258740697
25. Lin, C.Y.: ROUGE: A package for automatic evaluation of summaries. In: Text Summarization Branches Out. pp. 74–81. Association for Computational Linguistics, Barcelona, Spain, July 2004. https://aclanthology.org/W04-1013
26. Lin, T.Y., et al.: Microsoft coco: Common objects in context (2015)
27. Liu, F., Lin, K., Li, L., Wang, J., Yacoob, Y., Wang, L.: Mitigating hallucination in large multi-modal models via robust instruction tuning (2023)
28. Liu, H., et al.: A survey on hallucination in large vision-language models (2024). https://arxiv.org/abs/2402.00253
29. Liu, H., Li, C., Li, Y., Lee, Y.J.: Improved baselines with visual instruction tuning (2023)
30. Liu, H., Li, C., Wu, Q., Lee, Y.J.: Visual instruction tuning (2023)
31. Lovenia, H., Dai, W., Cahyawijaya, S., Ji, Z., Fung, P.: Negative object presence evaluation (NOPE) to measure object hallucination in vision-language models. In: Gu, J., Fu, T.J.R., Hudson, D., Celikyilmaz, A., Wang, W. (eds.) Proceedings of the 3rd Workshop on Advances in Language and Vision Research (ALVR), pp. 37–58. Association for Computational Linguistics, Bangkok, Thailand, August 2024. https://doi.org/10.18653/v1/2024.alvr-1.4, https://aclanthology.org/2024.alvr-1.4
32. Lymperaiou, M., Filandrianos, G., Thomas, K., Stamou, G.: Counterfactual edits for generative evaluation (2023)
33. Lymperaiou, M., Manoliadis, G., Menis Mastromichalakis, O., Dervakos, E.G., Stamou, G.: Towards explainable evaluation of language models on the semantic similarity of visual concepts. In: Calzolari, N., et al. (eds.) Proceedings of the 29th International Conference on Computational Linguistics, pp. 3639–3658. International Committee on Computational Linguistics, Gyeongju, Republic of Korea, October 2022. https://aclanthology.org/2022.coling-1.321/
34. Manevich, A., Tsarfaty, R.: Mitigating hallucinations in large vision-language models (LVLMs) via language-contrastive decoding (LCD). In: Ku, L.W., Martins, A., Srikumar, V. (eds.) Findings of the Association for Computational Linguistics: ACL 2024. pp. 6008–6022. Association for Computational Linguistics, Bangkok, Thailand, August 2024. https://doi.org/10.18653/v1/2024.findings-acl.359, https://aclanthology.org/2024.findings-acl.359
35. Miller, G.A.: Wordnet: a lexical database for English. Commun. ACM **38**(11), 39–41 (1995)
36. OpenAI: Gpt-4 technical report (2023)
37. Papineni, K., Roukos, S., Ward, T., Zhu, W.J.: Bleu: a method for automatic evaluation of machine translation. In: Isabelle, P., Charniak, E., Lin, D. (eds.) Proceedings of the 40th Annual Meeting of the Association for Computational Linguistics, pp. 311–318. Association for Computational Linguistics, Philadelphia, Pennsylvania, USA, July 2002. https://doi.org/10.3115/1073083.1073135, https://aclanthology.org/P02-1040

38. Petryk, S., Chan, D., Kachinthaya, A., Zou, H., Canny, J., Gonzalez, J., Darrell, T.: ALOHa: A new measure for hallucination in captioning models. In: Duh, K., Gomez, H., Bethard, S. (eds.) Proceedings of the 2024 Conference of the North American Chapter of the Association for Computational Linguistics: Human Language Technologies (Volume 2: Short Papers), pp. 342–357. Association for Computational Linguistics, Mexico City, Mexico, June 2024. https://doi.org/10.18653/v1/2024.naacl-short.30, https://aclanthology.org/2024.naacl-short.30/
39. Pillutla, K., et al.: Mauve: measuring the gap between neural text and human text using divergence frontiers (2021)
40. Qu, X., Chen, Q., Wei, W., Sun, J., Dong, J.: Alleviating hallucination in large vision-language models with active retrieval augmentation (2024). https://arxiv.org/abs/2408.00555
41. Radford, A., Wu, J., Child, R., Luan, D., Amodei, D., Sutskever, I.: Language models are unsupervised multitask learners (2019)
42. Rohrbach, A., Hendricks, L.A., Burns, K., Darrell, T., Saenko, K.: Object hallucination in image captioning (2019)
43. Tonmoy, S.M.T.I., Zaman, S.M.M., Jain, V., Rani, A., Rawte, V., Chadha, A., Das, A.: A comprehensive survey of hallucination mitigation techniques in large language models (2024)
44. Touvron, H., et al.: Llama: open and efficient foundation language models (2023)
45. Vedantam, R., Zitnick, C.L., Parikh, D.: Cider: Consensus-based image description evaluation (2015)
46. Wang, J., et al.: Git: A generative image-to-text transformer for vision and language. ArXiv abs/2205.14100 (2022). https://api.semanticscholar.org/CorpusID:249152323
47. Wang, J., et al.: Evaluation and analysis of hallucination in large vision-language models (2023)
48. Wang, W., et al.: Image as a foreign language: Beit pretraining for all vision and vision-language tasks. ArXiv abs/2208.10442 (2022). https://api.semanticscholar.org/CorpusID:251719655
49. Wu, M., Ji, J., Huang, O., Li, J., Wu, Y., Sun, X., Ji, R.: Evaluating and analyzing relationship hallucinations in large vision-language models (2024). https://arxiv.org/abs/2406.16449
50. Wu, Z., Palmer, M.: Verb semantics and lexical selection. arXiv preprint cmp-lg/9406033 (1994)
51. Xiao, Y., Wang, W.Y.: On hallucination and predictive uncertainty in conditional language generation. In: Merlo, P., Tiedemann, J., Tsarfaty, R. (eds.) Proceedings of the 16th Conference of the European Chapter of the Association for Computational Linguistics: Main Volume. pp. 2734–2744. Association for Computational Linguistics, Online, April 2021. https://doi.org/10.18653/v1/2021.eacl-main.236, https://aclanthology.org/2021.eacl-main.236/
52. Zhang, R., Zhang, H., Zheng, Z.: Vl-uncertainty: Detecting hallucination in large vision-language model via uncertainty estimation (2024). https://arxiv.org/abs/2411.11919
53. Zhang, S., et al.: Opt: Open pre-trained transformer language models (2022). https://arxiv.org/abs/2205.01068
54. Zhang, Y., et al.: Siren's song in the ai ocean: A survey on hallucination in large language models (2023)

55. Zhao, Z., Wang, B., Ouyang, L., Dong, X., Wang, J., He, C.: Beyond hallucinations: Enhancing lvlms through hallucination-aware direct preference optimization (2023)
56. Zhou, Y., et al.: Analyzing and mitigating object hallucination in large vision-language models. ArXiv abs/2310.00754 (2023). https://api.semanticscholar.org/CorpusID:263334335

Open Access This chapter is licensed under the terms of the Creative Commons Attribution 4.0 International License (http://creativecommons.org/licenses/by/4.0/), which permits use, sharing, adaptation, distribution and reproduction in any medium or format, as long as you give appropriate credit to the original author(s) and the source, provide a link to the Creative Commons license and indicate if changes were made.

The images or other third party material in this chapter are included in the chapter's Creative Commons license, unless indicated otherwise in a credit line to the material. If material is not included in the chapter's Creative Commons license and your intended use is not permitted by statutory regulation or exceeds the permitted use, you will need to obtain permission directly from the copyright holder.

Diffusion Counterfactuals for Image Regressors

Trung Duc Ha and Sidney Bender

Technische Universität Berlin, Straße des 17. Juni 135, 10623 Berlin, Germany
{t.ha,s.bender}@tu-berlin.de

Abstract. Counterfactual explanations have been successfully applied to create human interpretable explanations for various black-box models. They are handy for tasks in the image domain, where the quality of the explanations benefits from recent advances in generative models. Although counterfactual explanations have been widely applied to classification models, their application to regression tasks remains underexplored. We present two methods to create counterfactual explanations for image regression tasks using diffusion-based generative models to address challenges in sparsity and quality: 1) one based on a Denoising Diffusion Probabilistic Model that operates directly in pixel-space and 2) another based on a Diffusion Autoencoder operating in latent space. Both produce realistic, semantic, and smooth counterfactuals on CelebA-HQ and a synthetic data set, providing easily interpretable insights into the decision-making process of the regression model and reveal spurious correlations. We find that for regression counterfactuals, changes in features depend on the region of the predicted value. Large semantic changes are needed for significant changes in predicted values, making it harder to find sparse counterfactuals than with classifiers. Moreover, pixel space counterfactuals are more sparse while latent space counterfactuals are of higher quality and allow bigger semantic changes.

Keywords: Counterfactual Explanations · Diffusion Models · Image Regression

1 Introduction

Interpreting the results of deep learning (DL) models is still challenging due to the black-box nature of the predictions. In particular, the model might be using features that indicate good performance while completely relying on spurious correlations, commonly referred to as the "clever hans effect" [1,35,51,52]. In addition, understanding these results is critical for ethical and safety reasons in fields such as healthcare, credit scoring, and more. DL models must guarantee trustability, transparency, and fairness to be deployed in these areas [12].

This paper will focus on the post hoc explanation method called *counterfactual explanations*. The goal is to provide a "what-if" scenario of an alternate input that changes the prediction of the model while constraining the changes to be minimal and semantically meaningful [16]. This creates counterexamples that are more likely to be intuitive and easily interpretable [59]. Thus, users may arrive at natural conclusions such as "had I only changed X, the system would have predicted Y' rather than Y."

Particular interest has been given to image counterfactuals using generative models, guided by gradients toward altering the prediction. These methods can be divided into two categories: Using latent representations [14,48] or derivatives of diffusion models [2,24–26] to create changes along the data manifold. The effectiveness of these methods hinges on image quality, leading to increased adoption of diffusion models.

Most CE methods focus on image classification, as in the previous work mentioned. However, many important image tasks involve regression, especially in pathology [10,17,53,58]. Explainable AI for Regression (XAIR) methods have emerged to form a theoretical foundation [29,36–38]. Specifically, selecting an appropriate reference point is essential for producing the right explanations. In the context of XAIR, this is referred to as the *reference value* [38]. It serves as an important parameter for the context of a regression explanation, e.g. "what would this person look like if they were 20 or 80 years old?". This approach allows for more targeted explanations, distinguishing it from classifier explanations.

Some counterfactual approaches for image regression exist [2,14]. However, these approaches either use low-resolution generative models or do not use pretrained regressors. Moreover, they do not consider reference values. This gap forms the foundation of the contributions of this paper. Image regression counterfactuals present unique challenges: How do we achieve minimal, meaningful, and realistic changes while applying them effectively to regression? Moreover, defining minimality through pixel footprint may decrease interpretability [13].

To address these issues, our contributions are twofold: (1) We present two methods to create counterfactual explanations for image regression tasks using diffusion-based generative models. We adapt Adversarial Counterfactual Explanations (ACE) [25] that operate directly in pixel space and the Diffusion Autoencoder (Diff-AE) [45] that operates in latent space. (2) Regression-specific adaptations that allow us to produce counterfactuals with higher granularity, inspecting specific regions of the predicted values.

Our experiments on CelebA-HQ and a synthetic dataset demonstrate that both methods produce realistic, semantic, and smooth counterfactuals. We can reveal spurious correlations and observe that feature changes depend on the prediction region, with larger semantic alterations required for significant value shifts. Furthermore, we find a trade-off between sparsity and quality, with pixel-space changes offering greater sparsity, and latent-space edits providing higher quality and semantic flexibility.

The remainder of this paper is organized as follows. Section 2 reviews the relevant literature on counterfactual explanations and existing regression explanation techniques. Section 3 includes an overview of diffusion models and their derivatives and elaborates on our two novel approaches. Section 4 details our experimental setup with datasets, evaluation methods, and their results. It also includes implementation details, an ablation study, and regression-specific explanation analysis with spurious correlation identification. Finally, Sect. 5 concludes the paper with a summary of our findings and a discussion of potential future research directions.

2 Related Work

We contextualize our work by reviewing key studies on XAI, counterfactual explanations, and regression explanations relevant to our approach. Furthermore, we highlight the position of our work within the limited research of image regression counterfactuals.

2.1 Counterfactual Explanations for XAI

XAI methods generally align themselves by a mixture of the following properties [12,16,44,51]: The scope of a method describes whether it is applicable to the *global* behavior of the model or to a single *local* data point. Its usage categorizes it as interpretable by design (*intrinsic*) or architecture independent, applying to outputs of pre-trained models (*post-hoc*).

Local post-hoc methods are highly useful in areas such as healthcare and finance [12] as they can be directly applied to deployed blackbox models to explain highly critical decisions. Although common methods belonging to this class [3,4,42,47,56,61,62] visualize the importance of features of a particular prediction, they do not suggest *actionable* insights. Counterfactual explanations (CE) [60] have been developed to solve this gap. CEs create a counterexample of an input that alters the model's prediction, restricting the changes to be minimal and semantically meaningful. They reveal the most sensitive features in an intuitively interpretable manner. This allows users to understand patterns that influence the model's decision-making and identify potential vulnerabilities or biases. Moreover, CEs are suitable for finding and removing spurious correlations [5,25].

In image applications, generated counterfactuals must be realistic and lie on the data manifold. Several approaches exist; DiVE [48] employed Variational Autoencoders [31] to perform modifications in its latent space, restricting it to the data manifold. Diffeomorphic Counterfactuals [14] also followed this approach, additionally using Generative Adversarial Networks (GAN) to do this task, supplementing it with strong theoretical guarantees. Similarly, STEEX [23] used GANs in conjunction with a semantic map to restrict edits. However, these methods are limited by their generative models, which struggle to create high-resolution images.

Diffusion models [19] addressed this problem, leading to adoption for generating counterfactual images. DiME [24] uses diffusion models to partially noise the image and then guide the denoising process using a classifier. Similarly, ACE [25] starts by only partially noising the image. However, they based their method on adversarial attacks [57] using the diffusion process to filter out non-semantic components. In addition, the authors employ RePaint [41] for further refinement.

Counterfactual generation shares goals with semantic editing: making meaningful changes while maintaining overall structure and coherence. Methods involve GANs [9,40] and more recently diffusion models [11,21,33]. We highlight the Diffusion Autoencoder (Diff-AE) [45], which encodes high-resolution images into an editable semantic latent space while accurately reconstructing them. For interpretability, semantic edits are favored by humans, compared to minimal edits enforced by counterfactual search [13].

2.2 Regression Explanations

Several works apply classification-based attribution methods to regression problems either directly [29,58] or by first converting the regression task into multiclass classification [6,34]. Letzgus *et al.* [38] suggest that regression explanation methods need adaptation from classification. Since regression involves real-valued predictions, specifying a *reference value* for the explanation method is crucial to align it with the intention of the user. For example, "why an item is currently valued at 1200 dollars compared to its usual 1000 dollars price" [38]. Therefore, the user can provide context and precisely target the explanation. In addition, the reference value can be integrated into the measurement unit of the regression problem. Applications of this methodology include [36,37].

Regression counterfactual explanations have also been employed for regression tasks on structured [55] and multivariate time series [46] data. Applied to images, Dombrowski *et al.* [14] generate counterfactuals on the Mall dataset [8], only minimizing/maximizing the predicted number of pedestrians, and do not cover interpolation between explanations.

Several works cover counterfactuals for ordinal regression on pathological images [10,32,53]. We highlight the work of Atad *et al.* [2], who apply this to diffusion models by using the Diff-AE and a regressor predicting in the latent space.

This distinction discerns our contribution: using diffusion models to generate high-quality counterfactual images, and explaining a regressor operating in pixel space while considering reference values.

3 Methodology

In this section, we discuss our methods for the generation of regression counterfactuals. We first briefly summarize and review Denoising Diffusion Probabilistic Models (DDPM) and the relevant derivatives, the Denoising Diffusion Implicit Models (DDIM), and the Diffusion Autoencoder (Diff-AE). Lastly, we suggest two novel approaches to create regression counterfactuals: adaptations for ACE to form Adversarial Counterfactual Regression Explanations (AC-RE) and Diff-AE Regression Explanations (Diff-AE-RE).

3.1 Diffusion Models and Their Derivatives

Denoising Diffusion Probabilistic Models (DDPMs) [19] belong to a family of models that learn to model a data distribution through a forward and reverse noising process. The forward process gradually adds Gaussian noise to a data sample $\mathbf{x}_0$ over timesteps $1 \leq t \leq T$, creating a sequence of increasingly noisy samples. It is possible to directly infer the noised state $\mathbf{x}_t$ from any timestep t as

$$\mathbf{x}_t = \sqrt{\alpha_t}\mathbf{x}_0 + \sqrt{1-\alpha_t}\epsilon, \quad \epsilon \sim \mathcal{N}(\mathbf{0}, \mathbf{I}). \tag{1}$$

where α_t is the time-dependent noise schedule and ϵ is a noise variable.

A network then learns to reverse this noising process through a Markovian process, starting from $t = T$ and finally reaching $\mathbf{x}_0$. This process is computed by

$$\mathbf{x}_{t-1} = \boldsymbol{\mu}_\theta(\mathbf{x}_t, t) + \sigma_t \mathbf{z}, \quad \mathbf{z} \sim \mathcal{N}(\mathbf{0}, \mathbf{I}) \tag{2}$$

where $\boldsymbol{\mu}_\theta(\mathbf{x}_t, t)$ predicts the forward process posterior mean with a network with parameters θ and $\sigma_t \mathbf{z}$ is its deviation at timestep t. We refer the reader to [19] for an in-depth explanation.

Denoising Diffusion Implicit Models (DDIMs) [54] enhance DDPMs by introducing a deterministic approach, while allowing optimization towards the same objective. It modifies the reverse process to only depend on the input and the noise prediction network $\epsilon_\theta(x_t, t)$, directly computing the denoised observation $\mathbf{f}_\theta$:

$$\mathbf{f}_\theta(\mathbf{x}_t, t) = \frac{1}{\sqrt{\alpha_t}}(\mathbf{x}_t - \sqrt{1-\alpha_t}\epsilon_\theta(\mathbf{x}_t, t)) \tag{3}$$

and resulting in the inference distribution

$$q(\mathbf{x}_{t-1}|\mathbf{x}_t, \mathbf{f}_\theta(\mathbf{x}_t, t)) = \mathcal{N}\left(\sqrt{\alpha_{t-1}}\mathbf{f}_\theta(\mathbf{x}_t, t) + \sqrt{1-\alpha_{t-1}}\frac{\mathbf{x}_t - \sqrt{\alpha_t}\mathbf{f}_\theta(\mathbf{x}_t, t)}{\sqrt{1-\alpha_t}}, \mathbf{I}\right). \tag{4}$$

Because it is deterministic, the noise map $\mathbf{x}_T$ can be used to reconstruct images back to their original state, which implies inversion capabilities. This property is suitable for image editing tasks [21] and is advantageous for the generation of accurate counterfactuals.

Diffusion Autoencoders (Diff-AE). A Diffusion Autoencoder (Diff-AE) [45] is an extension of the DDIM and learns a meaningful and decodable representation of an image while leveraging diffusion models for high-quality reconstruction. It encodes an image into a lower-dimensional *semantic subcode* $\mathbf{z}_{\text{sem}}$ that captures high-level structured information and a *stochastic subcode* $\mathbf{x}_T$ that encodes fine-grained stochastic details, taking advantage of the deterministic generative process of the DDIM. The DDIM serves as both the encoder for the stochastic code and the decoder for image reconstruction.

The semantic latent code $\mathbf{z}_{\text{sem}}$ is computed by the learnable encoder function Enc_ϕ with parameters ϕ

$$\mathbf{z}_{\text{sem}} = \text{Enc}_\phi(\mathbf{x}_0) \tag{5}$$

mapping an input image $\mathbf{x}_0$ to its high-level semantic representation. The reverse process of the DDIM is then conditioned on this semantic latent code. The authors extend the expression of the denoised observation $\mathbf{f}_\theta$ in Eq. 3 and the inference distribution in Eq. 4 to:

$$\mathbf{f}_\theta(\mathbf{x}_t, t, \mathbf{z}_{\text{sem}}) = \frac{1}{\sqrt{\alpha_t}}(\mathbf{x}_t - \sqrt{1-\alpha_t}\epsilon_\theta(\mathbf{x}_t, t, \mathbf{z}_{\text{sem}})) \qquad (6)$$

To compute the complete denoising process, we use the mean of the inference distribution $q(\mathbf{x}_{t-1}|\mathbf{x}_t, \mathbf{f}_\theta(\mathbf{x}_t, t, \mathbf{z}_{\text{sem}}))$ for $1 \leq t < T$ and refer to the complete reconstruction at $t=1$ as

$$\hat{\mathbf{x}} = \mathbf{f}_\theta(\mathbf{x}_1, 1, \mathbf{z}_{\text{sem}}) \qquad (7)$$

The stochastic code $\mathbf{x}_T$ is obtained by rewriting the generative process such that it predicts the last noise state [45]:

$$\mathbf{x}_T = \sqrt{\alpha_T}\mathbf{f}_\theta(\mathbf{x}_{T-1}, T-1, \mathbf{z}_{\text{sem}}) + \sqrt{1-\alpha_T}\epsilon_\theta(\mathbf{x}_{T-1}, T-1, \mathbf{z}_{\text{sem}}) \qquad (8)$$

As $\mathbf{z}_{\text{sem}}$ is a lower-dimensional vector, it possesses a limited capacity to encode stochastic details. Therefore, $\mathbf{x}_T$ is inclined to represent information that was not covered by $\mathbf{z}_{\text{sem}}$, focusing on encoding local variations to optimize the training objective.

Preechakul et al. [45] use the semantic latent code $\mathbf{z}_{\text{sem}}$ to allow for semantic editing of images. Even when facial features are fit using only linear models, alterations in $\mathbf{z}_{\text{sem}}$ produce meaningful transitions. This property forms the basis for generating counterfactuals on this latent code.

3.2 Adversarial Counterfactual Explanations (ACE)

Jeanneret et al. [25] utilize the DDPM as a regularizer to transform adversarial attacks into semantically meaningful counterfactual explanations. Adversarial Counterfactual Explanations (ACE) generate counterfactual images by optimizing adversarial perturbations in the image space while filtering high-frequency and out-of-distribution artifacts using a diffusion model.

More specifically, consider $L_{\text{class}}(\mathbf{x}, y)$ as a function that quantifies the match between a sample $\mathbf{x}$ and a class y, typically the cross-entropy loss, which we aim to minimize. Consider a *filtering function* F that constrains a counterfactual $\mathbf{x}'$ to the data manifold of the training images. ACE implements this filtering function using the DDPM. It forward and reverse processes the counterfactual (Eq. 1 and 2) only to a certain depth $t = \tau$ with $1 < \tau < T$. This function is then referred to as F_τ. Applied to the optimization problem, we arrive at $L_{\text{class}}(F_\tau(\mathbf{x}'), y)$. The adversarial attack is applied through F_τ, filtering unwanted artifacts, and keeping the structure of the image in tact. The result of the optimization is called the *pre-explanation*.

To further refine the pre-explanation, the authors use the RePaint in-painting strategy [41]. Pixel changes are first thresholded with a binary mask to only include the areas highest in magnitude. Then the transitions between the original image and the counterfactual are smoothed out using the DDPM.

ACE provides coherent explanations without requiring modifications to the examined classifier. It surpasses state-of-the-art counterfactual generation techniques across multiple datasets in terms of validity, sparsity, and realism.

3.3 Diffusion Counterfactuals for Image Regressors

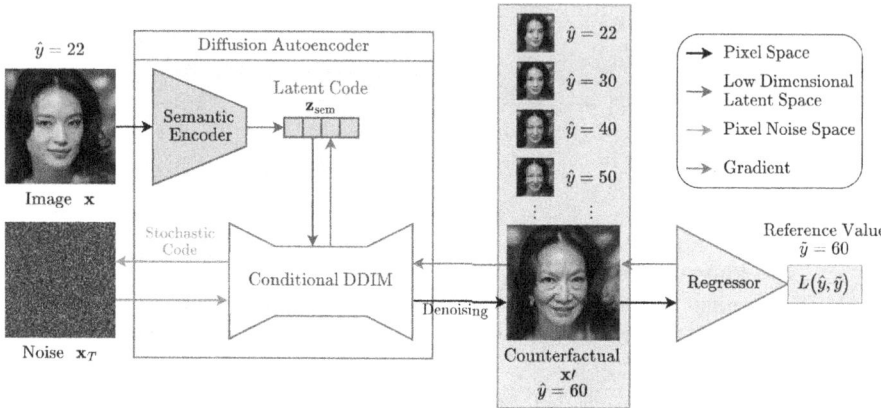

Fig. 1. Diff-AE Regression Explanations (Diff-AE-RE). The Diff-AE encodes an image into two distinct vectors: high-level semantics in the latent code z_{sem} and low-level features in the stochastic code x_T. The adversarial attack creates the gradients that only flow towards the latent code. Diff-AE-RE allows for a smooth transition between the counterfactuals across regression values offering fine-grained inspection of changed features.

We present the key contribution of this paper: The generation of counterfactual images tied to a regression problem using diffusion models. In Sect. 2 we discuss two CE generation methods using diffusion-based models: pixel-based and latent space-based. For the pixel space problem we adapt ACE [25], and for the semantic space we use the Diff-AE [45]. Figure 1 presents an overview of the Diff-AE-based method. We refer the reader to [25] for an overview of ACE.

Both methods introduce a loss function targeting the reference value $\tilde{y}$ as described in Sect. 2, along with a measure of difference from the reference value. We use the Mean Square Error (MSE) for its commonality in regression tasks and the Mean Absolute Error (MAE) for its clarity in interpretation.

Let r_ψ be a regression model with parameters ψ, x be a data point, x' its current counterfactual, initialized to be a copy of x. The initial prediction of the regressor is given by $\hat{y} = r_\psi(x')$ and we assign a designated reference value $\tilde{y}$. The regression loss function $L_{reg}(\hat{y}, \tilde{y}) = MSE(\hat{y}, \tilde{y})$ is the objective of adversarial attacks and $c(\hat{y}, \tilde{y}) = MAE(\hat{y}, \tilde{y})$ is the difference to the reference value. We empirically choose an early stopping criterion $c \leq 0.05$, similar to the validation error of CelebA-HQ dataset regressors. It balances explanation proximity to $\tilde{y}$, while limiting optimization steps.

Hence, to produce the counterfactuals $\mathbf{x}'$ we perform the adversarial attack and optimize

$$\arg\min_{\mathbf{x}'} L_{\text{reg}}(\hat{y}, \tilde{y}) \quad \text{s.t.} \quad c(\hat{y}, \tilde{y}) \leq 0.05 \tag{9}$$

To assess the performance of our methods, we use a novel, regression specific metric and established metrics used in ACE [25] and STEEX [23]. We elaborate on the specific details of these metrics in Sect. 4.

Adversarial Counterfactual Regression Explanations. We adapt ACE using the regression loss described previously L_{reg}. This algorithm performs the prediction on the pre-explanation, $\hat{y} = \mathbf{r}_\psi(F_\tau(\mathbf{x}'))$. The optimized loss function becomes $L_{\text{reg}}(\hat{y}, \tilde{y})$, using the mentioned early stopping criterion. The final refinement stage is performed after a successful adversarial attack. We refer to this regression-specific adaption as *AC-RE*. We expect the same properties of ACE to apply to AC-RE as well, namely semantic changes in the images on the data manifold with filtered out-of-distribution noise. In contrast to ACE, we cannot use a distance function for enhanced sparsity. During empirical testing, we found that the distance function is too limiting to produce counterfactuals that change the predicted value.

Diff-AE Regression Explanations. To adapt Diff-AE we use only the semantic code $\mathbf{z}_{\text{sem}}$ to optimize toward the reference value. For the counterfactual $\mathbf{x}'$ we produce its reconstruction $\hat{\mathbf{x}}'$ using the denoising process explained in Sect. 3.1. With this, the predicted regression value becomes $\hat{y} = \mathbf{r}_\psi(\hat{\mathbf{x}}')$. We then perform an adversarial attack w.r.t. $\mathbf{z}_{\text{sem}}$ using the regression loss $L_{\text{reg}}(\hat{y}, \tilde{y})$ until we reach the early stopping criterion. We call this method *Diff-AE-RE*. As we are only attacking the latent space of $\mathbf{z}_{\text{sem}}$, we aim to change only the high-level features of the images.

To enforce semantic sparsity, we add a distance function d between the latent code of the input image and the counterfactual to the objective of the adversarial attack. Through empirical tests elaborated in Sect. 4.7, we choose the distance function to be the ℓ_1-distance with its regularization constant $\lambda_d = 10^{-5}$. Let $\mathbf{z}_{\text{sem}}$ be the latent code of the input image $\mathbf{x}$ and $\mathbf{z}'_{\text{sem}}$ the latent code of the counterfactual $\mathbf{x}'$. We arrive at the following extended objective:

$$\arg\min_{\mathbf{z}'_{\text{sem}}} L_{\text{reg}}(\hat{y}, \tilde{y}) + \lambda_d \, d(\mathbf{z}_{\text{sem}}, \mathbf{z}'_{\text{sem}}) \quad \text{s.t.} \quad c(\hat{y}, \tilde{y}) \leq 0.05 \tag{10}$$

This approach is similar to and heavily inspired by approximate diffeomorphic counterfactuals [14], which demonstrate strong theoretical properties for autoencoders. We suggest an analysis of the implications for Diff-AE as future work.

4 Experiments

We experimentally evaluate the effectiveness of our methods in both synthetic and real-world scenarios. We compare their performance against classifier-based approaches and analyze their ability to provide meaningful regression-specific explanations.

First, we describe the datasets used in our experiments, which include a synthetic dataset and CelebA-HQ. We elaborate on the metrics evaluated on these datasets, covering validity, realism, and sparsity. We then outline the implementation details of our methods, specifying how we use the diffusion and regression models. Next, we present quantitative results, comparing our algorithms with classifier-based counterfactual generation approaches. We complement this with qualitative results, providing visual examples of our generated counterfactuals. Additional examples illustrate our models' ability to reveal spurious correlations and produce fine-grained regression-specific explanations. Finally, we conduct an ablation study that examines the contributions of key components to our methods.

4.1 Datasets

We first test the algorithms on a synthetic dataset called the square dataset. It consists of 64×64 images that have a uniform background from black to white and contains a square of size 8×8 in varying shades of red, enclosed by a gray border. The regression task is to predict the red intensity of the square. This results in a latent space with two dimensions that we can directly control. A minor amount of random Gaussian noise is added to the images to serve as regularization. The objective is to achieve a gradual transition in the color of the square, either from dark to bright red or the reverse. We choose the reference value inversely to the square's red intensity: darker red squares have bright red reference values, and vice versa. This ensures a balanced contrast for evaluating transitions. By construction, this dataset allows for precise control of particular evaluation aspects, as detailed in Sect. 4.2.

Following recent literature on generative CE [23–25], we evaluate our algorithms using the CelebA-HQ dataset [27]. It contains images of size 256×256 of cropped human faces. We choose the attribute "age" to generate the counterfactuals. If a face is marked as "young" we choose the reference value $\tilde{y} = 80$, while we assign "old" $\tilde{y} = 10$ to create CEs that are sufficiently distinct. We normalize ages to a 0-1 range for model training and evaluation.

To train a regression model for age prediction, we use the imdb-wiki-clean dataset [39], a cleaned version of the imdb-wiki dataset [50]. It consists of more than 500,000 face images with gender and age labels, with the latter being the target of the regressor. The images were cropped to match the CelebA-HQ format.

4.2 Evaluation Methods

We follow Jeanneret et al. [25] and assess CEs validity, sparsity, and realism.

The *validity of the explanations* for classification tasks is commonly measured by the flip rate of the CE produced. As there are no fixed thresholds for regression tasks, we choose the oracle score [22] and adapt it to the regression case. We introduce a secondary regressor with the same architecture as an oracle and compute the MAE between the predictions of the original regressor and the oracle. We refer to this as the *Oracle MAE*, suggesting the adversarial potency between the chosen models. A low score indicates the semantic and model-independent nature of the generated counterfactuals.

We determine *sparsity or proximity* by measuring changes in the 40 binary attributes of the CelebA-HQ dataset between the input image and the CE. The VGGFace2 model [7] predicts all attributes of the image pair and computes the mean number of attributes changed (MNAC). Like Jeanneret et al. [25], we use face verification accuracy (FVA) [7] and Face Similarity (FS) [25] to assess facial similarity through the deep features of the VGGFace2 model [7]. FS is defined as the cosine distance between the deep features of a pair of images, while FVA thresholds FS to create a binary output.

We evaluate the *realism* of the counterfactual images employing the commonly used FID [18] between the set of input images and the respective CEs.

For the square dataset, we evaluate CE with the same categories of metrics. However, since we can directly control the underlying parameters of the dataset, we can directly extract the MAE of the color values of the square and the background. The first evaluates validity, while the second evaluates sparsity. To assess realism, we also use the FID.

4.3 Implementation Details

This subsection covers technical details of our two approaches and the utilized regression models. We make our code and models available on GitHub[1].

Algorithms. To reduce the computational requirements for propagating gradients through the iterative process of the DDPM, ACE employs a "time-step re-spacing mechanism" [25]. This approach reduces the number of steps needed at the cost of decreased quality. Hence, AC-RE uses the same hyperparameters as ACE, using 25 steps to noise and 5 steps to de-noise the image, i.e. $\tau = 5$. We reuse the CelebA-HQ DDPM by ACE for AC-RE. To optimize the counterfactual objective, we follow ACE and use projected gradient descent [43] with a learning rate of $\frac{1}{255}$.

---

[1] https://github.com/DevinTDHa/Diffusion-Counterfactuals-for-Image-Regressors.

Similarly, we balance this tradeoff with Diff-AE-RE. By default, the underlying DDIM uses 250 implicit forward steps and 20 backward steps. Through empirical observations, we choose $T = 10$ for the reverse process to maintain high quality while allowing larger batch sizes. We use the pre-trained Diff-AE by Preechakul et al. [45], which was trained on FFHQ [28]. The cropping methods of FFHQ and CelebA-HQ overlap, allowing us to use the model without further modifications. We optimize the counterfactual objective using Adam [30] with a learning rate of 0.002, further elaborated in Sect. 4.7.

Regression Models. To train the regression models, we fine-tune the pre-trained classification model used by ACE [25], which is based on DenseNet [20]. To adapt this model to a regression task, we replace the final classification layer of the network with a fully connected layer with a single continuous output while freezing all other model weights during training. Hence, the model reuses its feature extraction capabilities, creating explanations comparable to those of the related works.

We also base the oracle model for the Oracle MAE on the DenseNet architecture. Hvilshoj et al. [22] argue that the choice of oracle has a major influence on the final score. We aim to ensure comparability with related works by selecting the same architecture for the oracle. However, adversarial vulnerabilities may transfer between the models if we choose to freeze layers. Hence, we decide to fine-tune the entire model, minimizing this risk.

4.4 Quantitative Comparisons

We analyze our methods with the metrics described in Sect. 4.2. First, we examine the results of the synthetic square data. Afterward, we assess how the methods compare to the classifier-based methods on CelebA-HQ.

Table 1 shows the results for the square dataset. We observe that AC-RE generally performs better in this task. It produces much sparser CE due to the limitations that ACE imposes on the changes: The structure of the image is mostly intact because of the lower amount of noising, and the final refinement stage further limits the areas that are changed.

In contrast, Diff-AE-RE reconstructs the image only from the semantic and stochastic code from a completely noised image. Because of this, the CEs lose their noise pattern, resulting in a higher FID. Figure 2 shows such an example. Moreover, as the structure of the image is expressed with the semantic code, alterations to it naturally lead to broader changes than AC-RE's pixel-based approach.

Table 2 shows the CelebA-HQ results for the attribute "age" with the evaluation metrics discussed in Sect. 4.2 and compares them to related classification methods. Compared to the classification-based methods, the FID of our methods is much higher. This is expected; since the CE for classification only need to cross the decision boundary to be considered successful, regression CE need

Table 1. Quantitative Results for the Square dataset. We show the best performance in bold. AC-RE performs much better in sparsity than Diff-AE-RE

Method	Square MAE	FID	Background MAE
AC-RE	**0.13**	**38.1**	**0.012**
Diff-AE-RE	0.167	121.9	0.032

to traverse a significant distance on the loss surface to approach the chosen reference values. Despite this, AC-RE still produces sparse CEs, indicated by the low MNAC score and the high facial similarity indicated by FVA and FS.

In contrast, Diff-AE-RE seems to produce CEs that are more semantically meaningful and realistic, indicated by the lower Oracle MAE and FID scores. Diff-AE-RE is limited to modifications in the latent space, restricting non-semantic adversarial components in the explanations and enabling wider changes in facial structure and properties.

This factor significantly decreases the performance of FVA and FS in the specific task of age regression. In Fig. 2, we present CEs from Diff-AE-RE that provide more convincing explanations than AC-RE when creating a CE for an old person turning young. Aging significantly alters facial structure and skin color due to numerous biological processes. Representing these age-related changes in the counterfactual results in larger pixel changes. This affects the extracted deep facial features of the VGGFace2 model, thus lowering the scores.

Table 2. Quantitative Results for CelebA-HQ. We show the best-performing regression-based method in bold. For reference, we compare the quantitative results of ACE [25] on the "age" attribute and show them in italics. Our methods perform similarly to classifier-based methods. AC-RE again produces much sparser CEs, keeping facial features intact, while Diff-AE-RE produces CEs that are more semantically sound and realistic

Method	Oracle MAE	FID	FVA	FS	MNAC
DiVE [48]	-	*33.8*	*98.2*	-	*4.58*
DiVE^{100} [48]	-	*39.9*	*52.2*	-	*4.27*
STEEX [23]	-	*11.8*	*97.5*	-	*3.44*
DiME [24]	-	*4.15*	*95.3*	*0.6714*	*3.13*
ACE ℓ_1 [25]	-	*1.45*	*99.6*	*0.7817*	*3.20*
ACE ℓ_2 [25]	-	*2.08*	*99.6*	*0.7971*	*2.94*
AC-RE	0.260	30.9	**93.1**	**0.666**	**2.68**
Diff-AE-RE	**0.184**	**26.7**	80.1	0.599	3.61

4.5 Qualitative Results

We show a selection of qualitative results in Fig. 2 for the squares and CelebA-HQ datasets, with their respective reference values. Similarly to the observations

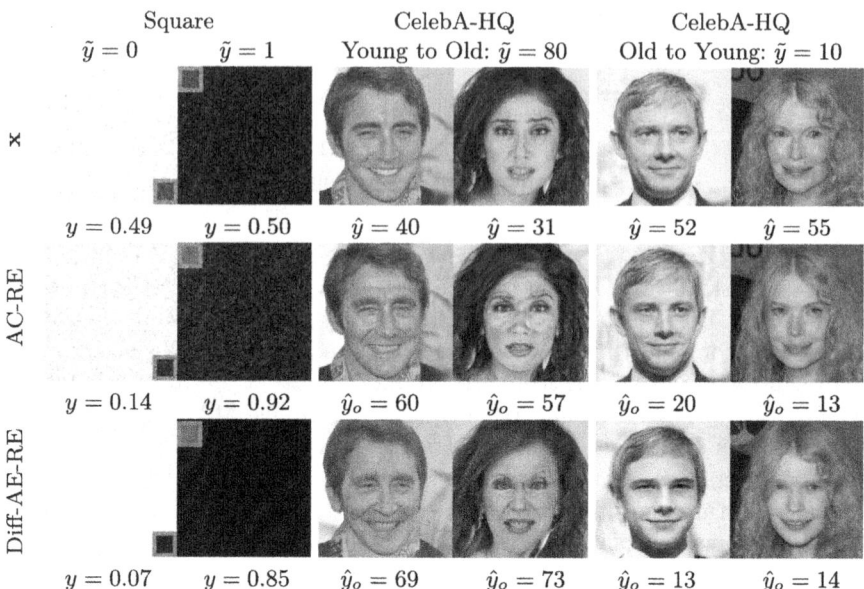

Fig. 2. Qualitative Results. The first row shows the input images x and their reference values $\tilde{y}$, while the following rows show the CEs of AC-RE and Diff-AE-RE. The captions indicate the extracted color of the square y, the regressor prediction $\hat{y}$, or the oracle prediction $\hat{y}_o$. AC-RE creates sparse explanations, while Diff-AE-RE creates broader and more realistic modifications. For the synthetic dataset, AC-RE creates more accurate counterfactuals. For CelebA-HQ, AC-RE primarily changes the textures in the face. In contrast, Diff-AE-RE alters facial shape, skin and teeth color, and accessories. Its oracle score indicates more realistic changes, aligning closely with the reference values.

of the quantitative results in Sect. 4.4, we see that AC-RE produces sparser CEs, while Diff-AE-RE produces broader changes.

For the square dataset, AC-RE creates a uniform color for the square and even reconstructs the noise patterns. Diff-AE-RE cannot reproduce these patterns, as previously described in Sect. 4.4. Moreover, the algorithm slightly shifted the location of the square of the image with the darker background (the border is no longer aligned with the edge of the image). Both algorithms perform similarly well regarding altering the actual color of the square.

For CelebA-HQ, AC-RE focuses on texture alterations, such as adding wrinkles and smoothing the skin, staying sparse in the pixel space. Diff-AE-RE introduces more distinct and realistic changes. This is reflected in the predictions of the Oracle model. They align more closely with the reference values, indicating fewer adversarial components. Although these changes are less minimal concerning the changed pixels, we see them as an advantage in creating additional features for interpretability. Specifically, we observe changes in facial shape, skin, and teeth color, and the presence of accessories.

The final point stands out significantly in our observations. For many CEs, we observe that Diff-AE-RE adds glasses or earrings. We investigate these phenomena in more detail to uncover spurious correlations in Sect. 4.5 and age-range-specific explanations in Sect. 4.6.

Spurious Correlations of the Regressor. Counterfactual explanations are the most effective when the changes are minimal and actionable. However, the definition of minimality changes depending on the context [16]. While ACE favors minimal pixel changes [25], enforcing it may not faithfully represent the behavior of the model and limit intuitive counterfactuals [13].

Although adding an accessory such as glasses introduces a significant pixel footprint in the image, it is a simple feature to understand for humans. As we observed in Sect. 4.5, Diff-AE-RE frequently adds glasses to the faces of CelebA-HQ to create a counterfactual of a young person to appear old.

Using this information, we conduct an experiment on a subset of the CelebA-HQ validation set: We use the getimg.ai Image Editor [15] to mask the area around the eyes and inpaint the image with the prompt "a person wearing glasses". This way, we precisely control the modifications to the image while creating realistic-looking images. Afterward, we compute the difference between the predictions of the regressor for the original and the edited image. We show the results in Fig. 3.

We observe that the modifications increase the predicted age by at least about five years, on average seven years. Notably, the edit of the first example has a particularly strong response, increasing the prediction by eleven years. However, the effect seems to be more pronounced for male faces, indicating a potential bias in the training dataset. Using our counterfactuals, we show that suggested feature changes can be directly applied in a very intuitive way ("putting on glasses") to alter the result of the regression model.

4.6 Regression Specific Explanations

To illustrate the differences between classification- and regression-based CEs, we explain a single image for various reference values, showing granular explanations between age regions. We choose five representative reference values $\tilde{y}$ in the target domain, specifically 10, 20, 40, 60, and 80, and analyze the main feature changes between each.

Figure 4 presents the results of AC-RE and Diff-AE-RE for this experiment, including the reconstructed images and the counterfactuals for each reference value for the two algorithms. Underneath the explanations, we visualize the difference between the reconstruction and its counterfactuals by plotting a heatmap showing the mean pixel value differences across color channels. Red indicates an increase in brightness, while blue indicates a decrease in brightness. For this particular example, the initial prediction of the person is 20 years. This does not result in changes in the counterfactual for Diff-AE-RE for $\tilde{y} = 20$. However, AC-RE performs the refinement step regardless of the predicted value, always producing minor changes in the image.

Fig. 3. Spurious Correlation. We reveal a spurious correlation in the regressor for sample images from the CelebA-HQ validation set. We use the getimg.ai Image Editor [15] to add glasses to each person via inpainting. On average, the person appears to be 7 years older than the model, with the first example showing an especially strong change. The effect seems to be more pronounced for male faces.

We first analyze the explanations for AC-RE. As this algorithm produces sparse and subtle changes, the colors of the heatmap are naturally faint. As shown in Sect. 4.5, texture changes primarily influence prediction values. The algorithm mostly changes the area around the eyes and eyebrows to reach the reference values $\tilde{y} = 10$ and $\tilde{y} = 40$ from age 20. For the younger age, it smoothens the skin, while for the older age, it darkens the skin and adds texture. The most apparent changes with increasing age to $\tilde{y} = 60$ and $\tilde{y} = 80$ occur around the eyes the intensity of the smile lines, and also the darkening of the skin. Moreover, we observe one of the same key features of the predictor as observed in the original ACE paper [25]: The cheek color gets redder with increasing reference value.

Diff-AE-RE in contrast produces heatmaps that are much more intuitively interpretable. We first observe that for $\tilde{y} = 10$, the regressor favors darker, rounder eyes and darker hair and skin. In addition, the neck seems to get slimmer. Noticeably, the whole image appears to be darker, which shows the problem of maintaining sparsity for this method. However, changes appear to be sparser for the latter reference values.

The transition from $\tilde{y} = 20$ to $\tilde{y} = 40$ strongly suggests the presence of a spurious feature, as the main modification is the addition of an earring, consistent with the findings in Sect. 4.5. Beyond this, the strongest changes appear to be in the shape of the smile and nose, along with minor changes to the lips and the width of the neck. As age progresses to $\tilde{y} = 60$, these features become even more pronounced. In addition, the jaw and neck shape gain importance, as well as the decrease in hair volume and the number of wrinkles. For $\tilde{y} = 80$, further modifications include thinning of the lips and eyebrows, complete disappearance of the second row of teeth, rounder chin, and even wider neck. The explanations provided by Diff-AE-RE reflect a combination of natural progressive aging processes and potential dataset biases.

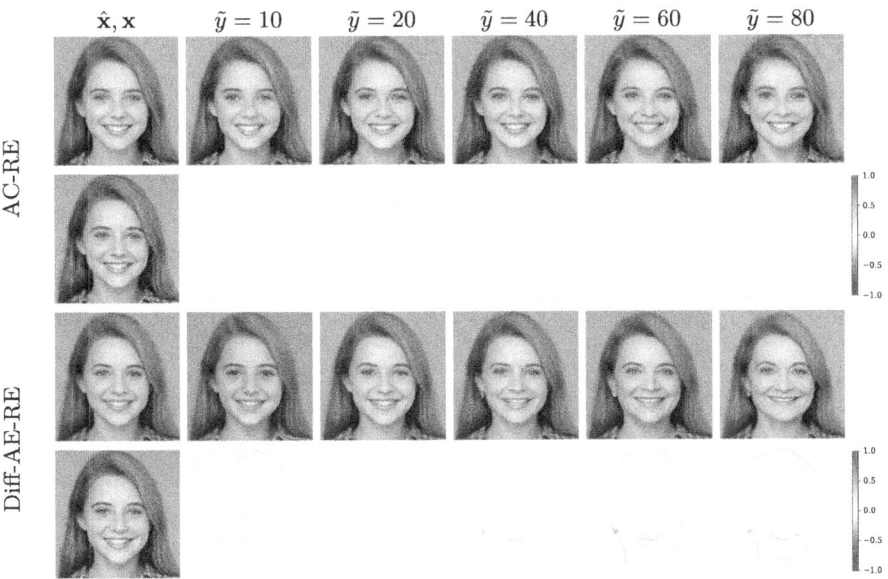

Fig. 4. Granular reference values. Counterfactual explanations generated by AC-RE and Diff-AE-RE for different reference values $\tilde{y} \in \{10, 20, 40, 60, 80\}$ for an image with an initial predicted age of 20. For each algorithm, we show the reconstructed image $\hat{x}$ with corresponding counterfactuals in the first row. The second row shows the input image x and heatmaps visualizing mean pixel-wise differences. AC-RE produces sparse, subtle changes. In contrast, Diff-AE-RE exhibits more intuitive but less sparse modifications for the lower age. The approach highlights key facial transformations associated with aging as well as a spurious feature.

4.7 Ablation Study

To better understand the contribution of each component of Diff-AE-RE, we conduct an ablation study. For an applicable study on AC-RE, we refer to the ablation study on ACE [25].

First, we explore the choice and distance function and its regularization constant λ_d. For this we empirically tested combinations of the ℓ_1 and ℓ_2 distance functions in the pixel and latent space, as well as a range of regularization constants $10^{-6} \leq \lambda_d \leq 10^{-2}$. We find that using no distance constraint resulted in aggressive image changes with some non-semantic changes. Applying the distance function on the pixel space results in counterfactuals with minimal changes in the image and the predicted age. Although the ℓ_2 distance limited the alterations somewhat, applying the ℓ_1 distance on the latent space produces more semantically meaningful and higher-quality counterfactuals. Regarding the regularization constant, we find that choosing $\lambda_d = 10^{-5}$ strikes a balance between generating expressive changes and preventing domination of the loss. We show examples of these effects with $\lambda_d = 10^{-5}$ in Fig. 5.

Second, we evaluated the choice of the optimization algorithm. Stochastic Gradient Descent (SGD) and SGD with momentum struggled to effectively navigate the latent space, requiring impractically low learning rates. In contrast, Adam [30] efficiently optimized towards the reference value. Finally, we examine the learning rate, observing that lower rates yielded smoother and more realistic counterfactuals, while higher rates risked exiting the data manifold, leading to poor image quality. This leads us to empirically choose a learning rate of 0.002 for Adam.

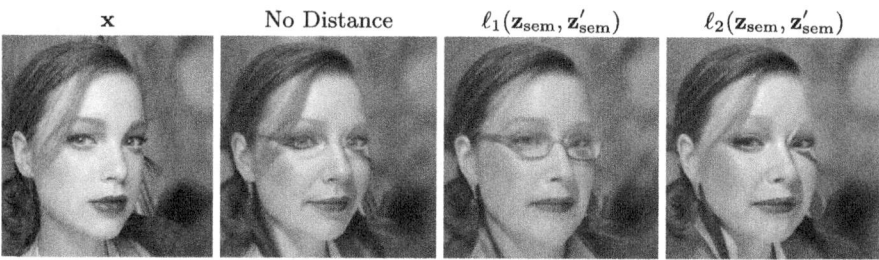

Fig. 5. Effect of distance function in the latent space with $\lambda_d = 10^{-5}$ We show the input image **x** and the generated counterfactuals with either no, ℓ_1- or ℓ_2-distance for the latent codes of the input z_{sem} and counterfactual z'_{sem}. Without a distance function, alterations are aggressive, with some non-semantic changes. While the ℓ_2-distance somewhat limits this, ℓ_1-distance limits changes to be semantically meaningful while increasing the quality of the explanation.

5 Conclusion

In this paper, we addressed the underexplored area of counterfactual explanations for image regression tasks by proposing two novel methods utilizing diffusion-based generative models: Adversarial Counterfactual Regression Explanations (AC-RE) operating in pixel space and Diffusion Autoencoder Regression Explanations (Diff-AE-RE) operating in latent space. Our methods perform similarly to classification-based counterparts and successfully generate realistic, semantic, and smooth counterfactuals. They provide valuable insights into the decision-making process of regression models and reveal spurious correlations. We demonstrated that feature changes in regression counterfactuals are dependent on the prediction region, with larger semantic alterations required for significant value shifts. Furthermore, we observed a trade-off between sparsity and quality, with AC-RE offering greater sparsity and Diff-AE-RE providing higher quality and semantic flexibility. This research paves the way for a better understanding of image regression models. Future work can apply these techniques to state-of-the-art diffusion models [49] and examine the theoretical implications of the Diffusion Autoencoder for Diffeomorphic Counterfactuals [14].

Acknowledgments. This work was supported by **BASLEARN**—TU Berlin/BASF Joint Laboratory, co-financed by TU Berlin and BASF SE.

Disclosure of Interests. The authors have no competing interests to declare that are relevant to the content of this article.

References

1. Anders, C.J., Weber, L., Neumann, D., Samek, W., Müller, K.R., Lapuschkin, S.: Finding and removing Clever Hans: using explanation methods to debug and improve deep models. Inform. Fusion **77**, 261–295 (2022). https://doi.org/10.1016/j.inffus.2021.07.015
2. Atad, M., et al.: Counterfactual explanations for medical image classification and regression using diffusion autoencoder. Mach. Learn. Biomed. Imaging **2**(iMIMIC 2023 special issue), 2103–2125 (2024). https://doi.org/10.59275/j.melba.2024-4862, https://www.melba-journal.org/papers/2024:024.html
3. Bach, S., Binder, A., Montavon, G., Klauschen, F., Müller, K.R., Samek, W.: On pixel-wise explanations for non-linear classifier decisions by layer-wise relevance propagation. PloS one **10**(7), e0130140 (2015). https://journals.plos.org/plosone/article?id=10.1371/journal.pone.0130140
4. Baehrens, D., Schroeter, T., Harmeling, S., Kawanabe, M., Hansen, K., Müller, K.R.: How to Explain Individual Classification Decisions. J. Mach. Learn. Res. **11**(61), 1803–1831 (2010), http://jmlr.org/papers/v11/baehrens10a.html
5. Bender, S., Anders, C.J., Chormai, P., Marxfeld, H.A., Herrmann, J., Montavon, G.: Towards fixing clever-hans predictors with counterfactual knowledge distillation. In: Proceedings of the IEEE/CVF International Conference on Computer Vision, pp. 2607–2615 (2023), https://openaccess.thecvf.com/content/ICCV2023W/CVAMD/html/Bender_Towards_Fixing_Clever-Hans_Predictors_with_Counterfactual_Knowledge_Distillation_ICCVW_2023_paper.html
6. Binder, A., Bockmayr, M., Hägele, M., Wienert, S., Heim, D., Hellweg, K., Ishii, M., Stenzinger, A., Hocke, A., Denkert, C., Müller, K.R., Klauschen, F.: Morphological and molecular breast cancer profiling through explainable machine learning. Nature Mach. Intell. **3**(4), 355–366 (2021). https://doi.org/10.1038/s42256-021-00303-4
7. Cao, Q., Shen, L., Xie, W., Parkhi, O.M., Zisserman, A.: VGGFace2: A Dataset for Recognising Faces across Pose and Age. In: 2018 13th IEEE International Conference on Automatic Face & Gesture Recognition (FG 2018), pp. 67–74. IEEE Press, Xi'an, China, May 2018. https://doi.org/10.1109/FG.2018.00020

8. Chen, K., Loy, C.C., Gong, S., Xiang, T.: Feature mining for localised crowd counting. In: Bmvc. vol. 1, p. 3 (2012). http://personal.ie.cuhk.edu.hk/~ccloy/files/bmvc_2012b.pdf
9. Cherepkov, A., Voynov, A., Babenko, A.: Navigating the GAN Parameter Space for Semantic Image Editing. In: 2021 IEEE/CVF Conference on Computer Vision and Pattern Recognition (CVPR). pp. 3670–3679. IEEE, Nashville, TN, USA, June 2021. https://doi.org/10.1109/CVPR46437.2021.00367, https://ieeexplore.ieee.org/document/9577554/
10. Cohen, J.P., Brooks, R., En, S., Zucker, E., Pareek, A., Lungren, M.P., Chaudhari, A.: Gifsplanation via Latent Shift: A Simple Autoencoder Approach to Counterfactual Generation for Chest X-rays. In: Proceedings of the Fourth Conference on Medical Imaging with Deep Learning, pp. 74–104. PMLR (Aug 2021). https://proceedings.mlr.press/v143/cohen21a.html
11. Couairon, G., Verbeek, J., Schwenk, H., Cord, M.: DiffEdit: Diffusion-based semantic image editing with mask guidance. In: The Eleventh International Conference on Learning Representations, September 2022. https://openreview.net/forum?id=3lge0p5o-M-
12. Das, A., Rad, P.: Opportunities and Challenges in Explainable Artificial Intelligence (XAI): A Survey, June 2020. https://doi.org/10.48550/arXiv.2006.11371, http://arxiv.org/abs/2006.11371
13. Delaney, E., Pakrashi, A., Greene, D., Keane, M.T.: Counterfactual Explanations for Misclassified Images: How Human and Machine Explanations Differ, December 2022. http://arxiv.org/abs/2212.08733
14. Dombrowski, A.K., Gerken, J.E., Müller, K.R., Kessel, P.: Diffeomorphic counterfactuals with generative models. IEEE Trans. Pattern Anal. Mach. Intell. **46**(5), 3257–3274 (2024). https://doi.org/10.1109/TPAMI.2023.3339980
15. Image Editor | getimg.ai. https://getimg.ai/image-editor
16. Guidotti, R.: Counterfactual explanations and how to find them: Literature review and benchmarking. Data Min. Knowl. Disc. **38**(5), 2770–2824 (2022). https://doi.org/10.1007/s10618-022-00831-6
17. Hesse, L.S., Dinsdale, N.K., Namburete, A.I.: Prototype Learning for Explainable Brain Age Prediction. In: 2024 IEEE/CVF Winter Conference on Applications of Computer Vision (WACV), pp. 7888–7898. IEEE, Waikoloa, HI, USA, January 2024. https://doi.org/10.1109/WACV57701.2024.00772, https://ieeexplore.ieee.org/document/10484288/
18. Heusel, M., Ramsauer, H., Unterthiner, T., Nessler, B., Hochreiter, S.: GANs trained by a two time-scale update rule converge to a local nash equilibrium. In: Advances in Neural Information Processing Systems, vol. 30. Curran Associates, Inc. (2017). https://papers.nips.cc/paper/2017/hash/8a1d694707eb0fefe65871369074926d-Abstract.html
19. Ho, J., Jain, A., Abbeel, P.: Denoising diffusion probabilistic models. In: Proceedings of the 34th International Conference on Neural Information Processing Systems, pp. 6840–6851. NIPS '20. Curran Associates Inc., Red Hook, December 2020
20. Huang, G., Liu, Z., Van Der Maaten, L., Weinberger, K.Q.: Densely Connected Convolutional Networks. In: 2017 IEEE Conference on Computer Vision and Pattern Recognition (CVPR). pp. 2261–2269. IEEE, Honolulu, HI, July 2017, https://doi.org/10.1109/CVPR.2017.243, https://ieeexplore.ieee.org/document/8099726/
21. Huberman-Spiegelglas, I., Kulikov, V., Michaeli, T.: An Edit Friendly DDPM Noise Space: Inversion and Manipulations, April 2024. http://arxiv.org/abs/2304.06140

22. Hvilshøj, F., Iosifidis, A., Assent, I.: On Quantitative Evaluations of Counterfactuals, October 2021. http://arxiv.org/abs/2111.00177
23. Jacob, P., Zablocki, É., Ben-Younes, H., Chen, M., Pérez, P., Cord, M.: STEEX: steering Counterfactual Explanations with Semantics, July 2022. http://arxiv.org/abs/2111.09094
24. Jeanneret, G., Simon, L., Jurie, F.: Diffusion Models for Counterfactual Explanations, March 2022. https://doi.org/10.48550/arXiv.2203.15636, http://arxiv.org/abs/2203.15636
25. Jeanneret, G., Simon, L., Jurie, F.: Adversarial Counterfactual Visual Explanations. In: 2023 IEEE/CVF Conference on Computer Vision and Pattern Recognition (CVPR). pp. 16425–16435. IEEE, Vancouver, BC, Canada, June 2023. https://doi.org/10.1109/CVPR52729.2023.01576, https://ieeexplore.ieee.org/document/10205255/
26. Jeanneret, G., Simon, L., Jurie, F.: Text-to-Image Models for Counterfactual Explanations: A Black-Box Approach, November 2023. http://arxiv.org/abs/2309.07944
27. Karras, T., Aila, T., Laine, S., Lehtinen, J.: Progressive Growing of GANs for Improved Quality, Stability, and Variation, February 2018. https://doi.org/10.48550/arXiv.1710.10196, http://arxiv.org/abs/1710.10196
28. Karras, T., Laine, S., Aila, T.: A style-based generator architecture for generative adversarial networks. In: Proceedings of the IEEE/CVF Conference on Computer Vision and Pattern Recognition (CVPR), June 2019
29. Khan, T., Ahmad, K., Khan, J., Khan, I., Ahmad, N.: An Explainable Regression Framework for Predicting Remaining Useful Life of Machines, April 2022. http://arxiv.org/abs/2204.13574
30. Kingma, D.P., Ba, J.: Adam: A Method for Stochastic Optimization, January 2017. https://doi.org/10.48550/arXiv.1412.6980, http://arxiv.org/abs/1412.6980
31. Kingma, D.P., Welling, M.: Auto-Encoding Variational Bayes, December 2022. https://doi.org/10.48550/arXiv.1312.6114, http://arxiv.org/abs/1312.6114
32. Klauschen, F., Dippel, J., Keyl, P., Jurmeister, P., Bockmayr, M., Mock, A., Buchstab, O., Alber, M., Ruff, L., Montavon, G., Müller, K.R.: Toward explainable artificial intelligence for precision pathology. Annu. Rev. Pathol. **19**(1), 541–570 (2024). https://doi.org/10.1146/annurev-pathmechdis-051222-113147
33. Kwon, M., Jeong, J., Uh, Y.: Diffusion Models already have a Semantic Latent Space, March 2023. http://arxiv.org/abs/2210.10960
34. Lapuschkin, S., Binder, A., Muller, K.R., Samek, W.: Understanding and comparing deep neural networks for age and gender classification. In: Proceedings of the IEEE International Conference on Computer Vision Workshops, pp. 1629–1638 (2017). https://openaccess.thecvf.com/content_ICCV_2017_workshops/w23/html/Lapuschkin_Understanding_and_Comparing_ICCV_2017_paper.html
35. Lapuschkin, S., Wäldchen, S., Binder, A., Montavon, G., Samek, W., Müller, K.R.: Unmasking Clever Hans predictors and assessing what machines really learn. Nat. Commun. **10**(1), 1096 (2019). https://doi.org/10.1038/s41467-019-08987-4
36. Letzgus, S., Müller, K.R.: An explainable AI framework for robust and transparent data-driven wind turbine power curve models. Energy AI **15**, 100328 (2024). https://doi.org/10.1016/j.egyai.2023.100328, https://www.sciencedirect.com/science/article/pii/S2666546823001003
37. Letzgus, S., Müller, K.R., Montavon, G.: XpertAI: Uncovering model strategies for sub-manifolds, March 2024. https://doi.org/10.48550/arXiv.2403.07486

38. Letzgus, S., Wagner, P., Lederer, J., Samek, W., Müller, K.R., Montavon, G.: Toward explainable AI for regression models. IEEE Signal Process. Mag. **39**(4), 40–58 (2022). https://doi.org/10.1109/MSP.2022.3153277
39. Lin, Y., Shen, J., Wang, Y., Pantic, M.: FP-age: Leveraging face parsing attention for facial age estimation in the wild. arXiv (2021)
40. Ling, H., Kreis, K., Li, D., Kim, S.W., Torralba, A., Fidler, S.: EditGAN: High-Precision Semantic Image Editing, November 2021.https://doi.org/10.48550/arXiv.2111.03186. http://arxiv.org/abs/2111.03186
41. Lugmayr, A., Danelljan, M., Romero, A., Yu, F., Timofte, R., Van Gool, L.: RePaint: inpainting using Denoising Diffusion Probabilistic Models. In: 2022 IEEE/CVF Conference on Computer Vision and Pattern Recognition (CVPR), pp. 11451–11461. IEEE, New Orleans, LA, USA, June 2022. https://doi.org/10.1109/CVPR52688.2022.01117, https://ieeexplore.ieee.org/document/9880056/
42. Lundberg, S.M., Lee, S.I.: A unified approach to interpreting model predictions. In: Advances in Neural Information Processing Systems, vol. 30. Curran Associates, Inc. (2017). https://proceedings.neurips.cc/paper/2017/hash/8a20a8621978632d76c43dfd28b67767-Abstract.html
43. Madry, A., Makelov, A., Schmidt, L., Tsipras, D., Vladu, A.: Towards Deep Learning Models Resistant to Adversarial Attacks, September 2019. https://doi.org/10.48550/arXiv.1706.06083, http://arxiv.org/abs/1706.06083
44. Molnar, C.: Interpretable Machine Learning. A Guide for Making Black Box Models Explainable. Leanpub, 2 edn. (2022) https://christophm.github.io/interpretable-ml-book
45. Preechakul, K., Chatthee, N., Wizadwongsa, S., Suwajanakorn, S.: Diffusion Autoencoders: Toward a Meaningful and Decodable Representation. In: 2022 IEEE/CVF Conference on Computer Vision and Pattern Recognition (CVPR), pp. 10609–10619. IEEE, New Orleans, LA, USA June 2022, https://doi.org/10.1109/CVPR52688.2022.01036, https://ieeexplore.ieee.org/document/9878402/
46. Raman, C., Nonnemaker, A., Villegas-Morcillo, A., Hung, H., Loog, M.: Why Did This Model Forecast This Future? Information-Theoretic Saliency for Counterfactual Explanations of Probabilistic Regression Models. Advances in Neural Information Processing Systems **36**, 33222–33240 (2023). https://papers.nips.cc/paper_files/paper/2023/hash/694ec0018b9fd0ebe863ec29fa5a89b9-Abstract-Conference.html
47. Ribeiro, M.T., Singh, S., Guestrin, C.: "Why Should I Trust You?": Explaining the Predictions of Any Classifier. In: Proceedings of the 22nd ACM SIGKDD International Conference on Knowledge Discovery and Data Mining, pp. 1135–1144. KDD '16, Association for Computing Machinery, New York, August 2016. https://doi.org/10.1145/2939672.2939778
48. Rodríguez, P., et al.: Beyond trivial counterfactual explanations with diverse valuable explanations. In: Proceedings of the IEEE/CVF International Conference on Computer Vision, pp. 1056–1065 (2021). https://openaccess.thecvf.com/content/ICCV2021/html/Rodriguez_Beyond_Trivial_Counterfactual_Explanations_With_Diverse_Valuable_Explanations_ICCV_2021_paper.html
49. Rombach, R., Blattmann, A., Lorenz, D., Esser, P., Ommer, B.: High-Resolution Image Synthesis with Latent Diffusion Models, April 2022. https://doi.org/10.48550/arXiv.2112.10752, http://arxiv.org/abs/2112.10752
50. Rothe, R., Timofte, R., Gool, L.V.: DEX: deep expectation of apparent age from a single image. In: 2015 IEEE International Conference on Computer Vision Workshop (ICCVW), pp. 252–257. IEEE, Santiago, Chile, December 2015, https://doi.org/10.1109/ICCVW.2015.41, http://ieeexplore.ieee.org/document/7406390/

51. Samek, W., Montavon, G., Lapuschkin, S., Anders, C.J., Müller, K.R.: Explaining deep neural networks and beyond: a review of methods and applications. Proc. IEEE **109**(3), 247–278 (2021). https://doi.org/10.1109/JPROC.2021.3060483
52. Samek, W., Müller, K.R.: Towards Explainable Artificial Intelligence. In: Samek, W., Montavon, G., Vedaldi, A., Hansen, L.K., Müller, K.R. (eds.) Explainable AI: Interpreting, Explaining and Visualizing Deep Learning, pp. 5–22. Springer, Cham (2019). https://doi.org/10.1007/978-3-030-28954-6_1
53. Singla, S., Eslami, M., Pollack, B., Wallace, S., Batmanghelich, K.: Explaining the black-box smoothly—a counterfactual approach. Med. Image Anal. **84**, 102721 (2023). DOIurlhttps://doi.org/10.1016/j.media.2022.102721, https://www.sciencedirect.com/science/article/pii/S1361841522003498
54. Song, J., Meng, C., Ermon, S.: Denoising Diffusion Implicit Models. In: International Conference on Learning Representations, October 2020. https://openreview.net/forum?id=St1giarCHLP
55. Spooner, T., Dervovic, D., Long, J., Shepard, J., Chen, J., Magazzeni, D.: Counterfactual Explanations for Arbitrary Regression Models. ArXiv (Jun 2021). https://www.semanticscholar.org/paper/Counterfactual-Explanations-for-Arbitrary-Models-Spooner-Dervovic/ff2f098e2ad415841836e985ee6dfa2fbad7e0c7
56. Sundararajan, M., Taly, A., Yan, Q.: Axiomatic Attribution for Deep Networks. In: Proceedings of the 34th International Conference on Machine Learning. pp. 3319–3328. PMLR (Jul 2017). https://proceedings.mlr.press/v70/sundararajan17a.html
57. Szegedy, C., et al.: Intriguing properties of neural networks (Feb 2014). https://doi.org/10.48550/arXiv.1312.6199, http://arxiv.org/abs/1312.6199
58. Velden, B.H.M., Janse, M.H.A., Ragusi, M.A.A., Loo, C.E., Gilhuijs, K.G.A.: Volumetric breast density estimation on MRI using explainable deep learning regression. Sci. Rep. **10**(1), 18095 (2020). https://doi.org/10.1038/s41598-020-75167-6
59. Verma, S., Dickerson, J., Hines, K.: Counterfactual Explanations for Machine Learning: A Review. NeurIPS 2020 Workshop: ML Retrospectives, Surveys & Meta-Analyses (ML-RSA) (2020)
60. Wachter, S., Mittelstadt, B., Russell, C.: Counterfactual Explanations Without Opening the Black Box: Automated Decisions and the GDPR (2017). https://doi.org/10.2139/ssrn.3063289
61. Zeiler, M.D., Fergus, R.: Visualizing and understanding convolutional networks. In: Fleet, D., Pajdla, T., Schiele, B., Tuytelaars, T. (eds.) ECCV 2014. LNCS, vol. 8689, pp. 818–833. Springer, Cham (2014). https://doi.org/10.1007/978-3-319-10590-1_53
62. Zhou, B., Khosla, A., Lapedriza, A., Oliva, A., Torralba, A.: Learning deep features for discriminative localization. In: Proceedings of the IEEE Conference on Computer Vision and Pattern Recognition, pp. 2921–2929 (2016). https://openaccess.thecvf.com/content_cvpr_2016/html/Zhou_Learning_Deep_Features_CVPR_2016_paper.html

Open Access This chapter is licensed under the terms of the Creative Commons Attribution 4.0 International License (http://creativecommons.org/licenses/by/4.0/), which permits use, sharing, adaptation, distribution and reproduction in any medium or format, as long as you give appropriate credit to the original author(s) and the source, provide a link to the Creative Commons license and indicate if changes were made.

The images or other third party material in this chapter are included in the chapter's Creative Commons license, unless indicated otherwise in a credit line to the material. If material is not included in the chapter's Creative Commons license and your intended use is not permitted by statutory regulation or exceeds the permitted use, you will need to obtain permission directly from the copyright holder.

Mitigating Text Toxicity with Counterfactual Generation

Milan Bhan[1,2(✉)], Jean-Noel Vittaut[2], Nina Achache[1], Victor Legrand[1], Annabelle Blangero[1,3], Nicolas Chesneau[1], Juliette Murris[4], and Marie-Jeanne Lesot[2]

[1] Ekimetrics, Paris, France
milan.bhan@ekimetrics.com
[2] LFI, LIP6, Sorbonne Université, Paris, France
[3] Aix-Marseille Université, Aix-Marseille, France
[4] Université Paris Cité, Paris, France

Abstract. Toxicity mitigation consists in rephrasing text in order to remove offensive or harmful meaning. Neural natural language processing (NLP) models have been widely used to target and mitigate textual toxicity. However, existing methods fail to detoxify text while preserving the initial non-toxic meaning at the same time. In this work, we propose to apply eXplainable AI (XAI) methods to both target and mitigate textual toxicity. We propose CF-Detox$_{\text{tigtec}}$ to perform text detoxification by applying local feature importance, counterfactual example generation and counterfactual feature importance methods to a toxicity classifier distinguishing between toxic and non-toxic texts. We carry out text detoxification through counterfactual generation on three datasets and compare our approach to three competitors. Automatic and human evaluations show that recently developed NLP counterfactual generators lead to competitive results in toxicity mitigation. This work is the first to bridge the gap between counterfactual generation and text detoxification and paves the way towards more practical applications of XAI methods.

1 Introduction

Online textual toxicity can be considered as rude, aggressive and degrading attitudes exhibited on online platforms, ranging from harmful to hateful speech. Hateful speech is defined as aggressive or offensive language against a specific group of people who share common characteristics, such as religion, race, gender, sexual orientation, sex or political affiliation [9]. Such toxic content has proliferated on the Internet in the recent years [46], raising concerns about its multi-faceted negative impact, such as the potential to threaten the psychological and physical well-being of victims [49] or to be used as a medium for criminal actions [37].

Toxic text data can also have a negative impact when used to train large language models (LLMs). Recent advances in natural language processing (NLP) and the development of LLMs such as GPT-3 [8] have been made possible by

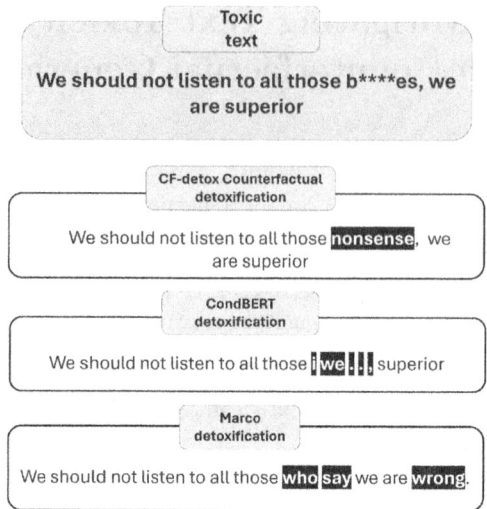

Fig. 1. Example of one text detoxification through counterfactual generation with our proposed CF-Detox$_{tigtec}$ compared to MaRCo [19] and CondBERT [12]. Text changes to mitigate toxicity are highlighted in blue. Explicitly toxic words have been censored with *.

utilizing vast quantities of textual data available on the Internet. These models have demonstrated a high capacity to generate plausible text, while raising several risks about harmful content generation [4] and bias amplification [15] coming from the training texts. Thus, by generating toxic content, LLMs may contribute to the rapid spread of online toxicity, as text is increasingly generated synthetically by chatbots [31].

To cope with the rapid development of online toxic content and curb its societal impact, automatic toxicity processing methods have been developed to detect and process hateful content in online communities and digital media platforms [14]. For example, such tools can be used to clean up language model training datasets, or to suggest interventions on toxic and hateful messages to the human-labor moderating online platforms. In particular, text detoxification (or toxicity mitigation) aims to rewrite toxic text in order to remove (or to mitigate) toxicity while preserving the initial non-toxic meaning and maintaining grammatical plausibility. Recent methods based on neural NLP models have been developed to perform text detoxification [12,19,26] by either generating text under constraint, or by detecting toxic content and modifying it. While these methods succeed in drastically lowering textual toxicity, they generally fail to preserve the initial non-toxic content. Besides, automatic online toxicity processing tools raise major ethical questions regarding the risks related to their robustness and their relationship with online human-labor.

In this paper we propose to address toxicity targeting and mitigation by applying eXplainable AI (XAI) methods [33]: more precisely Local Feature Importance (LFI) [3], counterfactual (CF) generators (see [18] for a survey) and Counterfactual Feature Importance (CFI) [6]. The former aims at detecting important input features to explain a model prediction. Instead, CF example generation explains a model prediction by identifying the minimal changes that enable flipping the outcome of a classifier. CFI measures token modification importance to explain label flipping related to CF explanations.

The main contributions of this work are as follows:

1. We show that LFI and CF generation can be applied to a toxicity classifier to target toxicity and to perform toxicity mitigation respectively,
2. We propose `CF-Detox`$_{\text{tigtec}}$, a detoxification method based on a recently developed CF generator: `TIGTEC` [7] and validated by both automatic and human experiments,
3. We illustrate how to apply CFI methods to make detoxified texts even more content preserving,
4. We discuss risks and opportunities related to automatic toxicity processing tools and define recommendations.

For illustrative purposes, Fig. 1 shows an initial toxic text and its detoxified versions obtained from our proposed method, `MaRCo` [19] and `CondBERT` [12] respectively. Here, counterfactual detoxification leads to more plausible, sparse and context preserving text as compared to the other methods.

The paper is organized as follows, in Sect. 2 we first recall basic principles about automatic toxicity processing and XAI. In Sect. 3 we propose methods to use common XAI approaches to (1) target toxicity and (2) generate plausible and content-preserving detoxified texts. Experimental results discussed in Sect. 4 highlight that text detoxification through CF generation achieves competitive results in terms of toxicity mitigation, content preservation and plausibility, as compared to state-of-the-art competitors. This section also compares the ability of different LFI methods to target toxic content. Experimental evaluation is performed, both automatically and with a human-grounded protocol. After discussion and conclusion, we finally discuss in Sect. 6 risks and opportunities around the use of toxicity mitigation methods. As a result, we discuss how to manage the diversity of toxicity perception and the risk of malicious use of detoxification tools and favor human-in-the-loop processes.

2 Background and Related Work

This section recalls the task of automatic toxicity detection and mitigation. We presents existing methods aiming to detoxify text using neural NLP models. We then introduce the XAI principles used in the next section to perform toxicity detection and mitigation. In the following, we employ *text detoxification* and *toxicity mitigation* interchangeably.

2.1 Automatic Toxicity Processing Background

Definition and Objective. Textual toxicity can be defined in multiple ways [14] and can take various forms, such as rude, offensive or hateful speech, potentially causing online harm to isolated people, minority groups or different ethnic, religious or racial groups [46]. Automatic toxicity processing can essentially take two forms: detection and mitigation. **Toxicity detection** can be either based on prior knowledge (vocabulary, regex) or obtained from a fine tuned toxicity classifier $f : \mathcal{X} \to \mathcal{Y}$ mapping an input text representation space $\mathcal{X}$ to an output space $\mathcal{Y}$ to distinguish toxic and non-toxic texts [11]. Training language models to perform this classification is difficult, as it requires access to datasets labeled based on an idiosyncratic definition of toxicity derived from human annotators [24]. **Toxicity mitigation** consists in rewriting a toxic text while preserving the non-toxic meaning. This task is even more difficult because it requires disentangling toxic and non-toxic meanings to modify the former plausibly while preserving the latter.

Evaluation Criteria of Text Detoxification. Numerous desirable properties have been proposed to assess automatically text detoxification. We organize them into three categories. When ground truth detoxified texts are unavailable, we use the previously introduced f classifier as an oracle to evaluate the toxicity level of the supposedly detoxified text. *Accuracy* (**ACC**) measures the extent to which the generated texts are accurately detoxified with respect to f. *Accuracy* can be measured by computing either the rate of successful changes or the average toxicity score of the generated texts using f. *Proximity* or *content preservation* (**CP**) evaluates how close two texts are. Textual similarity can be defined in two ways. The first one consists in evaluating textual proximity based on word sequence co-occurrences, with metrics such as self-BLEU [34] or the Levenshtein distance. The second consists in measuring semantic similarity from word-level embeddings [35] or sentence-level embeddings [50]. Finally, text *plausibility* is automatically evaluated by the perplexity (**PPL**) score usually obtained from generative language models such as GPT-2 [36].

2.2 Toxicity Mitigation with Neural NLP Models

This section describes two categories of methods leveraging neural NLP models to perform detoxification, namely Text Style Transfer (TST) and Masking and Reconstructing (M&R).

Text Style Transfer. TST (see [20] for a survey) aims to alter the stylistic attributes of an initial text while preserving its content that is unrelated to the target style. Text detoxification can be achieved through TST, where the initial style is characterized by the presence of toxicity, and the target style is defined by its absence. TST is usually performed by generating text with neural NLP decoders guided by an NLP toxicity classifier. In general, TST methods vary based on the language model used for autoregressive text generation and the heuristic of text generation steering.

A first TST approach [42] uses an encoder-decoder architecture based on recurrent neural networks to generate non-toxic text, using a toxicity convolutional neural network classifier to steer the style transfer. Another method [26] fine-tunes a text-to-text T5 model [38] by using a denoising and cyclic auto-encoder loss. ParaGeDi [12] uses a pre-trained T5-based paraphraser model and a class-conditioned language model to steer the text generation. TST methods generally detoxify text accurately but struggle to preserve its non-toxic meaning [19].

Masking and Reconstructing. Masking and Reconstructing (M&R) approaches perform toxicity mitigation by sequentially (1) targeting toxic content, (2) masking it, and (3) modifying it. Once the toxic content is targeted, mask infilling is usually performed with a neural NLP encoder. In general, M&R methods differ in the way they target toxic content, and the neural NLP model used to perform mask infilling.

A first M&R approach [47] detoxifies text by retrieving potential harmful Part-Of-Speech (POS) based on a predefined toxicity vocabulary, generating non-offensive POS substitution candidates, and editing the initial text through mask infilling with a RoBERTa encoder for unacceptable candidates. CondBERT [12] identifies tokens to be masked using a logistic bag-of-words classifier and performs mask infilling using a BERT encoder. The most recent M&R method called MaRCo [19] detects POS that could convey toxic meaning by comparing likelihoods from two BART encoder-decoders respectively fine-tuned on toxic and non-toxic content. The targeted potential toxic content is then replaced by non-toxic content by mixing token probabilities from these two encoder-decoders and a third neutral model. On average, M&R yields to better results than TST in terms of content preservation, and performs equally regarding toxicity mitigation [19].

2.3 XAI for NLP

In the following, we consider the neural NLP toxicity classifier $f : \mathcal{X} \rightarrow \mathcal{Y}$ introduced in the previous section, and a text $x = [t_1, ..., t_d] \in \mathcal{X}$ represented as a sequence of tokens of length d with $f(x) = y$. $\mathcal{Y}$ can either be a binary space that distinguishes toxic and non-toxic texts or a multi-class space that categorizes several levels of toxicity.

Local Feature Importance. A Local Feature Importance (LFI) function $g : \mathcal{X} \rightarrow \mathbb{R}^d$ explains a prediction by a vector $[z_1, ..., z_d]$ where z_i is the contribution of the i−th token to the prediction. The higher the contribution, the more important the token is to explain the prediction of the classifier f. Three types of LFI methods can be distinguished: *perturbation-based* such as KernelSHAP [29], *gradient-based* such as Integrated gradients [45] and *attention-based* such as self-attention in case of a Transformer classifier [5].

Counterfactual Explanations. Counterfactual (CF) explanations emphasize what should be different in an input instance to change the associated outcome of a classifier [2]. CF examples provide contrastive explanations by simulating alternative instances to assess whether a specific event (in our case the predicted class) still occurs or not [32]. The CF example generation can be formalized as a constrained optimization problem. For a given classifier f and an instance of interest x, a CF example x_{cf} must be close to x but predicted differently. It is defined as:

$$x_{\text{cf}} = \underset{z \in \mathcal{X}}{\operatorname{argmin}} \, c(x, z) \text{ s.t. } f(z) \neq f(x) \qquad (1)$$

where $c : \mathcal{X} \times \mathcal{X} \to \mathbb{R}$ is a cost function that aggregates several expected CF characteristics, such as the textual distance. The CF explanation is then the difference between the generated CF example and the initial data point, $x_{\text{cf}} - x$. Many desirable characteristics for CF explanations have been proposed [18], such as sparsity or plausibility to make sure that the CF example is not out-of-distribution [25]. In Sect. 3, we present several methods to generate textual CFs by comparing and relating them with the toxicity mitigation task.

Counterfactual Feature Importance. A Counterfactual Feature Importance (CFI) operator $h : \mathcal{X} \times \mathcal{X} \to \mathbb{R}^d$ computes token substitution importance between an instance of interest and its related CF explanation [6]. In the same way as common LFI, h_i is the contribution of the i-th token modification. CFI highlights the most important token modifications, making non-sparse CF explanations easier to read and more intelligible. A simple but effective way to compute CFI is to apply Integrated gradients to explain the difference between x_{cf} and x, by setting the baseline to the initial instance of interest x.

3 When XAI Meets Text Detoxification

In this section we show how LFI methods can foster toxic content targeting and discuss how to apply CF generation methods for performing text detoxification. We also propose a new method based on CFI to make detoxified texts even more content preserving.

3.1 Targeting Toxic POS with Local Feature Importance

Toxic POS targeting consists in identifying the elements in a toxic text that induce its toxicity. While toxicity can be easily defined partially by a predefined lexical field, it can also take on more complex forms implying specific cultural references or sarcasm that are difficult to detect automatically. Let f be a toxicity classifier and x is a toxic text with $f(x) = \texttt{toxic}$.

We propose to apply LFI to f to highlight important tokens that explain why x has been classified as toxic by f, enabling toxic POS detection. This way, toxic POS detection with LFI does not require the definition of a predefined toxicity vocabulary and is only based on a model that is trained to discriminate between toxic and non-toxic texts. Then, toxicity is detected in a *data-driven* manner based on a fine-tuned neural NLP model. Our proposition to apply LFI

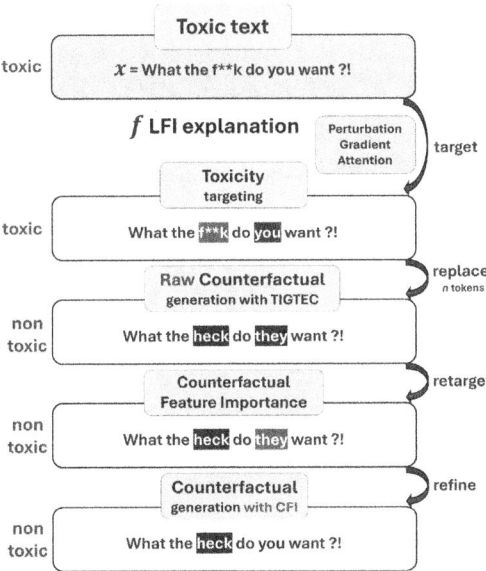

Fig. 2. Illustrative example of a toxic text and a CF detoxification process with our proposed *target-then-replace-then-refine* approach. (1) Toxic content (in red) is targeted and (2) then modified (in blue). To be more content preserving, the counterfactual example is finally refined (3) by restarting the counterfactual generation process, guided by counterfactual feature importance. Explicitly toxic words have been censored with *. The darker the shade of color (red for LFI, blue for CFI), the higher the importance.

methods to f makes it possible to detect complex forms of toxicity, as recent neural NLP models such as BERT can encode high level linguistic forms to make their predictions. Toxic POS detection through LFI depends on the ability of the f classifier to accurately discriminate between toxic and non-toxic texts. Consequently, a toxicity classifier with a low accuracy might misclassify toxic and non-toxic texts, leading to unreliable explanations.

The top part of Fig. 2 (toxicity targeting) shows an example of toxic POS targeting with LFI applied to a toxicity classifier: the token "**f**k**" is assessed as important to predict toxicity. In Sect. 4, we experimentally study the relevance of this approach by comparing *perturbation-based*, *attention-based* and *gradient-based* LFI methods.

3.2 Epistemic Similarities Between Text Detoxification and Counterfactual Generation

In the following, we disclose that toxicity mitigation and CF generation share common features in terms of objective, evaluation criteria and categories of approaches.

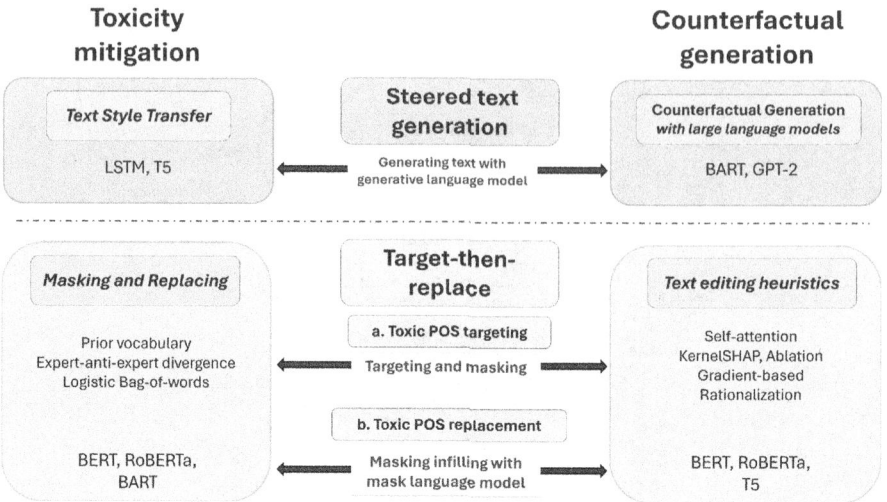

Fig. 3. Toxicity mitigation and counterfactual generation comparison by method category. Toxicity mitigation methods and counterfactual generators can be categorized as *steered text generation* and *target-then-replace* approaches. Neural NLP models used to generate text or replace tokens are similar or of the same nature.

Similarity of Objectives and Evaluation Criteria. Firstly, the aim of both toxicity mitigation and CF generation is to generate text close to an initial instance, while reaching a target state. For detoxification purpose, the target state is defined as non-toxicity, whereas the target state is defined by the f classifier label for CF generation. Secondly, as discussed in Sect. 2, toxicity mitigation methods share with CF generators several evaluation criteria, such as *accuracy*, *proximity* and *plausibility*. These evaluation criteria are measured with the same metrics, such as sparsity, embedding-based semantic similarity, BLEU score or perplexity measures.

Similarity of Constitutive Categories of Methods. Thirdly, methods detoxifying text and generating CFs can be grouped into two similar categories. As mentioned in [7], textual CF generators can be of two types: *Text editing heuristics* and *Counterfactual generation with large language models*.

Text editing heuristics is a family of CF generation methods that builds CF examples by slightly modifying the input text whose prediction is to be explained. Important tokens are targeted and modified with mask language models to switch the outcome of the classifier, making this approach very similar to the M&R way of detoxifying text. Text editing heuristics methods differ in the way they target important tokens and the language model used to modify the initial text. Regarding the former methods, they mostly target tokens to be modified by applying LFI methods to the classifier that has to be explained. For example, CLOSS [13] applies Ablation, MiCE [40] *gradient-based* approaches, CREST [48] leverages rationalization methods, and `TIGTEC` [7] employs KernelSHAP or Self-attention. Next, mask language models used to perform mask infilling are essentially T5, RoBERTa or BERT. This way, M&R methods and Text editing heuristics differ only in the way they target toxic POS. As mentioned in the previous section, the former detect tokens to change either by the use of prior knowledge (vocabulary), intrinsically interpretable model (logistic model) or expert-anti-expert disagreement, whereas Text editing heuristics apply LFI methods to a toxicity classifier. Finally, text is modified using the same kind of NLP encoder. We propose to group these two kinds of approaches together under the name of "**target-then-replace**" methods. Figure 2 shows the raw *target-then-replace* CF detoxification process, where the detoxification consists in performing the two following token changes: $\boxed{\text{f**k} \rightarrow \text{heck}}$ and $\boxed{\text{you} \rightarrow \text{they}}$, leading to a text certainly detoxified, but not perfectly content preserving.

Counterfactual generation with large language models (CF-LLM) approaches build CF examples by leveraging pre-trained generative language models in the same way as TST text detoxifiers. These methods differ in the language model applied to generate text and the heuristic used to steer the model towards a specific objective. For example, `CASPer` [30] learns perturbations to steer text generation with BART [27] and `Polyjuice` fine-tunes GPT-2 to generate CF examples. Thus, TST and CF-LLM methods differ in the way generative language models are steered towards a specific *style* or *label*. We group these two families of approaches together under the name of "**steered text generation**" methods. Figure 3 summarizes the connection between TST text detoxification and CF-LLM generation on the one hand, and M&R methods and Text editing heuristics on the other.

All in all, CF generation and text detoxification can be (1) defined in the same way with the objective to find a small change to reach a target state, (2) evaluated with common metrics and (3) categorized in two similar families of methods, namely *steered text generation* and *target-then-replace*.

3.3 Counterfactual Toxicity Mitigation Methodology

We propose to perform toxicity mitigation with a *target-then-replace* CF generator with respect to the f toxicity classifier. We postulate that, following the notations of Eq. 1, toxicity mitigation can be performed by setting x as a toxic instance of interest with $f(x) = \texttt{toxic}$. Therefore, the objective is to find x_{cf} that minimizes the cost function c such that $f(x_{\text{cf}}) = \texttt{non-toxic}$. This way, by denoting $\mathcal{M}$ as a *target-then-replace* CF generation method and h the LFI method used to target important tokens to be modified, x_{cf} is defined such as $x_{cf} = \mathcal{M}(x, h(x))$. The lack of ground truth detoxified texts is then overcome through the use of f as an oracle to guide text detoxification while keeping the non-toxic content. This way, text detoxification through CF generation consists in detecting texts classified as toxic by f and generating their related detoxified CF examples.

We also propose to use CFI to refine CF explanations (detoxified texts) and make them sparser, i.e. more content preserving. Since CF generation methods can generate explanations involving unnecessary token modifications (see token "you" in Fig. 2), we re-run the CF generator, guided by CFI to optimally target the tokens that have to be modified to perform detoxification. Formally, refining a CF example with a CFI operator consists in generating $\tilde{x}_{cf}$ such as $\tilde{x}_{cf} = \mathcal{M}(x, h(x_{cf}, x))$ with h a CFI operator. We categorize this methodology as a *target-then-replace-then-refine* approach. The entire Fig. 2 traces the whole *target-then-replace-then-refine* process of CF detoxification.

4 Experimental Settings

This section presents the experimental studies conducted across three datasets. We compare our approach performing CF toxicity mitigation named CF-Detox$_{\text{tigtec}}$ to three competitors: MaRCo, CondBERT and ParaGeDi.

4.1 Experimental Protocol

Datasets. We perform toxicity mitigation on three toxicity datasets from [19]. **Microagression.com** (MAgr) is a public blog containing socially-biased interactions with offending quotes. **Social Bias Frames** (SBF) is a corpus of offensive content from various online sources. We use a subset of SBF where the texts have been labeled as hateful by annotators. **DynaHate** is a dataset of hate comments that are difficult to detect for a hate-speech classifier. Toxicity mitigation is run on texts initially classified as toxic in all three cases. MAgr contains 425 toxic texts, SBF 557 and DynaHate 662. The three datasets are available in the Github project in the initial paper[1].

Counterfactual Generator and Competitors. We instantiate our method proposed in the previous section by setting as CF generation method TIGTEC [7]. The rationale behind this choice is that TIGTEC achieves the best compromise in terms of accuracy, content preservation and plausibility when compared with other major competitors [7]. TIGTEC is a *target-then-replace* textual CF generator that implements several LFI methods to target important tokens to be changed. It iteratively masks and replaces tokens with a BERT mask language model following a tree search policy based on beam search to minimize a cost function. We use the following settings to run TIGTEC, we first train a neural classifier (BERT or DistilBERT) on a toxic task dataset from Kaggle[2] to learn to distinguish toxic texts from non-toxic ones. The classifier performance after training is respectively 94.1% and 90.2% for BERT and DistilBERT. This way, CF text detoxification is performed with classifiers that have been trained on a different dataset from the ones used for the evaluation.

Toxicity mitigation is then performed by generating CF examples starting from toxic texts in order to reach a non-toxic state. In the following, we

---
[1] https://github.com/shallinan1/MarcoDetoxification/tree/main/datasets.
[2] https://www.kaggle.com/datasets/rounak02/imported-data.

call CF-Detox$_{\text{tigtec}}$ our new toxicity mitigation method based on CF generation. The cost function driving CF search is defined as in the TIGTEC paper as $c(x_{\text{cf}}, x) = -(p(y_{\text{non-toxic}}|x_{\text{cf}}) - \alpha d_s(x_{\text{cf}}, x))$ with $d_s(x, x') = \frac{1}{2}(1 - s(x, x'))$ where $p(y_{\text{non-toxic}})$ is the probability score of being non-toxic with respect to the trained classifier, s is a cosine similarity measure between text embeddings obtained from Sentence Transformers and α is a hyperparameter set to 0.3. This way, minimizing the cost function implies reaching a counterfactual state while staying semanticly close to the initial instance. The TIGTEC counterfactual search is performed in a beam search fashion, with beam_width = 4. For each neural model, CF-Detox$_{\text{tigtec}}$ is run in three different versions, targeting toxic POS with either KernelSHAP (kshap), Self-attention (attention) or Integrated gradients (IG). Self-attention is aggregated as in the original TIGTEC paper by averaging all the attention coefficients related to the CLS token over the attention heads in the last layer of the f classifier.

We compute CFI to refine the raw CF examples generated by CF-Detox$_{\text{tigtec}}$ by explaining the differences between the initial instances and their raw detoxified versions via Integrated gradients. CFI is only applied to CF examples (raw detoxified texts) initially involving at least two token modifications.

CF-Detox$_{\text{tigtec}}$ is compared to the three identified most recent text toxicity mitigation methods: MaRCo [19], CondBERT and ParaGeDi [12].

Automatic Evaluation. We use the 5 metrics previously introduced to assess toxicity mitigation. The toxicity metrics are based on a pre-trained toxicity classifier. The library used to import the pre-trained toxicity classifier is transformers and the model backbone is toxic-bert. This toxicity classifier is different from the one used to steer CF-Detox$_{\text{tigtec}}$ toxicity mitigation. The success rate is computed with the accuracy (**%ACC**) from the binary classifier to assess if the evaluated text is toxic or non-toxic. %ACC is defined as the number of non-toxic texts over the total number of evaluated texts, with respect to the pre-trained toxicity classifier. The average toxicity score (**SCORE**) is obtained from the last layer of the classifier.

The sparsity (**%S**) is computed with the normalized word-based Levenshtein distance. The content preservation (**%CP**) is computed with the cosine similarity between Sentence Transformer [39] embeddings to evaluate the semantic proximity between the initial toxic text and its detoxified version. The library used to import the Sentence Transformer is sentence_transformers and the model backbone is paraphrase-MiniLM-L6-v2.

Text plausibility is measured with the perplexity score [21] and compared to the perplexity of the original text (Δ**PPL**). This way, a ΔPPL score lower than 1 indicates than the text plausibility increases whereas ΔPPL greater than 1 means that the detoxified text is less plausible. This score is computed based on the exponential average cross-entropy loss of Gemma-2B [16], a recently developed small generative language model outperforming GPT-2. The library to import the pre-trained model is transformers and the backbone is gemma-2b. Due to the presence of outliers when calculating the entropy used to calculate perplexity, aggregation is performed with the median rather than the mean operator.

Human-Grounded Evaluation. In addition to automatic evaluation, we conduct a human-grounded experiment to compare CF-Detox$_{tigtec}$, MaRCo, CondBERT and ParaGeDi in terms of toxicity mitigation performance. It consists in asking 5 annotators to rank detoxified texts by toxicity level obtained by applying CF-Detox$_{tigtec}$, MaRCo, CondBERT and ParaGeDi on 20 randomly selected texts from each dataset. The order of appearance of the toxicity mitigation methods and the dataset is randomized, so that there is no spatial bias in information processing. Annotators can rank texts at the same level if necessary.

Before running the experiment, annotators are given the same instructions. To make sure that they annotate based on the same common knowledge, we define the textual toxicity as *"violent, aggressive or offensive language that may focus on a specific person or group of people sharing a common property. This common property can be gender, sexual orientation, ethnicity, age, religion or political affiliation."*. Annotators all have a MSc degree in data analytics or machine learning and have a good knowledge of English. None of the annotators are authors.

4.2 Results

Global Results. Table 1 shows the experimental results obtained by running each method on the same datasets. In this table, CF-Detox$_{tigtec}$ has been run using KernelSHAP to target toxic POS. For each dataset, CF-Detox$_{tigtec}$ leads to the most content preserving texts, with the highest %CP and %S scores. On the other hand, CF-Detox$_{tigtec}$ performs in average worse than CondBERT in terms of detoxification accuracy and score across all datasets. Still, the toxicity of texts generated by CF-Detox$_{tigtec}$ is in average lower than that of MarCo and similar to ParaGeDi over all text corpora. If CondBERT mitigates the most toxicity, the resulting detoxified texts are significantly different from the initial ones in terms of sparsity and semantic proximity. CondBERT generates the less plausible text across all datasets and degrades text plausibility whereas ParaGedi and MaRCo improve it. In particular, ParaGeDi produces the most plausible detoxified text. This result stems from the autoregressive properties of the paraphrase language model used by ParaGeDi to generate text that is intended to be plausible. However, the text generated by ParaGeDi diverges the most from the initial text in terms of sparsity and proximity.

The high perplexity level of the text generated by CF-Detox$_{tigtec}$ can be partially attributed to the mask language model used for generating new text. Indeed, it is significantly smaller than the encoder-decoder models used by ParaGeDi and MaRCo for text generation. The model used by CF-Detox$_{tigtec}$ is a *small* 66M parameters DistilBERT for masked language model, whereas each encoder-decoder model used by MaRCo and ParaGeDi to generate text are respectively a 139M parameters BART and a 220M parameters T5. Using a bigger mask language model such as BERT-base or BERT-large would improve the

Table 1. Counterfactual toxicity mitigation comparison to competitors on three datasets. Counterfactual toxicity mitigation is either based on a BERT or a Distil BERT classifier and target toxicity based on KernelSHAP.

Dataset	Metric	CondBert	MaRCo	ParaGeDi	CF-Detox$_{tigtec}$ Bert-kshap	Distilbert-kshap
Dynahate	ΔPPL ↓	1.37	0.70	**0.43**	1.24	1.25
	%CP ↑	68.8	68.4	71.2	86.4	**86.6**
	%S ↑	64.1	67.8	31.1	86.1	**86.3**
	%ACC ↑	**92.3**	70.2	89.9	82.9	81.9
	SCORE ↓	**0.10**	0.30	0.14	0.21	0.23
MAgr	ΔPPL ↓	2.59	0.72	**0.69**	2.04	2.16
	%CP ↑	66.2	65.2	78.4	84.6	**86.1**
	%S ↑	47.3	66.0	33.0	**70.1**	**70.1**
	%ACC ↑	**98.1**	82.1	91.6	95.1	91.8
	SCORE ↓	**0.05**	0.20	0.13	0.10	0.14
SBF	ΔPPL ↓	1.48	0.82	**0.59**	1.27	1.26
	%CP ↑	75.6	74.7	75.6	90.2	**90.4**
	%S ↑	68.1	68.1	37.3	87.6	**88.4**
	%ACC ↑	**95.9**	70.2	91.7	87.6	84.2
	SCORE ↓	**0.07**	0.31	0.12	0.16	0.21

plausibility of the text generated by CF-Detox$_{tigtec}$. CF-Detox$_{tigtec}$ still generates significantly more plausible texts as compared to CondBERT.

Human Evaluation. Figure 4 shows the results from the human-grounded experiment where human annotators rank methods' outputs by level of toxicity. CondBERT achieves the lowest level of toxicity on DynaHate and MAgr, which is consistent with the automatic analysis. CF-Detox$_{tigtec}$ and MaRCo produce less toxic texts as compared to ParaGeDi on the DynaHate dataset. Toxicity is overall at the same level across CF-Detox$_{tigtec}$, MaRCo and ParaGeDi on SBF.

This way, automatic and human evaluation underpin that CF-Detox$_{tigtec}$ offers another possible compromise between toxicity, meaning preservation and text plausibility as compared to other state-of-the-art existing methods.

Ablation Study. Table 2 shows the experimental results obtained by running three different versions of CF-Detox$_{tigtec}$ on the three datasets of interest. Each CF-Detox$_{tigtec}$ instance is defined by the LFI method used to target toxic POS. Table 2 shows that Self-attention, Integrated gradients and KernelSHAP lead to similar results in terms of toxicity mitigation, content preservation and text plausibility. These results highlight that LFI methods of a different nature (pertur-

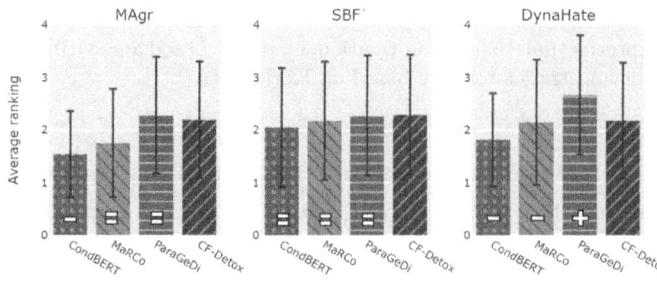

Fig. 4. Toxicity comparison on three test sets with a human-grounded experimental ranking evaluation. Competitor rank distributions are compared to CF-Detox$_{tigtec}$ using a one-tailed paired t-test with a 5% threshold risk. The sign "−" indicates that the rank is lower in average as compared to CF-Detox$_{tigtec}$, whereas "=" and "+" respectively indicate that the ranking is in average similar and greater.

bation, attention or gradient-based) can all yield good results, which underpins CF-Detox$_{tigtec}$ robustness.

Toxicity mitigation through CF generation methods like TIGTEC has to be performed by choosing the appropriate LFI method to target toxicity based on the available model information. For example, KernelSHAP is appropriate if no information (internal parameters, gradients) is available about the classifier f used to counterfactually mitigate toxicity, due to its *model-agnostic* nature. On the contrary, if f gradients are accessible, the use of Integrated gradients is recommended since it is less computationally costly than KernelSHAP. Finally, if all f parameters are accessible, using Self-attention is appropriate because it is available at no cost.

Since TIGTEC gradually masks and replaces tokens in the original toxic text based on LFI, we postulate that the sparser detoxified texts a LFI method induces, the better its performance, as it targets the most discriminating tokens of the initial text with respect to f. This way, integrated gradients give the most *faithful* explanations (i.e. target the most accurately toxicity).

CFI Enhancement. We refine detoxified texts using CFI following the *target-then-replace-then-refine* methodology previously introduced in Sect. 3.3. Table 3 shows similarity and sparsity growth rate obtained from CFs obtained by running CF-Detox$_{tigtec}$ with KernelSHAP to target toxic POS. On average, CFI increases both similarity and sparsity across all datasets, when CF-Detox$_{tigtec}$ is either based on BERT or DistilBERT. However, the gains are higher with the DynaHate dataset (respectively +4.7% and +4.8% uplift in sparsity for BERT and DistilBERT) containing the most toxic texts as compared to MAgr and SBF.

Figure 5 displays the relation between the gain induced by CFI and the number of tokens initially modified in the first version of the CF by focusing on the DynaHate dataset. The number of considered token modifications stops at

Table 2. CF-Detox$_{tigtec}$ counterfactual toxicity mitigation by LFI POS toxicity targeting method.

Dataset	Metric	CF-Detox$_{tigtec}$					
		Bert			Distilbert		
		attention	IG	kshap	attention	IG	kshap
Dynahate	ΔPPL $\downarrow$	1.34	1.26	**1.25**	1.43	**1.24**	1.25
	%CP $\uparrow$	**87.4**	86.3	86.4	**89.2**	87.0	86.5
	%S $\uparrow$	86.8	**87.4**	86.1	**87.4**	**87.4**	86.3
	%ACC $\uparrow$	81.6	**84.0**	82.9	79.0	81.4	**81.9**
	SCORE $\downarrow$	0.23	**0.20**	0.21	0.27	0.23	**0.23**
MAgr	ΔPPL $\downarrow$	2.38	2.14	**2.04**	2.76	2.26	**2.16**
	%CP $\uparrow$	**88.0**	85.8	84.6	**90.5**	87.1	86.1
	%S $\uparrow$	**70.7**	**70.7**	70.1	**71.4**	70.8	70.1
	%ACC $\uparrow$	94.4	**95.5**	95.1	89.0	**92.0**	91.8
	SCORE $\downarrow$	**0.13**	0.10	0.10	**0.19**	0.14	0.14
SBF	ΔPPL $\downarrow$	1.35	**1.26**	1.27	1.32	1.27	**1.26**
	%CP $\uparrow$	**91.5**	90.4	90.2	**92.3**	90.9	90.4
	%S $\uparrow$	88.7	**89.2**	87.6	89.0	**89.3**	88.4
	%ACC $\uparrow$	86.4	86.5	**87.6**	82.4	84.0	**84.2**
	SCORE $\downarrow$	0.19	0.17	**0.16**	0.24	**0.21**	0.21

Table 3. CFI-induced sparsity and similarity gains.

Model	Dataset	Similarity	Sparsity
BERT	MAgr	+0.5%	+1.2%
	SBF	+0.4%	+2.2%
	DynaHate	**+1.5%**	**+4.7%**
DistilBERT	MAgr	+0.3%	+0.9%
	SBF	+0.5%	+2.2%
	DynaHate	**+2.0%**	**+4.8%**

5, representing 95% of the CFs initially generated. It turns out that for Distil-BERT, the higher the number of initially modified tokens, the higher the sparsity and proximity gain (up to +11% for sparsity). Results are overall more stable for BERT across the number of tokens initially changed.

5 Discussion

In this work we showed that XAI methods can be applied to a toxicity classifier to target toxic POS with LFI and mitigate toxicity with CF generation.

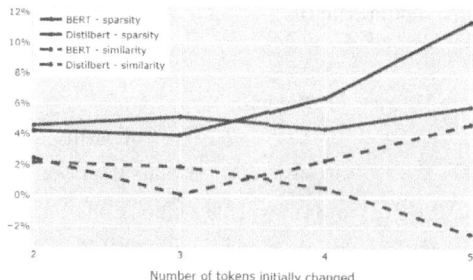

Fig. 5. Evolution of the gain in sparsity and similarity induced by CFI on Dynahate, according to the number of tokens initially modified, per model.

CF-Detox$_{\text{tigtec}}$ enables to find a new compromise in terms of toxicity lowering, content preservation, and textual plausibility. We also showed that CFI could be used to enhance detoxification in terms of proximity and sparsity by following a *target-then-replace-then-refine* approach. We believe that the latter concerns the XAI community in general, to make CF examples closer to the instance to be explained and sparser.

CF toxicity mitigation is highly dependent on the f toxicity classifier used to steer detoxification. If f is unreliable and only performs well on its training set, the risk of incorrectly indicating that the text has been detoxified is high. Therefore, the choice of f and the toxicity training data must be made with caution to avoid incorrect toxicity assessments during detoxification. The f classifier can be fine-tuned on a more specific dataset if the detoxification task is related to a precise kind of toxicity, such as racism or sexism.

CF detoxification has been tested by applying three different versions of TIGTEC with KernelSHAP, Integrated gradients, or Self-attention. There is a wide range of other LFI methods that could be used to target important tokens to explain a toxicity prediction. Besides, other CF generators such as MiCE [40], CREST [48] or CLOSS [13] could be used to perform toxicity mitigation. We believe that these CF generation methods could lead to other levels of compromise between toxicity lowering, text plausibility and content preservation.

Online toxicity is a systemic problem with complex and multiple roots [41]. Automatic toxicity processing does not in itself solve the factors *causing* online toxic content generation, but they offer technological means of *adaptation* to its rapid development. While CF toxicity mitigation may yield competitive results, it also raises ethical concerns that we discuss in Sect. 6.

6 Ethical Considerations

The use of automatic processing tools raises crucial ethical considerations. We identify some of the risks associated with the use of toxicity mitigation tools, and draw recommendations to limit them.

6.1 Managing Diversity of Values

In this work, we have considered a usual hate speech definition as *"aggressive or offensive language that can be focused on a specific group of people who share common property such as religion, race, gender, sexual orientation, sex or political affiliation"*. This definition is just one of many used by institutions and platforms to characterize hate speech [14]. In particular, hate speech characterization can focus either on violence and hate incentives or on the objective of directly attacking. The choice of a specific definition can have a tangible impact on the way online toxicity is automatically processed and perceived by web users. In addition, the perceived toxicity of language can vary based on identity and beliefs [1]. For instance, conservative annotators can show a higher propensity to label African American English dialect as toxic while being less likely to annotate anti-Black comments as harmful [43]. Such annotator biases can be reflected in the datasets used to detect toxicity. **Recommendation**: Toxicity training sets have to be built by annotators carefully selected to represent diversity of values. Besides, toxicity training sets have to be chosen in order to make sure that the values implicitly encoded in the classifier match those expected.

6.2 Against Malicious Use

A toxicity mitigation tool can be misused in various ways. One example is to use it as an adversarial attack generator to make a toxic text seem non-toxic. Adversarial attacks are small perturbations of data instances fooling a classifier with imperceptible changes [28], which bring them formally close to CFs. Since toxicity mitigation methods are based on the use of a toxicity classifier to steer the detoxification process, these methods are subject to adversarial attacks. In this manner, a dishonest user could hijack a detoxification tool to find small modifications to the initial texts, leading a toxicity classifier to falsely assess that a text is correctly detoxified. **Recommendation**: A recent work [10] proposes a method to detect textual adversarial attacks based on the computation of similarities between an input embedding and the training distribution. Toxicity mitigation methods can also be reverse engineered to discover the rules used by an online platform to process harmful contents. This can lead to a change in the terms used, expressed in a seemingly neutral way in order to continue to express hateful content online [23]. **Recommendation**: Toxicity classifiers have to be frequently retrained on updated datasets integrating changes in the vocabulary used to express toxicity to overcome toxicity concept drift.

6.3 Favoring Human-in-the-Loop to Overcome Detoxification Inaccuracy

State-of-the-art toxicity mitigation algorithms do not remove toxicity perfectly. Therefore, deploying a toxicity mitigation algorithm fully automatically is particularly risky since it could let harmful content spread. We propose to use these tools as the first layer of hate content processing before integrating humans into the loop. Behind any platform, online content must be reviewed and moderation is partly performed by human labor [17,22]. By being exposed to disturbing toxic content, human moderators can develop psychological and emotional distress [44]. Toxicity mitigation tools have the potential to induce a socio-technical change, suggesting textual intervention and reducing exposure for content moderators. **Recommendation**: We suggest using hate content detectors and mitigation methods based on the level of toxicity of the text. Text with the highest level of toxicity could simply be deleted, as it would be unlikely to be modified without completely altering its original meaning. Intermediate toxicity levels could be handled by a toxicity mitigation algorithm in order to preserve the general meaning of the text while proposing a softened version. This way, content moderators' exposure to the most hateful content would be significantly limited, and the more ambiguous content would be preprocessed by the mitigation algorithm to propose a more acceptable first version.

6.4 Personal Data

Each voluntary participant to the human evaluation signed an informed consent form outlining the project's purpose and details. The data were anonymized and processed only by the authors and stored in accordance with the General Data Protection Regulation (GDPR). It was possible to stop at any time. The Consent form used is anonymized and presented in Appendix A. This study was conducted for research purposes only.

7 Conclusion

This paper formalized how LFI and CF generation methods and CFI can be leveraged to accurately target textual toxic content and perform toxicity mitigation. $\text{CF-Detox}_{\text{tigtec}}$ leads to competitive results, with state-of-the-art performance in terms of content preservation while accurately detoxifying text and generating plausible text. $\text{CF-Detox}_{\text{tigtec}}$ is versatile since it can be used with various types of LFI methods (such as attention, gradient and perturbation) to target toxic POS and any kind of classifier allowing LFI computation.

This paper is the first to show the extent to which fields such as automatic toxicity processing and explainable AI, which have developed in parallel, actually share epistemic similarities and can be mutually beneficial, paving the way towards practical applications of XAI methods (Fig. 6).

A Appendix

A.1 Consent Form

A.2 Implementation Details

The code used to run the experiments is available on the github related to the TIGTEC paper[3].

---

[3] https://github.com/milanbhan/tigtec.

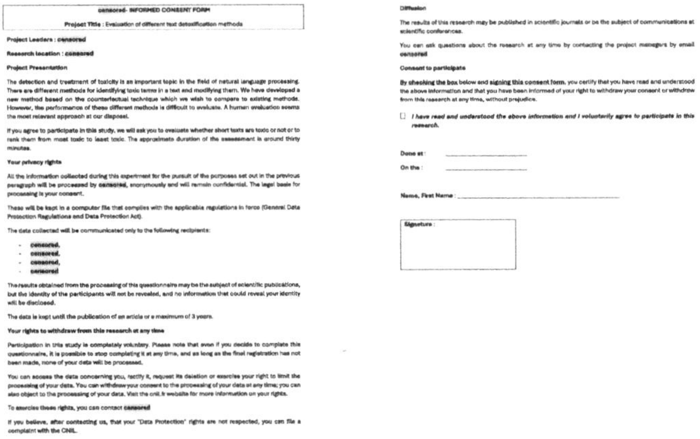

Fig. 6. Consent form

Pretrained Language Models. The library used to import pretrained language model to be finetuned to distinguish toxic and non-toxic content is `transformer`. In particular, the backbone version of BERT is `bert-base-uncased` the one of DistilBERT is `distilbert-base-uncased`. The library used to import the Sentence Transformer is `sentence_transformers` and the model backbone is `paraphrase-MiniLM-L6-v2`. The backbone of the pre-trained toxicity classifier is `toxic-bert`.

References

1. Al Kuwatly, H., Wich, M., Groh, G.: Identifying and measuring annotator bias based on annotators' demographic characteristics. In: Proceedings of the Fourth Workshop on Online Abuse and Harms, pp. 184–190. Association for Computational Linguistics (2020). https://doi.org/10.18653/v1/2020.alw-1.21, https://aclanthology.org/2020.alw-1.21
2. Ali, S., et al.: Explainable Artificial Intelligence (XAI): what we know and what is left to attain trustworthy artificial intelligence. Inf. Fus., 101805 (2023). https://doi.org/10.1016/j.inffus.2023.101805, https://www.sciencedirect.com/science/article/pii/S1566253523001148
3. Barredo Arrieta, A., Díaz-Rodríguez, N., Ser, D.: Explainable Artificial Intelligence (XAI): Concepts, taxonomies, opportunities and challenges toward responsible AI. Inf. Fus. **58**, 82–115 (2020). https://doi.org/10.1016/j.inffus.2019.12.012,
4. Bender, E.M., Gebru, T., McMillan-Major, A., Shmitchell, S.: On the dangers of stochastic parrots: can language models be too big? In: Proceedings of the 2021 ACM Conference on Fairness, Accountability, and Transparency, pp. 610–623. FAccT 2021, Association for Computing Machinery, New York, NY, USA (2021). https://doi.org/10.1145/3442188.3445922,
5. Bhan, M., Achache, N., Legrand, V., Blangero, A., Chesneau, N.: Evaluating self-attention interpretability through human-grounded experimental protocol. In: Proc. of the First World Conference on Explainable Artificial Intelligence xAI, pp. 26–46 (2023). http://arxiv.org/abs/2303.15190

6. Bhan, M., Vittaut, J.n., Chesneau, N., Lesot, M.j.: Enhancing textual counterfactual explanation intelligibility through counterfactual feature importance. In: Proceedings of the 3rd Workshop on Trustworthy Natural Language Processing (TrustNLP 2023), pp. 221–231. Association for Computational Linguistics, Toronto, Canada (2023). https://doi.org/10.18653/v1/2023.trustnlp-1.19, https://aclanthology.org/2023.trustnlp-1.19
7. Bhan, M., Vittaut, J.N., Chesneau, N., Lesot, M.J.: TIGTEC: token importance guided text counterfactuals. In: Proceedings of the European Conference on Machine Learning ECML-PKDD, pp. 496–512. Springer (2023). https://doi.org/10.1007/978-3-031-43418-1_30
8. Brown, T., Mann, B., Ryder, N., Sutskever, I.: Language models are few-shot learners. In: Advances in Neural Information Processing Systems, vol. 33, pp. 1877–1901 (2020)
9. Castaño-Pulgarín, S.A., Suárez-Betancur, N., Vega, L.M.T., López, H.M.H.: Internet, social media and online hate speech. systematic review. Aggression Violent Behav. **58**, 101608 (2021)
10. Colombo, P., Picot, M., Noiry, N., Staerman, G., Piantanida, P.: Toward stronger textual attack detectors. In: Findings of the Association for Computational Linguistics: EMNLP 2023, pp. 484–505 (2023)
11. Cook, D., Zilka, M., DeSandre, H., Giles, S., Maskell, S.: Protecting children from online exploitation: can a trained model detect harmful communication strategies? In: Proceedings of the 2023 AAAI/ACM Conference on AI, Ethics, and Society, pp. 5–14. AIES 2023, Association for Computing Machinery (2023). https://doi.org/10.1145/3600211.3604696,
12. Dale, D., Voronov, A., Dementieva, D.: Text detoxification using large pre-trained neural models. In: Moens, M.F., Huang, X., Specia, L., Yih, S.W.t. (eds.) Proceedings of the 2021 Conf. on Empirical Methods in Natural Language Processing, pp. 7979–7996. Association for Computational Linguistics (2021). https://doi.org/10.18653/v1/2021.emnlp-main.629
13. Fern, X., Pope, Q.: Text counterfactuals via latent optimization and shapley-guided search. In: Proceedings of the 2021 Conference on Empirical Methods in Natural Language Processing, pp. 5578–5593. Association for Computational Linguistics (2021). https://doi.org/10.18653/v1/2021.emnlp-main.452
14. Fortuna, P., Nunes, S.: A survey on automatic detection of hate speech in text. ACM Comput. Surv. **51**(4) (2018). https://doi.org/10.1145/3232676,
15. Gallegos, I.O., et al.: Bias and fairness in large language models: a survey (2023). http://arxiv.org/abs/2309.00770, arXiv:2309.00770
16. Gemma Team, G., Mesnard, T., Hardin, C., Dadashi, et al.: Gemma: open models based on Gemini research and technology. arXiv preprint arXiv:2403.08295 (2024)
17. Gillespie, T.: Custodians of the Internet: Platforms, Content Moderation, and the Hidden Decisions that Shape Social Media. Yale University Press (2018)
18. Guidotti, R.: Counterfactual explanations and how to find them: literature review and benchmarking. Data Min. Knowl. Disc. (2022). https://doi.org/10.1007/s10618-022-00831-6
19. Hallinan, S., Liu, A., Choi, Y., Sap, M.: Detoxifying text with MaRCo: controllable revision with experts and anti-experts. In: Proceedings of the 61st Annual Meeting of the Association for Computational Linguistics (Volume 2: Short Papers), pp. 228–242. Association for Computational Linguistics (2023). https://aclanthology.org/2023.acl-short.21

20. Hu, Z., Lee, R.K.W., Aggarwal, C.C., Zhang, A.: Text style transfer: a review and experimental evaluation. SIGKDD Explor. Newsl. **24**(1), 14–45 (2022). https://doi.org/10.1145/3544903.3544906
21. Jelinek, F., Mercer, R.L., Bahl, L.R., Baker, J.K.: Perplexity-a measure of the difficulty of speech recognition tasks. J. Acoust. Soc. Am. **62**(S1), S63 (2005). https://doi.org/10.1121/1.2016299
22. Jhaver, S., Zhang, A.Q., Chen, Q.Z., Natarajan, N., Wang, R., Zhang, A.X.: Personalizing content moderation on social media: User perspectives on moderation choices, interface design, and labor. Proc. ACM Hum. Comput. Interact. **7**(CSCW2) (2023). https://doi.org/10.1145/3610080,
23. Ji, H., Knight, K.: Creative language encoding under censorship. In: Brew, C., Feldman, A., Leberknight, C. (eds.) Proceedings of the First Workshop on Natural Language Processing for Internet Freedom, pp. 23–33. Association for Computational Linguistics (2018). https://aclanthology.org/W18-4203
24. Jigsaw: Toxic comment classification challenge. https://www.kaggle.com/c/jigsaw-toxic-comment-classification-challenge (2018). Accessed 30 Sep 2010
25. Laugel, T., Lesot, M.J., Marsala, C., Renard, X., Detyniecki, M.: The dangers of post-hoc interpretability: unjustified counterfactual explanations. In: Proceedings of the Twenty-Eighth International Joint Conference on Artificial Intelligence, pp. 2801–2807 (2019). https://doi.org/10.24963/ijcai.2019/388
26. Laugier, L., Pavlopoulos, J., Sorensen, J., Dixon, L.: Civil rephrases of toxic texts with self-supervised transformers. In: Proceedings of the 16th Conference of the European Chapter of the Association for Computational Linguistics: Main Volume, pp. 1442–1461 (2021)
27. Lewis, M., et al.: BART: denoising sequence-to-sequence pre-training for natural language generation, translation, and comprehension. In: Proceedings of the 58th Annual Meeting of the Association for Computational Linguistics, pp. 7871–7880. Association for Computational Linguistics, Online (2020). https://doi.org/10.18653/v1/2020.acl-main.703
28. Liang, H., He, E., Zhao, Y., Jia, Z., Li, H.: Adversarial attack and defense: a survey. Electronics **11**(8), 1283 (2022)
29. Lundberg, S.M., Lee, S.I.: A unified approach to interpreting model predictions. In: Proceedings of the 31st International Conference on Neural Information Processing Systems, pp. 4768–4777. NIPS 2017 (2017)
30. Madaan, N., Bedathur, S., Saha, D.: Plug and play counterfactual text generation for model robustness (2022). https://doi.org/10.48550/arXiv.2206.10429, arXiv:2206.10429
31. Martínez, G., Watson, L., Reviriego, P., Hernández, J.A., Juarez, M., Sarkar, R.: Combining generative artificial intelligence (AI) and the internet: heading towards evolution or degradation? arXiv preprint arXiv:2303.01255 (2023)
32. Miller, T.: Explanation in artificial intelligence: insights from the social sciences. Artif. Intell. **267**, 1–38 (2019). https://doi.org/10.1016/j.artint.2018.07.007
33. Molnar, C.: Interpretable machine learning. Lulu.com (2020). https://christophm.github.io/interpretable-ml-book/
34. Papineni, K., Roukos, S., Ward, T., Zhu, W.J.: BLEU: a method for automatic evaluation of machine translation. In: Proceedings of the 40th Annual Meeting on Association for Computational Linguistics, pp. 311–318. ACL 2002 (2002). https://doi.org/10.3115/1073083.1073135
35. Pennington, J., Socher, R., Manning, C.: GloVe: global vectors for word representation. In: Proceedings of the 2014 Conference on Empirical Methods in Natural

Language Processing (EMNLP), pp. 1532–1543. Association for Computational Linguistics (2014). https://doi.org/10.3115/v1/D14-1162
36. Radford, A., Wu, J., Child, R., Luan, D., Amodei, D., Sutskever, I.: Language models are unsupervised multitask learners (2018)
37. Rapp, K.: Social media and genocide: the case for home state responsibility. J. Hum. Rights **20**(4), 486–502 (2021)
38. Raffel, C., et al.: Exploring the limits of transfer learning with a unified text-to-text transformer (2019)
39. Reimers, N., Gurevych, I.: Sentence-BERT: sentence embeddings using siamese BERT-Networks. In: Proceedings of the 2019 Conf. on Empirical Methods in Natural Language Processing and the 9th International Joint Conference on Natural Language Processing (EMNLP-IJCNLP), pp. 3982–3992. Association for Computational Linguistics (2019). https://doi.org/10.18653/v1/D19-1410, https://aclanthology.org/D19-1410
40. Ross, A., Marasović, A., Peters, M.: Explaining NLP Models via Minimal Contrastive Editing (MiCE). In: Findings of the Association for Computational Linguistics: ACL-IJCNLP 2021, pp. 3840–3852. Association for Computational Linguistics, Online (2021). https://doi.org/10.18653/v1/2021.findings-acl.336
41. Salminen, J., Almerekhi, H., Milenković, M., Jung, S.g., An, J., Kwak, H.: Anatomy of online hate: developing a taxonomy and machine learning models for identifying and classifying hate in online news media. In: Proceedings of the International AAAI Conference on Web and Social Media, vol. 12 (2018)
42. Nogueira dos Santos, C., Melnyk, I., Padhi, I.: Fighting offensive language on social media with unsupervised text style transfer. In: Gurevych, I., Miyao, Y. (eds.) Proceedings of the 56th Annual Meeting of the Association for Computational Linguistics (Volume 2: Short Papers), pp. 189–194. Association for Computational Linguistics (2018). https://doi.org/10.18653/v1/P18-2031
43. Sap, M., Swayamdipta, S., Vianna, L., Zhou, X., Choi, Y., Smith, N.A.: Annotators with attitudes: how annotator beliefs and identities bias toxic language detection. In: Proc. of the 2022 Conf. of the North American Chapter of the Association for Computational Linguistics: Human Language Technologies, pp. 5884–5906. Association for Computational Linguistics, Seattle, United States (2022). https://doi.org/10.18653/v1/2022.naacl-main.431
44. Spence, R., Bifulco, A., Bradbury, P., Martellozzo, E., DeMarco, J.: The psychological impacts of content moderation on content moderators: a qualitative study. Cyberpsychology: J. Psychosoc. Res. Cyberspace **17**(4), 8 (2023)
45. Sundararajan, M., Taly, A., Yan, Q.: Axiomatic attribution for deep networks. In: Proceedings of the 34th International Conference on Machine Learning, ICML. ICML 2017, vol. 70, pp. 3319–3328. JMLR.org (2017). https://proceedings.mlr.press/v70/sundararajan17a/sundararajan17a.pdf
46. Thomas, K., Akhawe, D., Bailey, M., Boneh, D., Bursztein, E., Consolvo, S.: SOK: hate, harassment, and the changing landscape of online abuse. In: 2021 IEEE Symposium on Security and Privacy (SP), pp. 247–267 (2021). https://doi.org/10.1109/SP40001.2021.00028
47. Tran, M., Zhang, Y., Soleymani, M.: Towards a friendly online community: an unsupervised style transfer framework for profanity redaction. In: Scott, D., Bel, N., Zong, C. (eds.) Proceedings of the 28th International Conference on Computational Linguistics, pp. 2107–2114. International Committee on Computational Linguistics (2020). https://doi.org/10.18653/v1/2020.coling-main.190

48. Treviso, M., Ross, A., Guerreiro, N.M., Martins, A.: CREST: a joint framework for rationalization and counterfactual text generation. In: Rogers, A., Boyd-Graber, J., Okazaki, N. (eds.) Proc. of the 61st Annual Meeting of the Association for Computational Linguistics (Volume 1: Long Papers), pp. 15109–15126. Association for Computational Linguistics (2023). https://doi.org/10.18653/v1/2023.acl-long.842
49. Walther, J.: Social media and online hate. Curr. Opin. Psychol. **45** (2022). DOIurl-https://doi.org/10.1016/j.copsyc.2021.12.010
50. Zhang, T., Kishore, V., Wu, F., Weinberger, K.Q., Artzi, Y.: BERTscore: evaluating text generation with BERT. In: International Conference on Learning Representations (2019)

Open Access This chapter is licensed under the terms of the Creative Commons Attribution 4.0 International License (http://creativecommons.org/licenses/by/4.0/), which permits use, sharing, adaptation, distribution and reproduction in any medium or format, as long as you give appropriate credit to the original author(s) and the source, provide a link to the Creative Commons license and indicate if changes were made.

The images or other third party material in this chapter are included in the chapter's Creative Commons license, unless indicated otherwise in a credit line to the material. If material is not included in the chapter's Creative Commons license and your intended use is not permitted by statutory regulation or exceeds the permitted use, you will need to obtain permission directly from the copyright holder.

Guiding LLMs to Generate High-Fidelity and High-Quality Counterfactual Explanations for Text Classification

Van Bach Nguyen[1](✉)[ID], Christin Seifert[1][ID], and Jörg Schlötterer[1,2][ID]

[1] University of Marburg, Marburg, Germany
{vanbach.nguyen,christin.seifert,joerg.schloetterer}@uni-marburg.de
[2] University of Mannheim, Mannheim, Germany

Abstract. The need for interpretability in deep learning has driven interest in counterfactual explanations, which identify minimal changes to an instance that change a model's prediction. Current counterfactual (CF) generation methods require task-specific fine-tuning and produce low-quality text. Large Language Models (LLMs), though effective for high-quality text generation, struggle with label-flipping counterfactuals (i.e., counterfactuals that change the prediction) without fine-tuning. We introduce two simple classifier-guided approaches to support counterfactual generation by LLMs, eliminating the need for fine-tuning while preserving the strengths of LLMs. Despite their simplicity, our methods outperform state-of-the-art counterfactual generation methods and are effective across different LLMs, highlighting the benefits of guiding counterfactual generation by LLMs with classifier information. We further show that data augmentation by our generated CFs can improve a classifier's robustness. Our analysis reveals a critical issue in counterfactual generation by LLMs: LLMs rely on parametric knowledge rather than faithfully following the classifier.

1 Introduction

Counterfactual explanations identify minimal changes to the input that result in a changed prediction by a classifier. As such, they are a core tool for eXplainable AI (XAI), providing valuable insights into a classifier's decision-making process [21,31], thereby fostering interpretability. Counterfactual explanations in an XAI context differ from real-world counterfactuals: the latter describe hypothetical scenarios that contradict known facts [16], while the former aim to uncover a classifier's decision-making process. For example, given a negatively classified movie review, identifying minimal changes (adding, replacing or deleting words) that would turn the classifier's prediction into positive, while maintaining meaningful content (cf. Fig. 1) can provide insight into the classifier's reasoning and decision boundary. This insight can expose undesired model behavior, such as

---

Source code is available at https://github.com/bach1292/llm-cls.

© The Author(s) 2026

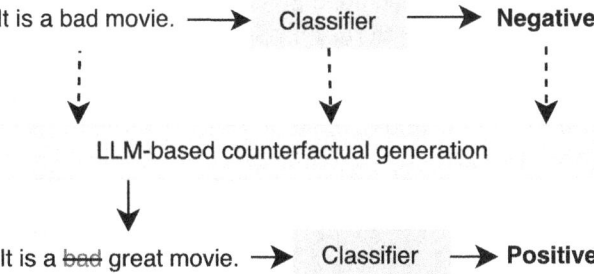

Fig. 1. Counterfactual explanations to explain a text classifier. Counterfactuals (CFs) are minimal changes to the input, such that the classifier assigns a different label. We propose and evaluate two approaches to generate CFs by LLMs that use information from the classifier (besides the original input and label) to guide the generation process post-hoc and ante-hoc.

biases against minorities [20], reliance on spurious correlations [11], or vulnerability to adversarial manipulations [12].
Counterfactual generation methods that access the classifier produce counterfactuals (CFs) with a high label-flip rate (i.e., they succeed in actually changing the prediction) and minimal changes [26,27,29]. However, they require task-specific fine-tuning and may generate low-quality text [22]. In contrast, Large Language Models (LLMs) are used for end-to-end generation without expensive fine-tuning and produce high-quality text [15,24]. However, they struggle to flip the labels with minimal changes [22,23], i.e., do not generate high-fidelity[1] CFs, because they do not have information about the classifier and its decision boundary.

In this paper, we aim to bridge the gap between fully supervised, costly CF generation methods and unsupervised, end-to-end text generation using LLMs. We present two simple yet effective approaches for incorporating classifier information to guide LLMs in CF generation (cf. Fig. 1), enabling high-quality text generation without the need for fine-tuning and offering broad applicability. In an ante-hoc approach, we first identify important words using an XAI method (saliency maps [28] and SHAP [18]). We then use the most important words and examples of factual-counterfactual pairs to prompt the LLM to generate counterfactual texts. Our second approach prompts the LLM to generate a set of candidate counterfactuals, evaluates their fidelity to the classifier, and selects the best candidate post-hoc based on minimality of changes and fidelity.

Specifically, the contributions of this paper are:

---

[1] The terms *fidelity* and *faithful* are sometimes used synonymously to describe how well an explanation aligns with the true reasoning of a classifier. In this paper, we use *fidelity* to refer to "true counterfactuals", i.e., counterfactuals that actually change a classifier's prediction and *faithful* to describe whether a counterfactual truly explains the classifier's actual reasoning.

- We show that LLMs can generate high-fidelity explanations with simple guidance signals, and can outperform fully-supervised state-of-the-art methods.
- We find that this performance depends on parametric knowledge of the LLM. LLMs generate high-fidelity counterfactuals for accurate classifiers, i.e., the counterfactuals reflect counterfactuals in the real-world, rather than faithfully explaining the classifier's true reasoning.
- Using the generated counterfactuals for data augmentation, we show that LLM-guided counterfactuals are an effective method to improve the robustness of text classifiers.

2 Related Work

Counterfactual text generation methods fall into three categories [22]: masking and filling approaches, sampling based on conditional distributions, and LLM-based generation.

Masking and Filling (MF): These methods involve (1) masking key words and (2) filling the masked words using a pretrained language model. MICE [27] and AutoCAD [30] use classifier gradients to identify important words, while DoCoGen [4] masks n-grams with scores exceeding a threshold. CREST [29] trains SPECTRA [13] to detect masking candidates. In step (2), these methods fine-tune T5 [25] to fill the blanks. Polyjuice [31] allows user-defined masking and fine-tunes a RoBERTa-based model using control codes to fill the blanks.

Conditional Distribution (CD): CF-GAN [26] and CLOSS [9] model a conditional distribution to generate counterfactuals based on the target label. CF-GAN adapts StarGAN [7] to produce realistic counterfactuals. CLOSS generates text counterfactuals by optimizing token embeddings, ranking impactful changes with Shapley values, and using beam search to select minimal, grammatically plausible edits that flip a model's prediction.

LLM-Based Generation: CORE [8] trains a counterfactual retriever using contrastive learning, where positive pairs consist of human-authored counterfactuals and negative pairs are paraphrases. The retriever selects relevant counterfactual excerpts from an unlabeled corpus, which are then incorporated into prompts to guide GPT-3 [3] in generating diverse counterfactual edits. CORE relies on counterfactual data and does not use classifier information. In contrast, DISCO [6] generates a large set of perturbations by masking spans identified by a neural syntactic parser and filling them using GPT-3. A filtering model then selects the most promising counterfactuals. However, DISCO is computationally expensive and therefore primarily suited for short-text tasks such as natural language inference (NLI). Additionally, DISCO focuses on generating CFs for data augmentation rather than explanations. FLARE [1] generates CFs by prompting LLMs in three steps: extracting latent features, identifying relevant words linked to those features, and minimally modifying these words to produce CFs.

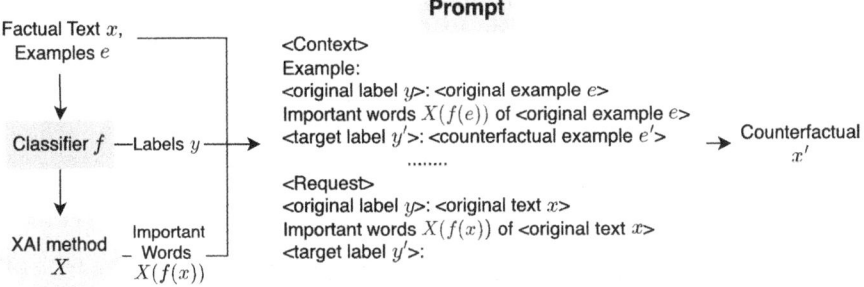

(a) Classifier-Guided Generation (CGG)

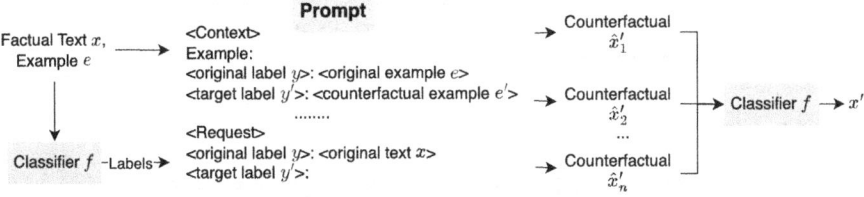

(b) Classifier-Guided Validation (CGV)

Fig. 2. Overview of two classifier-guided approaches for generating counterfactual explanations. a) Classifier-Guided generation (CGG) uses an XAI feature importance method to identify relevant words for the prediction, which are used to extend the prompt for generating a counterfactual example with an LM. b) Classifier-Guided Validation (CGV) is a post-hoc method and selects the best counterfactual example from a set of (unguided) generated candidates.

In summary, MF and CD methods require task-specific fine-tuning, while LLM-based generation lacks classifier integration and produces poor fidelity counterfactuals [22]. Our work not only addresses the limitations of both, fine-tuned and LLM-based methods, but also combines their strengths.

3 Guided LLM-Based Counterfactuals

Given a classifier f and an instance x, the original prediction is $f(x) = y$, and the counterfactual label is $y' \neq y$. Let p be a prompt containing instructions, context, and an example using the classifier's labels. $p(x, I)$ is the prompt applied to input x with external information I. Given input prompt p, an LLM M should generate a counterfactual $M(p) = x'$ such that $f(x') = y' \neq y$.

We propose two approaches that leverage information from the classifier f: **C**lassifier-**G**uided **G**eneration (**CGG**) and **C**lassifier-**G**uided **V**erification (**CGV**). These two approaches guide LLMs by classifier information through two distinct mechanisms. In CGG, the classifier's information is used only during the generation process by providing important words and the classifier's label for the example in the prompt, directly influencing the output. In CGV, the classifier's information is applied both during generation (by providing the classifier's label for the example, similar to CGG) and after generation (by using the classifier's label to validate the output). The two approaches can be applied independently or in combination.

3.1 Classifier-Guided Generation (CGG)

In **CGG**, the generation process is guided by information from the classifier. Specifically, we use an XAI method $X(f(x))$ to extract words from the input x that are important to the classifier's decision $f(x)$. These important words are then incorporated into the predefined prompt p to form $p(x, X(f(x)))$ (see Fig. 2a). A complete example of the prompt is provided in Appendix A. This prompt is input to the LLM M, which generates a counterfactual instance x', such that $M(p(x, X(f(x)))) = x'$.

3.2 Classifier-Guided Validation (CGV)

CGV uses the classifier after the generation process. Specifically, we use the LLM M with prompt p to generate n candidate samples $\{\hat{x}_i\}_{i=1}^n$. The classifier f is then used to validate the labels, assigning a label $\hat{y}_i$ to each sample, and we select the sample with the flipped target label y' that also minimizes the distance $d(\hat{x}_i, x)$ to the original input x (see Fig. 2b). Formally, we have

$$x' = \arg\min_{\hat{x}_i : f(\hat{x}_i) = y'} d(\hat{x}_i, x).$$

Thus, x' is the sample with the desired label and minimal distance to the original input. If no sample flips the label, we select the instance with minimal distance to the input.

4 Experimental Setup

We evaluate counterfactuals on the CEVAL benchmark [22], which includes two datasets: IMDB [19], a sentiment analysis dataset with binary labels (positive and negative), and SNLI [2], a natural language inference dataset with three labels (entailment, contradiction, and neutral). The benchmark assesses performance by counterfactual and text quality metrics. A benchmark run required approximately two hours per dataset on an A100 80GB GPU.

4.1 Models

Following the benchmark [22], we use BERT-based classifiers f that achieve 89% accuracy on IMDB and 90% on SNLI. We compare against MICE [27], the top method for counterfactual metrics according to the benchmark, CREST [29], a masking and filling method that uses SPECTRA [13] for masking and T5 [25] for filling in the blanks, and FLARE [1], an LLM-based method that generates counterfactuals through three steps by prompting LLMs. The baseline is *vanilla* 1-shot prompting without classifier guidance.

For the counterfactual generation LLM M, we compare Llama-3.1-8B-Instruct, Llama-2-7b-chat, and GPT-4o-mini[2]. Following [22], we use a temperature of 1.0 for all LLMs in the counterfactual generation task. For CGG, we adopt saliency maps [28] as the XAI method X, selecting the top 25% most important words with the highest gradients relative to the classifier's prediction, consistent with the benchmark (additional results with SHAP [18] are similar, cf. Appendix B). For CGV, we use Levenshtein Distance as distance measure d to select x' and set the number of samples $n = 5$ for IMDB and $n = 10$ for SNLI, as larger n values showed minimal differences in preliminary experiments. We use 1-shot prompts in our main experiments and analyze the impact of the number of shots with 5- and 10-shot prompts separately in Sect. 5.3).

4.2 Evaluation Metrics

We used the same set of metrics as in the CEVAL benchmark [22] to assess both counterfactual fidelity and text quality.

Counterfactual Metrics

Flip Rate (FR) measures how effectively a method can change labels of instances with respect to a pretrained classifier f. FR is defined as the percentage of generated instances where the labels are flipped over the total number of instances N [1]:

$$FR = \frac{1}{N} \sum_{i=1}^{N} \mathbb{1}[f(x_i) \neq f(x'_i)]$$

where $\mathbb{1}$ is the indicator function.

Token Distance (Dis) measures textual similarity by calculating the token-level Levenshtein distance $d(x, x')$ between the original instance x and the counterfactual x'. Levensthein distance is an ideal metric to assess minimality of edits as counterfactual generation involves specific edits (insertion, deletion, and substitution), rather than completely rewriting the text.

$$Dis = \frac{1}{N} \sum_{i=1}^{N} d(x_i, x'_i)$$

Perplexity (PP) evaluates whether the generated text is plausible, realistic, and follows a natural text distribution by calculating the perplexity of instance x with the length of n tokens using GPT-2:

$$PP(x) = \exp\left\{-\frac{1}{n} \sum_{i=1}^{n} \log p_\theta(z_i \mid z_{<i})\right\}$$

---

[2] Version: GPT-4o-mini-2024-07-18.

where $\log p_\theta(z_i \mid z_{<i})$ is the log-likelihood of token z_i given the previous tokens $z_{<i}$.

Text Quality Metrics. Grammar (GM) measures syntactical and grammatical accuracy.

Fluency (Flu) assesses whether the text is readable and has a natural flow.

Cohesiveness (Coh) assesses how logical and coherent the text structure is

Text quality metrics are assessed on a 5-point scale by prompting GPT-3.5 with a temperature of 0.2 in line with the benchmark [22].

5 Results

We investigated the impact of guidance signals for LLMs on the quality of generated counterfactuals (Sect. 5.1), analysed the impact of feature importance signals (Sect. 5.2), and the number of examples in few-shot prompting (Sect. 5.3). We used the generated examples to augment the training datasets (Sect. 5.4) and investigated whether the generated counterfactuals are faithful to the classifier's true reasoning (Sect. 5.5).

5.1 Incorporating Classifier Information Improves Performance on Counterfactual Metrics

Table 1 shows that our classifier-guided approaches improve key counterfactual metrics compared to the *vanilla* baseline across both datasets and for all LLMs.

For the combination of our two approaches (CGGV), we observe a consistent decrease of distance scores (Dis) and increase in flip rate (FR) in both datasets and across all LLMs. Among the language models in the combination of our two approaches (CGGV), Llama-3.1 achieves the best results, outperforming the flip rate of CREST and FLARE and closely matching MICE, the state-of-the-art counterfactual generation method in terms of flip rate. Notably, with more shots, Llama-3.1 even surpasses MICE in FR on the SNLI dataset (see Sect. 5.3). These results are particularly encouraging, as CREST, FLARE and MICE are dedicated counterfactual generation methods that require task-specific fine-tuning. In contrast, despite their simplicity, our approaches are equally (or even more) effective in generating high-fidelity counterfactuals. While text quality metrics (Grammar: GM, Fluency: Flu, Cohesiveness: Coh) show a slight decline – likely due to distribution shifts from forced word modifications – our approaches still outperform all other methods on these metrics except for FLARE on the IMDB dataset where performance is close. The high performance of CGV highlights that LLMs can generate high-quality counterfactuals with simple prompting, requiring only classifier-provided labels for guidance.

Table 1. Results for counterfactual metrics (FR: flip rate, Dis: token-level Levensthein Distance, PP: perplexity) and text quality metrics (GM: grammar, Coh: Cohesiveness, Flu: Fluency) on IMDB and SNLI. *Italic* denotes the best value within the same LLM, **bold** denotes the best value across all models, and the second-best value is underlined. *vanilla* indicates that no classifier information is used, and *CGGV* denotes the combination of CGG and CGV.

		IMDB						SNLI					
		FR ↑	Dis ↓	PP ↓	GM ↑	Coh ↑	Flu ↑	FR ↑	Dis ↓	PP ↓	GM ↑	Coh ↑	Flu ↑
	FLARE	0.89	39.4	<u>46</u>	3.06	3.14	3.07	0.2	**2.2**	61	3.25	2.99	3.19
	CREST	0.71	70.5	45	2.18	1.27	2.33	0.39	3.5	61	2.71	2.74	2.70
	MICE	**1.0**	38.5	62	2.71	2.81	2.79	**0.85**	5.6	100	3.33	3.31	3.33
Llama-3.1	vanilla	0.93	46.2	*46*	*3.10*	**3.19**	**3.16**	0.45	5.3	*51*	*3.63*	3.59	3.59
	CGG	0.94	45.4	56	2.85	2.93	2.95	0.40	4.4	58	3.62	*3.69*	*3.64*
	CGV	<u>0.99</u>	34.6	48	3.00	3.07	3.05	<u>0.84</u>	3.7	55	3.57	3.55	3.60
	CGGV	***1.0***	***32.7***	55	2.80	2.89	2.91	0.73	*3.3*	59	3.56	3.53	3.57
Llama-2	vanilla	0.78	81.9	59	***3.21***	<u>*3.15*</u>	2.70	0.41	5.2	***50***	***3.92***	3.90	3.91
	CGG	0.86	90.6	60	3.05	3.06	*3.03*	0.40	6.4	54	***3.92***	*3.91*	***3.95***
	CGV	0.94	65.5	***45***	2.84	2.90	2.89	*0.70*	*4.0*	56	3.84	3.83	3.81
	CGGV	*0.97*	*64.0*	68	2.91	2.96	2.94	0.65	5.0	56	3.89	*3.91*	3.87
GPT-4o-m	vanilla	0.94	47.5	***45***	*3.10*	*3.15*	*3.10*	0.50	3.7	58	<u>*3.90*</u>	3.93	*3.92*
	CGG	0.97	43.9	54	2.93	3.01	3.03	0.44	3.8	62	3.71	3.79	3.76
	CGV	<u>0.99</u>	*34.5*	47	3.06	3.12	*3.10*	0.75	*3.1*	61	3.87	***3.95***	*3.92*
	CGGV	<u>0.99</u>	36.6	54	2.87	2.99	2.97	0.63	*3.1*	64	3.67	3.72	3.72

5.2 Not All LLMs Benefit Equally from Feature Importance Guidance Signals

We investigate whether LLMs effectively use the words identified as important by the XAI method in CGG by measuring the *modification rate* (**MR**). MR is the percentage of important words that were changed, i.e., words present in the original text but missing from the generated text. As shown in Fig. 3a, CGG increases MR significantly from 0–40% to 70–75%. However, Fig. 3b shows that high MR does not guarantee flipping labels. While in LLama models, instances with flipped labels (true counterfactuals) are associated with higher MR than non-flipped instances, the opposite holds for GPT-4o-mini. Inspecting the flip rate for counterfactuals that rely heavily on important words (change at least 50% of them) shows that only Llama-2 benefits from this guidance signal, whereas flip rate decreases for the other two LLMs. This decrease could be the result of two potential reasons: (1) words that are important for the original prediction (label y) may not be relevant for counterfactuals, as noted in prior work [31], and (2) LLMs may fail to provide proper word substitutions.

Table 2. Examples where LLMs succeed (✓) or fail (✗) to flip the label by changing the important words (highlighted in bold).

Label	Text	Model
Natural Language Inference (SNLI)		
entailment → neutral	A young man ~~standing~~ stands outside ~~a laundromat~~. A man is standing.	✗ Llama-2
entailment → neutral	A smiling man and a baby girl posing for photo. A girl ~~poses for a selfie with her mother~~ is smiling and holding a toy.	✓ Llama-2
entailment → neutral	A man in ~~gray~~ black on a rocky cliff, overlooking the ~~mountains~~ ocean. A man can see mountains from where he stands.	✓ Llama-3.1
Sentiment Analysis (IMDB)		
Negative →Positive	...Did they even ~~try~~ consider someone like Danny Devito?!? ....OK , now get this they cast Jessica Simpson did anyone take a ~~look~~ glance at her husband? He ~~matches~~ fits Luke Duke to a tee!!!!!!...	✗ GPT-4o-m
Negative →Positive	being a NI ~~supporter~~ advocate, it's ~~hard~~ easy to ~~objectively~~ passionately ~~review~~ enjoy a movie ~~glorifying~~ celebrating **ulster** ~~nationalists~~ patriots...	✓ GPT-4o-m
Negative →Positive	... I ~~hate~~ have to ~~down talk~~ give a shout-out to another filmmaker so I'll just ~~use constructive criticism~~ share some praise. 1. Find ~~good~~ talented actors. Take the time. It ~~really helps~~ makes a huge difference. ...	✗ Llama-3.1

Table 2 presents examples where LLMs succeed or fail to flip the label. In failure cases, despite changing all important words the label remained unchanged, because the words were deleted or replaced by synonyms. In successful cases, LLMs not only changed important words but also modified other words to improve coherence, resulting in better text quality.

5.3 More Examples in Few-Shot Prompting Do Not Necessarily Improve Performance

Table 3 shows that increasing the number of shots improves the flip rate on SNLI (except for GPT-4o-mini), as well as distance and perplexity on IMDB, but has a minimal effect on the flip rate for IMDB. The impact of the number of shots varies by dataset and LLM type; for example, Llama-2 shows a strong decrease in distance when the number of shots increases on SNLI. On IMDB and across all other models on both datasets, differences are minimal or non-existent.

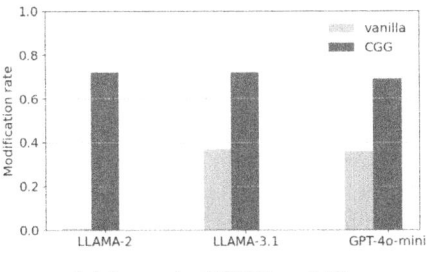
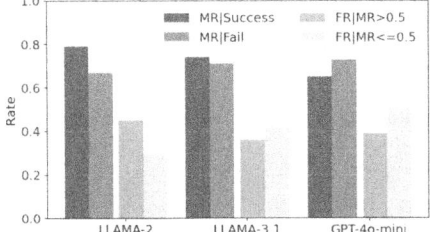

(a) Impact of CGG on MR.   (b) Dependencies between MR and FR

Fig. 3. Impact of CGG on modification rate (MR) and flip rate (FR) in the SNLI dataset. Figure 3a illustrates the MR for each LLM, with and without CGG. Figure 3b compares the MR for flipped (Success) and non-flipped (Fail) instances, alongside the FR for cases where MR > 0.5 and MR ≤ 0.5.

Additionally, increasing the number of shots can degrade LLM performance, especially for models with smaller context lengths like Llama-2. For instance, the flip rate on IMDB drops significantly with 5 shots, and Llama-2 cannot generate meaningful CFs with 10 shots on IMDB due to exceeding its 4096-token context limit. Therefore, we adopt a 1-shot setting for the representative results, even though n-shot settings may outperform it in certain cases.

5.4 LLM-Generated CFs Are Helpful for Data Augmentation

We evaluated whether the generated CFs improve model robustness by following the experimental setup from [14]. Specifically, we augmented the training data from [14] with our generated CFs and trained a BERT classifier on the augmented data. We then evaluated the classifier on three test sets: the original test set, a CF test set created through crowdsourcing [14], and a CF test set created by the dataset authors [10]. The latter two are considered out-of-distribution data [10], where models typically struggle. As Table 4 shows, the CFs generated by our methods improve classifier accuracy on all datasets, except for GPT-4o-mini on the IMDB dataset. On the original test set, our CF-augmented data outperformed human-augmented data. However, on the more challenging human-generated test sets, LLM-generated CFs perform worse than human-augmented data but still outperform models trained without data augmentation and also outperform other counterfactual generation methods such as FLARE and MICE. These results demonstrate that our methods not only enhance CF generation but also improve downstream task performance.

Table 3. Influence of the number of shots (# shots) for few-shot prompting. Results for counterfactual metrics (FR: flip rate, Dis: token-level Levensthein Distance, PP: perplexity) on IMDB and SNLI across different LLMs. **Bold** denotes the best value across all models, and the second-best value is underlined. 10-shot prompting is not applicable (n.a.) for Llama-2 since the prompt is larger than the size of the model's context.

# shots			IMDB			SNLI		
			FR ↑	Dis ↓	PP ↓	FR ↑	Dis ↓	PP ↓
1	Llama-2	CGG	0.86	90.6	60	0.40	6.4	54
		CGV	0.94	65.5	**45**	0.70	4.0	56
		CGGV	0.97	64.0	68	0.65	5.0	56
	Llama-3.1	CGG	0.94	45.4	56	0.40	4.4	58
		CGV	0.99	34.6	48	0.84	3.7	55
		CGGV	**1.0**	32.7	55	0.73	3.3	59
	GPT-4o-m	CGG	0.97	43.9	54	0.44	3.8	62
		CGV	0.99	34.5	47	0.75	3.1	61
		CGGV	0.99	36.6	54	0.63	3.1	64
5	Llama-2	CGG	0.77	35.2	89	0.40	5.5	56
		CGV	0.81	**25.0**	52	0.72	4.0	**53**
		CGGV	0.86	31.2	49	0.67	4.4	**53**
	Llama-3.1	CGG	0.94	38.0	49	0.38	3.8	58
		CGV	0.99	30.0	49	0.86	3.4	58
		CGGV	0.99	29.3	51	0.73	**2.8**	61
	GPT-4o-m	CGG	0.95	37.9	51	0.41	3.4	64
		CGV	0.98	32.7	47	0.69	3.5	59
		CGGV	0.99	31.1	50	0.53	3.1	65
10	Llama-2	CGG	n.a.	n.a.	n.a.	0.41	5.8	55
		CGV	n.a.	n.a.	n.a.	0.75	4.0	55
		CGGV	n.a.	n.a.	n.a.	0.66	4.5	**53**
	Llama-3.1	CGG	0.95	37.0	49	0.40	3.8	60
		CGV	0.98	29.1	48	**0.87**	3.4	58
		CGGV	**1.0**	29.0	50	0.72	**2.8**	61
	GPT-4o-m	CGG	0.95	36.6	50	0.42	3.3	64
		CGV	0.98	32.1	48	0.70	3.5	59
		CGGV	0.99	30.1	50	0.53	3.0	65

Table 4. Data augmentation performance. The original (baseline) training set is augmented with additional data (+) by multiple counterfactual generation methods. Orig is the original test set (in-distribution), Expert and Crowd are human-generated counterfactual test sets (out-of-distribution). *Italic* denotes the best value within the same LLM, **bold** denotes the best value overall, and the second-best value is underlined. We report the average accuracy over three runs (standard deviation is less than 0.01).

Augmentation Setup		IMDB			SNLI	
		Orig	Expert	Crowd	Orig	Crowd
Original (Baseline)		0.91	0.88	0.93	0.74	0.50
	+ Human	0.90	**0.93**	**0.96**	0.82	**0.71**
	+ FLARE	0.90	0.88	0.94	0.75	0.55
	+ MICE	0.89	0.88	<u>0.95</u>	0.78	0.61
Llama-2	+ vanilla	0.91	0.88	0.93	0.82	0.53
	+ CGG	*0.93*	0.87	0.92	0.81	0.63
	+ CGV	0.91	<u>0.90</u>	*0.94*	0.83	0.63
	+ CGGV	0.91	<u>0.90</u>	*0.94*	<u>0.84</u>	<u>0.65</u>
Llama-3.1	+ vanilla	0.91	0.86	0.92	**0.86**	0.55
	+ CGG	0.91	0.88	0.94	0.83	0.65
	+ CGV	<u>0.92</u>	<u>0.90</u>	<u>0.95</u>	0.75	0.54
	+ CGGV	0.90	<u>0.90</u>	0.94	0.83	<u>0.65</u>
GPT-4o-m	+ vanilla	*0.91*	0.88	*0.94*	0.80	0.57
	+ CGG	*0.91*	0.86	0.92	*0.82*	*0.62*
	+ CGV	*0.91*	0.87	0.93	0.74	0.49
	+ CGGV	0.90	*0.89*	0.93	0.81	*0.62*

5.5 LLMs Are Not Faithful to the Classifier, but Rely on Parametric Knowledge

When a classifier performs well, its decisions align with real-world logic, making it challenging to determine whether LLMs explain the classifier's reasoning or rely on real-world knowledge that coincidentally aligns with the classifier's decisions. Conversely, poorly performing classifiers often deviate from real-world logic. If LLMs can generate effective CFs for such classifiers, it indicates faithfulness to the classifier's reasoning rather than external knowledge. To evaluate this faithfulness, we tested LLMs using a low-accuracy classifier. Specifically, we trained a logistic regression classifier on the IMDB dataset with reversed labels (i.e., positive swapped with negative) while keeping the test set unchanged, resulting in 17% accuracy. This setup forces LLMs to explain a classifier that operates contrary to their parametric knowledge [32]. If LLMs could successfully explain this classifier, it would demonstrate faithfulness to any classifier, regardless of performance.

Table 5. Low-accuracy classifier. Results for counterfactual metrics (FR: flip rate, Dis: token-level Levenshtein Distance, PP: perplexity) on IMDB. Δ indicates the difference compared to the same setting with the high-accuracy classifier.

		FR ↑(Δ)	Dis ↓(Δ)	PP ↓(Δ)	MR
Llama-2	CGG	0.16 (-0.81)	69.3 (-0.24)	81 (+0.35)	0.33
	CGV	0.44 (-0.53)	44.9 (-0.31)	61 (+0.36)	0.21
	CGGV	0.38 (-0.60)	54.8 (-0.14)	59 (-0.13)	0.29
Llama-3.1	CGG	0.28 (-0.70)	48.1 (+0.06)	67 (+0.19)	0.47
	CGV	0.76 (-0.23)	**31.1** (-0.1)	49 (+0.02)	0.19
	CGGV	0.46 (-0.54)	39.0 (+0.19)	72 (+0.31)	0.42
GPT-4o-m	CGG	0.38 (-0.61)	45.7 (+0.04)	57 (+0.06)	0.53
	CGV	**0.79** (-0.20)	**31.1** (-0.1)	**47** (0)	0.19
	CGGV	0.54 (-0.45)	40.2 (+0.1)	57 (+0.06)	0.49

Table 5 shows that LLMs struggle to explain the low-accuracy classifier, with a significantly lower FR compared to the high-accuracy classifier. This suggests that LLMs heavily rely on their parametric knowledge, despite being prompted to adapt to reversed labels, aligning with prior findings in other tasks [5,17]. GPT-4o-mini performs best, reflecting better instruction understanding, though it still leans on parametric knowledge. CGV is the most robust method, maintaining moderate flip rates on Llama-3.1 and GPT-4o-mini, while Llama-2 and CGG show sharp declines, indicating an over-reliance on parametric knowledge. Distance and perplexity also worsen, further illustrating the difficulty of explaining low-accuracy classifiers. These results emphasize the importance of evaluating LLM-based counterfactual generation on both high- and low-accuracy classifiers. While low-accuracy classifiers are unlikely to be deployed in practice, they provide a proxy for wrong classifier decisions and more importantly, allow us to evaluate the faithfulness of counterfactual explanations, i.e., whether counterfactuals align with the classifier's true reasoning.

6 Conclusion

In this paper, we presented two simple yet effective approaches that use information from the classifier to guide counterfactual generation by LLMs. Our approaches improve the performance of multiple LLMs on counterfactual metrics by such margins that some even surpass state-of-the-art counterfactual generation methods, highlighting the value of leveraging classifier information. With our proposed approaches, we emphasize the important role of classifier information in improving counterfactual generation by LLMs and encourage its use for explanations or data augmentation in the future. Our experiments show that using the classifier's labels for validation is the most effective guidance to improve counterfactual metrics, while using important words as a guidance signal requires further research. We further show that augmenting the training data of a classifier with counterfactuals generated by our approach can improve model accuracy and robustness.

Our analysis uncovers a critical issue in counterfactual explanations by LLMs: LLMs are not fully faithful to the classifier, often relying more on parametric knowledge than the classifier's actual reasoning. Developers of future LLM-based counterfactual generation methods should pay attention to this issue. We strongly recommend evaluating counterfactuals with both high- and low-accuracy classifiers to ensure the faithfulness of counterfactual explanations.

A Example Prompts

```
Given a movie review with its original sentiment classified as either positive
or negative by a classifier, your task is to modify the text with minimal
edits to flip the sentiment prediction of the classifier. Please enclose the
generated text within <new> and </new> tags
You will be provided with a list of important words identified by the
classifier as influential in its prediction. Use these words as a guide for
your changes, ensuring that the
text remains fluent. Avoid making any unnecessary changes.
Example:
Positive: Long, boring, blasphemous. Never have I been so glad to see ending
credits roll.
Target sentiment: Negative
You must change these following important words: ['boring,', 'blasphemous.',
'glad'] to achieve the target sentiment.
Generated Text:
Negative: <new>Long, fascinating, soulful. Never have I been so sad to see
ending credits roll.</new>
Request: Similarly, given a movie review with its original sentiment
classified as either positive or negative by a classifier, your task is to
modify the text with minimal edits to flip the sentiment prediction of the
classifier.
Positive: A spoiler. What three words can guarantee you a terrible film? Cheap
Canadian Production. THE BRAIN fits those words perfectly. Terrible script,
idiotic acting and hilarious special effects make this a must for every BAD
movie fan. The horror is hilarious. The post production team looks like it
gave up. What makes THE BRAIN admirable is in the second half, it actually
tries to be good! Can a bit of ingenuity and consistency save what is already
a joke? It's around Christmas time. A mother and daughter are murdered by
one of the funniest looking villains ever. The day later, a rebel teen gets
into enough trouble that he is sent for a psychiatric analysis. If a cop's
head is chopped off and a stranger with blood on him and a bloody axe told
you some kids did it, who would you believe? What begins as funny turns dull
and tiring toward the end when THE BRAIN tries to be serious. A child cannot
be frightened by the scary moments. THE BRAIN is too funny a concept to try
and be gritty. The Psychological Research Institute is larger than major
manufacturing plants! Our ugly villain and its cohorts get credit for pulling
some of the worst acting I have seen. Viewer discretion advised heavily.
Target sentiment: Negative
You must change these following important words: ['worst', 'villain', 'dull',
'murdered', 'save', 'idiotic', 'concept', 'tries', 'tries', 'guarantee',
'terrible', 'joke', 'stranger', 'post', 'ugly', 'looking', 'looks', 'script',
'child', 'blood', 'scary', 'half', 'teen', 'fits', 'gave', 'told', 'special',
'horror', 'trouble', 'did', 'kids', 'funny', 'funny', 'make', 'daughter',
'cop', 'mother', 'believe', 'major', 'begins', 'gets', 'turns', 'end', 'axe',
'advised', 'movie', 'chopped', 'time', 'plants', 'like'] to achieve the target
sentiment.
You must enclose your generated text within opening '<new>' and closing
'</new>' tags, like the examples above. No further explanations are needed.
Your generated text:
```

Fig. 4. Prompt for CFs generation - IMDB - CGG.

Figure 4 and Fig. 5 present example prompts for sentiment analysis and NLI tasks used in the CGG approach.

```
Context: For NLI task, given two sentences (premise and hypothesis) and their
original relationship, determine whether they entail, contradict, or are
neutral to each other. Change the premise with minimal edits to achieve
the neutral relationship from the original one. Do not make any unnecessary
changes.
You will be provided with an ordered list of important words identified
by the classifier as influential in its prediction (First word is the most
important). Use these words as a guide for your changes.
Do not make any unnecessary changes. Make as few edits as possible. You must
enclose your generated text within opening '<new>' and closing '</new>' tags,
like the examples above. No further explanations are needed.
For example:
Original relationship: entailment
Premise: Seven people are racing bikes on a sandy track.
Hypothesis: The people are racing.
Target relationship: neutral
You must change these following words: ['racing'] in the premise to achieve
the target relation .
(Edited premise): <new>Seven people are riding bikes on a sandy track.</new>
Request: Similarly, given two sentences (premise and hypothesis) below and
their original relationship. Change the premise with minimal edits to achieve
the target neutral relationship.
You will be provided with an ordered list of important words identified
by the classifier as influential in its prediction (First word is the most
important). Use these words as a guide for your changes.
Original relationship: entailment
Premise: A man with a beard is talking on the cellphone and standing next to
someone who is lying down on the street.
Hypothesis: A man is prone on the street while another man stands next to him.
Target relationship: neutral
You must change these following words: ['cellphone', 'lying', 'beard',
'talking'] in the premise to achieve the target relation .
Do not make any unnecessary changes. Make as few edits as possible. You
must enclose your premise within opening '<new>' and closing '</new>' tags,
like the examples above. No further explanations are needed. Only return the
premise. (Edited premise):
```

Fig. 5. Prompt for CFs generation - SNLI - CGG.

B SHAP as Feature Importance Method

The results for CGG and CGGV using SHAP [18] in Table 6 indicate that using SHAP as the XAI method to identify important words performs similarly as saliency maps, reinforcing a limitation of XAI methods: words important for the current prediction are not necessarily important for counterfactual generation.

Table 6. SHAP as feature extractor. Results for counterfactual metrics (FR: flip rate, Dis: token-level Levensthein Distance, PP: perplexity) on IMDB and SNLI across different LLMs. **Bold** denotes the best value across all settings.

		IMDB			SNLI		
		FR ↑	Dis ↓	PP ↓	FR ↑	Dis ↓	PP ↓
	Llama-2	0.85	55.8	65	0.29	6.2	**56**
CGG	Llama-3.1	0.94	39.7	51	0.28	4.0	60
	GPT-4o-m	0.98	38.0	50	0.32	3.3	65
	Llama-2	0.95	33.6	**44**	0.53	4.7	61
CGGV	Llama-3.1	0.99	**30.2**	51	**0.62**	3.0	63
	GPT-4o-m	**1.00**	31.2	52	0.53	**2.9**	66

References

1. Bhattacharjee, A., Moraffah, R., Garland, J., Liu, H.: Towards LLM-guided causal explainability for black-box text classifiers. In: AAAI 2024 Workshop on Responsible Language Models, Vancouver, BC, Canada (2024)
2. Bowman, S.R., Angeli, G., Potts, C., Manning, C.D.: A large annotated corpus for learning natural language inference. In: Proceedings of the 2015 Conference on Empirical Methods in Natural Language Processing, pp. 632–642. Association for Computational Linguistics, Lisbon, Portugal (2015). https://doi.org/10.18653/v1/D15-1075, https://aclanthology.org/D15-1075
3. Brown, T., et al.: Language models are few-shot learners. Adv. Neural. Inf. Process. Syst. **33**, 1877–1901 (2020)
4. Calderon, N., Ben-David, E., Feder, A., Reichart, R.: DoCoGen: domain counterfactual generation for low resource domain adaptation. In: Proceedings of the 60th Annual Meeting of the Association for Computational Linguistics (Volume 1: Long Papers), pp. 7727–7746. Association for Computational Linguistics, Dublin, Ireland (2022). https://doi.org/10.18653/v1/2022.acl-long.533, https://aclanthology.org/2022.acl-long.533
5. Chen, H.T., Zhang, M., Choi, E.: Rich knowledge sources bring complex knowledge conflicts: Recalibrating models to reflect conflicting evidence. In: Proceedings of the 2022 Conference on Empirical Methods in Natural Language Processing, pp. 2292–2307. Association for Computational Linguistics, Abu Dhabi, United Arab Emirates (2022). https://doi.org/10.18653/v1/2022.emnlp-main.146, https://aclanthology.org/2022.emnlp-main.146
6. Chen, Z., Gao, Q., Bosselut, A., Sabharwal, A., Richardson, K.: DISCO: distilling counterfactuals with large language models. In: Proceedings of the 61st Annual Meeting of the Association for Computational Linguistics (Volume 1: Long Papers), pp. 5514–5528. Association for Computational Linguistics, Toronto, Canada (2023). https://doi.org/10.18653/v1/2023.acl-long.302, https://aclanthology.org/2023.acl-long.302
7. Choi, Y., Choi, M., Kim, M., Ha, J.W., Kim, S., Choo, J.: StarGAN: unified generative adversarial networks for multi-domain image-to-image translation. In: Proceedings of the IEEE Conference on Computer Vision and Pattern Recognition, pp. 8789–8797 (2018)

8. Dixit, T., Paranjape, B., Hajishirzi, H., Zettlemoyer, L.: CORE: a retrieve-then-edit framework for counterfactual data generation. In: Findings of the Association for Computational Linguistics: EMNLP 2022, pp. 2964–2984. Association for Computational Linguistics, Abu Dhabi, United Arab Emirates (2022). https://doi.org/10.18653/v1/2022.findings-emnlp.216, https://aclanthology.org/2022.findings-emnlp.216

9. Fern, X., Pope, Q.: Text counterfactuals via latent optimization and Shapley-guided search. In: Proceedings of the 2021 Conference on Empirical Methods in Natural Language Processing, pp. 5578–5593. Association for Computational Linguistics, Online and Punta Cana, Dominican Republic (2021). https://doi.org/10.18653/v1/2021.emnlp-main.452, https://aclanthology.org/2021.emnlp-main.452

10. Gardner, M., et al.: Evaluating models' local decision boundaries via contrast sets. In: Findings of the Association for Computational Linguistics: EMNLP 2020, pp. 1307–1323. Association for Computational Linguistics, Online (2020). https://doi.org/10.18653/v1/2020.findings-emnlp.117, https://aclanthology.org/2020.findings-emnlp.117

11. Geirhos, R., et al.: Shortcut learning in deep neural networks. Nat. Mach. Intell. **2**(11), 665–673 (2020)

12. Goodfellow, I.J., Shlens, J., Szegedy, C.: Explaining and harnessing adversarial examples. In: Bengio, Y., LeCun, Y. (eds.) 3rd International Conference on Learning Representations, ICLR 2015, San Diego, CA, USA, 7-9 May 2015, Conference Track Proceedings (2015). http://arxiv.org/abs/1412.6572

13. Guerreiro, N.M., Martins, A.F.T.: SPECTRA: sparse structured text rationalization. In: Proceedings of the 2021 Conference on Empirical Methods in Natural Language Processing, pp. 6534–6550. Association for Computational Linguistics, Online and Punta Cana, Dominican Republic (2021).https://doi.org/10.18653/v1/2021.emnlp-main.525, https://aclanthology.org/2021.emnlp-main.525

14. Kaushik, D., Hovy, E., Lipton, Z.: Learning the difference that makes a difference with counterfactually-augmented data. In: International Conference on Learning Representations (2020). https://openreview.net/forum?id=Sklgs0NFvr

15. Kojima, T., Gu, S.S., Reid, M., Matsuo, Y., Iwasawa, Y.: Large language models are zero-shot reasoners. Adv. Neural. Inf. Process. Syst. **35**, 22199–22213 (2022)

16. Kulakova, E., Aichhorn, M., Schurz, M., Kronbichler, M., Perner, J.: Processing counterfactual and hypothetical conditionals: an FMRI investigation. Neuroimage **72**, 265–271 (2013)

17. Longpre, S., Perisetla, K., Chen, A., Ramesh, N., DuBois, C., Singh, S.: Entity-based knowledge conflicts in question answering. In: Proceedings of the 2021 Conference on Empirical Methods in Natural Language Processing, pp. 7052–7063. Association for Computational Linguistics, Online and Punta Cana, Dominican Republic (2021). https://doi.org/10.18653/v1/2021.emnlp-main.565, https://aclanthology.org/2021.emnlp-main.565

18. Lundberg, S.M., Lee, S.I.: A unified approach to interpreting model predictions. In: Proceedings of the 31st International Conference on Neural Information Processing Systems, pp. 4768–4777. NIPS 2017, Curran Associates Inc., Red Hook, NY, USA (2017)

19. Maas, A.L., Daly, R.E., Pham, P.T., Huang, D., Ng, A.Y., Potts, C.: Learning word vectors for sentiment analysis. In: Proceedings of the 49th Annual Meeting of the Association for Computational Linguistics: Human Language Technologies, pp. 142–150. Association for Computational Linguistics, Portland, Oregon, USA (2011). https://aclanthology.org/P11-1015

20. Mehrabi, N., Morstatter, F., Saxena, N., Lerman, K., Galstyan, A.: A survey on bias and fairness in machine learning. ACM Comput. Surv. (CSUR) **54**(6), 1–35 (2021)
21. Miller, T.: Explanation in artificial intelligence: Insights from the social sciences. Artif. Intell. **267**, 1–38 (2019). https://doi.org/10.1016/j.artint.2018.07.007
22. Nguyen, V.B., Seifert, C., Schlötterer, J.: CEval: a benchmark for evaluating counterfactual text generation. In: Mahamood, S., Minh, N.L., Ippolito, D. (eds.) Proceedings of the 17th International Natural Language Generation Conference, pp. 55–69. Association for Computational Linguistics, Tokyo, Japan (2024). https://aclanthology.org/2024.inlg-main.6
23. Nguyen, V.B., Youssef, P., Schlötterer, J., Seifert, C.: LLMS for generating and evaluating counterfactuals: a comprehensive study. In: Findings of the Association for Computational Linguistics: EMNLP 2024. Association for Computational Linguistics, Miami, USA (2024). https://arxiv.org/html/2405.00722v1
24. Radford, A., Wu, J., Child, R., Luan, D., Amodei, D., Sutskever, I., et al.: Language models are unsupervised multitask learners. OpenAI Blog **1**(8), 9 (2019)
25. Raffel, C., et al.: Exploring the limits of transfer learning with a unified text-to-text transformer. J. Mach. Learn. Res. **21**(140), 1–67 (2020)
26. Robeer, M., Bex, F., Feelders, A.: Generating realistic natural language counterfactuals. In: Findings of the Association for Computational Linguistics: EMNLP 2021, pp. 3611–3625. Association for Computational Linguistics, Punta Cana, Dominican Republic (2021). https://doi.org/10.18653/v1/2021.findings-emnlp.306, https://aclanthology.org/2021.findings-emnlp.306
27. Ross, A., Marasović, A., Peters, M.: Explaining NLP models via minimal contrastive editing (MiCE). In: Findings of the Association for Computational Linguistics: ACL-IJCNLP 2021, pp. 3840–3852. Association for Computational Linguistics, Online (2021). https://doi.org/10.18653/v1/2021.findings-acl.336, https://aclanthology.org/2021.findings-acl.336
28. Simonyan, K.: Deep inside convolutional networks: visualising image classification models and saliency maps. arXiv preprint arXiv:1312.6034 (2013)
29. Treviso, M., Ross, A., Guerreiro, N.M., Martins, A.: CREST: a joint framework for rationalization and counterfactual text generation. In: Proceedings of the 61st Annual Meeting of the Association for Computational Linguistics (Volume 1: Long Papers), pp. 15109–15126. Association for Computational Linguistics, Toronto, Canada (2023). https://doi.org/10.18653/v1/2023.acl-long.842, https://aclanthology.org/2023.acl-long.842
30. Wen, J., Zhu, Y., Zhang, J., Zhou, J., Huang, M.: AutoCAD: automatically generate counterfactuals for mitigating shortcut learning. In: Findings of the Association for Computational Linguistics: EMNLP 2022, pp. 2302–2317. Association for Computational Linguistics, Abu Dhabi, United Arab Emirates (2022). https://doi.org/10.18653/v1/2022.findings-emnlp.170, https://aclanthology.org/2022.findings-emnlp.170
31. Wu, T., Ribeiro, M.T., Heer, J., Weld, D.: PolyJuice: generating counterfactuals for explaining, evaluating, and improving models. In: Proceedings of the 59th Annual Meeting of the Association for Computational Linguistics and the 11th International Joint Conference on Natural Language Processing (Volume 1: Long Papers), pp. 6707–6723. Association for Computational Linguistics, Online (2021). https://doi.org/10.18653/v1/2021.acl-long.523, https://aclanthology.org/2021.acl-long.523

32. Yu, H., Atanasova, P., Augenstein, I.: Revealing the parametric knowledge of language models: A unified framework for attribution methods. In: Ku, L.W., Martins, A., Srikumar, V. (eds.) Proceedings of the 62nd Annual Meeting of the Association for Computational Linguistics (Volume 1: Long Papers), pp. 8173–8186. Association for Computational Linguistics, Bangkok, Thailand (2024). https://doi.org/10.18653/v1/2024.acl-long.444, https://aclanthology.org/2024.acl-long.444

Open Access This chapter is licensed under the terms of the Creative Commons Attribution 4.0 International License (http://creativecommons.org/licenses/by/4.0/), which permits use, sharing, adaptation, distribution and reproduction in any medium or format, as long as you give appropriate credit to the original author(s) and the source, provide a link to the Creative Commons license and indicate if changes were made.

The images or other third party material in this chapter are included in the chapter's Creative Commons license, unless indicated otherwise in a credit line to the material. If material is not included in the chapter's Creative Commons license and your intended use is not permitted by statutory regulation or exceeds the permitted use, you will need to obtain permission directly from the copyright holder.

Exploring Ensemble Strategies for Graph Counterfactual Explanations

Mario Alfonso Prado-Romero[1,2(✉)], Bardh Prenkaj[3], and Giovanni Stilo[4]

[1] Gran Sasso Science Institute, L'Aquila, Italy
marioalfonso.prado@gssi.it
[2] Fondazione Gran Sasso Tech, L'Aquila, Italy
[3] Technical University of Munich, Munich, Germany
bardh.prenkaj@tum.de
[4] University of L'Aquila, L'Aquila, Italy
giovanni.stilo@univaq.it

Abstract. Recent advancements in graph neural networks (GNNs) have significantly enhanced the performance of AI systems in tasks such as community detection, user friendship prediction, and drug discovery. However, the opaque nature of these models undermines user trust, especially in sensitive domains like health and finance. Graph Counterfactual Explanation (GCE) methods aim to mitigate this issue by providing insights into model predictions and suggesting user actions for alternative outcomes. Yet, GCEs produced by different methods often vary in quality, diversity, and alignment with the original model's predictions. This work introduces an ensemble-based approach designed to address these inconsistencies by leveraging multiple GCE methods. Our approach comprises two main strategies: *Selection*, employing multi-criteria optimization to choose the optimal base explanation for each case, and *Aggregation*, combining multiple explanations to form a more robust overall explanation. We propose three selection strategies and six aggregation strategies. Our experimental evaluation demonstrates that these ensemble methods, particularly *Ideal-Point Multi-Criteria Selection*, consistently outperform individual GCE methods across diverse datasets in terms of quality, thereby significantly improving the interpretability of GNNs.

Keywords: Machine Learning · Graph Neural Networks · Explainable AI · Ensemble Learning · Counterfactual

1 Introduction

In today's digital age, where vast volumes of data are represented as graphs across diverse domains, the ability to harness this information to address real-world challenges has propelled significant advancements in machine learning (ML) techniques. At the forefront of these developments are Graph Neural Networks (GNNs) [32], which have substantially enhanced performance in key tasks such as molecular property prediction [39], protein-protein interaction prediction [15], community detection [42], and session-based recommendations [41]. Despite their notable success, GNNs continue to face the well-known "black-box" issue, which conceals the underlying mechanisms of their decision-making processes. As concerns about the risks associated with AI systems–particularly those handling sensitive data in domains such as healthcare, finance, and social networks–grow, this opacity poses significant challenges. Regulatory frameworks, such as the EU AI Act, underscore the critical need for AI systems to be interpretable as a means to foster privacy, trust, and fairness [21].

Graph Counterfactual Explanation (GCE) methods offer a robust means of explaining the decisions made by machine learning models by addressing the question: *"What changes in the graph structure or its elements would lead to a different outcome?"* For a comprehensive definition, see [29]. However, the heterogeneous nature of graph data–ranging from social networks to molecular structures and biological systems–presents a significant challenge in developing GCE methods that can produce high-quality explanations across diverse domains. To enhance both the versatility and the quality of explanations, GCE methods have evolved to become increasingly complex, incorporating techniques such as factual-counterfactual optimization [37], causality [19], and Generative Adversarial Networks (GANs) [26,28]. Yet, these methods still struggle to produce useful counterfactual explanations across different types of graphs. Furthermore, as GCE methods grow more sophisticated, they often become less intuitive for users, exacerbating the challenge of explaining a black-box model with another black box.

Ensemble learning, a methodology that integrates multiple machine learning models to enhance predictive accuracy, has achieved success across various applications, including explainability in artificial intelligence [13,35]. However, its application within the domain of Graph Counterfactual Explanations remains largely unexplored. In this paper, we introduce a novel approach that leverages ensembles of GCE methods to improve the quality of counterfactual explanations by integrating multiple, simpler explainers. This approach aims to address the challenges posed by the heterogeneous nature of graph data–ranging from molecular graphs to social networks–by enhancing the versatility and reliability of GCEs across diverse domains. Furthermore, our method seeks to minimize the need for users to possess extensive knowledge of specific domains or the underlying explanation techniques. The principal contributions of this research are as follows:

- Conducting the first extensive study of ensemble techniques within the GCE domain, exploring their applicability across diverse graph types and applications.
- Systematically applying ensemble techniques in GCE methods to enhance the robustness and accuracy of counterfactual explanations.
- Proposing innovative strategies for selecting and combining GCE methods effectively based on graph characteristics.

- Developing ensemble methods that integrate multiple GCE approaches to improve performance and generalizability.
- Performing a comprehensive empirical evaluation of the proposed strategies on synthetic and real-world datasets.
- Analyzing the strengths and limitations of the proposed strategies across different types of graph data and domains.

The remainder of this paper is structured as follows: Sect. 2 reviews related work on Graph Counterfactual Explanations, ensemble learning, and their applications. Section 3 covers key concepts in Graph Neural Networks (GNNs), explainability, and ensemble learning. In Sect. 4, we present our ensemble-based approach for improving GCE methods. Section 5 details the experimental setup, evaluates the proposed methods on synthetic and real-world datasets, and discusses the results. Finally, Sect. 6 summarizes contributions, key insights, and future research directions.

2 Related Works

This research is intricately connected to the fields of Graph Counterfactual Explainability (GCE) and Ensemble Learning (EL). A thorough review of the literature and relevant works in GCE is presented in Sect. 2.1. In contrast, Sect. 2.2 is dedicated to a detailed examination of the advancements and techniques within the domain of Ensemble Learning. Additionally, Sect. 2.3 outlines how our work builds upon and extends the existing body of knowledge, highlighting the novel aspects of our approach and its significance within the broader academic discourse. These sections collectively contextualize our contributions within the broader landscape of existing research.

2.1 Graph Counterfactual Explainability

While extensive research has been conducted on providing counterfactual explanations for images [46], text [20], and tabular data [24], the study of counterfactual explanations in graph-based models remains relatively underexplored. Specifically, only a limited number of works have addressed counterfactual explanations in the context of graphs [1,17,19,22,23,27,37,38]. According to [29], existing Graph Counterfactual Explanation (GCE) methods can be categorized into search-based, heuristic-based, and learning-based approaches. More recently, a new category has emerged, focusing on global (model-level) counterfactual explanations, which aim to provide insights at a broader, more systemic level [14].

Search- and Heuristic-Based Approaches: Search methods identify counterfactual explanations by leveraging predefined criteria, such as instance similarity, to search for suitable counterfactuals within a dataset. Conversely, heuristic-based methods iteratively modify the structure of the input graph until a valid counterfactual instance is obtained. These approaches are widely used across various domains where explainability in graph-based models is essential. Next, we briefly discuss notable methods that fall within these categories.

DCE [11] aims to find a counterfactual graph G' similar to the input graph G, but belonging to a different class, by searching within a given dataset $\mathcal{G}$. On the other hand, *DDBS* and *OBS* [1], which were initially designed for counterfactual explanations in brain networks, employ bidirectional search heuristics. These methods iteratively perturb edges of the input graph G until a counterfactual graph G' is obtained, then attempt to reverse perturbations to minimize changes while maintaining the counterfactual condition. *OBS* applies random edge perturbations, whereas *DDBS* leverages the edge statistics of $\mathcal{G}$ to guide the modifications. *MACCS* [38] is specifically designed for molecular data and employs the STONED method to explore only valid molecules by perturbing the SMILES representation. While molecular structures can naturally be modeled as graphs, this method operates on their string-based representations, limiting its applicability to broader graph domains. We direct the reader to [14,17,38] for further exploration of other search- and heuristic-based methods. Among heuristic-based approaches, *OBS* has demonstrated strong performance across diverse domains and datasets due to its generalizability. For this reason, we selected *OBS* as one of the base methods in our ensemble framework for generating counterfactual explanations in graph-based models.

Learning-Based Approaches: These methods typically follow a three-step pipeline. First, they generate masks highlighting relevant features based on a given input graph G. Next, these masks are applied to G to produce a modified graph G'. Finally, G' is evaluated by the oracle Φ, and the mask is updated based on the resulting prediction $\Phi(G')$. Learning-based strategies can be further categorized into perturbation matrix approaches [37], reinforcement learning-based methods [22,23], and generative approaches [19,26,27]. Generative approaches, in particular, leverage a learned latent space to sample plausible counterfactuals after training. More generally, generative methods capture both observed and estimated edge probabilities within this latent space, enabling efficient sampling strategies to generate counterfactual candidates tailored to the target input instance. We briefly describe these state-of-the-art methods next.

RCExplainer [4] can be considered a hybrid approach between heuristic and learning-based methods. It defines decision regions with linear boundaries using an underlying GNN. An unsupervised approach is used to identify these regions, helping to mitigate overfitting. *RCExplainer* employs a loss function on these linear boundaries to train a network that selects a subset of edges E^* from the original graph G. The resulting graph $G^* = (V^*, E^*)$ maintains the same class as G, and removing edges E^* from G produces a counterfactual graph G' outside this decision region, thereby satisfying the counterfactual condition. However, since it first identifies a factual explanation and then removes it to generate a counterfactual, *RCExplainer* does not explicitly optimize for minimal counterfactual modifications. On the other hand, *MEG* [23] employs multi-objective reinforcement learning (RL) models that are retrained for each input instance to generate minimal counterfactual explanations, particularly in molecular data.

The reward function in *MEG* incorporates a task-specific regularization term that guides the selection of perturbations to the input graph. However, it is challenging to generalize this model to other graph domains due to its domain-specific nature. Similarly, *MACDA* [22] leverages RL to generate counterfactual explanations for the drug-target affinity prediction problem, further illustrating the challenge of adapting such approaches beyond their intended applications.

CF^2 [37] aims to balance factual and counterfactual reasoning in generating explanations while minimizing the explanation size. However, similar to other factual-based approaches, it first identifies a subgraph within the input representing a factual explanation and then generates a counterfactual candidate by removing this subgraph from the target instance. This approach inherently limits the method's flexibility in generating counterfactuals in some domains. *CLEAR* [19] employs a Variational Auto-Encoder (VAE) to encode graphs into a latent representation Z, with the decoder generating counterfactuals based on Z, conditioned on the explainee class $c = \Phi(G)$. The resulting counterfactuals are complete graphs with stochastic edge weights, and a sampling process is applied to ensure their validity. However, the decoding process introduces node order inconsistencies between the original graph G and the counterfactual graph G', requiring a graph matching procedure, which is NP-hard [18].

RSGG-CE [27] employs a modified learning-based approach that utilizes Residual Generative Adversarial Networks (RGANs) in combination with a partial-order sampling strategy on the learned edge distribution to generate robust graph counterfactual candidates. The generator is trained to learn a graph representation that enables stochastic estimations of the graph's topology, thereby facilitating the generation of counterfactuals in a zero-shot manner. *RSGG-CE* has demonstrated strong performance among learning-based GCE methods, making it a compelling choice as one of the base methods in our ensemble framework for counterfactual explanations in graphs.

2.2 Ensemble Learning

Ensemble Learning (EL) [31] refers to a class of algorithms that combine multiple base models to enhance predictive performance and robustness. EL typically falls into three main categories: bagging [6], boosting [33], and stacking [40]. Bagging involves sampling with replacement to generate n different subsets of the dataset; each used to train an independent base model. The final prediction is obtained by aggregating the outputs of these models, often through majority voting or averaging [8]. Conversely, boosting employs an iterative training process where each subsequent base model is trained to correct the errors of the previous ones, thereby improving overall accuracy. On the other hand, stacking combines heterogeneous weak learners and utilizes a meta-model to learn the optimal way to integrate their predictions.

Ensembles of counterfactual explanations have been explored in the context of tabular data to improve the robustness of weak explainers by combining them into a more reliable model capable of explaining individual instances [13]. Dutta et al. [10] introduced *RobX*, a method that searches for robust counterfactuals in tabular data by iteratively refining those generated by base methods, employing a novel metric focused on counterfactual stability. Although not directly related to counterfactual ensembles, [3] examined the challenge of counterfactual uniqueness across different prediction models, wherein multiple valid counterfactuals can satisfy the desired condition. They formalized the concept of *ensemble consistent explanations*, which aims to generate a single, low-complexity counterfactual explanation that aligns with the decision boundaries of an ensemble of predictive models. Additionally, Stepka et al. [35] proposed a multi-criteria objective function for selecting the best explanation from an ensemble of counterfactual explainers using Pareto analysis. However, their approach is not designed for graph data, and it evaluates each explanation individually rather than leveraging graph-specific properties or relationships between counterfactual candidates.

2.3 Our Contribution to the Literature

Ensembles of explainers have been widely recognized for enhancing explanation quality across various learning tasks, such as clustering and anomaly detection [13]. While the potential of ensemble learning for Graph Counterfactual Explanations (GCEs) was discussed in a position paper [26], no prior work has introduced concrete methodologies for ensembling multiple GCE methods. Despite the increasing need for robust and adaptable counterfactual explanations in graph-based models, existing approaches remain confined to individual explainers, each with its own strengths and limitations. The ability to harness the diversity of counterfactual candidates generated by different methods remains an untapped opportunity in the field.

We take the first step toward addressing this gap by introducing an ensemble-based approach for GCEs. Unlike the method proposed in [3], which seeks a single consistent counterfactual across different predictive models, our approach actively integrates multiple base counterfactual explainers, all operating on the same underlying oracle. By doing so, we introduce novel strategies to select the most suitable base explanation or aggregate multiple candidates into a single, *robust counterfactual* that more effectively captures the underlying model's decision boundaries. Our work marks the first concrete exploration of ensemble methods for GCEs, opening the door to more reliable and adaptable counterfactual explanations in graph-based learning tasks.

3 Preliminaries

Given the black-box nature of deep learning systems, a fundamental challenge is understanding *what is happening under the hood*. The European AI Act [9] underscores the importance of interpretability in fostering safer digital environments while promoting privacy, trustworthiness, and fairness. Counterfactual Explanations (CE) are a powerful tool in this regard, providing actionable insights into how a system's decision could change given specific modifications to its input. As a specialization of CE, Graph Counterfactual Explanation (GCE) methods address the question: *"How should the input graph or its components (e.g., vertices, edges) be modified to obtain a different outcome?"* These methods are particularly relevant in graph-based learning tasks, where complex relational structures influence predictions. In the following, we outline the foundational concepts necessary for understanding how counterfactual explanations are generated in graph-based models.

Graphs and Adjacency Matrices. A graph, denoted as $G = (X, A)$, is a mathematical structure consisting of node features $X \in \mathbb{R}^{n \times d}$ and an adjacency matrix $A \in \mathbb{R}^{n \times n}$ which represents the connectivity between nodes. For an undirected weighted graph, the adjacency matrix A is symmetric, and its elements are defined as

$$A[v_i, v_j] = \begin{cases} w(v_i, v_j) & \text{if } (v_i, v_j) \text{ is an edge in } G \\ 0 & \text{otherwise} \end{cases} \quad (1)$$

where $w(v_i, v_j) \in \mathbb{R}$ is the weight vector of the edge incident to the nodes v_i and v_j. For directed graphs, the adjacency matrix may exhibit asymmetry, thereby indicating the directionality of the edges. We focus on undirected graphs and denote the graph dataset with $\mathcal{G} = \{G_1, \ldots, G_N\}$.

Graph Counterfactuals. Given a black-box (oracle) predictor $\Phi : G \to Y$, where, w.l.o.g., $Y = \{0, 1\}$, according to [29], a counterfactual for G is defined as

$$\mathcal{E}_\Phi(G) = \underset{G' \in \mathcal{G}', G \neq G', \Phi(G) \neq \Phi(G')}{\arg\max} \mathcal{S}(G, G') \quad (2)$$

where $\mathcal{G}'$ is the set of all possible counterfactuals, and $\mathcal{S}(G, G')$ calculates the similarity between G and G'.

Connectivity plays a fundamental role in many graph-based problems. Graph substructures in domains such as biochemistry, neurobiology, ecology, and engineering are intricately linked to their functionalities [2]. Moreover, the local neighborhood of a vertex is often crucial in determining its classification, as relational dependencies influence predictive models in graph-based learning. Consequently, as discussed in Sect. 2.1, most explanation methods developed for images and text cannot be directly applied to graphs, where structural information is propagated through message-passing mechanisms [16,43]. This distinction underscores the need for specialized techniques tailored to the unique properties of graph data.

Ensemble Learning. Ensemble learning is a machine learning paradigm in which multiple models (often referred to as *weak learners* or *base components*) are trained to solve the same problem and combined to form a stronger, more robust model that achieves superior performance. In the context of Graph Counterfactual Explanations (GCEs), the base components correspond to different explainers. Formally, we define the set of K individual GCE methods (base explainers) as $\mathbb{E} = \{\mathcal{E}_\Phi^1, \mathcal{E}_\Phi^2, \ldots, \mathcal{E}_\Phi^K\}$ where each explainer $\mathcal{E}_\Phi^k : G \to G'_k$ generates a counterfactual explanation G'_k for the input graph G, resulting in a set of generated counterfactuals $\mathbb{C} = \{G'_1, G'_2, \ldots, G'_K\}$.

It is important to note that GCEs differ significantly from traditional predictive tasks, as the problem cannot be neatly formulated with a single objective function. Instead, the output G^* of an ensemble method is obtained through two key operations: *selection* and *aggregation*, each of which can be specialized based on the chosen strategy (see Sect. 4). The selection function $\texttt{select} : 2^\mathbb{C} \to 2^\mathbb{C}$ returns a subset $\mathbb{C}' \subseteq \mathbb{C}$, while the aggregation function $\texttt{aggregate} : 2^\mathbb{C} \to \mathbb{C}$ composes a new counterfactual explanation from the selected candidates:

$$G^* = \texttt{aggregate}(\texttt{select}(\{G'_1, G'_2, \ldots, G'_K\})). \qquad (3)$$

If the *selection* function returns the full set $\{G'_1, G'_2, \ldots, G'_K\}$, the process reduces to an aggregation-only approach. Conversely, if the selection function outputs only a single explanation, no aggregation occurs, making the result equivalent to a pure selection method. In this study, we independently analyze selection and aggregation techniques to understand better their distinct contributions and potential impact on counterfactual explanation quality.

4 Ensembling Graph Counterfactual Explanations

In this section, we introduce our ensemble-based approach for Graph Counterfactual Explanations (GCEs), designed to harness the strengths of multiple explanation methods. Our approach is built on top of the GRETEL framework [25,30] and operates through multiple stages, integrating diverse counterfactual explainers to enhance the quality and robustness of explanations.

During training, all learning-based explainers are trained on the available dataset. Then, at inference time, given an instance to explain G, all base explainers $\mathbb{E} = \{\mathcal{E}^1_\phi, \mathcal{E}^2_\phi, \ldots, \mathcal{E}^K_\phi\}$ are queried to generate counterfactual examples, forming an initial set of candidates $\mathbb{C} = \{G'_1, G'_2, \ldots, G'_k\}$. Note that $k \neq K$ since an explainer may produce multiple counterfactual examples for a single instance. In the second stage, a *correctness selection* process is applied to filter $\mathbb{C}$, ensuring that only valid counterfactual instances remain in the refined set $\mathbb{C}'$. Finally, our ensemble method employs two distinct strategies to refine and improve the counterfactual explanations:

- **Explanation Selection**: Identifies the most suitable base explainer or counterfactual explanation for the given instance.
- **Explanation Aggregation**: Combines multiple counterfactual explanations generated by different GCE methods to construct a new, potentially superior, explanation.

In the next sections, we formally define these two strategies, starting with selection methods and then introducing our aggregation techniques.

4.1 Explanation Selection

The heterogeneous nature of graph data and its diverse applications make it difficult for a single GCE method to consistently outperform others across all datasets. In practice, different methods may provide the most suitable explanations depending on the class of the data instance and its specific structural properties. To address this variability, *Explanation Selection* aims to determine the most appropriate counterfactual explanation for a given target instance by selecting the most suitable GCE produced by a set of base explainers $\mathbb{E} = \{\mathcal{E}_\phi^1, \mathcal{E}_\phi^2, \ldots, \mathcal{E}_\phi^K\}$. In the following, we introduce the strategies we propose for selecting GCEs.

Ideal-Point Multi-Criteria Selection (IPMCS) evaluates the counterfactual explanations $G_i' \in \mathbb{C}$ generated by the base explainers in $\mathbb{E}$ using a set of criteria $H = \{h_1, h_2, \ldots, h_k\}$. The goal is to select the best explanation for $\Phi(G)$. However, in most cases, no single counterfactual explanation dominates all others across all evaluation criteria. Instead, multiple solutions may exist along a Pareto front, making direct selection challenging. To address this issue, we employ the *Ideal Point Method* [34,36], a computationally efficient approach widely recommended for scenarios where all criteria hold equal importance [5,35]. This method constructs an *ideal score point*:

$$Z = [z_1, z_2, \ldots, z_k], \quad \text{where } z_i = \max\{h_i(G') \mid G' \in \mathbb{C}\}, \quad \forall i = 1, \ldots, k. \quad (4)$$

Then, for each counterfactual $G_i' \in \mathbb{C}$, we compute its distance $d(Z, H(G_i'))$ from the ideal point Z. The explanation closest to Z is selected as the best counterfactual. While this approach ensures a balanced and optimal selection, applying all base explainers to every instance can be computationally expensive, particularly for large datasets.

Dataset-Level Explainer Selection (DLES) is designed to mitigate the computational cost associated with the *IPMCS* method. Instead of selecting the best explanation $G_i' \in \mathbb{C}$ for each instance, *DLES* focuses on selecting the most suitable explainer $\mathcal{E}_\phi^i \in \mathbb{E}$ for the entire dataset $\mathcal{G}$. During the training phase, this method follows a similar logic to multi-criteria selection but evaluates performance at the explainer level. Specifically, for each base explainer $\mathcal{E}_\phi^i$, we define its dataset-level performance score as:

$$s_{\mathcal{E}_i} = \sum_{G \in \mathcal{G}_\text{train}} \mathbb{1}(\mathcal{E}_\phi^i(G) = \arg\min_{G' \in \mathbb{C}} d(Z, H(G'))), \quad (5)$$

where $\mathbb{1}$ is the indicator function, and $d(Z, H(G'))$ represents the distance from the ideal point used in *IPMCS*. This score counts how many times each explainer provides the best counterfactual across the training set.

The explainer that maximizes $s_{\mathcal{E}_i}$ is selected as the dataset-optimal explainer:

$$\mathcal{E}_\phi^* = \arg\max_{\mathcal{E}_\phi^i \in \mathbb{E}} s_{\mathcal{E}_i}. \quad (6)$$

During inference, instead of evaluating all explainers, we directly apply $\mathcal{E}_\phi^*$ to a new instance G to generate its counterfactual $G' = \mathcal{E}_\phi^*(G)$. By automatically identifying the best explainer at the dataset level, *DLES* eliminates the need for manual analysis to determine the optimal base GCE method. However, its effectiveness is inherently limited by the performance of the best individual explainer, as it does not adapt to instance-specific variations.

Instance-Level Explainer Selection (ILES) is our proposed approach to overcome the limitations of the previous selection methods. Unlike *DLES*, which selects a single best explainer for the entire dataset, *ILES* dynamically determines the most suitable base explainer $\mathcal{E}_\Phi$ based on the structural properties of each individual instance G.

Training Phase: To train a selection model, we first construct a surrogate training set by sampling a subset of instances from the dataset $\mathcal{G}$. For each instance $G \in \mathcal{G}_{\text{train}}$, we apply the *Ideal-Point Multi-Criteria Selection (IPMCS)* method to determine the best-performing explainer:

$$y_G = \arg\min_{\mathcal{E}_\Phi^i \in \mathbb{E}} d(Z, H(\mathcal{E}_\Phi^i(G))), \tag{7}$$

where $d(Z, H(\mathcal{E}_\Phi^i(G)))$ represents the distance between the ideal score point and the evaluation criteria for the counterfactual explanation generated by explainer $\mathcal{E}_\Phi^i$. Each instance G in the training set is then labeled with the index of the explainer that produced the best explanation:

$$\mathcal{D}_{\text{train}} = \{(G, y_G) \mid G \in \mathcal{G}_{\text{train}}\}. \tag{8}$$

We then train a machine learning model Υ to predict the most suitable explainer based on the structure and features of G. Given the graph-based nature of the problem, we adopt a Graph Convolutional Network (GCN) as our reference model, leveraging its ability to capture complex relational dependencies in graph data.

Inference Phase: During inference, for a given target instance G, the trained model Υ predicts the most appropriate explainer $\mathcal{E}_\Phi^* = \Upsilon(G)$ where $\mathcal{E}_\Phi^* \in \mathbb{E}$ is the selected explainer. The corresponding counterfactual explanation is then generated as $G' = \mathcal{E}_\Phi^*(G)$.

By dynamically selecting the best explainer for each instance, *ILES* combines the efficiency of dataset-level selection with the adaptability of multi-criteria selection. However, its effectiveness depends on how well Υ generalizes to unseen instances and accurately associates them with their optimal explainer.

4.2 Explanation Aggregation

While selection-based methods identify the most suitable counterfactual explanation from a set of base explainers, they do not address cases where individual explanations are suboptimal. Even when a GCE method produces a valid counterfactual, the resulting explanation may lack practical utility if it introduces excessive modifications to the original instance. In such scenarios, selection alone is insufficient to overcome the inherent limitations of individual methods. To address this challenge, *Explanation Aggregation* methods aim to refine counterfactual explanations by integrating multiple candidates, leveraging the strengths of different base explainers. Instead of relying on a single method, these techniques construct improved counterfactuals by combining multiple explanations. By systematically aggregating counterfactual candidates, these methods effectively reduce the search space for counterfactual generation while enhancing explanation quality, robustness, and diversity. We propose the following explanation aggregation strategies:

Frequency Aggregation is a voting-based ensemble method that aggregates counterfactual explanations by identifying the most frequently proposed modifications across multiple base explainers. Instead of relying on a single counterfactual instance, this approach considers all valid counterfactuals and retains only the modifications that appear consistently across a predefined proportion of them. This method primarily focuses on edge additions and removals in graph structures. The process begins by querying all base explainers $\mathcal{E}_\Phi^k$ and filtering out any explanations that do not produce valid counterfactuals. This results in a refined set of valid counterfactuals $\mathcal{G}' = \{G'_1, G'_2, \ldots, G'_K\}$. Next, the method identifies consistent modifications across these counterfactuals. Let A be the adjacency matrix of the original instance G, and let A'_i be the adjacency matrix of the counterfactual explanation G'_i. We define the function $\Delta A(A, A'_i)$ that returns a binary matrix of the same dimensions as A, where:

$$\Delta A(A, A'_i)[u, v] = \begin{cases} 1, & \text{if edge } (u, v) \text{ is added or removed in } A'_i, \\ 0, & \text{otherwise.} \end{cases} \quad (9)$$

The frequency matrix ΔA_{freq} is then computed by summing the individual modification matrices across all valid counterfactuals:

$$\Delta A_{\text{freq}} = \frac{1}{|\mathcal{G}'|} \sum_{i=1}^{K} \Delta A(A, A'_i). \quad (10)$$

Once the frequency matrix is computed, a threshold τ is applied to retain only the most frequently occurring modifications. Specifically, edges in ΔA_{freq} with a frequency lower than τ are discarded:

$$A_{\text{perturb}}[u, v] = \begin{cases} 1, & \text{if } \Delta A_{\text{freq}}[u, v] \geq \tau, \\ 0, & \text{otherwise.} \end{cases} \quad (11)$$

The final counterfactual explanation G' is then obtained by applying the perturbation mask A_{perturb} to the original graph G.

The *Frequency Aggregation* approach leverages the collective knowledge of multiple base explainers, ensuring that only the most consistent modifications are retained. However, its effectiveness heavily depends on the user-defined threshold τ, which lacks flexibility and may require tuning based on the domain, the base explainers, and the specific instances involved.

Union and Intersection Aggregation are baseline methods that represent special cases of *Frequency Aggregation*, differing only in the choice of the threshold τ. In *Union Aggregation*, the final counterfactual explanation G'

retains all modifications that appear in at least one base explainer's output. This is equivalent to setting $\tau = 0$, ensuring that any proposed edge addition or removal across the explainers is included. Conversely, *Intersection Aggregation* produces a counterfactual explanation G' that retains only modifications that are consistently proposed by all base explainers. This corresponds to setting $\tau = 1$, meaning that only edge changes appearing in every counterfactual explanation are applied. These methods serve as intuitive baselines, providing lower and upper bounds on the number of modifications introduced by an aggregated counterfactual explanation.

Iterative Random Aggregation builds on the idea that base explainers act as filters, reducing the search space by producing a set of modifications that belong to valid, though not necessarily optimal, counterfactuals. This method enhances the likelihood of generating a counterfactual by conducting a new search within this constrained modification space. The process begins by querying all base explainers $\mathcal{E}_\Phi^k$ and constructing the union of all modifications proposed by the valid counterfactuals, defined as:

$$\Delta A = \bigcup_{i=1}^{K} \Delta(A, A'_i), \qquad (12)$$

where $\Delta(A, A'_i)$ extracts the differences between the adjacency matrices of the original instance A and each counterfactual explanation A'_i.

Then, the method behaves similarly to *iRand* [28], iterating up to a user-defined percentage of the target instance's edges. In the i-th iteration, i random modifications from ΔA are selected and applied to G, yielding a counterfactual candidate $\bar{G}$. If the prediction for the candidate differs from the one of the original instance $\Phi(\bar{G}) \neq \Phi(G)$, then $G' = \bar{G}$ is returned as the final counterfactual explanation. Otherwise, the process continues until either a valid counterfactual is found or the iteration limit is reached. To further increase the likelihood of generating a valid counterfactual, the method can explore different permutations of i modifications before proceeding to the next iteration. While this approach can yield highly effective counterfactuals in certain cases, it generally lacks stability due to its inherent randomness.

Stochastic Aggregation constructs counterfactual explanations by leveraging probabilistic sampling over an aggregated edge frequency matrix. This approach balances structure-driven modifications with randomness, enhancing both adaptability and robustness. The process begins by selecting all valid counterfactuals from $\mathbb{C}$ and aggregating their adjacency matrices into a cumulative matrix $A_{\text{sum}} = \sum_{G' \in \mathbb{C}} A_{G'}$. This matrix effectively represents an edge frequency distribution across the valid counterfactuals. The values in A_{sum} are then normalized to obtain an edge probability matrix $A_p = A_{\text{sum}}/|\mathbb{C}|$.

Next, the method performs a user-defined number of sampling iterations. In each iteration, a probabilistic sampler selects an edge based on the probabilities in A_p and applies it to construct a counterfactual candidate $\bar{G}$. The candidate is then evaluated based on whether it alters the model's prediction. If the prediction differs from that of the original instance ($\Phi(\bar{G}) \neq \Phi(G)$), the process terminates, and $G' = \bar{G}$ is returned as the final counterfactual explanation. Otherwise, the sampling continues until either a valid counterfactual is found or the iteration limit is reached.

This method synthesizes concepts from previous approaches. On the one hand, it is data-driven, utilizing edge probabilities to mitigate the instability of purely random changes. On the other hand, it benefits from a flexible iteration-based stopping criterion, making it more adaptable and easier to configure compared to methods that rely on fixed frequency thresholds.

Bidirectional Aggregation performs a heuristic search within a constrained modification space, leveraging the union of counterfactuals generated by the base explainers. This method refines counterfactual explanations by first introducing perturbations and then selectively reversing some of them to minimize unnecessary modifications.

The process begins by querying all base explainers to generate counterfactuals G'_i with adjacency matrices A'_i and constructing the perturbation matrix ΔA as in the *Iterative Random Aggregation* method. In the second stage, the method iteratively selects edges from ΔA randomly and perturbs them in G to generate a counterfactual candidate $\bar{G}$. Then, the candidate is evaluated based on whether it alters the model's prediction. If a valid counterfactual $\Phi(\bar{G}) \neq \Phi(G)$ is found, then $G' = \bar{G}$ and the process moves to the refinement stage. In the third stage, the method attempts to reverse some of the perturbations in G' to minimize the number of modifications while preserving the counterfactual condition. This reduction phase follows a strategy similar to *OBS* [1], ensuring that the final explanation G^* remains as close as possible to the original instance.

Although *Bidirectional Aggregation* initially behaves similarly to *Iterative Random Aggregation*, its refinement phase enables it to produce more compact and meaningful counterfactuals. By iteratively reducing unnecessary changes, this approach enhances interpretability while maintaining the validity of the counterfactual explanation (Table 1).

In general, aggregation ensembles have the potential to combine weak explanations into more robust counterfactuals, though their success is not always guaranteed. In cases where aggregation fails to produce a valid counterfactual, a reasonable fallback strategy would be to default to the best-performing individual explanation. However, we have not adopted this approach in this work, as it would introduce additional complexity and obscure a clear evaluation of the aggregation strategies' effectiveness. Similarly, explanation aggregation methods could theoretically be incorporated as base explainers within a selection process. While this could enhance the overall quality of the final explanation, it would significantly increase the computational cost of the selection procedure, making it less practical for large-scale applications.

Table 1. Summary of the proposed ensemble strategies.

Strategy	Type	Description	Strengths	Limitations
IPMCS	Selection	Selects the explanation closest to an ideal point across normalized evaluation metrics.	Balanced across metrics; consistently strong performance.	Computationally intensive; assumes uniform weighting of metrics.
DLES	Selection	Chooses the best base explainer based on average performance over the dataset.	Simple and efficient; stable at dataset level.	Ignores instance-level variation; performs as good as the best base explainer
ILES	Selection	Learns the best explainer for each instance based on its characteristics.	Adaptable to each instance; more efficient	Dependent on the accuracy of the underlying GNN
Frequency	Aggregation	Includes elements appearing in at least τ fraction of base explanations.	Generalizes Union/Intersection; flexible.	Sensitive to the selection of τ.
Union	Aggregation	Combines all unique changes from base explanations.	High recall; ensures inclusion.	May over-modify the graph structure.
Intersection	Aggregation	Retains only shared changes across all base explanations.	High confidence; minimal edit distance.	Too conservative; fails if no overlap exists.
Iterative Random	Aggregation	Samples perturbations iteratively and selects the best candidates over multiple rounds.	Lightweight and adaptable; explores solution space.	Dependent on p and t parameters; highly unstable.
Stochastic	Aggregation	Creates a new graph by selecting the most frequent edges in the base explanations	Simple; constitute a useful baseline.	May still have high variance; depends on edge distribution across base explanations.
Bidirectional	Aggregation	Uses the base explanations to build a counterfactual and then minimizes the changes	Can generate smaller counterfactuals.	Needs similar base counterfactuals.

5 Experimental Analysis

In this section, we leverage the GRETEL framework for evaluating the performance of the GCE methods integrated within our ensemble approach[1]. We begin by detailing the experimental setup, including the datasets, evaluation metrics, and base GCE methods used. Next, we present a comprehensive performance analysis of our proposed approaches. Finally, we conduct a qualitative assessment, comparing the explanations generated by different methods for a representative instance.

5.1 Experimental Setup

Datasets: The proposed methods were evaluated on one synthetic dataset, *Tree-Cycles*, and two real-world datasets, *ASD* and *IMDB-Binary*. These datasets present varying levels of complexity for the oracles, making it more challenging for the explainers to provide accurate counterfactual explanations. Table 2 summarizes key statistics of the datasets.

---

[1] The source code of the ensemble methods and the base explainers, as well as the configuration files for the experiments and the datasets are publicly available at https://github.com/aiim-research/GRETEL.

The *Tree-Cycles (TC)* dataset [44] is a well-known synthetic benchmark. Each instance consists of a graph containing a central tree motif and several cycle motifs, all connected to the tree via single edges. The dataset is divided into two classes: graphs without cycles (class 0) and graphs with cycles (class 1). The number of nodes, cycles, and nodes per cycle can be controlled when generating instances. For this study, we generated a dataset with 128 instances, each containing 28 nodes, ensuring that all explanation methods could be applied without computational constraints.

The *Autism Spectrum Disorder (ASD)* dataset [1] is a real-world graph classification dataset derived from functional magnetic resonance imaging (fMRI) data. In this dataset, nodes correspond to brain Regions of Interest (ROI), and edges represent co-activation between two ROIs. The dataset comprises two classes: individuals diagnosed with *Autism Spectrum Disorder* (ASD) and *Typically Developed* (TD) individuals as the control group. Notably, graph instances in this dataset may be disconnected.

The *IMDB-Binary* dataset is a widely used benchmark in graph classification, particularly within social network analysis. Each graph represents a movie, where nodes correspond to actors in ego-networks. Edges indicate collaborations between actors who have appeared in the same movie. Each graph is labeled as belonging to one of two classes, typically corresponding to different genres or categories (e.g., action vs. romance).

Table 2. Statistical description of the datasets.

Dataset	Tree-Cycles	ASD	IMDB-Binary
# of instances	500	101	1000
Avg # of nodes	28	116	19.77
Avg # of edges	27.566	655.624	96.53
Max # of nodes	28	116	136
# of classes	2	2	2
Class distribution	0.504 : 0.496	0.515 : 0.485	0.5 : 0.5
Graph type	Undirected	Undirected	Undirected
Connected components	One	Multiple	Multiple

Metrics: We evaluated the performance of our proposed methods using a variety of standard metrics, including *Correctness*, *Graph Edit Distance (GED)*, *Runtime*, *Oracle Calls*, *Fidelity*, *Sparsity*, and *Instability*. For detailed definitions of these metrics, refer to Prado-Romero et al. [29] and Guidotti [12]. Each metric provides insights into different aspects of the generated explanations, though their relative importance varies.

Correctness is the most critical metric, as it evaluates a method's ability to generate valid counterfactuals. It is defined as:

$$\text{Correctness}(G, G') = \mathbb{1}[\Phi(G) \neq \Phi(G')], \qquad (13)$$

where $\mathbb{1}[\cdot]$ is the indicator function that returns 1 if G' successfully changes the model's prediction and 0 otherwise.

Graph Edit Distance (GED) [7] measures the structural similarity between the original graph G and its counterfactual G'. Counterfactuals that introduce excessive modifications may be impractical or difficult to interpret. GED quantifies the minimum cost required to transform G into G' through a sequence of graph edit operations, including vertex and edge additions or deletions. Given a set of transformation paths $\mathcal{P}(G, G')$, where each path $\{p_1, p_2, \ldots, p_n\}$ consists of actions p_i with associated costs $\omega(p_i)$, GED is computed as:

$$\text{GED}(G, G') = \min_{\{p_1,\ldots,p_n\} \in \mathcal{P}(G,G')} \sum_{i=1}^{n} \omega(p_i). \tag{14}$$

Sparsity [45] is closely related to *GED* but specifically evaluates the proportion of modifications relative to the size of the original instance. Given a distance function $\mathcal{D}_{\text{inst}}(G, G')$ measuring the difference between G and G', and the instance size $|G|$, sparsity is defined as:

$$\text{Sparsity}(G, G') = \frac{\mathcal{D}_{\text{inst}}(G, G')}{|G|}. \tag{15}$$

The remaining metrics focus on additional aspects of computational efficiency and stability but are considered less central to evaluating the quality of counterfactuals. *Runtime* and *Oracle Calls* assess the computational cost of the methods, providing insights into their efficiency. *Instability* quantifies the variation in counterfactuals produced across multiple runs, offering a perspective on robustness; however, a method can exhibit high stability while still performing poorly in terms of *Correctness*. Lastly, *Fidelity* evaluates the explainers' dependency on the Oracle's quality, measuring their reliability in different scenarios. Since these metrics do not directly assess the validity or actionability of counterfactual explanations, we do not provide explicit mathematical definitions for them.

Base Explainers: We selected OBS [1], RSGG [27], and iRand [28] as base explainers for our ensemble methods.

OBS is a heuristic method that initially performs a random search to find a counterfactual and then iteratively reduces the size of the explanation by randomly undoing some modifications. Due to the non-deterministic nature of this approach, we employed three instances of OBS using default parameters to capture variability in its generated counterfactuals.

iRand is an explainer designed as a baseline GCE method. It generates counterfactuals by randomly perturbing the edges of the target graph. The method incrementally increases the number of perturbed edges up to a specified percentage of the total graph edges, denoted as p. For each iteration, it evaluates t different perturbation combinations. In our experiments, we set $p = 0.1$ and $t = 2$. Additionally, we considered three variants of *iRand* to analyze the effect of different perturbation strategies: one that performs only edge removals, another that performs only edge additions, and a third that applies both modifications.

RSGG is a generative approach that employs GANs to produce GCEs that conform to the data distribution of the target instance. We used the method's default parameters, modifying only the number of training epochs (e_p), with $e_p \in [300, 400, 500]$.

Parameters: The results reported for the *Frequency* aggregation strategy correspond to a fixed threshold of $\tau = 0.5$. The extreme cases $\tau = 0$ and $\tau = 1$ are reported as the *Union* and *Intersection* strategies, respectively. This choice illustrates the mid-point behavior of frequency-based voting while making explicit its relation to other aggregation variants. For the *Iterative Random* aggregation strategy, the perturbation budget p is set to 100%, meaning the method iteratively attempts to perturb i edges, where i ranges up to the total number of changes proposed by the base explainers. At each iteration, the method evaluates $t = 10$ candidate perturbations of size i.

5.2 Quantitative Performance Analysis

In the results, metrics are reported based on 10-fold cross-validation. A × is placed in table cells where the corresponding *Correctness* value is null, indicating no counterfactual was produced. Bold values highlight the best overall performance, while underlined values denote the second-best results. Additionally, a × may appear in the *Oracle Calls* column if the explainer does not query the oracle during inference.

Table 3. Results on TC@28. Training Oracle Accuracy = 100%

		Runtime↓	GED↓	Correctness↑	Oracle Calls↓	Sparsity↓	Fidelity↑	Instability↓
SoA	CF² [37]	0.011 ± 0.017	28.533 ± 0.234	0.531 ± 0.015	×	0.675 ± 0.004	0.531 ± 0.015	×
	CLEAR [19]	0.030 ± 0.040	52.408 ± 1.556	0.469 ± 0.015	×	1.263 ± 0.037	0.469 ± 0.015	1.292 ± 0.081
Base	OBS [1]	0.253 ± 0.171	1.326 ± 0.097	0.953 ± 0.051	408.287 ± 108.375	0.032 ± 0.002	0.953 ± 0.051	1.012 ± 0.007
	RSGG [27]	1.779 ± 0.870	14.465 ± 0.218	0.829 ± 0.074	157.822 ± 64.206	0.346 ± 0.005	0.829 ± 0.074	0.694 ± 0.029
	iRand	**0.005 ± 0.002**	1.000 ± 0.000	0.461 ± 0.039	9.103 ± 0.396	**0.024 ± 0.000**	0.461 ± 0.039	0.995 ± 0.002
Selection	DLES	0.127 ± 0.093	1.287 ± 0.122	0.977 ± 0.035	218.499 ± 89.559	0.031 ± 0.003	0.977 ± 0.035	1.013 ± 0.009
	IPMCS (Only GED)	6.386 ± 1.966	1.221 ± 0.113	**1.000 ± 0.000**	1651.650 ± 305.423	0.029 ± 0.003	**1.000 ± 0.000**	1.018 ± 0.008
	IPMCS	5.426 ± 2.150	1.213 ± 0.110	**1.000 ± 0.000**	1379.719 ± 116.237	0.029 ± 0.003	**1.000 ± 0.000**	1.019 ± 0.010
	ILES	0.279 ± 0.274	1.324 ± 0.153	0.969 ± 0.052	263.490 ± 172.193	0.032 ± 0.004	0.969 ± 0.052	1.017 ± 0.007
Aggregation	Intersection	6.126 ± 3.261	×	×	1520.701 ± 442.423	×	×	0.977 ± 0.002
	Frequency	7.602 ± 3.719	6.825 ± 1.191	0.477 ± 0.043	1758.019 ± 340.552	0.162 ± 0.028	0.477 ± 0.043	0.935 ± 0.015
	Union	7.765 ± 3.396	29.539 ± 3.578	0.594 ± 0.118	1496.044 ± 302.124	0.706 ± 0.087	0.594 ± 0.118	0.585 ± 0.054
	IRandom	5.560 ± 2.641	1.102 ± 0.085	0.858 ± 0.081	1475.080 ± 298.785	0.026 ± 0.002	0.858 ± 0.081	1.012 ± 0.009
	Stochastic	7.498 ± 3.880	6.616 ± 0.557	**1.000 ± 0.000**	1641.851 ± 384.278	0.158 ± 0.013	**1.000 ± 0.000**	0.896 ± 0.016
	Bidirectional	5.558 ± 1.972	1.197 ± 0.108	**1.000 ± 0.000**	1480.790 ± 319.196	0.029 ± 0.003	**1.000 ± 0.000**	1.018 ± 0.009

Table 3 presents the results of the proposed ensemble methods on the *Tree-Cycles* dataset. In this dataset, transitioning from a tree to a graph with cycles is relatively straightforward, as adding a single edge to the tree is sufficient. However, converting a graph with cycles into a tree requires identifying and removing the edges that form the cycles, making the task more challenging.

The proposed *IPMCS* selection method, along with the stochastic and bidirectional aggregation methods, outperforms the base explainers in terms of *Correctness*, achieving a perfect score of 100%.

In terms of structural distance, the base *iRand* explainer and the *IRandom-Aggregation* method achieve the best *GED* values. However, their lower *Correctness* suggests that these methods may perform well when transitioning from a tree to a graph with cycles but struggle with the reverse transformation. Since these methods default to returning the target instance when they fail to generate a counterfactual, the *GED* of such incorrect instances is not considered. In practice, the method that achieves the best overall *GED* value is *Bidirectional Aggregation*, followed closely by all proposed selection methods.

Regarding *Runtime* and *Oracle Calls*, the selection and aggregation methods are generally 3× to 5× more computationally expensive than the base methods. *ILES* was specifically designed to mitigate this issue, achieving a runtime and number of *Oracle Calls* comparable to its base explainers while also attaining a strong 96.9% *Correctness* and an improved *GED* score over its base counterparts.

In terms of stability, the base methods generally exhibit greater consistency compared to the ensemble methods. An exception is *Union Aggregation*, which, despite being stable, has lower *Correctness*. The reduced stability of ensemble methods can be attributed to the significant variations among the counterfactuals generated by different base explainers.

Overall, for this dataset, the selection and aggregation methods generate higher-quality explanations than individual explainers, balancing correctness, minimality, and computational cost.

Table 4. Results on ASD dataset. Training Oracle Accuracy = 77.4% ± 10.5%

		Runtime↓	GED↓	Correctness↑	Oracle Calls↓	Sparsity↓	Fidelity↑	Instability↓
SoA	CF² [37]	0.009 ± 0.018	655.544 ± 1.701	0.465 ± 0.158	×	1.477 ± 0.001	0.288 ± 0.085	×
	CLEAR [19]	0.131 ± 0.054	1179.439 ± 34.041	0.576 ± 0.187	×	2.659 ± 0.075	0.380 ± 0.240	1.274 ± 0.036
Base	OBS [1]	0.772 ± 0.233	9.716 ± 2.444	1.000 ± 0.000	665.918 ± 62.170	0.022 ± 0.006	0.542 ± 0.222	1.002 ± 0.001
	RSGG [27]	40.359 ± 17.743	349.689 ± 27.817	0.426 ± 0.136	626.314 ± 100.813	0.789 ± 0.063	0.206 ± 0.183	0.873 ± 0.044
	iRand	0.074 ± 0.034	27.408 ± 17.165	0.290 ± 0.145	211.307 ± 13.803	0.062 ± 0.038	0.010 ± 0.094	1.011 ± 0.005
Selection	DLES	0.870 ± 0.367	9.934 ± 2.710	1.000 ± 0.000	694.392 ± 93.110	0.022 ± 0.006	0.547 ± 0.210	1.002 ± 0.001
	IPMCS (Only GED)	109.273 ± 15.479	**9.035 ± 2.561**	1.000 ± 0.000	6363.050 ± 641.644	0.020 ± 0.006	0.547 ± 0.210	1.003 ± 0.002
	IPMCS	117.804 ± 34.266	9.119 ± 2.654	1.000 ± 0.000	6441.448 ± 590.034	1.072 ± 0.148	0.547 ± 0.210	1.002 ± 0.001
	ILES	0.857 ± 0.146	9.689 ± 2.533	1.000 ± 0.000	712.379 ± 90.594	0.022 ± 0.006	0.547 ± 0.210	1.002 ± 0.001
Aggregation	Intersection	132.224 ± 22.971	×	×	6443.386 ± 634.546	×	×	0.999 ± 0.000
	Frequency	134.653 ± 18.752	86.640 ± 19.530	0.405 ± 0.119	6435.220 ± 577.988	0.195 ± 0.044	0.289 ± 0.124	0.970 ± 0.008
	Union	136.229 ± 18.480	475.766 ± 65.861	1.000 ± 0.000	6441.448 ± 590.034	1.072 ± 0.148	**0.547 ± 0.210**	0.942 ± 0.106
	IRandom	149.888 ± 24.812	5.900 ± 8.549	0.079 ± 0.075	6635.115 ± 621.502	0.013 ± 0.019	0.021 ± 0.058	0.999 ± 0.000
	Stochastic	137.148 ± 19.681	98.207 ± 15.415	1.000 ± 0.000	6393.985 ± 576.919	0.221 ± 0.035	**0.547 ± 0.210**	0.988 ± 0.018
	Bidirectional	184.261 ± 27.957	**11.328 ± 2.541**	0.768 ± 0.126	7153.511 ± 673.567	0.026 ± 0.006	0.354 ± 0.191	1.003 ± 0.001

Table 4 presents the results on the *ASD* dataset. This dataset poses challenges for some oracles, as graph classification depends on the co-activation (edges) between brain regions, particularly when specific sets of regions exhibit stronger co-activation than others. The training oracle achieves an accuracy of 77.4% ± 10.5%, introducing an additional layer of uncertainty that may impact methods relying heavily on oracle queries. As observed in the results, *OBS* [1] significantly outperforms the other base methods, achieving perfect *Correctness* while maintaining a low *GED*. However, its dominance poses challenges within ensemble methods, particularly aggregation approaches, as its counterfactuals may overshadow those of weaker base explainers.

The selection methods demonstrate strong performance, achieving 100% *Correctness* while slightly improving *GED* compared to the base explainers. Among them, *ILES* achieves computational efficiency, maintaining a runtime comparable to the base methods (0.857 ± 0.146 seconds) while requiring significantly fewer oracle calls than IPMCS methods. *IPMCS* variants also perform well but at a higher computational costs. These results highlight the potential of *ILES* in balancing accuracy, efficiency, and structural similarity in counterfactual generation.

Aggregation methods, on the other hand, exhibit inconsistent performance on this dataset, suggesting that base explainers do not frequently share common counterfactual solutions. This lack of consistency among the base explanations limits the effectiveness of aggregation methods, preventing them from identifying reliable modifications. While *Union* and *Stochastic Aggregation* achieve 100% *Correctness* their explanations have a high structural dissimilarity with respect to the original instance. A notable case is *Bidirectional Aggregation*, which achieves a moderate *Correctness* of 76.8% while maintaining one of the best *GED* values (11.328). However, this improvement comes at the cost of efficiency, as it requires the most oracle calls.

Overall, the results indicate that selection-based ensembles provide a reliable approach to counterfactual generation on this dataset. While aggregation methods have the potential to refine explanations, their effectiveness appears to be dataset-dependent

Table 5. Results on IMDB-Binary dataset. Training Oracle Accuracy = 72.0% $\pm$ 4.1%

		Runtime↓	GED↓	Correctness↑	Oracle Calls↓	Sparsity↓	Fidelity↑	Instability↓
SoA	CF² [37]	**0.001 ± 0.000**	102.765 ± 16.001	0.212 ± 0.050	x	0.494 ± 0.038	0.082 ± 0.025	x
	CLEAR [19]	0.038 ± 0.005	1063.519 ± 99.552	0.416 ± 0.185	x	4.906 ± 0.870	0.215 ± 0.099	53.855 ± 6.183
Base	OBS [1]	2.814 ± 0.176	45.266 ± 9.152	0.492 ± 0.055	2445.426 ± 175.845	0.187 ± 0.023	0.233 ± 0.071	1.625 ± 0.119
	RSGG [27]	10.839 ± 1.350	95.674 ± 4.613	0.978 ± 0.012	**249.082 ± 22.744**	0.517 ± 0.029	0.450 ± 0.075	4.010 ± 0.345
	iRand	8.048 ± 0.243	97.483 ± 9.494	0.503 ± 0.056	2076.997 ± 148.520	0.471 ± 0.045	0.232 ± 0.062	4.982 ± 0.844
Selection	DLES	7.039 ± 1.007	94.742 ± 5.512	0.975 ± 0.013	250.458 ± 21.941	0.515 ± 0.031	0.447 ± 0.074	4.019 ± 0.332
	IPMCS (Only GED)	58.729 ± 5.934	73.571 ± 7.118	**0.999 ± 0.003**	12529.743 ± 823.316	0.397 ± 0.031	**0.471 ± 0.074**	3.796 ± 0.302
	IPMCS	62.804 ± 5.674	67.131 ± 4.921	0.932 ± 0.023	12533.799 ± 852.549	0.391 ± 0.030	0.420 ± 0.065	3.781 ± 0.296
	ILES	2.720 ± 0.219	45.598 ± 10.649	0.489 ± 0.046	2467.220 ± 161.522	0.188 ± 0.033	0.235 ± 0.067	1.600 ± 0.160
Aggregation	Intersection	65.134 ± 6.948	**2.679 ± 1.815**	0.536 ± 0.047	12525.067 ± 813.275	**0.010 ± 0.007**	0.235 ± 0.037	**1.045 ± 0.045**
	Frequency	66.673 ± 8.322	311.904 ± 32.202	0.931 ± 0.024	12529.632 ± 843.843	1.877 ± 0.198	0.415 ± 0.067	15.369 ± 1.496
	Union	64.825 ± 6.997	515.712 ± 38.445	0.827 ± 0.023	12523.969 ± 833.379	2.763 ± 0.187	0.388 ± 0.063	25.823 ± 2.841
	IRandom	99.005 ± 11.212	9.779 ± 7.548	0.553 ± 0.043	13799.622 ± 900.124	0.036 ± 0.025	0.246 ± 0.043	1.051 ± 0.039
	Stochastic	68.886 ± 6.524	77.343 ± 7.424	0.773 ± 0.051	12548.910 ± 835.415	0.428 ± 0.036	0.344 ± 0.058	4.974 ± 0.256
	Bidirectional	81.812 ± 9.153	35.827 ± 8.596	0.639 ± 0.044	13499.189 ± 911.300	0.142 ± 0.029	0.310 ± 0.053	1.393 ± 0.145

Table 5 presents the results on the *IMDB-Binary* dataset, where the oracle achieves a training accuracy of only 72.0% $\pm$ 4.1%. This relatively low accuracy introduces additional uncertainty, particularly affecting learning-based explainers. Among the base methods, *RSGG* [27] achieves the highest *Correctness*

(97.8%), but at the cost of a higher *GED*. Conversely, *OBS* [1] produces counterfactuals with lower *GED* but has a substantially lower *Correctness* (49.2%). The high instability observed across all methods is notable, with some aggregation strategies exhibiting extreme variance.

Selection methods generally perform well. *IPMCS (Only GED)* achieves the highest *Correctness* (99.9%) while maintaining a competitive *GED*, though at a significantly higher computational cost. *DLES* selects *RSGG* as the best explainer for the dataset, yielding performance identical to the base method. In contrast, *ILES*, which performed effectively in other datasets, struggled here due to the lower oracle accuracy affecting the selection model's reliability.

Aggregation methods exhibit mixed results. *Intersection Aggregation* achieves the lowest *GED* (2.679) but struggles with *Correctness* (53.6%). *Bidirectional Aggregation* offers a reasonable trade-off, attaining a *GED* of 35.8 while maintaining *Correctness* at 63.9%. However, most aggregation methods suffer from high instability, reducing their overall reliability.

Overall, *IPMCS* emerges as the most robust method across datasets, striking the best balance between correctness and explanation size. While aggregation methods can refine counterfactuals in structured domains, their effectiveness appears to diminish in settings with high oracle uncertainty. Despite these challenges, they demonstrate potential for generating improved explanations over individual base methods. A promising future direction could involve integrating selection and aggregation strategies to leverage the advantages of both approaches.

5.3 Qualitative Analysis

Fig. 1. (*Best viewed in color*) Counterfactuals generated by our aggregation methods and SoA approaches on a random TC@28 instance. Each block shows the adjacency matrix: black = unchanged edges, green = additions, red = deletions. (Color figure online)

To better understand the quality of the counterfactual graphs generated by our ensemble approach and state-of-the-art (SoA) methods, we present a visual comparison in Fig. 1. The figure illustrates the adjacency matrix of a randomly chosen instance from the Tree-Cycles dataset, which contains a single cycle and 28 nodes. Each pixel represents an edge: black pixels indicate edges retained from the original instance, red pixels denote removed edges, and green pixels correspond to newly added edges. This visualization provides a direct comparison of the explainers based on their structural modifications.

A correct counterfactual explanation for this instance should involve removing a single edge from the cycle (i.e., two red pixels for an undirected edge). Selection-based ensembles are omitted from the figure, as they replicate the behavior of OBS for this instance. As shown, CF^2 removes all edges, effectively destroying the graph structure. *CLEAR* removes and adds multiple edges, forming additional cycles, which contradicts the expected counterfactual transformation. *iRand* fails to generate a valid counterfactual and instead returns the original instance. While *RSGG* and *Union* produce valid counterfactuals, they remove more edges than necessary, leading to excessive perturbation. Among all methods, only *OBS* and the *Bidirectional Aggregation* approach produce correct and minimal counterfactual explanations.

This comparison highlights the limitations of existing base explainers, which often fail to generate satisfactory counterfactuals even in relatively simple graph datasets like Tree-Cycles. However, ensemble approaches demonstrate the potential to integrate the strengths of multiple methods, leading to improved explanation quality.

6 Conclusion

In this paper, we introduced and evaluated novel ensemble-based methods for generating Graph Counterfactual Explanations (GCEs) through selection and aggregation strategies. These approaches were designed to address the inherent limitations of individual explainers, improving the correctness, robustness, and diversity of counterfactual explanations across a variety of datasets.

Our experimental results demonstrated that the *Ideal-Point Multi-Criteria Selection (IPMCS)* method consistently achieved the highest correctness while preserving the structural similarity of counterfactuals to the original instance. This highlights its ability to systematically identify the most effective explainer for each case. The *DLES* and *ILES* methods offered a strong trade-off between performance and computational efficiency, but their effectiveness varied depending on the dataset. On the other hand, aggregation-based methods showed the potential to produce explanations that surpassed those of any individual base method. However, they exhibited greater variability, excelling under certain conditions while struggling in scenarios with high oracle uncertainty.

A promising avenue for future research is the integration of selection and aggregation techniques to harness the strengths of both approaches. Adaptive ensemble strategies, such as dynamic weighting or reinforcement learning-based selection, could further enhance the quality of counterfactual explanations. Additionally, more sophisticated aggregation mechanisms that account for structural consistency across multiple explainers may lead to even more interpretable and actionable counterfactuals. Enhancing the prediction model for the *ILES* method–potentially incorporating confidence-aware strategies that default to *IPMCS* when predictions are unreliable–could significantly improve its robustness. Moreover, expanding its capabilities beyond explainer selection to also determine the most suitable aggregation strategy represents an exciting direction for future work.

Ultimately, this work highlights the potential of ensemble learning to enhance counterfactual explanations for graph-based models. By evaluating diverse selection and aggregation strategies, we provide a foundation for advancing explainability in Graph Neural Networks. Our methods represent a step toward more robust and adaptable GCEs, paving the way for high-quality explanations across diverse domains.

Acknowledgments. The numerical simulations have been realized on the HPC cluster of the Department of Information Engineering, Computer Science and Mathematics (DISIM) at the University of L'Aquila. The work is partially funded by the European Union - NextGenerationEU under the Italian Ministry of University and Research (MUR) National Innovation Ecosystem grant ECS00000041 - VITALITY - CUP E13C22001060006, by National Recovery and Resilience Plan (Piano Nazionale di Ripresa e Resilienza, PNRR) - Project: "SoBigData.it - Strengthening the Italian RI for Social Mining and Big Data Analytics" - Prot. IR0000013 - Avviso n. 3264 del 28/12/2021, and by the "ICSC Centro Nazionale di Ricerca in High Performance Computing, Big Data and Quantum Computing."

Disclosure of Interests. The authors have no competing interests to declare that are relevant to the content of this article.

References

1. Abrate, C., Bonchi, F.: Counterfactual graphs for explainable classification of brain networks. In: Proceedings of the 27th ACM SIGKDD Conference on Knowledge Discovery & Data Mining, pp. 2495–2504 (2021)
2. Alon, U.: Network motifs: theory and experimental approaches. Nat. Rev. Genet. **8**(6), 450–461 (2007)
3. Artelt, A., Vrachimis, S., Eliades, D., Polycarpou, M., Hammer, B.: One explanation to rule them all–ensemble consistent explanations. arXiv preprint arXiv:2205.08974 (2022)
4. Bajaj, M., et al.: Robust counterfactual explanations on graph neural networks. Adv. Neural. Inf. Process. Syst. **34**, 5644–5655 (2021)
5. Branke, J., Deb, K., Miettinen, K., Słowiński, R. (eds.): Multiobjective Optimization. LNCS, vol. 5252. Springer, Heidelberg (2008). https://doi.org/10.1007/978-3-540-88908-3
6. Breiman, L.: Bagging predictors. Mach. Learn. **24**(2), 123–140 (1996)
7. Bunke, H.: Recent developments in graph matching. In: Proceedings 15th International Conference on Pattern Recognition, ICPR-2000, vol. 2, pp. 117–124. IEEE (2000)
8. Campagner, A., Ciucci, D., Cabitza, F.: Aggregation models in ensemble learning: a large-scale comparison. Inf. Fusion (2022)
9. Commission, E.: On artificial intelligence–a European approach to excellence and trust (2020)

10. Dutta, S., Long, J., Mishra, S., Tilli, C., Magazzeni, D.: Robust counterfactual explanations for tree-based ensembles. In: Chaudhuri, K., Jegelka, S., Song, L., Szepesvari, C., Niu, G., Sabato, S. (eds.) Proceedings of the 39th International Conference on Machine Learning. Proceedings of Machine Learning Research, vol. 162, pp. 5742–5756. PMLR, 17–23 July 2022
11. Faber, L., Moghaddam, A.K., Wattenhofer, R.: Contrastive graph neural network explanation. In: Proceedings of 37th Graph Representation Learning and Beyond Workshop at ICML 2020, p. 28. International Conference on Machine Learning (2020)
12. Guidotti, R.: Counterfactual explanations and how to find them: literature review and benchmarking. Data Mining and Knowledge Discovery, pp. 1–55 (2022)
13. Guidotti, R., Ruggieri, S.: Ensemble of counterfactual explainers. In: International Conference on Discovery Science, pp. 358–368. Springer (2021)
14. Huang, Z., Kosan, M., Medya, S., Ranu, S., Singh, A.: Global counterfactual explainer for graph neural networks. In: Proceedings of the Sixteenth ACM International Conference on Web Search and Data Mining, pp. 141–149 (2023)
15. Jha, K., Saha, S., Singh, H.: Prediction of protein-protein interaction using graph neural networks. Sci. Rep. **12**(1), 8360 (2022)
16. Kipf, T.N., Welling, M.: Semi-supervised classification with graph convolutional networks. In: 5th International Conference on Learning Representations, ICLR 2017, Toulon, France, 24–26 April 2017, Conference Track Proceedings. OpenReview.net (2017), https://openreview.net/forum?id=SJU4ayYgl
17. Liu, Y., Chen, C., Liu, Y., Zhang, X., Xie, S.: Multi-objective explanations of gnn predictions. In: 2021 IEEE International Conference on Data Mining (ICDM), pp. 409–418. IEEE (2021)
18. Livi, L., Rizzi, A.: The graph matching problem. Pattern Anal. Appl. **16**, 253–283 (2013)
19. Ma, J., Guo, R., Mishra, S., Zhang, A., Li, J.: CLEAR: generative counterfactual explanations on graphs. In: Oh, A.H., Agarwal, A., Belgrave, D., Cho, K. (eds.) Advances in Neural Information Processing Systems (2022), https://openreview.net/forum?id=YR-s5leIvh
20. McAleese, S., Keane, M.: A comparative analysis of counterfactual explanation methods for text classifiers. arXiv preprint arXiv:2411.02643 (2024)
21. Musch, S., Borrelli, M., Kerrigan, C.: The eu ai act as global artificial intelligence regulation. Available at SSRN 4549261 (2023)
22. Nguyen, T.M., Quinn, T.P., Nguyen, T., Tran, T.: Explaining black box drug target prediction through model agnostic counterfactual samples. IEEE/ACM Trans. Comput. Biol. Bioinf. (2022)
23. Numeroso, D., Bacciu, D.: Meg: Generating molecular counterfactual explanations for deep graph networks. In: 2021 International Joint Conference on Neural Networks (IJCNN), pp. 1–8. IEEE (2021)
24. Piaggesi, S., Bodria, F., Guidotti, R., Giannotti, F., Pedreschi, D.: Counterfactual and prototypical explanations for tabular data via interpretable latent space. IEEE Access (2024)
25. Prado-Romero, M.A., Prenkaj, B., Stilo, G.: Developing and evaluating graph counterfactual explanation with gretel. In: Proceedings of the Sixteenth ACM International Conference on Web Search and Data Mining, pp. 1180–1183 (2023)
26. Prado-Romero, M.A., Prenkaj, B., Stilo, G.: Revisiting countergan for counterfactual explainability of graphs. In: Maughan, K., Liu, R., Burns, T.F. (eds.) The First Tiny Papers Track at ICLR 2023, Tiny Papers @ ICLR 2023, Kigali, Rwanda, 5 May 2023. OpenReview.net (2023)

27. Prado-Romero, M.A., Prenkaj, B., Stilo, G.: Robust stochastic graph generator for counterfactual explanations. Proc. AAAI Conf. Artif. Intell. **38**(19), 21518–21526 (2024)
28. Prado-Romero, M.A., Prenkaj, B., Stilo, G.: Are generative-based graph counterfactual explainers worth it? In: Meo, R., Silvestri, F. (eds.) Machine Learning and Principles and Practice of Knowledge Discovery in Databases, pp. 152–170. Springer, Cham (2025)
29. Prado-Romero, M.A., Prenkaj, B., Stilo, G., Giannotti, F.: A survey on graph counterfactual explanations: definitions, methods, evaluation, and research challenges. ACM Comput. Surv. **56**(7) (2024)
30. Prado-Romero, M.A., Stilo, G.: Gretel: graph counterfactual explanation evaluation framework. In: Proceedings of the 31st ACM International Conference on Information and Knowledge Management, ACM (2022)
31. Sagi, O., Rokach, L.: Ensemble learning: a survey. Wiley Interdisc. Rev. Data Min. Knowl. Disc. **8**(4), e1249 (2018)
32. Scarselli, F., Gori, M., Tsoi, A., Hagenbuchner, M., Monfardini, G.: The graph neural network model. IEEE Trans. Neural Networks **20**(1), 61–80 (2008)
33. Schapire, R.E.: The strength of weak learnability. Mach. Learn. **5**(2), 197–227 (1990)
34. Skulimowski, A.: Applicability of ideal points in multicriteria decision-making. In: Proceedings of the 9th International Conference on Multiple Criteria Decision-Making, Fairfax, USA. pp. 5–8 (1990)
35. Stepka, I., Lango, M., Stefanowski, J.: A multi-criteria approach for selecting an explanation from the set of counterfactuals produced by an ensemble of explainers. Int. J. Appl. Math. Comput. Sci. **34**(1), 119–133 (2024)
36. Steuer, R.: Multiple Criteria optimization: theory, computation, and application. (WILEY SERIES IN PROBABILITY AND MATHEMATICAL STATISTICS), Wiley (1986), https://books.google.it/books?id=0H9jQgAACAAJ
37. Tan, J., Geng, S., Fu, Z., Ge, Y., Xu, S., Li, Y., Zhang, Y.: Learning and evaluating graph neural network explanations based on counterfactual and factual reasoning. In: Proceedings of the ACM Web Conference 2022, WWW 2022, pp. 1018–1027. ACM, New York, NY, USA (2022)
38. Wellawatte, G.P., Seshadri, A., White, A.D.: Model agnostic generation of counterfactual explanations for molecules. Chem. Sci. **13**(13), 3697–3705 (2022)
39. Wieder, O., et al.: A compact review of molecular property prediction with graph neural networks. Drug Discov. Today Technol. **37**, 1–12 (2020)
40. Wolpert, D.H.: Stacked generalization. Neural Netw. **5**(2), 241–259 (1992)
41. Wu, S., Tang, Y., Zhu, Y., Wang, L., Xie, X., Tan, T.: Session-based recommendation with graph neural networks. In: Proceedings of the AAAI Conference on Artificial Intelligence, vol. 33, pp. 346–353 (2019)
42. Wu, X., et al.: Clare: a semi-supervised community detection algorithm. In: Proceedings of the 28th ACM SIGKDD Conference on Knowledge Discovery and Data Mining, pp. 2059–2069 (2022)
43. Xu, K., Hu, W., Leskovec, J., Jegelka, S.: How powerful are graph neural networks? In: 7th International Conference on Learning Representations, ICLR 2019, New Orleans, LA, USA, 6–9 May 2019. OpenReview.net (2019), https://openreview.net/forum?id=ryGs6iA5Km
44. Ying, Z., Bourgeois, D., You, J., Zitnik, M., Leskovec, J.: Gnnexplainer: generating explanations for graph neural networks. In: Advances in Neural Information Processing Systems, vol. 32 (2019)

45. Yuan, H., Yu, H., Gui, S., Ji, S.: Explainability in graph neural networks: a taxonomic survey. IEEE Trans. Pattern Anal. Mach. Intell. (2022)
46. Zemni, M., Chen, M., Zablocki, E., Ben-Younes, H., Pérez, P., Cord, M.: Octet: object-aware counterfactual explanations. In: Proceedings of the IEEE/CVF Conference on Computer Vision and Pattern Recognition (CVPR), pp. 15062–15071, June 2023

Open Access This chapter is licensed under the terms of the Creative Commons Attribution 4.0 International License (http://creativecommons.org/licenses/by/4.0/), which permits use, sharing, adaptation, distribution and reproduction in any medium or format, as long as you give appropriate credit to the original author(s) and the source, provide a link to the Creative Commons license and indicate if changes were made.

The images or other third party material in this chapter are included in the chapter's Creative Commons license, unless indicated otherwise in a credit line to the material. If material is not included in the chapter's Creative Commons license and your intended use is not permitted by statutory regulation or exceeds the permitted use, you will need to obtain permission directly from the copyright holder.

Explainable Sequential Decision Making

Leveraging XAI Techniques for Context-Aware Energy Consumption Forecasting

Brígida Teixeira[1], Tiago Pinto[2], and Zita Vale[1(✉)]

[1] GECAD - Research Group on Intelligent Engineering and Computing for Advanced Innovation and Development, LASI - Intelligent Systems Associate LAboratory, ISEP, Polytechnic of Porto, R. Dr. António Bernardino de Almeida, 431, 4249-015 Porto, Portugal
{bct,zav}@isep.ipp.pt

[2] Universidade de Trás-os-Montes e Alto Douro e INESC-TEC, Quinta de Prados, 5000-801 Vila Real, Portugal
tiagopinto@utad.pt

Abstract. This study proposes a comprehensive framework integrating eXplainable Artificial Intelligence (XAI) techniques with clustering-based context extraction to enhance energy consumption forecasting in modern office buildings. By leveraging explanation vectors derived from state-of-the-art XAI methods such as SHAP and LIME, our framework identifies latent operational contexts from sensor data aggregated at 15-min intervals. These contexts enable the tailoring of predictive models through feature augmentation, context-specific training, and transfer learning strategies, thereby improving forecasting accuracy compared to conventional approaches. To identify the best-performing models for each context, hyperparameter optimization via grid search is employed across multiple algorithms–including Gradient Boosting, Random Forest, and K-Nearest Neighbors. Extensive experiments demonstrate that context-aware models significantly outperform baseline methods, achieving up to a 7% improvement in the coefficient of determination (R^2) and a marked reduction in error metrics. Our findings underscore the importance of integrating XAI with data-driven modeling to enhance predictive performance and model interpretability, which are critical for practical energy management and decision-making in complex building environments.

Keywords: Building Energy Management · Clustering · Energy Forecasting · eXplainable Artificial Intelligence (XAI) · LIME · SHAP

1 Introduction

The global energy sector is transforming and is driven by the urgent need for sustainability, efficiency, and integration of renewable energy sources. Buildings play a crucial role in this transition, accounting for approximately 40% of total energy consumption worldwide, making them one of the most significant contributors to carbon emissions [1]. The increasing electrification of heating and cooling systems and the growing adoption of distributed energy resources (DERs) further intensify the complexity of energy management in modern buildings [2]. To address these challenges, advanced forecasting techniques are necessary to optimize energy usage, enhance grid stability, and support proactive decision-making in Building Energy Management Systems [3].

Energy forecasting enables informed decision-making by anticipating future consumption patterns, allowing for efficient energy allocation and load balancing [4]. Short-term forecasts support real-time operational adjustments, anomaly detection, and demand-side management strategies [5]. Medium-term forecasting is critical for optimizing HVAC (Heating, Ventilation, and Air Conditioning) system scheduling, energy procurement, and facility maintenance [6]. At the same time, long-term forecasts guide infrastructure investments, energy policy planning, and capacity expansion [7]. Recent advancements in deep learning have significantly improved forecasting accuracy, with models such as Long Short-Term Memory (LSTM) networks and Convolutional Neural Networks (CNNs) surpassing traditional statistical methods in handling high-dimensional, nonlinear energy consumption data [8].

One of the main challenges in energy forecasting is accounting for the variability introduced by different operational contexts. Energy consumption patterns in buildings are influenced by occupancy levels, environmental conditions, equipment usage, and seasonal variations [9]. Clustering techniques have been increasingly adopted to segment energy data into meaningful operational contexts, enabling predictive models to be trained separately for different usage conditions [10]. This contextualization significantly enhances forecasting performance, allowing models to adapt to the unique characteristics of each context rather than relying on a single global model that may struggle with diverse patterns [11].

Explainable Artificial Intelligence (XAI) has become an indispensable tool in energy forecasting by providing transparency and interpretability to complex machine learning models. Advanced XAI techniques, such as Shapley Additive Explanations (SHAP) and Local Interpretable Model-Agnostic Explanations (LIME), allow for an in-depth analysis of feature importance, helping energy managers understand the key drivers behind energy consumption predictions [12]. These methods enhance trust in AI-driven decision-making by offering insights into the relationships between input variables and forecasted outputs. However, the effectiveness of explainability in energy forecasting can be further improved by incorporating context awareness. Context-aware XAI frameworks must consider various operational conditions, user roles, and targeted objectives to generate more meaningful explanations that align with real-world decision-making needs [13]. This approach ensures that explanations are interpretable and relevant to the surrounding environment, time-series dependencies, and system constraints. Furthermore, integrating mission contexts into explainability mechanisms allows for model refinement, debugging system errors, bias detec-

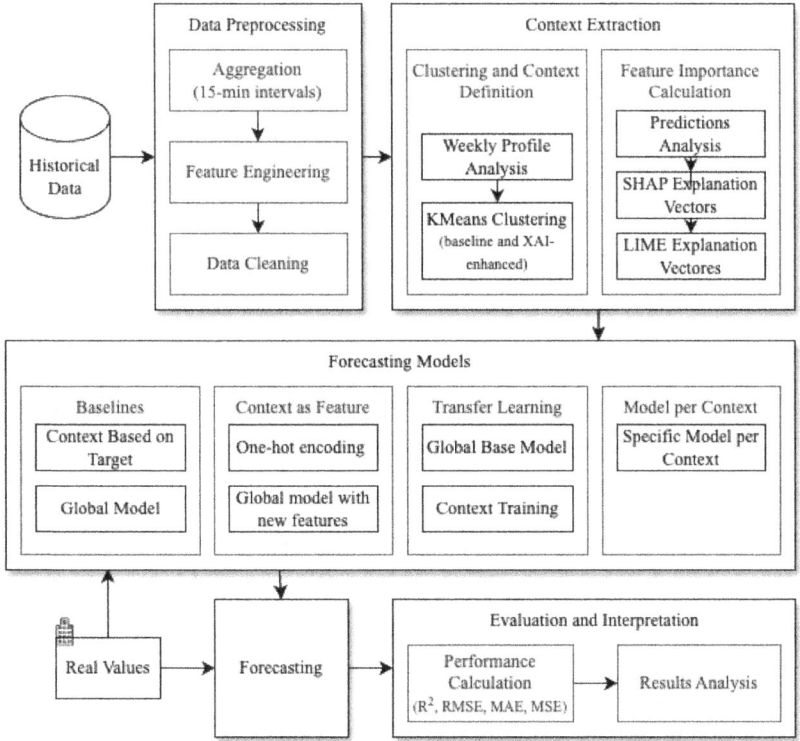

Fig. 1. Overview of the proposed methodology.

tion, and a deeper understanding of AI learning processes, making XAI a more practical and adaptive tool for energy management [14].

This paper proposes a framework built upon these insights by integrating XAI-derived explanation vectors into the clustering process to extract meaningful operational contexts. These contexts are then leveraged to enhance model training through feature augmentation, specialized context-dependent models, and transfer learning. Additionally, hyperparameter optimization via grid search is employed across multiple forecasting algorithms to ensure that each model variant is optimally configured.

The remainder of the paper is organized as follows: Sect. 2 details the methodology; Sect. 3 describes the case study setup and evaluation metrics; Sect. 4 presents the experimental results and a comprehensive discussion; and Sect. 5 concludes the paper with insights and directions for future research.

2 Methodology

The proposed methodology is organized as a multi-step process that integrates data acquisition, cleaning, aggregation, XAI-based context extraction, clustering, and the integration of contextual information into forecasting models. Figure 1 illustrates the entire workflow, detailed in the following stages.

2.1 Data Acquisition and Preprocessing

Energy consumption data and associated sensor readings are collected from building management systems at 5-minute intervals. The raw dataset is subjected to a cleaning process that includes: (i) Detecting and imputing missing values by computing the average of the adjacent periods; (ii) detecting anomalous consumption values using statistical measures and replacing outliers with interpolated averages from neighboring periods; (iii) aggregating data to meet the granularity requirements of the forecasting models (15-minutes intervals); and (iv) Feature engineering by extracting temporal features (e.g., hour, day-of-week) from timestamps to capture cyclical patterns, and additional features may be derived based on sensor readings to enhance model performance.

2.2 Baseline Forecasting Model

The baseline forecasting model is a reference to evaluate the effectiveness of incorporating contextual information into energy consumption predictions. It is designed to estimate future energy usage based on historical sensor data and environmental variables. The objective is to establish a benchmark before integrating clustering-based context extraction and XAI-driven feature augmentation.

A systematic model selection process is implemented rather than adopting a fixed predictive model. A grid search is conducted across multiple well-established machine learning algorithms, ensuring that the chosen model achieves optimal forecasting accuracy. The candidate models include:

- Gradient Boosting: A tree-based ensemble learning method that builds models sequentially, refining errors at each iteration. This technique is widely recognized for its strong predictive performance in structured datasets.
- Random Forest: An ensemble of decision trees that reduces overfitting by aggregating multiple predictions. This model is particularly effective in capturing complex, nonlinear relationships in energy consumption data.
- K-Nearest Neighbors (KNN): A non-parametric method that relies on similarity-based predictions, making it suitable for capturing localized consumption patterns that may not be well-represented by tree-based methods.

Each model is trained and evaluated using a cross-validation approach, ensuring that a specific train-test split does not bias the results. The selection criterion is based on standard performance metrics such as the coefficient of determination (R^2), root mean squared error (RMSE), and mean absolute error (MAE). The model demonstrating the highest predictive accuracy across validation sets is the baseline. Establishing a high-performing baseline makes it possible to assess the true impact of incorporating contextual information. The subsequent stages of this study compare the baseline model with context-aware variants, allowing for a rigorous evaluation of how operational contexts influence forecasting accuracy.

2.3 Context Identification Using XAI and Clustering

A context extraction process integrating explainability techniques and clustering is applied to improve forecasting models' adaptability to different operational conditions. The objective is to identify latent energy consumption patterns that reflect variations in occupancy levels, environmental factors, and building usage schedules.

The process begins with applying XAI techniques, namely SHAP [15], and LIME [16], to analyze the relative importance of input features for each weekly aggregated period. SHAP and LIME were selected due to their model-agnostic nature, compatibility with tabular data, and widespread adoption in XAI literature. SHAP offers consistent, theoretically grounded attributions based on cooperative game theory, providing global interpretability and robustness in capturing nonlinear feature interactions. LIME, on the other hand, is well-suited for localized explanations and produces sparse, human-readable attributions that facilitate instance-level understanding.

Based on these properties, both SHAP and LIME are employed to generate explanation vectors that characterize the contribution of each input feature to the model's prediction. Specifically, an explanation vector ϕ_j for each weekly sample a_j, where each component $\phi_{j,k}$ quantifies the contribution of the k-th feature to the energy consumption prediction, as shown in Eq. 1, where K represents the total number of features used in the forecasting model.

$$\phi_j = (\phi_{j,1}, \phi_{j,2}, ..., \phi_{j,K}), \tag{1}$$

To obtain a more robust measure of feature relevance across different weeks, Eq. 2 calculates the absolute contributions are averaged over all M weekly periods. This aggregation helps identify the most influential variables that drive energy consumption across distinct operational scenarios. The resulting importance scores I_k serve two primary purposes: (i) to identify the most influential features that drive energy demand across the full dataset, and (ii) to support the feature reduction process by ranking features based on their average absolute impact. This allows for a more informed and targeted feature selection strategy in subsequent modeling stages, enhancing both interpretability and computational efficiency.

$$I_k = \frac{1}{M} \sum_{j=1}^{M} |\phi_{j,k}|. \tag{2}$$

Once the explanation vectors $\{\phi_j\}_{j=1}^{M}$ are obtained, the K-means clustering algorithm is applied to segment the weekly periods into distinct operational contexts (Eq. 3), where C represents the total number of clusters, c_j is the cluster assignment for week j, and μ_c denotes the centroid of cluster c. The optimal number of clusters is determined using the silhouette score, ensuring each group represents a well-separated and meaningful context. To this end, the silhouette coefficient is computed for a range of candidate values $k \in [2, 10]$, and the configuration with the highest average silhouette score is selected.

$$\min_{\{c_j\},\{\mu_c\}} \sum_{j=1}^{M} \|\phi_j - \mu_{c_j}\|^2, \qquad (3)$$

Instead of computing abstract centroids, each cluster is represented by the data point closest to the mean (medoid), ensuring that the context corresponds to an actual, interpretable instance observed in the dataset. This approach enhances the practical interpretability of each context and avoids potential issues associated with centroids that may not correspond to any real-world configuration, which is particularly important when generating explanations or retraining models per context.

By integrating XAI techniques with clustering, this methodology allows for a data-driven segmentation of operational conditions. This enables the development of specialized forecasting models tailored to each identified context, ultimately improving prediction accuracy and interoperability. Moreover, the use of explanation vectors derived from XAI techniques, as opposed to raw input features or manually defined categories, offers a model-aligned view of feature relevance that reflects the actual internal decision logic of the predictor.

2.4 Integration of Contextual Information Into Forecasting Models

Once the operational contexts are identified, the final step involves incorporating this information into the forecasting models. The goal is to leverage the extracted contexts to improve predictive performance by tailoring the modeling approach to different operational scenarios. Three main strategies are considered:

- Feature Augmentation: The original feature set is extended by appending a one-hot encoded vector representing the context label. This allows the model to learn context-dependent patterns by explicitly incorporating the contextual classification into the input;
- Context-Specific Models: Instead of training a single global model, separate forecasting models f_c are trained for each context c. This approach enables each model to specialize in its respective operational condition, capturing nuances that may not be well represented in a global model;
- Transfer Learning: Instead of training separate models from scratch for each operational context, knowledge learned from a globally trained forecasting model is transferred and refined for specific contexts. Initially, a general forecasting model is trained using the complete dataset, capturing overall energy consumption patterns across different operational conditions. This model, referred to as the *global model*, has a set of learned parameters θ_{global}. For each identified context c, a new model is created by initializing it with the parameters of the global model. Instead of learning all parameters from scratch, only context-specific adjustments $\Delta\theta_c$ are learned, allowing the model to specialize while leveraging the general knowledge from the global mode.

Throughout these processes, hyperparameter optimization via grid search is continuously applied to ensure that each model configuration is optimally adapted to its respective context.

2.5 Feature Selection via XAI-Based Reduction

A feature selection process is applied to each of the three approaches described above, aiming to improve model efficiency and interpretability further. Instead of relying on the full feature set, the most relevant input variables are identified using the same XAI techniques (SHAP and LIME) used in the context extraction process. This step ensures that only the most influential features are retained for model training while reducing computational complexity, improving model interpretability, and preventing overfitting by eliminating redundant or low-impact variables. The feature selection process is conducted as follows:

- A reduced set of 100 representative samples is generated using KMeans clustering, effectively summarizing the full training set while preserving its distributional characteristics.
- XAI methods are applied to these representative samples, producing explanation vectors that quantify the contribution of each feature.
- Feature importance scores are computed by averaging absolute SHAP or LIME values across 100 representative samples:
- The final subset of features is determined by selecting those with the highest importance scores, ensuring that only the most informative variables are retained for training.

3 Case Study

The dataset used in this study consists of energy consumption measurements collected from a modern office building. To ensure consistency and meet the granularity requirements of the predictive models, all measurements were aggregated into 15-minute intervals, reducing noise while preserving essential consumption patterns. In addition to energy consumption values, the dataset includes environmental and occupancy-related variables, such as temperature, humidity, CO_2 concentration, and motion sensor activations. These contextual features provide valuable insights into the factors influencing energy demand.

For model training and evaluation, data from November 2018 to October 2019 were selected for training. The test period was defined as the entire month of November 2019, spanning from November 1, 2019, to December 1, 2019. This setup enables the evaluation of forecasting performance under real operational conditions, assessing how well the models generalize to unseen data over a complete monthly cycle. The forecasting performance was assessed using four standard error metrics: R^2, $RMSE$, MAE, MSE.

Hyperparameter optimization uses grid search to identify the best-performing configurations for the forecasting algorithms considered. The models considered included GB, RF, and KNN. Table 1 summarizes the hyperparameter values tested during optimization.

Table 1. Grid Search Parameters for Model Tuning

Model	Hyperparameter	Values Considered
Gradient Boosting	Learning Rate	0.01, 0.1, 0.2
	Max Depth	3, 5, 7
	n_estimators	50, 100
Random Forest	n_estimators	50, 100
	Max Depth	3, 5, 7
KNN Regressor	n_neighbors	3, 5, 7, 9

4 Results and Discussion

This section presents the experimental findings, starting with integrating the contextual information using XAI and clustering and concluding with the forecasting results and critical analysis.

Contextual information was integrated into the methodology by applying XAI techniques to generate explanation vectors for each 15-minute aggregated interval. These vectors were then subjected to KMeans clustering to segment the data into distinct operational contexts. Figure 2 compares the clustering outcomes obtained using three different approaches. The left panel illustrates the result of a baseline clustering that does not incorporate XAI-derived information, which identified only two broad clusters with limited contextual differentiation. The center panel presents the segmentation obtained using SHAP-based explanation vectors, revealing four well-defined and distinct operational contexts corresponding to patterns such as standard working hours, off-peak activity, and transitional periods. Finally, the right panel shows the clustering outcome based on LIME-derived vectors, which also resulted in two clusters, capturing broader usage patterns with less granularity compared to the SHAP-based approach. This contrast highlights that incorporating SHAP insights leads to a significantly more refined segmentation.

A feature reduction process was conducted to enhance model interpretability and computational efficiency. This process was applied to 100 representative samples extracted via KMeans, ensuring that the selected features represented the different operational contexts. The importance of each feature was computed based on the average absolute contribution across these samples, allowing for the identification of the most influential predictors. The final reduced feature set was determined by retaining only the highest-ranked features while discarding those with minimal impact.

Figure 3 illustrates the results of this reduction process for LIME approach, comparing feature importance scores before and after feature selection. The figure highlights that the most relevant variables were preserved.

Although the explanation vectors were generated using models that were previously optimized through grid search and validated using k-fold cross-validation, it is acknowledged that such vectors may still be influenced by characteristics

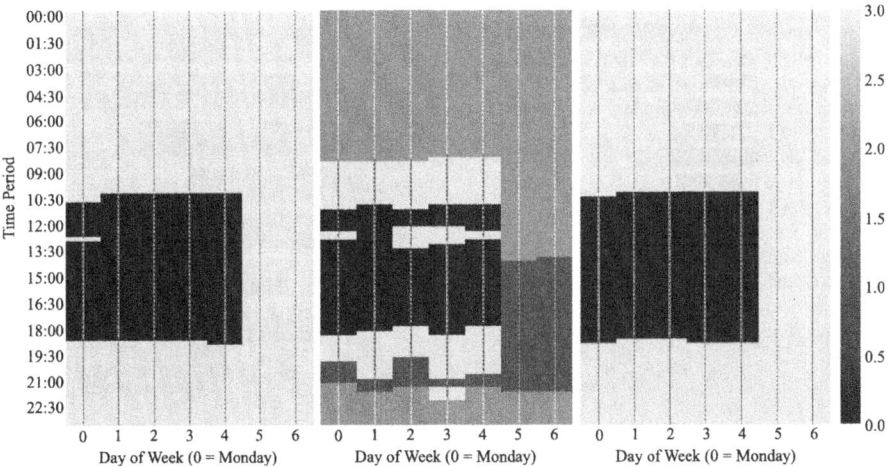

Fig. 2. Comparison of clustering approaches: Baseline clustering without XAI, identifying two contexts (Left); Clustering using SHAP-derived explanation vectors, identifying four contexts (Center); and Clustering using LIME-derived explanation vectors, identifying two contexts (Right).

specific to the model. To mitigate this, all explanations were produced from a single, consistently trained model and aggregated at the weekly level to minimize the impact of local noise. Nevertheless, future work will consider complementary validation approaches to further assess and mitigate potential biases in the context extraction process, ensuring that the identified patterns reflect genuine operational variability rather than model-driven artifacts.

Table 2 summarizes the experimental results obtained under various configurations, including the baseline approach, the integration of context through XAI (using both SHAP and LIME), context-specific modeling, and transfer learning.

The baseline model optimized through grid search without explicit context integration achieved an R^2 of 0.7247, RMSE of 162.50, and MAE of 108.00. In contrast, the conventional KMeans clustering model (without XAI-derived context) underperformed with an R^2 of 0.6424, $RMSE$ of 185.19, and MAE of 123.16. This discrepancy underscores the limitations of unsupervised segmentation when it is not complemented by an interpretative framework capable of identifying the key drivers of energy consumption.

By integrating contextual information as an additional feature, the SHAP-enhanced model reached an R^2 of 0.7265 and an $RMSE$ of 161.95 when using all features, with a slight increase in MAE (113.58). A similar configuration employing a reduced feature set yielded nearly identical results (R^2 of 0.7242, $RMSE$ of 162.63, MAE of 113.91), suggesting that the benefit of feature selection in this context is minimal. In contrast, the LIME-driven approach showed a decline in performance when using the reduced feature set (R^2 of 0.6750, $RMSE$ of 176.54, and MAE of 128.93) compared to its all-features scenario, which achieved an

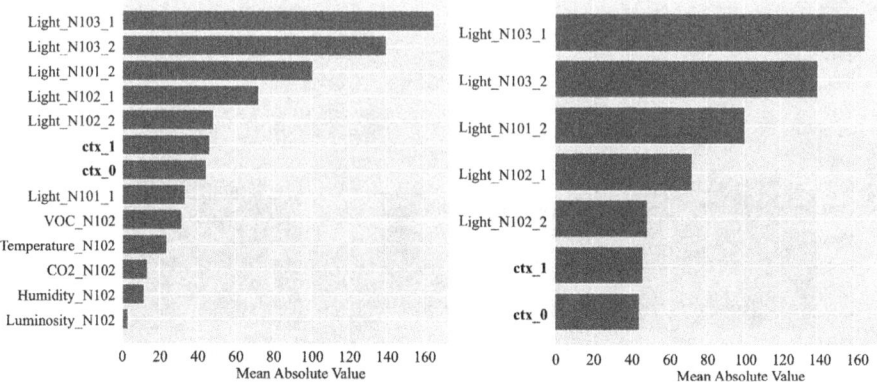

Fig. 3. Comparison of feature importance using LIME: Feature importance before reduction (Left); Feature importance after reduction (Right).

Table 2. Summary of Experimental Results

#	Approach	XAI	Contexts	Model	Features	RMSE	R^2
1	Model per Context	SHAP	4	{GB, GB, KNN, GB}	All	147.60	0.7728
2	Transfer Learning	LIME	2	{GB, GB}	All	153.57	0.7541
3	Model per Context	LIME	2	{GB, KNN}	All	156.61	0.7443
4	Context as Feature	LIME	2	GB	All	157.34	0.7419
5	Context as Feature	SHAP	4	GB	All	161.95	0.7265
6	Context as Feature	SHAP	4	GB	Sample	162.63	0.7242
7	Transfer Learning	SHAP	4	{GB, GB, GB, GB}	All	162.80	0.7236
8	Baseline	–	–	GB	All	162.50	0.7247
9	Baseline Cluster	–	–	GB	All	185.19	0.6424
10	Context as Feature	LIME	2	GB	Sample	176.54	0.6750

R^2 of 0.7419, $RMSE$ of 157.34, and MAE of 108.80. These findings indicate that for the LIME-based configuration retaining the full set of features is crucial for capturing the complex interactions that influence energy consumption.

Training separate models for each identified context led to the most significant performance enhancements. The SHAP-based specialized models, which segmented the data into four distinct operational contexts, achieved an R^2 of 0.7728, $RMSE$ of 147.60, and MAE of 97.90. This improvement suggests that tailoring models to the specific patterns within each context allows for a more effective capture of the underlying variability. Conversely, the LIME-derived context-specific models, which relied on a coarser segmentation into two contexts, exhibited a lower R^2 of 0.7443 with $RMSE$ and MAE of 156.61 and 99.00, respectively. The disparity in performance between SHAP and LIME approaches appears to stem from the granularity of the contextual segmentation, with the finer division provided by SHAP enabling better model specialization.

The transfer learning strategy, which involves fine-tuning a globally trained model for each context, yielded mixed results. In the SHAP-based scenario, the fine-tuned models achieved performance comparable to the baseline (R^2 of 0.7236, $RMSE$ of 162.80, MAE of 106.69), indicating that the transfer did not substantially enhance the model's ability to adapt to individual contexts. Conversely, the LIME-based transfer learning approach improved the R^2 to 0.7541 and reduced $RMSE$ and MAE to 153.57 and 101.87, respectively. Although less effective than dedicated context-specific models, transfer learning shows potential for leveraging global insights while allowing local adaptation. Context segmentation granularity proved critical: SHAP identified four operational contexts, enabling finer model tuning, whereas LIME's two-context split limited specialization. The results confirm that context-specific models outperform approaches that append context as a feature, as tailoring models to distinct consumption patterns leads to greater accuracy. While transfer learning can reduce training time and reuse global patterns, its effectiveness depends on context variability–fine-tuned global models may not capture local dynamics as well as fully specialized ones.

5 Conclusion

A novel framework integrating explainable artificial intelligence (XAI) techniques with clustering-based context extraction for energy forecasting has been presented. The proposed methodology leverages SHAP and LIME to generate explanation vectors to identify distinct operational contexts through clustering. Dedicated forecasting models tailored to these contexts achieved significantly improved predictive accuracy compared to conventional baseline approaches that either do not incorporate context or merely add context as an extra feature. The experimental results indicate that specialized models for each operational context outperform models using a global approach, emphasizing the importance of adapting to local consumption patterns. In addition, while transfer learning shows potential for reducing training time and utilizing global patterns, its effectiveness is highly contingent upon the granularity of the contextual segmentation. The feature reduction process driven by XAI further enhances model interpretability and computational efficiency. Future work will explore additional XAI techniques and the integration of real-time contextual data to refine model adaptability and extend the framework's applicability to other domains.

Acknowledgments. This work has been developed in the frame of PRECISE project (PTDC/EEI-EEE/6277/2020), DOI: 10.54499/PTDC/EEI-EEE/6277/2020, that receiving funding from FEDER Funds through the COMPETE program and from National Funds. The authors used the facilities and equipment provided by the GECAD research center (UIDB/00760/2020), DOI: 10.54499/UIDB/00760/2020. Brígida Teixeira is supported by national funds through FCT, Portugal government, with PhD grant reference 2020.08174.BD, DOI: 10.54499/2020.08174.BD.

References

1. IEA, U. Global status report for buildings and construction 2019. In: UN Eniroment Programme, vol. 224 (2019)
2. Mohammadi, M., Mohammadi, A.: Empowering distributed solutions in renewable energy systems and grid optimization. In: Distributed Machine Learning And Computing: Theory And Applications, pp. 141–155 (2024)
3. Markovics, D., Mayer, M.: Comparison of machine learning methods for photovoltaic power forecasting based on numerical weather prediction. Renew. Sustain. Energy Rev. **161**, 112364 (2022)
4. Muqeet, H., et. al. Sustainable solutions for advanced energy management system of campus microgrids: model opportunities and future challenges. Sensors (Basel, Switzerland) **22**, 2345 (2022)
5. Wang, X., Wang, H., Bhandari, B., Cheng, L.: AI-empowered methods for smart energy consumption: a review of load forecasting, anomaly detection and demand response. Int. J. Precis. Eng. Manuf.-Green Technol. **11**, 963–993 (2024)
6. Zhu, J., et. al.: Review and prospect of data-driven techniques for load forecasting in integrated energy systems. Appl. Energy. **321**, 119269 (2022)
7. Liu, T., et. al.: Study on deep reinforcement learning techniques for building energy consumption forecasting. Energy Build. **208**, 109675 (2020)
8. Masood, Z., Gantassi, R., Choi, Y.A.: A multi-step time-series clustering-based Seq2Seq LSTM learning for a single household electricity load forecasting. Energies **15**, 2623 (2022)
9. Zhuang, D., et. al.: Data-driven predictive control for smart HVAC system in IoT-integrated buildings with time-series forecasting and reinforcement learning. Appl. Energy **338**, 120936 (2023)
10. Ali, M., Prakash, K., Hossain, M., Pota, H.: Intelligent energy management: evolving developments, current challenges, and research directions for sustainable future. J. Clean. Prod. **314**, 127904 (2021)
11. Almusaylim, Z., Zaman, N.: A review on smart home present state and challenges: linked to context-awareness internet of things (IoT). Wirel. Networks **25**, 3193–3204 (2019)
12. Machlev, R., et. al.: Explainable artificial intelligence (XAI) techniques for energy and power systems: review, challenges and opportunities. Energy AI **9**, 100169 (2022)
13. Yang, W., et. al.: Survey on explainable AI: from approaches, limitations and applications aspects. Hum.-Centric Intell. Syst. **3**, 161–188 (2023)
14. Weber, L., et. al.: Beyond explaining: opportunities and challenges of XAI-based model improvement. Inf. Fusion **92**, 154–176 (2023)
15. Lundberg, S., Lee, S.: A unified approach to interpreting model predictions. In: Advances In Neural Information Processing Systems, pp. 4766–4775 (2017)
16. Ribeiro, M., et. al.: Why should i trust you?: Explaining the predictions of any classifier. In: NAACL-HLT 2016 - 2016 Conference Of The North American Chapter of The Association For Computational Linguistics: Human Language Technologies, Proceedings Of The Demonstrations Session, pp. 97-101 (2016)

Open Access This chapter is licensed under the terms of the Creative Commons Attribution 4.0 International License (http://creativecommons.org/licenses/by/4.0/), which permits use, sharing, adaptation, distribution and reproduction in any medium or format, as long as you give appropriate credit to the original author(s) and the source, provide a link to the Creative Commons license and indicate if changes were made.

The images or other third party material in this chapter are included in the chapter's Creative Commons license, unless indicated otherwise in a credit line to the material. If material is not included in the chapter's Creative Commons license and your intended use is not permitted by statutory regulation or exceeds the permitted use, you will need to obtain permission directly from the copyright holder.

ConformaSegment: A Conformal Prediction-Based, Uncertainty-Aware, and Model-Agnostic Explainability Framework for Time-Series Forecasting

Fatima Rabia Yapicioglu[1,2]($\boxtimes$), Meltem Aksoy[3], Tuwe Löfström[4], Fabio Vitali[1], and Alberto Rigenti[2]

[1] Department of Computer Science and Engineering, University of Bologna, Bologna, Italy
fatima.yapicioglu2@unibo.it
[2] Marketing and Sales, Automobili Lamborghini S.p.A, Sant'Agata Bolognese, Italy
[3] Research Center Trustworthy Data Science and Security, University Alliance Ruhr, Technical University Dortmund, Dortmund, Germany
[4] Jonkoping AI Lab, Department of Computing, Jonkoping University, Jönköping, Sweden

Abstract. Time-series forecasting is crucial for data-driven decisions across finance, healthcare, and environmental monitoring. Despite technological advances, identifying significant temporal segments impacting predictions remains challenging. We introduce ConformaSegment, a model-agnostic explainability framework that enhances time-series interpretability by identifying critical segments while quantifying prediction uncertainty. The framework integrates conformal prediction to generate reliable prediction intervals with guaranteed coverage rates, enabling users to understand which temporal segments most significantly influence forecasting outcomes. Our approach was validated across diverse real-world datasets using LSTM, RNN, and GRU models, demonstrating substantial performance improvements over existing techniques such as Saliency Maps and Integrated Gradients. ConformaSegment achieved mean R^2 improvements of 42% and 18% respectively over these methods, while enhancing prediction interval coverage by 25.73% and 40.15%. These results demonstrate that ConformaSegment effectively identifies critical time segments in forecasting tasks, improving both interpretability and uncertainty quantification, thus enhancing model trustworthiness for applications in healthcare, industrial maintenance, and other time-sensitive domains.

Keywords: Conformal Prediction · Model-Agnostic Explainability · Uncertainty-Aware Explainability · Reliable Time Series Explainability

1 Introduction

Time-series modeling, the analysis of sequential data points with temporal dependencies, is a foundational approach in both academia and industry. It plays a critical role in diverse domains such as healthcare [1], for monitoring physiological signals; finance [2], to forecast stock market trends; e-commerce [3], for predicting consumer behavior; autonomous driving [4], to anticipate trajectories; and aerospace [5], for system performance optimization. Beyond these, its applications extend to any field where understanding and forecasting temporal patterns are essential. The need for robust and scalable modeling techniques are increasing along with the growing volumes of time-series data.

To address the challenges and opportunities presented by the growing volume and complexity of time-series data, numerous models have emerged, ranging from classical statistical approaches like Auto-Regressive Integrated Moving Average (ARIMA) [6] and exponential smoothing [7], to advanced machine learning and deep learning methods such as Recurrent Neural Networks (RNNs) [8], Long-Short Term Memory Networks (LSTMs) [9], and transformer-based architectures [10]. These models aim to capture temporal dependencies, handle irregularities, and enhance predictive accuracy across various applications. Time-series modeling tasks can generally be divided into two categories: classification and regression (or forecasting for predicting future values). Classification tasks, such as predicting whether a stock will rise or fall based on historical data, involve assigning discrete labels to input data. In contrast, forecasting focuses on predicting continuous future values.

Despite significant advancements in time series modeling, many of the more advanced models, particularly deep learning-based methods, remain opaque in their decision-making processes, making it challenging for humans to understand how these models work. This phenomenon, known as *explainability* or *interpretability*, refers to the challenge of making complex models transparent and understandable to human users. In the classification task, explainability might highlight which features (e.g., past price movements or economic indicators) contributed most to the predicted class, while in forecasting it may show how different time windows or external factors influenced the predicted values. Explainability can be categorized into two main groups: *intrinsic explainability*, where the model is inherently designed to be interpretable and transparent, and *model-agnostic explainability*, which employs techniques that explain a model's behavior regardless of its internal structure.

Although explainability has recently become a key research area, studies focusing on enhancing interpretability within time-series modeling have been relatively scarce [11]. Most of the time-series explainability frameworks are instrinsic and limited to model structure [12]. This lack of transparency not only hinders interpretability, but also reduces the trust that users and stakeholders place in these models, particularly in critical applications such as healthcare, finance, and autonomous systems. Moreover, the trust and reliability of the produced explanations, commonly referred to as uncertainty-aware explanations, as highlighted in [13,14], have recently emerged as a critical area of research. However, this concept remains relatively underexplored, particularly in the context of time-series modeling.

Quantifying uncertainty, particularly epistemic uncertainty, is vital in determining the trustworthiness of the model outputs [15]. The uncertainty stems primarily from two sources: model uncertainty (epistemic), often caused by insufficient data collection, and data uncertainty (aleatoric), which arises from inherent noise in the data. Conformal prediction offers a rigorous framework for uncertainty quantification, with validity guaranteed under the exchangeability assumption, which ensures that data points are statistically indistinguishable in order [16,17]. This makes it a powerful and versatile tool across various research domains.

Consider a scenario where a machine learning model predicts the delivery time of urgent medical supplies to rural healthcare facilities, factoring in weather, distance, traffic, and vehicle type. Instead of a single estimate, a confidence interval improves reliability. For instance, an emergency airlift prediction of 45 minutes with a ±7-minute margin (95% confidence) results in a range of 38 to 52 min. This enhances transparency and supports informed decision-making in critical situations.

In this paper, we investigate the intersection of conformal prediction and transparency in time-series forecasting. We propose a novel algorithm that segments, weights, and highlights critical areas within a univariate time series, specifically tailored for forecasting tasks. The proposed algorithm leverages the conformal prediction framework to quantify changes in uncertainty measures, emphasizing the importance of these segments in improving interpretability. In an ECG-based healthcare application, the algorithm identifies segments with increased uncertainty, such as during arrhythmia episodes. By highlighting these, the model provides insights into potential health risks, offering more precise forecasts with confidence intervals for early diagnosis and timely intervention. Our main contributions can be listed as follows:

- *Novel Algorithm*: We introduce a model-agnostic algorithm that segments, weights, and highlights significant areas in time-series data, focusing on those areas where uncertainty critically changes. This approach improves the interpretability of the predictions by identifying key temporal segments that influence the outcomes of the prediction.
- *Uncertainty-Aware Forecasting*: By leveraging conformal prediction, our framework quantifies uncertainty and generates confidence intervals that capture variability from both the model and the data, offering a more reliable and transparent forecasting process.
- *Real-World Applications*: The proposed method is applied to critical domains, such as healthcare and industrial maintenance, enabling time-sensitive decision-making and demonstrating its practical relevance in high-stakes environments.
- *Validation*: The algorithm is rigorously evaluated on multiple datasets, confirming its robustness, effectiveness, and reliability in real-world forecasting scenarios.

The paper is organized as follows: Sects. 2 and 3 present the essential preliminaries and a review of related literature to provide the necessary background.

Section 4 delves deeper into the theoretical foundations of the proposed concept. Given the complexity of the theory, the experiments and evaluations are discussed separately in Sect. 5. Lastly, Sect. 6 interprets the results, draws conclusions, and suggests potential directions for future research.

2 Preliminaries

2.1 Time-Series Modeling

Time-series modeling focuses on analyzing sequential data to capture patterns, trends, and dependencies over time. In time series, *forecasting* aims to estimate the future value based on past observations in a time series. In contrast, *regression* involves predicting values, regardless of whether it is related to the past, present or future, based on the given data. Our study specifically focuses on the univariate *forecasting*, where the goal is to estimate future values.

In more scholarly terms, let $\mathbf{X} = \{x_1, x_2, \ldots, x_T\}$ represent a univariate time series of length T, where $x_t \in \mathbb{R}$ is the observation at time t.

The primary goal of time-series modeling, *forecasting*, involves predicting a future value x_{T+1}, based on historical observations. This is typically achieved by minimizing prediction error, such as Mean Absolute Error (MAE):

$$\mathcal{L}_{\text{MAE}} = \frac{1}{N} \sum_{i=1}^{N} |\hat{x}_i - x_i|, \tag{1}$$

where x_i and $\hat{x}_i$ denote the true and predicted values respectively, and N is the number of observations.

We can also use metrics such as R-Squared (R^2) for easier interpretation:

$$R^2 = 1 - \frac{\sum_{i=1}^{N}(x_i - \hat{x}_i)^2}{\sum_{i=1}^{N}(x_i - \bar{x})^2}, \tag{2}$$

where $\bar{x}$ is the mean of the actual values.

Statistical models like **ARIMA** [18] are often employed for simpler time-series forecasting, capturing linear relationships through autoregressive and moving average components. As data complexity increases, machine learning methods, including **RNNs** [19], offer greater flexibility by modeling nonlinear patterns. However, RNNs struggle with long-term dependencies, which are addressed by more advanced models such as **LSTM** [9] networks and **Gated Recurrent Units (GRUs)** [20], which incorporate mechanisms to retain important information over long sequences. In recent advancements, **Transformer-based models** [21] have set new benchmarks in forecasting. By utilizing self-attention mechanisms, these models are able to efficiently capture long-term dependencies, which enables them to process large-scale, high-dimensional time-series data.

2.2 Explainable Artificial Intelligence

Explainability in machine learning, particularly for time-series forecasting, refers to the ability to clarify the reasoning behind a model's predictions, thereby fostering trust in its outputs [22]. Time-series models, particularly complex ones such as RNNs or LSTMs, often operate as "black-boxes", making it difficult to interpret the factors driving predictions. Global explainability provides insights into model behavior, such as identifying common patterns in sensor data that predict vehicle failure. Local explainability focuses on individual predictions. For example, it can explain a forecast of the remaining lifespan of a vehicle component based on specific sensor readings at a given time. Reliable explanations are vital in high-stakes applications like autonomous vehicles, where small uncertainties can have major consequences. Trust indicators, including confidence and uncertainty measures, ensure accountability in areas like autonomous driving and real-time traffic prediction.

2.3 Uncertainty Estimation and Quantification

Predictive uncertainty in Artificial Intelligence (AI) modeling refers to the uncertainty associated with a model's predictions for future or unseen data points. It quantifies how confident the model is in its forecast, helping to understand not only the predictions but also the reliability of those predictions. This type of uncertainty is crucial for high-stakes applications, such as autonomous driving, predictive maintenance, or financial forecasting, where decision-making depends on the trustworthiness of the model.

Predictive uncertainty has two primary sources [15]:

1. **Aleatoric Uncertainty**: Represents irreducible noise in the data. For example, in automotive demand forecasting, factors such as sudden weather changes or supply chain disruptions can introduce variability that cannot be eliminated, even with more data.
2. **Epistemic Uncertainty**: Stems from limited model knowledge due to insufficient data. For instance, predicting rare vehicle failures or the behavior of newly introduced vehicle models can result in high epistemic uncertainty. Unlike aleatoric uncertainty, epistemic uncertainty can be reduced by incorporating additional data.

Predictive uncertainty is crucial in forecasting the remaining life of critical vehicle components, like brakes. A model may predict failure at 10,000 miles but with varying uncertainty. Aleatoric uncertainty signals noisy sensor data, while epistemic uncertainty suggests gaps in training data, reducing reliability. Our research focuses on epistemic uncertainty, which stems from limited knowledge due to insufficient data.

2.4 Conformal Prediction

Conformal prediction offers a framework for constructing prediction sets or confidence intervals (C) that reliably capture the true value at a specified error rate [16]. Unlike traditional methods that rely on specific distributional assumptions, it is distribution-agnostic and operates under the assumption of exchangeability, meaning that data points are treated as if they come from the same underlying distribution, regardless of order. Although standard conformal prediction assumes exchangeability, adaptations exist for time series data, preserving temporal dependencies while ensuring valid, uncertainty-aware prediction intervals.

The key principals of conformal prediction are efficiency and validity. Validity ensures that prediction intervals or sets maintain a specified coverage probability, while efficiency minimizes the interval sizes. The user-defined confidence level, denoted as $1 - \alpha$ ($a = error\ rate$), controls the desired assurance in the predictions, and the coverage rate measures the fraction of true instances contained within the prediction sets.

Here is a general overview of the process [17]:

1. **Data Splitting**: The dataset is divided into training, calibration, and test sets. The calibration set, separate from training, is used only to construct prediction sets. Ensuring it remains unseen during training preserves prediction integrity, prevents bias, and maintains validity. This approach enhances model generalization, providing accurate and reliable confidence intervals for new data.
2. **Calibration**: The calibration set $\{(\mathbf{X}_i, y_i)\}$ is used to construct a prediction set for new test points that maintains validity within the desired confidence level. Specifically, for a test input $\mathbf{X}_{test}$, the goal is to ensure the prediction set $C(\mathbf{X}_{test})$ satisfies:

$$1 - \alpha \leq \mathbb{P}(Y_{test} \in C(\mathbf{X}_{test})) \leq 1 - \alpha + \frac{1}{n+1}, \tag{3}$$

where Y_{test} is the actual label of the test point, α is the chosen error rate, and n is the total number of samples in the calibration set.
3. **Quantile Calculation**: For each pair in the calibration set, we calculate a score $A(x_i, y_i)$, which quantifies the degree of disagreement between the predicted and actual labels. The quantile $\hat{q}$ of these scores is determined using:

$$\hat{q} = \frac{(n+1)(1-\alpha)}{n}. \tag{4}$$

where n is the total number of samples in the calibration set and α is the error rate specified by the user.
4. **Prediction Set**: The prediction set $C(\mathbf{X}_{test})$ for a new test input $\mathbf{X}_{test}$ is formed by selecting the labels y such that:

$$C(\mathbf{X}_{test}) = \{y : A(\mathbf{X}_{test}, y) \leq \hat{q}\}.$$

This procedure guarantees that the prediction sets have valid coverage, meaning that the true label will be contained within the set with a probability at least $1 - \alpha$. Conformal prediction has been extended in various ways to address challenges such as risk control, covariate shift, and distribution shift [23]. For example, methods have been developed to handle known divergence shifts in the score approach [24].

3 Related Work

This section reviews studies at the intersection of time-series modeling and explainable AI, emphasizing uncertainty estimation and conformal prediction. Existing time-series AI tasks include uncertainty estimation, conformal prediction, and explainability, which involves tasks such as explaining individual time points, attributing outcomes, and analyzing event sequences [25]. Saliency maps generated by a two-stage CNN reveal contributions of features and intervals [26]. LIMESegment adapts LIME for time-series classification, addressing representation and perturbation challenges [27]. XCM, an explainable CNN for multivariate time series, improves both performance and interpretability by extracting relevant input features [28]. Explainable time-series tweaking proposes global and local transformations to alter classification decisions [29,30]. TS-CHIEF achieves state-of-the-art accuracy with effective embeddings and tree-based classifiers [31]. EBLR enhances forecasting accuracy and interpretability by leveraging nonlinear features and generating prediction intervals [32]. XTSTree [33] hierarchically segments time series using change detectors and stationarity tests, enhancing interpretability via symbolic regression, whereas ConformaSegment perturbs segments to assess their impact on predictive uncertainty. [34] classify time series for uncertainty and explainability, while ConformaSegment perturbs segments to assess their impact on predictive uncertainty. Uncertainty-aware frameworks include ConformaSight, which uses conformal prediction to improve transparency with robust feature importance estimates [13], and Fast Calibrated Explanations, which integrates ConformaSight's techniques for real-time uncertainty-aware explanations in classification and probabilistic regression [14]. Calibrated explanations employ prediction intervals for factual and counterfactual insights [35]. Conformal Predictive Systems (CPSs) and inductive Conformal Regression (CR) refine prediction intervals by leveraging nonconformity scores, enhancing efficiency and precision.

Despite advancements, no existing framework identifies the most influential segments in time-series forecasting. Our framework addresses this gap by leveraging uncertainty-aware conformal prediction to quantify uncertainty, ensure valid intervals, and highlight key segments driving forecast outcomes, enabling critical interval identification and retrospective analysis.

4 Problem Formulation and Presenting Our Approach

This section outlines the foundational principles, key components, practical guidelines, and validity requirements of the ConformaSegment framework, providing a clear roadmap for its application. It also presents a practical example scenario to illustrate the steps involved in splitting data, setting parameters, and using the explanation method.

4.1 ConformaSegment Structure and Working Mechanism

ConformaSegment is a novel framework based on conformal prediction to provide robust and interpretable segment-based explanations for time-series forecasting.

Traditional explanation methods rank features by importance but overlook temporal dynamics in sequential data. ConformaSegment addresses this by identifying key time segments through systematic noise introduction and measuring changes in uncertainty, revealing the most critical periods for accurate forecasting.

For instance, if a particular time segment has a significant impact on whether the true value falls within the prediction interval, this suggests that the interval plays a crucial role in shaping the confidence of the model. Therefore, providing explanations for the model's predictions requires not only identifying important segments but also clarifying how variations in uncertainty affect the predicted outcomes. We will now address key challenges that enables ConformaSegment for achieving reliable and interpretable forecasting as follows.

Adapting Conformal Prediction to Time-Series Forecasting: A univariate time series sample consists of a sequentially ordered set of observations, denoted as $x = [x_1, x_2, \ldots, x_T]$, where T is the number of time-steps. Consider a dataset of univariate time series samples $X \in \mathbb{R}^{N \times T}$, where N is the number of samples. Let $x \in \mathbb{R}^T$ be a specific sample to be analyzed. Given a black-box forecasting model $f : \mathbb{R}^T \to \mathbb{R}$, the predicted output for x is denoted as $Y_x = f(x)$.

In the context of **conformal prediction** for univariate time series forecasting, the goal is to generate prediction intervals that contain the true value with at least a user-defined coverage probability. To achieve this, nonconformity scores, denoted as $A(X_{\text{cal}}, Y_{\text{cal}})$, are calculated using the calibration data. Each score measures the residuals given by:

$$A(x_i, y_i) = |f(x_i) - y_i|. \tag{5}$$

Non-conformity scores, as defined in Eq. (5), are subsequently utilized to construct a prediction interval for a new test sample x_{new} at the desired confidence level. The resulting prediction interval is computed as follows:

$$\hat{I}_{1-\alpha}(x_{\text{new}}) = \big[f(x_{\text{new}}) - \text{quantile}_{1-\alpha}(A(X_{\text{cal}}, Y_{\text{cal}})), \\ f(x_{\text{new}}) + \text{quantile}_{1-\alpha}(A(X_{\text{cal}}, Y_{\text{cal}}))\big], \tag{6}$$

where $\text{quantile}_{1-\alpha}$ corresponds to the quantile value as formulated in Eq. (4) based on the confidence level $1 - \alpha$ as shown in Eq. (6).

To clarify, the expression $A(X_{\text{cal}}, Y_{\text{cal}})$ denotes the collection of nonconformity scores computed over the calibration set, where each element is obtained by applying the nonconformity function $A(x_i, y_i) = |f(x_i) - y_i|$ to each calibration point (x_i, y_i). The set $A(X_{\text{cal}}, Y_{\text{cal}}) = \{A(x_1, y_1), A(x_2, y_2), \ldots, A(x_n, y_n)\}$ is then used to compute the quantile$_{1-\alpha}$, which yields a single scalar value used in the prediction interval defined in Eq. (6).

Therefore, gaining insight into the factors that shape prediction intervals is essential to improve both the interpretability of the model and the trust in its predictions.

Thus, we define the following components:

Definition 1. Lower Bound: *The lower bound of the interval is $f(x_{\text{new}}) -$ quantile$_{1-\alpha}(A(X_{\text{train}}, Y_{\text{train}}))$, which provides the lower end of the predicted range.*

Definition 2. Upper Bound: *The upper bound of the interval is $f(x_{\text{new}}) +$ quantile$_{1-\alpha}(A(X_{\text{train}}, Y_{\text{train}}))$, which provides the upper end of the predicted range.*

Definition 3. The Coverage $(C(\alpha))$: *The coverage is defined as the proportion of test samples x_{test} for which the true value y_{test} lies within the prediction interval:*

$$C(\alpha) = \frac{1}{N_{\text{test}}} \sum_{i=1}^{N_{\text{test}}} \mathbb{I}\left(y_{\text{test},i} \in \hat{I}_{1-\alpha}(x_{\text{test},i})\right), \qquad (7)$$

where $\mathbb{I}(\cdot)$ is the indicator function, which takes the value 1 if the condition inside the parentheses is true (i.e., the true value is within the interval), and 0 otherwise.

In more scholarly terms, let $\hat{Y} = [\hat{L}_x, \hat{U}_x]$ as defined in Definition 1 and Definition 2 be the prediction interval, and define the change in coverage as:

$$\Delta\gamma = |\gamma(\hat{Y}_{\text{post}}) - \gamma(\hat{Y}_{\text{pre}})|, \qquad (8)$$

where $\gamma(\hat{Y})$ denotes the coverage probability of the prediction interval $\hat{Y}$, i.e., the probability that the true outcome lies within the interval, $\gamma(\hat{Y}) = \mathbb{P}(Y \in \hat{Y})$.

Coverage is a critical measure of the reliability of the prediction intervals. A model with high coverage ensures that the prediction intervals provide a good indication of where the true value will likely fall, allowing users to make more informed decisions. If the intervention causes a noticeable shift in $\hat{L}_x$ or $\hat{U}_x$, ultimately affecting the coverage as explained in Definition 3 and Eq. (7), it indicates that this segment plays a key role in shaping the prediction's uncertainty.

A large $\Delta\gamma$ (8) suggests that the intervention significantly influences the forecast value, highlighting the importance of the corresponding segment $\mathcal{I}_{\text{intervention}}$.

A Comprehensible View of a Time Series: To improve the interpretability of time series forecasting, we segment the time series $x = [x_1, x_2, \ldots, x_T]$ into meaningful nonoverlapping intervals (which we will call segments) $\{I_1, I_2, \ldots, I_K\}$, where each segment $I_k = [x_{\tau_{k-1}+1}, \ldots, x_{\tau_k}]$ is defined by change points $\{\tau_0, \tau_1, \ldots, \tau_K\}$, with $\tau_0 = 0$ and $\tau_K = T$. Here, K denotes the total number of segments, and $k \in \{1, \ldots, K\}$ represents the index of each segment.

To achieve this segmentation, we apply the PELT (Pruned Exact Linear Time) algorithm [36,37], which automatically identifies the optimal number of change points $\tau_1, \tau_2, \ldots, \tau_{K-1}$ that represent regime shifts in the time series. The algorithm minimizes a cost function $\mathcal{C}(I_1, I_2, \ldots, I_K)$, defined as:

$$\mathcal{C}(I_1, I_2, \ldots, I_K) = \sum_{k=1}^{K} \mathcal{C}_k(I_k), \tag{9}$$

where $\mathcal{C}_k(I_k)$ measures the cost of fitting a statistical model (e.g., constant mean, linear regression) to each segment I_k. The number of segments K is not fixed a priori but is determined by the PELT algorithm as part of the optimization process.

By segmenting the time series into distinct segments, we preserve its temporal structure, ensuring that each segment represents a unique pattern or regime. This segmentation improves localized interpretability, making it easier to understand how different time periods contribute to model predictions and confidence levels. Furthermore, each segment can be analyzed individually to assess its impact on the uncertainty of the prediction.

Quantifying the Segments Importance with ConformaSegment: The *Compute Feature Importance with ConformaSegment* (Algorithm 1) is formulated to evaluate the influence of distinct segments within a time series on the overall prediction uncertainty. By integrating conformal prediction, change point detection, and segment importance analysis, the algorithm provides a robust framework for quantifying localized contributions to uncertainty. This approach enables a deeper understanding of how specific temporal segments impact the predictive model's confidence and reliability. However, a key question remains: *How can we systematically determine the importance of each segment by quantifying its specific contribution to the overall prediction uncertainty?*

Initially, a baseline prediction interval $[\ell_{\text{base}}, u_{\text{base}}]$ is computed for the test sample x_{test} using conformal prediction at a predefined error level α, resulting in the prediction $\hat{y}$ (6). Subsequently, the signal is divided into distinct segments $\mathcal{I} = \{I_1, I_2, \ldots, I_k\}$ using the PELT algorithm as defined in Eq. (9) for change point detection in step (10). Each detected segment captures a specific temporal regime with unique characteristics.

For each perturbed segment $I_i \in \mathcal{I}$, updated prediction bounds $[\ell_i, u_i]$ are computed, reflecting the impact of local perturbations on the prediction uncertainty in step (11). The deviation of these updated bounds from the baseline

Algorithm 1. Compute Feature Importance with ConformaSegment

Require: Sample X_{test}, True value y_{test}, Error Rate α, PELT Penalty λ
Ensure: Importance values $\{s_i\}$ for each segment
1: Compute confidence interval for original signal:

$$(\hat{y}, \ell_{\text{base}}, u_{\text{base}}) \leftarrow \text{GetSingleConformalForecast}(\alpha, \mathbf{X}_{\text{cal}}, \mathbf{y}_{\text{cal}}, X_{\text{test}}, y_{\text{test}})$$

2: Detect change points with PELT:

$$\mathcal{I} \leftarrow \text{DetectChangePoints}(\mathbf{x}_{\text{test}}, \lambda) \tag{10}$$

3: Collect new bounds for each defined segment:

$$(\hat{y}', \{(\ell_i, u_i)\}) \leftarrow \text{GetBoundsForPerturbedSegments}(\mathcal{I}, x_{\text{test}}, y_{\text{test}}, \alpha) \tag{11}$$

4: Compute importance weights by using bounds retrieved:

$$\{s_i\} \leftarrow \text{ComputeImportanceWeights}(\ell_{\text{base}}, u_{\text{base}}, \{(\ell_i, u_i)\}) \tag{12}$$

5: Visualize segments and their importance weights retrieved:

$$\text{VisualizeFeatureImportance}(X_{\text{test}}, \hat{y}', \mathcal{I}, \ell_{\text{base}}, u_{\text{base}}, \{s_i\}) \tag{13}$$

6: **return** $\{s_i\}$

---

interval is used to calculate the significance weights s_i, as expressed in step (12). These weights quantify the contribution of each segment to the overall uncertainty, enabling a localized interpretability of the model's predictions.

Finally, the segments, importance values, and predictions are visualized to provide an intuitive representation of the results as shown in step (13) in Algorithm 1. This visualization highlights the segments most responsible for variations in prediction uncertainty, offering a pathway for a deeper analysis of the underlying data patterns. A key question arises: *How are these importance weights s_i calculated, and what makes them an effective measure of segment importance in explaining prediction uncertainty?* Two algorithms are designed to work in sequence to evaluate the significance of segments within a time series in terms of their impact on overall prediction uncertainty. These steps integrate perturbation methods, conformal prediction, and importance weight calculation.

The Algorithm 2, *Get Bounds for Perturbed Segments*, operates on the set of segments $\mathcal{I}$ obtained through change point detection. It starts by initializing empty lists for the lower bounds $\hat{l}_i$ and upper bounds $\hat{u}_i$ for each segment intervention. For each segment $\mathcal{I}_i \in \mathcal{I}$, the signal $\mathbf{x}_{\text{test}}$ is perturbed by adding uniform noise within a specified range n_r, as shown in Eq. (14).

Definition 4. (Uniform Noise). *Uniform noise [38] is generated by sampling from a uniform distribution $\mathcal{U}(a,b)$, where all values in $[a,b]$ have equal probability. Given a signal $\mathbf{x} = (x_1, \ldots, x_n)$ and an index set $\mathcal{I} \subseteq \{1, \ldots, n\}$, uniform noise replaces x_i at indices $i \in \mathcal{I}$ with $r_i \sim \mathcal{U}(a,b)$, yielding:*

$$\mathbf{x}' = (x_1, \ldots, x_{i-1}, r_i, x_{i+1}, \ldots, x_n), \quad \forall i \in \mathcal{I}. \tag{14}$$

This perturbed signal $\mathbf{x}_{\text{test}}'$ as demonstrated in Definition 4 is then used to perform conformal prediction, yielding the modified prediction $\hat{y}'$, as well as the corresponding lower and upper bounds $\hat{l}_i$ and $\hat{u}_i$, according to Eq. 16 . These bounds are stored in their respective lists, which are subsequently returned as outputs, capturing the uncertainty introduced by the perturbation in each segment.

Algorithm 2. Get Bounds For Perturbed Segments

Require: $\mathcal{I}$: Set of segments from change point detection, x_{test}: Input signal, y_{test}: True target value, α: Miscoverage level, n_r: Noise range for uniform noise addition
Ensure: $\hat{y}'$: Prediction for the modified signal, $\{\hat{l}_{ls}, \hat{u}_{ls}\}$: Lower and upper bounds for each segment
1: Initialize empty lists for storing lower and upper bounds:
$$\hat{l}_{ls} \leftarrow \emptyset, \quad \hat{u}_{ls} \leftarrow \emptyset$$
2: **for** each segment $\mathcal{I}_i \in \mathcal{I}$ **do**
3:     Modify the signal $\mathcal{I}_i$ by adding uniform noise within range n_r as in Eq. (14) :
$$\mathbf{x}_{\text{test}}' = \text{PerturbSegmentWithNoise}(\mathbf{x}_{\text{test}}, \mathcal{I}_i, n_r) \tag{15}$$
4:     Perform conformal prediction on the modified signal $\mathbf{x}_{\text{test}}'$:
$$(\hat{y}', \hat{l}_i, \hat{u}_i) \leftarrow \text{GetSingleConformalForecast}(\alpha, \mathbf{X}_{\text{cal}}, \mathbf{y}_{\text{cal}}, \mathbf{x}_{\text{test}}', y_{\text{test}}) \tag{16}$$
5:     Store the lower and upper bounds of the modified signal:
$$\hat{l}_{ls} \leftarrow \hat{l}_{ls} \cup \hat{l}_i, \quad \hat{u}_{ls} \leftarrow \hat{u}_{ls} \cup \hat{u}_i \tag{17}$$
6: **end for**
7: **return** $\hat{y}', \{\hat{l}_{ls}, \hat{u}_{ls}\}$: Modified prediction and bounds for each segment from (17)

The Algorithm 3, *Compute Importance Weights*, calculates the importance values for each segment based on the bounds obtained in Algorithm 2. It begins by computing the change in the upper bounds, $\Delta \hat{u}_i$, as the absolute difference between the base upper bound $\hat{u}_{\text{base}}$ and the perturbed upper bound $\hat{u}_i$, as expressed in Eq. (18). Similarly, it calculates the change in the lower bounds, $\Delta \hat{l}_i$, as the absolute difference between the base lower bound $\hat{l}_{\text{base}}$ and the perturbed lower bound $\hat{l}_i$, as shown in Eq. (19). These two changes are combined to compute the importance value s_i for each segment, as given by Eq. (20), where the importance value is the sum of the absolute changes in the upper and lower bounds. This final value, s_i, quantifies the contribution of each segment to the overall prediction uncertainty.

By following these two steps, the algorithms provide a measure of how each segment, when perturbed, affects the prediction bounds and ultimately the

Algorithm 3. Compute Importance Weights

Require: $\hat{u}_{\text{base}}$: Upper bound of the base prediction interval, $\hat{l}_{\text{base}}$: Lower bound of the base prediction interval, $\hat{u}_i$: Upper bound of the i-th segment, $\hat{l}_i$: Lower bound of the i-th segment (17)
Ensure: $\{s_i\}$: Significance values for each segment
1: Compute the change in the upper bound:

$$\Delta \hat{u}_i = |\hat{u}_{\text{base}}| - |\hat{u}_i| \quad \forall i \tag{18}$$

2: Compute the change in the lower bound:

$$\Delta \hat{l}_i = \left|\hat{l}_{\text{base}}\right| - \left|\hat{l}_i\right| \quad \forall i \tag{19}$$

3: Combine the changes in the upper bound, as defined in step (18), and the lower bound, as defined in step (19), to compute the significance values:

$$s_i = |\Delta \hat{u}_i| + \left|\Delta \hat{l}_i\right| \quad \forall i \tag{20}$$

4: **return** $\{s_i\}$: Importance values for each segment from (20)

---

uncertainty in the model's prediction. The first algorithm introduces noise to the signal and calculates the resulting modified bounds. The Algorithm 2 then evaluates the importance of each segment by analyzing changes in these bounds, offering insight into the localized impact of specific segments on overall prediction uncertainty. The importance values s_i, generated by the Algorithm 3 identify the segments that contribute most significantly to the model's uncertainty.

4.2 Efficiency and Computational Complexity of ConformaSegment

The computational complexity of *ConformaSegment* is determined by three components: perturbation, change point detection, and conformal prediction. Perturbing k intervals takes $O(n)$, change point detection with PELT is $O(k \cdot n)$, and conformal prediction requires $O(k \cdot m \log m)$. Therefore, the overall complexity is $O(k \cdot n + k \cdot m \log m)$, scaling linearly with the number of segments and signal length, and logarithmically with the calibration set size.

4.3 ConformaSegment in Practice: An Example Scenario

This section provides a practical example to showcase the interpretability and applicability of the proposed algorithm. Using the Sunspot dataset [39], we demonstrate how ConformaSegment generates model-agnostic, post-hoc explanations. Collected by NASA's Goddard Space Flight Center, this dataset captures monthly sunspot numbers over decades, reflecting solar activity trends. Its cyclical and seasonal nature makes it well-suited for assessing temporal forecasting models.

As a model-agnostic framework, ConformaSegment enables users to employ any forecasting model of their choice. An essential step in this process is to preserve a portion of the dataset as unseen calibration data, as described in Sect. 2.4. Although there is no strict rule for determining the exact number of calibration instances, the choice should be guided by the desired coverage metric. Setting N=1000 is often sufficient to achieve reliable results in various use cases [16].

Once trained and calibrated, the model generates predictions and explainability outputs. We used a four-layer LSTM regressor with dropout, designed to capture temporal dependencies and predict values from the *Monthly Mean Total Sunspot Numbers*. The current ConformaSegment explains univariate time series as a local explainer, targeting single sequences of $n = 50$ points. For segment importance analysis, we used `get_feature_importance()` as shown in Listing 1.1., which requires (i) the trained *model*, (ii) the *sample*, (iii) *alpha* for the conformal prediction error rate, (iv) calibration datasets *X_cal* and *y_cal*, and (v) *penalty* for the Pruned Exact Linear Time (PELT) change point detection algorithm [36]. This method ensures flexibility and reproducibility.

```
import conformasegment as cs
# Features and labels extraction
X, y = df.drop(["target"], axis=1), df["target"]
# Train, test, and calibration split
X_train, X_test, X_cal, y_train, y_test, y_cal = 
    data_split(X, y, split_rate=0.5, stratify=y)
# Defining and training your model
regressor = make_lstm().fit(X_train, y_train)
# Define parameters
sample = X_test[165] # 165 is sample index
alpha = 0.05 # error rate of conformal prediction
penalty = 4 # change point algorithm PELT penalty rate
cs.get_feature_importance(regressor, sample, X_cal,
    y_cal, alpha, penalty) # Call explainer for specific
    instance
```

Listing 1.1. How to use ConformaSegment package for explaining forecasting time-series sample?

Furthermore, as shown in Fig. 1, the output includes both the model's prediction and the confidence interval generated by the conformal prediction algorithm. The interval (highlighted in orange) signifies that, with the user-specified guarantee rate (set at 0.05, or 95% confidence in this case), the prediction is expected to fall within this range for the given sample. The vertical dashed lines in the figure represent the detected change points, which divide the time series into segments. In each segment (defined between consecutive change point lines), a rectangle indicates the importance weight assigned by the algorithm. The colors within the segments are aligned with these importance weights to facilitate interpretability.

For this specific sample, the time series consists of 50 data points. The forecasted value for the *Monthly Mean Total Sunspot Numbers* is 1.50. Although the predicted value is not correct, the confidence interval indicates that the true

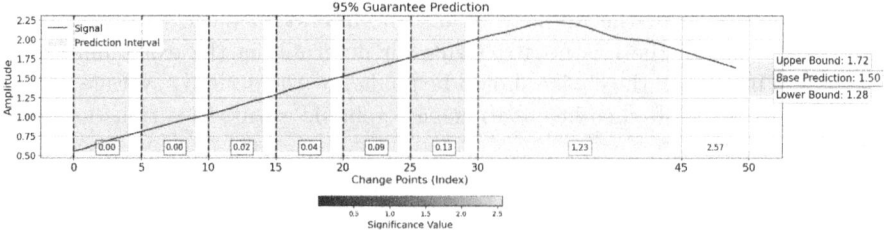

Fig. 1. Sample ConformaSegment Output. Base prediction is the value predicted by the conformal framework, with lower and upper bounds provided as in the confidence interval. Dashed lines represent the change points, while the rectangles between them indicate the importance weights calculated.

value will fall within the range of $lower\_bound = 1.28$ and $upper\_bound = 1.72$ with 95% confidence. The most significant segment, as indicated by the change points, is the last segment (between change points 45-50), which is weighted with an importance score of 2.57. The segment between change points 30-45 is assigned a weight of 1.23, while the segment between change points 25-30 has a weight of 0.13. These results suggest that the model relies most heavily on the recent data (the segment 45-50) when making predictions about the next sunspot numbers. For a more flexible analysis with an increased number of change points, the algorithm uses an adjustable PELT penalty parameter. This flexibility is crucial in scenarios where the time series is non-stationary, meaning its patterns and statistical properties change over time, requiring adaptive segmentation to capture varying importance levels accurately. The software package and implementation details can be found in the following link https://github.com/rabia174/ConformaSegment.

5 Experiments and Evaluations

5.1 Experimental Settings

Datasets. We evaluated the generalizability of our framework using five publicly available time-series datasets from diverse industries. Each dataset includes a designated target signal column, sequence length (measured in time steps), frequency, and unit, as summarized in Table 1. Following the framework's requirements, we selected the target numerical column and arranged it in sorted order. To train and meet the input dimensions required by sequential models, we segmented the data into smaller sequences and structured them accordingly.

Models. We selected three distinct models for the forecasting task, as outlined in Table 2. By employing diverse models, we harness their complementary strengths to capture varied patterns and estimating uncertainty, enhancing both the clarity and robustness of our analysis.

Table 1. Summary of Datasets for Time Series Analysis

Dataset	Target Signal	Sequences	Freq.	Unit
Sunspot [39]	Total Spot Numbers	50 ts	Monthly	Count (Spots)
Seattle Weather [40]	Max Temp	100 ts	Hourly	Celsius (°C)
ECG200 [41]	Abnormal ECG	140 ts	1 Hz	Millivolts (mV)
Strawberry [42]	Healthy Strawberries	235 ts	N/A	Wavenumbers (cm^{-1})
Yoga Pose [43]	Actor (Female)	300 ts	N/A	Pixels (one-dimensional)

Table 2. Summary of Model Architectures. Each model is trained using the Adam optimizer with Mean Squared Error as the loss function. The output layer for all models is a Dense layer with 1 unit. Dropout (rate: 0.2) regularization details are specified for each model. We utilized Tensorflow [44] for modeling.

Model Type	Details
LSTM	- Four LSTM layers with 100 units each
GRU	- Three GRU layers with 50, 25, and 10 units
Simple RNN	- Four RNN layers with 100 units each

Explainers. In this study, we compared our proposed framework, ConformaSegment, with Saliency Maps and Integrated Gradients, two well-suited methods for explaining deep sequential models such as LSTM and RNNs. These gradient-based methods leverage internal gradients to capture temporal dependencies and non-linear relationships in time-series data. They are computationally efficient, differentiable, and capable of providing fine-grained attributions for each timestep.

LIME [45] and SHAP [46] are not ideal for time-series forecasting, as they assume independent feature contributions and ignore temporal dependencies. Designed for single-instance tasks, they fail to consider the relevance of features across time steps. In contrast, ConformaSegment perturbs entire segments, preserving temporal dependencies critical for models like LSTM, RNN, and GRU, enabling more robust interpretability.

To ensure a robust and meaningful comparison, we focus on gradient-based methods that align with the characteristics of deep sequential models and the datasets under study. Table 3 summarizes the compared frameworks, highlighting that ConformaSegment is the only uncertainty-aware feature importance method specifically designed for time-series forecasting.

Experimental Setup. We evaluated the *effectiveness* and *robustness* of our method by comparing feature importance maps (weighted time-series segments) from ConformaSegment and other methods. All models in Table 2 were trained on datasets with identical training, calibration, and test set sizes, with varying sequence lengths as detailed in Table 1. Since ConformaSegment is segment-

Table 3. Comparison of Explainability Methods for Time Series Segment-Based Tasks

	Saliency Maps	Integrated Gradients	ConformaSegment
Handling Temporal Dependencies	No temporal consideration	Accounts for temporal relationships	Considers temporal dependencies through perturbation
Uncertainty Awareness	No uncertainty estimation	Can estimate uncertainty but lacks integration	Integrates uncertainty with coverage guarantees
Computational Complexity	Simple and fast	More computationally expensive	Moderately complex, optimized for segment detection
Model-Agnosticism	Dependent on model gradients	Dependent on model gradients	Model-agnostic
Robustness to Perturbations	Struggles with stability under random fluctuations	More stable than Saliency Maps but still affected by random fluctuations	Captures the effect of perturbations more precisely

based, we adapted other methods by averaging their feature importance values over segments defined by change points for consistent comparison.

To test *effectiveness*, we assessed the framework's ability to identify key intervals. The most important interval, based on feature importance, was perturbed with uniform noise, and model performance was re-evaluated on the same test set. Let $x_{t_1}, x_{t_2}, \ldots, x_{t_n}$ represent the time series with intervals $[t_i, t_j]$ as change points. The perturbed series is $x'_t = x_t + \mathcal{N}(x_{t_i}, x_{t_j})$, where $\mathcal{N}$ represents the added noise within the segment.

For time series forecasting, we chose **MAE** Eq. (1) for its accuracy and robustness against outliers, **R^2 score** Eq. (2) for evaluating model fit and trend capture, and **C(α)** Eq. (3) to ensure reliability within confidence intervals. These performance metrics for time-series models collectively balance accuracy, explanatory power, and reliability.

Definition 5. (Effectiveness). *Effectiveness is quantified by comparing the performance of the model in the perturbed series $\hat{y}(x'_t)$ with the baseline performance $\hat{y}(x_t)$. Let $x_t = \{x_{t_1}, x_{t_2}, \ldots, x_{t_n}\}$ represent the time series, and let $[t_i, t_j]$ denote the most significant segment defined by the explainability framework. The perturbed series x'_t is defined as:*

$$x'_t = \begin{cases} x_t + \mathcal{N}(t), & \text{if } t \in [t_i, t_j] \\ x_t, & \text{otherwise,} \end{cases} \quad (21)$$

where $\mathcal{N}(t)$ represents the uniform noise as explained in Definition 4 added to each individual time point x_t within the segment $[t_i, t_j]$. Effectiveness is quantified by analyzing the model's ability to maintain accurate predictions and proper coverage when the most significant segments are perturbed. This is assessed through three metrics:

– **Trend consistency (R^2):** Measured by the relative change in R^2 performance before and after perturbation. This is defined as:

$$\Delta_{trend}^{R^2} = \frac{|R^2(x_t) - R^2(x_t')|}{R^2(x_t)}, \qquad (22)$$

where $R^2(x_t)$ and $R^2(x_t')$ represent the R^2 scores on the original and perturbed series, respectively, given R^2's emphasis on how well the model maintains its ability to capture trends in the data.

– **Error consistency (MAE):** Measured by the relative change in MAE performance before and after perturbation. This is defined as:

$$\Delta_{error}^{MAE} = \frac{|MAE(x_t') - MAE(x_t)|}{MAE(x_t)}, \qquad (23)$$

where $MAE(x_t)$ and $MAE(x_t')$ represent the MAE values on the original and perturbed series, respectively, given the focus on the model's ability to maintain stable error margins.

– **Coverage consistency:** Evaluated by the relative change in coverage between the original and perturbed series. Coverage measures, as defined in Definition 7, the fraction of true target values y within the prediction intervals. Coverage consistency is quantified as:

$$\Delta_{coverage} = \frac{|Coverage(x_t) - Coverage(x_t')|}{Coverage(x_t)}, \qquad (24)$$

where a larger change indicates better consistency in maintaining reliable coverage across perturbations.

Larger changes in the measurements indicate that the framework is sensitive to significant segments when perturbed, maintaining consistency through larger performance gaps. To assess robustness, we tested the framework under varying α values, evaluating its ability to preserve stable feature importance maps.

Definition 6. (Robustness). Let $\alpha \in (0,1)$ be the error rate parameter used during calibration to control the miscoverage rate of the conformal prediction intervals. For a test set $\mathcal{D}_{test}$, the prediction interval $[\hat{y}_{lower}(x), \hat{y}_{upper}(x)]$ for each $x \in \mathcal{D}_{test}$ is defined as:

$$\Pr(y \in [\hat{y}_{lower}(x), \hat{y}_{upper}(x)]) \geq 1 - \alpha,$$

where y is the true target value. Robustness is evaluated by comparing feature importance maps at varying α values using the Pearson correlation coefficient [47] r, defined as:

$$r(F_\alpha, F_{\alpha'}) = \frac{\sum_{i=1}^{n}(F_\alpha(i) - \bar{F}_\alpha)(F_{\alpha'}(i) - \bar{F}_{\alpha'})}{\sqrt{\sum_{i=1}^{n}(F_\alpha(i) - \bar{F}_\alpha)^2 \sum_{i=1}^{n}(F_{\alpha'}(i) - \bar{F}_{\alpha'})^2}},$$

where $F_\alpha(i)$ and $F_{\alpha'}(i)$ are the feature importance values at error rates α and α', and $\bar{F}_\alpha$, $\bar{F}_{\alpha'}$ are their means.

High correlations in the robustness measure (Definition 6) between feature importance maps across different α values indicate that the framework consistently identifies important features in a highly similar way, independent of α variations.

6 Results and Discussion

In this section, we present the results for *effectiveness*, as defined in Definition 5, and *robustness*, as formulated in Definition 6.

Table 4. Effectiveness: Performance and coverage on x_{test} using a model trained on x'_{train} with the most significant segment perturbed by uniform noise. Low values confirm correct segment identification, causing reduced test performance. Bold values highlight the best results per dataset.

Dataset	Technique	LSTM			RNN			GRU		
		R^2	Cov.	MAE	R^2	Cov.	MAE	R^2	Cov.	MAE
Seattle W.	Original Data	0.83	94.5%	2.38	0.82	93.1%	2.56	0.78	94.2%	2.61
	Saliency Map	0.82	92.2%	2.40	0.80	93.6%	2.56	0.76	93.9%	2.73
	Integrated Gradients	0.81	93.3%	2.47	0.68	92.8%	3.16	0.68	92.8%	3.31
	Random Segments	0.66	82.3%	3.44	-0.39	42.7%	7.56	0.64	87.8%	3.36
	ConformaSegment	**0.66**	**79.8%**	**3.36**	**-1.7**	**19.9%**	**10.6**	**0.56**	**84.2%**	**3.88**
Sunspot	Original Data	0.73	80.6%	26.1	0.76	91.4%	25.3	0.70	83.6%	28.1
	Saliency Map	0.67	80.8%	28.7	0.78	92.6%	23.4	0.66	78.4%	31.3
	Integrated Gradients	0.68	92.8%	27.3	0.74	91.4%	25.7	0.71	83.6%	29.7
	Random Segments	-0.03	42.4%	58.6	0.18	69.6%	47.9	-0.7	53.8%	66.3
	ConformaSegment	**0.66**	**78.4%**	**29.8**	**0.27**	**73.0%**	**43.2**	**-0.11**	**53.8%**	**49.6**
ECG200	Original Data	0.90	97.8%	0.14	0.92	98.4%	0.13	0.94	96.4%	0.11
	Saliency Map	0.69	93.6%	0.25	0.86	97.2%	0.24	0.92	95.0%	0.13
	Integrated Gradients	0.35	97.8%	0.53	0.51	98.4%	0.46	0.51	98.4%	0.46
	Random Segments	0.23	81.8%	0.58	0.43	86.4%	0.46	0.62	84.6%	0.40
	ConformaSegment	**0.26**	**84.8%**	**0.50**	**0.37**	**87.6%**	**0.54**	**0.30**	**72.4%**	**0.49**
Strawberry	Original Data	0.98	89.6%	0.08	0.95	89.0%	0.15	0.97	94.6%	0.10
	Saliency Map	0.92	75.6%	0.16	0.95	80.6%	0.15	0.96	88.6%	0.14
	Integrated Gradients	0.60	98.6%	0.40	0.85	89.0%	0.28	0.07	94.6%	0.57
	Random Segments	0.05	31.6%	0.59	0.66	42.6%	0.44	0.24	36.3%	0.54
	ConformaSegment	**0.01**	**22.6%**	**0.60**	**0.47**	**16.8%**	**0.62**	**0.11**	**27.4%**	**0.72**
Yoga Pose	Original Data	0.99	98.0%	0.05	0.97	97.2%	0.07	0.98	99.2%	0.08
	Saliency Map	0.87	66.2%	0.18	0.95	88.2%	0.14	0.98	99.2%	0.08
	Integrated Gradients	0.33	98.0%	0.65	0.04	97.2%	0.73	0.24	98.4%	0.66
	Random Segments	0.02	17.6%	0.74	0.01	32.4%	0.73	0.63	57.6%	0.42
	ConformaSegment	**0.28**	**14.2%**	**0.68**	**0.03**	**27.0%**	**0.73**	**-0.04**	**31.8%**	**0.77**

Table 5. Robustness: Pearson Correlation Analysis (6) for Diverse α Levels in Conformal Prediction Framework Across Datasets and Models

α	Model	Seattle Weather	Sunspot	ECG200	Strawberry	Yoga Pose
0.005 vs. 0.10	LSTM	0.9928	0.9789	0.9176	0.8211	0.8453
	RNN	0.9957	0.7809	0.9372	0.9096	0.9162
	GRU	0.9780	0.9951	0.8083	0.8467	0.9162
0.10 vs. 0.25	LSTM	0.9848	0.9702	0.9081	0.7951	0.9400
	RNN	0.9926	0.8070	0.9954	0.9562	0.8770
	GRU	0.9724	0.9953	0.7675	0.8211	0.8770
0.05 vs. 0.25	LSTM	0.9891	0.9745	0.8899	0.8788	0.9408
	RNN	0.9940	0.8035	0.9939	0.9990	0.9723
	GRU	0.9840	0.9962	0.8253	0.8262	0.9723

Evaluating Effectiveness. ConformaSegment's effectiveness is validated through an perturbation study (see Experimental Setup), where perturbing the most significant segment led to substantial performance degradation in all models (Table 4). Before generating explanations, models were trained for 50–500 epochs, depending on dataset complexity, to optimize performance and prevent overfitting. Each dataset was split into equal-sized training, calibration, and testing sets. When the key interval identified by *ConformaSegment* was perturbed, R^2, MAE, and Coverage ($C(\alpha)$) dropped significantly. In the Sunspot dataset, Coverage decreased 30.27x, and MAE increased 13.45x compared to Integrated Gradients. In the Seattle W. dataset, coverage fell 13.39x, and MAE increased 1.81x. The largest drop in R2 was 16.99x compared to Saliency Maps and 8.50x versus Integrated Gradients. Furthermore, the consistency analysis between the performance metrics (R^2) of the original data and the data with uniformly added noise, where the highest-ranking segment was identified by ConformaSegment, revealed a t-statistic of 5.0007 ($p = 1.9 \times 10^{-4} < 0.001$), a mean difference of 0.7393, and a Cohen's d of 1.8221. These results indicate both statistical significance and practical relevance. Figure 2 shows that the framework outperforms Saliency Maps and Integrated Gradients in identifying critical segments.

Evaluating Robustness. Using the models listed in Table 2, training was performed on the original data and then feature importance maps were generated at different user-specified error rates (α), as required by the conformal prediction framework in ConformaSegment.

The high Pearson correlation rates across α levels indicate consistent feature importance patterns across models Table 5. A one-way ANOVA ($F = 0.375, p = 0.690$) found no significant differences among LSTM, RNN, and GRU, suggesting highly similar interpretability.

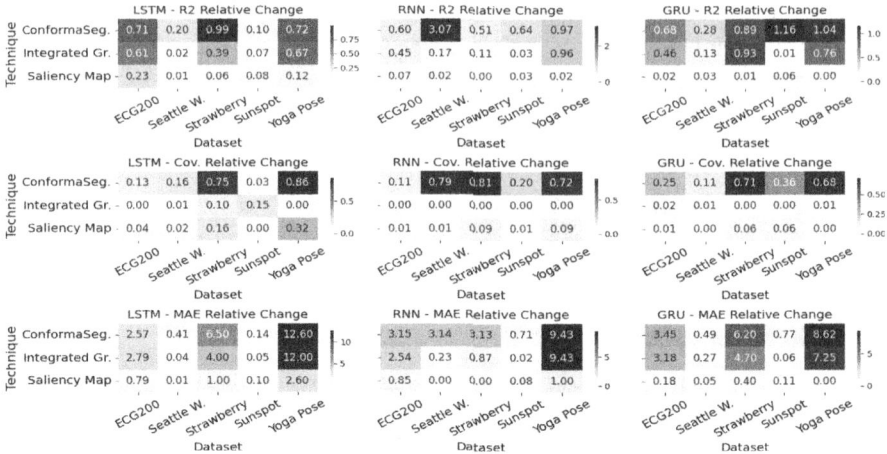

Fig. 2. Effectiveness with respect to MAE, R2, and Coverage. In the first row *Trend Consistency* (22), third row *Error Consistency* (23), and in the middle row *Coverage Consistency* (24) results have been measured and visualized on heatmaps.

7 Conclusions, Limitations, and Future Work

We introduced ConformaSegment, a novel algorithm for identifying and quantifying significant segments in time-series forecasting, leveraging conformal prediction for robust uncertainty estimation. ConformaSegment provides domain-specific insights, such as in ECG analysis, where it identifies key weeks or days affecting heart rate variations, aiding healthcare analysis, pattern recognition, diagnosis, and treatment. This demonstrates its broader applicability beyond traditional feature importance methods. By detecting change points and systematically perturbing segments, the algorithm assesses their contribution to predictive uncertainty through variations in the confidence interval bounds. This approach enhances interpretability while ensuring reliable performance with formal guarantees on prediction uncertainty.

Evaluations on five real-world datasets, employing diverse sequential models such as LSTM, RNN, and GRU, demonstrate the effectiveness and robustness of our approach. Comparative analysis with Saliency Maps and Integrated Gradients, highlights the superior performance of ConformaSegment in accurately identifying, quantifying, and prioritizing significant segments while addressing predictive uncertainty. Using the distribution-free nature of conformal prediction, the feature importance maps generated under varying user-specified error rates, corresponding to the coverage guarantees of the conformal framework, exhibited strong correlations. This consistency underscores the robustness and reliability of the proposed framework.

While conformal prediction provides strong coverage guarantees, the quality of explanations is influenced by the model architecture, highlighting a trade-off between interpretability and computational complexity.

For future improvements, we propose allowing users to integrate their own change point detection algorithms and extending the framework to support multivariate time-series forecasting explanations, enhancing its applicability.

Acknowledgments. The author Fatima Rabia is a PhD student at the University of Bologna, DISI, funded by PNRR (Piano Nazionale di Ripresa e Resilienza) & Automobili Lamborghini S.p.A, Italy. Tuwe Löfström acknowledges the Swedish Knowledge Foundation and industrial partners for funding the SPARK research and education environment at Jönköping University, Sweden (Project: PREMACOP, grant no. 20220187).

Disclosure of Interests. We declare no competing interests for this study.

References

1. Bui, C., Pham, N., Vo, A., Tran, A., Nguyen, A., Le, T.: Time series forecasting for healthcare diagnosis and prognostics with the focus on cardiovascular diseases. In: 6th International Conference on the Development of Biomedical Engineering in Vietnam (BME6), pp. 809–818. Springer, Singapore (2018)
2. Sezer, O.B., Gudelek, M.U., Ozbayoglu, A.M.: Financial time series forecasting with deep learning: a systematic literature review: 2005–2019. Appl. Soft Comput. **90**, 106181 (2020)
3. Chniti, G., Bakir, H., Zaher, H.: E-commerce time series forecasting using LSTM neural network and support vector regression. In: Proc. Int. Conf. Big Data Internet Things, pp. 80–84 (2017)
4. Dixit, A., Jain, M.: Driving style based trajectory prediction of the surrounding vehicles using LSTM & ARIMA in autonomous driving. J. Electr. Syst. **20**(2), 2631–2640 (2024)
5. Riesgo, J.M.R., Cabrera Fernández, J.L.: Reservoir neural network computing for time series forecasting in aerospace: potential applications to predictive maintenance. Eng. Proc. **68**(1), 17 (2024)
6. Box, G.E., Jenkins, G.M., Reinsel, G.C.: Time Series Analysis: Forecasting and Control. Holden-Day (1976)
7. Holt, C.C.: Forecasting Trends and Seasonals by Exponentially Weighted Averages. Office of Naval Research Memorandum (1957)
8. Rumelhart, D.E., Hinton, G.E., Williams, R.J.: Learning representations by back-propagating errors. Nature **323**(6088), 533–536 (1986)
9. Hochreiter, S., Schmidhuber, J.: Long short-term memory. Neural Comput. **9**(8), 1735–1780 (1997)
10. Vaswani, A., et al.: Attention is all you need. In: Adv. Neural Inf. Process. Syst. (NeurIPS) (2017)
11. Pan, J., Chen, J.: Explainable time-series forecasting models: a survey. arXiv preprint arXiv:2305.14582 (2023)
12. Zhao, Z., Shi, Y., Wu, S., Yang, F., Song, W., Liu, N.: Interpretation of time-series deep models: a survey. arxiv preprint arXiv:2305.14582 (2023)
13. Yapicioglu, F.R., Stramiglio, A., Vitali, F.: ConformaSight: conformal prediction-based global and model-agnostic explainability framework. In: World Conference on Explainable Artificial Intelligence, pp. 270–293. Springer, Cham (2024)

14. Löfström, T., Yapicioglu, F.R., Stramiglio, A., Löfström, H., Vitali, F.: Fast calibrated explanations: efficient and uncertainty-aware explanations for machine learning models. arXiv preprint arXiv:2410.21129 (2024)
15. Wang, T., et al.: From aleatoric to epistemic: exploring uncertainty quantification techniques in artificial intelligence. arXiv preprint arXiv:2501.03282 (2025)
16. Vovk, V., Gammerman, A., Saunders, C.: Machine-learning applications of algorithmic randomness. In: International Conference on Machine Learning (ICML), pp. 444–453 (1999)
17. Angelopoulos, A.N., Bates, S.: A gentle introduction to conformal prediction and distribution-free uncertainty quantification. arXiv preprint arXiv:2107.07511 (2021)
18. Box, G.E.P., Jenkins, G.M.: Time series analysis: forecasting and control. Holden-Day (1976)
19. Rumelhart, D.E., Hinton, G.E., Williams, R.J.: Learning representations by back-propagating errors. Nature **323**(6088), 533–536 (1986). https://doi.org/10.1038/323533a0
20. Cho, K., Bengio, Y., Bengio, S., Vinyals, O., Schuster, M.: Properties of neural machine translation: Encoder-decoder approaches. arXiv preprint arXiv:1409.1259 (2014)
21. Vaswani, A., et al.: Attention is all you need. In: Advances in Neural Information Processing Systems (NeurIPS), vol. 30. Curran Associates, Inc. (2017)
22. Angelov, P.P., Soares, E.A., Jiang, R., Arnold, N.I., Atkinson, P.M.: Explainable artificial intelligence: an analytical review. Wiley Interdiscip. Rev. Data Min. Knowl. Discov. **11**(5), e1424 (2021)
23. Podkopaev, A., Ramdas, A.: Tracking the risk of a deployed model and detecting harmful distribution shifts. arXiv preprint arXiv:2110.06177 (2021)
24. Tibshirani, R.J., Foygel Barber, R., Candes, E., Ramdas, A.: Conformal prediction under covariate shift. In: Advances in Neural Information Processing Systems (NeurIPS), vol. 32 (2019)
25. Theissler, A., Spinnato, F., Schlegel, U., Guidotti, R.: Explainable AI for time series classification: a review, taxonomy and research directions. IEEE Access **10**, 100700–100724 (2022)
26. Assaf, R., Schumann, A.: Explainable deep neural networks for multivariate time series predictions. In: Proceedings of the 28th International Joint Conference on Artificial Intelligence (IJCAI), pp. 6488–6490 (2019)
27. Sivill, T., Flach, P.: Limesegment: meaningful, realistic time series explanations. In: International Conference on Artificial Intelligence and Statistics (AISTATS), pp. 3418–3433. PMLR (2022)
28. Fauvel, K., Lin, T., Masson, V., Fromont, É., Termier, A.: XCM: an explainable convolutional neural network for multivariate time series classification. Mathematics **9**(23), 3137 (2021)
29. Karlsson, I., Rebane, J., Papapetrou, P., Gionis, A.: Locally and globally explainable time series tweaking. Knowl. Inf. Syst. **62**(5), 1671–1700 (2020)
30. Karlsson, I., Rebane, J., Papapetrou, P., Gionis, A.: Explainable time series tweaking via irreversible and reversible temporal transformations. In: 2018 IEEE International Conference on Data Mining (ICDM), pp. 207–216. IEEE (2018)
31. Shifaz, A., Pelletier, C., Petitjean, F., Webb, G.I.: TS-CHIEF: a scalable and accurate forest algorithm for time series classification. Data Min. Knowl. Disc. **34**(3), 742–775 (2020). https://doi.org/10.1007/s10618-020-00679-8
32. Ilic, I., Görgülü, B., Cevik, M., Baydoğan, M.G.: Explainable boosted linear regression for time series forecasting. Patt. Recognit. **120**, 108144 (2021)

33. Castro Silva, V., Zarpelão, B.B., Medvet, E., Barbon, S.: Explainable time series tree: an explainable top-down time series segmentation framework. IEEE Access **11**, 120845–120856 (2023)
34. Kono, T., Yamaguchi, S., Nagao, T.: Time series prediction with dual reliability: uncertainty and explainability. In: 2020 IEEE International Conference on Systems, Man, and Cybernetics (SMC), pp. 4095–4102. IEEE (2020)
35. Löfström, T., Löfström, H., Johansson, U., Sönströd, C., Matela, R.: Calibrated explanations for regression. arXiv preprint arXiv:2308.16245 (2023)
36. Killick, R., Fearnhead, P., Eckley, I.A.: Optimal detection of changepoints with a linear computational cost. J. Am. Stat. Assoc. **107**(500), 1590–1598 (2012)
37. Truong, C., Oudre, L., Vayatis, N.: Selective review of offline change point detection methods. Sign. Process. **167**, 107299 (2020)
38. Proakis, J.G., Manolakis, D.G.: Digital Signal Processing: Principles, Algorithms, and Applications, 4th edn. Pearson, Upper Saddle River, NJ (2007)
39. NASA's Goddard Space Flight Center. Sunspot Data. NASA (2025). https://science.nasa.gov/sun/sunspots/, Accessed Jan 2025
40. Kaggle. Seattle Weather Dataset (2025). https://www.kaggle.com/datasets/RTGoldman/seattle-weather, Accessed 15 Jan 2025
41. Lichman, M.: UCI Machine Learning Repository: ECG200 dataset. University of California, Irvine (2013)
42. Szentgyorgyi, R.: UCI Machine Learning Repository: Strawberry dataset. University of California, Irvine (2018)
43. Hossain, M.S., Choi, J.H.: UCI Machine Learning Repository: Yoga dataset. University of California, Irvine (2019)
44. Abadi, M., et al.: TensorFlow: large-scale machine learning on heterogeneous systems. TensorFlow, Google (2016)
45. Ribeiro, M.T., Singh, S., Guestrin, C.: "Why should I trust you?" explaining the predictions of any classifier. In: Proc. of the 22nd ACM SIGKDD Int. Conf. on Knowledge Discovery and Data Mining, pp. 1135–1144 (2016)
46. Lundberg, S.M., Lee, S.I.: A unified approach to interpreting model predictions. In: Proc. of the 31st Int. Conf. on Neural Information Processing Systems, pp. 4765–4774 (2017)
47. Pearson, K.: Mathematical contributions to the theory of evolution. II. Skew variation in homogeneous material. Philosophical Transactions of the Royal Society of London **187**, 453–480 (1896)
48. Gosset, W.S.: The probable error of a mean. Biometrika **6**(1), 1–25 (1908). https://doi.org/10.1093/biomet/6.1.1
49. Cohen, J.: Statistical power analysis for the behavioral sciences. Academic Press (1969)

Open Access This chapter is licensed under the terms of the Creative Commons Attribution 4.0 International License (http://creativecommons.org/licenses/by/4.0/), which permits use, sharing, adaptation, distribution and reproduction in any medium or format, as long as you give appropriate credit to the original author(s) and the source, provide a link to the Creative Commons license and indicate if changes were made.

The images or other third party material in this chapter are included in the chapter's Creative Commons license, unless indicated otherwise in a credit line to the material. If material is not included in the chapter's Creative Commons license and your intended use is not permitted by statutory regulation or exceeds the permitted use, you will need to obtain permission directly from the copyright holder.

FLEXtime: Filterbank Learning to Explain Time Series

Thea Brüsch[1,3], Kristoffer Knutsen Wickstrøm[2(✉)], Mikkel N. Schmidt[1,3], Robert Jenssen[2,3,4], and Tommy Sonne Alstrøm[1,3]

[1] DTU Compute, Technical University of Denmark, Lyngby, Denmark
[2] Department of Physics and Technology, UiT The Arctic University of Norway, Tromsø, Norway
kristoffer.k.wickstrom@uit.no
[3] Pioneer Centre for AI, University of Copenhagen, Copenhagen, Denmark
[4] Norwegian Computing Center, Oslo, Norway

Abstract. State-of-the-art methods for explaining predictions from time series involve learning an instance-wise saliency mask for each time step; however, many types of time series are difficult to interpret in the time domain, due to the inherently complex nature of the data. Instead, we propose to view time series explainability as saliency maps over interpretable parts, leaning on established signal processing methodology on signal decomposition. Specifically, we propose a new method called FLEXtime that uses a bank of bandpass filters to split the time series into frequency bands. Then, we learn the combination of these bands that optimally explains the model's prediction. Our extensive evaluation shows that, on average, FLEXtime outperforms state-of-the-art explainability methods across a range of datasets. FLEXtime fills an important gap in the current time series explainability methodology and is a valuable tool for a wide range of time series such as EEG and audio. Code is available at https://github.com/theabrusch/FLEXtime.

Keywords: Time series explainability · Learnable masks · Filterbanks

1 Introduction

Explainability of black-box models is paramount for safe decision-making in critical domains such as health care [5,12] and finance [62]. Although recent years have seen an abundance of explainability methods developed for images [1,26,33,45,63], time series have been overlooked to a higher degree [22]. A possible reason is the inherently complex nature of time series [50] which makes it difficult for humans to disentangle salient information.

Explainability methods, in general, can be divided into local and global explanations. Our work focuses on local methods. Local explainability methods provide explanations for single samples of data. Local methods often produce explanations as saliency maps over input features [10,55,56], thereby leaving the interpretation of the explanation to the user. Moreover, many methods are based on smoothness and sparsity constraints, assuming localized and sparse information in the explained domain [19,26,33]. This behavior may not be suitable for explaining time series, where salient information may often be found in latent feature domains such as the frequency domain [52]. Consider, as an example, the case where a class is characterized by the presence of two specific frequency components. This characteristic would be neither localized nor sparse if represented in the time domain. The concept is illustrated in Fig. 1 where the explanations in time and frequency domains, respectively, are plotted as heatmaps.

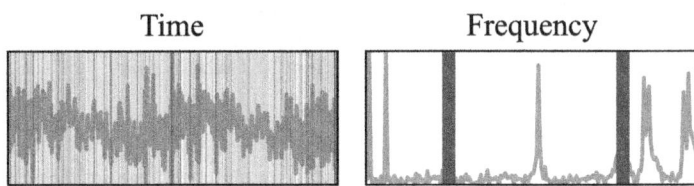

Fig. 1. Explainability methods that provide explanations (green heatmaps) in the time domain fail to parsimoniously explain time series data if the salient information is localized in the frequency domain. (Color figure online)

State-of-the-art methods for explaining time series often rely on learnable masks to create attribution maps in the time domain [19,24,35,36,47]. The masks are learned through gradient descent using an objective function that ensures that the model's output on the masked input aligns with the original output while masking out as much of the input as possible. However, while these methods yield high performance on time series where salient information is localized in the time domain, they are unable to describe salient features in the frequency domain.

In this work, we offer a novel perspective on time series explainability: Instead of saliency maps over the raw input space, we propose learning saliency maps over interpretable parts. Leveraging established signal processing methodology, we decompose the time series using a structured dictionary of interpretable components which serves as a basis for the explanations. Specifically, we propose to use a bandpass filterbank to learn explanations in the frequency domain, but we note that our methods can be adapted to other structured dictionaries. We combine all elements into a framework we refer to as FLEXtime (Filterbank Learning to EXplain time series). FLEXtime provides users the flexibility to define filter banks according to specific domain requirements, enhancing the interpretability of the learned explanations. We show that FLEXtime outperforms our developed baseline FreqMask (a frequency-oriented method based on Dynamask [19]), which learns explanations directly in the discrete Fourier domain. To the best of our knowledge, we are the first to develop a method for learnable explanations for time series in the frequency domain. Our contributions are as follows:

- We propose to reimagine time series explainability as explainability over interpretable parts to learn meaningful saliency maps.
- We propose FLEXtime, which leverages our proposed methodology by using a filterbank of bandpass filters to learn explanations in the frequency domain.
- We present the baseline FreqMask, inspired by Dynamask [19], that computes saliency maps directly on the frequency axis.
- We evaluate FLEXtime and FreqMask across a number of synthetic and real datasets with a range of descriptive metrics. FLEXtime outperforms all baselines, achieving the best average rank on faithfulness, robustness, and smoothness.

2 Previous Work on Time Series Explainability

Explainability for images has been a rapidly evolving field over the past years, whereas explainability for time series remains largely underexplored. While most natural images contain semantics that are easy for humans to decipher, the unintuitive nature of time series data makes interpretation difficult, even for experts [51]. Thus, time series represent unique challenges for the explainability community. Here, we present an overview of relevant work within the image domain and proceed to give an overview of the time series explainability field. Generally, explainability methods can be divided into intrinsic vs. post-hoc based on whether the explainability is build into the model, or if the explanation is computed after training. Additionally, explainability methods can be said to be either model-specific or model-agnostic. Model-agnostic methods can be applied to any model, while model-specific methods can only be applied to some models. We focus on local post-hoc explainability methods.

Explainability for Images. Generally, a number of gradient-based methods have been widely used for image explainability. This category includes Guided backpropagation [55], Layer-wise Relevance Propagation [10], and Integrated Gradients [56], which all use different techniques to distribute the gradient with respect to the model output in the input space. Since these methods require access to model gradients, all of them can be said to belong to the model-specific category. Gradient-based methods have been criticized for their unreliability in robustly determining importance [14].

Occlusion-based methods remove part of the input and assess the change in the model output. RISE is a model-agnostic method that samples masks and uses a weighted average to compute saliency maps [45]. Fong et al. [26] learn the mask using an optimization criterion. Kolek et al. [33] propose a rate-distortion framework to learn the mask. Both of the latter can be said to be model-specific, since they require us to backpropagate gradients from the output through the model to the input. Occlusion-based methods directly observe correlations between input perturbations and model responses.

Explainability in the Time Domain. Some recent work has focused on developing methods tailored for time series. Model-agnostic approaches include adopting methods such as LIME [49], SHAP [37], and RISE [45] to the time series domain [38,43,54]. However, the most successful approaches rely on the occlusion-based approach with learnable masks in the input domain. We base our work on these recent advances of learnable masks, noticing that none of these have explored learnable masks in the frequency domain.

The first method developed specifically for time series, Dynamask [19], poses a learning objective inspired by Fong. et al. [26] to learn extremal masks directly in the time domain. They adopt the method to the time domain, by adding a smoothness regularizer to avoid sudden jumps in saliency over time, and through dynamic perturbations of the input. ExtrMask [24] extends Dynamask by learning the perturbations through a neural network, while ContraLSP additionally applies contrastive learning when learning the perturbations [36]. TimeX recognizes that masking may lead to out-of-domain samples and instead trains a surrogate model that is more robust to masked inputs [47]. TimeX++ [35] uses an information bottleneck to learn the explanations and a neural network to produce in-domain masked samples.

While ExtrMask, TimeX, and TimeX++ all outperform Dynamask, the addition of neural networks for either mask or perturbation generation adds complexity and need for tuning of several hyperparameters - something that is not trivial to do for explainability tasks. Additionally, none of the methods can produce explanations in other domains than the time domain.

Modeling Time Series in the Frequency Domain. Recently, frequency modeling of time series has received more attention in the deep learning community. First, we examine recent uses in the general deep learning community. Second, we look at the few works that directly target time series explainability in the frequency domain.

Liu et al. [34] train a foundation model using a frequency-aware transformer architecture and show its superiority over models that do not consider the frequency domain. Crabbé et al. [20] show that the frequency domain better captures the data distribution for diffusion models. While none of this is directly related to explainability, it does indicate an increasing tendency to exploit frequency representations of time series in deep learning and related fields.

Few works have focused on explaining time series models in the frequency domain, but there are some notable recent works. Vielhaben et al. [61] use virtual inspection layers to propagate relevance from the time domain into the frequency domain. Gradient-based methods, though, have been outperformed by learnable masks in the time domain [19]. Finally, FreqRISE uses sampling of masks to estimate relevance in the frequency domain [15]. However, FreqRISE relies on computationally inefficient sampling and applies masks in the frequency domain by directly zeroing out frequency components, which may lead to artifacts.

In this work, we build on these recent trends in explaining time series in alternative domains by decomposing the signals into interpretable parts. We leverage the powerful concept of learnable masks to do so, and present a promising new direction for time series explainability that we call FLEXtime. FLEXtime is a local model-specific post-hoc method.

3 Explainability over Interpretable Parts

Instead of viewing the explainability of time series as a saliency map over the input, we propose instead the notion of explainability over interpretable parts. This new approach allows us to provide the user with saliency maps over elements of a more inherently interpretable nature for the time series in question. Additionally, due to the recent success of learnable masks, we propose to learn the saliency map over these interpretable parts. The section is organized as follows. First, in Sect. 3.1, we introduce the notion of learning a saliency map over interpretable parts. Section 3.2 proceeds to introduce our proposed method, FLEXtime. Finally, Sect. 3.3 establishes a simpler baseline, FreqMask inspired by Dynamask [19].

Notation. Let $X \in \mathbb{R}^{N \times V}$ be a uniformly sampled time series consisting of N time steps and V variables, drawn from the distribution $\mathcal{X}$, with the associated label or output $y \in \mathbb{R}^C$ with dimension, C. Here, y could be any regression or classification variable that is associated with X for the given task. For ease of notation, we will assume $V = 1$ without loss of generality, but the approach applies for any $V \in \mathbb{N}$.

We then assume a (black box) model $\mathbf{f}$ that predicts $\hat{y}$ from X, $\mathbf{f} : X \to \hat{y}$. The goal is now to explain the model's prediction in terms of the input X. The explanation should identify the most important features of the input X for $\mathbf{f}$ in predicting $\hat{y}$.

3.1 Learning a Mask over Interpretable Parts

We now lean on the signal processing methodology on sparse signal representations [58]. Many applications in signal processing rely on finding a sparse signal representation for the purpose of compression [64], denoising [23], and higher interpretability [32,42,59]. The sparse representation is a linear decomposition of the signal, X, into a suitable dictionary consisting of interpretable elements, $\{\psi_s\}_{n=1}^{S}$ [58]:

$$X = \sum_{s=1}^{S} \theta_s \psi_s. \tag{1}$$

where $\theta_s \in \mathbb{C}$. Notice here that the choice of dictionary and thus interpretable parts will be dependent on the signal in question and could be determined by domain experts.

In order to explain the prediction of our model $\mathbf{f}$ on input X in terms of our dictionary, we seek a mask $M = (m_s) \in [0,1]^S$. The value of m_s should indicate the saliency of element ψ_s, where m_s close to one indicates that element ψ_s is salient, while m_s close to zero indicates that element ψ_s is not salient. M is used to mask out elements of X via elementwise multiplication:

$$X^M = \sum_{s=1}^{S} (m_s \cdot (\theta_s \psi_s) + (1 - m_s) \cdot p_s). \tag{2}$$

Here, p_s is a perturbation applied for dictionary component s. We can obtain the resulting output of **f**:

$$\hat{y}^M = \mathbf{f}(X^M). \tag{3}$$

The goal is now to learn the mask M that optimally explains the output of the model. We will achieve the optimal mask, M, through optimization and thus need a set of desiderata to design the optimization objective.

For an optimal mask M that has identified all salient information, we expect $\hat{y}^M \approx \hat{y}$. As such, an objective should be to minimize the difference between $\hat{y}^M$ and $\hat{y}$. Generally, we can quantify this difference with some kind of distortion term, D. The distortion term, D, should be chosen according to the task at hand. I.e., for regression tasks the mean squared error would likely be a good choice, while for classification tasks the cross-entropy would be natural. However, minimizing D is not sufficient for providing useful explanations. Consider a mask, M where all elements $m_s = 1, s = 1, \ldots, S$. For this mask, we get $\hat{y}^M = \hat{y}$, since $X^M = X$ in this case.

Therefore, it is also necessary to control the sparsity of the mask. Generally, this is done with a regularization metric $R(M)$. Combining the minimization of D with the maximization of the sparsity of M through R allows us to define the optimization objective:

$$\min_{M} \; D(\hat{y}, \hat{y}^M) + \lambda R(M), \tag{4}$$

where λ controls the trade-off between D and R.

Generally, this objective can be interpreted from a rate-distortion perspective [18,33]. Here, for proper distortion measures, $D(\hat{y}, \hat{y}^M)$ acts as a proxy for the distortion of X caused by M, which we want to minimize. Similarly, the rate refers to the amount of signal in X being passed by M, which we also want to minimize. The objective can be optimized by initializing a mask M and optimizing the values of M via gradient descent [26].

3.2 Filterbank Learning to EXplain Time Series

How do we decide which dictionary to use to represent X? Clearly, this depends on the qualities and application of X. However, for many time series applications, the frequency domain is of particular interest [11,20]. Most natural signals do not carry frequency content on a single frequency but rather across a band of frequencies in an area of interest. We therefore propose composing the dictionary as a filterbank of bandpass filters, each with impulse response h_l, to split the

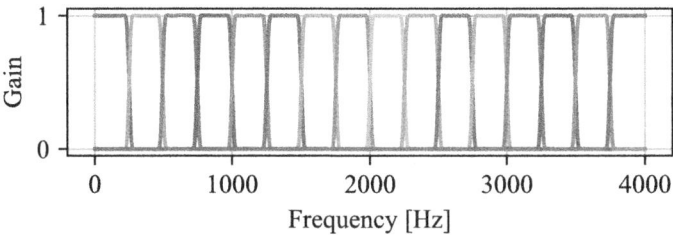

Fig. 2. Magnitude response of filterbank with 16 FIR filters with equal bandwidths.

signal into appropriate frequency bands:

$$X \approx \sum_{l=1}^{L} h_l * X, \qquad (5)$$

where $*$ denotes the convolution operation. Specifically, in this paper, we propose using a filter bank of L finite impulse response (FIR) filters that split the frequency axis into equally sized bins. This is chosen since FIR filters are stable and can easily be designed to have a linear phase response [44]. These properties allow for easy automatic design for a variety of datasets. An example of such a filterbank is shown in Fig. 2.

The filterbank design is inspired by the analysis filterbank framework such as [21,60]. Since we apply sparse masks, we do not need perfect reconstruction of our signals. Therefore, we use the window method to design the FIR filters and leave the number of filters, L, and filter length, N_h, as hyperparameters. In practice, however, the choice of filterbank could depend on the domain of choice. For audio, a natural choice could be an octave filterbank, where the frequency axis is divided into progressively wider frequency bands to more closely resemble human acoustics processing [46].

Independent of the design choice of the filterbank, the mask can now be learned as a combination of bandpass filtered versions of X. Combining the notation with the notation in Sect. 3.1, we can produce masked versions of X by masking out specific filters:

$$X^M = \sum_{l=1}^{L} \left(m_l \cdot (h_l * X) + (1 - m_l) \cdot p_l \right). \qquad (6)$$

Again, p_l denotes any applied perturbation. Generally, we set $p_l = 0$, but future work might investigate relevant perturbations to include.

We call this method Filterbank Learning to EXplain time series (FLEXtime). The FLEXtime framework is shown in Fig. 3.

The FLEXtime Learning Objective. In order to learn the mask, M, we need to define an appropriate learning objective. This is done by defining appropriate

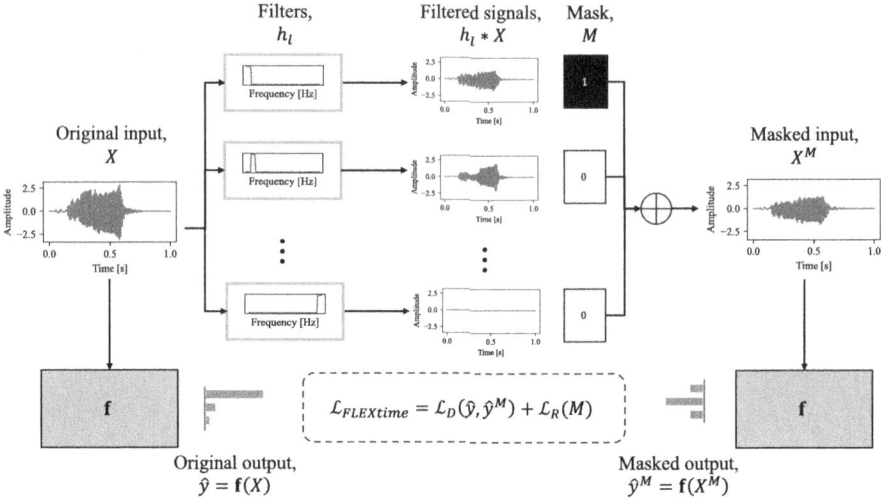

Fig. 3. FLEXtime: FLEXtime uses a filterbank to split the signal into frequency bands of a suitable bandwidth. It then optimizes a mask which chooses the frequency bands that best explains the signal X in terms of the prediction $\hat{y}$ of black box **f**. **f** is only used for inference and thus frozen during optimization.

expressions to insert into (4). Since we are focusing on classification tasks, we use the cross-entropy loss to measure the distortion caused by the mask:

$$\mathcal{L}_D(\hat{y}, \hat{y}^M) = -\sum_{c=1}^{C} \log\left(\hat{y}_c^M\right)\hat{y}_c, \tag{7}$$

where $\hat{y}_c^M$ is obtained using (6) and (3). To ensure that the method only focuses on the class, l, we wish to explain, we set all values of $\hat{y}_{c \neq l} = 0$ prior to computing $D(\hat{y}, \hat{y}^M)$.

For the sparsity constraint, we use the ℓ_1-norm. Additionally, to control the sparsity of the explanation, we introduce a ratio parameter, $r \in [0, 1]$, which acts as a threshold below which the sparsity constraint is ignored. Thus, we arrive at the following regularization metric:

$$\mathcal{L}_R(M) = \max\left(\frac{||M||_1}{L} - r, 0\right), \tag{8}$$

where L is the number of filters and therefore the length of the mask. The ratio parameter, r, will typically be chosen as a small value in the range of $0.05 - 0.15$, but can be tuned according to the user's need. We then arrive at the following objective function:

$$\mathcal{L}_{FLEXtime} = \mathcal{L}_D(\hat{y}, \hat{y}^M) + \lambda \mathcal{L}_R(M), \tag{9}$$

where λ determines the balance between the two loss terms.

3.3 Learning the Mask in the Fourier Domain

In FLEXtime, we use a filterbank of bandpass filters to learn explanations in the frequency domain. A simple baseline to measure this approach against, would be a masking strategy directly on the spectrum of the signal, i.e. removing individual frequency components. This can be achieved using another linear transform, namely the discrete Fourier transform (DFT). The DFT uses Fourier analysis to decompose the signal into sinusoids of different frequencies. As such, the Fourier spectrum describes how much energy each frequency component holds in the signal of interest. Using the inverse DFT, we can reconstruct the original signal as:

$$x_n = \frac{1}{N} \sum_{k=0}^{N-1} a_k e^{i\omega_k} e^{i2\pi \frac{k}{N} n}, \tag{10}$$

where n is the n-th time step and N is the total length of the signal. a_k and ω_k denote the magnitude and phase, respectively, of the k-th frequency component. Thus, we again arrive at a formulation equivalent to (1). We can then create masked versions of X as:

$$x_n^M = \frac{1}{N} \sum_{k=0}^{N-1} \left(m_k \cdot \left(a_k e^{i\omega_k} e^{i2\pi \frac{k}{N} n} \right) + (1 - m_k) \cdot p_k \right), \tag{11}$$

where p_k denotes a perturbation added to the masked out components in the frequency domain. For real signals, the DFT is even symmetric, which implies that $a_k = a_{-k \mod N}$, creating an effective mask size of length $N/2+1$ by letting $m_k = m_{-k \mod N}$.

The FreqMask Method. Inspired by the time series explainability method, Dynamask [19], we now present FreqMask, masks directly in the frequency domain as described above.

In accordance to the original Dynamask approach, we employ a windowed fading moving average perturbation. Naturally, here the windowed moving average is done in the frequency domain. By averaging the amplitudes a_k in a window centered at the current frequency, we obtain:

$$p_k = \frac{1}{2W+1} \sum_{k'=k-W}^{k+W} a_{k'}, \tag{12}$$

where $2W$ is a chosen window size. We set it to the default value of $W = 10$.

For easy comparability to FLEXtime, we use (7) and (8) for the distortion and rate terms in the optimization objective. In (8), we replace L with $N/2+1$, the size of the mask.

Finally, inspired by Dynamask [19], we use a smoothness constraint to avoid sudden jumps in saliency:

$$\mathcal{L}_S(M) = \sum_{k=0}^{N-1} |m_{k+1} - m_k|. \tag{13}$$

We therefore arrive at the following objective for the FreqMask method:

$$\mathcal{L}_{FreqMask} = \mathcal{L}_D(\hat{y}, \hat{y}^M) + \lambda_R \mathcal{L}_R(M) + \lambda_S \mathcal{L}_S(M). \tag{14}$$

FreqMask comes with a few significant limitations. By directly altering frequency components, FreqMask can only remove frequency content that aligns with the Fourier transform coefficients, e.g. if we have a signal of a one second duration, this is precisely the integer frequencies. Additionally, zeroing out frequency components can cause artifacts in the signal (see Section ?? for an example). Finally, it is worth noting that the artifacts become more prominent if the DFT does not have the same length as the signal [46].

4 Experimental Setup

Here, we describe practical details of the filterbank design and the critical components of our quantitative analysis, such as datasets, baselines, and metrics.

4.1 Hyperparameters of FLEXtime and FreqMask

For both FLEXtime and FreqMask, we always set $\lambda_R = \lambda_S = 1$ since we find that this balances the loss terms sufficiently and this choice limits the necessary tuning of hyperparameters. We always optimize FLEXtime and FreqMask using gradient descent for 1000 iterations with a step size of 1. When evaluating FLEXtime, we compute the collective frequency response of the filterbank after applying the learned mask.

For FLEXtime, we use a filterbank of L FIR filters that splits the frequency axis into equally sized bins. This leaves us with a number of design choices: the number of filters L, the length of the filters N_h, and the threshold r below which we ignore the sparsity constraint. For FreqMask, we need to choose the threshold r. Ideally, these parameters are chosen by domain experts who have knowledge of which resolution and sparsity may be necessary and sufficient.

Here, we instead use a cross-validation scheme to choose the optimal parameters based on faithfulness. Specifically, we loop through each split of each dataset and randomly sample 100 datapoints from each validation split. We then do a grid search over the number of filters, L, the filter length, N_h and the sparsity controlling ratio, r for FLEXtime. For FreqMask, we only need to choose the sparsity controlling ratio, r. We choose the hyperparameters that give the best faithfulness score on a 10% level. Given a tie, we choose the set with the lowest complexity. The chosen hyperparameters are shown in Table 1.

Table 1. Hyperparameters of FLEXtime and FreqMask for each dataset.

Dataset	FLEXtime			FreqMask
	L	N_h	r	r
Gender	128	501	0.10	0.10
Digit	128	501	0.10	0.05
PAM	32	95	0.10	0.05
Epilepsy	32	75	0.10	0.05
ECG	64	105	0.05	0.05
SleepEDF	256	901	0.10	0.10

4.2 Datasets

Here, we present the datasets on which we evaluate the explainability methods.

Synthetic Dataset. We generate a synthetic dataset with known localized salient information. We divide the frequency axis into $K = 32$ equally sized regions. We add frequency content within these regions, modulated by a Voigt profile [57]. This allows us to model a dataset with content that more closely resembles real-life signals, where frequency content is found in bands. We sample B of the K bins, where $B \sim \mathcal{U}(1, 10)$. Each bin, b, has a start frequency, $f_{b,start}$, and an end frequency, $f_{b,end}$. We linearly distribute 20 frequencies, $f_b \in [f_{b,start}, f_{b,end}[$ on which we add frequency content. We therefore generate the data within each sampled bin, b, as:

$$x_n^b = \sum_{f_b \in [f_{b,start}, f_{b,end}[} \left(a_{f_b}^b \sin\left(\frac{2\pi n}{N f_b} + \psi^b\right) \right), \tag{15}$$

where a_f^b is determined by the Voigt profile with peak location sampled within the bin. ψ^b is the phase, which is sampled from a uniform distribution for each bin, $\psi^b \sim \mathcal{U}(0, 2\pi)$. Finally, we create x_n by summing the frequency content of all bins:

$$x_n = \sum_{b=1}^{B} X_n^b + \epsilon, \tag{16}$$

ϵ is random noise sampled from a normal distribution, $\epsilon \sim \mathcal{N}(0, \sigma^2)$. We then choose four regions as salient, where the class labels are the powerset of the salient regions, i.e. there is a total of 16 classes. We generate 5 training sets of 10^4 samples and train a convolutional neural network on each split. We then generate 5 balanced test sets of 992 samples (i.e. 62 samples from each class) on which we test the methods.

Real-Life Datasets. We evaluate on five different datasets with a total of six different tasks when testing the model in a real-life setting.

Adhering to previous research on time series explainability [35,47], we use **PAM** for human activity recognition [48], **MIT-BIH (ECG)** for arrythmia detection [41], and **Epilepsy (EEG)** for seizure detection [7] datasets. We use the same transformer-based model architectures and data preprocessing pipelines as in [47]. All datasets are divided into five splits, and one model is trained for each split.

Additionally, we use the **AudioMNIST** dataset [11], which contains spoken digits from 0–9. This dataset has been shown to have salient information in the frequency domain [11,61]. The dataset contains two tasks: gender and digit classification, divided into four and five splits, respectively. We use the same preprocessing pipeline and convolutional model architecture as in the original work [11]. We train a model for each split.

Finally, we also include the **SleepEDFx** dataset [27,31]. The dataset contains whole-night EEG data annotated for sleep stages. Frequency bands are an important discriminator for sleep stages [3]. We divide the subjects into 5 splits to ensure no leakage. We use the same convolutional architecture as for the AudioMNIST dataset to train a sleep staging model for each split.

For all datasets we sample 1,000 samples from each test set for evaluation of the explainability methods. However, when computing the robustness scores, we use only 100 samples from each test due to the high computational complexity associated with this evaluation. Table 2 contains details on the size and dimensions of all datasets as well as the F1 score of the trained models on the sampled test sets.

Table 2. Overview of the real-life datasets used. The F1 score refers to the performance of the trained models on the dataset in question.

Dataset	# samples	Length	Dimension	Classes	Fs (Hz)	F1 score
Gender	30,000	8,000	1	2	8,000	.97(.03)
Digit	30,000	8,000	1	10	8,000	.96(.01)
PAM	5,333	600	17	8	100	.88(.02)
Epilepsy	11,500	178	1	2	178	.95(.01)
ECG	92,511	360	1	2	360	.93(.05)
SleepEDF	92,511	3,000	1	5	100	.90(.05)

4.3 Baselines

We use six different XAI baselines to compare our methods. For gradient-based explanations, we use **saliency** [53], **gradient times input** (G×I) [6], **guided backpropagation** (GB) [55], and **integrated gradients** (IG) [56]. We equip all of these with a virtual inspection layer to propagate the explanations into the frequency domain, see [61]. All methods that have been adapted to the frequency domain is marked by an *. Additionally, we compare to **FreqRISE** [15], which is directly designed to provide explanations in the frequency domain. Finally, when computing the faithfulness scores (see Sect. 4.4), we add a **random baseline** by randomly sampling frequency components to zero out.

4.4 Metrics

Quantitative evaluation of explainability is challenging due to the lack of ground truth explanations [29], and is an active field of research. Since ground truth explanations are not available, the quality of an explanation can be estimated by measuring different desirable properties [28]. In the time series explainability literature, most evaluations have been limited to only considering few desirable properties [19,35,47]. In this work, we strive towards evaluating a more comprehensive set of desirable properties. These properties that make up the basis for our evaluation metrics are described below.

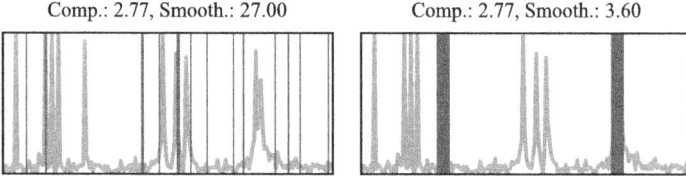

Fig. 4. Complexity and smoothness of two different saliency maps.

Localization. Localization measures to what degree the explanation is centered around a known region of interest [8,9]. For the synthetic dataset with known ground truth, we can directly assess the localization abilities of each method. Here, we follow previous work and compute the area under the recall curve (AUR) and precision curve (AUP), as well as the area under the precision-recall curve (AUPRC) [35,47].

Faithfulness. Faithfulness measures how aligned an explanation is with the prediction of a model [4,13]. Specifically, given an explanation, we keep only the 10% most important features as identified by the explanation. We then measure the mean true class probability of the model on this importance-masked data. For an explanation, where the most important information has been identified, we expect a high mean true class probability.

Complexity. An explanation should be as simple as possible such that it is easy for humans to understand. This can be measured by estimating the complexity of the saliency map [13,16]. We measure the complexity as the entropy of the fractional importance of feature m_i to the overall magnitude following [13]. Low complexity is better, but looking at complexity alone can be misleading. A saliency map that only highlights a single frequency component will have minimal complexity, but might not be informative. Therefore, complexity should be considered in conjunction with metrics that are connected to known regions of interest (localization) or the predictions of the model (faithfulness).

Smoothness. While complexity measures the sparsity of the signal, it yields no information on the smoothness of the saliency map. As such, a saliency map with 10% of the features marked as salient will have the same complexity independent of whether these features are scattered across the signal or placed in two localized peaks. We therefore suggest considering the smoothness of the saliency maps in conjunction with the complexity. Specifically, we propose using the total variation of the saliency map as a measure of smoothness:

$$S(M) = \sum_{i=1}^{N-1} |m_{i+1} - m_i|, \qquad (17)$$

where M is the saliency map with length N. We illustrate the difference between complexity and smoothness in Fig. 4 where both saliency maps have the same complexity but vastly different smoothness scores.

Robustness. A good explainability method should be robust to small changes in the input [2,4]. Here, we measure the robustness of the saliency map using the relative output stability (ROS) [2]. The ROS considers the behavior of the underlying model, by measuring the normalized change in the saliency map in response to small perturbations, *relative* to the change in the model output. We create 10 perturbed inputs by adding normally distributed noise with standard deviation $\sigma = 0.05 \cdot \sigma_{data}$, where σ_{data} is the standard deviation across the test set. The noise is added in the time domain, while the saliency maps are still computed in the frequency domain. We follow the original work [2] and report the log ROS.

5 Results

All results are computed across all splits of the data and models and reported as the mean and standard error of the mean across splits. We bold and underline the best result and any others whose 95% confidence interval overlaps with that of the best result. If the second-best result's confidence interval does not overlap with the best result's, we underline it. We compute the rank by ranking all methods by mean within each dataset and computing the average across all.

5.1 Synthetic Data

The localization scores on the synthetic data are reported in Table 3. We see that the FLEXtime method achieves the highest recall, closely followed by FreqRISE, while IG gets a very high precision. FreqRISE and FLEXtime have the highest AUPRC with no significant difference.

An example of explanations produced by IG, FreqRISE, and FLEXtime is shown in Fig. 5. The figure shows that IG gives very parsimonious

Table 3. Localization(↑) on synthetic data

	AUPRC	AUP	AUR
Saliency*	.19(.04)	.43(.12)	.08(.01)
G×I*	.21(.04)	.43(.12)	.07(.01)
GB*	.19(.04)	.42(.12)	.09(.01)
FreqRISE	**.94**(.02)	.62(.02)	**.81**(.04)
IG*	.62(.04)	**.99**(.01)	.09(.01)
FreqMask	.10(.01)	.73(.11)	.22(.09)
FLEXtime	**.90**(.09)	.86(.06)	**.84**(.07)

explanations, giving less relevance to the peak at the left. On the other hand, FLEXtime marks the entire ground truth region but also exceeds beyond the bounds due to the by-design fixed bandwidth. The same is true for FreqRISE, although yielding results with a more noisy baseline. As such, FLEXtime correctly highlights relevant regions with a very clear explanation.

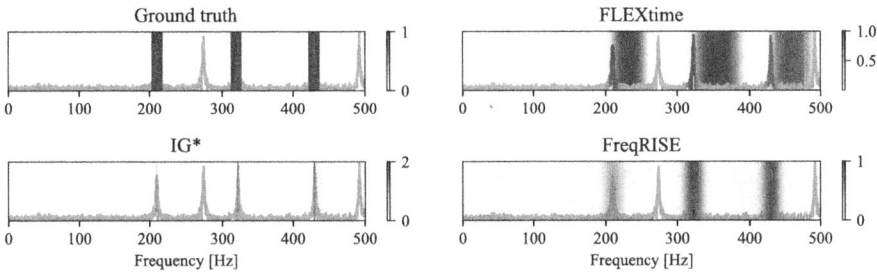

Fig. 5. Examples of explanations (green heatmaps) on a synthetic dataset example. (Color figure online)

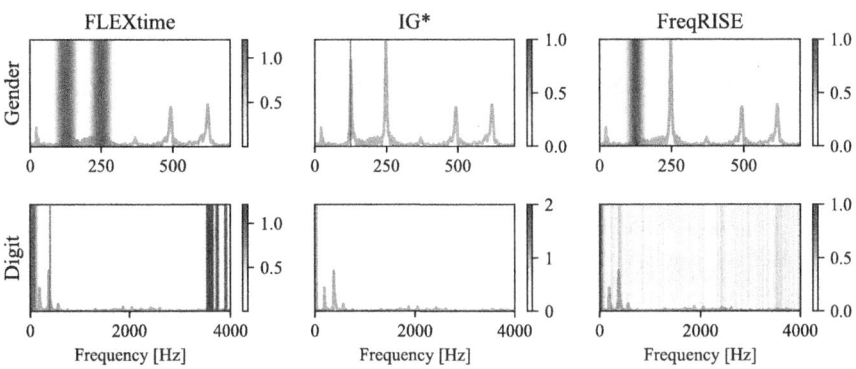

Fig. 6. Explanations (green heatmaps) produced by FreqRISE, IG, FLEXtime on both AudioMNIST tasks. Top row is the Gender task and bottom row is the Digit task. (Color figure online)

5.2 Real-Life Datasets

For the real-life datasets, the faithfulness scores are reported in Table 4. The table shows that FLEXtime always gives the best or joint best faithfulness score (considering confidence intervals). Additionally, FLEXtime gives the best average rank. The competing methods are FreqRISE, IG, and FreqMask, however, all of them have cases where they perform significantly worse than the best method. This is the Digit task for Dynamask, SleepEDF for FreqRISE, and ECG for IG. FLEXtime gives competitive performance on all datasets.

Additionally, we measure the complexities of the explanations given by the different methods. These results are reported in Table 5. FreqMask almost always gives the least complex solution. However, in most cases FLEXtime gives the second best complexity score and overall FLEXtime yields the second best average rank. Here, we should note that while FreqMask has a lower complexity, the faithfulness is much worse than FLEXtime. As such, we must remember that neither of these metrics should be considered without the other.

Table 4. Faithfulness (↑): Mean true class probability after inserting the 10% most important features. We report mean and standard error of the mean in parentheses. Best result and any result with overlapping 95% CI of the best result are bolded. Second best is underlined if CI is not overlapping with that of the best result.

Method	Gender	Digit	PAM	Epilepsy	ECG	SleepEDF	Rank
Random	.606(.013)	.207(.019)	.245(.007)	.819(.002)	.811(.006)	.289(.006)	7.3
Saliency*	**.943**(.024)	.414(.023)	.511(.024)	**.925**(.005)	.781(.015)	.409(.016)	5.5
G×I*	.713(.063)	.383(.011)	.516(.018)	**.880**(.027)	.793(.023)	.356(.014)	6.3
GB*	**.947**(.025)	.442(.022)	.533(.040)	.906(.008)	.738(.018)	.388(.017)	5.3
FreqRISE	**.970**(.013)	<u>.858</u>(.010)	**.836**(.013)	**.933**(.004)	**.862**(.045)	.638(.019)	<u>2.3</u>
IG*	**.970**(.014)	.604(.023)	**.814**(.025)	**.937**(.004)	.715(.067)	**.714**(.021)	3.2
FreqMask	.795(.050)	.557(.025)	**.845**(.012)	.861(.013)	**.888**(.020)	.619(.022)	4.0
FLEXtime	**.968**(.013)	**.907**(.011)	**.854**(.009)	**.928**(.003)	**.868**(.020)	**.746**(.022)	**1.8**

Table 5. Complexity scores (↓) across all methods and datasets. We report mean and standard error of the mean in parentheses. Best result and any result with overlapping 95% CI of the best result are bolded. Second best is underlined if CI is not overlapping with that of the best result.

Method	Gender	Digit	PAM	Epilepsy	ECG	SleepEDF	Rank
Saliency*	5.22(0.04)	5.71(0.07)	5.38(0.05)	2.38(0.01)	2.75(0.07)	5.42(0.03)	3.7
G×I*	5.48(0.10)	<u>5.59</u>(0.04)	5.53(0.01)	1.59(0.24)	2.71(0.16)	**4.88**(0.05)	3.3
GB*	5.40(0.12)	6.37(0.06)	5.46(0.04)	2.50(0.02)	2.83(0.01)	5.45(0.03)	5.5
FreqRISE	8.00(0.02)	8.17(0.00)	8.51(0.00)	4.30(0.00)	5.10(0.00)	7.21(0.00)	7.0
IG*	4.74(0.08)	6.25(0.04)	5.79(0.02)	1.68(0.07)	2.80(0.10)	<u>5.13</u>(0.04)	4.2
FreqMask	**1.96**(0.42)	**3.94**(0.15)	**3.58**(0.09)	**0.42**(0.05)	**0.94**(0.15)	5.44(0.01)	**1.5**
FLEXtime	<u>4.72</u>(0.44)	6.07(0.04)	<u>4.91</u>(0.11)	<u>0.69</u>(0.07)	**1.28**(0.34)	5.44(0.02)	2.7

Table 6. Smoothness scores (↓) across all methods and datasets. We report mean and standard error of the mean in parentheses. Best result and any result with overlapping 95% CI of the best result are bolded. Second best is underlined if CI is not overlapping with that of the best result.

Method	Gender	Digit	PAM	Epilepsy	ECG	SleepEDF	Rank
Saliency*	30.42(0.96)	42.53(3.23)	13.18(0.22)	5.05(0.04)	6.22(0.21)	35.21(1.12)	5.7
G×I*	23.09(2.19)	27.78(1.35)	7.24(0.22)	3.01(0.22)	4.67(0.34)	18.74(0.53)	3.8
GB*	33.12(2.74)	84.19(5.07)	12.69(0.25)	5.89(0.08)	7.34(0.30)	37.31(1.06)	6.3
FreqRISE	6.70(0.61)	**10.33**(0.14)	7.21(0.07)	7.40(0.05)	7.44(0.50)	**13.96**(0.54)	4.2
IG*	8.71(0.61)	43.91(2.54)	6.54(0.16)	3.27(0.11)	6.12(0.54)	32.96(1.31)	4.2
FreqMask	**2.49**(0.52)	**8.88**(1.12)	**0.75**(0.07)	<u>0.78</u>(0.08)	**1.48**(0.28)	42.29(1.47)	<u>2.5</u>
FLEXtime	**4.11**(0.49)	**9.51**(0.18)	**0.61**(0.06)	**0.48**(0.04)	**1.00**(0.28)	<u>16.60</u>(0.50)	**1.5**

Table 7. Robustness scores (↓) across all methods and datasets. We report mean and standard error of the mean in parentheses. Best result and any result with overlapping 95% CI of the best result are bolded. Second best is underlined if CI is not overlapping with that of the best result.

Method	Gender	Digit	PAM	Epilepsy	ECG	SleepEDF	Rank
Saliency*	**14.09**(0.27)	**8.88**(1.01)	23.61(0.34)	17.37(0.24)	15.35(0.41)	18.80(0.46)	4.2
G×I*	16.59(0.78)	**8.96**(0.50)	**16.26**(0.62)	16.00(0.77)	**13.22**(0.76)	15.37(0.12)	<u>3.0</u>
GB*	**14.83**(0.63)	**9.56**(0.28)	22.56(0.18)	17.18(0.21)	15.57(0.64)	18.87(0.35)	5.0
FreqRISE	19.13(0.29)	**10.65**(0.15)	**14.88**(0.19)	21.99(0.21)	18.48(0.49)	<u>14.39</u>(0.11)	5.0
IG*	16.60(0.49)	**9.43**(0.20)	16.45(0.23)	<u>14.65</u>(0.24)	**12.73**(0.67)	15.64(0.20)	3.5
FreqMask	16.41(0.65)	12.28(0.16)	<u>16.18</u>(0.26)	17.65(0.11)	15.99(0.34)	17.45(0.09)	5.0
FLEXtime	**11.89**(1.22)	**9.34**(0.27)	17.12(0.34)	**11.33**(0.76)	**14.50**(1.25)	**10.88**(0.41)	**2.3**

Table 6 shows the smoothness scores. The table shows that while FreqMask and FLEXtime typically have the two best scores, FLEXtime achieves the best average rank, with FreqMask coming in second.

Finally, the robustness scores indicate how stable the methods are against minor perturbations to the input data. Table 7 shows the robustness results. Again, FLEXtime has a stable, good performance. FLEXtime gets the best score on 3 datasets and is within the confidence interval on the best score on 2 other datasets. The remaining dataset, PAM, differs from the remaining datasets by having multiple channels (17 channels). This may affect the optimization procedure if some of the channels carry redundant information. Overall, FLEXtime again achieves the best overall rank.

Figure 6 shows two examples on the AudioMNIST dataset, one for the Gender task of a male speaker, and one for the Digit task of the digit 6. On the Gender task, all methods find the first large peak around 125 Hz, adhering to expert knowledge that the male fundamental frequency typically lies in the range of 90-150 Hz [25]. FLEXtime and IG additionally mark the first harmonic. While all methods pick up on a low frequency component on the Digit task, FLEXtime also puts emphasis on the high frequency content of the signal. Upon closer examination, we find that when applying only the high-pass filter of the learned explanation to the signal, the model still correctly classifies the signal as the digit 6. This behavior indicates that the high frequency content is indeed relevant for the model's classification. The saliency maps of IG and FreqRISE are both more scattered, making it difficult to identify the most relevant part of the signal. This indicates that FLEXtime picks up on important components in the signal unidentified by other methods.

5.3 Case Study on Sleep Staging

In this section, we perform a deeper qualitative assessment on the SleepEDF dataset. Sleep data is often described in terms of its frequency content in different sleep stages [3]. As such, we can use it to qualify whether we can discover similar patterns as described in the literature by using our explainability methods. The aim is therefore to show the benefit of using explanations in the frequency content to explain signals with known frequency-specific characteristics.

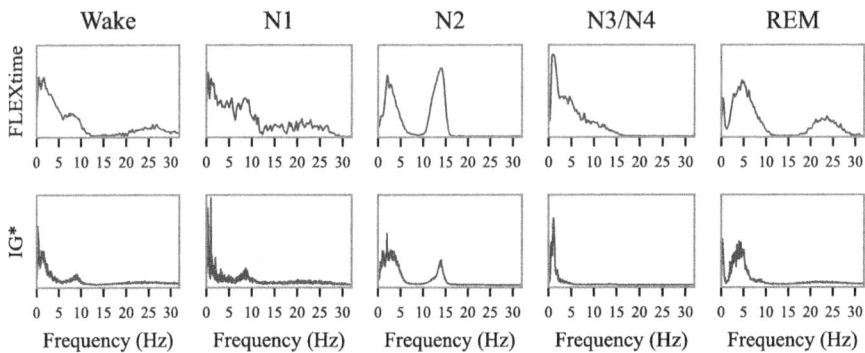

Fig. 7. Average saliency maps across all correctly classified samples within each of the five classes for one of the SleepEDF test sets.

To get an understanding of the global model behavior across an entire class, we look at one of the SleepEDF test sets. We inspect the explanations produced by FLEXtime and IG since they yield the highest faithfulness scores. We average the saliency maps produced by each method across all correctly classified samples within each class. The resulting plots are shown in Fig. 7.

First, the figure shows that each of the classes has characteristic traces in the frequency domain, indicating that the model is indeed using specific patterns in the frequency domain to classify the data into sleep stages. IG finds that the *Wake* class and the *N1* sleep stage have very similar traces. For FLEXtime, they are slightly more distinguishable. In the literature, the *N1* class is characterized by mixed-frequency activity with a slight increase in the 4-7 Hz band [30]. This aligns with the explanations provided by both FLEXtime and IG. The *Wake* class typically contains alpha activity (8-13 Hz) [30], which is not apparent in IG or FLEXtime explanations. This may be due to the fact that alpha waves are typically best recorded by occipital leads [3] (EEG leads located on the back of the skull), whereas this dataset only contains the Fpz-Cz lead (EEG lead located to the front of the skull).

The *N2* sleep stage contains two clear peaks around 3 Hz and 13 Hz for both IG and FLEXtime. The *N2* stage is characterized by the presence of K-complexes or sleep spindles [30]. The K-complexes are mainly localized in time, whereas the sleep spindles are oscillations of 12-14 Hz [30] and thus align perfectly with the second peak, which is more prominent for FLEXtime. The *N3/N4* sleep stage is also known as slow wave sleep [3]. The patterns found by both IG and FLEXtime clearly represent this with a large peak around 2 Hz.

Finally, for *REM* sleep, both IG and FLEXtime have a peak at 5 Hz. However, FLEXtime has a second prominent peak around 24 Hz. *REM* sleep is known to contain saw-tooth waves in the 2–6 Hz range, which could explain the first peak. However, *REM* sleep can also contain beta activity (16–32 Hz) [39], which could explain the second prominent peak seen in the FLEXtime explanation.

Lastly, we investigate the addition of a smoothness regularizer to the FLEXtime objective. Specifically, we add the smoothness regularizer from FreqMask presented in (13) to the objective function in (9). Figure 8 shows examples of explanations on the *N2*, *N3/N4*, and the *REM* class using FLEXtime with and without the smoothness regularizer. The two versions highlight similar areas, that is, for *N2*, we see a prominent band around 12–14 Hz, for *N3/N4* the importance is concentrated on low frequency content (<5 Hz), and for *REM* there is a highlighted section around 23 Hz. All of this is consistent with the characteristics mentioned previously. However, the smoothness regularized version of FLEXtime removes some of the noise, making the explanations more easily comprehendible. When evaluating the smoothness regularized version of FLEXtime across the entire test set and across the five seeds, we achieve better complexity, 5.38(0.01), and smoothness, 7.04(0.11). However, faithfulness drops to 0.724(0.021).

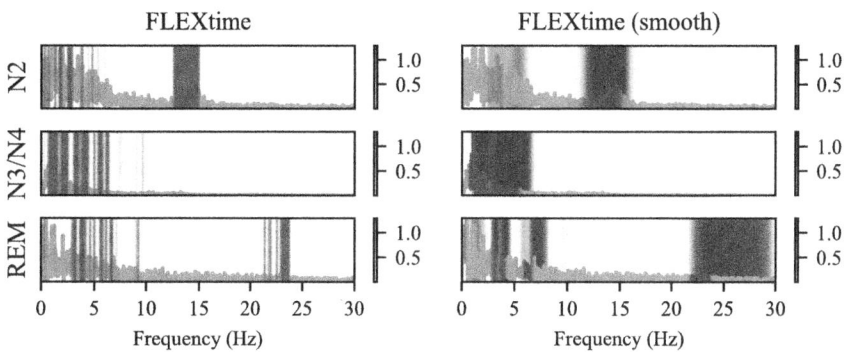

Fig. 8. Examples of explanations produced by FLEXtime and a smoothness regularized version of FLEXtime on samples from the *N2*, *N3/N4* and *REM* classes.

6 Discussion and Conclusion

We proposed to reimagine time series as explainability over interpretable parts. In particular, we presented FLEXtime, an approach to time series explainability that utilizes the powerful notion of filterbanks to learn relevant explanations in the frequency domain.

FLEXtime outperforms state-of-the-art baselines on faithfulness, smoothness and robustness on a range real-life datasets. The datasets cover a variety of domains and comprise time series of variable signal length and number of variables. FLEXtime also has competitive performance on localization. Simultaneously, FLEXtime outperforms the simpler baseline FreqMask also developed for this study. This is likely because FLEXtime reduces the dimensionality of the problem to make for easier optimization by leveraging the fact that frequency information is often localized in bands.

Additionally, due to the filtering approach, FLEXtime is able to handle streaming time series more smoothly, compared to the remaining methods which would have to rely on windowing to transform the data into the frequency domain.

Faithfulness vs. Complexity. FLEXtime achieves the best rank on the faithfulness score, but only second best on the complexity score, where it is outperformed by FreqMask. It is, however, important to note that the complexity can only be interpreted while simultaneously considering the faithfulness scores since a sparse solution is irrelevant if it does not highlight the correct regions. E.g., while FLEXtime has higher complexity score than FreqMask on the Digit task, it also achieves the best faithfulness score. This indicates that a more complex solution is needed to adequately describe this dataset.

Towards Different Filter Bank Designs. In this work, we used FIR filterbanks with parameters tuned through cross-validation to model our explanations. This means that not all filterbanks are able to perfectly reconstruct the signals. This will rarely be an issue since we are looking for sparse masks that highlight relevant regions of interest. However, we believe that future work should focus on investigating the effect of perfect reconstruction filterbanks on the results [60]. Additionally, using tailored filterbanks for the different domains will allow domain experts to utilize prior knowledge to extract meaningful explanations from the data [17,40]. Finally, considering alternative ways to split the signals into interpretable parts may shed light on new avenues for time series explainability.

Metrics and Qualitative Assessment. Quantifying the quality of the explanations is difficult. This, for instance, becomes apparent when considering FLEXtime with and without smoothness regularization. On the SleepEDF dataset, the smoothness regularized version gives an explanation that is easier to comprehend, but with a lower faithfulness. This may be due to the computation of faithfulness, which assigns pointwise importance in the frequency domain. This approach will likely favor sharper and more precise explanations at the cost of a more noisy looking importance map. Here, we have optimized for faithfulness, but we find that optimizing for other metrics yields different results. We therefore believe future work should investigate how to properly quantify and balance different qualities when building new explainability methods for time series.

Case-Study on Sleep Data. Using FLEXtime we were able to identify known markers for different sleep stages. This shows the benefit of moving to the frequency domain, where we can use known identifiers of class-specific characteristics to explain the models. Confirming existing knowledge using FLEXtime is a valuable tool for model debugging and validation. However, a more exciting avenue for explainability in general is to shed new light in understanding underlying mechanisms in the data. We hope that the case study can increase trust in FLEXtime and be a tool for domain experts to formulate new hypotheses for gaining a deeper understanding of disease patterns using data such as EEG.

Limitations. Although FLEXtime has clear competitive advantages across a range of metrics, it still comes with potential for future work. One current limitation of the method is that it requires tuning or choice of hyperparameters for the filterbank. Especially, if no expert knowledge is available. Automatic filterbank design could be a fruitful future direction for development. Additionally, as of now, the filterbank design of FLEXtime offers only insights into the frequency domain, and no explanation of time relevant features. Future work should focus on exploring the trade-off between the two and potentially incorporating insights from both domains via new filterbank designs.

6.1 Conclusion

Our new method, FLEXtime, bridges an important gap in time series explainability, where multiple works have successfully applied learnable masks in the time domain, but none in the frequency domain. Additionally, we highlight that naive masking over the DFT, in effect, means that we would mask out single frequencies, and this goes against established signal processing theory. FLEXtime instead learns the mask over a sufficiently expressive filterbank. This leads to a much more computationally stable procedure with a clear learning objective while having the flexibility to tailor the filterbank to the application at hand. This point is furthered by the superior performance of FLEXtime over FreqMask. Combined with the competitive performance of FLEXtime, outperforming all established state-of-the-art baselines across a range of metrics, we hope that this work will inspire future research in this direction.

Acknowledgments. This work was supported by the Pioneer Centre for AI, DNRF grant number P1, as well as the Research Council of Norway via Visual Intelligence grant no. 309439 and grant no. 303514.

Disclosure of Interests. The authors have no competing interests to declare that are relevant to the content of this article.

References

1. Achtibat, R., et al.: From attribution maps to human-understandable explanations through concept relevance propagation. Nat. Mach. Intell. **5**(9) (2023)
2. Agarwal, C., et al.: Rethinking stability for attribution-based explanations. In: ICLR 2022 Workshop on PAIR2Struct (2022)
3. Altalag, A., Road, J., Wilcox, P., Aboulhosn, K.: Pulmonary function tests in clinical practice, chap. Diagnostic tests for sleep disorders. Springer International Publishing, 2nd edn. (2019)
4. Alvarez-Melis, D., Jaakkola, T.S.: Towards robust interpretability with self-explaining neural networks. In: Proceedings of the 32nd International Conference on Neural Information Processing Systems. NIPS'18 (2018)

5. Amann, J., Blasimme, A., Vayena, E., Frey, D., Madai, V.I.: Explainability for artificial intelligence in healthcare: a multidisciplinary perspective. BMC Med. Inform. Decis. Mak. **20**(1), 310 (2020)
6. Ancona, M., Ceolini, E., Oztireli, C., Gross, M.: Towards better understanding of gradient-based attribution methods for deep neural networks. In: International Conference on Learning Representations (2018)
7. Andrzejak, R., Lehnertz, K., Mormann, F., Rieke, C., David, P., Elger, C.: Indications of nonlinear deterministic and finite-dimensional structures in time series of brain electrical activity: Dependence on recording region and brain state. Phys. Rev. E Stat. Nonl. Soft Matt. Phys. **64** (2002)
8. Arias-Duart, A., Parés, F., Garcia-Gasulla, D., Giménez-Ábalos, V.: Focus! rating Xai methods and finding biases. In: IEEE International Conference on Fuzzy Systems (2022)
9. Arras, L., Osman, A., Samek, W.: CLEVR-XAI: A benchmark dataset for the ground truth evaluation of neural network explanations. Inf. Fusion **81** (2022)
10. Bach, S., Binder, A., Montavon, G., Klauschen, F., Müller, K.R., Samek, W.: On pixel-wise explanations for non-linear classifier decisions by layer-wise relevance propagation. PLOS ONE **10**(7), 1–46 (07 2015)
11. Becker, S., Vielhaben, J., Ackermann, M., Müller, K.R., Lapuschkin, S., Samek, W.: AudioMNIST: exploring explainable artificial intelligence for audio analysis on a simple benchmark. J. Franklin Inst.**361**(1) (2024)
12. Beger, J.: The crucial role of explainability in healthcare AI. Eur. J. Radiol. **176**, 111507 (2024)
13. Bhatt, U., Weller, A., Moura, J.M.: Evaluating and aggregating feature-based model explanations. IJCAI International Joint Conference on Artificial Intelligence (2020)
14. Bilodeau, B., Jaques, N., Koh, P.W., Kim, B.: Impossibility theorems for feature attribution. Proc. National Acad. Sci. **121**(2) (2024)
15. Brüsch, T., Wickstrøm, K.K., Schmidt, M.N., Alstrøm, T.S., Jenssen, R.: FreqRISE: explaining time series using frequency masking. In: Northern Lights Deep Learning Conference (2025)
16. Chalasani, P., Chen, J., Chowdhury, A.R., Wu, X., Jha, S.: Concise explanations of neural networks using adversarial training. In: Proceedings of the 37th International Conference on Machine Learning. PMLR (2020)
17. Chandra, S., Sharma, A., Singh, G.K.: Computationally efficient cosine modulated filter bank design for ECG signal compression. Irbm **41**(1) (2020)
18. Cover, T.M., Thomas, J.A.: Elements of Information Theory, 2nd edition, chap. 10. Wiley (2005)
19. Crabbé, J., Van Der Schaar, M.: Explaining time series predictions with dynamic masks. In: Meila, M., Zhang, T. (eds.) Proceedings of the 38th International Conference on Machine Learning. PMLR (2021)
20. Crabbé, J., Huynh, N., Stanczuk, J., van der Schaar, M.: Time series diffusion in the frequency domain (2024)
21. Crochiere, R.E., Rabiner, L.R.: Multirate digital signal processing, chap. 7. Prentice-hall Englewood Cliffs, NJ (1983)
22. Di Martino, F., Delmastro, F.: Explainable AI for clinical and remote health applications: a survey on tabular and time series data. Artif. Intell. Rev. **56**(6) (2023)
23. Elad, M., Aharon, M.: Image denoising via sparse and redundant representations over learned dictionaries. IEEE Trans. Image Process. **15**(12) (2006)

24. Enguehard, J.: Learning perturbations to explain time series predictions. In: Proceedings of the 40th International Conference on Machine Learning. Proceedings of Machine Learning Research, vol. 202. PMLR (2023)
25. Fitch, J., Holbrook, A.: Modal vocal fundamental frequency of young adults. Arch. Otolaryngol. **92**(4) (1970)
26. Fong, R., Patrick, M., Vedaldi, A.: Understanding deep networks via extremal perturbations and smooth masks. In: IEEE/CVF International Conference on Computer Vision (2019)
27. Goldberger, A.L., et al.: Physiobank, physiotoolkit, and physionet: components of a new research resource for complex physiologic signals. Circulation **101**(23) (2000)
28. Hedström, A., et al.: Quantus: an explainable AI toolkit for responsible evaluation of neural network explanations and beyond. J. Mach. Learn. Res. **24**(34) (2023)
29. Hedström, A., Bommer, P., Wickstrøm, K.K., Samek, W., Lapuschkin, S., Höhne, M.M.C.: The meta-evaluation problem in explainable AI: identifying reliable estimators with MetaQuantus. Trans. Mach. Learn. Res. (2023)
30. Jafari, B., Mohsenin, V.: Polysomnography. Clin. Chest Med. **31**(2) (2010)
31. Kemp, B., Zwinderman, A.H., Tuk, B., Kamphuisen, H.A., Oberyé, J.J.: Analysis of a sleep-dependent neuronal feedback loop: the slow-wave microcontinuity of the EEG. IEEE Trans. Biomed. Eng. **47**(9) (2000)
32. Kim, T., Shakhnarovich, G., Urtasun, R.: Sparse coding for learning interpretable spatio-temporal primitives. Adv. Neural Inf. Process. Syst. **23** (2010)
33. Kolek, S., Nguyen, D.A., Levie, R., Bruna, J., Kutyniok, G.: A Rate-Distortion Framework for Explaining Black-Box Model Decisions. Springer International Publishing (2022)
34. Liu, R., et al.: Frequency-aware masked autoencoders for multimodal pretraining on biosignals. In: ICLR Workshop (2024)
35. Liu, Z., et al.: Timex++: learning time-series explanations with information bottleneck. In: Proceedings of the 41st International Conference on Machine Learning (2024)
36. Liu, Z., et al.: Explaining time series via contrastive and locally sparse perturbations. In: The International Conference on Learning Representations (2024)
37. Lundberg, S.M., Lee, S.I.: A unified approach to interpreting model predictions. In: Proceedings of the 31st International Conference on Neural Information Processing Systems. NIPS'17, Curran Associates Inc., Red Hook, NY, USA (2017)
38. Mercier, D., Dengel, A., Ahmed, S.: TimeREISE: time series randomized evolving input sample explanation. Sensors **22**(11), 4084 (2022)
39. Merica, H., Blois, R.: Relationship between the time courses of power in the frequency bands of human sleep EEG. Neurophys. Clin. **27**(2) (1997)
40. Mittal, R., Prince, A.A., Nalband, S., Robert, F., Fredo, A.R.J.: Modified-mamemi filter bank for efficient extraction of brainwaves from electroencephalograms. Biomed. Sig. Process. Control **69** (2021)
41. Moody, G., Mark, R.: The impact of the MIT-BIH arrhythmia database. IEEE Eng. Med. Biol. Mag. **20**(3) (2001)
42. Morante, M., Østergaard, J., Theodoridis, S.: Interpretable nonnegative incoherent deep dictionary learning for FMRI data analysis. In: 2023 IEEE International Conference on Acoustics, Speech and Signal Processing (ICASSP) (2023)
43. Nayebi, A., Tipirneni, S., Reddy, C.K., Foreman, B., Subbian, V.: WindowSHAP: a efficient framework for explaining time-series classifiers based on shapley values. J. Biomed. Inform. (2023)
44. Oppenheim, A.V., Schafer, R.W.: Discrete-time signal processing. Pearson Education, 3rd edn. (2010)

45. Petsiuk, V., Das, A., Saenko, K.: RISE: Randomized input sampling for explanation of black-box models. British Machine Vision Conference 2018, BMVC 2018 (2019)
46. Proakis, J., Manolakis, D.: Digital signal processing, chap. 11. Macmillan, 4th edn. (2007)
47. Queen, O., Hartvigsen, T., Koker, T., Huan, H., Tsiligkaridis, T., Zitnik, M.: Encoding time-series explanations through self-supervised model behavior consistency. In: Proceedings of Neural Information Processing Systems, NeurIPS (2023)
48. Reiss, A., Stricker, D.: Introducing a new benchmarked dataset for activity monitoring. In: 2012 16th International Symposium on Wearable Computers (2012)
49. Ribeiro, M.T., Singh, S., Guestrin, C.: "Why should i trust you?": Explaining the predictions of any classifier. In: Proceedings of the 22nd ACM SIGKDD International Conference on Knowledge Discovery and Data Mining (2016)
50. Rojat, T., Puget, R., Filliat, D., Ser, J., Gelin, R., Díaz-Rodríguez, N.: Explainable Artificial Intelligence. XAI) on timeseries data, A survey (2021)
51. Schlegel, U., Arnout, H., El-Assady, M., Oelke, D., Keim, D.A.: Towards a rigorous evaluation of xai methods on time series. In: 2019 IEEE/CVF International Conference on Computer Vision Workshop (ICCVW). IEEE (2019)
52. Schröder, M., Zamanian, A., Ahmidi, N.: Post-hoc saliency methods fail to capture latent feature importance in time series data. Lect. Notes Comput. Sci. **13932** (2023)
53. Simonyan, K., Vedaldi, A., Zisserman, A.: Deep inside convolutional networks: visualising image classification models and saliency maps (2014)
54. Sivill, T., Flach, P.: LIMESegment: meaningful, realistic time series explanations. In: Camps-Valls, G., Ruiz, F.J.R., Valera, I. (eds.) Proceedings of The 25th International Conference on Artificial Intelligence and Statistics. Proceedings of Machine Learning Research, PMLR (2022)
55. Springenberg, J.T., Dosovitskiy, A., Brox, T., Riedmiller, M.: Striving for simplicity: the all convolutional net (2015)
56. Sundararajan, M., Taly, A., Yan, Q.: Axiomatic attribution for deep networks. In: Proceedings of the 34th International Conference on Machine Learning. Proceedings of Machine Learning Research, vol. 70. PMLR (2017)
57. Tepper García, T.: Voigt profile fitting to quasar absorption lines: an analytic approximation to the voigt-hjerting function: A new method to compute Voigt profiles. Monthly Notices of the Royal Astronomical Society **369**(4) (2006)
58. Theodoridis, S.: Machine Learning: a Bayesian and Optimization Perspective, Second Edition, chap. 9. Elsevier (2020)
59. Tolooshams, B., Ba, D.E.: Stable and interpretable unrolled dictionary learning. Trans. Mach. Learn. Res. (2022)
60. Vaidyanathan, P.P.: Quadrature mirror filter banks, m-band extensions and perfect-reconstruction techniques. IEEE ASSP Mag. **4**(3) (1987)
61. Vielhaben, J., Lapuschkin, S., Montavon, G., Samek, W.: Explainable AI for time series via Virtual Inspection Layers. Pattern Recogn. **150** (2024)
62. Weber, P., Carl, K.V., Hinz, O.: Applications of explainable artificial intelligence in finance—a systematic review of finance, information systems, and computer science literature. Manag. Rev. Quarterly **74**(2) (2024)
63. Wickstrøm, K.K., et al.: RELAX: Representation learning explainability. Int. J. Comput. Vision **131**(6) (2023)
64. Zhang, X., Lin, W., Ma, S., Wang, S., Gao, W.: Rate-distortion based sparse coding for image set compression. In: Visual Communications and Image Processing (2015)

Open Access This chapter is licensed under the terms of the Creative Commons Attribution 4.0 International License (http://creativecommons.org/licenses/by/4.0/), which permits use, sharing, adaptation, distribution and reproduction in any medium or format, as long as you give appropriate credit to the original author(s) and the source, provide a link to the Creative Commons license and indicate if changes were made.

The images or other third party material in this chapter are included in the chapter's Creative Commons license, unless indicated otherwise in a credit line to the material. If material is not included in the chapter's Creative Commons license and your intended use is not permitted by statutory regulation or exceeds the permitted use, you will need to obtain permission directly from the copyright holder.

From Text to Space: Mapping Abstract Spatial Models in LLMs During a Grid-World Navigation Task

Nicolas Martorell[1,2]

[1] Faculty of Exact and Natural Sciences, University of Buenos Aires,
Buenos Aires, Argentina
nmartorell@fbmc.fcen.uba.ar
[2] National Scientific and Technical Research Council (CONICET),
Buenos Aires, Argentina
https://exactas.uba.ar/

Abstract. Understanding how large language models (LLMs) represent and reason about spatial information is crucial for building robust agentic systems that can navigate real and simulated environments. In this work, we investigate the influence of different text-based spatial representations on LLM performance and internal activations in a grid-world navigation task. By evaluating models of various sizes on a task that requires navigating toward a goal, we examine how the format used to encode spatial information impacts decision-making. Our experiments reveal that cartesian representations of space consistently yield higher success rates and path efficiency, with performance scaling markedly with model size. Moreover, probing LLaMA-3.1-8B revealed subsets of internal units—primarily located in intermediate layers—that robustly correlate with spatial features, such as the position of the agent in the grid or action correctness, regardless of how that information is represented, and are also activated by unrelated spatial reasoning tasks. This work advances our understanding of how LLMs process spatial information and provides valuable insights for developing more interpretable and robust agentic AI systems.

Keywords: Spatial Navigation · LLM Agents · Abstract World Models

1 Introduction

Large language models (LLMs) have demonstrated impressive capabilities in processing and generating text [9,11], yet a critical question remains: do these models develop abstract internal representations of the world, or do they simply memorize typical reasoning paths? This debate is particularly heated in non-textual domains—such as spatial or perceptual tasks—where the models have only been exposed to such concepts indirectly through text [5,6,8]. While several studies have shown that LLMs can learn and solve tasks in these domains [28,

38,52], and that their internal representations can be linearly mapped to those external structures [21], a clear understanding of how these internal models are composed and how they influence behavior is still lacking.

This question is of increasing importance as LLMs are being deployed as agents that interact with environments by taking sequential actions based on textual inputs [48,55]. In non-multimodal settings, the representation of spatial information as text is crucial, as language models are known to be highly sensitive to prompting [4,25,41]; the format in which this information is encoded may profoundly influence a model's ability to extract relevant knowledge and make correct decisions. Furthermore, studying distinct representations of spatial information can help unveil if and how LLMs encode abstract models of space (i.e. internal activations that contain spatial information and are invariant to changes in prompting and context), and whether they leverage those internal world models to make decisions.

To address these issues, we investigated how LLM behavior and understanding of space change based on how spatial information is provided in the prompt, and whether there exists an internal model of space that is invariant to how that information is represented. We evaluated the LLaMA-3 family of models [16], spanning model sizes from 1B to 90B parameters, on a Grid-World Spatial Orientation Task (GWSOT). In this task, models were required to navigate a 2D grid toward a goal by selecting one of four possible moves. We tested several different Spatial Information Representations (SIRs) in text form. We categorized these representations into three types: Cartesian representations, in which the (x, y) coordinates of both the agent and the goal are explicitly encoded; Topographic representations, which preserve the grid-like spatial structure in the text; and Textual representations, which describe the world state in prose. Across model sizes, we found that Cartesian representations consistently yielded better performance.

Furthermore, to gain insight into the internal processing of spatial information, we probed the activations of the LLaMA-3.1-8B model during the GWSOT. Our analysis revealed parameters that significantly predicted the position of the agent in the grid, as well as parameters that predicted action correctness in the subsequent step, regardless of how spatial information was represented in the prompt. Intriguingly, a subset of these units, primarily located in the model's middle layers, were also more active when the model tackled spatial reasoning questions in unrelated contexts. These findings point to the existence of core units that form an internal spatial model invariant to prompt variations, context, and task specificity.

Our contributions can be summarized as follows:

- We demonstrate that spatial orientation performance scales with model size.
- We show that specific ways of encoding spatial information have significant effects on model performance, even when the conveyed information is equivalent.
- We reveal that LLMs can represent the position of an agent in 2D space in ways that are partially invariant to prompting, with units that encode specific spatial features abstractly.
- We find specific units that predict action correctness during spatial navigation, which are also activated in unrelated spatial reasoning contexts.

2 Related Work

World Models in LLMs. World models have been defined as a compact, coherent, and interpretable representation of the generative process underlying the training data [21,22,47]. Some authors argue that LLMs lack internal world models capable of predicting world states and simulating action outcomes, which can impair their performance in agentic and planning tasks [5,8]. On the other hand, some studies have identified specific neurons that encode space and time, demonstrating internal models that remain robust to variations in prompting [21]. Other investigations have found evidence for internal models of the non-linguistic world—ranging from perceptual structures such as color to spatial orientation concepts, cardinal directions, and object properties [1,28,38]. Implicit world models have also been described in goal-oriented contexts where the representation is influenced by an agent's objectives [30].

Internal Representations and Mechanistic Interpretability. Mechanistic interpretability has emerged as a promising avenue for understanding the inner workings of LLMs [18,37,46]. Linear probing [3] and other methods have been used to analyze emergent behaviors in larger models and to trace how internal representations influence output, providing essential insights for causality and AI safety [7,34,50]. For example, research has shown that neurons across different layers tend to specialize, with middle layers often containing neurons that represent higher-level contextual features [17,19,20,33]. Furthermore, some neurons exhibit task-specific activations and can be predictive of model performance on these tasks [26,33,44,51].

Prompting Techniques and Prompt Influence on Outcome. A growing body of work has established that LLM performance is highly sensitive to the specific prompting techniques employed, across a variety of benchmarks and tasks [4,25,41]. Even variations in prompt formatting have been found to lead to notable differences in model behavior [43]. This has driven the development of a wide range of prompting techniques which become highly relevant when attempting to improve LLM performance [40,53].

LLMs for Spatial Navigation. LLMs have also been applied to spatial navigation tasks despite being trained solely on text [14,24]. These tasks have commonly been represented as text-based sequences, where models are asked to provide information about the environment or actions that have effects in the world [31,54,57]. Previous studies have evaluated LLMs as agents navigating gridworld environments, where models must plan a full path in advance to locate goals and avoid obstacles [2,32]. These approaches demonstrate that LLMs can solve spatial navigation tasks, although small models have shown limited generalization to variations such as differing grid sizes or obstacle configurations [2].

Spatial Maps in Neuroscience. The neuroscience literature provides a foundational perspective on spatial representations through studies of spatial maps in the brain. Early work on place cells in the hippocampus of rats revealed that specific neurons encode an animal's position in a two-dimensional space [35,36]. Subsequent research identified other spatially tuned cells—such as grid cells, which encode grid-like patterns; head-direction cells, which signal the direction of gaze; and boundary cells, which respond to environmental edges [23,27,45]. The specialization observed in biological systems suggests that generalist artificial systems, including LLMs, might similarly develop internal representations for spatial orientation and navigation.

3 Evaluating LLMs in a Spatial Orientation Task

To evaluate spatial orientation in an agentic context, we designed the Grid-World Spatial Orientation Task (GWSOT), as illustrated in Fig. 1. This is a simple variation of a classic reinforcement learning task [12,13], where an agent and a goal are placed in an 5×5 grid. The two left-most panels of Fig. 1 depict example trials, where green arrows indicate a correct path leading to the goal, whereas red arrows show a path that result in failure by reaching a maximum number of steps.

At every step, the agent is provided with the current world state in a conversation-style prompt—where user messages describe the grid state and assistant messages record previous decisions. The LLM is required to respond with a JSON object containing a single key, "action", whose value is one of four commands: "UP", "DOWN", "LEFT", or "RIGHT". An action is defined as correct if it reduces the Manhattan distance between the agent and the goal. A trial ends when the agent reaches the goal or when it exceeds a maximum step limit.

We use different Spatial Information Representations (SIRs) to convey the current world state to the LLM. We categorized SIRs into three classes:

- Cartesian representations: The LLM receives explicit (x, y) coordinates for the agent and the goal, along with the grid size.
- Topographic representations: The two-dimensional structure of the grid is preserved by representing cells and objects using characters or words. This requires LLMs to be able to interpret the text layout as structure, which previous research has shown these models are able to achieve [29].
- Textual representations: The world state is described in prose-like language.

To ensure that our findings are attributable to the SIR class rather than to a specific formatting style, we implemented two variants for each class: JSON and Chess Notation for Cartesian, Symbol and Word Grid for Topographic, and Row and Column Description for Textual (see Fig. 1, right panels). Despite their differences, all six SIR types encode identical spatial information.

For additional details on the task configuration and system prompt see Appendix A.

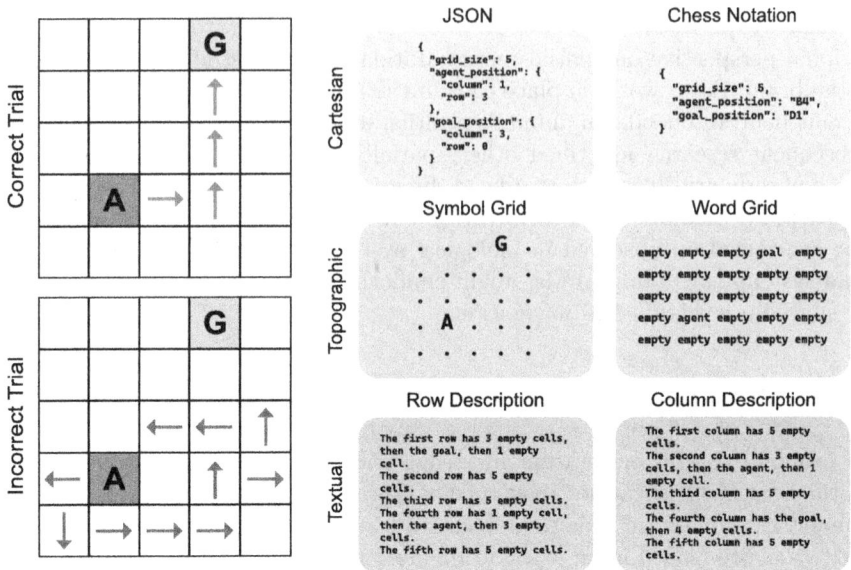

Fig. 1. The Grid-World Spatial Orientation Task (GWSOT). A Goal (G, yellow) is placed in a random position in a 5 × 5 grid (left-most panels). An Agent (A, blue) is placed in a semi-random location in the same grid, at least two steps away from the Goal. Green arrows (top panel) show a correct path which leads to the goal. Red arrows (bottom panel) shows an incorrect path which leads to task failure. The six panels on the right show examples of the three SIR classes and six SIR types used across this study (Color figure online).

4 Prompting and Scale as Factors in Performance

We evaluated the LLaMA 3 family of models—specifically the 3.2-1B, 3.2-3B, 3.1-8B, 3.2-11B, 3.1-70B, and 3.2-90B variants—in the 5 × 5 GWSOT. For each model and each of the six SIR types, we conducted 100 trials, resulting in a dataset of 3,600 trials. In addition, we ran 100 trials with a random policy agent that uniformly selected one of the four possible actions at each step, providing a baseline for comparison. A complete account of each experiment performed in this work, along with their features and number of trials per condition can be found in Appendix B.

Model performance was quantified using three metrics. First, we computed the success rate as the proportion of trials in which the agent reached the goal. Second, for successful trials, we measured path efficiency by dividing the minimum number of steps required to reach the goal (i.e., the initial Manhattan distance) by the actual number of steps taken by the agent; an efficiency of 1 indicates a perfect, direct path. Third, for unsuccessful trials, we calculated the final distance ratio by dividing the final Manhattan distance from the agent to the goal by their initial Manhattan distance. A ratio of 1 implies no improvement, while lower ratios indicate that the agent moved closer to the goal despite not reaching it.

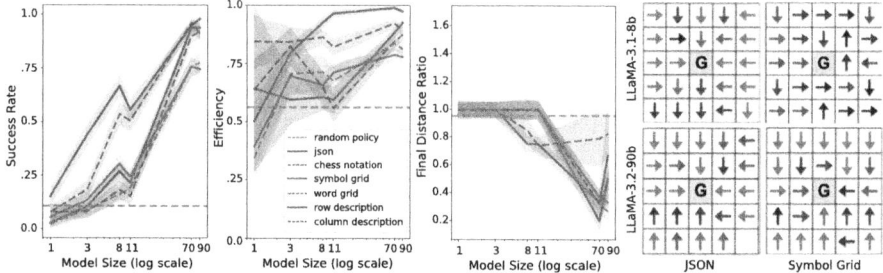

Fig. 2. Model performance improves with model size and is influenced by SIR type. The first three panels show performance metrics in the 5 × 5 GWSOT for Cartesian (green), Topographic (red) and Textual (blue) SIR classes. In all cases, the gray dashed line shows the performance of a random policy agent. Left-most panel shows the success rate of LLMs in this task as a function of model size. Second panel show the mean efficiency of LLMs in this task as a function of model size, only for trials where the goal was reached. Third panel shows the mean final distance ratio as a function of model size, only for trials where the goal was not reached. In all cases, the x axis (model size) is logarithmic and shadings represent standard error. The right-most four panels depict example policy maps for the LLaMA-3.1-8B and the LLaMA-3.2-90B models, for the JSON and Symbol Grid SIRs. Arrows represent the most common action chosen by the model in each relative position to the goal. Brighter red arrows represent more commonly taken actions, whereas darker arrows represent uncertain decisions (Color figure online).

The first three panels of Fig. 2 summarize how both model scale and SIR type influence these performance metrics. The left panel shows that success rates increase with model size for every SIR type (Linear Regression, $\beta = 0.008$, $p < .001$). The smallest models (1B and 3B) perform near chance level—around 10%—for all SIR types except for JSON, while the largest models (70B and 90B) always exceed a 74% success rate. Particularly, the 90B model receiving the JSON representation achieved an outstanding 98% success rate. Notably, Cartesian SIRs consistently outperformed Topographic and Textual SIRs across model sizes (Binomial GLM: success ~ representation + model_size, $\beta_{topographic} = 1.385, p < .001; \beta_{textual} = 1.270, p < .001$), although the mid-sized models (8B and 11B) exhibited the most pronounced performance differences between SIRs. For example, the 8B model achieves a 66% success rate with the JSON SIR but only 30% with its best non-cartesian SIR (Symbol Grid). Importantly, this pattern holds regardless of formatting variations within each SIR class (compare same-color curves in the left panel of Fig. 2—both JSON and Chess Notation outperform Topographic and Textual SIRs).

A similar trend was observed in the efficiency metric, shown in the second panel of Fig. 2. This metric also improved with the scale of the model (Gaussian

GLM: efficiency $\sim$ model_size, $\beta_{\text{model\_size}} = 0.001$, $p < .001$), and Cartesian SIRs consistently resulted in models taking more efficient paths to the goal during successful trials (Gaussian GLM: efficiency $\sim$ representation + model_size, $\beta_{\text{topographic}} = -0.159$, $p < .001$; $\beta_{\text{textual}} = -0.116$, $p < .001$), particularly in the mid-sized models where performance is above chance and not yet saturated. Notably, the largest models approached near-optimal efficiency in this task when receiving the JSON SIR (see green continuous curve).

Furthermore, the final distance ratio (third panel of Fig. 2) also improves with scale (Gaussian GLM: final_distance_ratio $\sim$ model_size, $\beta_{\text{model\_size}} = -0.006$, $p < .001$). Smaller models (1B and 3B) fail to improve their positions in unsuccessful trials regardless of SIR type, while in mid-sized models (8B and 11B) only Cartesian representations led to improvements (Welch's t-test; Cartesian: $t = -1.96$, $p = 0.053$, marginally significant; Topographic: $t = 1.06$, $p = 0.291$; Textual: $t = 1.41$, $p = 0.162$). For the largest models (70B and 90B), all SIR types demonstrated improvements relative to the random policy (Welch's t-test; Cartesian: $t = -3.055$, $p = 0.004$; Topographic: $t = -9.223$, $p < 0.001$; Textual: $t = -7.324$, $p < 0.001$). Overall, these metrics reveal a scaling law for spatial navigation performance, and show that Cartesian representations are better tuned to convey spatial information to the models.

To gain further insight into the models' spatial reasoning, we constructed policy maps—the four right-most panels of Fig. 2—where cells represent positions relative to the goal (recentered to the middle of the grid to allow visualization), and arrows indicate the most common action chosen in each cell, colored by the relative frequency with which that action was chosen at each position in the grid. For brevity, only maps for the LLaMA-3.1-8B and LLaMA-3.2-90B models using JSON and Symbol Grid SIRs are shown. Presenting the models with a Cartesian SIR resulted in a higher proportion of correct policies across positions and model sizes, compared to other SIR types. However, larger models found the correct policy in more positions and were more consistent in their behavior. This aligns with the quantitative performance metrics, reinforcing the conclusion that Cartesian representations (and especially the JSON SIR) lead to more reliable spatial decision-making.

5 Activations Encode Spatial Features in a Mid-Sized LLM

To investigate whether specific parameters within LLMs are involved in representing spatial information, we conducted a detailed analysis of the LLaMA-3.1-8B model—the smallest variant that demonstrated above-chance performance across all SIR types (see left-most panel of Fig. 2). Our primary aim was to determine whether activations in individual layers encode the grid configuration up to a linear transformation and, if so, what are the components of that spatial model and how it depends on the SIR type.

We trained linear regression models to predict the complete configuration of a 5 × 5 grid, represented as a 50-dimensional binary vector (with 25 dimensions

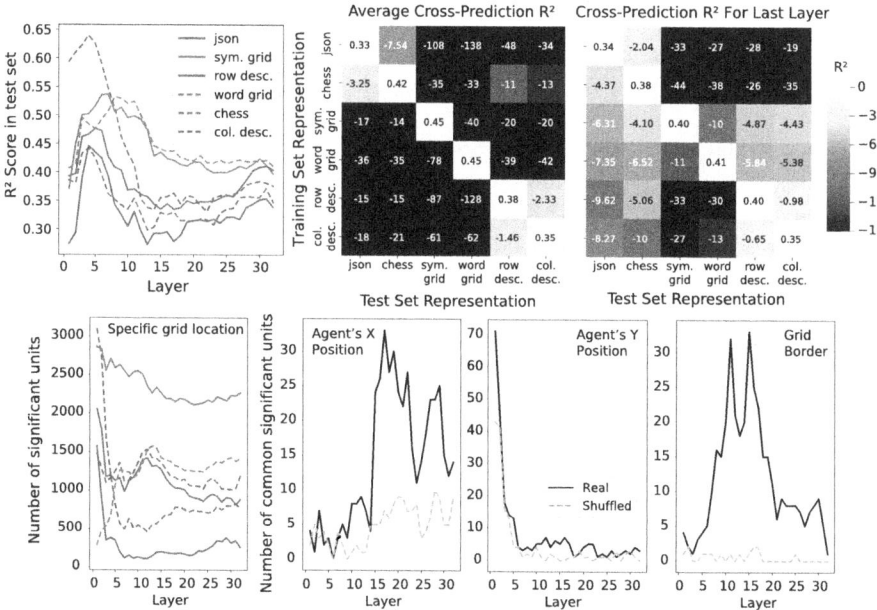

Fig. 3. Activations in LLaMA-3.1-8B predict grid configuration. Left-most top panel shows the R^2 of linear models trained on activations from individual layers to predict the full configuration of the 5 × 5 grid for each of the six SIR types. Second top panel shows the R^2 of linear models trained on each individual SIR type (rows) and evaluated on every individual SIR type (columns), averaged across models trained on each layer. The color scale is cut-off at -15 for visualization purposes. The third top panel shows the same cross-prediction R^2 measure but evaluated only for models trained on the last layer. The left-most bottom panel shows the number of parameters from each layer that were significantly correlated with the agent's position being in one specific cell from the 5 × 5 grid, for each SIR type. The last three bottom panels show the number of units in each layer that were significantly correlated with the agent's x position, y position or with border cells, for all six SIR types (black curves). Dashed gray lines shows the same calculation performed on shuffled parameter indices.

encoding the presence or absence of the agent and 25 for the goal—details on this analysis can be found on Appendix C). The R^2 values of these linear models generally peaked in early middle layers and then declined in later layers, as depicted in the left-most top panel of Fig. 3. This was the case for all SIR types. However, the layer at which the R^2 peaked depended on the SIR class. For Cartesian and Textual representations, R^2 peaked around layer 5, exhibited a dip, and then showed a modest recovery in the final layers. In contrast, Topographic representations reached their maximum performance deeper in the model (around layer 10) before declining monotonically. These observations suggest that the way the model represents spatial information, and how this representation changes across layers, depends on how that information is encoded in text. Despite these differences, the test-set performance of every layer for each SIR type consistently exceeded that of a null model (Permutation Test: one per model against 10 shuffles, p < .001 for all cases), indicating that information about the spatial configuration of the grid is present throughout the network regardless of SIR type.

To assess the generalizability of these internal representations, we performed cross-SIR predictions by training linear models on activations derived from one SIR type and evaluating its performance on activations from the others. Averaging R^2 scores across layers revealed that representations do not generalize fully between different SIR types—performance dropped markedly when the training and testing SIRs differed (top middle panel in Fig. 3). However, this drop was considerably smaller when evaluating within the same SIR class (for example, when training on JSON and testing on Chess Notation, or between different Textual variants). As the variance of R^2 values between SIR types decreased from superficial to deep layers (left-most top panel of Fig. 3), we wondered if grid representations might also become more consistent in deeper layers. Motivated by this hypothesis, we examined cross-SIR performance using only the final layer activations (right-most top panel in Fig. 3). Indeed, we found that R^2 values were generally larger for models trained on this layer than in the average case. Furthermore, the best performance for every SIR was achieved when training and testing on the same SIR type, with the second-best performance always occurring for the other member of the same SIR class. However, only R^2 values for same-SIR testing were found to be significantly larger than those obtained by evaluating a null model (Permutation Test: one per comparison against 10 shuffles, p <0.05 only for models tested on same-SIR activations). These findings suggest that the representation of grid space is mostly specific to each SIR, but there appears to be some component of that representation that is generalizable at least between SIRs of the same class. Based on this observation, we turned to look for abstract components of the model that could be representing spatial information irrespective of SIR type.

Inspired by the existence of place cells in biological systems, which activate only when an animal is in a specific position in space [35,36], we next explored whether individual units in the model exhibit spatial selectivity with respect to the agent's position in the grid. For each SIR type, we fitted a linear model per individual parameter, using activations as regressors for predicting whether the agent occupied a specific cell of the 5 × 5 grid. We performed this analysis for all model parameters and for all 25 grid cells, and adjusted p-values by the number of comparisons using the Bonferroni correction (see Appendix C for more details). We found hundreds to thousands of units per layer (depending on the SIR type—see left-most bottom panel in Fig. 3) that were significantly correlated with the agent's presence in specific grid cells. However, these correlations might reflect the encoding of particular textual motifs within a SIR rather than a true, abstract spatial model. To attempt to find units that encode spatial information in a general way, irrespective of how that information is represented in the input, we looked for parameters that showed a correlation with a specific grid cell across all SIR types. Interestingly, we found no such units, suggesting that the model does not represent the position of the agent by recognizing specific spatial locations, as is the case in biological systems.

We then wondered if the agent's position in the grid might instead be encoded continuously in the x and y axes. To evaluate this, we looked for units whose activations were correlated with the agent's x or y coordinates. We found 448 parameters that were significantly correlated with the agent's x position across all SIR types, predominantly in intermediate and deeper layers. Shuffling the parameter indices between SIR types markedly reduced the number of common significant units (compare black and gray curves in the bottom second panel of Fig. 4, Wilcoxon signed-rank test, $W = 7$, $p < .001$). In contrast, units encoding the agent's y coordinate regardless of SIR type were less common but still existed (258 in total) and tended to be concentrated in the most superficial layers (bottom third panel, Wilcoxon signed-rank test, $W = 27$, $p < .001$). Additional information on these analyses can be found in Appendix D.

Finally, motivated by the concept of boundary cells in neuroscience, which are activated when an animal is close to an environment's boundary [27], we next looked for units which consistently encoded whether the agent was located in a border cell. We identified 373 units that were significantly correlated with this condition for all SIR types—far exceeding the number observed in a shuffled control (compare black and gray curves in the right-most bottom panel of Fig. 4, Wilcoxon signed-rank test, $W = 2$, $p < .001$). These invariant units were primarily concentrated in intermediate layers (approximately layers 8–18).

Overall, our findings indicate that the LLaMA-3.1-8B model builds an internal representation of grid space that is partially dependent on how spatial information is represented, but also contains components that show a high level of abstraction in encoding spatial features such as the location of the agent in 2D space.

6 Robust Units Encode Spatial Reasoning Across Unrelated Tasks

Spatial reasoning does not only involve representing locations in space—it requires detecting relations between objects' positions to make predictions and guide decision-making. For an LLM to effectively navigate its environment, it must be able to understand whether its actions will move it closer to or farther from its target. This capability—predicting action correctness—requires an internal representation of the relative positions of objects within the environment. With this in mind, we next investigated whether the LLaMA-3.1-8B model exhibits this form of spatial reasoning representations.

We again fitted a linear model per parameter, this time using activations during the generation of the action keyword as predictors of action correctness (i.e., whether a selected action moves the agent closer to the goal) and applying a Bonferroni correction for the total number of parameters in the model. Our results revealed that all model layers contained hundreds to thousands of parameters

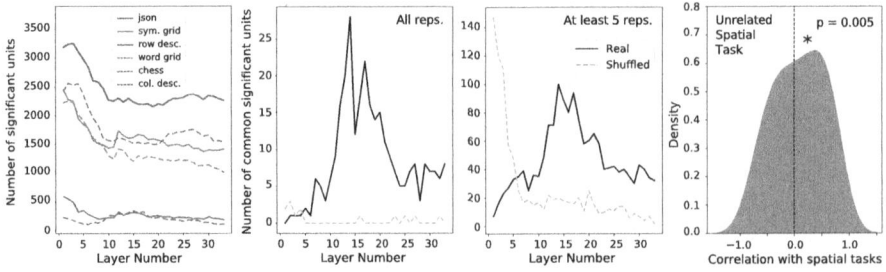

Fig. 4. Activations in LLaMA-3.1-8B predict action correctness across representation types. The left-most panel compares the total number of parameters per layer that are significantly correlated with action correctness for each SIR type. The second and third panels show the number of common significant parameters across all representation types and across at least 5 of the 6 representation types, respectively (black curves) compared to a shuffle between representations (gray dashed curves). The last panel shows the distribution of correlation coefficients between parameter activation and the spatial nature of a question in an unrelated task, for each parameter identified in the second panel as significantly correlated with action correctness for all SIR types in the GWSOT (Color figure online).

that were significantly correlated with action correctness (Fig. 4, first panel), paralleling results from the spatial features studied in the previous section. Interestingly, both Cartesian representations—and especially the JSON variant—yielded the highest number of significant parameters, followed by Topographic and then Textual representations. The number and distribution of these parameters was quite consistent between SIRs of the same class (compare curves of the same color in first panel), reinforcing the fact that differences between SIRs arise from the spatial encoding method rather than from specific prompt formatting. Interestingly, the parameter count for the JSON SIR was slightly higher than for the Chess Notation SIR, mirroring prior results from model's behavior (Fig. 2, compare green curves in the first three panels—success rate, efficiency and final distance ratio tend to be improved for JSON with respect to Chess Notation). This suggests that prompt formatting could be playing a smaller but significant role in the Cartesian case.

We then asked if the model contained units that showed this correlation with action correctness irrespective of how spatial information was represented. Indeed, we identified a subset of 286 units that were significantly correlated with action correctness for all six SIR types (Fig. 4, second panel), far exceeding the 12 units found in a shuffled control (Wilcoxon signed-rank test, $W = 12.5$, $p < .001$). These 286 units were predominantly located in the middle layers of the model (approximately layers 12–22), consistent with the distribution of units encoding the agent's position (Fig. 3) and with previous studies reporting that higher-level conceptual processing in LLMs tends to emerge in intermediate layers [17,19,20,33].

Given that this model had low performance in the GWSOT for some SIR types (i.e. both the Column Description and Word Grid SIRs had success rates below 20%), we considered that our inclusion criterion for this core group of parameters might be excluding units that nevertheless encode abstract spatial information. To explore this, we ran the same analysis using a more permissive threshold, identifying units that were significantly correlated with action correctness in at least five of the six SIR types. Under this relaxed criterion, we identified 1,560 units across all model layers (Fig. 4, third panel; there are more common units than expected by chance: Wilcoxon signed-rank test, $W = 81.5$, $p < .001$). Notably, even with this substantial increase in the number of detected parameters, their distribution remained strikingly consistent: most of these units were concentrated in the middle layers, and almost none were located in earlier layers where most of the significant parameters for single SIRs are found.

These findings, together with our results from Fig. 3, support the presence of a genuine spatial information encoding system within the model, characterized by a concentration of abstract, prompt-independent units in its middle layers. However, if these units are really functioning as a spatial world model, we would expect them to be involved in spatial reasoning regardless of the specific task. To test this, we examined the activation of the 286 core action-correctness encoding units in a different context. We presented the LLaMA-3.1-8B model with a set of spatial-reasoning and non-spatial-reasoning questions (200 each, examples in Appendix E) and averaged the activations of these core units across all input tokens. For each unit, we computed the correlation between its average activation and a binary indicator of whether the question was spatial or not. The resulting distribution of correlation coefficients was significantly higher than zero (Fig. 4, right-most panel, Wilcoxon signed-rank test, $W = 16634$, $p = 0.005$), indicating that these units are more active when receiving spatial-reasoning questions than when receiving questions that are not conveying information about space. In contrast, randomly chosen units—matching the number of core units per layer— did not exhibit this bias (Wilcoxon signed-rank test, $W = 19108$, $p = 0.31$). This suggests that these parameters, which predict action correctness in the GWSOT, are indeed processing spatial information in a task-independent way. Interestingly, when we performed the same analysis for the core units that encode the agent's position in the 2D space, correlations were not significantly higher than 0 (Wilcoxon signed-rank test, $W = 129291$, $p = 0.78$), supporting the hypothesis that abstract spatial reasoning is related with inner representations of outcome prediction rather than with the encoding of specific spatial features such as object locations.

Finally, we asked if silencing these core spatial units would decrease the performance of the model when navigating our spatial orientation task. To evaluate this, we conducted an ablation experiment in which we silenced these 286 neurons during the 5×5 GWSOT using the JSON SIR (more information on ablation experiments can be found in Appendices B and C). Interestingly, there was almost no impact in the performance of the model: it achieved 55% success rate during ablation trials compared to 59% for the intact model. The same was true when silencing units correlated with the agent's position for all SIR types (those found in Fig. 3): performance in this task was not reduced (62%). This suggests that abstract spatial units constitute only a minor component of the overall spatial encoding system in LLMs, and that SIR-specific units are enough to solve this task. To evaluate if SIR-specific units were indeed necessary, we attempted to test the model while ablating all units significantly correlated with action correctness for the JSON SIR. However, these comprised 59.7% of the total parameter count across all layers (see green curve in left-most panel of Fig. 4; also a discussion of this point in Appendix D). Consequently, the model was unable to output coherent actions in these trials. This was the case even when we restricted parameter ablation to the middle layers (12–22). Our results suggest that spatial information is widely distributed throughout the model, likely comprised mostly of polysemantic neurons (i.e. neurons that encode multiple features or concepts simultaneously) that cannot easily be perturbed without disrupting general model behavior and output coherence.

7 Discussion

Our results demonstrate that representing spatial information in Cartesian coordinates yields the best performance for LLMs in the GWSOT. Both Cartesian representations consistently outperform Topographic and Textual SIRs across a range of model sizes, showing that this advantage is not tied to a specific prompting style but rather reflects the effectiveness of this spatial encoding method. It's interesting, but perhaps expected, that LLMs prefer to process spatial information when it's presented mathematically, where the x and y dimensions can be operated separately to find the correct orientation, instead of relying on an intuitive understanding of topographical space like humans would. It is also interesting that the JSON variant usually outperforms the Chess Notation SIR, which might indicate a prevalence of such representations in the training data.

We designed a very simple spatial orientation task to be able to test spatial reasoning in smaller models, for which the 5×5 GWSOT is challenging. These models are easier to study and can be more realistically deployed in contexts where memory, energy and speed can be limiting. However, this reduces the generalizability of our findings to more complex scenarios. Preliminary work from our group using LLaMA-3.2-90B suggests that some results, such as the advantage in performance provided by Cartesian SIRs, also hold in other settings, such as adding more goals or obstacles to the GWSOT (not shown). Future work should extend these experiments to more challenging conditions and to models outside the LLaMA-3 family to determine whether the advantages of representing space in certain ways are robust and persist in real-world agentic tasks.

Another promising direction is the exploration of multimodality in spatial reasoning. Currently, our study compares distinct text-based representations of spatial information. Recent works have investigated how combining image and text prompts can impact performance in spatial reasoning tasks [39, 49], and some work has been done in integrating visual or other kinds of perceptual information with text in LLMs [15,42,56]. Future work should further explore how integrating visual cues with specific textual descriptions of space might provide complementary advantages in agentic frameworks.

Our analysis of the LLaMA-3.1-8B model provides compelling evidence that even relatively small LLMs develop abstract models of spatial information. We find that all layers contain representations of the grid state up to a linear transformation. Crucially, these representations are mostly dependent on how information is encoded in text, although we observe some degree of generalization, as SIRs from the same class produce more similar spatial encodings. We also find specific units that can represent the position of the agent in the grid by detecting its (x, y) coordinates, as well as detecting whether the agent is near the grid's boundary. These units are remarkably general, detecting these properties regardless of SIR type, which indicates that they are not encoding prompt-specific features but the abstract concept of spatial location in the grid. Notably, these units are mostly located in intermediate and deeper layers, matching results from previous research that show higher-level reasoning and conceptual encodings in LLMs can be found in these layers [17,19,20,33]. This information hierarchy might reflect how information is progressively abstracted in transformer architectures, with middle layers building representations that are independent of input and output format. Together, these findings point to inner models of space that are mostly prompt-dependent, with some elements encoding abstract spatial features, such as positions in 2D space.

Moreover, we demonstrate the existence of a subset of spatial units—also concentrated in intermediate layers—that can predict whether the selected action will get the agent closer to the goal, showing an understanding of spatial orientation regardless of how information is represented. Remarkably, these units are particularly active even during spatial reasoning tasks outside the grid-world context, suggesting that they can represent spatial information in a very abstract way, regardless of task and prompting. However, it's important to note that these units may not exclusively process spatial information (i.e. they might not be monosemantic [10,46]). Furthermore, it is interesting that they are not strictly necessary to perform well on a spatial orientation task, as shown by our ablation experiments. This suggests that they are the most abstract elements of a spatial information processing system that appears to be widely distributed throughout the network. This is supported by the fact that the number of neurons whose activity correlates significantly with action correctness can reach tens of thousands across all model layers for certain SIRs, as shown in Fig. 4. This wider representation of space appears to be less general (as it is SIR-specific) but sufficient to correctly navigate this simple 2D space. It also appears to be comprised of polysemantic neurons, which are necessary to preserve basic output coherence. Overall, the core abstract units we find may not be essential for spatial navigation in this simple task, but they show that the model is building a representation of space that is partially independent of input formatting. In the future, it would be interesting to investigate whether the abstract components of the spatial model are necessary when solving harder problems or trying to navigate different kinds of environments. Furthermore, this model of space could be quite different in larger LLMs. We were not able to probe larger models due to constraints in memory and compute, but future work should look for equivalent structures in these larger LLMs to study how these internal representations of space change or stay invariant with scale.

We introduce a framework for studying abstract representations in LLMs by defining abstractness as invariance to input formatting. Our method involves identifying diverse representations of a system of interest and employing linear probing and correlation analysis to detect network components that consistently represent system features, irrespective of input variations. This framework can be useful beyond navigation tasks, and could be applied to study abstract reasoning across various contexts and domains.

Our work aims to enhance the explainability of LLM-based agentic systems by elucidating how the representation of spatial information influences model behavior. These insights have practical implications for the design of agentic systems. For instance, when deploying LLMs in environments where spatial reasoning is critical, explicitly formatting spatial data in a Cartesian manner could lead to more robust and efficient decision-making. Moreover, understanding the internal structure of spatial representations may inform future strategies for mechanistic analysis and interventions. These might involve reweighing or isolating identifiable units to mitigate unexpected behaviors, as well as using information encoded in these specific groups of neurons to make agentic decision-making more transparent, thus leading to safer and more reliable AI systems.

Acknowledgments. This study was funded by a PhD Scholarship from the National Scientific and Technical Research Council (CONICET).

Disclosure of Interests. The authors have no competing interests to declare that are relevant to the content of this article.

A GWSOT Details

An agent and a goal are placed inside a grid of size 5×5. The agent is positioned semi-randomly, ensuring that it starts at least two steps away from the goal. At each step of a trial, the agent must choose one of four possible actions—up, down, left, or right. All actions remain available even when the agent is at the grid's boundary; if an action would move the agent outside the grid, its position is not updated. Prior to making a decision, the current world state is provided to the LLM as a user message. The full prompt given to the model is comprised of a conversation where user messages are world states and assistant messages represent past decisions. The prompt received by the LLM always starts with a user message (the initial world state) and alternates between user and assistant roles until a final user message (the current world state). This allows in-context learning, as the LLM can use information about how previous actions have altered the environment to adjust its strategy. The model is then required to output a JSON object containing a single field, "action", whose value is a string corresponding to the chosen move. Invalid responses result in the agent's position not being updated, although these were only infrequently observed in the 1B and 3B models.

We define an action as correct if it brings the agent closer to the goal and as incorrect otherwise. A trial terminates when the agent successfully reaches the goal or when the maximum number of steps is exceeded, which is defined as $2 \times N$ (where N is the grid size). In the 5×5 grid, the agent is allowed a maximum of 10 steps. This number is chosen so that the agent can always reach the goal via a non-optimal path, even if the agent and the goal start positioned at opposite corners of the grid.

The following system prompt accompanies all representations to help the models understand the task instructions:

```
You are a navigation assistant tasked with guiding an Agent
   to a Goal in a 5x5 grid world. The Agent will start in a
   random position, and your objective is to provide
   directions that bring the Agent to the Goal.

Each time you receive an updated state of the world, choose
   the optimal next move to bring the Agent closer to the
   Goal. You may only respond with a JSON object containing
   a single field named "action", which should contain one
   of the following strings in all capital letters: "UP", "
   DOWN", "LEFT", or "RIGHT".

Ensure that your response is strictly in this format, with no
    additional text or commentary, since it will be used
   automatically and with no human supervision by a Python
   script to get the next world state.
Remember:
Your goal is to bring the Agent closer to the Goal as
   efficiently as possible.
Only respond with the JSON object in the exact format
   specified, using one of the four allowed action strings.
```

Examples of SIRs are provided in the right panels of Fig. 1.

The full code to build and execute the GWSOT, as well as for all statistical analysis, is open source and available on GitHub.

B Summary of Experiments

In this appendix, we provide a detailed summary of all experiments conducted for the Grid-World Spatial Orientation Task (GWSOT). For each experiment, we specify the models used, the spatial information representations (SIRs) applied, and the number of trials run under each condition. A random policy agent was also evaluated as a baseline. When analyzing experimental results, a statistical threshold of 0.05 was used throughout this study.

B.1 Standard GWSOT Across Model Sizes

We evaluated six LLaMA-3 models (3.2-1B, 3.2-3B, 3.1-8B, 3.2-11B, 3.1-70B, and 3.2-90B) on the standard 5×5 grid. For each model, every single SIR was tested individually. Each model was evaluated on 100 trials per representation (JSON, Chess Notation, Symbol Grid, Word Grid, Row Description, and Column Description), with 100 total trials for the Random Policy.

B.2 Probing

For probing analyses, we focused on the LLaMA-3.1-8B model using all SIR conditions. The final dataset comprised individual world-state/action pairs (between 3 and 10 per trial) along with their corresponding hidden-state activations. For each SIR representation (JSON, Chess Notation, Symbol Grid, Word Grid, Row Description, and Column Description), we ran 50 trials.

B.3 Ablation Studies

We conducted ablation experiments on the LLaMA-3.1-8B model using only the JSON SIR. We silenced either units correlated with action correctness across all SIRs (100 trials) or units correlated with agent position across all SIRs (50 trials). We also evaluated the effect of silencing all units correlated with action correctness only in JSON SIR trials, but this disrupted basic output coherence, so we only conducted a small number of trials for this condition (10 trials). We also ran 100 trials each for a control condition (no ablation).

C Linear Probing and Identification of Feature-Predicting Units

In this appendix, we describe in detail the methods used to probe internal representations of spatial information in the LLaMA-3.1-8B model. Our analyses include (1) training linear regression models to decode the full grid configuration, (2) analyzing individual neurons for significant correlations with specific spatial features, (3) determining common significant units across different SIR types, and (4) silencing groups of units in ablation experiments while evaluating the model on a GWSOT. In all cases, activation values were sampled by providing the model with the full conversation history (i.e., all previous world states and decisions), as in non probing trials.

C.1 Linear Regression for Grid Configuration

For each SIR, we first extracted activations from every layer of the model. Activations were averaged over all input tokens before each step and then used to predict the complete configuration of the grid. Specifically, the target was a 50-dimensional binary vector—25 dimensions indicating the presence (1) or absence (0) of the agent and 25 for the goal. For each SIR and for each layer separately, a standard linear regression model was trained on 90% of the data (training set) and evaluated on the remaining 10% (test set). A total of (layers × SIRs) = 32 × 6 = 192 models were trained. The performance of these linear models was quantified by the coefficient of determination (R^2), both for the training and the test set. Training set R^2 was always 1.0 for every model we trained.

To assess the invariance of the internal representations across different SIRs, we performed cross prediction experiments. Linear models trained on activations from one SIR were evaluated on the test sets of each of the other SIRs separately (i.e., each model was evaluated on six test sets, always receiving activations from the layer they were trained on). R^2 scores were computed for each evaluation and averaged across layers when applicable.

For each layer, we created a null baseline by shuffling the target values (i.e., permuting Y_{train}) to break the true relationship between activations and grid configuration. The null models consistently produced highly negative R^2 values (i.e., extremely poor predictive performance), confirming that the true models captured meaningful spatial information.

C.2 Analysis of Individual Units

To identify which units are predictive of specific spatial features, we fitted a simple linear model for each model parameter using each parameter's activations when producing the first decision token to predict the spatial feature we cared about. In these analyses, the length of the predictor vector X and the target vector Y was the total number of world-state/action pairs in the dataset of a specific SIR type. X was built from parameter activations in each step and Y contained the spatial feature of interest (e.g., a binary indicator of whether the agent is in a particular grid location, or near the grid's border, etc.). P-values for each unit were adjusted by using a Bonferroni correction to account for multiple comparisons (usually by $n_{\text{layers}} \times n_{\text{params\_per\_layer}}$, except when doing comparisons for every grid cell, where the number of comparisons was $5 \times 5 \times n_{\text{layers}} \times n_{\text{params\_per\_layer}}$). A significance threshold of 0.05 was used to determine whether a specific parameter was significantly correlated with the spatial feature of interest after correction.

C.3 Identification of Common Significant Units

To isolate units that reliably encode spatial features regardless of the representation, we determined common units across all SIRs. For each SIR, a binary mask was created indicating whether a parameter's corrected p-value (after Bonferroni adjustment) was below the significance threshold. Parameters that were significant for all SIRs were identified by taking the logical AND across the masks for all SIRs. To evaluate whether this overlap was greater than expected by chance, we compared the number of common units to a shuffle control, in which parameter indices within each layer were randomly permuted between SIRs. This allowed us to test whether the observed overlap exceeds what would be expected from random alignment of SIR-specific units.

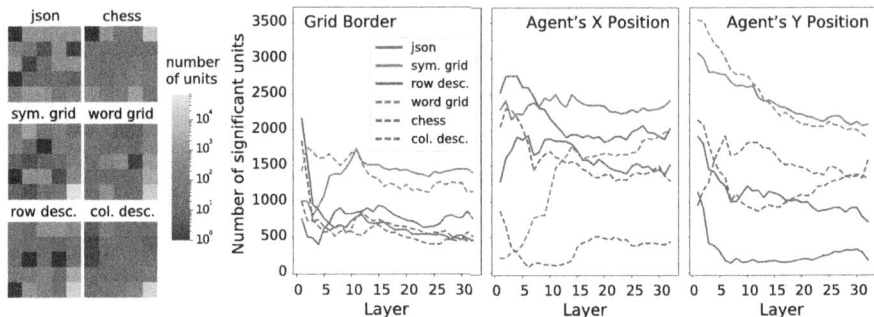

Fig. 5. Supplementary results from probing analysis. Left-most panel shows six heatmaps displaying the number of units that were significantly correlated with the position of the agent being a specific grid cell, for each SIR type. Gray cells denote places where no units were significantly correlated with that position. Note the color scale is logarithmic. The last three panels show the number of parameters per layer significantly correlated with a spatial feature of interest, for each SIR type. The features displayed are whether the agent is located on the grid border, the agent's x coordinate and the agent's y coordinate, respectively.

C.4 Ablation Experiments

In our ablation experiments, we silenced specific groups of units—identified as significantly correlated with spatial features—by applying a binary mask during the model's forward pass. This procedure effectively zeroed out the contributions of the selected parameters while leaving the remainder of the network intact. We then evaluated the model on the 5×5 GWSOT, always using the JSON SIR, to compare its performance with and without ablation and computed the Success Rate for each condition.

D Additional Results from Probing Experiments

In this appendix, we present supplementary analyses from our probing experiments on the LLaMA-3.1-8B model, focusing on the internal encoding of spatial information. The results summarized in Fig. 5 provide further insight into how different SIRs influence the model's activations.

First, when attempting to identify parameters correlated with specific grid locations, we observed that no individual unit was consistently correlated with the same grid cell across all SIR types. However, for single SIRs, we found that some grid positions were associated with thousands of significantly correlated units, while others had few or none (Fig. 5, left-most panel, heatmaps). Although this pattern varied across different SIRs, it was relatively consistent when comparing SIRs within the same class (compare pairs of heatmaps in the same row). This might indicate differences in how the model processes the 2D environment, or it could simply reflect differences in the textual formulation of each SIR rather than a true abstraction of spatial features.

Furthermore, considering that each layer of the LLaMA model comprises 4096 parameters, it is notable that in certain layers and for specific SIRs more than half of these parameters show significant correlations with a spatial feature (last three panels of Fig. 5). It is important to note that many of these parameters are likely not representing space directly, but rather correlating with the form of the input for each specific SIR (i.e. similar prompts should yield similar activations). If this was the case, we would expect the number of significant parameters to be larger in more superficial layers, where representations are closer to the input. This is indeed what we see, in contrast to the distribution of parameters significantly correlated to the spatial feature of interest across all SIRs, which usually peaks in intermediate and deep layers. This suggests that many of these hundreds to thousands of significantly correlated parameters per layer for single SIRs are not truly encoding spatial information but rather representing basic features of the input text.

E Alternative Spatial/Non-spatial Reasoning Task

To investigate if units identified as processing spatial information in the GWSOT are also activated in an unrelated spatial context, we designed an additional task to compare spatial and non-spatial reasoning. We created a dataset of reasoning prompts that fall into two categories:

- Spatial Reasoning Examples: These prompts describe everyday scenarios with explicit spatial cues (e.g., directions, relative positions) and require the model to reason about object locations.
- Non-Spatial Reasoning Examples: These prompts focus on abstract or personal reflections, descriptions, or general reasoning that do not emphasize spatial layout.

We used the following system prompt across all examples:

```
You have been tasked with answering reasoning questions.
    Please answer precisely and briefly.
```

Table 1. Example Prompt and Response Pairs for Alternative Task

Condition	Prompt	Response
Spatial	You are in a library, you see a table to your left and a bookshelf to your right. You need to find the book which should be on the shelf next to the window.	To find the book, I would walk to the bookshelf next to the window, which is to my right.
Spatial	I'm in my office with my desk in front of me. To the right of the desk is a filing cabinet, and behind me is a bookshelf. I think I left my stapler near the filing cabinet; could you help me locate it?	Since the stapler is near the filing cabinet, and the filing cabinet is to the right of the desk, the stapler should be located to the right of the desk.
Non-Spatial	You are a hardworking person who has been told you often overwork yourself, and you wonder if that leads to burnout.	I often put in long hours, prioritizing work over self-care and relaxation. This constant push to be productive might be contributing to burnout. I've noticed I'm more irritable and exhausted lately, and my motivation has been wavering. Maybe it's time to reevaluate my work-life balance.
Non-Spatial	I live in the jungle, have a long tail, and often swing from trees. I enjoy eating bananas. What animal could I be?	You are likely a monkey.

For each prompt, the model generated a response and we extracted corresponding hidden state activations for further analysis. Table 1 shows some examples of prompt/response pairs for the spatial and non-spatial conditions.

References

1. Abdou, M., Kulmizev, A., Hershcovich, D., Frank, S., Pavlick, E., Søgaard, A.: Can language models encode perceptual structure without grounding? a case study in color (2021). arXiv preprint arXiv:2109.06129
2. Aghzal, M., Plaku, E., Yao, Z.: Can large language models be good path planners? a benchmark and investigation on spatial-temporal reasoning (2023). arXiv preprint arXiv:2310.03249
3. Alain, G., Bengio, Y.: Understanding intermediate layers using linear classifier probes (2016). arXiv preprint arXiv:1610.01644
4. Anagnostidis, S., Bulian, J.: How susceptible are llms to influence in prompts? (2024). arXiv preprint arXiv:2408.11865
5. Bender, E., Gebru, T., McMillan-Major, A., Shmitchell, S.: On the dangers of stochastic parrots: Can language models be too big? In: Proceedings of the 2021 ACM Conference on Fairness, Accountability, and Transparency, pp. 610–623 (2021)
6. Bender, E., Koller, A.: Climbing towards NLU: on meaning, form, and understanding in the age of data. In: Proceedings of the 58th Annual Meeting of the Association for Computational Linguistics, pp. 5185–5198 (2020)

7. Bereska, L., Gavves, E.: Mechanistic interpretability for AI safety–a review (2024). arXiv preprint arXiv:2404.14082
8. Bisk, Y., Holtzman, A., Thomason, J., Andreas, J., Bengio, Y., Chai, J., et al.: Experience grounds language (2020). arXiv preprint arXiv:2004.10151
9. Bommasani, R., Hudson, D., Adeli, E., Altman, R., Arora, S., von Arx, S., et al.: On the opportunities and risks of foundation models (2021). arXiv preprint arXiv:2108.07258
10. Bricken, E.A.: Towards monosemanticity: Decomposing language models with dictionary learning (2023). Transformer Circuits Thread
11. Brown, T., Mann, B., Ryder, N., Subbiah, M., Kaplan, J., Dhariwal, P., et al.: Language models are few-shot learners. In: Advances in Neural Information Processing Systems, vol. 33, pp. 1877–1901 (2020)
12. Chevalier-Boisvert, M., Dai, B., Towers, M., Perez-Vicente, R., Willems, L., Lahlou, S., et al.: Minigrid & miniworld: modular & customizable reinforcement learning environments for goal-oriented tasks. In: Advances in Neural Information Processing Systems, vol. 36 (2024)
13. Chevalier-Boisvert, M., Willems, L., Pal, S.: Minimalistic gridworld environment for gymnasium. In: Advances in Neural Information Processing Systems, pp. 8024–8035 (2018)
14. Côté, M., Kádár, A., Yuan, X., Kybartas, B., Barnes, T., Fine, E., et al.: Textworld: a learning environment for text-based games. In: Computer Games: 7th Workshop, CGW 2018, held in conjunction with the 27th International Conference on Artificial Intelligence, IJCAI 2018, Stockholm, Sweden, July 13, 2018, Revised Selected Papers 7, pp. 41–75. Springer International Publishing (2019)
15. Driess, D., et al.: Palm-e: an embodied multimodal language model (2023). arXiv preprint arXiv:2303.03378
16. Dubey, A., Jauhri, A., Pandey, A., Kadian, A., Al-Dahle, A., Letman, A., et al.: The llama 3 herd of models (2024). arXiv preprint arXiv:2407.21783
17. Durrani, N., Dalvi, F., Sajjad, H.: Discovering salient neurons in deep NLP models. J. Mach. Learn. Res. **24**, 362:1–362:40 (2022)
18. Elhange, E.A.: A mathematical framework for transformer circuits (2021). Transformer Circuits Thread
19. Geva, M., Schuster, R., Berant, J., Levy, O.: Transformer feed-forward layers are key-value memories (2020). arXiv preprint arXiv:2012.14913
20. Gurnee, W., Nanda, N., Pauly, M., Harvey, K., Troitskii, D., Bertsimas, D.: Finding neurons in a haystack: Case studies with sparse probing (2023). arXiv preprint arXiv:2305.01610
21. Gurnee, W., Tegmark, M.: Language models represent space and time (2023). arXiv preprint arXiv:2310.02207
22. Ha, D., Schmidhuber, J.: World models (2018). arXiv preprint arXiv:1803.10122
23. Hafting, T., Fyhn, M., Molden, S., Moser, M., Moser, E.: Microstructure of a spatial map in the entorhinal cortex. Nature **436**(7052), 801–806 (2005)
24. Huang, W., Abbeel, P., Pathak, D., Mordatch, I.: Language models as zero-shot planners: extracting actionable knowledge for embodied agents. In: International Conference on Machine Learning, pp. 9118–9147. PMLR (2022)
25. Leidinger, A., Van Rooij, R., Shutova, E.: The language of prompting: What linguistic properties make a prompt successful? (2023). arXiv preprint arXiv:2311.01967
26. Leng, Y., Xiong, D.: Towards understanding multi-task learning (generalization) of LLMs via detecting and exploring task-specific neurons (2024). arXiv preprint arXiv:2407.06488

27. Lever, C., Burton, S., Jeewajee, A., O'Keefe, J., Burgess, N.: Boundary vector cells in the subiculum of the hippocampal formation. J. Neurosci. **29**(31), 9771–9777 (2009)
28. Li, B., Nye, M., Andreas, J.: Implicit representations of meaning in neural language models (2021). arXiv preprint arXiv:2106.00737
29. Li, W., Duan, M., An, D., Shao, Y.: Large language models understand layout (2024). arXiv preprint arXiv:2407.05750
30. Li, Z., Cao, Y., Cheung, J.: Do LLMs build world representations? probing through the lens of state abstraction. In: Proceedings of the 38th Annual Conference on Neural Information Processing Systems (2021)
31. Lin, J., Gao, H., Xu, R., Wang, C., Guo, L., Xu, S.: Advances in embodied navigation using large language models: a survey (2023)
32. McDonald, C., Malloy, T., Nguyen, T., Gonzalez, C.: Exploring the path from instructions to rewards with large language models in instance-based learning. In: Proceedings of the AAAI Symposium Series, vol. 2, pp. 334–339 (2023)
33. Meng, K., Bau, D., Andonian, A., Belinkov, Y.: Locating and editing factual associations in GPT. In: Advances in Neural Information Processing Systems, vol. 35, pp. 17359–17372 (2022)
34. Nanda, N., Chan, L., Lieberum, T., Smith, J., Steinhardt, J.: Progress measures for grokking via mechanistic interpretability (2023). arXiv preprint arXiv:2301.05217
35. O'Keefe, J.: Place units in the hippocampus of the freely moving rat. Exp. Neurol. **51**(1), 78–109 (1976)
36. O'Keefe, J., Dostrovsky, J.: The hippocampus as a spatial map: preliminary evidence from unit activity in the freely-moving rat. Brain Research (1971)
37. Olah, C., Cammarata, N., Schubert, L., Goh, G., Petrov, M., Carter, S.: Zoom in: an introduction to circuits. Distill **5**(3), e00024–001 (2020)
38. Patel, R., Pavlick, E.: Mapping language models to grounded conceptual spaces. In: International Conference on Learning Representations (2022)
39. Ranasinghe, K., Shukla, S., Poursaeed, O., Ryoo, M., Lin, T.: Learning to localize objects improves spatial reasoning in visual-LLMs. In: Proceedings of the IEEE/CVF Conference on Computer Vision and Pattern Recognition, pp. 12977–12987 (2024)
40. Sahoo, P., Singh, A., Saha, S., Jain, V., Mondal, S., Chadha, A.: A systematic survey of prompt engineering in large language models: Techniques and applications (2024). arXiv preprint arXiv:2402.07927
41. Salinas, A., Morstatter, F.: The butterfly effect of altering prompts: How small changes and jailbreaks affect large language model performance (2024). arXiv preprint arXiv:2401.03729
42. Schumann, A., Agarwal, S., Batra, D.: Velma: verbalization embodiment of LLM agents for vision and language navigation in street view (2023). arXiv preprint arXiv:2302.05739
43. Sclar, M., Choi, Y., Tsvetkov, Y., Suhr, A.: Quantifying language models' sensitivity to spurious features in prompt design or: How i learned to start worrying about prompt formatting (2023). arXiv preprint arXiv:2310.11324
44. Song, R., et al.: Does large language model contain task-specific neurons? In: Proceedings of the 2024 Conference on Empirical Methods in Natural Language Processing, pp. 7101–7113 (2024)
45. Taube, J., Muller, R., Ranck, J.: Head-direction cells recorded from the postsubiculum in freely moving rats. i. description and quantitative analysis. J. Neurosci. **10**(2), 420–435 (1990)

46. Templeton, E.A.: Scaling monosemanticity: extracting interpretable features from claude 3 sonnet (2024). Transformer Circuits Thread
47. Vafa, K., Chen, J., Kleinberg, J., Mullainathan, S., Rambachan, A.: Evaluating the world model implicit in a generative model (2024). arXiv preprint arXiv:2406.03689
48. Wang, G., Xie, Y., Jiang, Y., Mandlekar, A., Xiao, C., Zhu, Y., et al.: Voyager: an open-ended embodied agent with large language models (2023). arXiv preprint arXiv:2305.16291
49. Wang, J., et al.: Is a picture worth a thousand words? delving into spatial reasoning for vision language models (2024). arXiv preprint arXiv:2406.14852
50. Wang, K., Variengien, A., Conmy, A., Shlegeris, B., Steinhardt, J.: Interpretability in the wild: a circuit for indirect object identification in GPT-2 small (2022). arXiv preprint arXiv:2211.00593
51. Wang, X., Wen, K., Zhang, Z., Hou, L., Liu, Z., Li, J.: Finding skill neurons in pre-trained transformer-based language models (2022). arXiv preprint arXiv:2211.07349
52. Wei, J., Tay, Y., Bommasani, R., Raffel, C., Zoph, B., Borgeaud, S., et al.: Emergent abilities of large language models (2022). arXiv preprint arXiv:2206.07682
53. Wei, J., Wang, X., Schuurmans, D., Bosma, M., Xia, F., Chi, E., et al.: Chain-of-thought prompting elicits reasoning in large language models. In: Advances in Neural Information Processing Systems, vol. 35, pp. 24824–24837 (2022)
54. Yamada, Y., Bao, Y., Lampinen, A., Kasai, J., Yildirim, I.: Evaluating spatial understanding of large language models (2023). arXiv preprint arXiv:2310.14540
55. Yao, S., et al.: React: synergizing reasoning and acting in language models (2022). arXiv preprint arXiv:2210.03629
56. Zheng, S., Liu, J., Feng, Y., Lu, Z.: Steve-eye: Equipping LLM-based embodied agents with visual perception in open worlds (2023). arXiv preprint arXiv:2310.13255
57. Zhu, X., et al.: Ghost in the Minecraft: generally capable agents for open-world environments via large language models with text-based knowledge and memory (2023). arXiv preprint arXiv:2305.17144

Open Access This chapter is licensed under the terms of the Creative Commons Attribution 4.0 International License (http://creativecommons.org/licenses/by/4.0/), which permits use, sharing, adaptation, distribution and reproduction in any medium or format, as long as you give appropriate credit to the original author(s) and the source, provide a link to the Creative Commons license and indicate if changes were made.

The images or other third party material in this chapter are included in the chapter's Creative Commons license, unless indicated otherwise in a credit line to the material. If material is not included in the chapter's Creative Commons license and your intended use is not permitted by statutory regulation or exceeds the permitted use, you will need to obtain permission directly from the copyright holder.

Class-Dependent Perturbation Effects in Evaluating Time Series Attributions

Gregor Baer[1,2(✉)], Isel Grau[1,2], Chao Zhang[2,3], and Pieter Van Gorp[1,2]

[1] Information Systems, Eindhoven University of Technology, Eindhoven, The Netherlands
g.baer@tue.nl
[2] Eindhoven Artificial Intelligence Systems Institute, Eindhoven University of Technology, Eindhoven, The Netherlands
[3] Human-Technology Interaction, Eindhoven University of Technology, Eindhoven, The Netherlands

Abstract. As machine learning models become increasingly prevalent in time series applications, Explainable Artificial Intelligence (XAI) methods are essential for understanding their predictions. Within XAI, feature attribution methods aim to identify which input features contribute the most to a model's prediction, with their evaluation typically relying on perturbation-based metrics. Through systematic empirical analysis across multiple datasets, model architectures, and perturbation strategies, we reveal previously overlooked class-dependent effects in these metrics: they show varying effectiveness across classes, achieving strong results for some while remaining less sensitive to others. In particular, we find that the most effective perturbation strategies often demonstrate the most pronounced class differences. Our analysis suggests that these effects arise from the learned biases of classifiers, indicating that perturbation-based evaluation may reflect specific model behaviors rather than intrinsic attribution quality. We propose an evaluation framework with a class-aware penalty term to help assess and account for these effects in evaluating feature attributions, offering particular value for class-imbalanced datasets. Although our analysis focuses on time series classification, these class-dependent effects likely extend to other structured data domains where perturbation-based evaluation is common (Code and results are available at https://github.com/gregorbaer/class-perturbation-effects.).

Keywords: Feature attribution · Perturbation analysis · XAI evaluation · Time series classification

1 Introduction

Explainable Artificial Intelligence (XAI) has emerged as a critical paradigm for understanding complex machine learning models, particularly in domains where trust and explainability are essential, such as finance or healthcare. Within XAI, feature attribution methods quantify how input features contribute to model predictions, with their often model-agnostic nature enabling application across different architectures and data types. These methods are increasingly being applied to structured data domains, such as time series, where temporal dependencies pose unique challenges. In such contexts, ensuring reliable evaluation of attribution quality becomes crucial [22].

The evaluation of feature attribution methods faces a fundamental methodological challenge: the absence of a ground truth for explanations. Although human-centered evaluation offers a direct assessment of the utility of explanations [11], it suffers from scalability limitations and potential domain-specific biases. Consequently, functional evaluation approaches have emerged as primary validation frameworks, with the aim of computationally verifying whether attribution methods satisfy certain desirable properties [2,9]. Perturbation analysis represents one such framework that evaluates attribution correctness by measuring how modifying features impacts model predictions. This approach rests on a key assumption: perturbing important features should yield proportional changes in model output.

Although perturbation analysis has gained traction for evaluating attribution methods in structured data domains like time series, previous work has mainly focused on aggregate performance metrics. Studies note that perturbation effectiveness can vary substantially with data characteristics, leading to recommendations to evaluate multiple ways of perturbing features [14,17]. However, how this effectiveness varies with specific data characteristics remains largely unexplored. A closer examination of reported results reveals an intriguing pattern: substantial portions of datasets can remain unaffected by perturbation when using a single strategy uniformly across all instances [14,18]. This observation suggests underlying methodological challenges that have not yet been systematically investigated.

Our analysis of these empirical patterns points to an important methodological limitation: the effectiveness of perturbation-based evaluation can vary substantially across different predicted classes, which we refer to as *class-dependent perturbation effects*. These effects manifest when perturbation strategies effectively validate feature attributions for some classes while showing limited or no sensitivity for others. We hypothesize that such behavior emerges from classifier biases, where models learn to associate certain perturbation values with specific classes, potentially compromising the reliability of current evaluation practices.

Our research examines how class-dependent effects influence perturbation-based evaluation of attributions. Through extensive empirical analysis, we show that these effects appear more pronounced with perturbation strategies that show strong aggregate performance, and persist across different perturbation strategies, model architectures, and attribution methods. This asymmetry in perturbation effectiveness has important implications: data set imbalance may influence evaluation results, and evaluation metrics might reflect specific model behaviors rather than attribution quality. Although our evidence stems from time series classification, similar considerations may extend to other structured data domains such as computer vision.

This paper makes several contributions to existing XAI evaluation methodologies. First, we identify and characterize class-dependent effects in the evaluation of feature attributions with perturbation, supported by comprehensive empirical evidence across four commonly used benchmark datasets. Second, we introduce a penalty term that can be applied to any aggregate XAI evaluation metric to investigate the extent of class-dependent effects. Third, we provide recommendations for evaluation protocols that consider these effects, including how to assess whether attribution methods are affected by class-specific perturbation behaviors.

The remainder of this paper is organized as follows. Section 2 discusses related work on perturbation analysis for time series classification. Section 3 introduces the notation and a formal definition of perturbation analysis, as well as the metrics used to measure explanation correctness and class differences. Section 4 presents our experimental setup to investigate class-dependent perturbation effects. Section 5 analyzes our results and discusses their implications for XAI evaluation. Finally, Sect. 6 concludes with recommendations for future research directions.

2 Related Work

The evaluation of explanations remains a critical challenge in XAI research. To address this, functional evaluation techniques have emerged as key computational methods for assessing the quality of explanations without human intervention [2,9].

We focus on perturbation analysis as a computational method to measure the correctness and compactness of explanations, properties identified as key quality criteria for XAI methods [9]. This approach was first introduced by Samek et al. [12] to evaluate feature attribution methods in the image domain. It involves sequentially perturbing pixels in order of the most relevant features first by replacing them with noninformative values and observing the impact on model predictions. This process generates a perturbation curve that tracks these prediction changes, allowing the calculation of metrics such as the area under or over the curve to jointly measure the correctness and compactness of explanations.

In this context, correctness refers to whether an explanation faithfully identifies features that truly influence the model's prediction. Compactness captures how concisely the explanation represents the model's behavior. A compact explanation would show a quick degradation of predictions when perturbing just a few highly-ranked features, indicating that the model relies on a small subset of input features. The fundamental assumption underlying this approach is that perturbing important features should degrade model predictions proportionally to their attributed importance, while perturbing irrelevant features should have minimal effects on the model output.

Within time series classification, there are various explanation methods, categorized into approaches based on time points, subsequences, instances, and others [22]. Our work focuses on feature attribution at the level of time points, examining how each point within a time series contributes to model predictions. As illustrated in Fig. 1, these explanations identify the most influential parts of a time series for a prediction, visualized as a heatmap where darker regions indicate minimal contribution and lighter regions indicate stronger contribution to the prediction. The figure also demonstrates how different attribution methods can yield varying explanations for the same instance, highlighting the need for robust evaluation methods that answer the question of which explanation is correct.

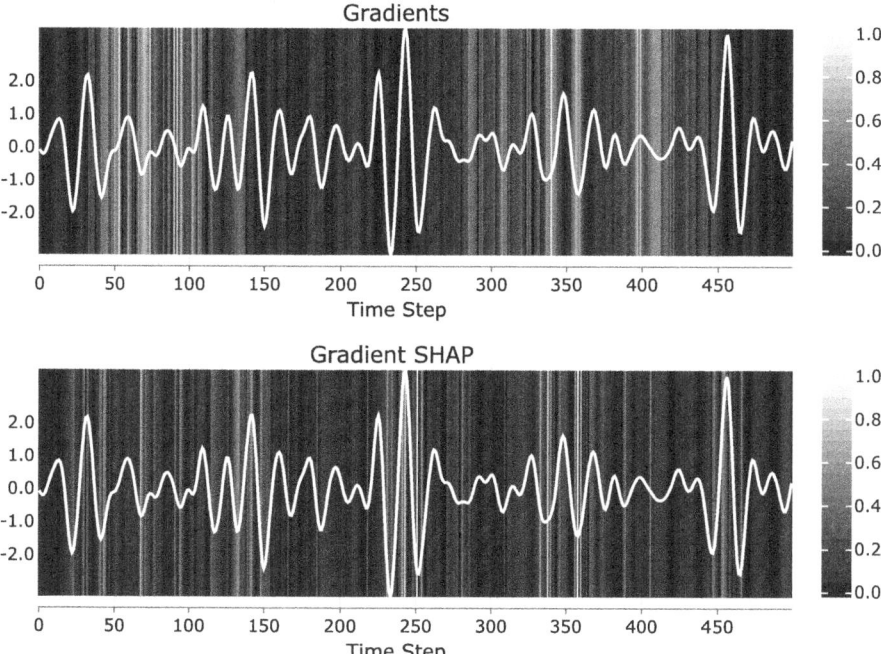

Fig. 1. Output from Gradients [19] and Gradient SHAP [7] attribution methods for InceptionTime [6] classifier on one FordB dataset sample. The white line represents the input time series, while the heatmap indicates feature importance for the predicted class over time, with lighter colors denoting higher importance. Attributions were normalized to [0,1].

Figure 2 demonstrates how feature attributions can guide the perturbation process, where important time points or segments of a time series (indicated by darker red) are replaced with non-informative values like zero. This approach forms the basis of perturbation-based evaluation methods discussed below. Schlegel et al. [13] were the first to apply perturbation analysis to time series classification, evaluating the quality of attributions by measuring the average change in accuracy over the perturbed samples with four perturbation strategies, including zero and mean value replacement. Mercier et al. [8] expanded on this framework by evaluating attributions with additional metrics from image explanations, such as sensitivity and infidelity, revealing that no single attribution method consistently outperforms others in all aspects of evaluation.

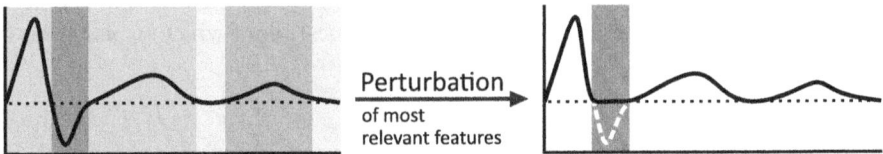

Fig. 2. Schematic illustration of time series perturbation based on feature attributions. Reddish rectangles represent feature attribution importance (darker red indicates higher importance). This example shows one perturbation approach: replacing values in the most important region with a constant value (e.g. zero). (Color figure online)

Another methodological advance came from Šimić et al. [18], who introduced a metric that compares perturbations of features ordered by their attributed importance. Their approach addressed a key limitation: perturbation strategies can affect predictions regardless of the relevance and location of the feature. By measuring the difference between most and least relevant feature perturbations, they provided a more robust assessment of attribution quality. Their metric builds upon the degradation score introduced for image explanations [16], adapting it with cubic weighting to emphasize the early divergence between perturbation orders.

Further developments focused on understanding the effectiveness of perturbations. Schlegel et al. [14] introduced a novel visualization method to qualitatively assess the effectiveness of perturbations by showing class distribution histograms and distances between the original and perturbed time series, among others. They also benchmarked the effectiveness of 16 perturbation strategies by recording the number of flipped class labels. Building on this, Schlegel et al. [15] introduced the AttributionStabilityIndicator, which incorporates the correlation between original and perturbed time series to ensure minimal data perturbations while maintaining a significant prediction impact.

Recent work explored additional methodological refinements. Turbé et al. [23] incorporated perturbations into model training to mitigate distribution shifts, while Nguyen et al. [10] developed a framework to recommend optimal explanation methods based on aggregate accuracy loss across perturbed samples. Furthermore, Serramazza et al. [17] evaluated and extended InterpretTime [23] on various multivariate time series classification tasks by averaging different perturbation strategies and applying said strategies in chunks.

However, an important question has remained unexplored: how do the characteristics of different classes affect perturbation-based evaluation methods? Perturbation strategies may be influenced by classifier biases. For example, if a classifier learned to associate certain perturbation values (such as zero) with specific classes, the effectiveness of perturbation-based evaluation could vary between different predicted classes. This phenomenon occurs when perturbation values inadvertently match features the model has associated with a specific class. As a result, substituting "important" features with these values might paradoxically reinforce rather than disrupt the prediction, regardless of attribution correctness.

This consideration may help explain some findings in the literature. For example, Schlegel et al. [14] evaluated 16 different perturbation approaches and found that for most datasets, only up to 60% of the samples changed their predicted label under perturbation, regardless of the strategy employed. These results suggest that the effectiveness of perturbations might be influenced by factors beyond the perturbation strategy itself. Our work investigates whether class-dependent effects could explain these observed patterns, examining how the relationship between perturbation strategies and learned class representations might affect evaluation outcomes.

3 Class-Adjusted Perturbation Analysis

Feature attribution methods for time series classification identify the time points that influence a model's predictions. Since there is usually no ground truth for evaluating attributions, perturbation analysis is commonly used to assess attribution quality by modifying input features and observing the impact on model predictions. The assumption is that destroying information at important time points should cause the predictions to change, while perturbing irrelevant time points should have minimal impact.

Let $\mathbf{x} = [x_1, \ldots, x_N]$ represent a univariate time series of length N. A classifier $f(\mathbf{x})$ outputs predicted probabilities over C classes, where q_c denotes the probability of class c. An attribution method produces relevance scores $\mathbf{r} = [r_1, \ldots, r_N]$ of the same length as $\mathbf{x}$, where r_i quantifies the importance of time point i to the model's prediction. To evaluate whether attributions correctly identify relevant features, we perturb the time series $\mathbf{x}$ using a perturbation strategy p. The perturbed value at time point i is denoted as x'_i. Common perturbation strategies include replacing values with constants ($x'_i = 0$), statistical aggregates ($x'_i = \text{mean}(\mathbf{x})$), or transformations based on local statistics.

We evaluate attribution quality using the degradation score (DS) [16,18]. This metric compares two perturbation sequences: most relevant features first (MoRF), where features are perturbed in descending order of attributed importance, and least relevant features first (LeRF), where features are perturbed in ascending order. An effective attribution method should show strong prediction changes under MoRF perturbation but minimal impact under LeRF perturbation. This aligns with the intuition that modifying truly important features should significantly disrupt the model's decision-making process, while perturbing irrelevant features should leave the core signal intact. Figure 3 illustrates these expected behaviors.

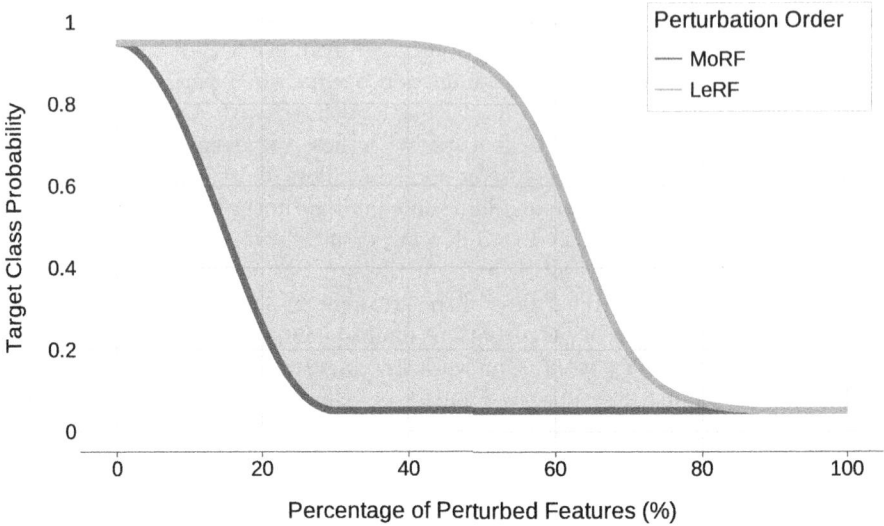

Fig. 3. Example of MoRF and LeRF perturbation curves. Here, we show a desirable outcome, where PC$_{\text{MoRF}}$ drops quickly as a result of perturbation whereas PC$_{\text{LeRF}}$ stays unaffected when perturbing the first 40% of least important features, resulting in a high DS, or area between both perturbation curves.

Formally, for a given instance **x** belonging to class c, a perturbation strategy p, and a number of perturbed features m, we track the prediction changes through the perturbation curve, which is obtained from interpolating the vector:

$$\text{PC}_{\mathbf{x}}(c, p, m) = [q_{cp1}, \ldots, q_{cpm}], \tag{1}$$

where q_{cpi} represents the predicted probability of class c after perturbing i features. If all time points are perturbed, then $m = N$. Without loss of generality, we denote the vectors $\text{PC}_{\mathbf{x}}(c, p, m)$ describing the perturbation curves in the MoRF and LeRF order as PC$_{\text{MoRF}}$ and PC$_{\text{LeRF}}$, respectively. Then, the DS measures the sum of the signed difference between the LeRF and MoRF perturbation curves at each perturbation step:

$$\text{DS} = \frac{1}{m} \sum_{i}^{m} (\text{PC}_{\text{LeRF}_i} - \text{PC}_{\text{MoRF}_i}). \tag{2}$$

The DS ranges from -1 to 1, where positive values suggest correct feature attributions (MoRF perturbations impact predictions more than LeRF), zero indicates non-discriminative attributions (equal impact regardless of perturbation order), and negative values suggest flawed attributions (LeRF perturbations have a stronger impact than MoRF).

To evaluate attribution methods for multiple instances, we usually compute the mean degradation score $\overline{\text{DS}}$. However, this aggregate metric can mask important class-specific behaviors. Therefore, we extend this evaluation framework by introducing the class-adjusted degradation score DS_c that balances overall attribution accuracy with consistent performance across classes. This metric rewards attribution methods that achieve both high aggregate performance and uniform behavior across different classes. Formally, we define:

$$\mathrm{DS}_c(\alpha) = \overline{\mathrm{DS}} - \alpha \cdot \Delta, \tag{3}$$

where α is a parameter in $[0, 1]$ that controls the penalty strength. The penalty term Δ quantifies the performance differences between classes. For example, for the trivial case of binary classification, it measures the absolute difference in attribution performance between the two classes:

$$\Delta = \frac{1}{2}|\overline{\mathrm{DS}}_1 - \overline{\mathrm{DS}}_0|. \tag{4}$$

For multi-class problems, we extend this concept by computing the mean absolute difference across all possible class pairs:

$$\Delta = \frac{1}{2}\frac{1}{\binom{C}{2}}\sum_{i<j}|\overline{\mathrm{DS}}_i - \overline{\mathrm{DS}}_j| = \frac{1}{C(C-1)}\sum_{i<j}|\overline{\mathrm{DS}}_i - \overline{\mathrm{DS}}_j|, \tag{5}$$

where i, j are class indices and C is the number of classes. Since the maximum possible value of the mean absolute difference in all pairs is 2, we introduce a factor $\frac{1}{2}$ that normalizes the penalty to the interval $[0,1]$. This ensures that the class-adjusted degradation score DS_c remains on the $[-1,1]$ scale, conserving its interpretation. Setting $\alpha = 1$ assigns equal importance to overall attribution correctness ($\overline{\mathrm{DS}}$) and consistency between classes (Δ), ensuring that both aspects are weighted equally in the final evaluation metric. For example, in a binary classification task where $\overline{\mathrm{DS}}_1 = 1$ and $\overline{\mathrm{DS}}_0 = 0$, then $\overline{\mathrm{DS}} = 0.5$, which can be interpreted as a moderately good degradation score value. However, the MoRF and LeRF curves behave perfectly for all instances of class 1, while for class 0, no differences are observed in the curves on average. Assuming $\alpha = 1$, the penalty $\Delta = 0.5$ allows us to account for this difference in class behavior, resulting in a more strict class-adjusted degradation score $\mathrm{DS}_c = 0$.

Although we apply this penalty framework to the mean DS, it generalizes to any evaluation metric. This allows a systematic investigation of class-dependent effects in attribution evaluation by comparing base metrics against their class-adjusted variants while requiring minimal additional computation, as it utilizes class information already collected during the standard perturbation process. We use this framework to analyze how perturbation-based evaluation methods can exhibit different behaviors across classes.

4 Experiment Set-up

We design our experiments to systematically investigate the effectiveness of attribution methods for time series data, with a particular focus on class-specific differences in perturbation behavior. Our investigation addresses three key aspects: (1) the general effectiveness of attribution methods across architectures and datasets, (2) the presence and characteristics of class-dependent perturbation effects, and (3) the relationship between perturbation strategy selection and these effects.

We use four univariate time series datasets from the UCR Time Series Classification Archive [1]: *FordA*, *FordB*, *ElectricDevices* (ElecDev) and *Wafer*. Table 1 presents the characteristics of these datasets along with the achieved accuracy of the classifiers used in this study. For visualizations of representative samples and detailed class distributions, see Appendix A. These datasets are among the largest in the UCR Archive and are commonly used to evaluate feature attributions with perturbations [8,8,13–15,18,23], making our results comparable to previous work.

Table 1. Dataset characteristics and model performance across architectures. Accuracy metrics (Train, Val, Test) are reported in decimal format.

Dataset	Train Size	Test Size	Length	Classes	ResNet Train	Val	Test	InceptionTime Train	Val	Test
FordA	3,601	1,320	500	2	0.999	0.931	0.937	1.000	0.945	0.952
FordB	3,636	810	500	2	1.000	0.930	0.804	0.997	0.938	0.849
Wafer	1,000	6,164	152	2	1.000	1.000	0.993	1.000	1.000	0.998
ElecDev	8,926	7,711	96	7	0.981	0.913	0.716	0.987	0.895	0.702

For model training, we select two distinct and widely-adopted deep learning architectures: ResNet [24] and InceptionTime [6] for their strong performance baselines [3] and different feature extraction approaches. Following the predefined UCR splits, we train each model with a batch size of 256 using the AdamW optimizer with cosine annealing learning rate scheduling for up to 500 epochs, implementing early stopping with patience of 25 epochs to ensure stable model convergence. The validation set for early stopping consists of 20% of randomly selected observations from the train set, stratified by the class label. As shown in Table 1, both architectures achieve performance comparable to previous perturbation studies [14,18] and approach the performance of state-of-the-art deep learning models [3]. Although we observe some performance disparity between training and test sets, indicating potential model capacity for further optimization through hyperparameter tuning, the achieved performance levels are sufficient for our objective of evaluating feature attributions.

We evaluate five widely adopted attribution methods.[1] These include four gradient-based methods: Gradients (GR) [19], Integrated Gradients (IG) [21], SmoothGrad (SG) [20], and Gradient SHAP (GS) [7]. We also include a method based on perturbation, Feature Occlusion (FO) [4]. While gradient-based methods compute feature importance by analyzing how changes in inputs affect model outputs through gradient calculations, perturbation-based methods systematically modify input features and observe the resulting changes in predictions. To ensure balanced class representation while maintaining computational feasibility, we compute attributions on a stratified sample of 300 instances per class from the test set. Attributions always explain the predicted class label.

Our experimental design incorporates six established perturbation strategies from previous work [14,18] and extends them with a systematic framework of constant-value perturbations. The details of the different strategies are described in Table 2. Although previous studies primarily focus on mean and zero value substitution among other more sophisticated strategies, we also evaluate a comprehensive grid of constant perturbation values ranging between -2 and 2. This extension provides an interpretable baseline for understanding class-dependent perturbation effects, especially given the normalization of the UCR datasets to zero mean and unit standard deviation.

Table 2. Perturbation strategies investigated in our experiments. Each strategy transforms an input time series, represented as vector $\mathbf{x} = [x_1, \ldots, x_N]$ where x_i represents the value at time step i. The perturbed value is denoted as x'_i. For strategies involving subsequence length k, we set $k = 0.1$ in our experiments, corresponding to 10% of the time series length.

Strategy	Description	Modification procedure
Gauss	Random noise from distribution	$x'_i \sim \mathcal{N}(\text{mean}(\mathbf{x}), \text{std}(\mathbf{x}))$
Unif	Random values within range	$x'_i \sim \mathcal{U}(\min(\mathbf{x}), \max(\mathbf{x}))$
Opp	Flip sign	$x'_i = -x_i$
Inv	Invert around maximum	$x'_i = \max(\mathbf{x}) - x_i$
SubMean	Local subsequence average	$x'_i = \frac{1}{|W_i|} \sum_{j \in W_i} x_j$, where $W_i = \{j : \max(0, i - k + 1) \leq j \leq i\}$
Zero	Replace with zero	$x'_i = 0$
Constant	Replace with predefined values	$x'_i = c$ where $c \in \{-2, -1.5, -1, -0.5, 0, 0.5, 1, 1.5, 2\}$

We apply these perturbation strategies systematically following the MoRF and LeRF orders, as determined by the feature attributions. For both orders, features are perturbed incrementally in steps of 2% of the time series length (rounded up) until 50% perturbation coverage is reached, recording the predicted probabilities at each perturbation step. This bounded perturbation approach ensures computational efficiency by excluding the latter half of features, which typically exhibit minimal discriminative power.

To analyze both overall attribution quality and potential class-dependent effects, we employ two evaluation approaches. First, we compute the DS (Eq. 2)

---

[1] We implement all attribution methods using the TSInterpret package [5].

from these perturbation curves, providing a normalized measure between -1 and 1 for each sample that enables consistent comparison across datasets with varying time series lengths and perturbation step sizes. We establish overall performance by averaging DS metrics across all experimental conditions, allowing comparison with previous perturbation studies. To capture class-dependent effects, we extend this analysis using class-adjusted penalties (Eqs. 4 and 5) to calculate the class-adjusted metric, DS_c (Eq. 3) with $\alpha = 1$.

5 Results and Discussion

5.1 Evaluating Attribution Quality

To establish baseline performance and enable comparison with previous work, we begin by evaluating the overall effectiveness of different attribution methods and perturbation strategies. Table 3 presents the mean DS metrics aggregated across all experimental conditions. The observed DS ranges align with previous findings by Šimić et al. [18], suggesting consistent behavior in different experimental settings.

Examining these results in detail, we find that the perturbation strategies exhibit varying levels of performance, with notable dependencies on model architectures and datasets. Zero and SubMean perturbations often achieve the highest DS scores across the different experimental configurations, though Gauss occasionally outperforms them in specific contexts. Importantly, optimal perturbation selection appears highly contingent on model architecture, even when controlling for the dataset. For instance, on the FordB and Wafer datasets, Gauss perturbations perform relatively well for InceptionTime on several attribution methods, but for ResNet, SubMean or Zero yield better results.

We also observe substantial performance variations among the attribution methods. FO, IG and GS tend to achieve the highest DS values across datasets and perturbation strategies, indicating better feature importance identification. While FO frequently demonstrates marginally superior performance compared to IG and GS, this advantage is not consistent across all experimental settings. In contrast, GR shows poor discriminative ability, frequently yielding negative or near-zero DS values, suggesting that its feature importance assignments are often not better than random ordering. Between these extremes, GS typically outperforms GR but falls short of the effectiveness demonstrated by IG, GS and FO, depending on the experimental condition.

Although these aggregate metrics provide valuable insights into overall method effectiveness, they potentially mask important variations in performance distributions. To better understand these underlying patterns, we examine the distribution of DS metrics through a more detailed case study.

5.2 Distribution Patterns in Attribution Quality

To understand how attribution performance varies between individual instances, we analyze the distributional characteristics of DS scores. For this analysis, we

Table 3. Mean degradation scores ($\overline{DS}$) for named perturbation strategies across datasets, models, and attribution methods. $\overline{DS}$ measures the average differential impact between perturbing most and least relevant features. Positive values indicate correct feature identification, values near zero suggest non-discriminative attributions, and negative values indicate reversed feature importance. The largest values for each dataset and model-attribution column pair are highlighted in bold.

Dataset	Perturbation	ResNet					InceptionTime				
		GR	IG	SG	GS	FO	GR	IG	SG	GS	FO
FordA	Gauss	−.006	.058	.021	−.040	.088	**−.004**	.109	.012	−.025	.141
	Inv	**−.002**	.014	.008	.012	.015	**−.004**	.016	.001	.011	.018
	Opp	−.027	.031	.011	.027	.040	−.052	.058	.018	.044	.061
	SubMean	−.041	.074	**.026**	.071	.127	−.092	.167	**.051**	.143	.198
	Unif	−.013	.008	.004	.009	.011	−.014	.020	.010	.017	.019
	Zero	−.041	**.075**	.025	**.072**	**.130**	−.096	**.173**	**.051**	**.149**	**.205**
FordB	Gauss	−.002	.021	−.002	−.026	.030	−.029	**.130**	**.014**	−.025	**.182**
	Inv	**.000**	.001	.000	.001	.002	**−.007**	.017	.007	.011	.021
	Opp	−.012	.020	.003	.015	.025	−.045	.035	−.022	.026	.034
	SubMean	−.022	**.041**	.007	**.032**	**.062**	−.071	.090	−.070	**.081**	.102
	Unif	−.003	.003	.002	.003	.007	−.009	.008	.004	.003	.007
	Zero	−.023	.040	**.008**	.031	.058	−.072	.091	−.069	**.081**	.103
Wafer	Gauss	−.060	−.105	.006	.084	−.164	.016	−.098	**.119**	**.177**	−.204
	Inv	.022	.065	.037	.043	.139	−.013	**.093**	.026	.072	.244
	Opp	−.020	.012	.013	.011	.021	−.009	.059	.044	.047	.134
	SubMean	**.117**	**.198**	.013	**.172**	**.329**	**.060**	.054	.031	.067	.058
	Unif	−.011	.012	.035	.019	.034	.030	.024	.066	.023	.102
	Zero	−.019	.064	**.045**	.050	.138	.024	.079	.044	.050	**.278**
ElecDev	Gauss	−.004	−.010	.009	.006	−.008	.029	−.001	.079	.050	−.036
	Inv	.014	.059	.080	.052	.071	−.026	.060	.010	.056	.028
	Opp	.023	.180	.061	.144	.220	.073	.183	.087	.179	.197
	SubMean	**.143**	**.236**	**.220**	**.222**	**.272**	**.148**	**.217**	**.113**	**.201**	**.290**
	Unif	.052	.094	.052	.057	.156	.038	.103	.048	.070	.107
	Zero	.035	.156	.075	.122	.271	.085	.187	.076	.164	.269

focus on the FordB dataset, InceptionTime architecture, and SubMean perturbation strategy, as these demonstrate patterns typical of our broader findings. Figure 4 presents these distributions, revealing both overall performance patterns and, crucially, class-specific effects.

The aggregate distributions shown in Fig. 4a reveal notable variation in the effectiveness of attribution methods. IG, GS, and FO exhibit positively skewed distributions with extended tails toward higher DS values, indicating better attribution quality. In contrast, GR and SG demonstrate negative skewness with tails extending toward lower DS values, suggesting less reliable feature identification. Critically, we observe a concentration of scores around zero, implying limited discriminative power in feature ordering for many instances, even among the better-performing methods.

Figure 4b presents a class-stratified analysis that uncovers substantial heterogeneity in attribution quality across classes. For IG, GS, and FO, instances from class 1 consistently achieve higher DS scores with pronounced positive tails and minimal negative values. The same methods show markedly different behavior for class 0, where DS scores cluster tightly around zero, indicating minimal perturbation impact. GR and SG show an inverse pattern, with class 1 showing predominantly negative scores while class 0 maintains a more balanced distribution centered near zero.

These pronounced class-dependent variations in attribution performance raise questions about the generalizability of perturbation-based evaluation methods. To determine whether this phenomenon extends beyond our case study, we now examine class-dependent behavior across all experimental conditions.

5.3 Class-Dependent Effects in Perturbation Analysis

We apply the proposed class-adjusted DS (DS_c) metric to all experimental conditions to investigate class-dependent behaviors. Table 4 presents these adjusted scores, which balance average attribution correctness with consistency between classes. Our results show that incorporating class consistency penalties substantially reduces performance metrics across most experimental conditions, particularly for previously high-performing perturbation strategies.

Zero, SubMean and Gauss perturbations, which demonstrated superior performance before, show marked degradation under class-adjusted evaluation, with most DS scores shifting toward zero or even becoming negative. The extent of this impact differs among experimental conditions, particularly across various datasets. Wafer and ElecDev generally show more resilience to class adjustment compared to FordA and FordB, though we still see reduced scores. For ElecDev, the interpretation of these results requires additional context: as the only multiclass dataset in our evaluation, the pairwise averaging of class differences may underestimate class-specific effects due to the higher dimensionality of the classification space.

To examine the mechanisms underlying these class-specific effects, Fig. 5 presents a detailed analysis of perturbation impacts across classes on the FordB dataset. Figure 5a, which focuses on named perturbation strategies with InceptionTime and FO attribution, reveals systematic class-dependent behavior. Class 0 instances exhibit minimal response to perturbation across all strategies, with DS scores tightly clustered around zero, while Class 1 instances demonstrate substantial variability in perturbation response. For Class 1, Gauss is the most effective, followed by Zero and SubMean strategies. This asymmetric response pattern may explain the earlier observed degradation in class-adjusted metrics: perturbation strategies succeed primarily by exploiting class-specific model behaviors.

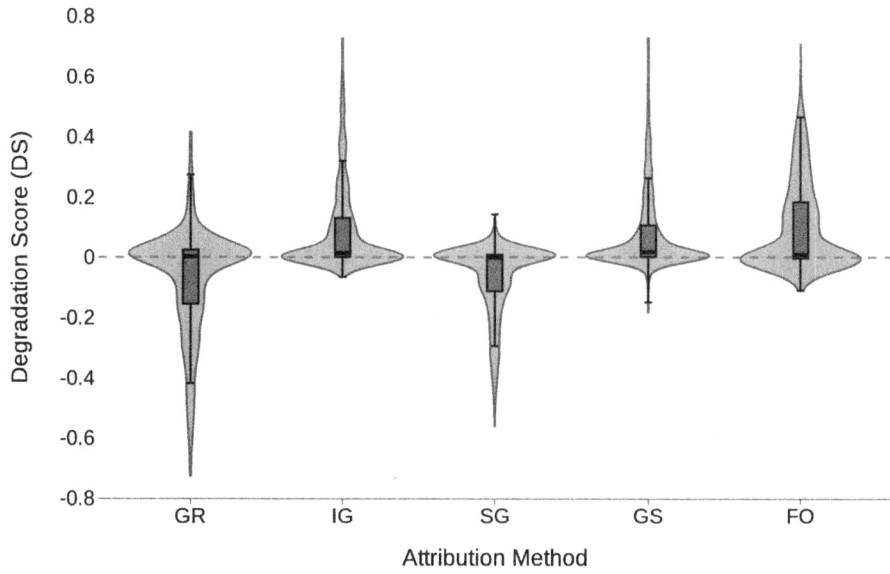

(a) Overall DS distributions per attribution method

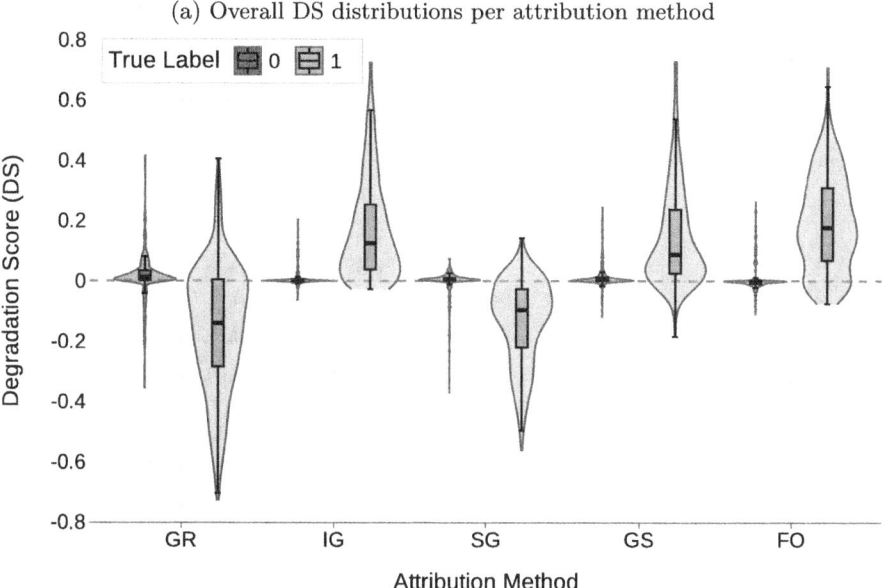

(b) Class-specific DS distributions per attribution method

Fig. 4. Distributions of DS for different attribution methods on the FordB dataset (classifier: InceptionTime, perturbation strategy: SubMean).

Table 4. Class-adjusted mean degradation scores (DS_c with $\alpha = 1$) for named perturbation strategies across datasets, models, and attribution methods. DS_c measures both attribution quality and cross-class consistency of perturbations. Positive values indicate good attribution quality with consistent behavior across classes, while lower values suggest either poor attribution quality or inconsistent performance between classes. The largest values for each dataset and model-attribution column pair are highlighted in bold.

Dataset	Perturbation	ResNet					InceptionTime				
		GR	IG	SG	GS	FO	GR	IG	SG	GS	FO
FordA	Gauss	−.011	**.003**	**.001**	−.078	.003	−.008	**.001**	.000	−.049	**.002**
	Inv	**−.005**	.000	.000	.000	.001	**−.007**	.000	.000	**.000**	.000
	Opp	−.053	.001	.000	.001	.001	−.104	.000	.000	**.000**	.000
	SubMean	−.082	**.003**	.000	**.002**	**.005**	−.188	.000	**.001**	**.000**	.000
	Unif	−.025	.000	.000	.000	.000	−.028	.000	.000	**.000**	.000
	Zero	−.082	**.003**	**.001**	**.002**	**.005**	−.197	.000	**.001**	**.000**	−.001
FordB	Gauss	−.004	.003	−.003	−.049	.006	−.068	**.015**	**.009**	−.046	**.026**
	Inv	**−.001**	.000	−.001	.000	.000	**−.013**	.003	.001	.002	.003
	Opp	−.023	.003	**.001**	.002	.004	−.091	.004	−.041	.004	.005
	SubMean	−.044	**.006**	.000	**.005**	**.010**	−.158	.013	−.134	.014	.014
	Unif	−.007	.001	.000	.001	.001	−.017	.001	.001	.001	.001
	Zero	−.044	**.006**	.000	**.005**	**.010**	−.159	.013	−.134	**.015**	.015
Wafer	Gauss	−.149	−.214	**.001**	.003	−.367	.003	−.201	−.004	.033	−.419
	Inv	.008	.003	.000	.002	.002	−.026	.001	−.012	.008	.009
	Opp	−.042	.002	−.001	.003	.003	−.021	.002	−.011	.010	.008
	SubMean	**.034**	**.018**	−.005	**.037**	**.038**	.014	**.048**	**.000**	.018	**.028**
	Unif	−.020	.001	**.001**	.002	.001	.002	.002	−.014	.008	.008
	Zero	−.047	.007	−.001	.011	.013	.012	.009	−.023	**.036**	.016
ElecDev	Gauss	−.039	−.036	−.020	−.029	−.044	.011	−.015	.045	.027	−.091
	Inv	−.024	.012	.047	.009	.025	−.082	.018	−.045	.027	−.036
	Opp	−.029	.104	.001	.096	.156	.039	.140	.041	.116	.122
	SubMean	**.078**	**.130**	**.141**	**.136**	.219	**.075**	**.151**	**.081**	**.134**	**.229**
	Unif	.026	.031	−.003	.020	.082	−.004	.055	.026	.041	.022
	Zero	−.010	.089	.031	.063	**.226**	.053	.118	.038	.104	.162

Analyzing the constant-value perturbations in Fig. 5b reinforces these findings while providing additional information. The evaluation of perturbation values between -2 and 2 reveals optimal effectiveness at moderate positive values, particularly around 0.5. We now extend the investigation of the constant perturbation strategies to all experimental conditions.

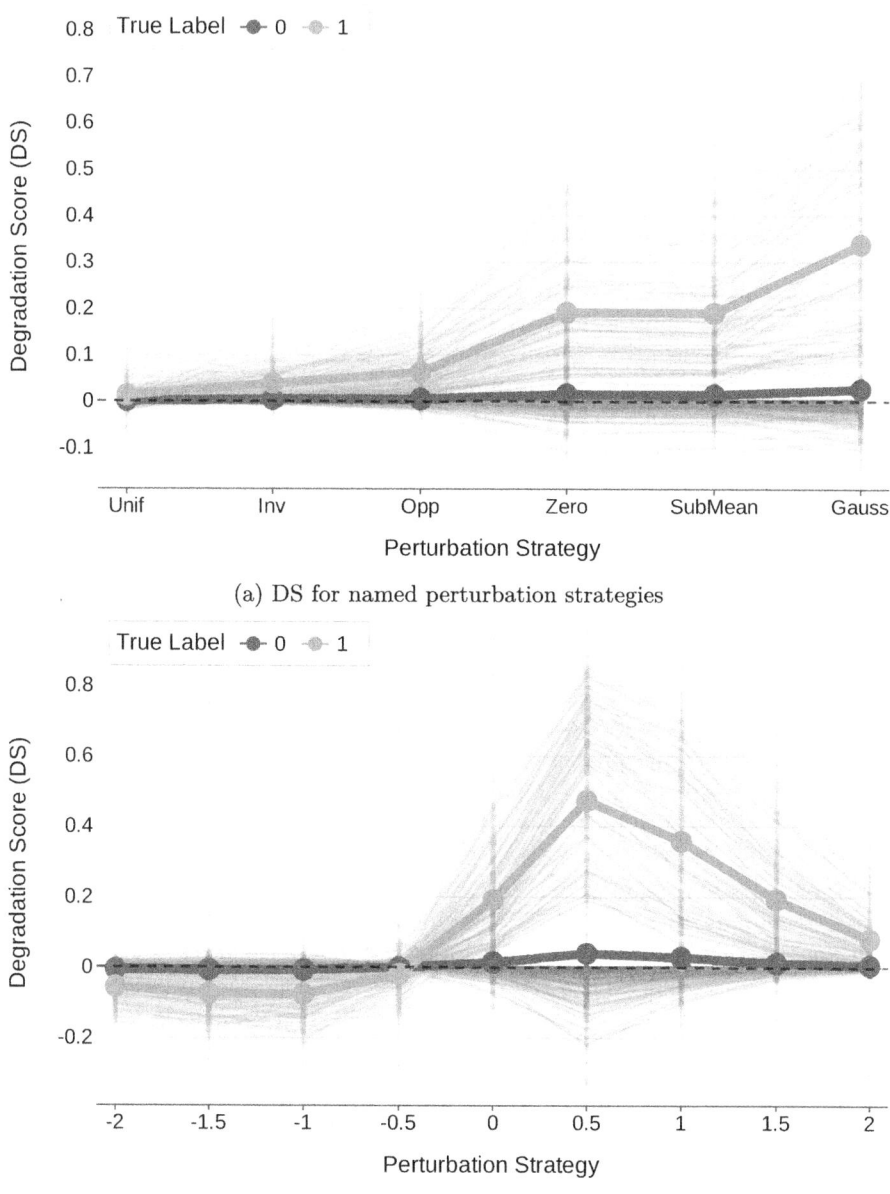

Fig. 5. Class-stratified analysis of DS for different perturbation strategies on the FordB dataset (classifier: InceptionTime, attribution method: FO). Thin lines show individual observations, while thick lines indicate class means.

5.4 Evaluating Constant Perturbation Values

Table 5 shows the class-adjusted DS for the constant perturbation strategies, revealing significant domain-specific variations. The effectiveness of constant perturbations varies significantly by dataset and classifier architecture. FordA and FordB often show the best performance with 0.5 perturbation. Wafer demonstrates inconsistent responses, where optimal perturbation constants vary across attribution methods. ElecDev exhibits the best performance with a perturbation constant of 0.5 for ResNet, and different constants between −0.5 and 0.5 for InceptionTime, though its multiclass nature introduces additional complexity in interpreting class-adjusted metrics.

Interestingly, negative perturbation values generally yield negative class-adjusted scores for most datasets, indicating asymmetric class responses to the perturbation direction. However, this effect varies by attribution method, classifier, and dataset. For example, GR, SG and GS on ElecDev exclusively show positive scores for negative perturbation constants. These results suggest that the effectiveness of perturbation-based evaluation depends on the alignment between perturbation values and the learned class representations in the feature space.

5.5 Synthesis and Implications

Our investigation reveals three key findings on perturbation-based evaluation of feature attributions. First, the effectiveness of perturbation strategies can vary substantially between classes, with performance often showing asymmetric impacts. This pattern appears particularly in binary classification tasks, where perturbation strategies may validate attributions effectively for one class while showing limited sensitivity to the other.

Second, we observe that perturbation strategies that show strong aggregate performance often demonstrate the most pronounced class-dependent effects. When examining these strategies using our class-adjusted framework, we find that much of their effectiveness stems from strong performance in specific classes rather than consistent behavior across all classes. This observation suggests the importance of examining class-specific responses when evaluating perturbation strategies.

Table 5. Class-adjusted mean degradation scores (DS_c with $\alpha = 1$) for constant-value perturbation strategies across datasets, models, and attribution methods. DS_c measures both attribution quality and cross-class consistency of perturbations. Positive values indicate good attribution quality with consistent behavior across classes, while lower values suggest either poor attribution quality or inconsistent performance between classes. The largest values for each dataset and model-attribution column pair are highlighted in bold.

Dataset	Perturbation	ResNet					InceptionTime				
		GR	IG	SG	GS	FO	GR	IG	SG	GS	FO
FordA	−2	−.045	−.068	−.008	−.067	−.083	−.016	−.077	.000	−.042	−.083
	−1.5	−.066	−.093	−.012	−.092	−.094	−.027	−.100	.000	−.056	−.106
	−1	−.098	−.102	−.013	−.104	−.086	−.054	−.091	.000	−.054	−.091

continued

Table 5. continued

Dataset	Perturbation	ResNet					InceptionTime				
		GR	IG	SG	GS	FO	GR	IG	SG	GS	FO
	−0.5	−.129	−.011	.000	−.016	.001	−.136	.000	**.001**	.000	.000
	0	−.082	.003	**.001**	.002	.005	−.197	.000	**.001**	.000	−.001
	0.5	−.032	**.005**	**.001**	**.004**	**.010**	−.040	**.001**	.000	**.001**	**.002**
	1	−.012	.003	**.001**	.003	.004	−.009	**.001**	.000	.000	**.002**
	1.5	**−.009**	.001	**.001**	.001	.001	−.005	**.001**	.000	.000	.001
	2	**−.009**	.000	.000	.000	.001	**−.004**	.000	.000	.000	.000
FordB	−2	−.011	−.038	**.001**	−.043	−.015	**−.004**	−.045	.000	−.039	−.056
	−1.5	−.017	−.045	**.001**	−.054	−.018	−.007	−.060	−.002	−.054	−.074
	−1	−.026	−.033	**.001**	−.043	−.009	−.017	−.063	−.017	−.060	−.076
	−0.5	−.040	.000	**.001**	.000	.003	−.054	−.016	−.062	−.023	−.020
	0	−.044	.006	.000	.005	.010	−.159	.013	−.134	.015	.015
	0.5	−.024	**.008**	.000	**.007**	**.018**	−.096	**.022**	−.021	**.020**	**.039**
	1	−.005	.003	−.003	.003	.006	−.069	.015	**.009**	.013	.028
	1.5	**−.001**	.001	−.002	.001	.002	−.053	.009	.006	.008	.013
	2	**−.001**	.000	−.001	.000	.000	−.034	.005	.003	.004	.005
Wafer	−2	−.035	−.054	**.001**	−.053	−.125	.001	−.116	-.002	−.155	−.374
	−1.5	−.087	−.166	**.001**	−.191	−.289	.002	−.169	−.004	−.250	−.423
	−1	−.204	−.202	.000	−.267	−.309	.006	−.226	−.006	−.314	−.337
	−0.5	−.142	−.048	−.004	−.075	−.048	**.018**	−.177	−.006	−.224	.018
	0	−.047	.007	−.001	**.011**	.013	.012	.009	−.023	.036	.016
	0.5	.008	**.008**	.000	.008	**.017**	.005	**.014**	−.029	**.047**	.047
	1	.025	.002	**.001**	.003	.016	−.014	.004	−.027	.031	**.056**
	1.5	**.031**	−.003	−.001	−.001	.006	.000	.003	−.016	.017	.040
	2	.019	−.006	−.003	−.003	−.001	−.001	.003	−.013	.014	.030
ElecDev	−2	−.055	−.040	−.032	−.037	−.054	.004	−.028	.044	.007	−.114
	−1.5	−.023	−.039	−.010	−.031	−.029	.016	−.010	.048	.024	−.074
	−1	**.017**	−.069	.000	−.027	−.005	.021	.003	.054	.036	−.021
	−0.5	.002	−.028	.018	.011	.049	**.054**	.055	**.075**	.092	.104
	0	−.010	.089	.031	.063	.226	.053	**.118**	.038	.104	**.162**
	0.5	.005	**.147**	**.100**	**.129**	**.269**	.013	.106	.019	**.106**	.144
	1	.006	.114	.076	.098	.193	.005	.112	.027	.094	.123
	1.5	.005	.087	.078	.086	.139	.015	.098	.032	.066	.063
	2	.003	.067	.078	.068	.078	.024	.041	.036	.029	−.005

Third, our analysis of constant perturbation strategies shows that optimal perturbation values can vary across datasets and architectures, indicating that perturbation effectiveness may be influenced by the specific characteristics of learned model representations. This finding suggests that the choice of perturbation values warrants careful consideration for each specific application context.

6 Conclusion and Future Work

This paper presents a systematic investigation of class-dependent effects in perturbation-based evaluation of feature attributions for time series classification. Through empirical evaluation across four datasets, five attribution methods, and multiple perturbation strategies, we demonstrate that perturbation-based evaluation methods can exhibit class-specific behaviors that warrant careful consideration in validation procedures. Namely, we show that: (1) perturbation effectiveness can vary substantially between classes; (2) strategies with stronger aggregate performance often exhibit more pronounced class-dependent effects; and

(3) optimal perturbation strategies can vary considerably across datasets and model architectures, suggesting that perturbation effectiveness is influenced by specific characteristics of learned model representations and that domain-specific calibration may be necessary.

We recommend several evaluation approaches to address potential class-dependent effects. First, supplementing aggregate metrics with more detailed class-stratified analysis can help identify when dominant classes disproportionately influence results. Second, applying penalty frameworks like the one proposed in this study quantifies class-dependent effects without additional computational burden, allowing researchers to systematically compare attribution methods while accounting for class biases. Third, evaluating individual instances with multiple perturbation strategies targeting different class predictions may help validate attribution robustness beyond the limitations of any single approach.

The generalizability of our findings faces two primary constraints. Our investigation encompasses only four datasets and two classifier architectures, potentially limiting broader applicability. Additionally, the observed perturbation response patterns may reflect specific characteristics of our experimental configuration rather than fundamental properties of the evaluation approach. Nevertheless, the alignment with previous literature suggests wider relevance of our methodology.

Future research directions emerge from these findings. One promising avenue involves developing perturbation strategies that systematically account for class-specific model behaviors, particularly focusing on methods that can push predictions toward different classes. Additionally, investigating methods to adaptively select perturbation strategies for individual instances could improve evaluation effectiveness, as our results suggest that different instances may require different perturbation approaches to effectively validate their attributions.

Acknowledgments. This paper is supported by the European Union's HORIZON Research and Innovation Program under grant agreement No. 101120657, project ENFIELD (European Lighthouse to Manifest Trustworthy and Green AI).

Disclosure of Interests. All authors declare that they have no conflicts of interest.

A Dataset Visualizations and Class Distributions

Table 6. Class distribution across datasets. Values represent the proportion of samples in each class for training and test sets.

Dataset	Train							Test						
	C0	C1	C2	C3	C4	C5	C6	C0	C1	C2	C3	C4	C5	C6
FordA	.513	.487	–	–	–	–	–	.516	.484	–	–	–	–	–
FordB	.512	.488	–	–	–	–	–	.495	.505	–	–	–	–	–
Wafer	.097	.903	–	–	–	–	–	.108	.892	–	–	–	–	–
ElecDev	.081	.250	.095	.165	.270	.057	.082	.087	.254	.098	.151	.242	.096	.072

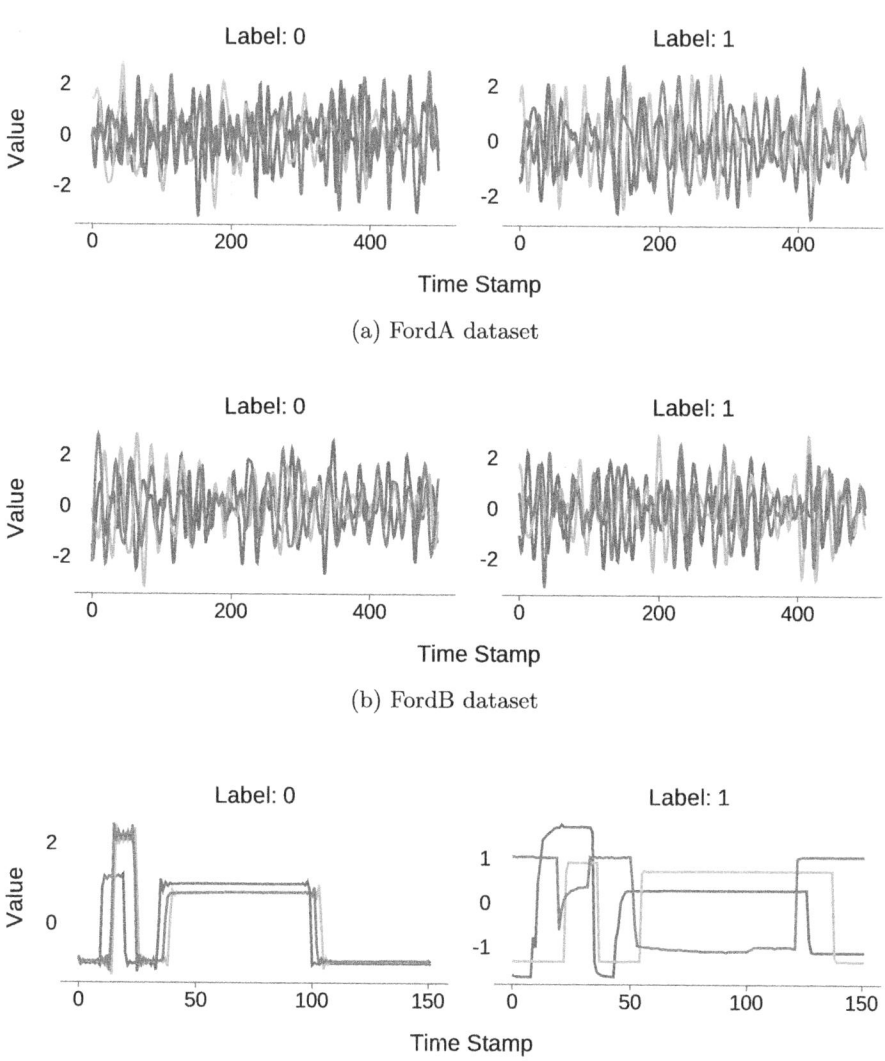

Fig. 6. Representative samples from the three binary classification datasets used in this study. For each dataset, three randomly selected instances per class are shown to illustrate the characteristic patterns and variability between classes. If datasets had labels not starting from 0, they were remapped to start from 0 (ranging from 0 to $C-1$), preserving the existing order.

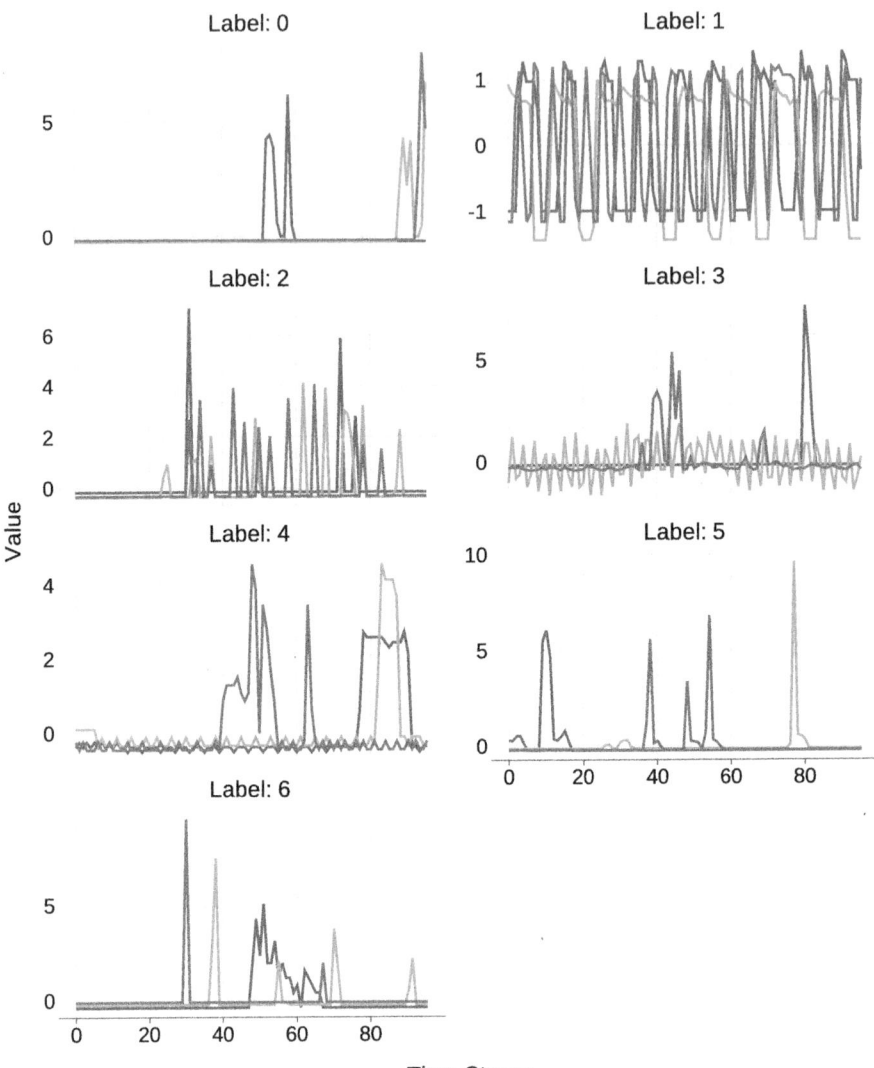

Fig. 7. Representative samples from the one multiclass classification dataset used in this study, ElecDev. Three randomly selected instances per class are shown to illustrate the characteristic patterns and variability between classes. If datasets had labels not starting from 0, they were remapped to start from 0 (ranging from 0 to $C-1$), preserving the existing order.

References

1. Dau, H.A., et al.: The UCR time series archive. IEEE/CAA J. Automatica Sinica **6**, 1293–1305 (2019). https://doi.org/10.1109/JAS.2019.1911747
2. Doshi-Velez, F., Kim, B.: Considerations for evaluation and generalization in interpretable machine learning. In: Escalante, H.J., Escalera, S., Guyon, I., Baró, X., Güçlütürk, Y., Güçlü, U., van Gerven, M. (eds.) Explainable and Interpretable Models in Computer Vision and Machine Learning, pp. 3–17. Springer (2018). https://doi.org/10.1007/978-3-319-98131-4_1
3. Fawaz, H.I., Forestier, G., Weber, J., Idoumghar, L., Muller, P.A.: Deep learning for time series classification: a review. Data Mining Knowl. Disc. **33**, 917–963 (2019). https://doi.org/10.1007/s10618-019-00619-1
4. Fong, R.C., Vedaldi, A.: Interpretable explanations of black boxes by meaningful perturbation. In: Proceedings of the IEEE International Conference on Computer Vision, pp. 3429–3437 (2017). https://openaccess.thecvf.com/content_iccv_2017/html/Fong_Interpretable_Explanations_of_ICCV_2017_paper.html
5. Höllig, J., Kulbach, C., Thoma, S.: TSInterpret: a python package for the interpretability of time series classification. J. Open Source Softw. **8**, 5220 (2023). https://doi.org/10.21105/joss.05220
6. Fawaz, I.H., et al.: InceptionTime: finding AlexNet for time series classification. Data Mining Knowl. Disc. **34**, 1936–1962 (2020). https://doi.org/10.1007/s10618-020-00710-y
7. Lundberg, S.M., Lee, S.I.: A Unified approach to interpreting model predictions. In: Guyon, I., Luxburg, U.V., Bengio, S., Wallach, H., Fergus, R., Vishwanathan, S., Garnett, R. (eds.) Advances in Neural Information Processing Systems, vol. 30 (2017). https://proceedings.neurips.cc/paper_files/paper/2017/file/8a20a8621978632d76c43dfd28b67767-Paper.pdf
8. Mercier, D., Bhatt, J., Dengel, A., Ahmed, S.: Time to Focus: A Comprehensive Benchmark Using Time Series Attribution Methods (2022). https://doi.org/10.48550/arXiv.2202.03759
9. Nauta, M., et al.: From anecdotal evidence to quantitative evaluation methods: a systematic review on evaluating explainable AI. ACM Comput. Surv. **55**, 1–42 (2023). https://doi.org/10.1145/3583558
10. Nguyen, T.T., Le Nguyen, T., Ifrim, G.: Robust explainer recommendation for time series classification. Data Mining Knowl. Disc. **38**, 3372–3413 (2024). https://doi.org/10.1007/s10618-024-01045-8
11. Rong, Y., et al.: Towards human-centered explainable AI: a survey of user studies for model explanations. IEEE Trans. Pattern Anal. Mach. Intell. **46**(4), 2104–2122 (2024). https://doi.org/10.1109/TPAMI.2023.3331846
12. Samek, W., Binder, A., Montavon, G., Lapuschkin, S., Müller, K.R.: Evaluating the visualization of what a deep neural network has learned. IEEE Trans. Neural Netw. Learn. Syst. **28**, 2660–2673 (2017). https://doi.org/10.1109/TNNLS.2016.2599820
13. Schlegel, U., Arnout, H., El-Assady, M., Oelke, D., Keim, D.A.: Towards a rigorous evaluation of XAI methods on time series. In: 2019 IEEE/CVF International Conference on Computer Vision Workshop (ICCVW), pp. 4197–4201 (2019). https://doi.org/10.1109/ICCVW.2019.00516
14. Schlegel, U., Keim, D.A.: A deep dive into perturbations as evaluation technique for time series XAI. In: Longo, L. (ed.) Explainable Artificial Intelligence, vol. 1903, pp. 165–180. Springer Nature Switzerland, Cham (2023). https://doi.org/10.1007/978-3-031-44070-0_9

15. Schlegel, U., Keim, D.A.: Introducing the attribution stability indicator: a measure for time series XAI attributions. In: ECML-PKDD Workshop XAI-TS: Explainable AI for Time Series: Advances and Applications (2023). https://doi.org/10.48550/arXiv.2310.04178
16. Schulz, K., Sixt, L., Tombari, F., Landgraf, T.: Restricting the flow: information bottlenecks for attribution. In: International Conference on Learning Representations (2020). https://openreview.net/forum?id=S1xWh1rYwB
17. Serramazza, D.I., Nguyen, T.L., Ifrim, G.: Improving the evaluation and actionability of explanation methods for multivariate time series classification. In: Bifet, A., Davis, J., Krilavičius, T., Kull, M., Ntoutsi, E., Žliobaitė, I. (eds.) Machine Learning and Knowledge Discovery in Databases. Research Track, pp. 177–195 (2024). https://doi.org/10.1007/978-3-031-70359-1_11
18. Šimić, I., Sabol, V., Veas, E.: Perturbation effect: a metric to counter misleading validation of feature attribution. In: Proceedings of the 31st ACM International Conference on Information and Knowledge Management, pp. 1798–1807 (2022). https://doi.org/10.1145/3511808.3557418
19. Simonyan, K., Vedaldi, A., Zisserman, A.: Deep inside convolutional networks: visualising image classification models and saliency maps. In: Proceedings of the International Conference on Learning Representations (ICLR) (2014). https://doi.org/10.48550/arXiv.1312.6034
20. Smilkov, D., Thorat, N., Kim, B., Viégas, F., Wattenberg, M.: SmoothGrad: removing noise by adding noise (2017). https://doi.org/10.48550/arXiv.1706.03825
21. Sundararajan, M., Taly, A., Yan, Q.: Axiomatic attribution for deep networks. In: Proceedings of the 34th International Conference on Machine Learning, pp. 3319–3328 (2017). https://proceedings.mlr.press/v70/sundararajan17a.html
22. Theissler, A., Spinnato, F., Schlegel, U., Guidotti, R.: Explainable AI for time series classification: a review, taxonomy and research directions. IEEE Access **10**, 100700–100724 (2022). https://doi.org/10.1109/ACCESS.2022.3207765
23. Turbé, H., Bjelogrlic, M., Lovis, C., Mengaldo, G.: Evaluation of post-hoc interpretability methods in time-series classification. Nat. Mach. Intell. **5**, 250–260 (2023). https://doi.org/10.1038/s42256-023-00620-w
24. Wang, Z., Yan, W., Oates, T.: Time series classification from scratch with deep neural networks: a strong baseline. In: 2017 International Joint Conference on Neural Networks (IJCNN), pp. 1578–1585 (2017). https://doi.org/10.1109/IJCNN.2017.7966039

Open Access This chapter is licensed under the terms of the Creative Commons Attribution 4.0 International License (http://creativecommons.org/licenses/by/4.0/), which permits use, sharing, adaptation, distribution and reproduction in any medium or format, as long as you give appropriate credit to the original author(s) and the source, provide a link to the Creative Commons license and indicate if changes were made.

The images or other third party material in this chapter are included in the chapter's Creative Commons license, unless indicated otherwise in a credit line to the material. If material is not included in the chapter's Creative Commons license and your intended use is not permitted by statutory regulation or exceeds the permitted use, you will need to obtain permission directly from the copyright holder.

Explainable AI in Finance & Legal Frameworks for XAI Technologies

XAI In Fraud Detection: A Causal Perspective

Katiuscka van Veen, Faizan Ahmed[(✉)], and Maurice van Keulen

University of Twente, Enschede, Netherlands
k.y.vanveen@student.utwente.nl, {faizan.ahmed,m.vankeulen}@utwente.nl

Abstract. Fraud detection systems powered by machine learning (ML) often lack transparency, raising concerns about trustworthiness and interpretability. While Explainable AI (XAI) addresses these issues, many methods rely on correlation rather than causation, potentially overlooking true fraud patterns. This study integrates causal discovery with XAI to propose a novel evaluation framework for fraud detection, validated on synthetic and real-world datasets. Our pipeline combines ML models, SHAP-based explanations, and causal feature selection via CD-NOD. Results show that models trained on causally selected features achieve slightly higher XAI alignment on quantitative metrics compared to correlation-based methods, particularly on synthetic data. However, real-world data challenges such as anonymization has lead to limited causal interpretability. This work lays groundwork for trustworthy AI in high-stakes finance, highlighting the need for dynamic causal methods and improved causality-specific evaluation metrics.

Keywords: Fraud Detection · Explainable Artificial Intelligence (XAI) · Causal Discovery · CD-NOD · SHAP · Trustworthy AI · Machine Learning

1 Introduction

Explainable Artificial Intelligence (XAI) is a growing field that is becoming more relevant with the increasing popularity and awareness of machine learning and AI as tools for everyday use [1]. One of the major issues with classical AI is that despite high performance and reliable output, reasoning often cannot be accurately explained or even observed at all. XAI solves this issue by providing transparency into the workings of the model or framing the output in a way that allows a user to understand its conclusions. This explainability is especially vital when AI is used in financial and commercial contexts where fraud detection techniques might use inherent biases in historical data in order to draw conclusions instead of finding the real fraudulent patterns [2]. The performance of existing fraud detection techniques are already impressive and could help minimize overall fraud in privately owned businesses as well as public institutions. However, the risk of implementing a highly complex model with low transparency is too great, as it becomes very difficult to justify in a judicial setting or directly to clients.

Fraud can be defined as the practice of intentional deception to secure an unfair (or unlawful) gain for the perpetrator [3]. This is often a financial gain, but could also be in the form of status or information, among other possible benefits. AI and machine learning solutions have therefore been sought after because of their ability to classify and identify fraudulent outliers within large collections of data that might be overlooked by manual detection methods [4]. Catching fraud in its initial stages could save an organization or an individual a significant amount of money, time, and could prevent further instances of it. While recent advancements in technology and models have caused the average performance to be high, an important issue remains the lack of transparency and context in decision-making and final outputs [5].

XAI could be a solution for this, as it provides the transparency that is required to be able to use these methods in practice. However, existing works and studies have shown that the current use of XAI in fraud detection research is still limited, and often not substantiated by quantitative evaluation but rather anecdotally or not at all [5]. Alongside this, many current AI and XAI methods rely on correlations to draw conclusions. This is difficult to verify as there is not always a clear ground truth [6]. Traditional fraud detection systems often rely on historical data patterns, which may inadvertently amplify biases or fail to adapt to evolving fraud tactics. For instance, correlation-based models might flag transactions based on superficial similarities to past fraud cases, rather than identifying novel, causal indicators of fraud. Causal discovery techniques, which infer cause-effect relationships from data, offer a promising solution. By identifying features with direct causal links to fraud, these methods could enhance both model accuracy and explanation quality, while reducing reliance on spurious correlations.

This study investigates the potential of integrating causal discovery with XAI to improve the explainability and trustworthiness of fraud detection models. Our central hypothesis is that models trained on causally selected features will produce more reliable and actionable explanations, aligning with real-world fraud dynamics rather than superficial data patterns. This was done through the implementation of a pipeline that includes a machine learning model with an explainability module. In the feature selection step of the pipeline, a simple filtering technique and a causal discovery based technique were both implemented and fed separately to the ML model. These methods were compared to observe the XAI output and gauge whether the causality based method affected the overall interpretability.

The introduction briefly describes the relevant literature for brevity of space. The rest of the paper is organized as follows: Sect. 2 describes the methodology adopted, while the results are presented in Sect. 3. The discussion and conclusions are presented in Sect. 4 and Sect. 5, respectively.

2 Methodology

2.1 Pipeline Architecture

The overall architecture is designed to systematically compare the effects of causal and correlation-based feature selection on both model performance and explanation quality. This structure allows for direct comparison of causal and correlation-based approaches across identical experimental conditions, as the only difference is in the feature selection phase.

The overall architecture consists of five distinct phases: the data preprocessing phase, the feature selection phase, the prediction phase, the explanation phase, and the evaluation phase. In Fig. 1 the basic architecture can be observed.

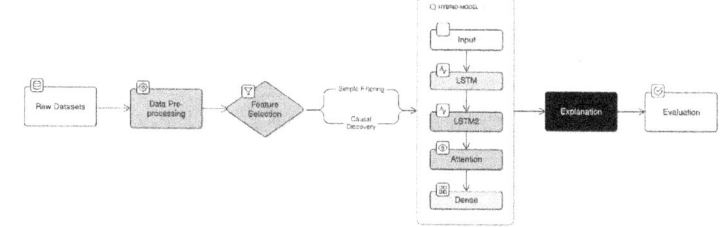

Fig. 1. Pipeline architecture.

2.2 Implementation and Setup

For all of the sections of the pipeline, the Python programming language was used. The causal discovery phase utilized the CD-NOD [8] algorithm from the causal-learn package[1], which identifies causal relationships among variables while accounting for temporal dependencies in transaction data. For machine learning, a hybrid LSTM-attention model was implemented using TensorFlow, combining the sequential pattern recognition capabilities of LSTMs with the noise-reduction strengths of attention mechanisms. SHAP values were computed to quantify feature contributions to model predictions. Data preprocessing, including cleaning, feature engineering, encoding, and scaling, was performed using Pandas and NumPy.

2.3 Data Description

Synthetic Dataset. The first dataset is a synthetic dataset that consists of transactions, customer details, and card data of an unnamed banking institution

---

[1] https://causal-learn.readthedocs.io/en/latest/index.html.

across the 2010's. The dataset was downloaded from Kaggle[2], and consisted of 5 separate files. All files were tabular which made merging and converting between file types possible without any significant structural changes. The data is merged based on the transaction, client, and merchant id's as primary keys. The distribution of fraudulent vs. non-fraudulent transactions was very imbalanced. There are 8901631 regular transactions and 13332 fraudulent ones. This means that only 0.1% of the transactions are actually fraudulent. The dataset's rich features allowed for direct interpretation of causal relationships as they were left in their original state.

Real Dataset. The second dataset is a credit card transaction dataset which contains European transactions made over a two day timespan in September of 2013. The Université Libre de Bruxelles collected this data in collaboration with Wordline and the Machine learning group and contains real data from European cardholders. This dataset was also downloaded from Kaggle[3] and contains one file. Due to privacy concerns of the cardholders, the original features that were included in the dataset were anonymized, and transformed using principal component analysis (PCA). Only the timestamps, fraud labels, and transaction amounts were kept in their original state. Since the transformed features no longer directly represent one feature but rather a combination, a direct explanation based on the information that the features provide is no longer possible. Finally, the dataset is also highly imbalanced, with 284315 legitimate transactions and only 492 fraudulent ones. The percentage of fraud is therefore only 0.172% which is similar to that of the other dataset. The inclusion of this real dataset is to compare the performance and outputs of the pipeline on an anonymized dataset.

2.4 Data Pre-processing and Feature Selection

In Fig. 2 the simplified steps of these phases are shown. The start is the raw dataset while the end is the input dataset. The data cleaning step includes de-duplication, and filling missing values (such as an unknown location or zip code). That was followed by feature engineering, where new features such as debt to income ratio, day, month, and geo_cluster (among others) were extracted from

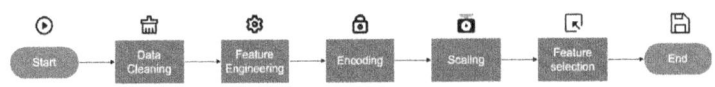

Fig. 2. Data pre-processing steps.

---

[2] https://www.kaggle.com/datasets/computingvictor/transactions-fraud-datasets.
[3] https://www.kaggle.com/datasets/mlg-ulb/creditcardfraud/data.

the existing features and added to the dataset. What followed was the encoding step, where categorical string features were transformed into numerical categories. The final step before feature selection is the scaling step, which is included to limit the influence that large ranges and outliers have on the analysis of the data. Scaling has also been shown to increase stability in the calculations when performing back propagation, which is valuable when working with an RNN based model [7]. The feature engineering and encoding steps were not applied to the real dataset as they were not applicable to the anonymized numerical data.

Finally, the feature selection was done in two ways(cf. Figure 1): using simple, filtered based techniques and causal relationship based techniques. The simple method included Chi-squared (for the categorical features) and ANOVA (for the continuous features) tests. The causal feature selection relies on CD-NOD causal discovery to determine the relationships that variables have with each other. It is important to note that the algorithm takes into account the timestamps of the transactions and does not assume that the relationships remain constant throughout the entire dataset. For both methods, the features with the closest relation to the fraud label were chosen.

2.5 Machine Learning Model

Before the data was used as input to the model, the dataset was first ordered by timestamp to make sure the model was able to register the transactions in the proper order. Additionally, an under sampling technique was used in order to minimize the effects of the class imbalance for the large synthetic dataset. For the real dataset the SMOTE oversampling method was used in order to increase the amount of fraudulent data points. The model architecture is comprised of five layers which leads to a final output (as can be seen in Fig. 1). There is a combination of LSTM, attention, and dense layers which makes this a hybrid model that enhances the natural capabilities of the LSTM with an attention layer that is commonly used in transformers. The attention layer is helpful when avoiding noise and volatility, and has been used for time-series predictions with the use of LSTM models before [10].

2.6 Explanation

SHAP values are computed to quantify each feature's contribution to model predictions. Violin plots are then used to visualize feature importance, as they can show both magnitude and directionality (positive/negative impact on fraud likelihood). For the synthetic dataset, SHAP explanations were directly interpretable due to their detailed features. For the real dataset, PCA-transformed features limit direct interpretability but allows analysis of feature influence.

2.7 Evaluation

For the machine learning model the AUC-ROC was used as the primary evaluation method. For the XAI evaluation, various metrics identified in the CO-12 framework were used to measure a few of the CO-12 properties (correctness, contrastivity, compactness, confidence, and coherence) [9]. The metrics used are single deletion, data randomization, redundancy, confidence accuracy, and alignment with domain knowledge. Evaluations were conducted separately for features selected via causal and correlation-based methods, enabling direct comparison of their impact on explainability.

3 Results

3.1 Synthetic Dataset

When the feature selection was performed, the features with the highest scores were selected to train the ML model. For the non-causal features, the AUC was 91.22% while the validation AUC (on unseen data) was 90.37%. The causal features had an AUC of 89.73% while the validation AUC was 90.52%. This does not indicate a significant difference in performance. In table 1 further ML evaluation details are shown. Notably, the recall improved with the causal features while the precision worsened.

Table 1. ML result summary (left: non-causal, right: causal)

	Precision	Recall	F1-score		Precision	Recall	F1-score
0 - No Fraud	0.85	0.95	0.90	0 - No Fraud	0.87	0.91	0.89
1 - Fraud	0.86	0.67	0.76	1 - Fraud	0.80	0.72	0.76
accuracy			0.85	accuracy			0.85
macro avg	0.86	0.81	0.83	macro avg	0.84	0.82	0.82
weighted avg	0.86	0.85	0.85	weighted avg	0.84	0.85	0.84

In Fig. 3, a violin summary plot is depicted which is ordered by the overall amount of influence of that feature on the model. Based on the plots(see Fig. 3), the most influential features remain the same, but most of the irrelevant features were not selected by the causal method, and the hour feature (which appears influential) was not present in the non-causal features at all. For the evaluation of SHAP, the quantitative evaluation methods discussed in the methodology were conducted. These will be listed per the CO-12 property that they belong to [9]. A summary of the evaluation metrics can be observed in table 2. Overall, the model trained on the causal features did improve slightly in each of the categories.

3.2 Real Dataset

This section will cover the results of the pipeline when applied to the real dataset. Since this dataset does not have labeled features, the overall analysis and evaluation of the results is more limited than that of the synthetic dataset. Since

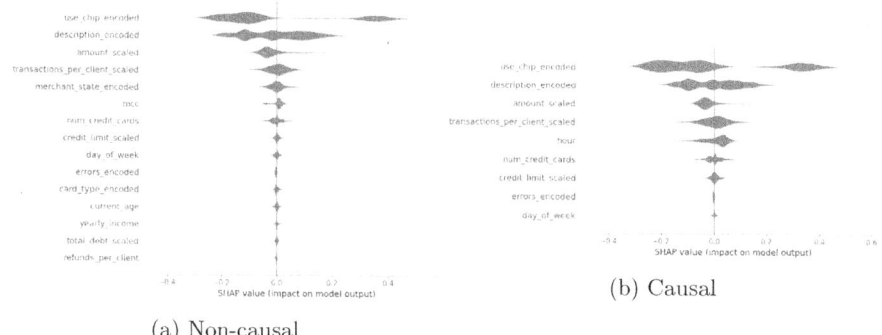

Fig. 3. Violin plots based on SHAP values.

Table 2. XAI Evaluation summary per CO-12 property

	Non-causal	Causal
Correctness	Highest correlation: 0.9216	Highest correlation: 0.9305
	Lowest correlation: 0.7145	Lowest correlation: 0.8626
Contrasivity	Larger SHAP differences for top features	Smaller SHAP differences for same features
Compactness	High mutual information (MI) among top features	Lower MI between features
Confidence	Widest confidence intervals for top features	Similar intervals but more stable for lower-ranked features.
Coherence	Rank correlation: 0.4242	Rank correlation: 0.4848

the feature names by themselves are not meaningful, the coherence metric was not measured. An interesting outcome is that neither the simple filtering nor the causal feature selection method includes the Amount feature, which would have been expected based on previous fraud detection systems. However, since the remaining features are unknown, it is possible that they include a combination of amount and another feature which increases its informational value compared to the amount by itself.

Table 3. ML result summary (left: non-causal, right: causal)

	Precision	Recall	F1-score		Precision	Recall	F1-score
0 - No Fraud	0.97	0.99	0.98	0 - No Fraud	0.99	0.98	0.99
1 - Fraud	0.99	0.95	0.97	1 - Fraud	0.97	0.98	0.97
accuracy			0.98	accuracy			0.98
macro avg	0.98	0.97	0.98	macro avg	0.98	0.98	0.98
weighted avg	0.98	0.98	0.98	weighted avg	0.98	0.98	0.98

The training AUC was 99.39% on the non-causal set while the validation AUC was 99.81%. For the causal set the training AUC was 99.35% while the validation AUC was 99.82%, which is a minimal difference. In table 3 further details about the ML evaluation are shown. The scores are much higher than those of the synthetic dataset, making few mistakes, but also not showing much of a difference between causal and non-causal sets.

In Fig. 4, the violin summary plots are depicted.

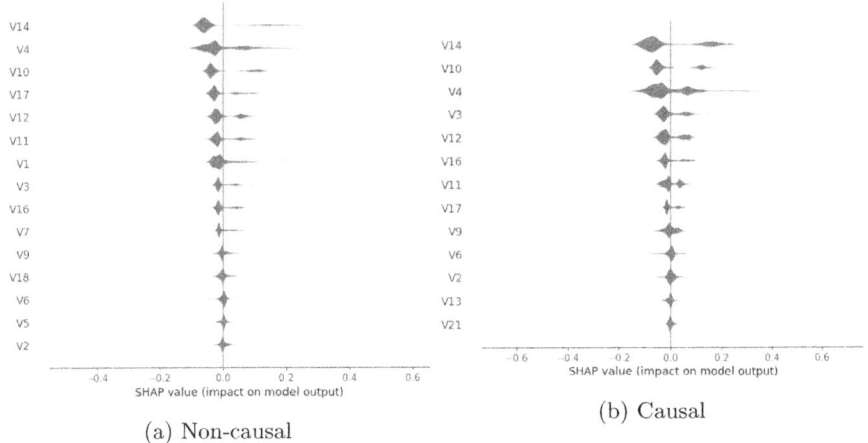

Fig. 4. Violin plots based on SHAP values.

Since all of the features are dimensionality reduced combinations of features, there is not a lot of insight that we can derive directly from the variable names themselves. However, an interesting observation that can be seen on the violin plot is that the most influential features all tend to have a negative impact, meaning that they make it more likely that a transaction is not fraud rather than that it is. The SHAP values also seem to be limited in the -0.2 to 0.2 range, which is more restricted than the values of the synthetic dataset. The XAI evaluation metrics for this dataset can be seen in table 4.

The results here are more mixed. The outcome on contrasivity and confidence are worse with the causal features, while the correctness and compactness are still improved. The stability of the SHAP explanations across both sets is relatively low compared to the synthetic dataset.

3.3 Stakeholder Feedback

Besides the rankings that were collected to evaluate the coherence property, some qualitative feedback was also collected. A group of sixteen stakeholders (who work in an industry that directly deals with detecting fraud) were anonymously surveyed on whether they would be open to using the SHAP explanations to

Table 4. XAI Evaluation summary per CO-12 property

	Non-causal	Causal
Correctness	Highest correlation: 0.2093	Highest correlation: 0.26
	Lowest correlation: 0.5698	Lowest correlation: 0.6612
Contrasivity	SHAP differences mostly align with feature importance	Mismatch between SHAP value differences and feature importance
Compactness	Very high mutual information (MI) among features	Slightly lower MI between features
Confidence	Moderate confidence intervals	Wider intervals for most features

assist in fraud detection and if it would assist in their understanding of data or a model. Of the respondents, 88% answered that they felt the plots of the SHAP output would increase their understanding of a dataset. Additionally, 75% of respondents thought that their understanding of the model would be improved and that they would use the plots to assist in fraud detection. Furthermore, 62.5% thought that the XAI plots could help them draw better conclusions about fraudulent behaviors and patterns, however, 25% did believe that they would need additional information to be able to use the plots in a practical setting. SHAP was easy to understand as 13% of the respondents indicated that they would not have understood the plot's purpose without an additional explanation, even though 38% of respondents were not previously familiar with XAI explanations at all. The majority of the respondents were able to gauge the main idea of the plots and gave fairly accurate descriptions of what information was being shown despite being given no context further than that it was fraud-related. The earlier coherence score was also calculated using the user ratings, and showed that there is certainly an overlap in terms of the expectations and the XAI output, but that the pipeline could potentially provide new insights. Overall, this means that the structures and layouts of the graphs themselves were clear enough for the meaning to come across.

4 Discussion

4.1 Influence of Causal Methods on Outcomes

Causal discovery based feature selection demonstrated some potential for identifying the most relevant features without sacrificing interpretability. The performance of the machine learning model stayed consistent despite the fact that the amount of features were reduced by one-third (fifteen vs. nine features), which shows that while the correlational feature selection might find the most relevant features, it also includes redundant ones. By using a causal method, the complexity is reduced due to the decrease of features, while the XAI explanations are also simplified by making them more compact.

It is important to note however, that generating the causal graph and establishing the relationships is more computationally expensive than calculating them in a correlational way. This would create hurdles when designing a system that aims for, for example, real-time analysis. The benefit is that once the relationships are established based on a dataset, the model can be taught to focus on these features for future transactions. However, a re-evaluation of the causal relationships would be necessary over time in order to capture emerging patterns of fraudsters.

The integration of causal discovery techniques into the feature selection process demonstrated the potential to enhance the explainability of fraud detection models. On the synthetic dataset, the causal feature selection method led to a slight improvement in the quantitative XAI metrics, as evaluated by the CO-12 framework. This suggests that causal discovery can help identify more relevant features, reducing redundancy and improving the reliability of the explanations. However, on the real dataset, the benefits of causal feature selection were less pronounced. The anonymized features in the real dataset limited the interpretability of the causal relationships, making it more challenging to distinguish the impact of causal discovery on the model's explanations. This indicates a limitation of the XAI method when dealing with data that has been significantly transformed or that causally selected features are not a reliable method of improving the XAI outputs across datasets.

4.2 Evaluation Methods

The effect that the causal features had on the evaluation of the XAI technique showed an increase in the metrics that were chosen. However, this effect was limited when looking at the real dataset. This suggests that the current evaluation methods may not fully capture the benefits of causal discovery, particularly in datasets with transformed features. Many of these evaluation methods match the XAI technique that they evaluate, and since they are largely based on correlational methods, the evaluation methods also focus on it. While it is clear that there is an indirect way to measure causality that is linked to the better XAI metrics, there is a gap when it comes to metrics that can directly measure cause and effect.

SHAP explanations have been a target of manipulation before, where it has been shown that adversaries could perturb or adapt the data in order to get an inflated feature importance on certain features. This knowledge alone could affect the trust that stakeholders have in the explanations of a model, and therefore limit the use of them in practice. Using the causal features shows an improvement in evaluation methods that test the robustness against perturbations and switches in labels, which do not cover the entirety of the manipulation tactics, but are promising.

4.3 Limitations

Due to the time and resource constraints of this study there were certain trade-offs that had to be made. The first being that there was a limit on the techniques that could be tested. This pipeline was fitted to a specific machine learning model as well as SHAP as the only XAI technique. The pipeline could have been enriched by an extension of the methods, as well as the inclusion of multiple causal discovery techniques to see whether this had a different effect. Some proposed causal methods in literature have also not been implemented yet in a usable programming module, which also limited their direct use. These do represent opportunities for further research however.

Another important consideration is that since there is no ground truth causal graph for the datasets used, the causal relationships that were inferred might not be 100% accurate. There is no way of knowing whether or not the fraud relationships are truly present and represent the actions of the actual malevolent parties. The current assumption is that the generated causal graph is accurate enough to be able to represent true patterns, but cannot be taken at face value without review – which is why expert stakeholders can use it as a tool but not a replacement of fraud detection work.

Currently, the ML model only looks at one transaction at a time, but ideally, sequential patterns could be analyzed and flagged in groups so that the progression of events could be identified as fraud. One difficulty here would be determining the length of these sequences, and what to do in case the client details are not known. This increased complexity would cause increased processing and training time for the model, but could also lead to more information and knowledge that is currently not available.

4.4 Future Directions

In terms of future research directions, it would be sensible to keep the stakeholders in mind. If improvements could help work towards a more practical way of using XAI in fraud detection it would be valuable for any possible users. Real-time fraud detection would be one of the applications that could be useful for institutions. While this would be possible by using the existing trained model, this method would degrade the performance over time as fraud patterns change. Finding a way to dynamically update and generate the causal graph based on more recent data would allow for the real-time detection to correspond to the current trends. Since the CD-NOD causal technique is quite time consuming, another causal method could be tested, or a representative subset of the dataset could be used to generate the causal graph instead. Another method could be pruning the irrelevant edges while calculating the causal graph.

An interesting direction could be the focus on metrics that are able to evaluate causality directly. A possible way could be by blocking the identified causal pathways and seeing how this affects the model and the XAI explanations. This is challenging without a ground truth causal structure however, which is why it could be difficult to implement in a changing environment. Integrating the causal graph structures with the XAI explanations at the end could also be an interesting step that goes beyond the scope of this study. Seeing whether causality is more effective before or after the training of the model could lead to some insights on where it is most useful to integrate causal methods.

Finally, this framework could be extended to other types of fraud that might not use transactional data. Seeing the effect of causal discovery on areas like insurance fraud, or language based frauds would give a better indication on how robust this method is for fraud detection systems outside of the financial sector, and whether causality has a broader effect.

5 Conclusion

This study addresses the research question of how causal discovery techniques can improve the explainability of fraud detection models. The results indicate that integrating causal discovery with XAI methods can enhance the alignment of model explanations with underlying causal relationships, particularly in datasets with rich and interpretable features. The synthetic dataset demonstrated improved XAI metrics and more reliable explanations when using causally selected features. However, the real dataset, due to anonymization and feature transformation, showed limited benefits from causal discovery, highlighting the uncertainty of the benefits and the further need of causal research. The study also identified limitations such as the computational cost of causal discovery and the lack of a ground truth causal graphs for validation. Future research should focus on developing more efficient causal discovery algorithms, refining evaluation metrics for XAI techniques, and exploring the application of causal methods in other fraud detection contexts. Further to this, it would be interesting to investigate how causal relationship evolves or updates over time. This could be done, for example, by using a sliding window approach or automated re-training cycles."

References

1. Černevičienė, J., Kabašinskas, A.: Explainable artificial intelligence (XAI) in finance: a systematic literature review. Artif. Intell. Rev. **57**(8) (2024)
2. Sahoh, B., Choksuriwong, A.: The role of explainable Artificial Intelligence in high-stakes decision-making systems: a systematic review. J. Ambient. Intell. Humaniz. Comput. **14**(6), 7827–7843 (2023)
3. Oxford: Oxford English Dictionary. Oxford University Press, United Kingdom (2020)
4. Bello, O., Olufemi, K.: Artificial intelligence in fraud prevention: exploring techniques and applications challenges and opportunities. Comput. Sci. IT Res. J. **5**(6), 1505–1520 (2024)
5. Charmet, F.: Explainable artificial intelligence for cybersecurity: a literature survey. Ann. Telecommun. **77**(11), 789–812 (2022)
6. Carloni, G., Berti, A., Colantonio, S.: The role of causality in explainable artificial intelligence. (2023)
7. Vanishing and Exploding Gradients Problems in Deep Learning. https://www.geeksforgeeks.org/vanishing-and-exploding-gradients-problems-in-deep-learning/ Accessed 25 Jan 2025
8. Huang, B.: Causal discovery from heterogeneous/nonstationary data. J. Mach. Learn. Res. **21**(89), 1–53 (2020)

9. Nauta, M.: From anecdotal evidence to quantitative evaluation methods: a systematic review on evaluating explainable AI. ACM Comput. Surv. **55**(13s), 1–42 (2023)
10. Hollis, T., Viscardi, A., Yi, S. E.: A Comparison of LSTMs and Attention Mechanisms for Forecasting Financial Time Series. (2018)

Open Access This chapter is licensed under the terms of the Creative Commons Attribution 4.0 International License (http://creativecommons.org/licenses/by/4.0/), which permits use, sharing, adaptation, distribution and reproduction in any medium or format, as long as you give appropriate credit to the original author(s) and the source, provide a link to the Creative Commons license and indicate if changes were made.

The images or other third party material in this chapter are included in the chapter's Creative Commons license, unless indicated otherwise in a credit line to the material. If material is not included in the chapter's Creative Commons license and your intended use is not permitted by statutory regulation or exceeds the permitted use, you will need to obtain permission directly from the copyright holder.

Detecting Fraud in Financial Networks: A Semi-supervised GNN Approach with Granger-Causal Explanations

Linh Nguyen[1](✉)[iD], Marcel Boersma[1,2][iD], and Erman Acar[1][iD]

[1] University of Amsterdam, 1098, XH Amsterdam, The Netherlands
nguyenthidieulinh276@gmail.com
[2] KPMG Netherlands, 1186, DS Amstelveen, The Netherlands

Abstract. Fraudulent activity in the financial industry costs billions annually. Detecting fraud, therefore, is an essential yet technically challenging task that requires carefully analyzing large volumes of data. While machine learning (ML) approaches seem like a viable solution, applying them successfully is not so easy due to two main challenges: (1) the sparsely labeled data, which makes the training of such approaches challenging (with inherent labeling costs), and (2) lack of explainability for the flagged items posed by the opacity of ML models, that is often required by business regulations. This article proposes SAGE-FIN, a semi-supervised graph neural network (GNN) based approach with Granger causal explanations for Financial Interaction Networks. SAGE-FIN learns to flag fraudulent items based on weakly labeled (or unlabelled) data points. To adhere to regulatory requirements, the flagged items are explained by highlighting related items in the network using Granger causality. We empirically validate the favorable performance of SAGE-FIN on a real-world dataset, Bipartite Edge-And-Node Attributed financial network (Elliptic++), with Granger-causal explanations for the identified fraudulent items without any prior assumption on the network structure.

Keywords: semi-supervised learning · financial fraud · bipartite graph · graph neural network · causal explanation

1 Introduction

Fraudulent activities in transaction data present a critical yet challenging issue within the financial industry. Financial fraud arises in various areas, such as insurance, banking, taxation, and corporate sectors [1,2]. Mitigating efforts are often labor intensive, requiring significant time, effort, and resources, costing billions annually; for example, Know-Your-Customer (KYC) departments within banks are estimated to cost 500 million dollars each year per bank. Machine learning (ML) approaches could alleviate this labor-intensive task, analyzing many data points for fraud characteristics. However, there remain two main challenges to tackle: (1) the labels of the financial transactions (fraud or non-fraud) are often expensive to obtain for model training [3–6], and (2) the outcomes of the ML models often lack interpretability when it comes to justifying the detected anomalous items for further investigation. Motivated by these challenges, we propose a model that leverages the sparsely labeled data points and explains why the detected activities are flagged as fraudulent.

Transactions can naturally be represented as graphs whose nodes correspond to involved parties and the edges correspond to money flows between them [7–9]. The model must incorporate the graph structure to detect novel fraudulent patterns. Graph Neural Networks (GNNs) offer a framework for analyzing such structures and detecting novel patterns. Despite their demonstrated efficiency, most GNNs function as a black box without explicit knowledge representations, limiting their capability to provide necessary explanatory medium. This limitation, in turn, undermines their adoption in critical domains such as the financial sector [10]. Rather necessary is the transparency of models to ensure traceable decision-making processes [10], comply with legal regulations [11] to maintain accountability while adhering to privacy [12]. A desirable (informal) property of these explanations is that the generated explanations should reflect an intuition of causal relevance [13]. That is, the explanation should answer a question of sort *when a GNN yields an outcome, which part of the input graph is causally relevant?*

Another challenge is the so-called *class imbalance* which stems from the fact that fraudulent activities only correspond to a small fraction of the total activities within a financial system. As a result, only limited examples of fraudulent activities are available to learn from, which makes them more challenging to detect. Interestingly enough, Motie and Raahemi. [14] reveal in their review that research on GNN applications to financial fraud detection themselves carry an imbalanced rate of exploration; that is, supervised learning approaches make 88% of all approaches, with semi-supervised and unsupervised approaches correspond to 9% and 3%, respectively. A semi-supervised approach here would mean learning a classifier from the labeled data points while learning structural properties from unlabeled data points.

This paper aims to bridge the research gaps in applying GNN for anomaly detection in the financial domain by creating the first semi-supervised GNN model on the bipartite graph while simultaneously providing causal explanations for the identified anomalies. The unsupervised GraphBEAN model [29] is the most closely related work to ours in the context of anomaly detection, as it compresses a bipartite social media network input graph. However, it lacks explainability in its model outputs. Our work extends the GraphBEAN architecture to adapt it for real-world financial transaction datasets and incorporates Granger causal explanations for model outputs, which is crucial to use a deep learning model in the financial domain.

To highlight, we make the following contributions:

1. We propose a semi-supervised architecture, called SAGE-FIN, for financial fraud detection, and show its potential on generalizing beyond bi-partite graphs (i.e., k-partite graphs).
2. We evaluate SAGE-FIN on a publicly available real-world dataset: Elliptic++.
3. We offer insights into financial anomalies identified by SAGE-FIN through the lens of Granger causality, aligning with the specific needs of the financial sector.

The rest of the paper is organized as follows. Next section presents the problem definition and key notations; Sect. 3 illustrates our main contribution – the SAGE-FIN architecture with the Granger causal explanation; Sect. 4 presents experimental setup, Elliptic++ dataset and the results; Sect. 5 is the discussion section, sharing gained insights and the limitations; Sect. 6 is the related work; Sect. 7 (Conclusion) closes the paper.

2 Background Knowledge and Notation

In this section, we formally define the problem definition, provide relevant background knowledge and introduce the key notations upon which our proposed SAGE-FIN model is based.

2.1 Problem Definition

In our scenario, a monetary transfer between wallets is a transaction. This can be represented by a (bipartite) graph in which both wallets and transactions are represented by nodes; each having its own set of features. See Fig. 1 for an example sub-graph of the Bitcoin transaction dataset. More formally, we define a bipartite graph as $G = (V, U, E)$. For each node $v \in V$ and $u \in U$, a feature vector $x_v \in R^n$ and $x_u \in R^m$, sets U and V represent transactions and wallets, respectively. Further, $e \in E$ represents an edge that connects a wallet to a transaction. For some nodes, we have class labels $y \in \{0, 1\}$. For example, in Fig. 1, we have Wallet *address 8* that sends some Bitcoin to Wallet *address 4*. This transaction is shows as *transaction 3*. Here *address 4* is labeled as an fraudulent address and *transaction 3* is labeled as a non-fraudulent transaction. The objective is to learn a model that predicts the classes of transactions and wallets, and provides an explanation for the predicted instance.

2.2 Message Passing and Graph Convolution

This research studies the heterogeneous bipartite graph structure which has different feature vectors for each node partition. This fills up the research gap that

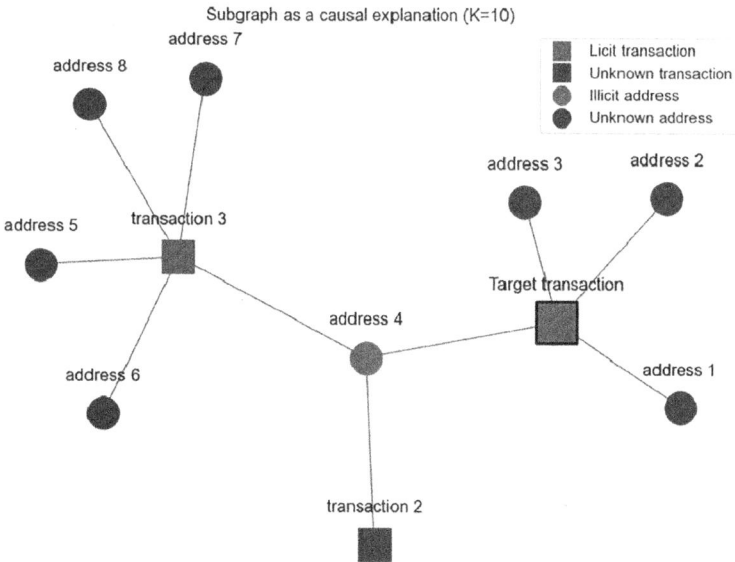

Fig. 1. An example graph of the Bitcoin wallets-transactions network.

most of the literature worked on the monopartite graph whereas the financial transaction networks often exhibit the bipartite nature. To use all the feature vectors of both node types and edges, the message passing algorithm is designed such that it aggregates all information from the two node types and the edges.

The SAGE-FIN network follows the GraphBEAN architecture proposed by [29] which comprises P (even number) convolution layers, where half of these layers are allocated for the encoder and the remaining half are utilized for the feature decoder. The q-th layer representation for node u_i within set U, node v_j within set V, and edge $e_{i,j}$ within set E are presented as $h_i^{u(q)}$, $h_j^{v(q)}$, and $h_{i,j}^{e}{}^{(q)}$ accordingly.

According to the GraphBEAN architecture proposed by [29], to compute the new representations $h_i^{u(q)}$, $h_j^{v(q)}$, and $h_{i,j}^{e}{}^{(q)}$, the messages are collected and passed to the particular node and edge. The messages to a node u_i within set U come from the aggregator functions (average) over the neighboring node representations, the aggregator functions (average) over the edge representations connected to u_i, and its own previous representations. A similar process is followed for the messages to node v_i within set V. Messages are also collected and passed to edge $e_{i,j}$ within set E, which are simply derived from the nodes connected to the edge, namely u_i and v_j, and its own previous representation. The computations of messages passed to u_i, v_j, $e_{i,j}$ are formulated as follows:

$$\mathbf{h}_i^{u(q)} = \gamma_\Theta \left(\phi_\Theta(\mathbf{x}_i^u), \bigoplus_{v_j \in \mathcal{N}(u_i)} \phi_\Theta(\mathbf{x}_j^v), \bigoplus_{e_{i,j} \in \mathcal{M}(u_i)} \phi_\Theta(\mathbf{x}_{i,j}^e) \right) \qquad (1)$$

$$\mathbf{h}_i^{v(q)} = \gamma_\Theta \left(\phi_\Theta(\mathbf{x}_j^v), \bigoplus_{u_i \in \mathcal{N}(v_j)} \phi_\Theta(\mathbf{x}_i^v), \bigoplus_{e_{i,j} \in \mathcal{M}(v_j)} \phi_\Theta(\mathbf{x}_{i,j}^e) \right) \qquad (2)$$

$$\mathbf{h}_{i,j}^{e\;(q)} = \gamma_\Theta \left(\phi_\Theta(\mathbf{x}_j^u), \phi_\Theta(\mathbf{x}_j^v), \phi_\Theta(\mathbf{x}_{i,j}^e) \right) \qquad (3)$$

where ϕ_Θ denotes the differentiable function to learn the features, $\bigoplus$ represents the mean, max aggregation of the encoded features within each node partition and edge set, γ_Θ concatenates the aggregated encoded feature vectors of both node partition and edge set together.

The message flows presented in the Eqs. 1, 2, 3 are depicted in Fig. 2. In each convolution layer, the message to the first node partition is aggregated from the information of this node in the previous layer, the information of the other node partition, and the information of the edges connecting these nodes. The same rule applies to the other node partition. For the edge, the message is passed from the information of that edge in the previous layers and the information of both node partitions on that edge.

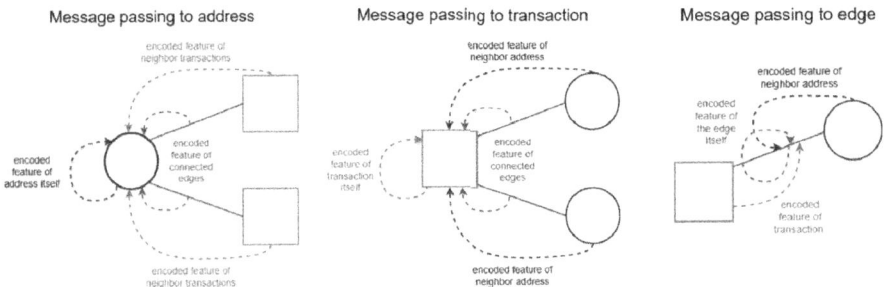

Fig. 2. Illustration of the message passing process for nodes and edges adapted from [29].

After the messages are collected and passed to each node and edge, the subsequent representations are computed. The messages are passed to a linear operation and then the output of the linear operation is normalized using batch normalization. Subsequently, this normalized output is passed through a ReLU activation function.

2.3 Granger Causality

Granger causality, as originally proposed by Clive Granger [37], is a statistical hypothesis test for determining whether one time series is useful in forecasting another. Specifically, a time series X_t is said to Granger-cause another time series Y_t if past values of X_t have a statistically significant effect on predicting future values of Y_t, given past values of Y_t itself [37]. Formally, X_t Granger-causes Y_t if:

$$\text{Var}(Y_{t+1}|Y_t, Y_{t-1}, ..., X_t, X_{t-1}, ...) < \text{Var}(Y_{t+1}|Y_t, Y_{t-1}, ...) \qquad (4)$$

where:

- $\text{Var}(Y_{t+1}|Y_t, Y_{t-1}, \ldots, X_t, X_{t-1}, \ldots)$ is the variance of the prediction error of Y_{t+1} using past values of both Y and X.
- $\text{Var}(Y_{t+1}|Y_t, Y_{t-1}, \ldots)$ is the variance of the prediction error of Y_{t+1} using only past values of Y.

Within the context of this paper (i.e., Granger causality for Graph neural network), the Granger causal explainer algorithm generates a subgraph S for a node prediction from the original graph G. The subgraph S would then contain relevant information to make a prediction (classification) of an instance if it is fraudulent or non-fraudulent. Fundamentally, the Granger causal explainer algorithm finds the edges in the graph G that significantly affect the outcome of the classifier (fraud or not) in the neural network. All these significant edges form the subgraph S. The Granger causal explainer also implies that the outcome of the classifier does not change significantly when using the entire graph G or only a subgraph S. The ultimate objective of the Granger causal explainer is to find a subgraph of the original network with a significant causal influence on the outcome of classifier in the graph neural network.

3 Methodology

This SAGE-FIN model first employs the message passing algorithm that propagates also the edge attributes together with the node attributes to the graph convolution layers. The binary classification loss is added to the loss function. Here, the ground-truth labels of some data points guide the model to learn the anomalous patterns in conjunction with the node features and topological patterns of the entire graph, which includes a substantial amount of unlabeled data points. Building upon the SAGE-FIN model, a Granger causal explainer algorithm is implemented to extract the most critical nodes and edges. These elements significantly influence the classification of fraud versus non-fraud by the SAGE-FIN model, guided by the principle of Granger causality. From here onward, within this paper, we name Granger causal explanation as Causal explanation in short.

3.1 Graph Neural Network Architecture for Anomalies Detection

We propose a semi-supervised neural network architecture for anomaly detection in bipartite graphs with two main components: 1) unsupervised structure learning and 2) supervised classification learning. The first component consists of a (a) graph convolutional autoencoder that reconstructs the node's features and (b) an edge reconstruction module that predicts whether an edge exists between a pair of nodes. This aligns with the GraphBEAN model proposed by [29]. The second part, supervised learning, is the new element added to the GraphBEAN model. It is a linear classification head that classifies the node as fraudulent and non-fraudulent. The supervised part is only used for the limited data points with a label. This enhancement enables the architecture to function within a semi-supervised learning paradigm, as illustrated in Fig. 3.

Adopted and modified from [29], the training objective function is the combination of the reconstruction loss from the feature decoder, the binary classification loss of the structure decoder's edge prediction and the binary classification loss of the node classification decoder for the labeled nodes.

3.2 Causal Explanation for Anomaly Detection Outcomes

After the model's classification stage, a Causal explainer algorithm extracts the nodes and edges that have the largest Granger causal contribution to the model's fraud/non-fraud classification. The distillation algorithm introduced by [36] is modified to be compatible with the bipartite graph instead of the unipartite graph. Each specific node being classified by the SAGE-FIN model is examined. To quantify the influence of individual edges on the model output, the loss function produced by the model when operating on the entire graph G is compared with the loss function produced by the model when excluding a particular edge of the original graph. The Granger causal effect of that particular edge on the SAGE-FIN's output is then assessed by the reduction in the loss function, representing the change in loss function due to the removal of that edge. Formally,

$$C_j = L_2 - L_1 \tag{5}$$

where,

- C_j is the Granger causal effect of edge e_j
- L_1 is the loss function of the node classification decoder in SAGE-FIN for the entire graph
- L_2 is the loss function of the node classification decoder in SAGE-FIN when excluding edge e_j from the original graph

Essentially, C_j reflects the individual causal impact of the edge e_j within the original graph G on the resulting classified nodes. By ordering the edges based on their causal contributions C_j, the top K edges which constitutes a connected subgraph S signify the most influential connections and can be extracted to provide a causal explanation for the SAGE-FIN's predictions.

To identify a subgraph S that serves as a causal explainer for a node Y labeled by the pre-trained SAGE-FIN model, an algorithm is employed. First, we define a set N comprising all nodes within an n-hop neighborhood of Y. The parameter n is determined based on the application-specific requirements, balancing the comprehensiveness of the subgraph S and the follow-up investigation complexity. Secondly, a list of edges of each node in the set N is constructed based on the graph's adjacency matrix. After that, the causal explainer algorithm iterates over

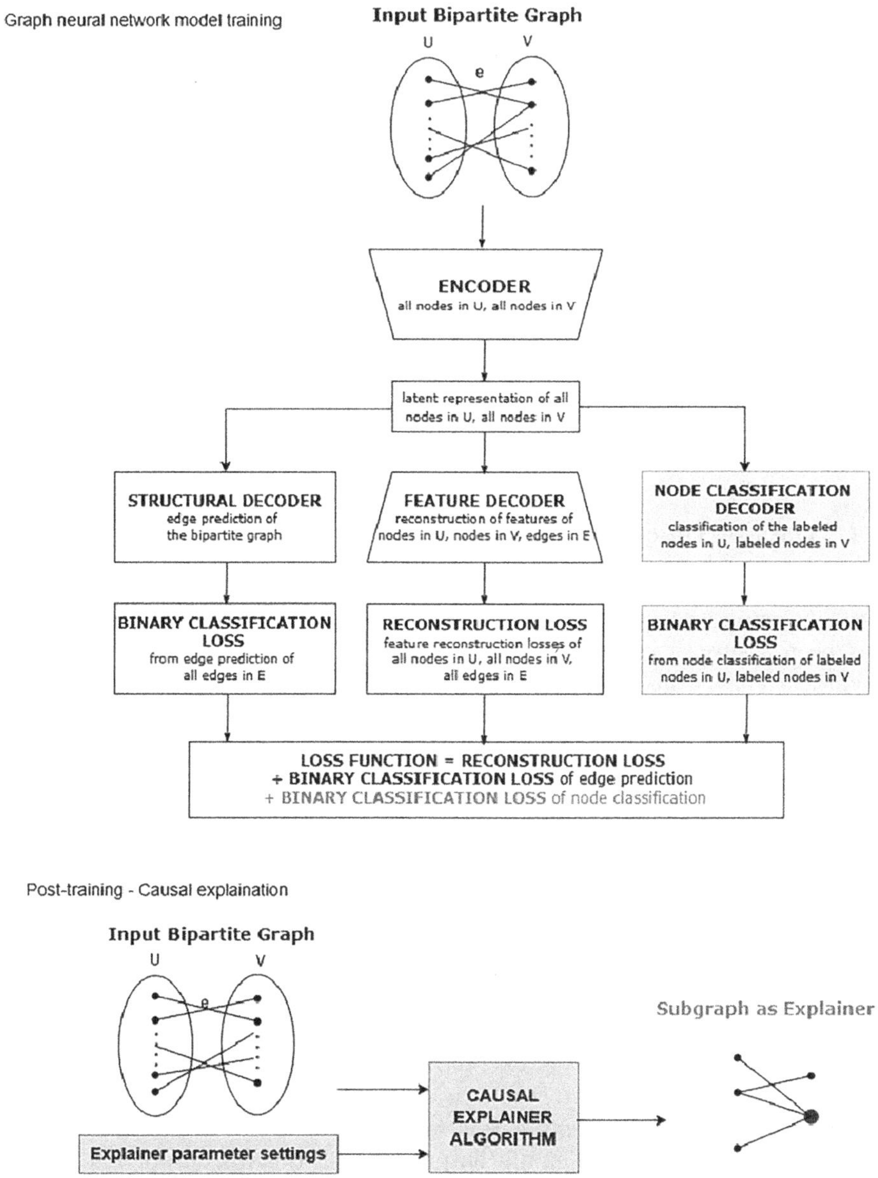

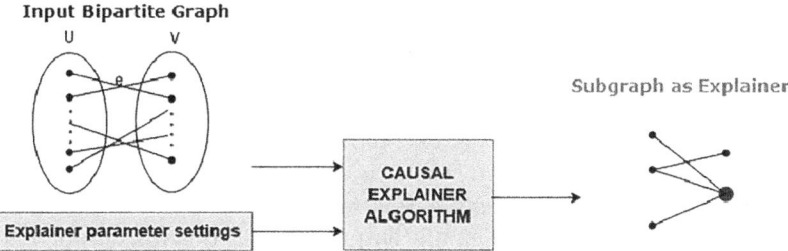

Fig. 3. The SAGE-FIN architecture adds a node classification decoder to the unsupervised GraphBEAN architecture [29] and supplement the neural network with Causal explanation layer after the model training. The new elements contributed by this paper are highlighted in orange. (Color figure online)

the neighborhood of Y, proceeding from the first to the nth hop. For each node encountered, and for each edge linked to this node, the algorithm calculates the loss function L_2 representing the loss when this edge is excluded and compares it with the initial loss function L_1 in the pre-trained SAGE-FIN model using the entire graph G. If L_2 is bigger than L_1, it indicates a causal influence of this edge on the model's classification and this edge is appended to a list $\mathcal{C}$. This process is repeated for all nodes within n-hop neighborhood. Finally, the algorithm selects the top K edges from the list $\mathcal{C}$ with the most significant causal contribution C_j, ensuring that these edges form a connected subgraph containing node Y. This resulting subgraph S is then designated as the causal explainer for the target node Y.

4 Experimental Setup and Evaluation

In this section, we describe the Elliptic++ dataset and outline the data preprocessing steps we performed.

4.1 Dataset Description and Analysis

Blockchain network offers a unique and accountable channel for financial forensics by mining its transparent and immutable transaction data. Recently, there has been a surge in the application of machine learning models trained with cryptocurrency transaction data for anomaly detection, such as money laundering and other fraudulent activities. For the task of anomaly detection using semi-supervised learning techniques within the GNN framework, the real-world Elliptic++ Bitcoin data is utilized. The dataset is presented in a bipartite format, where monetary flows from wallets to specific transactions are presented as edges, wallet addresses and transactions are depicted as two different node partitions. The address-transaction graph is visualized in Appendix A. This representation facilitates the detection of fraudulent transactions and wallets addresses within the Bitcoin network. The source and detailed description of the data collection pipeline can be found in the paper [15].

The Elliptic++ dataset resembles the heterogeneous graph structure of many real-world financial networks where each node partition has different features size. Within the Elliptic++ dataset, the Bitcoin transactions node set comprises 203,769 transactions (nodes), each characterized by 165 features. These features include 93 local features representing local information about the transaction (for example, the number of inputs/outputs, transaction fee, output volume) and 72 aggregated features derived by aggregating transaction information one-hop forward/backward[1]. The Bitcoin wallet addresses node set consists of 822,942 wallet addresses, each described by 56 features related to transactions, such as total Bitcoin transacted (sent and received), total fees in Bitcoin, and temporal

---

[1] Due to intellectual property issues, the data source does not provide an exact description of all the features in the dataset.

features such as the number of blocks between transactions and the number of interactions among addresses. The Elliptic++ dataset is set up with high quality, ensuring no missing values within its comprehensive set of features. The main properties of the graph are shown in the Table 1

Table 1. Key properties of Elliptic++ dataset

	Transaction set	Wallet set
#Features	165	56
#Non-fraudulent nodes	42019 (21%)	251088 (31%)
#Fraudulent nodes	4545 (2%)	14266 (2%)
#Unknown nodes	157205 (77%)	557588 (67%)

The bipartite graph, containing Bitcoin transaction and wallet node sets, spans over 49 timestamps. The interval between two timestamps is two weeks. The labels of the fraudulent/non-fraudulent for nodes are provided by the author [15] based on the original Elliptic dataset published on Kaggle. The node features and labels are proprietary but publicly accessible.

4.2 Data Preprocessing and Parameter Settings

First, the features and classes of wallet addresses and transactions are integrated with the addresses-transactions edge list to create a comprehensive list of nodes and edges for the graph construction. Among 165 transaction features, 72 aggregated features are removed from the model training because they are derived by aggregating transaction information one-hop forward/backward, which functions as the propagation of the message in the graph convolution layers. Therefore, only 93 local transaction features are merged into the wallets-transactions edge list. Subsequently, the dataset is divided into training, validation, and test sets using a random split with a ratio of 70%–15%–15%. All features in the wallet addresses dataset are scaled using the standardization transformation. The normalized features of all nodes and edges are then used by the SAGE-FIN model. The SAGE-FIN architecture consists of four layers: two convolution layers for the encoder and two convolution layers for the feature decoder. The structure decoder and node classification decoder include Multilayer Perceptrons with four dense layers. For training SAGE-FIN model, the Adam optimizer is used with a learning rate of 0.005. The dimension of latent variables and hidden layers is set to 32. Finally, for the edge prediction in the structure decoder, the negative cases (non-connected node pairs) are set to five times the number of edges (connected node pairs) in the graph. These hyperparameters were selected after several experiments and the combination of these values yielded optimal performance in the validation set. The SAGE-FIN model is trained for 200 epochs. The model performance is evaluated using the following metrics: precision, recall, and F1 score. After the SAGE-FIN model identifies the anomalies, a causal explainer algorithm is implemented to extract the causality explanation for the GNN's classification. The goal is to identify a subgraph S, determined by the number of hops (n-hop) and number of edges (K) from the target node, that significantly influences the output of the model. Since the ground-truth motif for the Elliptic++ dataset is unavailable, the values of n-hop and K are selected qualitatively to ensure that the subgraph S is human-interpretable and suitable for further investigation. A K value that is too small may yield insignificant explanations, while a K value that is too large may result in an overly complex subgraph S. From Fig. 4 and Fig. 5, it can be observed that the majority of the wallet addresses and transactions have no more than five direct edges and a minimal number of addresses and transactions possess more than ten direct edges. Therefore, it has been determined that the nodes within a 4-hop radius from the target node are considered, and the causal explainer algorithm retrieves the K (i.e., in our case $K = 10$) edges that exhibit the most significant causal contribution to the classification of the target nodes.

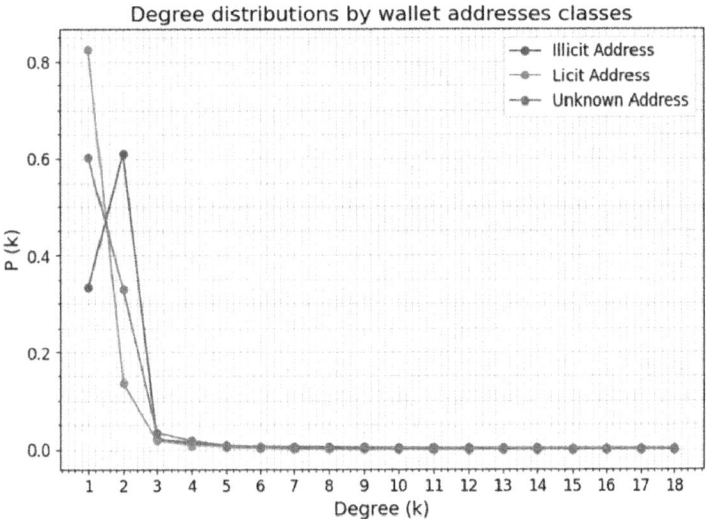

Fig. 4. Degree distribution of wallet address node set

5 Results

Our evaluation consists of two parts: anomaly detection and their Granger causal explanations.

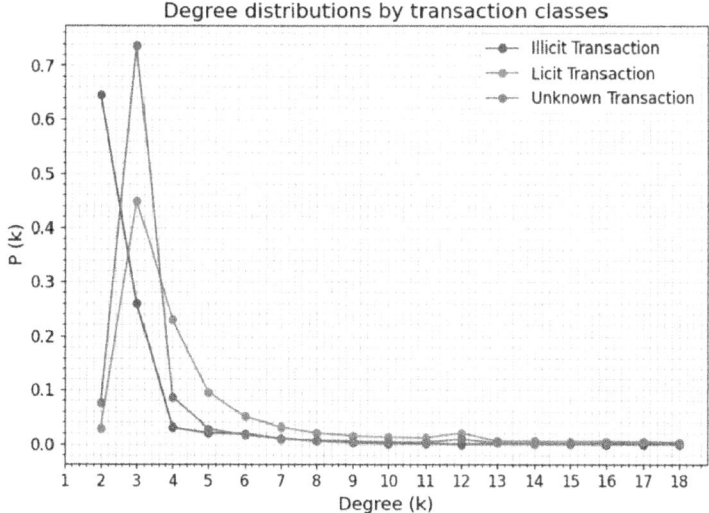

Fig. 5. Degree distribution of transaction node set

5.1 Anomaly Detection

To evaluate the anomaly detection of the SAGE-FIN model on the Elliptic++ dataset, metrics including precision, recall, and F1-score were employed to evaluate the anomaly detection on the labeled data with ground-truth annotations. The performance of the SAGE-FIN model stabilized after 40 epochs and achieved its optimal F1-score for the labeled nodes at epoch 190. The training set attained F1 scores of 0.908 and 0.918 for the wallet addresses and transactions, respectively. The validation set recorded F1 scores of 0.798 and 0.812 for the wallet addresses and transactions. With those settings, the F1 scores for the test set are 0.806 and 0.807. The performance of the SAGE-FIN is benchmarked against the state-of-the-art (SOTA) machine learning models on the labeled dataset. We consider the following SOTA models: Logistic Regression (LR), Random Forest (RF), Multilayer Perceptrons (MLP), and Extreme Gradient Boosting (XGB), as examined in the study by [15]. The classification performances on the labeled data by the SAGE-FIN model and the four state-of-art machine learning models are presented in Table 2:

For the unlabeled nodes, since ground-truth annotations are unavailable for evaluation, address-transaction edge prediction accuracy can be used as a proxy for the evaluation. Anomalies can be interpreted as nodes involved in unexpected edges, where interactions between particular wallet addresses and transactions should not occur. The F1-score convergences for edges in the training and test sets after 190 epochs. The training set achieved an F1-score of 0.908 for the address-transaction edge. The validation set recorded an F1-score of 0.874 for the address-transaction edge. Under those settings, the F1-score for the test set is 0.883.

Table 2. Fraudulent wallet and transaction detection results

	Wallet			Transaction		
Model	Precision	Recall	F1 score	Precision	Recall	F1 score
SAGE-FIN	0.802	0.775	0.806	0.753	0.792	0.807
LR	0.491	0.049	0.089	0.649	0.091	0.159
RF	0.968	0.793	0.872	0.986	0.829	0.899
MLP	0.823	0.414	0.551	0.850	0.856	0.853
XGB	**0.958**	**0.826**	**0.887**	**0.974**	**0.872**	**0.920**

In summary, the SAGE-FIN model propagates the node's features through the neural network architectures and learns the graph topological structure, thereby enabling the detection of both node and edge anomalies.

5.2 Causal Explanation for Anomalies

Following the identification of node anomalies by the SAGE-FIN model, the subsequent objective is to extract causal explanations for the trained model's outcomes. Causal explanations aim to answer the question: when a graph neural network makes a prediction, which parts of the input graph are relevant? To verify the causal explanations derived from the causal explainer algorithm on the Elliptic++ dataset, given the detected anomalies, the following evaluation metrics are employed:

1. Within the test set containing labeled data, $p(y|S)$ should be close to $p(y|G)$. A good explainer should be able to generate more compact subgraphs yet maintain the prediction accuracy,
2. The causal explanations should be visualized to allow qualitative performance analysis.

Due to the substantial size of the dataset, this subsection demonstrates representative causal explanations for a detected anomalous wallet address in 6 and a non-fraudulent transaction in 7 for illustration purposes. The model's node classification decoder estimated a 0.84 probability that a particular wallet address is fraudulent and a 0.83 probability that a particular transaction is non-fraudulent. The causal explainer algorithm identified the top 10 edges that most significantly influenced the classifier's decision, as depicted in Fig. 6 for the fraudulent wallet address and Fig. 7 for the non-fraudulent transaction. By removing the other edges within a 4-hop radius from this identified fraudulent wallet address, the model's node classification decoder still estimated a 0.891 probability of fraud for this wallet address, close to the original probability of 0.84 without removing any edges. For the non-fraudulent transaction, the 10-edge subgraph led to a 0.91 probability of non-fraud, which is also close to the original probability of 0.83 without removing any edges. This proves that these top 10 edges primarily drove the classifier's decision from a casual perspective.

6 Discussion

In this section, we reflect upon the evaluation of the performance of the SAGE-FIN model, the nature of explanations of the identified frauds, and some limitations.

6.1 On the Performance of SAGE-FIN Model

We used the Elliptic++ dataset to detect fraudulent transactions and wallet addresses using the SAGE-FIN model. The edge prediction served as a proxy for detecting fraudulent nodes for unlabeled data. The model's performance for edge prediction across different datasets was compared. The model achieved an F1-score of 0.883 on the Elliptic++ test set, comparable to the original unsupervised GraphBEAN performance in [29] on the social media Wikipedia dataset, where the edge prediction F1-score was 0.902, demonstrating the stability of the model. For the labeled data, the semi-supervised version of the model demonstrated strong performance, with an F1-score of 0.806 for wallet addresses and 0.807 for transactions. The causal explainer algorithm extracts the subgraph S which is human-interpretable and suitable to investigate the fraudulent instance further.

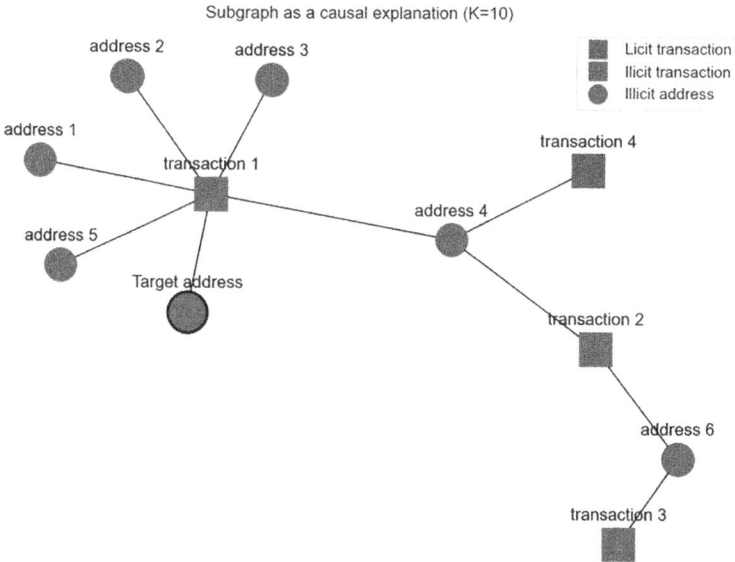

Fig. 6. Top 10 edges as the causal explanation for a target fraudulent wallet address (circles present addresses while squares present transactions)

The model is benchmarked against the SOTA machine learning algorithms, as shown in Table 2. Across different node partitions, the SOTA models themselves resulted in substantially better predictions for the transaction dataset in general,

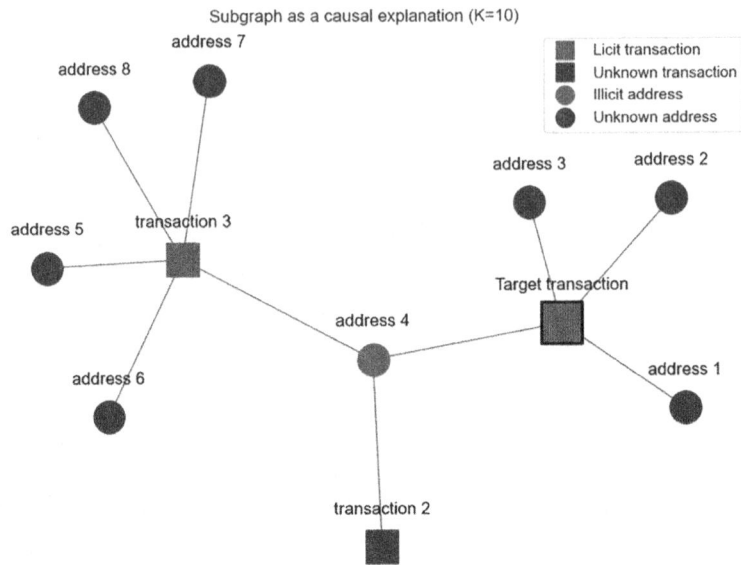

Fig. 7. Top 10 edges as the causal explanation for a target non-fraudulent transaction (circles present addresses while squares present transactions)

which has fewer nodes than the wallet address dataset. Moreover, our SAGE-FIN model integrates the features of wallet addresses and transactions within a single graph, thereby achieving comparable prediction performance for both node sets. Noteworthy is that GNN is also capable of handling larger datasets, whereas the performance of the SOTA methods deteriorates when the data size grows. Across several model choices, the model significantly outperformed the Logistic Regression model but did not surpass RF and XGB, primarily due to the latter model's noticeably higher precision. Overall, XGB is the best-performing model for fraud detection. The Logistic Regression model, which assumes a linear relationship between the input features and the log probabilities of the output, often fails for complex data, particularly in cases involving complex relationships such as those in graph-structured data. In contrast, XGB builds the trees sequentially, with each new tree correcting errors from the previous ones. These approaches prevent overfitting and enhance effectiveness and accuracy on the Elliptic++ dataset. There are also explainability methods for these SOTA models. Explainable Boosting Machine introduced by [39] combines cyclic gradient boosting with automatic interaction detection, resulting in models that are both accurate and inherently understandable. Similarly, SHAP (SHapley Additive exPlanations) developed by [40] is a unified approach to interpreting model predictions, which has been applied to GBDTs to provide clear local explanations by attributing the contribution of each feature to the final prediction. However, while methods like SHAP and Explainable Boosting Machine provide clear, additive attributions for feature importance, these methods struggle to capture dependencies between features. Overall, although the GNN did not perform as well as RF and XGB in anomalies detection, it can offer causal explanations for the identified fraud cases based on the graph structure which is the main advantage of our work. They are specifically designed to identify critical subgraphs, nodes, and edges that influence predictions. These explainers go beyond traditional feature importance scores by uncovering relational patterns and hierarchical dependencies in graph data, which is crucial for domains like financial fraud detection. This capability helps auditors to investigate the group associated with the identified fraud and its interactions, thereby providing a comprehensive understanding of the anomaly under investigation.

To evaluate the anomalies detection for unlabeled data, the address-transaction edge prediction accuracy can be used as a proxy. Anomalies can be interpreted as nodes involved in unexpected edges, where interactions between particular wallet addresses and transactions should not occur. However, edge prediction typically achieves higher accuracy than node anomaly detection because it directly leverages structural patterns and historical transaction behaviors, making it easier to identify likely connections. In contrast, node anomaly detection requires distinguishing between normal and abnormal behaviors at the entity level, which is inherently more complex due to the diverse transaction patterns of different users. Moreover, anomalies often represent rare or novel cases that lack sufficient historical data for reliable classification, whereas edge prediction benefits from abundant observed relationships that improve learning and generalization. Consequently, while edge prediction can serve as a useful proxy for node anomaly detection, its superior accuracy highlights the challenge of precisely identifying anomalous nodes solely based on their individual attributes and sparse interactions.

6.2 Causal Explanation for the Identified Frauds

The causal explanation for a representative fraudulent wallet address and a non-fraudulent transaction in the Elliptic++ dataset are illustrated in Fig. 6 and Fig. 7. The causal explainer algorithm effectively identifies the essential components—neighboring nodes—that contribute to the fraud label of a particular identified fraudulent activity. In Fig. 6, the fraudulent activity (denoted by the red node) was determined by a fraudulent transaction (denoted by the red squares), which was associated with multiple fraudulent wallet addresses (denoted by red circles). One non-fraudulent transaction (the green square) was included in the subgraph because it connected to a fraudulent wallet address and contained relevant information for the model decision. On the other hand, in Fig. 7, the non-fraudulent transaction (denoted as the green square) was decided by three unknown wallet addresses (denoted by blue circles) and a fraudulent address (the red circle). Even though the associated addresses were unknown, their features did not exhibit any suspicious patterns. Moreover, the fraudulent address played a role in the Granger causal explanation of the non-fraudulent transaction. Because this fraudulent address was linked to a non-fraudulent transaction, which suggests that the target transaction is classified based on the features of multiple nodes and edges in its neighborhood. For the sensitivity analysis, the subgraphs with ten edges for a fraudulent wallet and a non-fraudulent transaction were reduced further to smaller subgraphs with only six edges, as shown in Fig. 8 and Fig. 9. This analysis reveals that the classification of the identified fraud was predominantly driven by a single fraudulent transaction connected to the other five non-fraudulent wallet addresses. Even after further edge removal, the model's node classification decoder estimated a probability of 0.96 for the fraud label of this wallet address. This probability was less aligned with the original probability of 0.84 when no edges were removed, compared to the 10-edge subgraph with an estimated probability of 0.891. For the non-fraudulent transaction, the classification was mainly driven by the cluster with some labeled nodes, leading to a probability of 0.90 for the non-fraud label of this transaction which is close to subgraph of size 10-edge with an estimated probability of 0.91. This emphasizes the importance of the labeled nodes in deciding whether a node is a fraud or not. Such finding also indicates that a subgraph with ten edges is likely to offer a more comprehensive view of the causal explanation for the GNN classification.

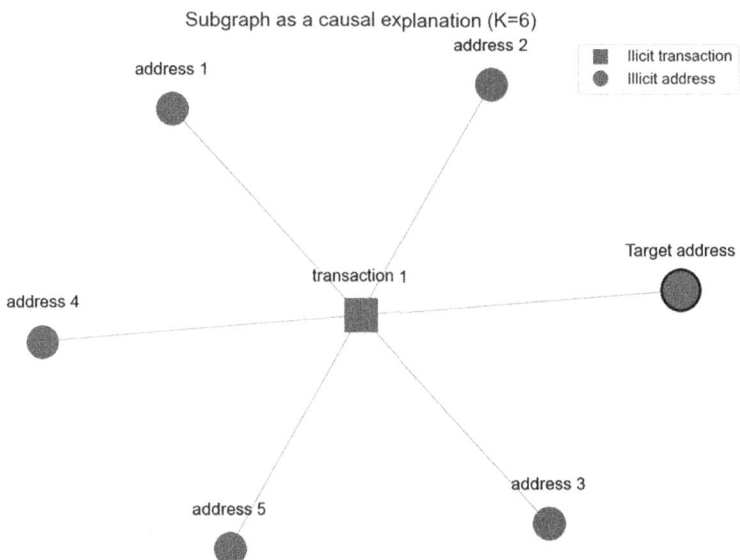

Fig. 8. Top 6 edges as the causal explanation for a target fraudulent wallet address (circles present addresses while squares present transactions)

6.3 Limitations

In this study, the application of the SAGE-FIN neural network for detecting fraudulent activities within a financial dataset is explored. The model is designed

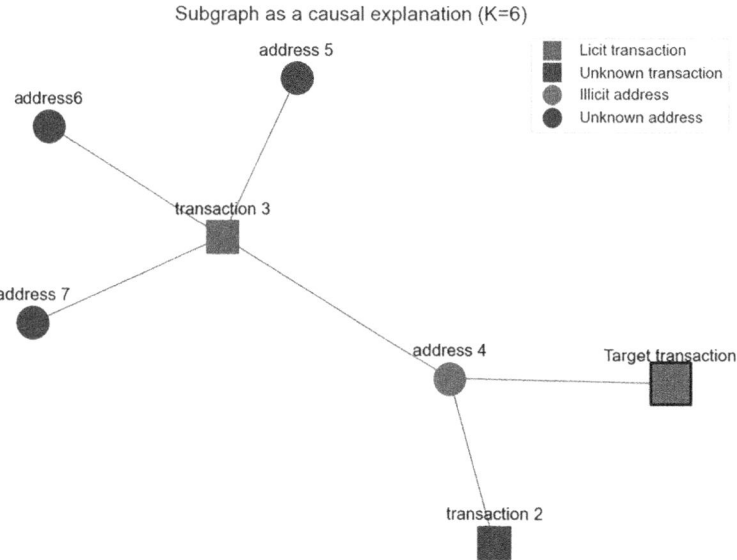

Fig. 9. Top 6 edges as the causal explanation for a target non-fraudulent transaction (circles present addresses while squares present transactions)

to utilize the rich information inherent in the nodes as well as the overall structure of the graph. However, the model neglected the graph's temporal dimension. The Elliptic++ dataset includes time step information, which could be crucial for understanding the evolution of fraudulent activities over time. Incorporating temporal graph neural network such as Temporal Graph Attention Network or Dynamic Graph Neural Network could allow the model to capture temporal dependencies and evolving transaction patterns, potentially improving anomalies detection accuracy. Moreover, looking at the explanatory subgraph can still be difficult to interpret to some extent in particular cases. On the causality side, it should be noted that unlike Pearlian causality [41], the notion of Granger causality is still based on correlation, and there can be undesirable hidden confounders which misguide the process of explaining actual causation. Methods like structural causal models or causal representation learning could be used to identify confounding variables and enhance the causal interpretability of the anomalies detection explanation.

7 Related Work

We provide an overview of relevant literature, which consists of two aspects: GNNs for anomaly detection and causal explanations for GNNs.

7.1 Graph Neural Networks for Anomaly Detection

In many domains, the financial data forms a bipartite (or more generally k-partite) graph, such as bookkeeping in auditing, banking transaction and Bitcoin trading. Such bipartite graphs have distinct and rich node-and-edge attributes. Thus, the capability of an employed ML model to operate on bipartite node-and-edge-attributed graphs is crucial for real-world applications.

Supervised Learning on Real-World Financial Data. Bitcoin Elliptic dataset [15,16] is a widely used public dataset containing transactional data of the Bitcoin blockchain network. Graph Convolutional Networks are often used to detect fraudulent instances in graphs. Kipf et al. [17] popularized the applications of such models in the machine learning domain. The methods can be categorized into spatial and spectral-based methods [18,19]. For example, [20] employs metapath-based heterogeneous GNNs for collusion fraud detection, [21] predicts mutual fund returns with GNNs, [22] proposes two neural networks to prevent financial contagion, [23–25] apply financial networks to study contagion effects and systemic risks. However, prior studies on Elliptic rely on supervised learning methods, which is impractical in the financial industry.

Semi-supervised Learning on the Uni-Partite Financial Graphs. [27] applied GraphSAGE for semi-supervised fraud detection in credit card transactions. [28] introduced a Knowledge-Guided Semi-Supervised GNN, using expert-designed rules to label data and train fraud detectors. However, these models work only with unipartite graphs without capturing the interaction of the financial network. Financial data can be modeled as bipartite graphs with distinct features for each partition and rich node and edge attributes, which are essential for accurate anomaly detection and explainability. A model limited to unipartite graphs would miss crucial information, making bipartite node-and-edge-attributed graph processing vital for such applications.

Unsupervised Learning for Bipartite Non-financial Graph. [29] introduced the unsupervised GraphBEAN model, which compresses a bipartite social network input graph into low-dimensional (node-only) latent representations, utilizing a series of customized graph convolution layers. Subsequently, the topological structure of the graph, as well as its node and edge attributes, are reconstructed. To improve the learning process on the unlabeled data, the domain knowledge can be used to first label the frauds, followed by a semi-supervised approach.

7.2 Causal Explanation for Graph Neural Networks

At the intersection of XAI and Graph Neural Networks, we recognize two main categories: (a) instance-level explanations and (b) model-level explanations [30].

The instance-level explanations depend on the input, such as gradient, perturbation, decomposition, and surrogate methods. In contrast, model-level explanations provide input-independent explanations, resulting in high-level understanding e.g., the XGNN model proposed by [31] which was designed to scrutinize graph patterns that lead to a specific class, the Bayesian graphic networks model by [32,33] which takes into account the multivariate conditional dependencies among the nodes in the graph. We focus on **instance-level explanations** to explain why a particular instance is flagged as fraudulent. Examples include GNNExplainer [34], which offers a local explanation for an instance (a node/ an edge/ a graph) by identifying a compact subgraph that leads to its prediction, PGM-Explainer [35] which models feature dependencies via conditional probability, Gem [36] a model-agnostic method for various graph tasks, Shapley values [42] which provides the explanations for the predictions generated by a machine learning model. The Granger causality [37] determines if one variable improves the prediction of another, providing transparent causal insights without relying on a specific model structure. On the other hand, function-based Causal discovery like Neural Granger Causality [38] leverages deep learning to model complex, high-dimensional, and nonlinear relationships, which allows it to uncover more intricate causal dependencies. However, this comes at the cost of higher computational demands and reduced interpretability. While more flexible, its black-box nature limits its suitability in finance, where transparency is crucial for regulatory and policy decisions.

8 Conclusion

This paper proposed a semi-supervised model SAGE-FIN for anomaly detection in bipartite node-and-edge-attributed graphs, capable of detecting anomalies at both the node and the edge levels. The model leverages a small amount of labeled data to identify anomalies within a large volume of unlabeled data. The SAGE-FIN model has demonstrated commendable performance in terms of precision, recall, and F1-score metrics when applied to real-world datasets. It achieved F1 scores of 0.806, 0.807, and 0.883 for wallet addresses, transactions, and edges, respectively. While the SAGE-FIN model significantly outperformed the Logistic Regression model, it did not surpass the performance of Random Forest and XGBoost. However, the SAGE-FIN model's ability to provide (causal) explanations for identified fraud based on graph structure is a notable advantage. This capability has the potential to help auditors to investigate the implicated group and its interactions thoroughly, offering a rich enough medium to pinpoint the reason for anomalies.

Additionally, the research introduced a Granger causal explanations for the SAGE-FIN model identified frauds cases. This is essential in domains like finance to ensure accountability in decision-making process.

Based on the identified limitations of the SAGE-FIN model as discussed in Sect. 6, we recommend to incorporate the temporal dimension to develop a dynamic graph anomaly detection algorithm, and potentially extend it to go beyond Granger causality (i.e., Pearlian causality [41]).

Disclosure of Interests. The authors report no conflicts of interest, and declare that they have no relevant or material financial interests related to the research in this paper. The authors alone are responsible for the content and writing of the paper, and the views expressed here are their personal views and do not necessarily reflect the position of their employer.

A Appendix A

The Elliptic++ dataset presents a bipartite address-transaction graph that illustrates the flow of Bitcoin across transactions and addresses. This structure enables the evaluation of transaction purposes and the relationships among addresses within the same transaction (Fig. 10):

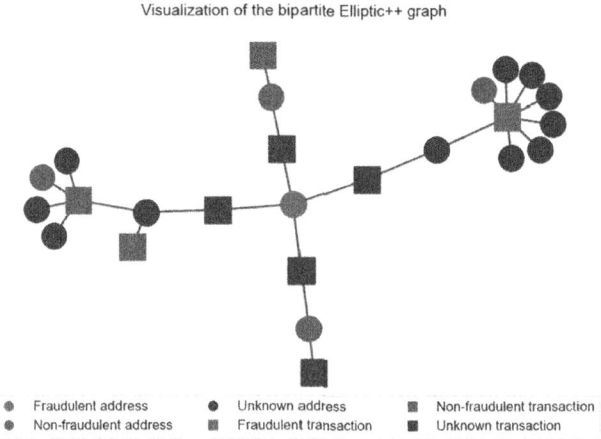

Fig. 10. Illustration of Bitcoin wallet addresses-transactions network as a bipartite graph

References

1. Albashrawi, M.: Detecting financial fraud using data mining techniques: a decade review from 2004 to 2015. J. Data Sci. **14**, 553–570 (2016)
2. Ngai, T., Hu, Y., Wong, H., Chen, Y., Sun, X.:The application of data mining techniques in financial fraud detection: a classification framework and an academic review of literature. J. Decis. Support Syst. **50**, 559–569 (2011)
3. Chandola, V.,Banerjee, A., Kumar, V.:Anomaly detection: a survey. ACM Comput. Surv. (CSUR) **41**(3), 1–58 (2009)
4. Thilakarathna, K., Fukuda, K., Seneviratne, A., Hu, Y., Seneviratne, S.: Characterizing and detecting money laundering activities on the bitcoin network. preprint arXiv:1912.12060 (2019)

5. Monamo, P., Marivate, V., Twala, B.: A multifaceted approach to Bitcoin fraud detection: global and local outliers. In: 15th IEEE International Conference on Machine Learning and Applications (ICMLA), pp. 188–194. IEEE (2016)
6. Visbeek, S., Acar, E., Hengst, F.: Explainable fraud detection with deep symbolic classification. In: World Conference on Explainable Artificial Intelligence, pp. 350–373. Springer (2024). https://doi.org/10.1007/978-3-031-63800-8_18
7. Azarm, C, Zeelt, M., Acar, E.: On the potential of network-based features for fraud detection (2024)
8. Boersma, M.: Complex networks in audit: a data-driven modelling approach. Universiteit van Amsterdam (2024)
9. Sourabh, S., Hoogduin, L., Kandhai, D., Boersma, M.: Financial statement networks: an application of network theory in audit. J. Netw. Theory Finan. **4**, 59–85 (2018)
10. Bussmann, N., Giudici, P., Marinelli, D., Papenbrock, J.: Explainable AI in fintech risk management. Front. Artif. Intell. **3**, 26 (2020)
11. Gomber, P., Kauffman, RJ., Parker, C., Weber, B.W.: On the fintech revolution: interpreting the forces of innovation, disruption, and transformation in financial services. J. Manag. Inf. Syst. **35**(1), 220–265 (2018)
12. Weber, P., Carl, KV., Hinz, O.: Applications of explainable artificial intelligence in finance—a systematic review of finance, information systems, and computer science literature. Manag. Rev. Q. **74**(2), 867–907 (2024)
13. Yablo, S.: Causal relevance. Philos. Issues **13**, 316–328 (2003)
14. Motie, S., Raahemi, B.: Financial fraud detection using graph neural networks: a systematic review. J. Expert Syst. Appl. **240**, 122156 (2024)
15. Elmougy, Y., Liu, L.: Demystifying fraudulent transactions and illicit nodes in the bitcoin network for financial forensics. In: Proceedings of the 29th ACM SIGKDD Conference on Knowledge Discovery and Data Mining (2023)
16. Weber, M., et al: Anti-money laundering in bitcoin: experimenting with graph convolutional networks for financial forensics. ArXiv abs/1908.02591 (2019)
17. Kipf, TN., Welling, M.: Semi-supervised classification with graph convolutional networks. arXiv (2016)
18. Zhang, S., Tong, H., Xu, J., Maciejewski, R.: Graph convolutional networks: a comprehensive review. Comput. Soc. Netw. **6**, 1 (2019)
19. Zhou, J., et al.: Graph neural networks: a review of methods and applications. arXiv (2018)
20. Ghosh, S., Anand, R., Bhowmik, T., Chandrashekhar, S.: GoSage: heterogeneous graph neural network using hierarchical attention for collusion fraud detection. In 4th ACM International Conference on AI in Finance. ACM, New York, NY, USA (2023)
21. Jiang, S., Uddin, A., Wei, Z, Yu, D.: The network of mutual funds: a dynamic heterogeneous graph neural network for estimating mutual funds performance. In 4th ACM International Conference on AI in Finance. ACM, New York, NY, USA (2023)
22. Cao, Z., Chen, Z., Mishra, P, Amini, H., Feinstein, Z.: Modeling inverse demand function with explainable dual neural networks. In 4th ACM International Conference on AI in Finance. ACM, New York, NY, USA (2023)
23. Giudici, P., Spelta,A.: Graphical network models for international financial flows. J. Bus. Econ. Stat. **34**, 128–138 (2016)
24. Billio, M., Getmansky, M., Lo, A., Pelizzon, L.: Econometric measures of connectedness and systemic risk in the finance and insurance sectors. J. Finan. Econ. **104**(3), 535–559 (2012)

25. Battiston, S., Puliga, M, Kaushik, R., Tasca, P., Caldarelli, G.: DebtRank: too central to fail? Financial networks, the FED and systemic risk. Nat. Sci. Rep. **2**, 541 (2012)
26. Akoglu, L., Tong, H., Koutra, D.: Graph based anomaly detection and description: a survey, DMKD J. (2015). https://doi.org/10.1007/s10618-014-0365-y
27. Jing, R., et al.: A graph-based semi-supervised fraud detection framework. In: 4th IEEE International Conference on Cybernetics (Cybconf), pp. 1–5 (2019)
28. Rao, Y., et al.: Knowledge guided fraud detection using semi-supervised graph neural network. In: Web Information Systems Engineering–WISE 2021: 22nd International Conference, pp. 385–393 (2021)
29. Fathony, R., Ng, J., Chen, J.: Interaction-focused anomaly detection on bipartite node-and-edge-attributed graphs. In: International Joint Conference on Neural Networks (IJCNN) (2023)
30. Yuan, H., Yu, H., Gui, S., Ji, S.: Explainability in graph neural networks: a taxonomic survey. IEEE Trans. Pattern Anal. Mach. Intell. **45**(5), 5782–5799 (2023)
31. Yuan, H., Tang, J., Hu, X., Ji, S.: XGNN: towards model-level explanations of graph neural networks. In: Proceedings SIGKDD ACM (2020)
32. Giudici, P.: Learning in Graphical Gaussian Models, Bayesian Statistics, vol. 5, pp. 621–628 (1996)
33. Ahelegbey, A., Giudici, P.: NetVIX - a network volatility index for financial markets. Physica A: Stat. Mech. Appl. **594**, 127017 (2022)
34. Ying, Z., Bourgeois, D., You, J., Zitnik, M., Leskovec, J.: Generating explanations for graph neural networks. In: Proceedings of Advances in Neural Information Processing Systems Conference, pp. 9244–9255 (2019)
35. Vu, N. Thai, T: Probabilistic graphical model explanations for graph neural networks. In: Proceedings of Advances in Neural Information Processing Systems Conference (2020)
36. Li, B., Lin, W., Lan, H.: Generative causal explanations for graph neural network (2021)
37. Granger, C.: Investigating causal relations by econometric models and cross-spectral methods. Econometrica: J. Econ. Soc. **37**, 424–438 (1969)
38. Tank, A., Covert, I., Foti, N., Shojaie, A., Fox, E.: Neural Granger causality. IEEE Trans. Pattern Anal. Mach. Intell. **44**(8), 4267–4279 (2021)
39. Caruana, R., Lou, Y., Gehrke, J., Koch, P., Sturm, M., Elhadad, N.: Intelligible models for healthcare: predicting pneumonia risk and hospital 30-day readmission. In: Proceedings of the 21th ACM SIGKDD International Conference on Knowledge Discovery and Data Mining, pp. 1721–1730 (2015)
40. Lundberg, S. M., Lee, S.I.: A unified approach to interpreting model predictions. In: Advances in Neural Information Processing Systems (NeurIPS), pp. 4765–4774 (2017)
41. Pearl, J., Glymour, M., Jewell, NP.: Causal Inference in Statistics: A primer. Wiley (2016)
42. Babaei, G., Giudici, P., Raffinetti, E.: Explainable artificial intelligence for crypto asset allocation. Finance Res. Lett. **47**, 102941 (2022)

Open Access This chapter is licensed under the terms of the Creative Commons Attribution 4.0 International License (http://creativecommons.org/licenses/by/4.0/), which permits use, sharing, adaptation, distribution and reproduction in any medium or format, as long as you give appropriate credit to the original author(s) and the source, provide a link to the Creative Commons license and indicate if changes were made.

The images or other third party material in this chapter are included in the chapter's Creative Commons license, unless indicated otherwise in a credit line to the material. If material is not included in the chapter's Creative Commons license and your intended use is not permitted by statutory regulation or exceeds the permitted use, you will need to obtain permission directly from the copyright holder.

Legal Requirements, Trust Issues and Engineering Challenges - A Multi-disciplinary Case for User-Specific Explainability

Merle Fairhurst[1], Katharina Kaesling[1], and Verena Klös[2]

[1] Centre for Tactile Internet with Human-in-the-Loop (CeTI), Technische Universität Dresden, Dresden, Germany
{merle.fairhurst,katharina.kaesling}@tu-dresden.de
[2] Carl von Ossietzky Universität Oldenburg, Oldenburg, Germany
verena.kloes@uol.de

Abstract. When it comes to explainability, clearly one size does not fit all. But what factors should be considered when designing novel technologies for domestic use? Based on an interdisciplinary workshop held in March 2024 in Dresden, we discuss explainability in human-machine interaction with regard to user autonomy and trust. Analysing the webs of stakeholders, we highlight the need to consider both the context of the human-machine interaction and the specific needs of the various stakeholders. Legal requirements and positions of the stakeholders are considered, as well as current research on trust in cognitive neuroscience. Both suggest that Explainability Engineering should tailor explanations to the specific person concerned. Like the workshop, the paper draws on the use case of AI-powered domestic robots and health wearables. How are explanations in that context shaped by current regulations and inhowfar do they address user needs? What role does trust play within the web of different regulations and for user reliance? How should explanations vary depending on the duration of use of the technology? Based on current cognitive neuroscience and legal research, we highlight interdisciplinary requirements for Explainability Engineering that fosters understanding and trust in a Human-Machine Interaction.

Keywords: legal requirements on XAI · digital autonomy and XAI · explainability and trust · User-specific explainability

1 Introduction

Robots and wearables, combined with artificial intelligence, have great potential to empower humans. Specifically, home robots with their diverse application areas, including health assistance, can enable humans to live at home and autonomously shape their daily life and improve well-being. When it comes to defining the central role of the human, explainability is key. Human empowerment in the context of social and collaborative robotics presupposes a certain understanding of machine decisions and their backgrounds. Different disciplines work with different concepts of understanding and, consequently, define the information needed for such an understanding differently. Specific rights to information and explanations are provided, for example, in data protection and AI regulation. Recent advances in robotics and wearables were not yet considered when drawing up the General Data Protection Regulation of 2016, making its interpretation with regard to the goals pursued vital for the empowerment of the humans whose data is processed. This contribution is the result of a close interdisciplinary dialogue focused on data protection law, explainability of robot behaviour, and neuroscience.

Drawing on the use case of domestic health assistance devices, such as a physiotherapy haptic feedback device [29], which are used long-term rather than short term, we discuss the possibilities and potential of user-specific explanations. Rather than focusing on the straightforward cases of human-machine interactions, here we consider how user-specific explainability varies as a function of use duration, comparing long-term versus short-term use only. In particular, this interdisciplinary endeavour focuses on detailing the special consideration of long-term interactions of humans and social and collaborative robots. Explanations for robot behaviour can foster understanding and increase acceptance of robots if they answer the user's needs [52]. Papagni and Koeszegi explore how explainable robots can be designed to be both understandable and trustworthy for non-expert users by addressing three key challenges: the approximate nature of explanations, their dependence on interaction contexts, and human cognitive limitations. The authors propose a framework based on sense-making that emphasizes establishing contextual boundaries, using plausibility rather than accuracy as a key evaluation criterion, and integrating interactive and multimodal explanations to enhance human-robot trust and interpretability.

Personalization would allow explanations not only to be tailored to the situation, but also to the recipient's role, level of expertise and prior experiences, thereby fulfilling the legal requirements and applying them according to the spirit of the law. Cognitive neuroscience is currently investigating the role of explanations in trust in machines. In particular, based on advances in our understanding of the dynamics of trust in interpersonal settings, there is evidence that more evolving conceptualizations of trust in technology are required [50,55]. Additionally, extending research on multi-agent-systems (MAS), specifically in the case of a developed technology proposed by a healthcare provider, cognitive neuroscience may be able to shed light on how estimations of trust in these more complex cases may be processed. In this paper, we provide a multi-disciplinary view on requirements for personalized explainability of robots in a domestic setting, taking into account the diverse human needs for explainability in the domain of AI powered domestic robots and wearables for care and health assistance.

In the following, we first describe an interdisciplinary workshop on explanation needs of different stakeholders that we held 2024 in Dresden. Based on these preliminary discussions at the workshop, we use this as a springboard to consider the challenges regarding tailored explainability from an interdiscilinary perspective. In Sect. 3, we focus on legal requirements for explanations. We discuss questions related to trust and explainability in Sect. 4, and summarise the findings and analyse open challenges for XAI in Sect. 5.

2 Interdisciplinary Workshop on Stakeholder Needs

In March 2024, we held a small interdisciplinary workshop with attendees ranging from master students to postdocs on the topic of tailoring explanations for AI powered health and care assistant systems to different stakeholders. It should be noted that attendees were academics and not stakeholders themselves. This clear limitation points towards an important need to include diverse stakeholders into these conversations surrounding XAI (see for an example in healthcare comparing the views and needs of clinicians and patients [38]. The workshop took place in the context of the cluster of excellence *Centre for Tactile Internet with Human-in-the-Loop (CeTI)* at the Technische Universität Dresden and was entitled "Personalizing Explainability: What information for whom?". We selected the context of physical care and physiotherapy due to the critical role trust plays in decision-making processes within this context and because this setting includes an interesting web of stakeholders. Clinical and care scenarios are unique in that they involve direct human well-being, requiring a high degree of transparency, reliability, and accountability in decision-making processes [60]. For example, the inclusion and reliance on AI-driven or automated systems in physiotherapy introduces challenges related to explainability, as patients/users and clinicians must understand and trust the recommendations made by such technologies [5,27]. Moreover, in these settings, trust must be established among multiple stakeholders, including human clinicians, patients, medical device manufacturers, and increasingly, technology-driven decision-making systems [41]. We are therefore driven to consider the trust ecosystem and who in fact needs to be trusted: a human manufacturer, human clinician or technology and what level of explainability is required by the different stakeholders within the ecosystem. Importantly, in the case of care, in this complex network of stakeholders the decision maker may be different to the end user.

In the workshop, we presented four vignettes -short descriptions of usage scenarios - for a care robot assistant, specifically a smart walker, and a physiotherapy vest that provides haptic feedback (see Table 1). For our vignettes, we conceived of a factorial design to investigate how context (neutral vs. negative) and usage duration (short-term vs. long-term) influence the necessity and depth of explanations as a function of the different stakeholders within the trust ecosystem. In clinical settings, the nature of the context—whether neutral or negative, due to malfunctions or unmet user expectations—can significantly impact patient trust and the perceived importance of detailed explanations. Similarly, the duration of technology use may alter expectations for explanation depth, with long-term use potentially necessitating more comprehensive information to maintain trust and adherence. In each case, the vignettes present a user, their need for a particular digital assistant device and details of how the device functions and controlled. The two devices chosen fall within the care category: one a smart walker, the other an automated physiotherapy vest used to provide haptic feedback to improve exercise performance and thereby compliance. Across these two devices, we compare technologies that would be used for a short duration, the physiotherapy vest, with other devices that might be used more long-term, such as the smart walker. We further challenged workshop participants to consider contexts in which either the care device functioned as it was supposed to (neutral) versus negative contexts, in which the technology either could not be controlled by the user or did not function as desired.

AI-driven healthcare technologies involve multiple stakeholders, each with distinct needs for explainability based on their role, expertise, and familiarity with AI. Data holders and processors, such as hospitals or research institutions, require explainability for compliance with data governance frameworks and to ensure AI models align with regulatory standards. Service providers, including AI developers and vendors, need technical transparency to validate model performance, detect biases, and enhance interoperability with clinical systems. Clinicians rely on interpretable AI outputs to support medical decision-making, preferring actionable explanations that align with their domain knowledge while maintaining trust in automated recommendations. Nasarian et al. systematically review the challenges and methodologies associated with interpretable machine learning (IML) and explainable artificial intelligence (XAI) in healthcare, emphasizing their importance in enhancing clinician-AI collaboration and trust [49]. Their findings highlight the need for a structured approach to implementing XAI in digital health interventions, addressing concerns such as bias and interpretability trade-offs noting however that there is no scientific evidence supporting a general balance between accuracy and explainability. Looking beyond the clinician, the explainability requirements of patients vary widely—adult patients may need concise, patient-friendly interpretations to understand treatment suggestions, while elderly patients (70 years) might benefit from simpler, non-technical explanations due to cognitive and sensory limitations [64]. A young child (7 years old) may require visual or narrative-based explanations tailored to their cognitive development, while their parents seek transparent and comprehensive justifications to make informed decisions on their behalf [59]. A legal guardian of an adult patient faces similar concerns, needing clarity on AI-driven recommendations to advocate for the patient's best interest. Additionally, patients' prior exposure to AI affects their expectations—tech-savvy patients may prefer detailed insights into model mechanics, while those unfamiliar with AI may need reassurance through high-level, intuitive explanations to foster trust. These diverse explainability needs underscore the importance of designing AI-driven systems with adaptive, stakeholder-specific explanation strategies to ensure ethical, effective, and patient-centred healthcare AI adoption.

In Table 1, we summarise the vignettes provided to participants of the workshop. Attendees were asked to consider these four scenarios and then in groups to consider the explainability needs by stakeholder. In Table 2, we summarise some of the key outcomes of the workshop activity. Common themes can be identified including degree of control over the system, details of how the system works, opportunities to interact/communicate with the system, what can be done in the case of malfunction, the level of intelligence of the system and whether the system could learn about the user.

Due to the size of the workshop, we are only able to report the suggestions of our small group of participants as to the considerations of different stakeholders. These were captured based on the interactive discussion both before and after the vignette activity, as seen in Table 2. The workshop provided not only a list of specific stakeholder needs for the discussed scenarios but also highlighted the need for further interdisciplinary research and discussions to be able to answer questions like *How is explainability in that context shaped by current regulations and do they fall short of recognizing user needs? What role does trust play within the web of different (legal) relationships? How does explainability and thus trust vary depending on the duration of use of the technology? How can we improve XAI based on the answers to those questions?* Obviously, there are clear limitations to this initial stage workshop, as described notably the number of attendees and the participation of not only experts involved in designing XAI, but also the very stakeholders we discuss. Furthermore, it should be noted that the list of stakeholders is far from exhaustive but illustrates the broad range of individuals whose needs and profiles should be considered when determining the levels and format of explainability. For example, we did not distinguish between a very young child (2 and below) and a 7-year-old child, where the latter is actually typically able to communicate things like pain, while the former is not. We therefore use this initial workshop discussion as a springboard to consider three different perspectives related to creating tailored explainability solutions for different stakeholders. In the remainder of the paper, we discuss questions raised within the workshop in further detail specifically as they relate to the legal requirements for explanations, questions related to trust and explainability and finally consider open challenges for XAI.

3 Legal Requirements for Explanations Under the GDPR

Some of these stakeholder needs have been taken up by the legislator. Generally, private persons are under no obligation to explain their decisions or behaviour to other private persons [6, Rn. 155]. Both the General Data Protection Regulation (GDPR) and the AIA (Artificial Intelligence Act) contain rights to explanations for certain decisions. Explanations enable the data subject, i.e. the person to whom the data relates, to check the lawfulness of the data processing (see Recital 63 GDPR) and to challenge it. Following on from this idea, the fundamental rights background, namely Articles 1, 7 and 8 of the European Charter of Fundamental Rights, undermines the relevance of rights to explanation [30, p. 444]. Here, the focus is on explanations relating to the processing of data for automated decision-making under the GDPR, which remains the primary legal source securing the data subject's data autonomy [17, Art. 1 Rn. 3 f.]

Table 1. Workshop Activity Vignettes

	Care Robot (physical care)	Physio Vest
Neutral Context	A 80-year old woman, Anna, who needs some assistance to get into a seating position and some support when walking, received a novel smart walker four weeks ago. The device can be controlled via voice, via remote control and with buttons on the device. It helps her to get up from a chair or a sofa, enables her to walk to the nearby supermarket and suggests a rest whenever it senses that the walk is too exhausting for her. While using it, the device also tracks her health status and creates a daily report for the caretaker Bob who comes every morning and evening. In case of emergencies, the device can call an alarm service. Anna, Bob and also Anna's children are happy that Anna uses the smart walker.	A 70-year old patient is referred to a physiotherapist for a lower back injury. After the first introductory sessions, the physiotherapist suggests the use of a novel remote haptic feedback device (VEIIO Shirt) to ensure practice of exercises at home are more like those done in the context with the physio. The patient returns home and starts to use the device. The patient receives haptic feedback and completes the exercises as instructed.
Negative Context	A 80-year old woman, Anna, who needs some assistance to get into a stand from a seating position and some support when walking, has received a novel smart walker four weeks ago. The device can be controlled via voice, via remote control and with buttons on the device. It helps her to get up from a chair or a sofa,, enables her to walk to the nearby supermarket and suggests a rest whenever it senses that the walk is too exhausting for her. Usually, Anna agrees and happily takes a rest whenever the device suggests it. One day, Anna is in a rush because her grandchildren will visit her in the afternoon and she wants to buy their favourite cookies for them. Thus, she refuses to take a rest and continues walking to the supermarket instead. The device continues suggesting a rest every 2 min now and Anna gets angry. She wants to turn this functionality off but don't know how.	A 25-year old patient is referred to a physiotherapist for a lower back injury. After the first introductory sessions, the physiotherapist suggests the use of a novel remote haptic feedback device (VEIIO Shirt) to ensure practice of exercises at home are more like those done in the context with the physio. The patient returns home and starts to use the device. The patient receives haptic feedback but finds the feedback unpleasant. Moreover, the feedback is either too strong or too weak and the patient feels they have little or no control over the device. The patient abandons practice of their exercises.

even after full applicability of the AI Act. Most AI powered domestic robots and wearables in the domain of care and health assistance will not amount to high-risk AI systems triggering the explanation requirement of Art. 86 AIA. In legal literature, requirements for explanations under the GDPR are generally

Table 2. Stakeholder Explainability Needs

Persons	Identified Needs/ Stakeholder Questions
Data holder/Data Processor	Legal certainty and transparency: What explanations do I have to give? How can I give them in a way that facilitates use and strengthens user trust?
Service Provider	How is the current/past performance? What were the causes for malfunctions? What are possible solutions?
Physiotherapist	How to use the system? Why this action? How to explain the system to a patient?
"Regular" User	How does this work? How can I communicate? What control do I have? How do I use it? What can I do if something unforeseen happens?
Young User (Child, 7 years)	How can I communicate (without reading/writing/...)? What control do I have (and what can I decide for myself?) How can I understand why the wearable/robot behaves a certain way? Can I talk to it? What does it show me?
Parents of the Child User	How can I understand what the technology does (in order for me to explain it to the child)? What choices should I leave to my child? Can I talk to it? What does it show me?
Old User (Senior Citizen, 70 years)	How can I communicate (without reading small print/typing/...)?
Legal Guardian (of an adult)	How can I understand what the technology does (in order for me to be able to decide if it is safe to use with my ward or recommend its use?)? What choices should I leave to the ward? What does it show me?
User with AI/ Technology-Affinity	What kind of training data was used for the technology? Will it learn from me? Is it reliable and safe?
User without AI/ Technology experience	How does it know what to do? Can I trust it?

divided into explanation requirements "ex ante", meaning before an automated decision, and "ex post", meaning after such a decision. As the "decision" as part of the automated decision making process is a legally relevant category, defined in Art. 22 (1) GDPR, the legal categories are not congruent with the post-hoc vs. ante-hoc categories in computer science. This differentiation stems from the GDPR's focus on automated decision making. Only certain decisions qualify as decisions within the meaning of Article 22 (1) GDPR, so that the categories are not identical to the classification of explanations referred to as "post-hoc" in computer science. It will be analysed in how far the rights to explanation mirror the diversity of stakeholders identified in the workshop both with regard to the persons obligated to give explanations and to those entitled to receive one. The obligations under the GDPR are interpreted differently, with rights to ex post declarations being discussed particularly controversially. According to the interpretation suggested here, the GDPR does guarantee rights to explanation after a so-called "automated decision", based both on Art. 15 and on Art. 22 para. 3 in conjunction with recital 74 sentence 2 GDPR.

3.1 What Is "Automated Decision-Making" Under the GDPR?

The GDPR of 2016 does not use the term AI, but addresses the broader legal concept of automated decision making (ADM). In principle, decision-making is automated if it is based on algorithms and takes place without significant human involvement. The regulatory objective is not to allow humans to become the mere object of automated decisions made by a machine. Art. 22 GDPR does not contain any more detailed requirements for the algorithm, so it also applicable to AI systems. The automated decision is characterised by an output producing legal effects or similar significant effects (Art. 22 para. 1 GDPR). A legal effect presupposes that the legal status of the data subject is changed in some way by the decision, e.g. by affecting contractual relationships. "Similar effects" have to be comparable to these legal effects, so they are seen as limited to 'only serious effects', putting someone at a 'serious disadvantage [3, p. 22f]. However, in line with the concept of protection, the threshold for a 'decision' must not be set too high (see Court of Justice of the European Union (CJEU), 7.12.2023 (C-634/21) - OQ/Land Hessen)). The additive impact of, for example, false guidance from health wearables - e.g. constant overcorrection for physical therapy - or robot behaviour detrimental to the health of the user overtime - should also suffice for the finding of a significant effect on the data subject.

3.2 Explanations as Part of the Data Subject's Right to Access

The GDPR foresees certain rights to information and - in case of automated decision-making - explanation in Art. 13–15 GDPR. Under Art. 13 and 14 GDPR, the data subject has to be informed when personal data are obtained (see Art. 13 para. 2 lit. f and Art. 14 para. 2 lit. f and 3 GDPR). The data subject's right of access under Art. 15 GDPR depends on the data subject's request, which can be made at any point in time, i.e. both before and after a decision. Both the information obligations under Art. 13 and 14 GDPR and the right of access under Art. 15 GDPR contain the data controller's obligation to give "meaningful information about the logic involved, as well as the significance and the envisaged consequences of such processing for the data subject" (Art. 13 para. 2 lit. f; Art. 14 para. 2. lit. g, Art. 15 para. 1 lit. h GDPR). Despite the repetitive use of the wording in the GDPR, what constitutes such meaningful information remains largely unclear and depends on the individual case.

A distinction can be made between 'general logic', such as the type of data, the characteristics taken into account, etc., and ex post explanations for specific decisions, i.e. the reasons for a particular automated decision [63, p. 78]. Before a specific decision has been made - as is the case for the rights under Art. 13 and 14 GDPR - the content of the ex ante declaration obligation can only refer to abstract information [63, p. 84]. Accordingly, general information to be provided on the functionality of the system can, e.g. include information on the logic, the meaning, the intended consequences and the general functionality [63, p. 78]. A decision tree, for example, can and should be disclosed [63, p. 78]. There is legal uncertainty as to whether only the context, e.g. possible results, or also the actual mechanics are to be communicated [56, p. 291], [12, Rn. 55]. In any case, the explanation of the logic involved has to include information about the connections between the data processing and the decision made in each case [56, p. 291].

The right of access under Art. 15 GDPR contains a right to explanation, as recently asserted by the Court of Justice of the European Union (CJEU, 27.02.2025 (C-203/22 - Dun and Bradstreet Austria). The CJEU held that Art. 15 lit. h GDPR"affords the data subject a genuine right to an explanation as to the functioning of the mechanism involved in automated decision-making of which that person was the subject and of the result of that decision." (para. 57). The explanation has to allow the user to challenge the automated decision. The court also shed light on the interpretation of the term "meaningful information about the logic involved" by stating that this includes information on the procedure and principles actually applied in order to use, by automated means, the personal data of the data subject with a view to obtaining a specific result (para 58). It goes on to specify that the legal requirements for explanations cannot be satisfied by the mere communication of a complex mathematical formula, such as an algorithm (para. 59). It also does not deem a detailed description of all the steps in automated decision-making sufficient since not sufficiently concise and intelligible (para. 59). The CJEU takes up the guidelines of the Article 29 Working Party on automated individual decision-making, including profiling, for the purposes of Regulation 2016/679, according to which real, tangible examples must be given [2, p. 26]. The authors of the Working Group explicitly mention the use of additional tools to illustrate such effects, e.g. visual techniques to explain how a past decision was made. This recommendation thus reflects Recital 58 GDPR, according to which the principle of transparency requires the use of additional visual elements where appropriate. In any case, the requirement of a certain minimum level of comprehensibility of the information for the data subject must be observed. This can pose considerable challenges for Explainability Engineering, as there is a trade-off between simplification and meaningfulness.

3.3 Explanations as Part of Suitable Measures to Safeguard the Position of Data Subjects

Furthermore, under Art. 22 para. 3 GDPR, the controller must also take suitable measures to safeguard the rights and freedoms as well as the legitimate interests of the data subject, including at least the right to obtain the intervention of a person on the part of the controller, to express his or her point of view and to contest the decision. The measures should also extend to the preliminary stages of the decision [36, Rn. 15], [43, Rn. 39c]. This is necessary to ensure the effectiveness of these measures. The data subject should be able to assert the right to human intervention in accordance with Art. 22 para. 3 GDPR both before and after the decision. Recital 71 sentence 4 GDPR expressly states: 'In any case, such processing should be subject to suitable safeguards, which should include specific information to the data subject and the right to obtain human intervention, to express his or her point of view, to obtain an explanation of the decision reached after such assessment and to challenge the decision'. While this is only a recital, as many authors have rightly pointed out, the recital will still guide the interpretation of EU law. The teleological and systematic interpretation that goes beyond the recital also speaks in favour of including explanations in the category of minimum measures under Art. 22 para. 3 GDPR. Explanations are not only a necessary prerequisite for the other minimum measures mentioned in the wording of Art. 22 para. 3 GDPR, but also for the rights of data subjects as a whole. For the interpretation, the function of the right to explanation in the overall structure of the legal protection of data subjects and the system of the GDPR has to be considered, notably the interplay of Art. 22 with the data subject's rights in Art. 13, 14 and in particular Art. 15 GDPR. This function speaks in favour of the requirement of explanations also under Art. 22 para. 3 GDPR, despite the CJEU not mentioning it as part of the suitable measures in its judgment of 27.02.2025 (C-203/22 - Dun and Bradstreet Austria).

3.4 Web of Data Subjects and Data Controllers

Under the GDPR, it is the data controller(s)' obligation to provide explanation(s) to the data subject(s) concerned. Due to the lack of further categories, all stakeholder positions are considered with regard to these two legal positions. There can be more than one person who determines the purposes and means of the data processing and thus several data controllers within the meaning of Art. 4 No. 7 GDPR. Several entities can be joint controllers together (Art. 26 para. 1 GDPR) and thus jointly responsible for the fulfilment of the explanation requirements. In light of the CJEU's broad approach to joint control (see only C-210/16, ECLI:EU:C:2018:388 paras 26–28; C-272/19 ECLI:EU:C:2020:535, para 66), there will be considerable joint control in scenarios with more than one person deciding on the use [19]. Despite the apparent assumption of the CJEU, more controllers do not necessarily equal more protection - here: targeted explanations - for the data subjects [28, p. 333]. Finck aptly speaks of "Cobwebs of Control" [28]. Joint controllers should expressly regulate how they will fulfill their obligations. They are free to divide responsibilities [28, pp. 334–335], e.g. for giving explanations. As the European Data Protection Board suggested, it has to be considered who will be best situated to answer the data subjects requests [25, pp. 41–42]. The GDPR does not specifically deal with scenarios with chains of explanations, as they are created by law, e.g. for relationships between medical personnel and patients or between legal guardians and their subjects. Both medical personnel and legal guardians are examples for persons who have to give explanations while relying on explanations themselves. With regard to legal guardians, it has been discussed, to what extent the legal guardian (see §1814 German Civil Code) is also a data controller, which would give the charge the right of access - including the right to explanation, as argued above. The District Court of Hanover took the view that a legal guardian is not a "controller" within the meaning of Art. 4 No. 7 GDPR (28.06.2022, 17 T 19/22, para. 31), as the legal guardian processes the data on behalf of the person being cared for. In July 2024, the CJEU decided, however, that a former guardian who has professionally performed his duties in relation to a person under his care is to be classified as the "controller" for the processing of the personal data concerning that person that is in his possession (11.07.2024 (Rs. C-461/22), para. 30), as the guardian decides on the purposes and means of processing the personal data of the person under his care. The guardian's power of representation does not change the fact that he or she then processes data for his or her own sphere in his own name. This recent development of case law illustrates the practical challenges that come with the GDPR's conception of all relationships between stakeholders as bipolar ones between data controller(s) and data subject.

3.5 Tailoring Explanations to Data Subjects

When gearing the explanation towards the average member of the intended audience, the data controller faces the challenge of identifying the intended audience and ascertain the average member's level of understanding [4, pp. 7f.]. For technologies benefiting the public at large, the "average user" will likely not represent the diverse needs. Insofar AI technologies in combination with robotics and wearables can be used specifically to meet the needs of specific persons, e.g. for care or support in physical therapy. Specific needs also exist with regard to the explanations. The personalization of health wearables and care robots can include explanations, specifically for cases of long-term use. What makes an explanation intrinsically valuable, and "meaningful" under the GDPR, differs from person to person [1, p. 236]. Explanation requirements can benefit different stakeholders, e.g. the child doing physiotherapy or the senior citizen. The EU Commission calls for adaptive explainability of the algorithmic decision-making process to the extent possible [16]. In that communication, user-specific explainability is expressly linked to user trust, which is supposedly increased by tailored explanations, as underpinned by research on explainable AI [33, p. 50]. While it might generally be challenging to implement that, the context of continually used home robots and personalized health wearables allows for personalized explanations. These explanations can build on user profiles, as home robots interact recurrently with the same persons, who might be children or older adults, technically versed or not. Explanations can also build on previous ones given to the same person. With regard to long-term use, relevant data for explanations can be collected to improve explanations and continued use. The GDPR recognizes specific needs and vulnerabilities of certain groups. It specifically provides special requirements for children (Recital 38, Recital 71, Art. 12 para. 1, Recital 58 GDPR, which is linked to Art. 13 UNCRC). For children as subgroup of AI users, specific methods have been developed, relying heavily on Diagrams, cartoons, graphics, video and audio content, gamified or interactive content [34, 37] and direct language [8, p. 372]. Yet, vulnerabilities in the context of human-machine-interaction are not limited to children and not only specific to groups, but to individuals. Here, recommendations based on the data subject's legal position go beyond the letter of the law.

3.6 Legally Motivated Recommendations

Despite the fundamental relevance for the position of the stakeholders, there is considerable legal uncertainty as to the explanation requirements. It has been argued here that such automated decisions have to be explained under the GDPR not just by providing general information on the functioning, but also by specifically explaining decisions after they affected data subjects, as recently affirmed by the CJEU in C-203/22 (Judgement of 27 February 2025, ECLI:EU:C:2025:117). Data subjects can make use of their rights to access at this point in time and request, inter alia, "meaningful information about the logic involved, as well as the significance and the envisaged consequences" of the data processing (Art. 15 para. 1 lit h GDPR). Also, it has been explained why explanations should be considered part of the suitable measures to safeguard the position of data subjects under Art. 22 (3) GDPR, which means it has to be foreseen by the data controller and built in as part of Requirement Engineering. Even if one disagrees with that interpretation, such explanations can [39, p.282], [54, Rn. 77] and should [1, pp. 241 f.], [22, Rn. 25] be given. The GDPR requirements also presuppose a decision with a legal or significant effect on the data subject. It has been argued here that additive effects, e.g. of continued detrimental physiotherapy guidance, can also amount to a significant effect, here for the health of the user. Notwithstanding this view, explanations for data subjects using home robots and health wearables should also be given if the effects of automated data processing do not exceed the threshold of significance. As the EU Commission underlines, explanations are linked to the trust of users, which also hinges on the personalization of the explanations [16]. The legal uncertainty as to what constitutes meaningful information under Art. 15 para. 1 lit h GDPR and explanations under Art. 22 (3) GDPR can only be reduced with a view to specific use cases and in an interdisciplinary manner with regard to trust not only in interpersonal relationships in the web of data controllers and subjects, but specifically with regard to AI as part of robots and wearables.

4 Trust and Explainability

4.1 Trust in Humans Versus Trust in Technology

Acceptance and long-term use of domestic robots and health wearables will depend on establishing and maintaining a sense of trust in these autonomous agents [47]. Moreover the adoption of AI systems, particularly in healthcare, is significantly hindered by a lack of trust. Shan et al. emphasize that trust is conditioned by both human factors and the inherent properties of AI systems [57]. This assertion is supported by the findings of Stanley and Dorton, who argue that trust is mediated by various factors beyond mere performance, including the utility of AI within the broader sociotechnical system [23]. Such insights suggest that fostering trust requires a holistic approach that considers user experiences and the contextual impact of AI technologies. Much of our understanding of the basis of trust in non-human agents is based on the research on interpersonal trust [15]. However, existing studies typically explore trust in social settings, technology, and AI separately but often lack integration [41]. While trust in people involves volition and moral agency, trust in technology relies on functionality, reliability, and helpfulness. As such, we can say that for both human-human (interpersonal) and human-computer relations, trust is thought to revolve around the reliance on others to act predictably and beneficially [44].

4.2 Explainability and Trust in Technology

This conception of trust in technology is extended by McKnight and colleagues who put forward a theoretical framework distinguishing different types of trust in technology [45]. Specifically they distinguish between an individual's propensity to trust technology (general belief in technology's reliability), institution-based trust in technology (belief in the structural safeguards surrounding technology) and trust in specific technology (belief in the attributes of a particular system, e.g., Microsoft Excel). Markus et al. assert that transparency and interpretability are essential for users to assess the trustworthiness of AI systems, particularly when integrated into health care contexts [42]. This aligns with the findings of Dhuliawala et al., who discuss how users develop mental models of AI systems [21]. Therefore, implementing XAI methodologies can help bridge the gap between user expectations and AI capabilities, fostering a more trustworthy relationship. Specifically, users will assess these agents based on their performance, safety, and alignment with their expectations. In other words, trust will be grounded more in technical competency and some level of understanding of the consistent, error-free operation of these technologies.

The relationship between performance and trust however is not linear. One of the foundational aspects of trust in AI is the distinction between calibrated trust, distrust, and overtrust. He et al. highlight that users may exhibit distrust towards AI systems, preferring human providers even when AI demonstrates superior capabilities [35]. Specifically, Dhuliawala and colleagues have noted that incongruence between models of how technology should behave and actual experiences can undermine trust [21]. This mismatch can also lead to overtrust which occurs when users place excessive faith in AI, often beyond its actual capabilities [35]. This nuanced understanding of trust dynamics is crucial, as it underscores the need for AI systems to be designed with user perceptions in mind, ensuring that trust is appropriately calibrated. Additionally, it should be noted that users can exhibit a transfer of trust, with their trust in one AI system (e.g., an autonomous car) affecting trust in similar technologies. As such tailoring of explanations will need to take into account not only a user's general propensity to touch but also their familiarity with similar technologies.

4.3 The Trust Ecosystem

The Foundational Trust Framework put forward by Lukyanenko and colleagues provides a comprehensive approach to understanding AI trust dynamics and guides future research efforts [41]. The framework extends our conceptualisation of isolated AI systems and instead suggests that trust is affected by AI's relationships with users, organizations, and regulations. The framework describes interactions between these different systems in a broader trust ecosystem.

One can also consider the trust ecosystem to encompass multiple actors or stakeholders. In the healthcare setting (as detailed in Sect. 2), and borrowing the concept of networked trust [24], we consider this complex web of actors ranging from the developer of the technology and the prescribing clinician through to the end user and potentially their legal guardian. The idea of additional stakeholders and the relationship between these stakeholders brings to the fore the idea of tailored explanations of the technology. Moreover, as discussed in the workshop, as a function of factors such as the level of dependence and duration of the relationship between the user and the technology, we need to consider not only what information people need to appropriately trust automation, but also to explore its competence envelope, to adjust automation parameters, and to track and learn from norm deviations over time.

4.4 Short-Term Versus Long-Term Use of AI-Based Technologies: an Evolving Sense of Trust

Besides identifying the parameters that determine a sense of trust, additional challenges to the current framework of trust include a shift in considering a one-shot decision to trust versus an evolving sense of trust that is shaped by interpersonal dynamics [50]. Initial trust forms before or during the first interaction and is influenced by the user's propensity to trust, the human-like characteristics of AI with users perceiving AI as more trustworthy if it exhibits competence, benevolence, and fairness [32] and lastly, the perceived integrity of AI (Fairness, Transparency, Accountability) with algorithms that provide explanations for their decisions and appear fair and unbiased likely to be trusted more [58]. Additionally, in the initial phase of establishing trust, trust is stronger if AI is perceived as useful and intuitive [18]. As users interact with AI repeatedly, trust is influenced by social influence where trust increases when AI is recommended by peers or organizations [61]. Additionally, with increasing familiarity and understanding, users trust AI more [31]. Lastly, over time, users trust AI based on continued reliability, predictability, and performance [45]. Specifically considering MAS, Cheng and colleagues propose that an agent's trustworthiness is updated using long-term and short-term observations of the agent's behaviour [14]. Relatedly, Chio and Lee suggest a relational and responsive model of trust which not only describes how trust is established but how this dynamic process supports long term trusting relationships [15]. The authors go further to describe how this is relevant for technology that adapts to its environment without human intervention—i.e., autonomous agents. One can, for example, envision technologies where automation shifts roles over the lifespan of a relationship as a function of changing needs (e.g., the care robot provides a greater range of assistance as the elderly user's capacity diminishes).

4.5 Trust in the Special Case of Care

From a conceptual perspective, trust is relevant to any interaction involving vulnerability and uncertainty [40]. Interpersonal trust within the special case of care, in which a patient is particularly vulnerable, presents additional considerations. In a recent article, McParlin and colleagues put forward the idea of a therapeutic alliance: a collaborative working relationship between a clinician and patient which is a critical component of person-centred care [46]. Specifically, strengthening this alliance contributes to positive clinical outcomes across multiple healthcare disciplines [48,53]. In the case of care-robots or wearables prescribed or suggested by healthcare professionals, the alliance extends beyond the single dyad. Instead, we must consider trust not only between the clinician and the patient but also trust in the proposed technology by both the clinician and the patient. Future work should consider so-called networked trust [24] within a more complex ecosystem and how to model and moderate trust. Within this ecosystem, it is not only important to understand changes in levels of trust in the AI technology but also how a greater reliance on AI may influence the patient-clinician bond of trust [51].

4.6 Future Considerations of Explainability and Trust in Technology

To date, our conceptualisation of trust in technology and the need for explainability has been adequate to cover the simple cases of single use, direct interactions between an individual user and an AI-assisted technology. Based on the outcomes of the workshop, it becomes clear that considering the more complex cases will require an interdisciplinary approach. In particular, with insight from cognitive neuroscience, future work may include the development of mixed multi-agent models [13] of the so-called web or ecosystem of trust involving multiple stakeholders to determine how to optimise transparency, decision making and trust [5]. Beck et al. in their systematic review have identified three key areas in which research in trust in AI is lacking: (1) limited diversity as current conceptualisations are dominated by studies from Western, Educated, Industrialized, Rich, and Democratic (WEIRD) countries [7], (2) conceptual and theoretical gaps in studies that result from a lack of a consistent theoretical frameworks, leading to poor generalizability, (3) , related to our Vignette study, methodological issues with many studies using single-timepoint measurements of trust failing to examine long-term interactions with AI. Relatedly, specific to long-term use of AI technologies, as trust waxes and wanes during the extended relationship, a greater understanding of a user's need or request for further explanations should be investigated. For example, this request could signal either a lack of trust in the technology (over time) in general, a lack of knowledge about a new function or role the technology now plays in the relationship, or, within the trust ecosystem, a lack of trust in a recommendation by either the AI technology or the prescribing healthcare professional.

5 Requirements and Open Challenges for Transdisciplinary Explainability Engineering

In this section, we summarize and classify the findings and requirements on explanations that we have identified in the previous sections and link them to approaches and open challenges in XAI and Explainability Engineering.

5.1 What Needs to Be Explained?

The GDPR mandates information be given to the data subject, the person to whom the processed data relates. This information takes the shape of explanations specifically with regard to automated decision-making. The legal requirements are linked to the data subject's data autonomy. It has been shown, with regard to this rationale, that the preferable interpretation of Article 15 as well as Article 22 (3) in conjunction with Recital 71 Sentence 4 GDPR is to assert rights to explanations not only before, but also after decisions affecting the data subject have occurred.

Data subjects can at any point in time request "meaningful information about the logic involved as well as the significance and the envisaged consequences of such processing for the data subject" under Art. 15 para. 1 lit. h GDPR, so this information has to be available. While there are some legal specifications as to what meaningful information means, there is still considerable legal uncertainty. While it is discussed in legal literature whether the obligation extends to disclosing the algorithm itself, its disclosure as such would not be beneficial to the users of AI-powered domestic robots and health wearables, be the user one with affinity towards (AI) technologies or not.

The GDPR rights to explanation are geared towards the data subject's understanding of a certain decision, which has an impact on its legal status or similar significance for the user. Thus, there is a certain threshold for the applicability of the legal requirement. However, it has been argued that the significance can also come from an additive impact, which can, for example, occur when using health wearables which consistently over-correct the user's physiotherapy positions. Furthermore following the principle of caution, which should guide practical decisions on implementing legal requirements, behaviour should be explained beyond these decisions with significant consequences.

In order to explain an automated decision, information must be provided on the functionality of the system, i.e. on the logic, the meaning, the intended consequences and the general functionality. It has been suggested that a decision tree should be shared with users as this allows for identifying the relevant factors for a decision, as well as to identify which changes in the input would enable a different branch in the tree, and thus a different decision. However, in modern AI algorithms such a tree does not exist and thus XAI methods aim to construct interpretable surrogate models. Others argue that it would suffice to reveal possible decision results. In any case, the logic involved must be explained by providing both general information on the functioning and information on the connections between the data processing and the decision made in each case. Single algorithmic decisions within the meaning of the GDPR can be explained using existing XAI techniques. However, there is still research needed to fully address this requirement. Additionally, for every use case, an interdisciplinary assessment of their potential and compliance with GDPR requirements is necessary, which is not feasible in practice. The AI Act implements comparable requirements for decisions based on output of certain high-risk AI systems mentioned in Art. 86 AI Act. In the area of physical care and physiotherapy, AI systems would, e.g., be considered high-risk if they use biometrics for emotion recognition. In any case, the GDPR right to explanation takes precedence for data processing. The legal regulations aim at fostering trust, without, however, linking specific requirements to it.

From research on human's trust in technology (cf. Section 4), we know that users develop mental models of AI systems and that incongruence between these models and actual experiences can undermine trust. Humans assess these systems based on their performance, safety, and alignment with their expectations. Thus, explanations that are given with the aim of increasing trust should provide information that helps to align the mental model of the user with the actual behaviour of the system, provides missing situational information, or justifies malfunctions or situations with poor performance. However, how to provide these types of explanations is still ongoing research. While there is already a lot of research on how to increase situational awareness without increasing the cognitive workload of human operators too much [62], identifying the missing information to provide tailored explanations requires modelling of the user's knowledge and thought process. This is a fascinating field of research that requires interdisciplinary collaboration between psychology that can help to identify models that are able to predict the user's needs, and different disciplines of computer science, i.e. user modelling, knowledge modelling, logics or AI. To identify causes for malfunctions, techniques from quality assurance can be investigated, e.g. runtime monitoring, anomaly detection and root cause analysis as exemplarily done in [9]. In the workshop, we identified explanation needs regarding the general functionality, usability and controllability of the system. This is also supported by current research on the impact of explainability on User Experience (UX) [20]. We also identified a need for transparency concerning performance, reliability and safety, including justifications for decisions and malfunctions, as supported by research on trust in technology. Due to the privacy-sensitive topic of health, additional questions regarding data processing and privacy need to be addressed by explanations. Brunotte et al. showed that users indeed like to get privacy explanations and that these can increase trust and privacy awareness of users [11]. There also exist many open challenges for cybersecurity research regarding AI systems as summarized by the ENISA report [26].

This summary shows that the need for explanations goes beyond explaining individual AI decisions based on the input data or testing the robustness of the learned model (local XAI methods) or how the model of the AI system works in general, e.g., which features are important for decisions (global XAI methods). While XAI methods help to understand and improve AI models and thus help to answer questions about the inner logic of the system, justify decisions, produce contrastive explanations that enable a certain controllability, and test the robustness and reliability of the learned models, we have to broaden the scope of explanations and (interdisciplinary) develop new solutions in order to provide information about

1. the data collection for AI decisions (Which data is collected, when, how and why?; What are the consequences for the data subjects? How can an understanding be reached while including all the legally required information? Which factors were considered when designing the data set, i.e. is it balanced, are relevant minorities/special cases included?).
2. the preprocessing of input data for AI decisions (How is the data obtained and processed, e.g., which sensors are used? Is the data filtered? Are the sensors and processing algorithms reliable?),
3. the post-processing of AI decisions (How are AI decisions used in the system?, How do they influence further (non-AI) algorithmic decisions?),
4. usage and reliability of the system (How to use the system?, How to achieve my goals with the system?, How reliable is the system?, Which measures ensure safety?).

5.2 How to Explain?

While the legal requirements only contain very broad requirements as to how to explain the data processing (see Art. 12 GDPR), the CJEU (27.02.2025- C-203/22, ECLI:EU:C:2025:117, para. 45) refers to the guidelines from the data protection working group suggesting to provide tangible examples. Those examples shall allow the data subject to really understand the potential impact of the automated decision system on themselves. The GDPR also advises the use of illustrative means, e.g. visual techniques to explain how a past decision was made. The explanations have to be given in a concise, transparent, intelligible and easily accessible form, using clear and plain language, in particular for any information addressed specifically to a child (Art. 12 para. 1, Recital 58). But it is not just children whose understanding is fostered by clear and plain language. Recital 58 Sentence 1 adds that the principle of transparency requires that any information addressed to the public or to the data subject be concise, easily accessible and easy to understand, and that clear and plain language and, additionally, where appropriate, visualisation be used. However this requirement poses considerable challenges for Explainability Engineering, as we have to find a good trade-off between simplification and meaningfulness.

When providing explanations to improve trust in AI systems, we have to be careful and aim for calibrated trust, i.e. a level of trust that is aligned with the capabilities of the AI system, rather than achieving overtrust where users place excessive faith in AI beyond its capabilities. This does not only require to give information about the AI's capabilities but also to design the explanations with user perceptions in mind to ensure that the tone and appearance of information does not mislead the users perceived trustworthiness of the system which leads us to the research challenge of tailoring explanations. This should also be considered when interpreting the GDPR's and AI Act's right to explanations.

5.3 Tailoring to Stakeholders and User Types

Our workshop results show that different stakeholders require different information in order to successfully fulfil their role-specific tasks with the AI system. *Service Providers* have to guarantee a certain level of performance and reliability, and thus require transparency with respect to those quality attributes. In case of malfunctions they need explanations about the cause and also actionable suggestions on how to solve the problem. In case of health wearables, possible *users* of the system are both the *physiotherapists* and the *patients*. The *physiotherapists* need to understand the system to decide in which cases the system can be beneficial and its limitations. Furthermore, they need to understand how the system works and how it will affect the patients in order to explain that to patients, and require detailed explanations for individual decisions to monitor the treatment and to answer questions from patients, who will most likely address their physiotherapists if they feel insecure with the device. The *patients* need a basic understanding of the functionality of the system to make an informed decision whether to use the system, how to use it and what to expect from it. The latter is especially important to calibrate trust and expectations to avoid frustration resulting from high expectations. Young patients, i.e. children, additionally need to understand what they can decide on their own and where to get help from an adult.

In our analysis of the GDPR, we found that this is partly reflected in the term "meaningful information" as this is a subjective term that needs to be specified for each person, and thus also stakeholder, individually. However, the GDPR only distinguishes between data controller(s) and data subject(s) without considering further relationships between stakeholders. Thus all stakeholders have to be mapped to these two legal positions, which are, however, not fixed, but stakeholders can switch between both roles or even have both. In cases of joint control of the data, several entities share the obligation to provide explanations.

If we consider the different stakeholders as different user types, the GDPR acknowledges specific needs and vulnerabilities of certain groups like children and requires adapted explanations that rely more on visual explanations like videos or cartoons that were made for young children. This is an example of well-defined requirements for user-specific explanations but limited to one user group. Although not explicitly stated in legal regulations, it is clear that we need to provide similar adjusted explanations for other user groups, and even individuals, as well. This is also acknowledged by the call of the EU Commission for user-specific explanations to increase trust in AI systems. One challenge that also needs to be addressed in future research then, is how to evaluate user-specific explanations. Here, we propose to foster transdisciplinary research together with HCI experts that already have experience with user-adaptive interfaces and neuroscientists that understand how humans perceive explanations.

When we consider the principle of transparency, i.e. that any information addressed to the public or to the data subject has to be easy to understand, it is clear that we also need to consider the prior knowledge of the addressees. However, this itself varies between individual users and probably needs to be learned with AI techniques. However, if we use AI techniques to explain AI systems, do we then need to explain the explaining AI system?

From trust research, we learned that explanations also need to be adapted over time to support an evolving trust relationship with technology that is designed for long-term use, e.g. home assistant robots or care robots. While initial explanations help to align the user's mental model with the system, over time explanations can be reduced. However, because user trust still relies on continued reliability, predictability, and performance, exceptional behaviour still requires an explanation to maintain the user's trust. Additionally, long-term use enables adaptation of the autonomous system to changing needs of the user, e.g. providing a greater range of assistance as the elderly user's capacity diminishes. However, this adaptation needs to be accompanied with explanations in order to align the user's mental model with the novel system behaviour and to explain the reasoning process that led to the adaptation, as this is based on user data. This allows a definition of meaningful information for the specific person rather than for an average group of envisioned users.

We have shown that explainability needs from different stakeholders are diverse and concern various aspects of the system which cannot fully be addressed by classical XAI approaches, but require transdisciplinary solutions (within computer science and beyond) and a new engineering discipline which we call Explainability Engineering [10] to elicit user- and context-specific explainability requirements and design methods for constructing interactive explanations that can adapt to users, address various aspects and provide insights on system behaviour that go beyond pure data processing. Explainability Engineers should then work with neuroscientists and legal scholars throughout the AI lifecycle in order to calibrate trust-inducement and fulfill legal requirements for meaningful explanations.

Acknowledgments. Authors in alphabetic order. This work was supported by the DFG under the project EXC 2050/1 (CeTI, project ID 390696704, as part of Germany's Excellence Strategy). M. Fairhurst also acknowledges the financial support by the Federal Ministry of Education and Research of Germany in the programme of "Souverän. Digital. Vernetzt.". Joint project 6G-life, project identification number: 16KISK002.

Disclosure of Interests. The authors have no competing interests to declare that are relevant to the content of this article.

References

1. A., S., Powles, J.: Meaningful information and the right to explanation. In: International Data Privacy law, vol. 7, pp. 233–242 (2017)
2. Article 29 Data Protection Working Party: Guidelines on automated individual decision-making and profiling for the purposes of Regulation 2016/679, wP251rev.01, Adopted on 3 October 2017 As last Revised and Adopted on 6 February 2018, pp. 1–30 (2018). https://ec.europa.eu/newsroom/article29/items/612053
3. Article 29 Data protection working party: guidelines on transparency under regulation 2016/679, wP251rev.01, Adopted on 3 October 2017, As last Revised and Adopted on 6 February 2018, pp. 1–30 (2018). https://ec.europa.eu/newsroom/article29/items/612053
4. Article 29 data protection working party: guidelines on transparency under regulation 2016/679, wp260rev.01, Adopted on 29 November 2017 As last Revised and Adopted on 11 April 2018, pp. 1–40 (2018). https://ec.europa.eu/newsroom/article29/items/622227/en
5. Asan, O., Bayrak, A.E., Choudhury, A., et al.: Artificial intelligence and human trust in healthcare: focus on clinicians. J. Med. Internet Res. **22**(6), e15154 (2020)
6. Bachmann, G.: §241 BGB. In: Saecker, F., Rixecker, R., Oetker, H., Limberg, B., Schubert, C. (eds.) Münchener Kommentar zum BGB, 9. Auflage (2022)
7. Benk, M., Kerstan, S., von Wangenheim, F., Ferrario, A.: Twenty-four years of empirical research on trust in AI: a bibliometric review of trends, overlooked issues, and future directions. AI & Society, pp. 1–24 (2024)
8. Berger-Walliser, G., Barton, Thomas Haapio, H.: From visualization to legal design: a collaborative and creative process. Am. Bus. Law J. **54**, 347–392 (2017)
9. Brito, L.C., Susto, G.A., Brito, J.N., Duarte, M.A.: An explainable artificial intelligence approach for unsupervised fault detection and diagnosis in rotating machinery. Mech. Syst. Signal Process. **163**, 108105 (2022)
10. Brunotte, W., Chazette, L., Klös, V., Speith, T.: Quo vadis, explainability?–A research roadmap for explainability engineering. In: Requirements Engineering : Foundation for Software Quality, pp. 26–32. Springer (2022). https://doi.org/10.1007/978-3-030-98464-9_3
11. Brunotte, W., Specht, A., Chazette, L., Schneider, K.: Privacy explanations – a means to end-user trust. J. Syst. Softw. **195**, 111545 (2023)
12. Bäcker, M.: Article 13 DSGVO. In: Kühling, Buchner (eds.) Datenschutz-Grundverordnung, Bundesdatenschutzgesetz: DS-GVO / BDSG, 4. Auflage (2024)
13. Calvaresi, D., Mualla, Y., Najjar, A., Galland, S., Schumacher, M.: Explainable multi-agent systems through blockchain technology. In: Calvaresi, D., Najjar, A., Schumacher, M., Främling, K. (eds.) EXTRAAMAS 2019. LNCS (LNAI), vol. 11763, pp. 41–58. Springer, Cham (2019). https://doi.org/10.1007/978-3-030-30391-4_3
14. Cheng, M., Yin, C., Zhang, J., Nazarian, S., Deshmukh, J., Bogdan, P.: A general trust framework for multi-agent systems. In: Proceedings of the 20th International Conference on Autonomous Agents and MultiAgent Systems, pp. 332–340 (2021)
15. Chiou, E.K., Lee, J.D.: Trusting automation: designing for responsivity and resilience. Hum. Factors **65**(1), 137–165 (2023)
16. Commission, E.: Building trust in human centric artificial intelligence. Communication from the Commission to the European Parliament, the Council, the European Economic and Social Committee and the Committee of the Regions (COM), vol. 168 (2020)

17. Dalby, L.: Article 1 GDPR. In: Spindler, G., Schuster, F., Kaesling, K. (eds.) Recht der elektronischen Medien, 5. Auflage, Bd. 1. C.H.Beck (2025)
18. Davis, F.D.: Perceived usefulness, perceived ease of use, and user acceptance of information technology. MIS Q. **13**, 319–340 (1989)
19. De Conca, S.: Between a rock and a hard place: Owners of smart speakers and joint control. SCRIPTed **17**, 238–268 (2020)
20. Deters, H., et al.: The x factor: On the relationship between user experience and explainability. In: Proceedings of the 13th Nordic Conference on Human-Computer Interaction, pp. 1–12 (2024)
21. Dhuliawala, S., Zouhar, V., El-Assady, M., Sachan, M.: A diachronic perspective on user trust in AI under uncertainty. arXiv preprint arXiv:2310.13544 (2023)
22. Dix, A.: Kommentierung zu Art. 15. In: Simitis, S., Hornung, G., Spiecker gen. Döhmann, I. (eds.) Datenschutzrecht DS-GVO, BDSG, 2. Auflage (2025)
23. Dorton, S.L., Stanley, J.C.: Minding the gap: tools for trust engineering of artificial intelligence. Ergon. Des. **33**, 142–147 (2024)
24. Durante, M.: What is the model of trust for multi-agent systems? whether or not e-trust applies to autonomous agents. Knowl. Technol. Policy **23**, 347–366 (2010)
25. European Data Protection Board: Guidelines 07/2020 on the concepts of controller and processor in the GDPR, adopted on 02 September 2020, pp. 1–48 (2020)
26. European union agency for cybersecurity: artificial intelligence and cybersecurity research. In: Pascu, C., Barros Lourenco, M. (eds.) – ENISA research and innovation Brief (2023). https://doi.org/10.2824/808362
27. Ferrario, A., Loi, M.: How explainability contributes to trust in AI. In: Proceedings of the 2022 ACM Conference on Fairness, Accountability, and Transparency, pp. 1457–1466 (2022)
28. Finck, M.: Cobwebs of control: the two imaginations of the data controller in EU law. In: International Data Privacy Law, vol. 11 (2021)
29. Floessel, P., et al.: Evaluating user perceptions of a vibrotactile feedback system in trunk stabilization exercises: a feasibility study. Sensors **24**(4), 1134 (2024)
30. Fresz, B., Dubovitskaya, E., Brajovic, D., Huber, M.F., Horz, C.: How should AI decisions be explained? Requirements for explanations from the perspective of european law. In: Proceedings of the AAAI/ACM Conference on AI, Ethics, and Society, vol. 7, pp. 438–450 (2024)
31. Gefen, D.: E-commerce: the role of familiarity and trust. Omega **28**(6), 725–737 (2000)
32. Glikson, E., Woolley, A.: Human trust in artificial intelligence review
33. Grochowski, M., Jablonowska, A., Lagioia, F., Sartor, G.: Algorithmic transparency and explainability for EU consumer protection: unwrapping the regulatory premises. In: Critical Analysis of Law (CAL), vol. 8, pp. 43–63 (2021)
34. Haapio, H., Passera, S.: Transforming contracts from legal rules to user - centered communication tools: a human-information interaction challenge. In: Communication Design Quarterly, vol. 1 (2013)
35. He, X., Zheng, X., Ding, H.: Existing barriers faced by and future design recommendations for direct-to-consumer health care artificial intelligence apps: Scoping review. J. Med. Internet Res. **25**, e50342 (2023)
36. Horváth: Artikel 22 DS-GVO. In: Spindler, G., Schuster, F., Kaesling, K. (eds.) Recht der elektronischen Medien 5. Aufl., Bd. 1. C.H.Beck (2025)
37. Information Commissioner's Office of the UK: Age appropriate design: a code of practice for online services (2020)

38. Kim, M., Kim, S., Kim, J., Song, T.J., Kim, Y.: Do stakeholder needs differ?-Designing stakeholder-tailored explainable artificial intelligence (XAI) interfaces. Int. J. Hum Comput Stud. **181**, 103160 (2024)
39. Kumkar, L., Roth-Isigkeit, D.: Erklärungspflichten bei automatisierten Datenverarbeitungen nach der DSGVO. In: JuristenZeitung, vol. 75, pp. 277–286 (2020)
40. Lee, J.D., See, K.A.: Trust in automation: designing for appropriate reliance. Hum. Factors **46**(1), 50–80 (2004)
41. Lukyanenko, R., Maass, W., Storey, V.C.: Trust in artificial intelligence: from a foundational trust framework to emerging research opportunities. Electron. Mark. **32**(4), 1993–2020 (2022)
42. Markus, A.F., Kors, J.A., Rijnbeek, P.R.: The role of explainability in creating trustworthy artificial intelligence for health care: a comprehensive survey of the terminology, design choices, and evaluation strategies. J. Biomed. Inform. **113**, 103655 (2021)
43. Martini, M.: Artikel 22 DS-GVO. In: Paal, B., Pauly, D. (eds.) DS-GVO | BDSG Kommentar, 3. Aufl. (2022)
44. Mayer, R.C., Davis, J.H., Schoorman, F.D.: An integrative model of organizational trust. Acad. Manag. Rev. **20**(3), 709–734 (1995)
45. Mcknight, D.H., Carter, M., Thatcher, J.B., Clay, P.F.: Trust in a specific technology: an investigation of its components and measures. ACM Trans. Manage. Inf. Syst. (TMIS) **2**(2), 1–25 (2011)
46. McParlin, Z., Cerritelli, F., Friston, K.J., Esteves, J.E.: Therapeutic alliance as active inference: the role of therapeutic touch and synchrony. Front. Psychol. **13**, 783694 (2022)
47. Meyer, J., Lee, J.D.: Trust, Reliance, and Compliance. In: The Oxford Handbook of Cognitive Engineering, pp. 109–124 (2013)
48. Miciak, M., Mayan, M., Brown, C., Joyce, A.S., Gross, D.P.: A framework for establishing connections in physiotherapy practice. Physiother. Theory Pract. **35**(1), 40–56 (2019)
49. Nasarian, E., Alizadehsani, R., Acharya, U.R., Tsui, K.L.: Designing interpretable ml system to enhance trust in healthcare: a systematic review to proposed responsible clinician-AI-collaboration framework. Inf. Fus. **108**, 102412 (2024)
50. Nooteboom, B.: Trust: forms, foundations, functions, failures and figures. Edward Elgar Publishing (2002)
51. Nundy, S., Montgomery, T., Wachter, R.M.: Promoting trust between patients and physicians in the era of artificial intelligence. JAMA **322**(6), 497–498 (2019)
52. Papagni, G., Koeszegi, S.: Understandable and trustworthy explainable robots: a sensemaking perspective. Paladyn, J. Behav. Robot. **12**(1), 13–30 (2020)
53. Ryu, J., Banthin, D.C., Gu, X.: Modeling therapeutic alliance in the age of telepsychiatry. Trends Cogn. Sci. **25**(1), 5–8 (2021)
54. Schmidt-Wudy, F.: Art. 15 DS- GVO. In: Wolff, Brink, v. Ungern-Sternberg (eds.) BeckOK Datenschutzrecht, 50. Edition (2024). Stand: 01.11.2024
55. Schuetz, S., Kuai, L., Lacity, M.C., Steelman, Z.: A qualitative systematic review of trust in technology. J. Inf. Technol. **40**(1), 55–76 (2025)
56. Sesing, A.: Grenzen systemischer Transparenz bei automatisierter Datenverarbeitung. In: MMR Zeitschrift für IT-Recht und Recht der Digitalisierung, pp. 288–292 (2021)
57. Shan, Y., Ji, M., Xie, W., Lam, K.Y., Chow, C.Y.: Public trust in artificial intelligence applications in mental health care: topic modeling analysis. JMIR Hum. Factors **9**(4), e38799 (2022)

58. Shin, D., Park, Y.J.: Role of fairness, accountability, and transparency in algorithmic affordance. Comput. Hum. Behav. **98**, 277–284 (2019)
59. Sisk, B.A., Antes, A.L., Burrous, S., DuBois, J.M.: Parental attitudes toward artificial intelligence-driven precision medicine technologies in pediatric healthcare. Children **7**(9), 145 (2020)
60. Topol, E.J.: High-performance medicine: the convergence of human and artificial intelligence. Nat. Med. **25**(1), 44–56 (2019)
61. Venkatesh, V., Morris, M.G.: Why don't men ever stop to ask for directions? Gender, social influence, and their role in technology acceptance and usage behavior. MIS Q. **24**, 115–139 (2000)
62. Vered, M., Howe, P., Miller, T., Sonenberg, L., Velloso, E.: Demand-driven transparency for monitoring intelligent agents. IEEE Trans. Hum. Mach. Syst. **50**(3), 264–275 (2020)
63. Wachter, S., Mittelstadt, B., Floridi, L.: Why a right to explanation of automated decision-making does not exist in the general data protection regulation. Int. Data Priv. Law **7**(2), pp. 76–99 (2017)
64. Wong, A.K.C., Lee, J.H.T., Zhao, Y., Lu, Q., Yang, S., Hui, V.C.C.: Exploring older adults' perspectives and acceptance of AI-driven health technologies: Qualitative study. JMIR Aging **8**, e66778 (2025)

Open Access This chapter is licensed under the terms of the Creative Commons Attribution 4.0 International License (http://creativecommons.org/licenses/by/4.0/), which permits use, sharing, adaptation, distribution and reproduction in any medium or format, as long as you give appropriate credit to the original author(s) and the source, provide a link to the Creative Commons license and indicate if changes were made.

The images or other third party material in this chapter are included in the chapter's Creative Commons license, unless indicated otherwise in a credit line to the material. If material is not included in the chapter's Creative Commons license and your intended use is not permitted by statutory regulation or exceeds the permitted use, you will need to obtain permission directly from the copyright holder.

Explainable Fairness in Mortgage Lending

Golnoosh Babaei[1(✉)], Paolo Giudici[1], and Lunshuai Wu[2]

[1] University of Pavia, Pavia, Italy
{golnoosh.babaei,paolo.giudici}@unipv.it
[2] Business School, Ningbo University, Ningbo, China

Abstract. In this paper we employ explainable artificial intelligence methods to identify unfairness in mortgage lending. Our aim is to reproduce credit lending decisions via explainable machine learning models and, then, assess whether such decisions are fair, particularly in terms of race. To this end, the paper employs data from New York state, deriving from the Home Mortgage Disclosure Act (HMDA). We contribute to the existing literature in two main ways. First, we assess fairness marginally, by means of parity measures based on the recently proposed S.A.F.E. AI metrics; but also conditionally, comparing the explanations in different population groups. Second, we extend the Shapley value approach measuring the contribution of each explanatory variable not to the predicted values but to precision and recall, thereby better taking into account data unbalancedness.

Our empirical findings indicate the presence of racial disparities in loan approval rates. This underscores the need for increased efforts and targeted interventions to promote fair and equitable lending practices.

Keywords: Credit Lending · SAFE AI Metrics · Precision and Recall · Responsible AI

1 Introduction

In recent years, with the development of financial technologies, ensuring fairness and transparency within the financial system has become an urgent and critical issue. A model is considered as a fair model if it performs equally across the observations in different specific demographic groups such as male/female, black/white and etc. Loan approval, as a core component of financial services, directly affects both individuals' and enterprises' financing capabilities and development opportunities. Discrimination in any form during the loan approval process not only harms the interests of affected groups, but can also lead to social inequality and imbalanced economic development.

This study is dedicated to analyzing data related to loan approval rates with the aim of thoroughly evaluating the critical role of these rates in community service. Specifically, this research focuses on identifying the presence and extent of racial discrimination in the loan approval process, an issue that has long been contentious within the financial sector. By assessing whether financial institutions equitably meet the loan needs of community residents, we aim to uncover potential discriminatory lending practices that disproportionately affect certain racial groups.

The topic of assessing fair credit lending has been examined in recent literature. For example, [11] examined the racial controversy in mortgage lending since the enactment of the Home Mortgage Disclosure Act (HMDA). Although loan data have been collected since 1977, lenders were not required to report applicant characteristics until 1990. The data reveal significant disparities in loan rejection rates among races, suggesting potential discriminatory practices. Despite a supplementary survey by the Federal Reserve Bank of Boston, most banks still received satisfactory compliance ratings, with scant direct evidence of discriminatory practices, highlighting the complexity of detecting and addressing potential discrimination.

[2] explored policy issues concerning racial and ethnic differences in home loan rejection rates, noting that the pronounced racial disparities in the loan market have put pressure on regulatory agencies. Given that these disparities are often attributed to discrimination, there is a growing demand of resolving this issue. However, not all causes of these disparities are fully understood and policymakers must evaluate the costs and benefits of various interventions under incomplete information to reduce unfairness without imposing unnecessary burdens on the market.

[12] investigated the role of race in home loans and the sensitivity of racial estimates to changes in model specifications. By comparing parameter estimates from statistical models used by the Federal Reserve Bank of Boston, which utilized subsets of data corresponding to FDIC regulators and alternative variants reflecting information from loan application reviews, the study found that estimates of racial effects are highly sensitive to model assumptions; minor modifications can eliminate the racial effect. Empirical results suggest that statistical models that assess the impact of race on mortgage lending may not provide reliable bias information, underscoring the importance of model construction and selection to avoid misleading policy conclusions. [9] investigated the adverse impact of neighborhood racial composition on mortgage lending, even after controlling for income, housing conditions, and related neighborhood and housing characteristics. Industry representatives argued that the racial distribution of mortgages was an unintended consequence of profit-driven lending activities. However, Gotham's analysis of 1991 Home Mortgage Disclosure Act (HMDA) data for the Kansas City metropolitan area showed that minority applicants faced higher rejection rates than whites, including high-income minorities being rejected at similar or even higher rates compared to low-income whites, indicating that race played a crucial role in loan approval decisions independent of financial status.

[6] examined racial dynamics during the peak of subprime mortgage lending, using HMDA data and regression models to illustrate home purchase loans in 2006. The findings indicate that African Americans and Latinos were more

likely to receive subprime loans, particularly higher-income minorities, supporting the view that affluent minorities were targeted as subprime loan recipients. The study also revealed systematic issues within financial markets, showing that minorities could not leverage high social status in the same way as whites. [20] specifically reviewed the racial and ethnic disparities in the loan approval process in Mississippi, emphasizing how institutional practices controlled by privileged groups perpetuated discriminatory behaviors, particularly against African Americans, hindering their ability to accumulate wealth through home ownership.

To summarise the available literature, Table 1 highlights the research background and the results from thirteen papers which have discussed a problem similar to ours. In this paper, we will utilize Random Forest (RF), Gradient Boosting Trees (GBT), as well as Stacked Ensemble Model (SEM) and Voting Ensemble Model (VEM), to identify the drivers of loan decisions. We will then extend the Sustainable, Accurate, Fair, and Explainable (SAFE) metrics framework proposed by [3] to conduct a comprehensive quantitative assessment of loan decisions.

The SAFE framework encompasses four core metrics: Accuracy, Robustness, Explainability, and Fairness, collectively referred to as the Rank Graduation Box (RGB), specifically Rank Graduation Accuracy (RGA), Rank Graduation Robustness (RGR), Rank Graduation Explainability (RGE), and Rank Graduation Fairness (RGF). The original contribution of this paper is the extension of the S.A.F.E. framework to ensemble models such as SEM and VEM, and their application to assess loan approval decisions, where they have not yet been applied. Through the application of the S.A.F.E. metrics, we also shed new light on the assessment of racial biases in loan approval.

The remainder of this paper is organized as follows: Sect. 2 presents the data we consider; Sect. 3 introduces the proposed approach; Sect. 4 discusses the application of proposal. Finally, Sect. 5 concludes the paper.

2 Data

The data utilized in this study are sourced from the Home Mortgage Disclosure Act (HMDA), widely recognized as the most comprehensive publicly available resource in the USA mortgage market. Enacted by the U.S. Congress in 1975 and implemented through Regulation C, HMDA mandates that numerous financial institutions collect, report, and publicly disclose detailed information about individual mortgage loans. These data serve several critical purposes. For community assessment, they provide valuable insight into whether lenders are adequately serving the housing needs of their communities. With respect to policy development, public officials rely on these data to inform policy decisions and develop initiatives aimed at fostering a fair and effective housing market. With regard to revealing lending patterns, the data help identify potential discriminatory lending practices, promoting more equitable financial practices.

In this dataset, there are 157171 observations among which 70% are utilized for training and the rest for testing the models explained in Sect. 3. In our study,

Table 1. Research Background

No.	Citation	Summary	Conclusion
1	[14] (1994)	The impact of race on home mortgage lending decisions had been a complex and controversial issue requiring careful empirical analysis.	Multiple case studies needed to establish robust evidence concerning the existence and nature of discrimination
2	[11] (1994)	Since the enactment of the Home Mortgage Disclosure Act (HMDA), the role of race in mortgage lending had sparked controversy.	Data revealed significant racial disparities in loan outcomes, with limited direct evidence of discriminatory practices, highlighting the complexity of detecting and addressing potential discrimination
3	[2] (1995)	Pronounced racial and ethnic differences in loan rejection rates had put pressure on regulatory agencies.	Policymakers had to evaluate the costs and benefits of various interventions under incomplete information
4	[18] (1996)	The paper explored the theoretical foundations and limitations of using racial differences in loan defaults as an indicator of mortgage lending discrimination.	Tests based on the loan approval process should have been prioritized as the primary method for assessing whether mortgage lending discrimination existed
5	[12] (1997)	The study investigated the role of race in home loans and the sensitivity of racial estimates to changes in model specifications.	Estimates of racial effects had been highly sensitive to model assumptions; minor modifications could eliminate the racial effect
6	[19] (1997)	The research analyzed the impact of sample selection on mortgage default propensity using simulation methods.	Previous criticisms of default-based discrimination tests confirmed, indicating that such tests might produce biases due to omitted variables
7	[9] (1998)	The adverse impact of neighborhood racial composition on mortgage lending had been evident, even after controlling for income, housing conditions, and related characteristics.	Minority applicants faced higher rejection rates than whites, including high-income minorities being rejected at similar or even higher rates compared to low-income whites
8	[16] (2000)	The discussion on racial discrimination in mortgage markets expanded by introducing loan performance metrics such as default rates and administrative costs.	Minorities experienced higher administrative costs and default rates relative to whites, suggesting the presence of credit market discrimination

(*continued*)

Table 1. (*continued*)

No.	Citation	Summary	Conclusion
9	[6] (2013)	Racial dynamics during the peak of subprime mortgage lending had been examined.	African Americans and Latinos were more likely to receive subprime loans, especially higher-income minorities, supporting the view that affluent minorities were targeted as subprime loan recipients
10	[17] (2019)	The importance of home ownership in the American Dream and how government policies supported this through subsidies and housing finance systems had been highlighted.	Substantial market reforms were necessary to address the persistent wealth gap caused by cumulative disadvantages of race and racism
11	[8] (2020)	The interaction effect of gender and ethnicity in loan approval had been investigated through field experiment data from Bolivia.	Microcredit policies targeting women should consider social expectations and structural barriers to financial inclusion
12	[20] (2023)	Racial and ethnic disparities in the loan approval process in Mississippi had been reviewed.	Institutional practices perpetuated discriminatory behaviors against African Americans, hindering their ability to accumulate wealth through home ownership
13	[4] (2023)	Racial disparities in the auto loan market documented lower approval rates for black and Hispanic applicants even after controlling for creditworthiness.	Lower approval rates found for black and Hispanic applicants, leading to approximately 80,000 fewer minority loans annually, with lower default rates but higher interest rates, indicating racial bias

the description of variables can be seen from Table 2. The response variable 'action_taken' indicates whether a loan application was approved or declined, while control and explanatory variables capture demographic, economic, and geographic information about the applicants and their environments. Binary variables help categorize specific attributes of the borrower or the loan, whereas continuous variables offer detailed insights into income levels and loan amounts.

Figure 1 illustrates that there are differences in the distribution of income across various combinations of race and gender. The median and interquartile range of income for White and Black/African American women and men may differ, suggesting that both gender and race could have an impact on income levels. The central tendency of income for different groups is represented by

Table 2. Summary of Variables

Variable	Description	Values
Response Variable		
action_taken	Loan approval outcome	1 = declined, 0 = approved
Control Variable		
race_1	First Applicant's race	1 = Black/African American, 0 = White
Binary Variables		
gender	Gender of the applicant	1 = male, 0 = female
loan_purpose	Purpose of seeking the loan	1 = refinancing, 0 = home purchase
lien_status	Status of the lien securing the loan	1 = first lien, 0 = subordinate lien
loan_type	Type of loan insurance	1 = FHA insured, 0 = GSE insured
Continuous Variables		
log(income)	Natural logarithm of applicant's gross annual income	Continuous
log(loan)	Natural logarithm of loan amount	Continuous

Note: FHA = Federal Housing Administration; GSE = Government-sponsored enterprise

the median line (middle line) and mean (white box) within the box plot. If the median or mean of a particular group is significantly higher or lower than those of other groups, it may indicate that the group holds an advantage or disadvantage in terms of income. The scatter plots illustrating the relationship between income and loan amount reveal a positive correlation, indicating that individuals with higher incomes tend to receive larger loan amounts. In terms of group trends, dashed trend lines depict the linear relationship between income and loan amount for each group. The slope and position of these trend lines provide additional insights into the loan behavior of different groups.

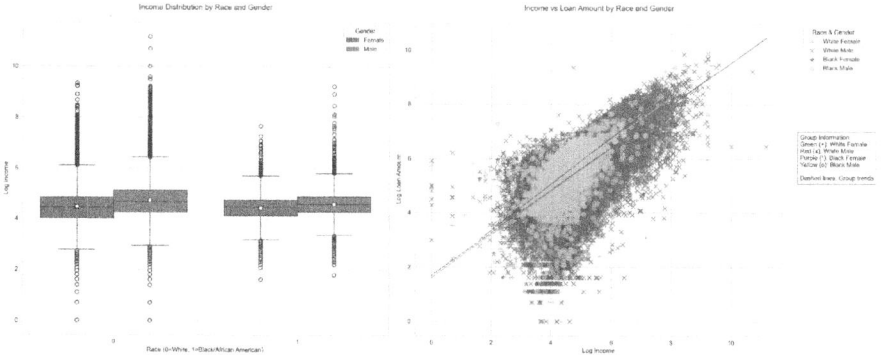

Fig. 1. Loan amount by Race and Gender

Figure 2 represents the rejection rates for males and females with different race categories. As it can be seen, the rejection rate for the black race group is higher for both male and female categories. This stresses the importance of the fairness evaluation for the decision making models based on this dataset.

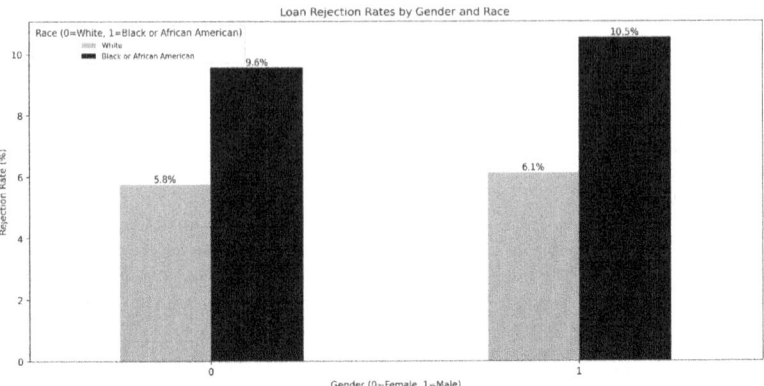

Fig. 2. Rejection Rates

3 Methods

3.1 Ensemble Models

In the context of credit rating prediction, ensemble tree models such as random forests and gradient boosting have demonstrated a good performance, both in accuracy and in detecting explainability and fairness (see e.g. [5]). Other ensemble techniques, which average different types of models, such as SEM and VEM, have not yet been employed, and we propose to do so in this paper. We now briefly recall, in a comparative manner, the four considered machine learning models. The Random Forest (RF) model is an average of tree models. It aggregates predictions from all trees via majority voting to determine the final class. A Gradient Boosting Tree (GBT) is also an average of tree models. Differently from Random Forest, this approach iteratively adds new models to gradually enhance the performance of the existing model. In each iteration, a new tree is trained to minimize the residuals of the prediction from the previous tree. A Stacked Ensemble Model (SEM) is an ensemble learning approach that combines multiple base learners of different types and uses a meta-estimator to integrate their predictions, effectively leveraging the strengths of diverse models to enhance overall performance. Base learners are initially trained to generate predictions on validation sets, which are then used as input features for training the meta-estimator.

In the implementation of this paper, we use two base learners: Random Forest and Gradient Boosting Trees. As the final estimator, we employ the Logistic Regression model which takes in input the predictions from the base learners and produces in output the final prediction.

A Voting Classifier Ensemble Model (VEM) is an ensemble learning method that combines multiple classifiers and makes final decisions based on their aggregated predictions. Voting Classifiers are available in two forms: hard voting, where the final prediction is based on the majority class, and soft voting, which averages the probability estimates from all classifiers. In this paper, we employ soft voting, wherein the final class prediction is determined by calculating the weighted average of the probability estimates provided by each classifier for each class. In the implementation of this paper, we use two base machine learning models also for VEM: Random Forest and Gradient Boosting Trees.

3.2 SAFE Metrics

To assess the reliability and the fairness of the credit decisions, reproduced in terms of Random Forests, Gradient Boosting, SEM and VEM, we employ the recently proposed Rank Graduation Box approach (RGB, [3]), which has introduced a suite of metrics aimed to measure the Sustainability, Accuracy, Fairness, and Explainability (S.A.F.E.) of any machine learning output.

In this paper, we aim to extend the metrics to ensemble machine learning models, with the final aim of evaluating the fairness of credit acceptance decisions, conditionally on different personal characteristics. To this end, we will provide a reformulation of the RGB metrics but before, we provide a brief definition of them.

Let Y be a statistical variable to be predicted. In the machine leaning context, we observe n observations of Y in a test set, which will be employed to assess whether the predictions for the same observations, obtained from a machine learning model trained on a set of m observations, are Sustainable, Accurate, Fair and Explainable. To this aim, the observed Y in the test set can be employed to build their Lorenz curve L, arranging the Y values in a non-decreasing sense. For $i = 1, \ldots, n$, the Lorenz curve ([15]) can be defined by the pairs: $(i/n, \sum_{j=1}^{i} y_{r_j}/(n\bar{y}))$, where r_j indicates the non-decreasing ranks of Y and $\bar{y}$ indicates the mean of Y. The same Y values can also be used to build the dual Lorenz curve, L'_Y, ordering the Y values in a non-increasing sense. For $i = 1, \ldots, n$, the dual Lorenz curve can be defined by the pairs: $(i/n, \sum_{j=1}^{i} y_{r_{n+1-j}}/(n\bar{y}))$, where r_{n+1-j} indicates the non-increasing ranks of Y. Now considering the predicted values for the Y values which are obtained from a machine learning model, we can denote them by Y^*. Let r_i^*, for $i = 1, \ldots, n$, indicate the non-decreasing ranks of Y^*. To measure the divergence between Y and Y^*, with a function which is based on the data and model independence, [7] proposes to calculate a concordance curve $C = C(Y, Y^*)$ ordering the Y values not in terms of their ranks, but with respect to r_i^*, the ranks of the Y^* values. More formally, for $i = 1, \ldots, n$, a concordance curve is defined by the pairs: $(i/n, \sum_{j=1}^{i} y_{r_j^*}/(n\bar{y}))$, where r_i^* indicates the non-decreasing ranks of Y^*.

Figure 3 displays the concordance curve of Y^*, along with the Lorenz curve and the dual Lorenz curve of Y. Note that the area between L'_Y and L_Y is the Lorenz Zonoid, equivalent to the Gini coefficient when the Y variable is unidimensional.

Note that, when $r_i^* = r_i$, for all $i = 1, \ldots, n$, the concordance curve coincides with the Lorenz curve; when $r_i^* = r_{n+1-i}$, for all $i = 1, \ldots, n$, the concordance curve coincides with the dual Lorenz curve. In general, the concordance curve is lower than L'_Y and greater than L_Y, by construction. Furthermore, $RGA = 0$

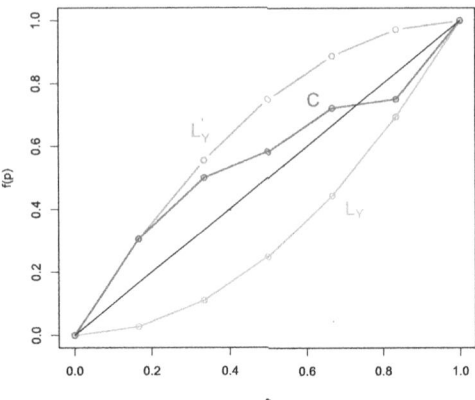

Fig. 3. The Lorenz Curve L_Y, the dual Lorenz Curve L'_Y, and the concordance curve C.

when $C = L_Y$ and is restricted within the range $0 \leq RGA \leq 1$. These results indicate that RGA can be interpreted as a divergence between Y and Y^*.

These properties have led [7] to introduce a Rank Graduation Accuracy measure (RGA), defined by the area between the L'_Y and the C curve, divided by the area of the Lorenz Zonoid. They also show that RGA is equivalent to the well-known Area Under the Curve (AUC), when Y is binary, with the advantage that RGA can be calculated in a similar way and also when Y is ordinal or continuous. This is possible essentially by replacing the thresholds that originate the coordinates of the ROC Curve (True Negatives and False Positives) with the observed (ordered) Y values.

[3] extended the construction behind RGA to different types of comparison between pairs of variables that arise from the assessment of machine learning models. In summary: the comparison between the predicted Y^* and the predicted Y^* under data perturbations lead to a Rank Graduation Robustness (RGR) measure, which can be employed to assess Sustainability of AI, particularly under cyber attacks; the comparison between the predicted Y^* and the predicted $Y*$, when one or more explanatory variables are eliminated from a machine learning model lead to a Rank Graduation Explainability (RGE) measure, which can be employed to assess the interpretability of the AI output; the comparison between the predicted Y^* conditionally and unconditionally to a protected attribute, such as gender or race, lead to a Rank Graduation Fairness (RGF) measure, which can be employed to assess the degree of discrimination of AI. RGF measures the effect of removing the protected variable on the model's predictions.

All these measures can be interpreted as divergence measures of a statistical variable Y^* from a "reference" variable Y, and lead to the general "Rank Graduation" (RG) divergence, defined as:

$$RG(Y^*, Y) = \frac{\sum_{i=1}^{n} \left\{ \frac{1}{n\bar{y}} \left(\sum_{j=1}^{i} y_{n+1-j} - \sum_{j=1}^{i} y_{r_j^*} \right) \right\}}{\sum_{i=1}^{n} \left\{ \frac{1}{n\bar{y}} \left(\sum_{j=1}^{i} y_{n+1-j} - \sum_{j=1}^{i} y_j \right) \right\}} \quad (1)$$

We now reformulate the RG divergence to improve its interpretation and, in particular, to assess fairness conditionally on the different characteristics of the loan applicants. To this end, we can arrange the numerator of (1) with the coordinates of the Lorenz Curve. Recalling that

$$Gini(Y) = \sum_{i=1}^{n} \left\{ \frac{1}{n\bar{y}} \left(\sum_{j=1}^{i} y_{n+1-j} - \sum_{j=1}^{i} y_j \right) \right\},$$

we obtain that:

$$RG(Y^*, Y) = \frac{Gini(Y) - \sum_{i=1}^{n} \left\{ \sum_{j=1}^{i} y_j - \sum_{j=1}^{i} y_{r_j^*} \right\}}{Gini(Y)}. \quad (2)$$

The expression in (2) is the main theoretical result of this paper. When assessing predictive accuracy, the divergence of RG can be interpreted as the percentage of the Gini inequality present in the Y observations to be predicted "explained" by a machine learning model that produces predictions $Y*$. The "best" model leads to a concordance curve that coincides with the Lorenz curve: in this case $RG(Y^*, Y) = 1$, it means that the model explains all the inequality of Y. The "worst" model leads to a concordance curve that coincides with the Dual Lorenz curve: in this case $RG(Y^*, Y) = 0$, meaning that the model explains nothing of the inequality of Y.

A similar reasoning can be carried out when we assess explainability, fairness or sustainability. In the case of explainability, which will be the most important focus of this paper, the divergence in (2) indicates the percentage of inequality that is lost when a explanatory variable is removed from the predictor set: the higher the RG divergence, the more important (explainable) is that variable. Note that (2) can be applied to all types of Y variables, including continuous ones. In this case, the accuracy measurement most employed are based on the Euclidean distance between Y and Y^*, leading to the well-known mean squared error of the predictions:

$$RMSE(Y^*, Y) = \sum_{i=1}^{n} (y_i - y_i^*)^2 \quad (3)$$

To help interpret RMSE, which is not normalized, an often employed quantity is the percentage of variability of Y explained by the variability of the predictions Y^* which, in analogy with regression model fitting, is called R^2:

$$R^2(Y^*, Y) = \frac{\sum_{i=1}^n (y_i - \bar{y})^2 - \sum_{i=1}^n (y_i - y_i^*)^2}{\sum_{i=1}^n (y_i - \bar{y})^2} \quad (4)$$

Comparing 4 with 2, and recalling that $Var(Y) = \sum_{i=1}^n (y_i - \bar{y})^2$, the analogy is clear: RG and R^2 describe, respectively, the percentage of "true" inequality or variability that is maintained when Y is replaced with Y^*. In the case of explainability, both indicate how much information is lost when a predictor is eliminated: in terms of variability (R^2) or inequality (RG). Both measures have advantages and disadvantages. The RG divergence is applicable to different types of variables: binary, ordinal or continuous (albeit non-negative). The R^2 can be calculated for all types of continuous response variables, including those defined on negative values.

We remark that this similarity is not surprising, and it extends the well-known measurement of the dispersion of a statistical distribution, which can be measured either in terms of the mean deviation from the mean or in terms of the mean difference between its observations.

The former setting leads to the coefficient of variation, a scale invariant measure that summarises with a scalar value the variability of a statistical distribution in terms of the mean distances from the mean, normalised by the mean itself:

$$CV(Y) = \frac{\sigma}{|m|}, \quad (5)$$

where σ and m are the standard deviation and mean, respectively, of a statistical distribution Y. The latter setting leads to the Gini index, a scale invariant measure that summarizes with a scalar value the inequality of a statistical distribution in terms of the mean difference between its values, normalized by their mean:

$$G(Y) = \frac{1}{2m} \int\int |x - y| \mu(dx)\mu(dy). \quad (6)$$

where m is the mean of a statistical distribution Y supported over $[0, \infty)$.

While the coefficient of variation is well defined for every distribution that has non-null mean, the Gini index requires μ to be supported only on the positive half-line in order to attain a value between 0 and 1. On the other hand, the Gini index is easier to interpret than the coefficient of variation: it is always between 0 and 1, where 0 represents a status of perfect equality, while 1 represents the maximum inequality.

4 Empirical Analysis

Initially, we use logistic regression to assess unfairness in loan approvals. Table 3 presents the results of two logistic regression models, one without including the control variable 'race_1'(race), and the other incorporating race as a control variable.

From Table 3, we can observe several key insights regarding the overall performance of logistic regression models with and without the control variable 'race_1'. In particular, Table 3 shows that all variables are significant, and that the sign and values of the regression coefficients of the two models including and excluding 'race_1', are very similar.

Table 3. Logistic Regression Results Comparison

Without Control Variable					With Control Variable				
Var	coef	std	z	P	[CI]	Var	coef	std	z	P	[CI]
const	−3.6488***	0.082	−44.742	0.000	[−3.809, −3.489]	const	−3.7205***	0.082	−45.434	0.000	[−3.881, −3.560]
v1	0.0586***	0.022	2.610	0.009	[0.015,0.103]	v1	0.0857***	0.023	3.791	0.000	[0.041,0.130]
v2	1.0372***	0.021	48.604	0.000	[0.995,1.079]	v2	1.0255***	0.021	47.975	0.000	[0.984,1.067]
v3	0.3801***	0.080	4.770	0.000	[0.224,0.536]	v3	0.4088***	0.080	5.124	0.000	[0.252,0.565]
v4	0.4530***	0.027	17.070	0.000	[0.401,0.505]	v4	0.4102***	0.027	15.281	0.000	[0.358,0.463]
v5	−0.0962***	0.015	−6.274	0.000	[−0.126,−0.066]	v5	−0.0796***	0.015	−5.166	0.000	[−0.110,−0.049]
v6	0.1267***	0.016	7.963	0.000	[0.095,0.158]	v6	0.1008***	0.016	6.293	0.000	[0.069,0.132]
						v7	0.4140***	0.034	12.354	0.000	[0.348,0.480]

Notes:
1. Significance levels: ***p<0.01, **p<0.05, *p<0.1
2. v1: gender, v2: loan_purpose, v3: loan_type, v4: lien_status
3. v5: log(income), v6: log(loan)
4. v7: race_1 (control variable only)
5. [CI] represents the 95% confidence interval
6. P values less than 0.001 are reported as 0.000

We then fit four different machine learning models: RF, GBT, SEM and VEM, using the same train/test split. For each model, we calculate the S.A.F.E. metrics and, in particular, the RGF metric to assess fairness with respect to race and gender. The results, in terms of RGA, RGR and RGF, are reported in Table 4.

Table 4. SAFE metrics: RGA, RGR, RGF

Model	RGA	RGR	RGF(Gender)	RGF(Race)
RF	0.628	0.564	0.922	0.927
GBT	0.682	0.503	1.000	0.998
SEM	0.681	0.520	0.989	0.990
VEM	0.662	0.504	0.956	0.959

Table 4 shows that the GBT model is the most accurate, followed by SEM, VEM and RF. All accuracies are not very high, reflecting the difficulty in predicting with a machine learning model so many credit decisions, which often have a strong subjective component.

Concerning fairness, note that all models, and especially GBT, indicate a high level of fairness with the RGF metric always greater than 90%. This result is not aligned with previous empirical findings on the same data, discussed in the literature review Section, which indicate racial discrimination. To better understand whether credit decisions are fair with respect to race, we now follow the standard parity approach (see e.g. [13]), comparing the S.A.F.E: metrics across the protected variable. In practice, this means that we have run the four considered machine learning models separately in two population groups: a protected group (Black=African American) and a non-protected group (White = White American). We can compare the values of the SAFE metrics in the two groups. The results of the comparison are included in Table 5.

Table 5. Empirical results

Comparison between White and Black applicants

Model	RGA	RGR	RGE1	RGE2	RGE3	RGE4	RGE5	RGF
White Subsample								
RF	0.622	0.571	0.177	0.069	0.090	0.123	0.139	0.073
GBT	0.681	0.502	0.253	0.003	0.016	0.005	0.026	0.002
SEM	0.679	0.516	0.191	0.010	0.031	0.021	0.037	0.010
VEM	0.659	0.503	0.189	0.040	0.058	0.070	0.089	0.042
Black Subsample								
RF	0.609	0.580	0.160	0.064	0.081	0.106	0.093	0.072
GBT	0.660	0.508	0.165	0.000	0.016	0.025	0.020	0.012
SEM	0.655	0.514	0.146	0.008	0.023	0.037	0.026	0.018
VEM	0.636	0.509	0.155	0.034	0.048	0.067	0.057	0.040

Note: This table presents a comprehensive analysis of model performance across different conditions. RF = Random Forest, GBT = Gradient Boosting Trees, SEM = Stacking Ensemble Model, VEM = Voting Ensemble Model. RGE1 = RGE(loan purpose), RGE2 = RGE(lien status), RGE3 = RGE (loan type), RGE4 = RGE (income), RGE5 = RGE (loan amount).

From Table 5, we can see that RGA for the RF model is slightly higher for the White group: at 0.622, compared to 0.609 for the Black group, with a difference of −0.013. The GBT model shows a more pronounced disparity, where the RGA for Whites is 0.681 versus 0.660 for Blacks, resulting in a difference of −0.021. The differences for SEM and VEM are slightly larger, with discrepancies reaching −0.024 in both cases. All models indicate a slight difference in accuracy between the models trained in the two population groups, which does not indicate a clear bias. Rather, the difference is negative for all models, and this may be the result of the smaller dimension of the Black sample which is compared to the White one.

The latter finding is consistent with the difference in the RGR metrics. In fact, in terms of RGR, the RF model exhibits a slightly higher RGR when applied to the Black sample, with a value of 0.580 compared to 0.571 for the White sample, resulting in a difference of 0.010. GBT and VEM show a similar result, with a difference of 0.006. In contrast, the SEM model shows a slightly lower RGR for the Black sample at 0.514, compared to 0.516 for the White sample, but the difference is only −0.002. Overall, it seems that the parity approach leads to the same result as before: there is no clear evidence of discrimination. These results are in line with those of [1] who analysed the same data using a RF and a logistic regression model.

We thus follow another route and proceed in line with the individual approach to fairness, which, for credit lending, implies that similar people should have similar credit scores. The RGE statistics, which we have formulated in this paper in terms of reduction in Gini inequality, are particularly suited for this purpose, as they can be calculated separately for Whites and Blacks. A substantial difference in RGE for a predictor variable will indicate a type of conditional fairness, as two individuals, who differ only in race, should have a similar explanation for that variable. From Table 5, columns 4–8 we can see the results of this further analysis. In addition to the RGE values for all predictor variables in Table 2, we present the values of RGF(gender), this time calculated separately for Blacks and Whites. Table 5 shows that:

RGE(loan purpose) stands out in the GBT model, revealing a significant discrepancy: the importance of loan purpose for the Black group is 0.165, while it is 0.253 for the White group, resulting in a notable difference of −0.088. This indicates that loan purpose plays a less critical role in the Black population's model.

RGE(lien status) is almost negligible for the Black group whereas it has a slight importance for the White group, indicating that property status is less relevant for Blacks.

RGE(loan type) is almost negligible for GBT, and it is less important in RF, SEM and VEM.

RGE(income) is significantly more important for the Black group in the GBT model, with a value of 0.025 compared to 0.005 for the White group, demonstrating that income is a more crucial factor for Blacks.

RGE(loan amount) exhibits a marked difference in the RF model, where it is much less important for the Black group (0.093) compared to the White group (0.139), with a difference of -0.046, suggesting that loan amounts have a lesser impact on the Black population.

Finally, the Rank Graduation Fairness appears slightly more important for the Black group in both the RF and VEM models, with differences of 0.005 and 0.006, respectively.

In summary, two variables show a high difference in RGE between the White and Black group: loan amount and income. While loan amount matters more for Whites, income matters more for Blacks. These difference explain discrimination:

Black people are rejected more, regardless of the amount they ask; and they are more penalised by their income.

As a final robustness check, it is important to assess whether the four different machine learning models are aligned with each other, as it seems from the discussion so far. To this aim, Table 6 reports the Spearman correlation coefficients among the prediction ranks of the four models.

Table 6. Correlation Matrix Among the Machine learning Models

White Subsample					Black Subsample				
	RF	GBT	SEM	VEM		RF	GBT	SEM	VEM
RF	1.000	0.917	0.984	1.000	RF	1.000	0.983	0.992	0.998
GBT	0.917	1.000	0.956	0.917	GBT	0.983	1.000	0.992	0.987
SEM	0.984	0.956	1.000	0.984	SEM	0.992	0.992	1.000	0.992
VEM	1.000	0.917	0.984	1.000	VEM	0.998	0.987	0.992	1.000

Table 6 shows that all models exhibit high levels of correlation across both subsamples, particularly in the black subsample where the correlation coefficients are generally higher. Regarding differences, although the correlations among the models are generally high, the GBT model shows relatively lower correlations with other models in the white subsample. However, this discrepancy diminishes in the black subsample, where the correlations involving GBT align more closely with those of other models. Finally, the RF model demonstrates very high correlations with other models in both the white and black subsamples, reinforcing its robust performance across different demographic groups.

We now extend the previous analysis trying to take unbalancedness of the response into account. To this aim, we focus on the F1 score, the harmonic mean of precision and recall, more sensitive to model performance for the less represented response values (loan rejection).

Without loss of generality, we focus this more detailed analysis on the output from the Random Forest classifier, and we study the value of the F1 score for different classification thresholds. Table 7 represents the F1 values for a set of thresholds that ranges from 0.1 to 0.9.

As we expect, having highly unbalanced data, the F1 scores are relatively low, and the highest F1 value is reached in correspondence of the smallest threshold (0.1).

To assess fairness, considering the two protected groups of race: "Black" and "White", and using a default threshold (i.e. 0.5), we find that the F1 score for the black group is equal to 0.069 while the F1 score for the white group is 0.068.

These results indicate that, using a fairness parity measure, based on the F1 score, the difference between the protected groups is small. As the data is unbalanced, the comparison between the two race groups can be extended to F1 score values at various thresholds, from 0.1 to 0.9, as shown in Fig. 4.

Table 7. F1 score values for different thresholds.

Threshold	F1 score
0.1	0.149
0.2	0.135
0.3	0.116
0.4	0.094
0.5	0.069
0.6	0.058
0.7	0.026
0.8	0.013
0.9	0.002

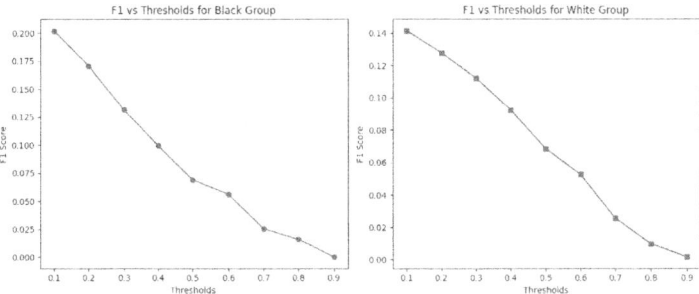

Fig. 4. F1 score values for different thresholds in "Black" and "White" groups.

Figure 4 shows that the F1 score decreases when the threshold increases, in both white and black groups. Furthermore, the difference in F1 score values between the two protected groups is larger for smaller thresholds. Thus, the comparison at different thresholds indicates a small imparity, confirming the result obtained at the 0.5 threshold. Overall, these results indicate that a marginal measure of fairness (F1 at different thresholds) is not able to identify evidence of discrimination, consistently with what obtained using the SAFE accuracy, robustness and fairness metrics. Unfairness may be found working conditionally on the control variables, as was done previously using RGE. We now extend RGE better taking into account the correlations between the control varaiables, in a manner that resembles the construction of Shapley values.

First we find the additional contribution of the control variables, using the F1 score values, calculated separately for the white and black categories, at the default threshold. the additional contribution is obtained, for each control variable, taking the difference between the F1 value with that variable and without that variable. This in line with the calculation of the RGE metrics. Table 8 shows the results of this analysis.

Table 8 shows that the contribution of some variables such as 'loan_purpose', 'loan_type', 'log(loan)', and 'log(income)' are different between white and black

Table 8. F1 contribution of the variables in the "Black" and "White" protected groups.

Variable	F1 contribution (Black)	F1 contribution (White)
gender	−0.000737	0.000024
loan_purpose	0.002914	0.002214
loan_type	−0.000438	0.000544
lien_status	−0.000153	0.000035
log(income)	0.000619	0.001747
log(loan)	0.000675	0.000802

groups. This is in line with what found using the RGE measure, with the additional advantage of taking unbalancedness into account.

The previous analysis considers the additional contribution of each variable, independently of the others. We can further improve the measurement of fairness calculating the average F1 contribution of race in different coalitions of variables, similarly to what is done for Shapley values [10].

To this aim, we calculate the F1 score for the RF model based on different coalitions of variables, including race, and we repeat the calculation for all thresholds between 0.1 and 0.9. Figure 5 shows the results of the calculation, with the F1 scores of all the 64 coalitions that include race.

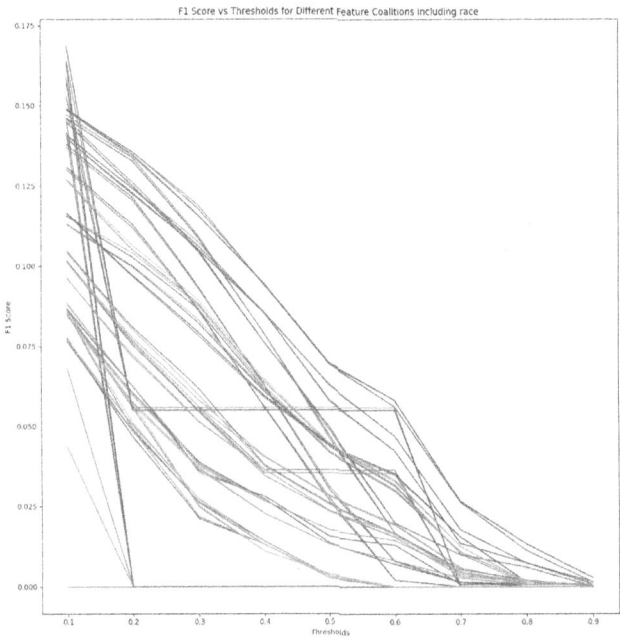

Fig. 5. F1 scores for the models based on different coalitions including race

From Fig. 5 note that the highest F1 score is equal to 0.169, and it occurs for the ('race_1', 'gender', 'loan_purpose','lien_status') coalition, using a threshold equal to 0.1. The results illustrated in Fig. 5 can be employed to calculate the contribution of race to different coalitions and different thresholds. To this aim, Table 9 exemplifies the contribution of race based on F1 score for four feature coalitions in different thresholds.

Table 9. F1 based contribution of race to four different coalitions in various thresholds

Feature coalition	0.1	0.2	0.3	0.4	0.5	0.6	0.7	0.8	0.9
(race_1, loan_type)	0.068068	0.000000	0.000000	0.000000	0.000000	0.000000	0.000000	0.000000	0.000000
(race_1, gender, loan_purpose, loan_type, lien_status, log(income), log(loan))	0.003151	0.001478	0.004539	0.000252	−0.000986	−0.000537	0.000607	0.001314	0.000000
(race_1, gender, loan_purpose, loan_type, log(income), log(loan))	0.003129	0.002140	0.005018	0.000592	−0.000506	−0.000553	0.000607	0.001314	0.000000
(race_1, loan_purpose, log(income), log(loan))	0.005605	0.006183	0.008844	0.005590	0.004503	0.003178	0.001231	−0.000007	0.000000

Table 9 shows that the contribution of race is higher when we consider a threshold of 0.1, with other thresholds indicating less contribution. This is the case for all coalitions, as we expect, being 0.1 the "optimal" threshold for accuracy.

Note that the coalition with the highest contributions for race is that which contains loan purpose, log(income) and log(loan). This is in line with our previous results from RGE, indicating a high interaction between race and these three variables. We can finally average the additional contribution of race to all coalitions, for all thresholds. This leads to a measure that extends the RGF metrics in a Shapley-like manner, taking dependencies into account. In our application, the value of the average additional contribution of race for each threshold is reported in Table 10.

Table 10. Average marginal contribution of Race

Threshold	Average contribution of race
0.1	0.008865
0.2	0.008359
0.3	0.008108
0.4	0.006519
0.5	0.005077
0.6	0.004297
0.7	0.000919
0.8	0.000145
0.9	0.000000

Table 10 shows that the average contribution of race decreases, as expected, when the threshold increases. However, all average contributions are low, and do not indicate a potential sign of unfairness. Once more, marginal measures of fairness are not able to identify a bias. Differently, when we condition on specific control variables, such as loan purpose, log(income) and log(loan), as in Table 9, bias appears, depending on the levels of the control variables.

Thus, to carefully address the issue of whether a bias exists in the analysed credit lending data, in Table we report the ten coalitions with the highest F1 score, at the 0.1 threshold and, for each of them, we report the corresponding additional contribution of Race to the score itself: the lower the contribution the higher the fairness.

Table 11. Top ten feature coalitions based on F1 score and their corresponding race contribution. The reported values are calculated based on threshold equal to 0.1.

Feature coalition	F1 score	Race contribution
(race_1, gender, loan_purpose, lien_status)	0.168498	−0.005959
(race_1, gender, loan_purpose)	0.163974	−0.006302
(race_1, loan_purpose, lien_status)	0.163373	−0.011083
(race_1, loan_purpose)	0.158843	−0.011433
(race_1, gender, loan_purpose, loan_type, lien_status)	0.156840	−0.000723
(race_1, gender, loan_purpose, loan_type)	0.152795	−0.001173
(race_1, loan_purpose, loan_type, lien_status, log(income), log(loan))	0.148962	0.002462
(race_1, gender, loan_purpose, loan_type, lien_status, log(income), log(loan))	0.148756	0.003151
(race_1, loan_purpose, loan_type, log(income), log(loan))	0.148710	0.002652
(race_1, gender, loan_purpose, loan_type, log(income), log(loan))	0.148653	0.003129

Table 11 indicate that all coalitions that include income or loan amount have a certain degree of unfairness, with a positive contribution of race. Among them is the coalition that includes loan purpose, income and loan amount, that we already commented. Differently, the coalitions that do not include those variables are fair, as the contribution of race to them is negative.

5 Conclusions

Our study confirms the significant impact of ethnicity in loan approval rates. It has reached this conclusion using different ensemble machine learning models, aimed to learn credit decisions from the observed data. The conclusion has been reached by means of an appropriate reformulation of the S.A.F.E. AI metrics and, in particular, comparing the values of the Rank Graduation Explainability metric (RGE) for different variables across the White and Black population groups. Since credit datasets are usually imbalanced, we have also utilized the F1 score to measure the fairness of the considered models.

From a methodological viewpoint, this study has proposed a reformulation of the Rank Graduation metrics proposed in the S.A.F.E. machine learning context. In particular, the Rank Graduation Explainability metrics, which have helped to identify racial discrimination for the analysed data, can be interpreted as the percentage reduction in Gini inequality due to the removal of each variable or group of variables. Furthermore, we have shown how, in the presence of unbalanced data, other metrics can be calculated, such as the F1 score, to enhance robustness of the results. We have shown how F1 scores can be extended in a conditional manner, to measure both accuracy and fairness.

From an empirical viewpoint, our results indicate that loan approval in the state of New York has a degree of unfairness by race, which is evident when the effect of race is conditional on the amount of loan requested and on the income of the applicant. Our results are similar to those available in the literature, for the same data, as Table 1 shows. We however present more insights on explainability and fairness. Future research should focus on the application of the S.A.F.E. AI metrics to other data and field domains. From a technical view point, the paper can be improved in several directions. First, random effects or multiplicative effects should be added to the considered models and in particular to logistic regression. Second, RGA and RGE could be tested also against an increasing level of noise in input features, as done in [3]. Third, statistical tests based on resampling can be applied to assess statistical significance of the metrics as shown in [3]. We also remark that cross validation can be used although it might reduce the interpretability of the results.

Acknowledgement. This study was funded by: the European Union - NextGenerationEU, in the framework of the GRINS- Growing Resilient, INclusive and Sustainable (GRINS PE00000018). The views and opinions expressed are solely those of the authors and do not necessarily reflect those of the European Union, nor can the European Union be held responsible for them.

Disclosure of Interests. The authors have no competing interests to declare that are relevant to the content of this article.

References

1. Agarwal, S., Muckley, C.B., Neelakantan, P.: Countering racial discrimination in algorithmic lending: a case for model-agnostic interpretation methods. Econ. Lett. **226**, 111117 (2023)
2. Ambrose, B.W., Hughes, W.T., Simmons, P.: Policy issues concerning racial and ethnic differences in home loan rejection rates. J. Hous. Res. **6**(1), 115–135 (1995)
3. Babaei, G., Giudici, P., Raffinetti, E.: A rank graduation box for safe AI. Expert Syst. Appl. (2025)
4. Butler, A.W., Mayer, E.J., Weston, J.P.: Racial disparities in the auto loan market. Rev. Financ. Stud. **36**(1), 1–41 (2023)
5. Chen, Y., Giudici, P., Kailang, L., Raffinetti, E.: Measuring fairness in credit ratings. Expert Syst. Appl. 285 (2024)
6. Faber, J.W.: Racial dynamics of subprime mortgage lending at the peak. Hous. Policy Debate **23**(2), 328–349 (2013)
7. Giudici, P., Raffinetti, E.: RGA: a unified measure of predictive accuracy. Adv. Data Anal. Classif. 1–27 (2024)

8. Gonzales Martinez, R., Aguilera-Lizarazu, G., Rojas-Hosse, A., Aranda Blanco, P.: The interaction effect of gender and ethnicity in loan approval: a Bayesian estimation with data from a laboratory field experiment. Rev. Dev. Econ. **24**(3), 726–749 (2020)
9. Gotham, K.F.: Race, mortgage lending and loan rejections in a US city. Sociol. Focus **31**(4), 391–405 (1998)
10. Hart, S.: Shapley value. In: Game theory, pp. 210–216. Springer (1989)
11. Horne, D.K.: Evaluating the role of race in mortgage lending. FDIC Bank. Rev. **7**(1), 1–16 (1994)
12. Horne, D.K.: Mortgage lending, race, and model specification. J. Financ. Serv. Res. **11**(1), 43–68 (1997)
13. Hurlin, C., Pérignon, C., Saurin, S.: The fairness of credit scoring models. arXiv preprint arXiv:2205.10200 (2022)
14. Leven, C.L., Sykuta, M.E.: The importance of race in home mortgage loan approvals. Urban Affairs Quarterly **29**(3), 479–489 (1994)
15. Lorenz, M.O.: Methods of measuring the concentration wealth. Publ. Am. Stat. Assoc. **9**(70), 209–219 (1905). https://doi.org/10.2307/2276207
16. Martin, R.E., Hill, R.C.: Loan performance and race. Econ. Inq. **38**(1), 136–150 (2000)
17. Perry, V.G.: A loan at last? Race and racism in mortgage lending. In: Race in the marketplace: Crossing critical boundaries, pp. 173–192 (2019)
18. Ross, S.L.: Mortgage lending discrimination and racial differences in loan default. J. Hous. Res. **7**, 117–126 (1996)
19. Ross, S.L.: Mortgage lending discrimination and racial differences in loan default: a simulation approach. J. Hous. Res. **8**(2), 277–297 (1997)
20. Smith, J.A., Fulgham, G.G.: Investigating racial/ethnic disparities in loan approval: a Mississippi perspective. Am. Res. J. Econ. Financ. Manag. **11**(4), 77–93 (2023)

Open Access This chapter is licensed under the terms of the Creative Commons Attribution 4.0 International License (http://creativecommons.org/licenses/by/4.0/), which permits use, sharing, adaptation, distribution and reproduction in any medium or format, as long as you give appropriate credit to the original author(s) and the source, provide a link to the Creative Commons license and indicate if changes were made.

The images or other third party material in this chapter are included in the chapter's Creative Commons license, unless indicated otherwise in a credit line to the material. If material is not included in the chapter's Creative Commons license and your intended use is not permitted by statutory regulation or exceeds the permitted use, you will need to obtain permission directly from the copyright holder.

Cyber Risk Management with Time Varying Artificial Intelligence Models

Paolo Giudici[1], Marco Pirra[2], and Rasha Zieni[1]

[1] Department of Economics and Management, University of Pavia, Pavia, Italy
rasha.zieni@unipv.it
[2] Department of Economics, Statistics and Finance, Universitá della Calabria, Rende, (CS), Italy

Abstract. The aim of this paper is to employ explainable artificial intelligence methods to prioritize cyber risks. To achieve this, we compare alternative machine learning models that predict the evolution of cyber attacks while accounting for time dependence. Subsequently, we apply explainable AI techniques to identify the most significant types of cyber attacks based on their occurrence.

We illustrate our approach using data from the Hackmanac website, which categorizes worldwide cyber attacks by severity. The empirical findings reveal two distinct periods: before and after 2023. In both cases, eXtreme Gradient Boosting emerges as the best-performing model. Furthermore, the most relevant explanatory features remain relatively consistent across different explainable artificial intelligence methods but vary over time, reflecting the recent evolution of cyber threats.

Keywords: Explainable machine learning · Markov Switching Models · Cyber Risks

1 Introduction

The rapid expansion of AI applications has heightened the importance of cyber risk management, which focuses on detecting, monitoring, and mitigating threats posed by cyber attacks. Traditional cyber risk assessment methods have primarily relied on standardized frameworks such as the Common Vulnerability Scoring System (CVSS) [9] and guidelines from organizations like the National Institute of Standards and Technology (NIST) [10]. While these approaches provide a valuable baseline for measuring risk, they often struggle to capture the complexity and evolving nature of modern cyber threats [11]. Recent studies have leveraged advanced statistical and stochastic modeling techniques to analyze cyber risk, particularly the frequency and severity of data breaches in high-risk sectors like healthcare. Traditional approaches, such as hurdle Poisson models, effectively address excess zeros in breach datasets, while log-normal distributions capture the skewed nature of breach sizes ([5]; [12]).

In addition to these methods, recent work by Agosto and Giudici [2] introduces a multivariate negative binomial score-driven model that explicitly accounts for interdependence across economic sectors in cyber risk events. Their findings reveal significant time and cross-sector contagion, particularly with the information and communication technology (ICT) and government sectors acting as sources of cyber risk spread, and the education sector being notably vulnerable. This contagion-based approach adds an important systemic dimension to cyber risk modeling, emphasizing the need to consider both temporal dynamics and relational dependencies when assessing threats. We remark that contagion may lead to persistence in the frequency time series as shown by Agosto et al. [1].

However, newer methodologies, including Markov switching models, have gained traction for their ability to capture dynamic, time-varying characteristics in count data. Originally applied in transportation safety and epidemiology, these models outperform traditional zero-inflated approaches by accounting for regime shifts and non-linear dependencies ([8]; [3]). Their integration into cyber risk assessment could enhance predictive accuracy, particularly when incorporating external factors such as policy interventions and technological advancements [7]. Additionally, stochastic processes like integer-valued GARCH models have been employed to model overdispersion and temporal clustering in count data, providing a robust framework for breach frequency analysis [4]. These insights underscore the interdisciplinary nature of cyber risk modeling and the ongoing need for innovative analytical tools to address the evolving cybersecurity landscape.

One of the primary challenges in cyber risk management modeling is the limited availability of data, largely due to the confidential nature of cyber attacks. Recently, cyber data providers that aggregate news from the Internet have gained traction, with Hackmanac [6] emerging as a key player. Hackmanac's fourth annual Global Cyber Attacks Report offers an in-depth analysis of thousands of cyber incidents from 2023. To provide a comprehensive view of the global cybersecurity landscape and highlight key trends, the report examines over 7,000 documented attacks from 2023, comparing them with data from the past five years. In its 2024 edition, Hackmanac introduced the Estimated Severity Index, a proprietary algorithm designed to measure the severity of each attack consistently. This innovative metric enables a systematic assessment of cyber-attack impacts, allowing for the first-time ranking of cyber threats based on their effects on various victim types.

In this paper, we integrate Markov switching models with explainable AI techniques to interpret the dynamics of cyber attacks and prioritize interventions where risks are highest. We test our proposed methodology on the latest Hackmanac dataset, generously provided by its creators. Our contributions to the literature are threefold. First, we employ Markov switching models to determine whether cyber attack data should be analyzed as a whole or segmented into distinct time periods. Second, we compare alternative machine learning models conditioned on the time periods identified by the Markov switching model using metrics computed at optimal thresholds. Third, we leverage Shapley values to identify the key drivers of cyber risk, focusing on the attacker, target, and technique classes.

The remainder of the paper is structured as follows. In Sect. 2, we describe the available data and its relevance to our study. Section 3 introduces our proposed explainable machine learning models and applies them to the full dataset. In Sect. 4, we conduct an exploratory econometric analysis. Section 5 presents the application of Markov switching models. In Sect. 6, we analyze the data by conditioning the explainable machine learning models on the time periods identified by the Markov switching models. Finally, Sect. 7 concludes the paper.

2 Data

The Hackmanac dataset comprises a set of time series representing monthly cyber event counts from January 2018 to December 2023.

Figure 1 illustrates the total number of cyber events over time.

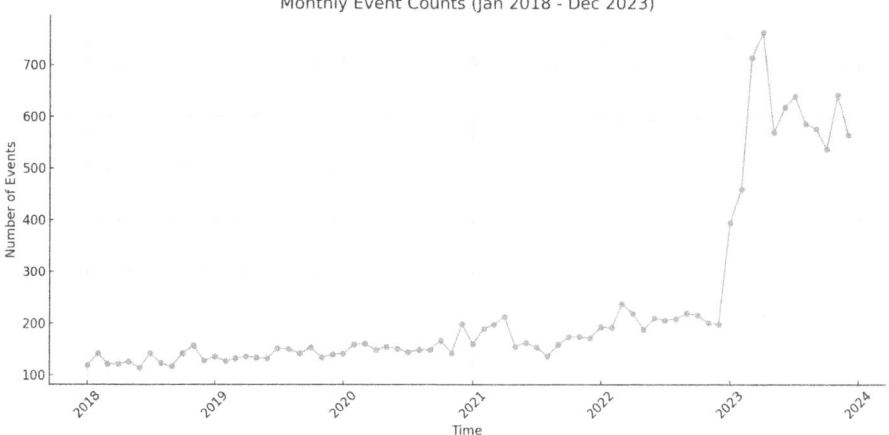

Fig. 1. Monthly Event Counts (Jan 2018 - Dec 2023)

Figure 1 reveals distinct patterns across two primary periods. From 2018 to early 2022, event counts remained relatively stable, fluctuating between 100 and 200 per month, with only minor short-term variations and no significant trends. However, in early 2023, the series experiences a sharp surge, peaking at over 700 events per month, indicating a regime shift. Following this peak in mid-2023, event counts decline but exhibit irregular fluctuations. Despite the decrease, post-2023 levels remain significantly higher than in the pre-2023 period. This trend suggests structural changes or external factors influencing the data-generating process.

To accurately describe the data, it is essential to consider the distribution of cyber events by severity, as shown in Table 1.

Table 1. Distribution of Events by Severity

Severity	Total Count	Percentage
Critical	3,871	23.2%
High	8,850	53.0%
Medium	3,138	18.8%
Low	829	5.0%
Total	16,688	100.0%

Table 1 indicates that the dataset is quite imbalanced, with the "High" category accounting for more than 53% of events, while the "Low" category represents only about 5%. The evolution of event counts for each severity type is shown in Fig. 2.

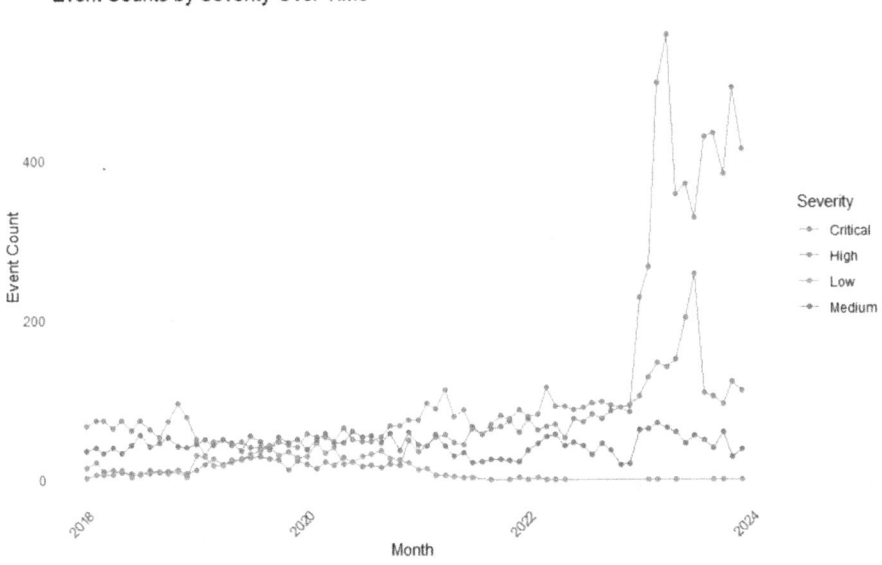

Fig. 2. Monthly Event Counts, Different Severities (Jan 2018 - Dec 2023)

Figure 2 highlights a significant surge in high-severity events beginning around 2022, suggesting a sharp increase in critical incidents requiring heightened attention. Critical-severity events follow a similar upward trend during this period, albeit with a more gradual trajectory, possibly indicating an escalation of high-severity incidents or a shift in reporting dynamics. In contrast, medium- and low-severity events remain relatively stable, exhibiting consistent patterns over time with minor fluctuations, reflecting steadier, lower-impact occurrences.

These differences suggest distinct underlying factors influencing each severity level. The notable spikes in higher-severity categories may signal shifts in organizational priorities, emerging external threats, or changes in incident reporting protocols. This analysis underscores the importance of closely monitoring and addressing high-severity incidents to enhance risk management and maintain operational stability.

In addition to the severity breakdown, it is useful to understand the distribution of key categorical variables. Table 2 provides the frequency distributions for the main explanatory variables, including attacker class, target class, technique class, and geographical region (continent).

Table 2. Frequency distributions of explanatory variables

Variable	Category	Frequency
Continent	AM	7742
Continent	EU	3636
Continent	–	3043
Continent	AS	1694
Continent	OC	361
Continent	AF	188
Continent	INT	29
Attacker Class	Cybercrime	14483
Attacker Class	Espionage/Sabotage	1324
Attacker Class	Hacktivism	555
Attacker Class	Information Warfare	332
Target Class	Multiple Targets	2488
Target Class	ICT	1929
Target Class	Healthcare	1747
Target Class	Gov/Mil /LE	1721
Target Class	Manufacturing	1433
Target Class	Financial/Insurance	1309
Target Class	Education	1112
Target Class	Professional/Scientific/Technical	1049
Target Class	Wholesale/Retail	667
Target Class	Transportation/Storage	506
Target Class	News/Multimedia	489
Target Class	Organizations	380
Target Class	Arts/Entertainment	348

(*continued*)

Table 2. (*continued*)

Variable	Category	Frequency
Target Class	Energy/Utilities	320
Target Class	Other Services	315
Target Class	Construction	301
Target Class	Hospitality	270
Target Class	Telco	227
Target Class	Agriculture/Forestry/Fishing	60
Target Class	Mining/Quarrying	23
Technique Class	Malware	8820
Technique Class	Unknown	2794
Technique Class	Vulnerabilities	1870
Technique Class	Phishing/Social Engineering	1496
Technique Class	Multiple Techniques	624
Technique Class	Identity Theft/Account Cracking	477
Technique Class	DDoS	457
Technique Class	Web Attack	156

These distributions indicate a significant skew in the dataset towards certain attack types and geographical areas. For example, the majority of attacks are attributed to cybercrime actors and primarily occur in America and Europe. This imbalance may influence model performance and feature importance rankings in the subsequent analysis.

3 Explainable Machine Learning

In this section, we apply explainable machine learning models to the dataset introduced in the previous section to identify key features that contribute to classifying attack severity. We train seven machine learning models on the entire dataset, framing the problem as a binary classification task. For this purpose, instances labeled as High and Critical are assigned to class 1, while those labeled as Medium and Low are assigned to class 0. The dataset is imbalanced, with 12,720 observations in class 1 and 3,967 in class 0.

To address class imbalance without compromising explainability, we adjust the decision threshold to balance precision and recall across both classes. We propose using a balance metric (see Fig. 3), defined as the arithmetic mean of precision and recall, for threshold optimization, as shown in (1). Each model undergoes hyperparameter tuning to enhance performance, and the optimal decision threshold is selected accordingly.

$$AM = \frac{1}{2} \left(\frac{\text{Precision}_0 + \text{Recall}_0}{2} + \frac{\text{Precision}_1 + \text{Recall}_1}{2} \right) \quad (1)$$

Table 3 summarizes the performance of all trained classifiers based on accuracy and Area Under the ROC Curve (AUC). Among them, eXtreme Gradient Boosting (XGBoost) achieves the best overall performance and is selected as the final classifier.

Table 3. Performance of different classifiers on the whole dataset. The table presents the optimal threshold, accuracy, per-class accuracy, and AUC for each classifier.

Classifier	Threshold	Accuracy	Accuracy by Class		AUC
			Class 0	Class 1	
RF	0.49	0.83	0.75	0.86	0.88
XGBoost	**0.59**	**0.85**	**0.67**	**0.91**	**0.89**
LR	0.79	0.72	0.79	0.70	0.81
KNN	0.60	0.81	0.64	0.87	0.81
SVM	0.81	0.79	0.72	0.81	0.82
Voting	0.69	0.82	0.75	0.84	0.88
Stacking	0.67	0.84	0.68	0.89	0.88

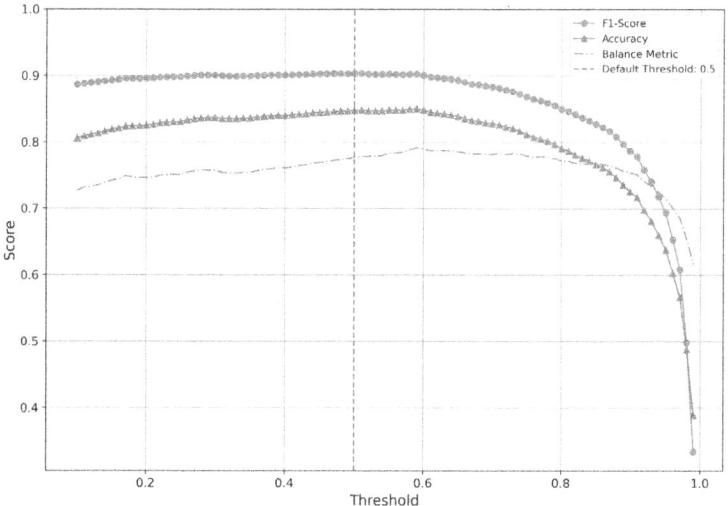

Fig. 3. Threshold optimization for XGboost applied on the entire dataset

To enhance the interpretability of XGBoost, we use Shapley values to identify key features influencing its predictions. The top 15 contributing features, as shown in Fig. 4, include: *Technique Class_ Malware, Continent_ , Target Class_ Multiple Targets* and *Attacker Class_ Cybercrime*. The Shapley value analysis reveals key drivers of cyber risk severity. Technique Class_Malware is consistently the most influential feature, highlighting the prevalence and destructive potential of malware-based attacks. Attacker Class_Cybercrime ranks second, indicating the dominant role of financially motivated actors. The importance of Target Class_Multiple Targets suggests that generalized, broad-scale attacks significantly influence severity classification.

Interestingly, Continent_ (especially values representing AM and EU) also carries substantial weight, indicating either geographic concentration of attacks or potential regional differences in reporting practices.

The results are insightful but can be further improved by leveraging the observed patterns in Figs. 1 and 2, which suggest a possible regime shift in the nature of cyber attacks in recent periods. To investigate this, in Sect. 5, we propose using Markov switching models to determine whether a regime change has occurred and, if so, when it took place. Before proceeding, the next section presents a preliminary econometric analysis of the data.

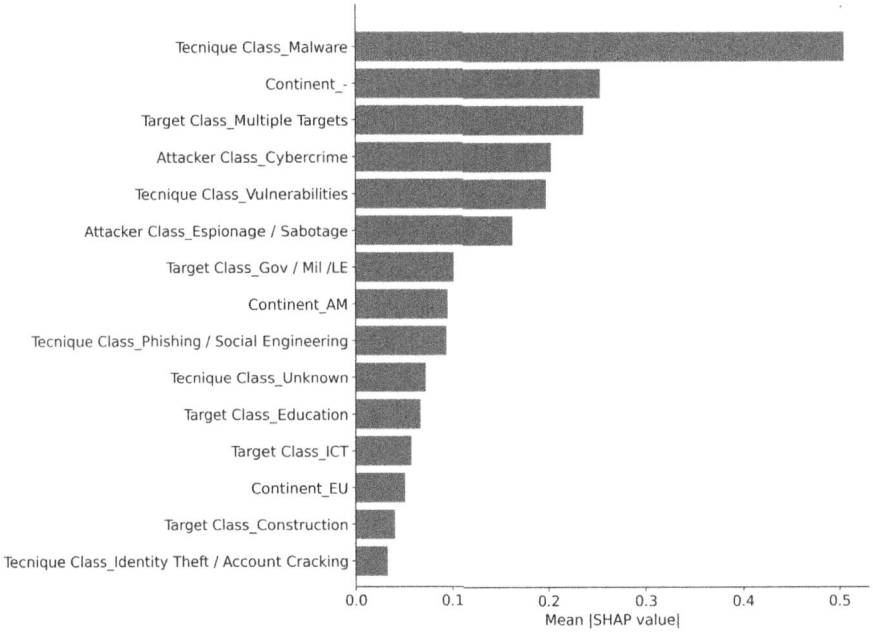

Fig. 4. The 15 most important explanatory variables identified using Shapley values applied to the XGBoost model on the entire dataset

4 Econometric Analysis

This section presents a time series econometric analysis of the available count data. We explore various models, incorporating linear and nonlinear trends, seasonality, and autoregressive properties.

Intercept-Only Model

We begin with the simplest possible model, which includes only an intercept. This model estimates the mean event count without accounting for time trends or seasonality, as described by the following equation:

$$\hat{Y} = \beta_0 + \epsilon \qquad (2)$$

Using the available data, the estimated intercept is 231.9 with a standard error of 19.8. The corresponding t-value is 11.71, with a highly significant p-value ($p < 2e-16$). The residual standard error is 168, suggesting substantial fluctuations in event counts. While this model serves as a baseline, it is too simplistic to capture time-dependent patterns effectively.

Linear Trend Model

This model includes time as a predictor, as follows:

$$\hat{Y} = \beta_0 + \beta_1 \cdot \text{Time} + \epsilon \qquad (3)$$

The estimated intercept is 17.78 with a standard error of 27.52. The time coefficient is 5.87 with a standard error of 0.66 and a highly significant p-value ($p < 0.001$), indicating a strong increasing trend. The residual standard error is 115.6, which is lower than in the intercept-only model, suggesting an improved fit. The R^2 value is 0.5337, meaning that time explains 53.4% of the variance in event counts. The F-statistic is 80.12 on 1 and 70 degrees of freedom, with a p-value of $3.255e-13$, confirming that time is a significant predictor.

From this model, we conclude that the increasing trend is statistically significant, but the model does not account for potential seasonality or nonlinear patterns.

Quadratic Trend Model

We now consider adding a quadratic term to capture nonlinearity:

$$\hat{Y} = \beta_0 + \beta_1 \cdot \text{Time} + \beta_2 \cdot \text{Time}^2 + \epsilon \qquad (4)$$

The estimated intercept is 206.40 with a standard error of 29.80 ($p = 1.81e-09$), indicating statistical significance. The linear term, -9.43 (standard error: 1.88, $p = 4.10e-06$), suggests that event counts initially decline over time. The quadratic term, 0.2095 (standard error: 0.0250, $p = 4.08e - 12$), indicates a U-shaped trend, meaning event counts first decrease before increasing. The residual standard error is 81.95, lower than that of the linear trend model, suggesting an improved fit. The R^2 value is 0.7688, meaning this model explains 76.9% of the variance— a significant improvement over the linear model. The F-statistic is 114.7 on 2 and 69 degrees of freedom, with $p < 2.2e - 16$, confirming strong model significance.

We conclude that the quadratic model better captures the curved trend in event counts than the linear model. However, it does not explicitly model seasonality, which may still influence the data. Incorporating seasonal components (e.g., ARIMA) could further improve accuracy.

ARIMA Model (SAR(1) with Drift)

As previously suggested, we now apply an ARIMA model that incorporates seasonal autoregressive (SAR) terms:

$$\text{ARIMA}(0,1,0)(1,0,0)_{12} + \text{drift} \tag{5}$$

Applying this model to our data reveals that the seasonal autoregressive term ($\phi_1 = 0.4046$, standard error: 0.1941) suggests moderate seasonality. The drift term ($\delta = 8.0898$, standard error: 9.0206) indicates a steady long-term increase. The model's accuracy is summarized by the following goodness-of-fit measures:

- AIC = 764.43
- RMSE = 49.40
- MAE = 27.13
- MAPE = 10.42%

Based on these metrics, we conclude that the model effectively captures both trend and seasonality, making it a strong candidate for forecasting.

Alternative ARIMA Model (SMA(1))

We now explore an alternative ARIMA model by replacing the seasonal autoregressive (SAR) term with a seasonal moving average (SMA) term:

$$\text{ARIMA}(0,1,0)(0,0,1)_{12} \tag{6}$$

The estimated parameters indicate that the seasonal moving average coefficient ($\theta_1 = 0.3132$, standard error: 0.1730) suggests modest seasonal smoothing. The accuracy metrics for this model are as follows:

- AIC = 764.2, slightly lower than the previous ARIMA model.
- RMSE = 50.34
- MAE = 26.99
- MAPE = 10.03%

Based on these accuracy metrics, we conclude that this model performs similarly to the SAR(1) model, capturing seasonality through a moving average component instead.

Exponential Smoothing (ETS Model)

We now consider an exponential smoothing model:

$$\text{ETS}(M, N, N) \tag{7}$$

Applying this model to our data reveals that the smoothing parameter ($\alpha = 0.8781$) indicates a strong reliance on recent values. The model fit metrics are as follows:

- AIC = 821.92, higher than the ARIMA models, indicating a poorer fit.
- RMSE = 52.24
- MAE = 26.78
- MAPE = 9.64%

We conclude that this model is useful for short-term forecasting due to its emphasis on recent data. However, its lack of seasonal adjustments makes it less suitable for datasets with strong seasonal patterns.

Model Comparison

We conclude the presentation of econometric models with a comparison table (Table 4):

Table 4. Comparison of Econometric Models

Model	Trend	Seasonality	Fit Quality (R^2/AIC)	Best For
Intercept-Only	None	None	Very Poor ($R^2 = 0$)	Baseline comparison
Linear Trend	Increasing	None	Moderate ($R^2 = 0.53$)	Basic trend analysis
Quadratic Trend	Nonlinear	None	Strong ($R^2 = 0.77$)	Capturing curved trends
ARIMA (SAR 1, Drift)	Increasing	Yes (SAR)	Good (AIC = 764.43)	Time series forecasting
ARIMA (SMA 1)	Increasing	Yes (SMA)	Slightly better than ARIMA (SAR)	Alternative seasonal modeling
ETS Model	Smoothing	None	Higher AIC (worse fit)	Short-term predictions

From Table 4, we conclude that ARIMA models (SAR(1) and SMA(1)) perform best, as they capture both trend and seasonality. Additionally, the quadratic model effectively detects acceleration and deceleration in event counts.

5 Regime-Switching Models (MSM)

This section introduces Markov-Switching Models (MSMs) to detect structural shifts and model time-dependent behavior in the monthly count of cyber events. While a visual inspection of Figs. 6 and 7 suggests a clear shift in event dynamics around early 2023, the use of Markov-Switching Models (MSMs) provides a formal and statistically grounded approach to identifying and characterizing structural changes in the data. Unlike a manual split, MSMs estimate regime changes based on like-lihood optimization, allowing for reproducible and objective segmentation. Additionally, MSMs capture temporal dependence and regime persistence through transition probabilities, which enhances our understanding of the underlying dynamics. This is particularly valuable for cyber risk analysis, where abrupt shifts may stem from external shocks (e.g., major vulnerabilities or geopolitical events) and have lasting effects. By modeling each regime with distinct parameters—including intercepts, AR terms, and residual variances—MSMs reveal deeper differences in data-generating processes. These regime assignments then inform our explainable machine learning pipeline, enabling time-aware model calibration and more meaningful interpretation of feature importance over time. Thus, MSMs contribute not only to better segmentation but also to richer explanation and predic-tive insight.

We begin with a two-regime MSM without autoregressive dynamics:

$$\text{MSM}(k=2, p=0) \tag{8}$$

This model identifies two regimes with distinct characteristics. Regime 1 has an intercept of 160.43 and a residual standard error of 30.99, while Regime 2 shows a much higher in-tercept of 589 and a residual standard error of 95.85. The model fit is acceptable (AIC = 912.81, BIC = 925.92, log-likelihood = -454.41). Transition probabilities are nearly deter-ministic:

$$\begin{bmatrix} P_{11} & P_{12} \\ P_{21} & P_{22} \end{bmatrix} = \begin{bmatrix} 1.0000 & 0.0833 \\ 4.99 \times 10^{-40} & 0.9167 \end{bmatrix}$$

These extreme values reflect a strong persistence within regimes, supporting the presence of a dominant structural shift—consistent with the findings from visual inspection and econometric analysis.

To enhance the model's ability to capture internal dynamics, we incorporate an AR(1) structure:

$$\text{MSM}(k=2, p=1) \tag{9}$$

The MSM with AR(1) significantly improves model performance (AIC = 667.87, BIC = 693.97, log-likelihood = -329.94). In Regime 1, the intercept is 29.48 with a strong AR(1) coefficient of 0.8241, and $R^2 = 0.82$. In Regime 2, the intercept is 362.97 with a more moderate AR(1) coefficient of 0.4077. The residual standard errors are lower in this model (18.13 and 76.83, respectively). Transition probabilities are slightly more flexible:

$$\begin{bmatrix} P_{11} & P_{12} \\ P_{21} & P_{22} \end{bmatrix} = \begin{bmatrix} 0.9943 & 0.0859 \\ 0.0057 & 0.9141 \end{bmatrix}$$

The inclusion of the AR(1) term allows the model to capture temporal dependence within regimes and yields more realistic regime transitions. This model provides a more nuanced view of regime behavior and enhances the interpretability of the regime-specific dynamics.

We also estimated a three-regime MSM to explore more complex structures. While feasible, the third regime often captured transient noise rather than a meaningful phase, offering no consistent gains in AIC or BIC. Its inclusion complicated interpretation, misaligned with key figures, and hindered integration into our explainable ML pipeline. Therefore, we retained the two-regime model for its superior balance of fit, simplicity, and clarity. That said, higher-order MSMs may still be valuable for datasets with finer-grained dynamics or multiple structural breaks.

Model Comparison

Table 5 summarizes key results from both two-regime models. While the base MSM highlights the existence of two structural regimes, the AR(1) model provides additional insight into within-regime dynamics.

Table 5. Comparison of Markov-Switching Model Specifications

Metric	MSM (p = 0)	MSM with AR(1)
AIC	912.81	667.87
BIC	925.92	693.97
Log-Likelihood	−454.41	−329.94
Regime 1 Intercept	160.43	29.48
Regime 1 AR(1)	—	0.8241
Regime 2 Intercept	589.00	362.97
Regime 2 AR(1)	—	0.4077
Transition Prob. P_{11}	1.0000	0.9943
Transition Prob. P_{22}	0.9167	0.9141

Introducing an autoregressive component in the Markov-Switching Model (MSM) significantly enhances model performance. The first model, MSM with $p = 0$, assumes that event counts depend solely on the regime, allowing only the intercepts to vary across states. In contrast, the second model, MSM with $p = 1$, includes an AR(1) term, capturing temporal dependence within each regime. This structural difference results in a substantial improvement in model fit.

Overall, the Markov-Switching Model with AR(1) provides a more comprehensive representation of event count dynamics by capturing both regime-dependent shifts and within-regime temporal dependencies. The reduced residual variance, improved model fit, and more flexible transition dynamics suggest that event counts exhibit significant temporal dependence within regimes, particularly in the lower-variance regime. Incorporating an autoregressive component not only enhances forecasting accuracy but also offers a more realistic depiction of regime shifts in time series data.

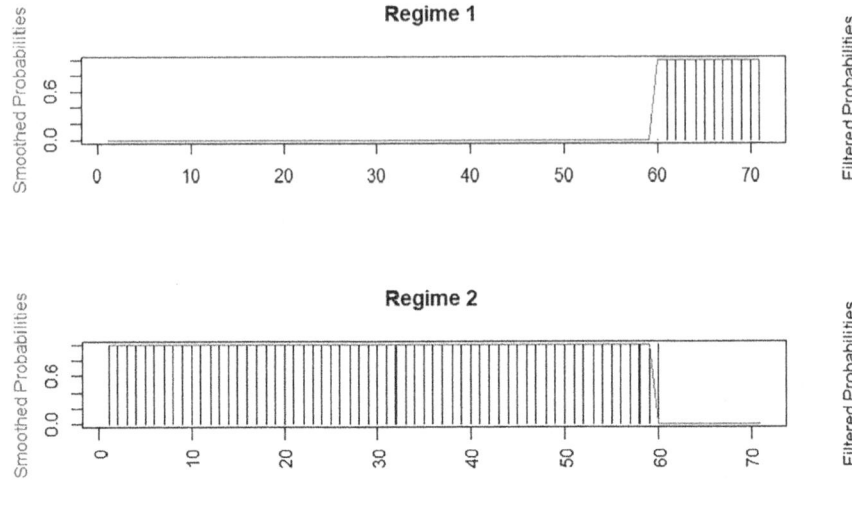

Fig. 5. Regime Probabilities

The plots in Fig. 5 illustrate the smoothed and filtered probabilities for the two regimes of the model. Figure 5 illustrates the evolution of regime probabilities over time. Regime 1 becomes dominant in the latter part of the series, as indicated by a sharp increase in smoothed probabilities around observation 60, corresponding to a period of high event counts. In contrast, Regime 2 prevails in the earlier part of the series, with high smoothed probabilities until around observation 60, reflecting periods of low and stable event counts.

The sharp transitions highlight structural changes in the data-generating process, consistent with the observed increase in event counts, as shown in Fig. 6. From Fig. 6, we observe that the shaded region highlights the period where Regime 1 becomes dominant, with probabilities nearing 1. This transition coincides with a sharp increase in event counts, indicating that Regime 1 captures a high-variance state associated with elevated event activity. In contrast, the earlier part of the series shows negligible probability for Regime 1, corresponding to periods of low and stable event counts. This visualization confirms a structural shift in the data-generating process during the latter part of the time series.

To complement the previous visualization, Fig. 7 illustrates the relationship between event counts and the smoothed probabilities for Regime 2. Figure 7 illustrates the dominance of Regime 2 during the earlier part of the series, as indicated by the shaded region where probabilities remain close to 1. This regime corresponds to periods of low and stable event counts, reflecting a calm and predictable state. Around observation 60, the smoothed probabilities for Regime 2 drop significantly, aligning with a sharp rise in event counts as Regime 1 takes over. This transition from a stable regime (Regime 2) to a high-variance regime (Regime 1) reflects a significant structural change in the data.

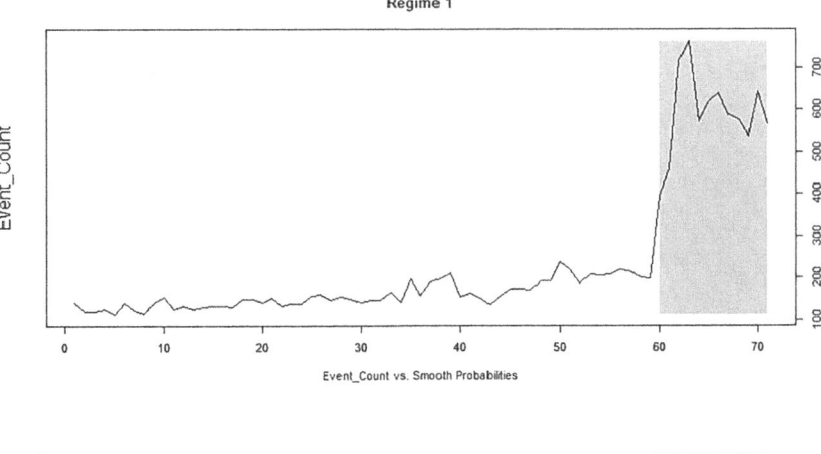

Fig. 6. Event Counts and Regime 1 Probabilities

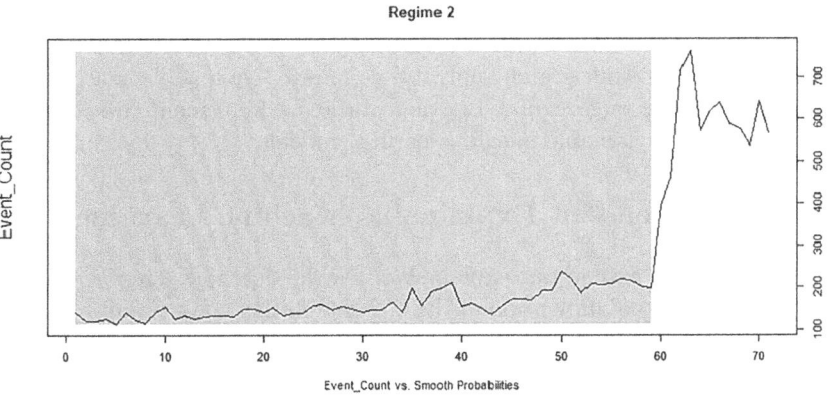

Fig. 7. Event Counts and Regime 2 Probabilities

We conclude that the selected MSM model with an AR(1) trend provides the best balance between capturing long-term structural shifts and short-term persistence while avoiding the instability observed in quadratic models. The AR(1) component ensures that past values contribute meaningfully to current estimates, while the linear trend maintains interpretability without introducing excessive complexity. This model is recommended for forecasting event counts, as it effectively captures both underlying trends and autoregressive dependencies. In the next section, we build on the results obtained from the selected

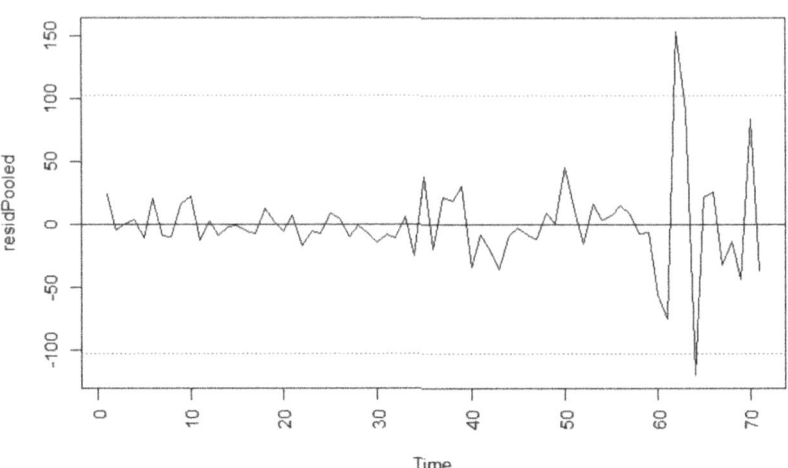

Fig. 8. Pooled Residuals

Markov-Switching models and apply two separate explainable machine learning models, one for each regime. In other words, we implement two conditional, time-dependent explainable machine learning models.

6 Time-Dependent Explainable Machine Learning

In this section, we extend our explainable machine learning approach by incorporating the temporal dimension of the dataset. Rather than training models on the entire dataset, we divide the data into two distinct periods: 2018–2022 and 2023, aligning with the regimes identified by the Markov-Switching model in the previous section.

By training separate classifiers for each period, we aim to capture temporal variations in the key features influencing attack severity classification. Following the methodology in Sect. 3, we apply seven machine learning classifiers to both time periods, treating the problem as a binary classification task. Instances are labeled as 1 (high and critical) and 0 (medium and low). We perform hyperparameter tuning for each classifier and optimize the decision threshold to address dataset imbalance using the same balance metric (Equation (1)), ensuring a fair trade-off between precision and recall across both classes. As shown in Tables 6 and 7, XGBoost achieves the best overall performance in both time periods, making it the final selected classifier for feature importance analysis.

Our analysis reveals that the key features influencing classification decisions vary across time periods. Certain attack attributes and techniques become more prominent in one period than in the other, highlighting the evolving nature of cyber threats. Without separating the dataset into these two periods, some important features affecting classification outcomes would remain unrecognized.

Table 6. Performance of different classifiers on the 2018–2022 dataset. The table presents the optimal threshold, overall accuracy, per-class accuracy, and AUC for each classifier.

Classifier	Threshold	Accuracy	Accuracy by Class		AUC
			Class 0	Class 1	
RF	0.60	0.80	0.71	0.85	0.85
XGBoost	**0.56**	**0.80**	**0.66**	**0.87**	**0.86**
LR	0.63	0.68	0.63	0.71	0.73
KNN	0.43	0.77	0.57	0.87	0.80
SVM	0.42	0.77	0.50	0.91	0.81
Voting	0.61	0.78	0.67	0.84	0.84
Stacking	0.62	0.79	0.67	0.86	0.85

Table 7. Performance of different classifiers on the 2023 dataset. The table presents the optimal threshold, overall accuracy, per-class accuracy, and AUC for each classifier.

Classifier	Threshold	Accuracy	Accuracy by Class		AUC
			Class 0	Class 1	
RF	0.88	0.84	0.83	0.84	0.89
XGBoost	**0.81**	**0.90**	**0.76**	**0.91**	**0.91**
LR	0.84	0.86	0.81	0.87	0.87
KNN	0.43	0.92	0.45	0.96	0.79
SVM	0.51	0.92	0.26	0.99	0.75
Voting	0.85	0.86	0.80	0.87	0.90
Stacking	0.84	0.89	0.72	0.91	0.90

To illustrate these temporal differences, we analyze the feature importance rankings obtained by applying Shapley values to the selected models for each period separately. Figure 9(a) and Fig. 9(b) present the top contributing features for the periods 2018–2022 and 2023, respectively, highlighting shifts in the importance of attacker and technique attributes over time. For reference, the overall feature importance when training on the entire dataset is shown in Fig. 4.

To further investigate the differences between the two periods, we analyze the decision threshold optimization process. Figure 10(a) and Fig. 10(b) show the variation of different performance metrics as a function of the decision threshold for the periods 2018–2022 and 2023, respectively. The results suggest that optimal thresholds vary between periods, reinforcing the need for time-aware model calibration. For reference, the threshold optimization for the entire dataset is shown in Fig. 3.

These findings underscore the importance of accounting for time-dependent variations in cyber threat classification. Training models on separate time periods improves the detection of evolving attack patterns and ensures that key

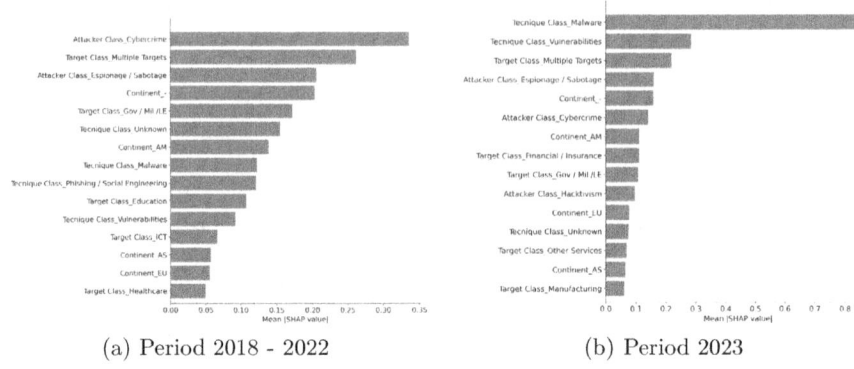

(a) Period 2018 - 2022   (b) Period 2023

Fig. 9. The 15 most important explanatory variables obtained by applying Shapley values to the XGBoost model for the 2018–2022 dataset (a) and the 2023 dataset (b).

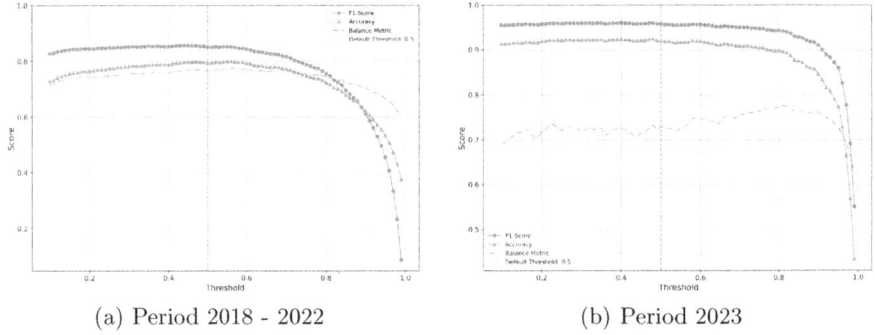

(a) Period 2018 - 2022   (b) Period 2023

Fig. 10. Threshold optimization for XGBoost applied to the 2018–2022 dataset (a) and the 2023 dataset (b).

features remain relevant. This approach enhances both the performance and interpretability of machine learning models in cybersecurity applications.

7 Conclusions

In this paper, we propose a hybrid methodology that combines explainable machine learning models with time series econometric techniques—specifically, Markov-Switching Models (MSMs)—to support time-dependent interpretation of cyber risk dynamics. Our findings demonstrate that segmenting the dataset using regime changes identified through MSMs enhances the interpretability of classification models. While a structural break is visually apparent in early 2023, MSMs offer a formal and data-driven approach to identifying and modeling this shift. Additionally, they capture regime persistence and intra-regime dynamics, which static or manually split models cannot. This structured segmentation enables more robust integration with explainable AI techniques. For example, applying Shapley values to eXtreme Gradient Boosting (the best-performing model) within each regime reveals meaningful temporal variation in feature importance, such as the decline of *Attacker Class_ Cybercrime* in the post-2023 period.

Future research will focus on: (i) extending the framework to rolling-window analyses to capture gradual or recurring shifts in cyber threat behavior; (ii) evaluating forecast performance once more data is available; (iii) exploring higher-order MSMs for richer regime structures; and (iv) validating the methodology on additional cyber attack datasets to assess its generalizability and robustness.

Acknowledgements. We sincerely thank the experts of the Hackmanac Project Sofia Scozzari and Andrea Zapparoli Manzoni for generously sharing the dataset used in this study.

This study was funded by: the European Union - NextGenerationEU, in the framework of the GRINS- Growing Resilient, INclusive and Sustainable (GRINS PE00000018). The views and opinions expressed are solely those of the authors and do not necessarily reflect those of the European Union, nor can the European Union be held responsible for them.

References

1. Agosto, A., Cavaliere, G., Kristensen, D., Rahbek, A.: Modeling corporate defaults: poisson autoregressions with exogenous covariates (PARX). J. Empir. Financ. **38**, 640–663 (2016)
2. Agosto, A., Giudici, P.: Cyber risk contagion. Risks **11**(9), 165 (2023)
3. Chen, C.W., Khamthong, K., Lee, S.: Markov switching integer-valued generalized auto-regressive conditional heteroscedastic models for dengue counts. J. R. Stat. Soc.: Ser. C: Appl. Stat. **68**(4), 963–983 (2019)
4. Doukhan, P., Fokianos, K., Rynkiewicz, J.: Mixtures of nonlinear poisson autoregressions. J. Time Ser. Anal. **42**(1), 107–135 (2021)
5. Edwards, B., Hofmeyr, S., Forrest, S.: Hype and heavy tails: a closer look at data breaches. J. Cybersecur. **2**(1), 3–14 (2016)
6. Hackmanac: Hackmanac Global Cyber Attacks Report (2024). https://hackmanac.com/wp-content/uploads/2024/07/Hackmanac_Global_Cyber_Attacks_Report-2024_PR.pdf. Accessed 05 Feb 2025
7. Li, Y., Mamon, R.: Modelling health-data breaches with application to cyber insurance. Comput. Secur. **124**, 102963 (2023)
8. Malyshkina, N.V., Mannering, F.L.: Zero-state markov switching count-data models: an empirical assessment. Accid. Anal. Prev. **42**(1), 122–130 (2010)
9. Mell, P., Scarfone, K., Romanosky, S.: Common vulnerability scoring system. IEEE Secur. Priv. **4**(6), 85–89 (2006)
10. Mell, P., Scarfone, K., Romanosky, S., et al.: A complete guide to the common vulnerability scoring system version 2.0. In: Published by FIRST-forum of incident response and security teams. vol. 1, p. 23 (2007)
11. Spring, J., Hatleback, E., Householder, A., Manion, A., Shick, D.: Time to change the CVSS? IEEE Secur. Priv. **19**(2), 74–78 (2021)
12. Sun, H., Xu, M., Zhao, P.: A multivariate frequency-severity framework for healthcare data breaches. Ann. Appl. Stat. **17**(1) (2023)

Open Access This chapter is licensed under the terms of the Creative Commons Attribution 4.0 International License (http://creativecommons.org/licenses/by/4.0/), which permits use, sharing, adaptation, distribution and reproduction in any medium or format, as long as you give appropriate credit to the original author(s) and the source, provide a link to the Creative Commons license and indicate if changes were made.

The images or other third party material in this chapter are included in the chapter's Creative Commons license, unless indicated otherwise in a credit line to the material. If material is not included in the chapter's Creative Commons license and your intended use is not permitted by statutory regulation or exceeds the permitted use, you will need to obtain permission directly from the copyright holder.

Author Index

A
Acar, Erman 330
Achache, Nina 135
Ahmed, Faizan 317
Aksoy, Meltem 218
Alstrøm, Tommy Sonne 243

B
Babaei, Golnoosh 378
Baer, Gregor 292
Bender, Sidney 112
Bhan, Milan 135
Blangero, Annabelle 135
Boersma, Marcel 330
Brüsch, Thea 243

C
Chaidos, Nikolaos 72
Chesneau, Nicolas 135

D
Danese, Danilo 3
Di Noia, Tommaso 3
Di Sciascio, Eugenio 3
Dimitriou, Angeliki 72, 87

F
Fairhurst, Merle 354
Fasano, Giuseppe 3
FIlandrianos, Giorgos 87

G
Gerolymatos, Stavros 45
Giudici, Paolo 378, 399
Grau, Isel 292

H
Ha, Trung Duc 112
Halilović, Amar 27

Hasić, Vahidin 27
Heinert, Edgar 45

J
Jenssen, Robert 243

K
Kaesling, Katharina 354
Keser, Mert 45
Klös, Verena 354
Knoll, Alois 45
Krivić, Senka 27

L
Legrand, Victor 135
Lesot, Marie-Jeanne 135
Löfström, Tuwe 218
Lombardi, Angela 3
Lymperaiou, Maria 87

M
Martorell, Nicolas 268
Mikriukov, Georgii 45
Murris, Juliette 135
Mütze, Annika 45

N
Nguyen, Linh 330
Nguyen, Van Bach 158

P
Pinto, Tiago 205
Pirra, Marco 399
Prado-Romero, Mario Alfonso 177
Prenkaj, Bardh 177

R
Rigenti, Alberto 218
Rottmann, Matthias 45

S

Schlötterer, Jörg 158
Schmidt, Mikkel N. 243
Schwalbe, Gesina 45
Seifert, Christin 158
Spanos, Nikolaos 72
Stamou, Giorgos 72, 87
Stilo, Giovanni 177

T

Teixeira, Brígida 205

V

Vale, Zita 205
Van Gorp, Pieter 292
van Keulen, Maurice 317
van Veen, Katiuscka 317
Vitali, Fabio 218
Vittaut, Jean-Noel 135
Voulodimos, Athanasios 72, 87

W

Wickstrøm, Kristoffer Knutsen 243
Wu, Lunshuai 378

Y

Yapicioglu, Fatima Rabia 218

Z

Zhang, Chao 292
Zieni, Rasha 399

Made in the USA
Monee, IL
03 May 2026